BOOKS BY JEFFREY MEYERS

BIOGRAPHY
A Fever at the Core: The Idealist in Politics
Married to Genius
Katherine Mansfield
The Enemy: A Biography of Wyndham Lewis
Hemingway
Manic Power: Robert Lowell and His Circle
D. H. Lawrence

CRITICISM
Fiction and the Colonial Experience
The Wounded Spirit: T. E. Lawrence's Seven Pillars of Wisdom
A Reader's Guide to George Orwell
Painting and the Novel
Homosexuality and Literature
D. H. Lawrence and the Experience of Italy
Disease and the Novel
The Spirit of Biography

BIBLIOGRAPHY
T. E. Lawrence: A Bibliography
Catalogue of the Library of the Late Siegfried Sassoon
George Orwell: An Annotated Bibliography of Criticism

EDITED COLLECTIONS
George Orwell: The Critical Heritage
Ernest Hemingway: The Critical Heritage
Wyndham Lewis by Roy Campbell
Robert Lowell: Interviews and Memoirs

EDITED ORIGINAL ESSAYS
Wyndham Lewis: A Revaluation
D. H. Lawrence and Tradition
The Legacy of D. H. Lawrence
The Craft of Literary Biography
The Biographer's Art
T. E. Lawrence: Soldier, Writer, Legend
Graham Greene: A Revaluation

D. H. LAWRENCE

D. H. LAWRENCE

A BIOGRAPHY

JEFFREY MEYERS

ALFRED A. KNOPF 🐎 NEW YORK 1990

THIS IS A BORZOI BOOK
PUBLISHED BY ALFRED A. KNOPF, INC.

Library of Congress Cataloging-in-Publication Data
Meyers, Jeffrey
D. H. Lawrence: a biography/Jeffrey Meyers.—1st ed.
p.   cm.
Includes bibliographical references.
ISBN 0-394-57244-0
1. Lawrence, D. H. (David Herbert), 1885–1930—Biography.
2. Authors, English—20th century—Biography.   I. Title.
PR6023.A93Z68118   1990
823'.912—dc20   89-43294
[B]   CIP

Manufactured in the United States of America
First Edition

FOR WILLIAM CHACE

Contents

Illustrations follow page 238

Illustrations

16. Dorothy Brett, self-portrait, 1922 (Special Collections, University of New Mexico)
17. Percy Lucas (from Audrey Lucas. *E. V. Lucas: A Portrait*. London: Methuen, 1939. Methuen publishers)
18. Lawrence, c.1917 (Nottinghamshire County Library Service)
19. Katherine Mansfield and Middleton Murry, 1918 (Alexander Turnbull Library, Wellington, New Zealand)
20. Robert Mountsier, 1918 (Silas Mountsier III)
21. Esther Andrews, c.1910 (Betsey Harries)
22. William Henry Hocking (Kitty Rogers)
23. Maurice Magnus, 1915 (Black Sparrow Press)
24. Achsah, Harwood and Earl Brewster, Capri, c.1921 (Harwood Brewster Picard)
25. Frieda and Lawrence, Chapala, Mexico, 1923 (University of Nottingham Library)
26. Mabel and Tony Luhan, New Mexico, 1940s (Photography Collection, Harry Ransom Humanities Research Center, University of Texas at Austin)
27. Lawrence, Mexico City, 1924 (photograph by Edward Weston. © 1981 Arizona Board of Regents Center for Creative Photography)
28. Aldous Huxley and Lawrence, Scandicci, 1926 (Margaret Needham)
29. Lawrence, Florence, 1928 (photograph by Robert Davis. Photography Collection, Harry Ransom Humanities Research Center, University of Texas at Austin)
30. Richard Aldington, 1929 (Special Collections, Morris Library, Southern Illinois University)
31. D. H. Lawrence, *Fauns and Nymphs,* 1928 (Saki Karavas)
32. D. H. Lawrence, manuscript of "The Ship of Death," 1929 (Harry Ransom Humanities Research Center, University of Texas at Austin)

Preface

Though Lawrence's life and works have been subject to intensive scrutiny, my own research—and the use of unpublished essays and letters of Lawrence and his circle—has revealed significant new information about the influence of coal mining and Congregationalism on Lawrence's life, his parents' background and social class, the circumstances of his mother's death, Lawrence's physical sterility, the reasons for the suppression of *The Rainbow* and his exhibition of paintings, his friendship with Robert Mountsier and Esther Andrews, his homosexual relationship with the Cornish farmer William Henry Hocking, Ford Madox Ford's role in Lawrence's expulsion from Cornwall, the origins of his connection with Alfred Knopf and the clinical history of his tuberculosis. I also provide new interpretations of several works, including "England, My England," "The Rocking-Horse Winner" and "The Princess."

I have tried to emulate Lawrence's great gift of perceiving and revealing the inner life of people, to illustrate his complex method of mingling autobiography and fiction, and to show (as F. R. Leavis observed) that there was no separation between the artist who wrote and the man who lived.

Acknowledgments

Biography is a cooperative enterprise, and I am pleased to acknowledge the assistance of a great many people and institutions. I had generous hospitality from Kenneth and Ellen Meyers in Berkeley, Ben and Judith Lindfors and Joan Sanger in Austin, Robert and Lynn Piper in Washington, William and Gladys Froggatt near Nottingham. Ross Parmenter was extremely helpful and sent many valuable pages about Lawrence in Mexico. Lewis Sawin and Gene DeGruson gave me copies of unpublished Lawrence letters. My wife, Valerie, rigorously criticized each chapter and compiled the index. The Inter-Library Loan office at the University of Colorado was extremely helpful. And a grant from the University of Colorado enabled me to visit libraries in America and England.

The librarians at the following archives allowed me complete access to their collections of Lawrence letters and manuscripts, and guided me through the complex task of reading them: in America, the University of California at Berkeley, UCLA, University of New Mexico, Stanford University and the Harry Ransom Humanities Research Center at the University of Texas in Austin; in England, the British Library, Greater London Record Office, National Sound Archive, Nottingham County Library, Public Record Office and University of Nottingham Library.

During the last decade I interviewed a number of people, no longer living, who knew Lawrence: Dorothy Brett, A. S. Frere, David Garnett, Sir Julian Huxley, Richard Murry, Montague Weekley and Rebecca West. For more recent interviews I would like to thank Michael Asquith,

Barbara Weekley Barr, John Carswell, Dr. Mary Saleeby Fisher, Walter Forster, John Geister, Brewster Ghiselin, Rachel Hawk, Enid Hopkin Hilton, Francis Huxley, Lady Juliette Huxley, Frederick Jeffrey, Jan Juta, Yvonne Kapp, Saki Karavas, Margaret King Needham, Harwood Brewster Picard, Roy Spencer and Julian Morrell Vinogradoff.

For letters about Lawrence I am grateful to Daniel Aaron, James Boulton, Matthew Bruccoli, Betty Bruce, Charlotte Cardon, Virginia Spencer Carr, Noel Carrington, Carlo Carlucci, David Cavitch, John Colmer, Dr. Sheldon Cooperman, Nora Crook, Dr. Mary Lou Cullinen, Keith Cushman, Paul Delany, Elizabeth Dos Passos, Leon Edel, Susan Ehrlich, Valerie Eliot, David Farmer, Eleanor Farnham, Maria Gibson, Johan Götzsche, Martin Green, Betsey Harries, Stanley Hocking, Mary Lago, Norman Levine, Muriel Lough, Townsend Ludington, John Martin, Mary McCarthy, Jørgen Mejer, Vibeke Merrild, Beatrice Moore, Polly Moore, Thomas Moser, Silas Mountsier III, Alan Munton, the Earl of Oxford and Asquith, Norman Page, Laurence Pollinger, Peter Quennell, Stefano Ravagli, Jeffrey Robinson (of London), Lois Rudnick, David Sanders, Helen Scholz, Michael Squires, C. J. Stevens, Ernest Tedlock, Valerie Thompson, Marlise Wälde, Andrews Wanning, Frank Waters, Dorothy Nehls Weida, Kingsley Widmer and George Zytaruk.

I received useful information from the following institutions: Academy of Motion Picture Arts and Sciences, American Jewish Archives, Bow Street Magistrates Court, Brandt & Brandt, BBC Written Archives Centre, British Coal Corporation (which arranged my trip down a mine near Doncaster), British Medical Association, Cornwall County Council, D. H. Lawrence Society of England, Fairchild Publications, Federal Records Office (St. Louis), General Medical Council (London), General Synod of the Church of England, *Hampstead and Highgate Express*, Harvard University Archives, Lake Erie College, Las Palomas de Taos, New Mexico State Records Center, Newspaper Guild, Radcliffe College Library, Royal Danish Academy of Art, Royal Danish Embassy, *Smith Alumni Quarterly*, Smith College Archives, Southern Illinois University Library, Taos County Clerk, United States Department of State, University of Tulsa Library, University of Virginia Library, University of Wisconsin Library, University of Wisconsin Press, Williams College, Writers Guild of America, Yale University Alumni Records Office and Yale University Library.

Life went straight into his work.

— JESSIE CHAMBERS

Very few books of DHL's are fully comprehensible unless one knows the personal circumstances; for, like Goethe's, nearly all DHL's "creative" writing is a projection of his own life. His opera omnia are huge autobiography embroidered.

— RICHARD ALDINGTON

D. H. LAWRENCE

CHAPTER ONE

Eastwood:
A Mining Village

D. H. LAWRENCE, known for his restless wanderings in later
years, spent the first half of his life in Eastwood, a coal-mining village in
the Erewash Valley, eight miles northwest of Nottingham. In this region,
the lovely countryside and traditional agricultural life still survived
amidst the depredations of Victorian industrialism. "In this queer jum-
ble of the old England and the new," Lawrence wrote in "Nottingham
and the Mining Countryside," "I came into consciousness."[1] The region
was also rich in legend and literary associations. The Sherwood Forest
of Robin Hood, and Newstead Abbey, where Byron had grown up, lay to
the north; and Derbyshire, where George Eliot had set her novels, to the
west. The conflict between the mechanical and the pastoral, centered in
the mines and farms near Eastwood, became one of the major themes of
Lawrence's fiction.

Coal mining—which dominated the life of Eastwood—had a powerful
effect on the formation of Lawrence's character. Freud, in a famous
analogy, compared the psychoanalyst's exploration of the unconscious to
the archeologist's excavation of the layers of the earth: "I had no choice
but to follow the example of those discoverers whose good fortune it is to
bring to the light of day after their long burial the priceless though
mutilated relics of antiquity."[2] Henry Moore, the son of a coal miner, was
influenced by the miner's close connection to the inner earth and the

intense dramas of underground life, and found similarities between coal
mining and sculpting. Lawrence, the first writer to use Freudian ideas
in the English novel, used mining for coal—the elemental substance
extracted from the dark subterranean regions—to symbolize his search
for the essential, instinctual unconscious.

The destructive and regenerative flood scenes in *The Rainbow* and
The Virgin and the Gipsy occur after the earth has been disturbed by
coal mining. In a letter of August 31, 1925, written just before his return
to the Midlands, Lawrence recalled his earliest emotions about coal,
exalted its poetic qualities and idealized the intimacy of the miners:
"What was there in the mines that held the boy's feelings? The darkness,
the mystery, the otherworldness, the peculiar camaraderie, the sort of
naked intimacy: men as gods in the underworld, or as elementals. . . . The
deathliness of steel, as against the comparative softness, silkiness, natu-
ralness of coal. . . . Coal is a symbol of something in the soul, old and dark
and silky and natural."[3]

Lawrence sympathized with the Luddites, who began their movement
in Nottingham, flourished between 1811 and 1816, and at the beginning
of the Industrial Revolution tried to destroy the machinery that was
dehumanizing the lives of urban workers. "Somewhere about 1820,"
Lawrence wrote, "the [local Barber, Walker coal] company must have
sunk the first big shaft—not very deep—and installed the first machinery of the real industrial colliery."[4] The first coal mine in the area was
actually sunk in 1841—two years after the first train had left Nottingham for Derby—when an investor excavated two seven-foot pits to a
depth of more than six hundred feet. By 1854 Nottingham had seventeen
collieries, and seven years later Thomas North held long leases of nearly
ten thousand acres in the Nottinghamshire coalfield. The years 1884 to
1888 were ones of economic depression; 1888 to 1893 were years of
prosperity, when the union came in and Lawrence's family (during the
first decade of his life) improved their housing; 1893 was the year of the
strike and the lockout.

Mechanical improvements were gradually introduced toward the end
of the century: winding gear and larger cages to lower and raise the men
in the mines, electricity for lighting, new cutting and hauling equip-
ment, machines at the pithead for sorting and washing the coal. But
"steam engines, lamps, cages, and handling gear did not affect the mode
of mining coal at the face. This continued to depend on the old way of
doing things, more intensely applied: blows deftly struck by hand
against the coal face, and underground transport very largely by human

muscle."[5] Coal mining remained a pick-and-shovel industry; as late as 1913 less than eight percent of British coal was cut by machine.

George Orwell, who went down a mine near Wigan, Lancashire, in 1936, idealized the miners, as Lawrence had done, and described conditions that had scarcely changed since the days of Zola's *Germinal* (1885): the infernal constriction, the agonizing toil, the imminent danger of extinction.

> Most of the things one imagines in hell are there—heat, noise, confusion, darkness, foul air, and, above all, unbearably cramped space.... [You see] the line of bowed, kneeling figures, sooty black all over, driving their huge shovels under the coal with stupendous force and speed....
>
> You have a tolerable-sized mountain on top of you; hundreds of yards of solid rock, bones of extinct beasts, subsoil, flints, roots of growing things, green grass and cows grazing on it—all this suspended over your head and held back only by wooden props as thick as the calf of your leg.[6]

Orwell's farmer's knowledge of the earth and his Swiftian ability to isolate the significant detail of the grazing cows standing on top of the pits reveal the depths and dangers of the mines.

The eight-hour day was finally granted in 1908 after years of labor unrest, decreasing productivity, technological advances, and fluctuations in wages and prices. In March 1912, during the first national coal stoppage, a million miners—fighting for higher wages and better working conditions—went on strike for six weeks. Despite significant improvements, the industry's major weakness before 1914 was the low rate of mechanization combined with the declining productivity of labor.

The coal owners responded to these serious problems with the peculiar mixture of paternalism and ruthlessness that Lawrence described in his coal-mining novels from *Sons and Lovers* to *Lady Chatterley's Lover.* As S. G. Checkland observes:

> By the third quarter of the [nineteenth] century, owners of very extensive enterprises had often lost touch with the mass of their employees. They knew that a minimum degree of ruthlessness was essential if the enterprise was to hold its own over the successive phases of the cycle. There seemed no other sensible rule but to resist claims for wage increases in good times and to enforce decreases in

bad. Many of them quite literally could not afford to become involved in the human effects of policy, for to do so would have meant the passing, first of wealth and power, and then of the vitality of the enterprise.[7]

In 1842, when the miners were still virtually slaves, a government official had reported: "I have met with pits where it rained so as to wet the children to the skin in a few minutes, and at the same time so hot that they could scarcely bear their clothes on to work in, and in this wet state they had to continue fourteen hours, and perhaps had to walk a mile or two at night without changing or drying their clothes."[8] The miners' efforts to ensure their safety and welfare led to a series of government inquiries and acts of Parliament from 1880 to 1914, and to stricter regulations about ventilation, safety lamps, shafts and winding, haulage, the support of roofs and sides, signaling, machinery, electricity and explosives. But coal mining remained the most dehumanizing and dangerous occupation in England.

In addition to the common perils of working with heavy machinery, the miners suffered the exceptional disasters of underground work: roof falls, flooding, explosive gases and the remorseless destruction of their respiratory systems. The men might be crushed or buried alive by sudden falls of earth that blocked their way out of the mine. The deep pits might suddenly be inundated with floods or choked with poison gas and fire damp. The miners' lungs were clogged with dust as they breathed the odors of stinking horses and sweating men. Almost all miners over forty suffered from asthma and chronic bronchitis. The mines were always dark, dirty and dusty as well as hot, wet and cramped. Eating, drinking, urinating and defecating all took place in a confined space, and rats ran through the stagnant water.

From 1850 until 1914 more than a thousand miners were killed annually. Between 1868 and 1919 a miner was seriously injured every two hours and killed every six hours. The 1930s poet Cecil Day Lewis, whose clergyman father had accepted a colliery vicarage in north Nottinghamshire in 1918, referred to Disraeli's description of the "two nations" (the rich and the poor) and recalled "that 'other nation' and the dangerous war they waged . . . men injured by falls of roof, maimed by runaway tubs [of coal], killed by an explosion or the cage dropping out of control from a pithead."[9]

The intimate, perilous work made the half-naked miners "very clannish, a form of group cohesion that manifested itself both in intense loyalty to their local combinations, friendly societies, and trade unions, and also in a distinctive world of folk-lore. These strong mutual bonds were reinforced by the almost unbreakable heredity of the trade."[10] The boys who were Lawrence's classmates in Eastwood looked forward to being initiated into pit work when they left school at thirteen or fourteen years old.

The subterranean conditions were reflected above ground in the mechanical squalor of furnaces, factories, smoking chimneys, polluted air and industrial waste. The miners lived within walking distance of the pits. From infancy Lawrence was familiar with the ragged, permanently coal-stained men, heard the rattling of the coal trains, saw the great gin wheels, the timberwork, the banks of coal heaped high next to the pits, which were sunk at close intervals throughout the countryside. Day Lewis remembered "the prevailing wind [that] brought the acrid smell of slag-tips from the Mansfield colliery. . . . Day and night the long coal trains clanked along the embankment. . . . I could hear already the hooters from the mines and the distant rattle of the pit-head winding gear as the cages went up and down."[11]

Lawrence's teenage girlfriend, Jessie Chambers, who lived on a farm near Eastwood, noted that "the quiet of the night was punctuated by the metallic rattle of the winding engine and the rhythmic sighing of the ventilating fans" and that "most of the district [was] naked industrialism, and depressing in the extreme."[12] But Lawrence had an ambivalent, even contradictory attitude toward the mines. He could not go as far as W. H. Auden, born in Birmingham but raised in York, who wrote: "Tramlines and slagheaps, pieces of machinery, / That was, and still is, my ideal scenery."[13] But never having been down a mine, and strangely attracted to the exciting landscape of his childhood, which reminded him of God guiding Moses to the Promised Land in Exodus 13:21, Lawrence observed in *Sons and Lovers:* "I like the pits here and there. I like the rows of trucks, and the headstocks, and the steam in the daytime, and the lights at night. When I was a boy, I always thought a pillar of cloud by day and a pillar of fire by night was a pit, with its steam, and its lights, and the burning bank—I thought the Lord was always at the pit-top."[14]

Enid Hilton, the daughter of Lawrence's middle-class Eastwood mentor, Willie Hopkin, remembered (after ninety years) lying in bed at the cold dawn, listening to the shuffle of miners' clogs on the cobblestones and to the hymns they sang on their way to work. In "Return to Bestwood," a late autobiographical essay, Lawrence also remembered the blackened faces of "the homeward-trooping colliers when I was a boy, the ringing of the feet, the red mouths and the quick whites of the eyes, the swinging pit bottles, and the strange voices of the men from the underworld calling back and forth." He concluded that the miners— prototypes of all the earthy, passionate gamekeepers, Gypsies, Celts, Mexicans and Indians who wander through his works—"are the only people who move me strongly, and with whom I feel myself connected in deeper destiny." In a crucial passage in his essay on the mining countryside, he explained his attraction to the instinctual, intimate, intuitional life he had observed in his father and his father's mates:

> The people lived almost entirely by instinct, men of my father's age could not really read. And the pit did not mechanize men. On the contrary. Under the butty system, the miners worked underground as a sort of intimate community, they knew each other practically naked, and with curious close intimacy, and the darkness and the underground remoteness of the pit "stall," and the continual presence of danger, made the physical, instinctive, and intuitional contact between men very highly developed, a contact almost as close as touch, very real and very powerful. This physical awareness and intimate *togetherness* was at its strongest down pit. . . . They brought with them above ground the curious dark intimacy of the mine.[15]

Yet Lawrence's return to Eastwood and observation of the harsh conditions of the general strike in 1926 marked a radical change in his attitude. It evoked childhood memories that confirmed his belief in male friendship but also emphasized the grim realities, the fact that "a coalmine remains a hole in the black earth, where blackened men hew and shovel and sweat." The dreariness and dirtiness, the smells and the sounds, were the same in 1926 as they had been in his youth: "The black-slate roofs beyond the wind-worn young trees at the end of the garden are the same thick layers of black roofs of blackened brick houses, as ever. There is the same smell of sulfur from the burning pit bank. Smuts fly on the white violas. There is a harsh sound of machinery." In his late "Autobiographical Fragment," he stressed the miners' slavery to industry and portrayed them as automatons, extinguishing their lamps and wandering into the twilight, accompanied by mechanical noise and by the sound of the exhausted pit pony dragging himself to death: "The shafts where we used to watch the cage-loads of colliers coming up suddenly, with a start: then the men streaming out to turn in their lamps, then trailing off, all grey, along the lane home; while the screens still rattled, and the pony on the sky-line still pulled along the tub of 'dirt,' to tip over the edge of the pit-bank."[16]

In his last novel, *Lady Chatterley's Lover,* Lawrence portrayed the miners as victims of the machine. He bitterly condemned their subjection to ugly clothes, furniture, surroundings, religion and ideals as well as the extinction of their intuitive faculty and of their vital connection to the earth:

> She took in the utter, soulless ugliness of the coal-and-iron Midlands. . . . She heard the rattle-rattle of the screens at the pit, the puff of the winding-engine, the clink-clink of the shunting trucks, and the hoarse little whistle of the colliery locomotives. Tevershall pit-bank was burning. . . . And when the wind was that way, which was often, the house was full of the stench of this sulphurous combustion of the earth's excrement. . . .
>
> The blackened brick dwellings, the black slate roofs, glistening their sharp edges, the mud black with coal-dust, the pavements wet and black. It was as if dismalness had soaked through and through everything. The utter negation of natural beauty, the utter negation of the gladness of life, the utter absence of the instinct for shapely beauty which every bird and beast has, the utter death of the human intuitive faculty was appalling.

Lawrence explained to his friend Catherine Carswell that mining villages were needlessly ugly because "miners through having to work underground had become blind to form values. They craved for 'a bit of colour,' and so loved and cultivated flowers with passion."[17]

The all-pervasive industrial ugliness was also reflected in the towns and houses of the miners. Polluted water and inefficient waste disposal made most mining villages very unhealthy; and the tiny windows and the lack of gas or electric lighting made most of the houses (built by and rented from the colliery) extremely dull and gloomy. As John Benson remarks: "The nineteenth-century miner and his wife faced enormous difficulties in their life together. The cramped, unhealthy home, the lack of privacy, the ways in which wages were paid, the early starts, the comings and goings, indeed the very fact of working at the pit, made it far from easy to enjoy a stable and comfortable home life."[18]

Before the first mines were sunk, the economy of Eastwood had been based on agriculture, the lace trade and the frame-knitting industry, but after 1850 coal production became dominant. At the time of Lawrence's birth, in 1885, Eastwood had about four thousand inhabitants; by 1910 the town had grown to about nine thousand. Eastwood had about fourteen public houses and beer shops in the 1890s, and heavy drinking was the principal diversion of the miners.

Drinking →

Lawrence's father, Arthur, and Lawrence's uncles Walter and James all worked at the Brinsley colliery. James was killed there in a mining accident in 1880. Arthur was a butty, a superior worker operating within a managerial hierarchy, who agreed with the colliery owner on a price per ton for extracting the coal. He then hired, supervised and paid the gang of stall men who worked with him. In the 1890s the miners' annual earnings at Brinsley were the highest in the five collieries owned by the Barber, Walker Company and fluctuated between a low of £75 and a high of £120.

The Brinsley mine had exploded, three years after James' death, on June 10, 1883. And on December 23, 1904, the local *Eastwood and Kimberley Advertiser* reported that Arthur Lawrence had suffered his second serious accident in one year:

> Mr. Arthur Lawrence, of Walker-street, a miner, was hurt whilst at work down the Brinsley Colliery on Monday. Whilst following his employment Mr. Lawrence was struck on the back by a fall of bind [hardened clay], and, falling on a quantity of debris, was badly crushed internally. Having been medically attended it was found that the injuries were of so serious a nature as to necessitate his removal to Nottingham Infirmary. A pathetic incident in connection with the case is the fact that Mr. Lawrence was suffering from a fractured leg exactly a year ago, and was an inmate of the Infirmary on Christmas Day as will be the case this year.[19]

Lawrence's mother was determined to keep her three sons out of the mines, and Arthur Lawrence was the last coal miner in the immediate family.

CHAPTER TWO

A Disastrous
Marriage

LAWRENCE came from a family of craftsmen and composers: tailors, miners, lacemakers and hymn writers. Though he vaguely claimed a great-grandfather who came to England as a refugee after the French Revolution, his family history actually began with his paternal grandfather, John Lawrence. He was a tall, silent, strange man, famous in his district as a dancer and a boxer. Trained as a military tailor, he supplied moleskin trousers for the Brinsley mine, near Eastwood, and lived to be eighty-six. Lawrence later remembered "the great rolls of coarse flannel and pit-cloth which stood in the corner of my grandfather's shop when I was a small boy, and the big, strange old sewing machine, like nothing else on earth, which sewed the massive pit trousers."[1]

John Lawrence had four sons. George and Arthur were considered well-to-do miners; James was killed in the Brinsley colliery; Walter was notorious for his drinking and violence. In March 1900, "Lawrence's Uncle Walter, his father's youngest brother, was charged with 'unlawfully wounding and committing grievous bodily harm upon Walter Lawrence junior on the 18th March.' After a teatime argument Walter senior had thrown at his fifteen-year-old son a sharpening steel which had penetrated the youth's ear causing 'brain trouble, paralysis, meningitis' and subsequent death."[2]

Lawrence's father, Arthur, the oldest son, was born in 1846 in a humble cottage near a quarry hole at the Brinsley railroad crossing. He left school when he could scarcely read and write, entered the colliery at the age of seven and worked from five in the morning until nine at night. He sang in the Newstead Abbey choir as a boy. Like his father, he was a well-known dancer and, in his youth, ran a dancing class. Enid Hilton remembered him from her childhood as a handsome, virile man with an imposing beard and impressive bearing. She thought him a nice rather than a fearful figure, and certainly no fool.

Arthur's coloring and voice gave Jessie Chambers an impression of richness and warmth. To her older sister, May, "he looked handsome in a rugged way: black curly hair and beard streaked slightly with silver; blue eyes smiling kindly in a rugged face, glancing over the [chapel] congregation with a friendly air; well-built and strong in figure; and a genial manner." May added that Lawrence's mother, by comparison, "appeared bitter, disillusioned, and austere." In *Sons and Lovers*, Lawrence first explains why his mother was immediately attracted to the vital and passionate miner. He then describes how the once genial man, after years of marriage to a bitterly disillusioned wife, had been transformed into a surly brute: he was "well set up, erect, and very smart. He had wavy black hair that shone again, and a vigorous black beard that had never been shaved. His cheeks were ruddy, and his red, moist mouth was noticeable because he laughed so often and so heartily. . . . He was so full of colour and animation, his voice ran so easily into comic grotesque, he was so ready and so pleasant with everybody."[3]

Lawrence and his younger sister, Ada, accepted and propagated their mother's version of her family history, which she invented to establish her superiority. Lydia Beardsall claimed descent from an old, prosperous Puritan family, who had fought with Cromwell and had been ruined by a depression in the lace trade. Her maternal grandfather, John Newton (1802–86), was a Methodist composer whose hymn "Sovereignty" was No. 356 in the *Methodist Hymnbook*. Lawrence claimed, with some significant qualifications: "My mother was, I suppose, superior. She came from town, and belonged really to the lower bourgeoisie. She spoke King's English, without an accent." Ada stated that Lydia's "father had worked as an engineer in the Sheerness dockyard, and she became a schoolteacher."[4]

Roy Spencer has discovered that George Beardsall was not an engineer, nor was Lydia a teacher, in the normally accepted sense of the words, and that she had absolutely no claim to class superiority. Lydia, one of six daughters, was born in 1851 and grew up in the slums of

industrial Manchester and in the squalid streets of the Isle of Sheppey in
Kent. Her father, who described himself as an engineer but was actually
a fitter who assembled machinery, had been permanently disabled in an
industrial accident in 1870. Lydia had been dismissed for incompetence
as a pupil teacher when she was an adolescent of fourteen. A school
inspector's report from Sheerness, Kent, dated July 1865, led directly to
Lydia's dismissal: "L. Beardsall's Examination Papers and H.M. Inspector's Report as to her qualifications for a Teacher are so unsatisfactory
that my Lords have had considerable hesitation in sanctioning her
continuance as a Pupil Teacher. Unless her next examination is passed
with credit her name will be removed from the Register of Pupil
Teachers."

After her father's accident and Lydia's brief, unsuccessful career as
an apprentice teacher, the Beardsall family moved to the slums of
Nottingham. Lydia was slaving away in a tedious job in the lace trade
when she met her future husband. Both of Lawrence's parents were in
fact "born into the working-class. . . . At the time they married Arthur
Lawrence was socially superior to his bride, for his father was a settled,
hard-working and respected man . . . and his mother ran a successful
shop."[5] Though Lydia came from town, Arthur had the comparative
advantage of a boyhood in Eastwood, which, unlike the urban slums of
the Midlands, was near the countryside and still connected to rural life
and traditions.

Ada's description of her rather frail mother suggests that she was
intellectually rather than physically impressive: "She was small and
slight in figure, her brown hair, sprinkled with grey, brushed straight
back from a broad brow; clear blue eyes that always looked fearless and
unfaltering, and a delicately shaped nose, not quite straight owing to an
accident which occurred when she was a girl; tiny hands and feet, and a
sure carriage." Jessie Chambers, who was cruelly victimized by Mrs.
Lawrence, noted a tinge of patronage in her voice, though "she struck me
as a bright, vivacious little woman, full of vitality, and amusingly
emphatic in her way of speaking." She also observed Lydia's energy,
sharp tongue, icy disdain and unshakable conviction of self-
righteousness:

Mrs. Lawrence, though small, was an arresting figure with shrewd
grey eyes in a pale face, and light-coloured hair. Her smallness was
more than compensated for by her vigour and determination. . . .
Her confidence in herself and her pronouncements upon people

and things excited my wonder. It was new to me to meet anyone so certain of herself and of her own rightness. But she could be vivid in speech, gay and amusing; and in spite of a keen edge to her tongue, she was warm-hearted. . . .

Mrs. Lawrence, in her black dress, would sit in the low rocking chair like a little figure of fate, coldly disapproving. . . . Her prestige was unchallenged; it would have seemed like sacrilege to question her authority.[6]

Enid Hilton, who also knew Lydia from childhood, thought she was superior in name only—and even more superior when ill; and was both respected and disliked for her haughty airs. The most incisive, hitherto unpublished, account of Lydia's character was recorded by William Ernest Lawrence. The son of her oldest son, George, he lived with his grandmother's family at the turn of the century, when his uncle D. H. Lawrence was in high school. William Ernest stresses Lydia's isolation in the village, her dominating personality, fanatical cleanliness, strict discipline and self-proclaimed superiority:

She was as unlike and unaccepted in Eastwood as I should imagine the devil would be in heaven. . . .

She was diminutive, but a very determined, autocratic, overbearing type. . . .

I had to be scrubbed like a ruddy cherub and my boots cleaned about ten times. I daren't hardly breathe when I went to chapel with her. . . . She insisted on her own pew in the church, and no one on God's earth would dare to go and sit in that pew. If they did, she stood and looked at the minister until he came and removed them like a shot. She wouldn't stand that at any price.[7]

Lydia Lawrence also had considerable refinement and culture. She read widely, wrote verse and loved serious intellectual discussions. In "Return to Bestwood," Lawrence's last word on his beloved mother, he addressed her directly and adopted a mildly satiric tone when describing her naive idealism and misguided respect for the ruling class: "You were so keen on progress: a decent working man, and a good wage! You paid my father's union pay for him, for so many years! You were at your Woman's Guild when they brought you word your father, the old tyrannus, was dead! At the same time you believed so absolutely in the ultimate benevolence of all the masters, of all the upper classes. One had to be grateful to them, after all!"[8]

Lydia's one claim to intellectual superiority (by association) was based on the marriage of her younger sister Ada to a man who, after an extraordinary career, became an internationally respected authority on Arabic language and literature. Lawrence's uncle Fritz Krenkow was born in Germany in 1872, came to England twelve years later, worked for a hosiery firm in Leicester beginning in 1899 and became a naturalized citizen in 1911. Though he had no formal academic training, he taught himself Arabic, received an honorary degree from the University of Leipzig in 1929, was professor of Islamic Studies at Muslim University, in Aligarh, India, during 1929–30 and professor of Arabic at the University of Bonn during 1931–35. Though Krenkow had an erect Prussian bearing, he was completely dominated by his prim and proper wife. She made him slavishly wait on her and cut some offensive pages from Lawrence's novel *The Rainbow* before she allowed the scholar to read it. She became ill when he taught in India, disliked the country and forced him to return to Europe.⁹ Krenkow, the first scholar and intellectual Lawrence had met, encouraged his nephew to use his impressive library during visits to Leicester and to retranslate Egyptian fellahin poetry from German into English. Lawrence was drawn to Germany when Krenkow was living in the Rhineland and visited him there in 1912.

Arthur Lawrence and Lydia Beardsall, though temperamentally and intellectually opposed, were distantly related by marriage. Jonathan Chambers, Jessie's younger brother, described their meeting, their mutual attraction and the first of Arthur's minor deceptions (quite possibly matched by Lydia's own). He also noted that Lydia was particularly responsive to Arthur after having been disappointed in love by a "refined" young man who decided to marry a wealthy older woman:

[Arthur Lawrence] was a collier, very skilled and highly respected and already a butty, which represented the climax of the average collier's ambitions. He was also an attractive character, lively and gay, with an infectious laugh and a good singing voice. . . . [He] was a keen dancer and it was as a result of a meeting in a dance-hall in Nottingham that he met his future wife. . . . [He] had dancing blue eyes, a long black curly beard, and [was] a lively talker, of course in the Eastwood dialect. Lydia Beardsall was also a clever and attractive woman trained as a teacher and lately jilted by a schoolmaster. They were drawn to one another from the first encounter, and he soon asked her to marry him. When she asked him what he did for a living he said he was a contractor. Now that was strictly true. He contracted to get coal.

Ada said that Lydia "was attracted by his graceful dancing, his musical voice, his gallant manner and his overflowing humour and good spirits. He, on his side, was drawn to the rather quiet, reserved and ladylike girl." They married, two days after Christmas, in 1875, when Arthur was twenty-nine and Lydia twenty-four. He passionately loved his wife, worshipped the ground she walked on and was proud to have married a "superior" woman. Lydia, who soon realized she had been deceived by passion and had made a terrible mistake, "despised his guts."[10]

Willie Hopkin, who liked Lawrence's father, acutely observed that "Arthur Lawrence was not of the material to mould into his wife's idea of a gentleman. He was one naturally. . . . She was a foolish woman to think she could alter her husband and force him into her ways."[11] But when she realized that her rough, uneducated husband had failed to match her expectations, she ruthlessly and relentlessly made him pay for her disappointment.

In *Sons and Lovers,* a violent argument breaks out when the mother refuses to serve dinner to the hungry, exhausted miner. Lydia also regarded as humiliating and degrading the wife's traditional task of washing her husband's back when he bathed in a tin tub on Saturday night. Jonathan Chambers wrote that she never forgave him for being a common man. "She considered she had been basely betrayed; she had been lowered in her own eyes and she would punish him as she was well able to do. She had a tongue like a whiplash and laid about her with such effect that Arthur Lawrence eventually became almost a stranger in his own house."[12]

The Lawrences were known throughout the village as an unhappy couple. Lydia had no tact or patience with her husband, taunted and provoked him, treated him with icy disdain, mocked his coarse habits, condemned his drinking, refused to sleep with him and taught the children to look down on their father. An Eastwood neighbor recalled that Arthur "had to listen to them but was never allowed to tell them what was in his mind. They were not interested in his work at all. . . . He was treated more like a lodger than a father."[13] If he tried to speak he would be ordered up to bed.

Arthur's faults came from a weak rather than a malevolent character. Lawrence's novel and his autobiographical essays portray Arthur as a handsome and vital man, a loving but frightening father, at his best when working with his hands. Though he was sometimes drunk and occasionally violent, he was faithful to his wife, worked hard and held a steady job. As a character in Lawrence's story "Jimmy and the Desperate Woman" exclaims: "If I give in to the coal face, and go down the mine every day to eight hours' slavery, more or less, somebody's got to give in to me." The constant struggle for dominance in his parents' marriage (as in Lawrence's own) made children and friends nervous and uneasy. "There seemed to be a tightness in the air," Jessie noted, "as if something unusual might happen any minute. It was somehow exciting, yet it made me feel a little sick."[14]

In an unpublished autobiographical essay, "That Women Know Best," written in the late 1920s, Lawrence recalled a vivid incident in which his father threatened his mother and insisted on domination. Though frightened, Lawrence felt this male assertiveness was entirely appropriate. But his mother undermined his father's claim to authority with a characteristically caustic remark. Though men pretend to dominate, Lawrence suggested, women really rule:

> When I was a small boy, I remember my father shouting at my mother: "I'll make you tremble at the sound of my footstep!"—To me it seemed a very terrible, but still perfectly legitimate thing to say, and though I'm sure I wept, I secretly felt it was splendid and right. Women and very small children should by nature tremble at the sound of the approaching wrath of the lord and master.
>
> But alas! My mother, even though she was furious, only gave one of her peculiar amused little laughs and replied: "Which boots will you wear?"[15]

The fiercest point of contention was drink. Lydia, a teetotaler, had persuaded Arthur to take the pledge when they married. When he broke his promise, she ruined their life with moral frenzy against John Barleycorn. Ada, though extremely sympathetic to her mother, confessed that Lydia "would wait up for him, at night, her rage seething, until on his arrival it boiled over into a torrent of biting truths which turned him from his slightly fuddled and pleasantly apologetic mood into a brutal and coarse beast." Lawrence was undoubtedly thinking of his comparatively tolerant father when, at the end of *Etruscan Places*, he sympathized with the prisoner who had murdered his wife: "He had a passion for the piano: and for thirty years his wife nagged him when he played. So one day he silently and suddenly killed her. So, the nagging of thirty years [was] silenced."[16]

George Neville, Lawrence's closest childhood friend, insisted that

Arthur "was no drunken reprobate" and agreed with Willie Hopkin and Jonathan Chambers that "he was quite a bit above the average collier of that district in those days." Since Arthur was virtually driven from his own house, he naturally fled to the pubs and drank with his friends. He occasionally got drunk, but never drank on Sundays or missed work, and was certainly not a habitual drunkard.

In December 1910, a week before his mother died of cancer, Lawrence synthesized his view of his parents' marriage and anticipated the themes of *Sons and Lovers:* "My mother was a clever, ironical, delicately moulded woman, of good, old burgher descent. She married below her. My father was dark, ruddy, with a fine laugh. He is a coal miner. He was one of the sanguine temperament, warm and hearty, but unstable: he lacked principle, as my mother would have said. He deceived her and lied to her. She despised him—he drank. Their marriage has been one carnal, bloody fight." He concluded by comparing Arthur, who was deeply distressed by Lydia's illness, to a burnt-out coal: "I look at my father—he is like a cinder. It is very terrible, mis-marriage."[17]

Toward the end of his life, Lawrence adopted a more sympathetic view of his father's character, praising the defiance of conventional behavior (a striking contrast to his mother's rigid respectability) that he himself had imitated:

To the end of his days his idea of life was to escape over the fringe of virtue and drink beer and perhaps poach an occasional rabbit. . . .

He wasn't even respectable, in so far as he got drunk rather frequently, [rarely] went near a chapel, and was usually rather rude to his little immediate bosses at the pit.

He practically never had a good stall all the time he was a butty, because he was always saying tiresome and foolish things about the men just above him in control at the mine.[18]

In the late 1920s Lawrence also told his friends Rhys Davies and Achsah Brewster that he now understood and respected his father—"a piece of the gay old England that had gone"—much more than he had when he wrote *Sons and Lovers.* He thought his parents' quarrels were caused more by his mother's malicious taunts than by his father's drunkenness. He believed he had not done justice to his father, grieved over the hostile portrait and felt like rewriting the novel. He remembered:

When children they had accepted the dictum of their mother that their father was a drunkard, therefore was contemptible, but that

as Lawrence had grown older he had come to see him in a different
light; to see his unquenchable fire and relish for living. Now he
blamed his mother for her self-righteousness, her invulnerable
Christian virtue within which she was entrenched. She had
brought down terrible scenes of vituperation on their heads from
which she might have protected them. . . . She would turn to the
whimpering children and ask them if they were not disgusted with
such a father. He would look at the row of frightened children, and
say: "Never mind, my duckies, you needna be afraid of me. I'll do ye
na harm."[19]   *Nehls, p. 276*

One of Lawrence's biographers, Emile Delavenay, writes with astonishing imperception that "in the formative years of Lawrence's personality, his father's influence was either non-existent or completely
negative."[20] On the contrary, Lawrence drew equally from his parents
during childhood. From his mother he absorbed artistic sensitivity,
intellectual curiosity, ambition, perfectionism, habits of study, a work
ethic and a notion of bourgeois respectability; from his father, intuition,
vitality, zest for life, love of nature, defiance of authority, scorn for
materialism and rejection of conventional values. He married a woman
whose personality and temperament were diametrically opposed to his
mother's narrow, genteel, respectable, rigid, repressed, puritanical,
sanctimonious and self-righteous character. Throughout his adult life
Lawrence nourished and advocated the qualities inherited from his
father, just as he rejected and suppressed those traits that came from his
mother.

CHAPTER THREE

Childhood and Chapel,
1885–1898

D A V I D   H E R B E R T   L A W R E N C E , the fourth of five children, was born on Victoria Street in Eastwood on September 11, 1885. The house was small; money was limited. As he later told a friend: "My mother never wanted me to be born." He barely recovered from an attack of bronchitis when he was two weeks old and suffered from pulmonary disease for the rest of his life. At the turn of the century, the highest incidence of tuberculosis occurred among the inhabitants of industrial towns. In the Eastwood district in 1898, the largest single killers were tuberculosis and bronchitis, which accounted for seventeen percent of the deaths.[1] D. H Lawrence Handbook, p. 139

Willie Hopkin first saw Lawrence when he was only a few weeks old and struggling to maintain a precarious hold on life. When Lydia "came out on the main road with her newest baby in a three-wheeled pram with ironbound wheels, I stopped and asked how the baby was faring. She uncovered his face and I saw a puny, fragile little specimen. I could understand the doubts expressed by Mrs. Lawrence about being able to 'rear' him. Years later Lawrence said to me: 'Before I went to school I was a snuffy-nosed little beggar, seldom without a cold.'" One of Lawrence's classmates recalled that Lydia was constantly telling her son: "wipe your nose, Bert." In his "Autobiographical Sketch," Lawrence described himself as "a delicate pale brat with a snuffy nose, whom most people treated quite gently as just an ordinary delicate little lad." His oldest brother, George Arthur, said: "We all petted and spoiled him from the time he was born—my mother poured her very soul into him."[2]

George Arthur, born in 1876 and only five feet four inches tall, began
as a rebellious boy who ran away to be a soldier and ended up as a
successful engineer and Baptist lay preacher, living to the age of ninety-
one. After leaving school, he worked at the High Park Colliery and then
apprenticed himself to a picture framer in Eastwood. In 1895 he impulsively joined the army. But he was desperately unhappy as a soldier
and, after fifteen months service, was bought out by his family at the
considerable cost of £18. He then got a job in Nottingham and moved to
the city. George Arthur, whom his son called "a terrible martinet,"
quarreled with Lawrence in 1914, soon after the war had broken out.
After George Arthur had been introduced to Lawrence's German wife,
Frieda, he was carried away with patriotic fervor and exclaimed: "I
would like to go and kill some of 'them Germans.'"[3]

William Ernest, born in 1878, was ambitious and successful. He was
Lydia's favorite son and died young. He obtained a position in a London
office, earned a handsome salary and was a legendary figure in Eastwood. A good student and keen reader as a boy, he got his first job at the
local Cooperative Society. Inspired by the Protestant work ethic and by
Samuel Smiles' *Self-Help* (1864), he studied typing and shorthand in
the evenings, and worked for the Shipley Colliery and the Griffiths
Cycle Company in Coventry. During his last four years, he was employed by John Holman and Sons, Solicitors, in Lime Street, London, as
a clerk and correspondent. A stilted obituary in the *Eastwood and
Kimberley Advertiser* on October 18, 1901, stressed his ambition and
reported that "London's gaiety could not wrest from him his love for
work and his keen desire to get on, and after business hours his evenings
were spent in the study of French and German languages, a knowledge
of which he acquired sufficient to converse and write letters. To undertake so much was too much, but his large mind, his keen desire for hard
work, his ambition to make himself thoroughly fitting to fill a high post,
to get on and be useful in the world was great."[4]

Lawrence also had two sisters: Emily, born in 1882, and Ada, born in
1887. Emily, whom Enid Hilton characterized as "cold and judgmental,"
married a shopkeeper in 1904. Lawrence mildly satirized her priggish-
ness by alluding to Richardson's heroine and calling her "Pamela, or
Virtue Rewarded." He was much closer to the more intellectual and
sympathetic Ada, who taught elementary school before her marriage in
1913. Ada, who published a book about Lawrence's youth in 1931, vainly
struggled with Frieda for Lawrence's love during his lifetime and for his
money after his death. Despite some inevitable disapproval of his life

and work, both sisters worshipped the adult Lawrence: "Anything 'our Bert' said was taken as gospel."[5]

Ada complained that the family was always conscious of poverty. In Victoria Street, Lydia kept a shop — which eventually failed — where she sold baby clothes and ribbons in order to supplement her husband's income. Arthur's wages varied considerably, depending on the quality of the coal face and on whether he was allowed to work full time. But, as Jonathan Chambers (who became a professor of economic history at Nottingham University) points out, Arthur "was a highly skilled man, bringing home good money, occupying a house with a bay window and separate 'entry' of which the Lawrences were immensely proud, and handing over to his wife enough money to give three of their five children [William Ernest, David and Ada] a good education."[6] Lawrence portrayed his father's decline in *Sons and Lovers.* The family actually moved twice in four years (1887–91) — from Victoria Street to the Breach to Walker Street — and always to much better houses. They moved to their best house, in Lynn Croft, in 1908 and took family holidays from 1906 to 1909 at seaside resorts: Mablethorpe, Robin Hood's Bay and Flamborough on the Lincolnshire and Yorkshire coasts, as well as the Isle of Wight.

Eastwood consisted of a drab main street and hundreds of mean miners' dwellings. The "little four-room houses," Lawrence wrote, "with the 'front' looking outward into the grim, blank street, and the 'back,' with a tiny square brick yard, a low wall, and a w.c. and ash-pit, looking into the desert of the square," allowed no privacy. "You can hear every word the next-door people say. . . . You can see everybody in the square if they go to the w.c.!" In the Breach, the family's second dwelling and the first one Lawrence remembered, the houses were in a hollow, and the backs looked out onto drab patches of garden. Though it was hideous, Lawrence claimed to have loved it. Lynn Croft, according to Jessie Chambers, was a considerable improvement: "It was a comfortable house, comfortably furnished, and Lawrence was justly proud of his home."[7] All this substantiates Jonathan Chambers' conclusion that the Lawrences were a relatively prosperous working-class family.

Lawrence was the first English novelist to profit from the Education Act of 1870, for which W. E. Forster, a minister in Gladstone's cabinet, was largely responsible. The act gave subsidies to existing schools and established new national "board schools" that taught academic subjects and provided basic instruction in the Bible. It added five thousand schools to the English system and laid the foundation for compulsory state education.

Lawrence was sent to the Beauvale Board School, like the other local lads, at the age of three and a half. But he was soon withdrawn, perhaps because of poor health, and did not return until he was seven. Lydia taught him to read and write, and kept him at her side. Lawrence was a weak and delicate child, who could not bear harsh criticism, rough sports or physical fights. He spent most of his time playing with girls. All his teachers and schoolmates agreed that he was girlish rather than manly. He suffered from the contempt of the boys at school and from the quarrels of his parents at home.

His aggressive friend George Neville said that "he was a thin, pale, weakly lad, always scrupulously clean, neat and tidy [as his nephew William Ernest had been while living with Lydia], with no energy for our oft-times over-robust games." Albert Limb insisted that "Lawrence was weak and puny, and the most cowardly boy I ever knew. Any little boy could go and punch him, and he would not retaliate."8 A teacher recalled that he "was a brilliant boy when he was here. . . . He struck me, though, as being rather effeminate, compared with his brother." Lawrence later wrote that the schoolmaster, W. W. Whitehead, "was an excellent, irascible old man with a white beard. My mother had the greatest respect for him. I remember he flew into a rage with me because I did not want to admit my first name, which is David. 'David! David!' he raved. 'David is the name of a great and good man.'"9

In a revealing scene in *Sons and Lovers,* Lawrence portrays Paul Morel's agonizing shyness (which he never manages to overcome) when he makes his weekly visit to the colliery office to collect his father's wages. Every Friday he is forced to confront the hostile miners, who mock his timidity and resent the education that will allow him to escape their harsh life. One of Lawrence's girlfriends reports that he was equally terrified at the annual party that the colliery owner gave for the miners' children:

On Boxing Day every year, the miners' children from many miles around were invited to Lamb Close House, the home of the colliery owner, Mr. Barber, and were given one new penny and one large orange each. On one occasion Bertie dared not go forward, so I took my presents, gave them to him, and then went back for his. The butler looked at me very hard, and I was afraid he would not give me another penny and orange. My words tumbled out: "Please, I am not taking two pennies for myself. One was for Bertie Lawrence."[10]

Willie Hopkin—a radical journalist, local politician and leading figure in Eastwood intellectual life—contributed significantly to Lawrence's education by encouraging his ambitions, by stimulating conversation and by introducing him to books, ideas and people. Hopkin, whom Lawrence kept in touch with throughout his life, was born in Castle Donnington in Nottinghamshire in 1862. His father was postmaster and proprietor of a boot shop, which employed an aged craftsman, Old William, who sat in a corner and made boots by hand for miners crippled by accidents. Hopkin, interested in promising sons of miners, kept an open house on weekends and was especially fond of Lawrence.

In the opening scene of Lawrence's play *Touch and Go* (1920), Willie Houghton, who is based on Willie Hopkin, tries to arouse the miners with a stirring speech. In *Mr. Noon* (published in 1984), Lawrence sympathetically describes Lewis Goddard, also based on Willie, as "handsome, with a high forehead and a small beard, a socialist, something like Shakespeare's bust to look at, but more refined. He had an attractive, boyish nape of the neck, for a man of forty-five, no longer thin. So he crouched gazing into the hot, spurting, glowing fire. He was a pure idealist, something of a Christ, but with an intruding touch of the goat. His eyelids dropped oddly, goat-like, as he remained abstracted before the fire." Willie died on his feet, at the age of eighty-nine, while giving a lecture in 1951.

Willie's daughter, Enid, first met Lawrence at the turn of the century, when she was five and he fifteen. She remembered him as a gangling youth with a trace of down on his cheeks, a few adolescent spots and extraordinary, all-seeing eyes. Lawrence did not pay much attention to Enid at first. But he later visited her during a childhood illness and opened new worlds to her with his intellectual curiosity and his understanding of the natural world.[11]

Tragedy struck the Lawrence family in 1901. After a weekend visit in Eastwood, William Ernest returned to London and went to work. "But the following day he was too ill to get up. A doctor was sent for, and he pronounced the case hopeless. A second doctor was called in, but their skill was to no avail, deceased having contracted erysipelas [an acute infectious disease], and pneumonia afterwards set in."[12] After William Ernest's death, Lydia rooted her life in Bert and became obsessively, destructively devoted to her son.

In *Leonardo da Vinci,* Freud writes of the artist's mother: "In the manner of all ungratified mothers she thus took her little son in place of her husband, and robbed him of a part of his virility by maturing too early his erotic life." For similar reasons and with similar results, Lydia Lawrence tried to stifle in her son the sexual passion that had led to her own unhappy marriage. As May Chambers wrote: "she dreaded the years when only she and her husband were left together [in antagonistic silence], and at any cost she would fight to keep her son for herself."[13]

After portraying his parents' incompatibility in a famous letter to the Scottish poet Rachel Taylor, Lawrence went on to describe his extreme hostility to his father and abnormal attachment to his mother:

> I was born hating my father: as early as ever I can remember, I shivered with horror when he touched me. He was very bad before I was born.
>
> This has been a kind of bond between me and my mother. We have loved each other, almost with a husband and wife love, as well as filial and maternal. We knew each other by instinct. She said to my aunt—about me: "But it has been different with him. He seemed to be part of me."—and that is the real case. We have been like one, so sensitive to each other that we never needed words. It has been rather terrible, and has made me, in some respects, abnormal.[14]

But no one is born hating his father. Lawrence was *taught* by his mother to hate and fear his father, who was "bad" before he was born because their fourth child was unwanted. In *Sons and Lovers,* Lawrence describes how his hungry, frustrated and drunken father flung a table drawer at his pregnant mother and cut her forehead while the unborn baby, baptized by his mother's blood, boiled inside her; how the father then pushed the mother into the cold walled garden and locked her out of the house. Lydia complained bitterly about this as soon as her youngest and last remaining son could understand such cruel and potentially dangerous treatment. He was trained to loathe "the smell of pit dirt and his father's crude habits, which were gradually cultivated to annoy his 'superior' children." He told Jessie Chambers, in a tone of deep chagrin, "'I've never really had a father.'" His father existed; but he was denied, virtually destroyed by his mother, and Lawrence confessed: "'I have to hate him for Mother's sake.'"[15] Though Lawrence was in some respects abnormal, his mother's cultivation of the feminine side of his personality gave him an astonishing insight into women and enabled him to create a brilliant series of female characters.

After his parents, the greatest influence in Lawrence's youth was the Congregational Church. Lydia had been brought up as a Methodist. But both she and Lawrence criticized the crude, emotional revival meetings of Primitive Methodism and were attracted to the more austere, intellectual aspects of Congregationalism. In the essay "Hymns in a Man's Life," Lawrence emphasized the difference between his stable, respectable institution and the more militant, fanatical Dissenters from the Church of England: "The Primitive Methodists, when I was a boy, were always having 'revivals' and being 'saved,' and I always had a horror of being saved.... The Congregationalists are the oldest Nonconformists, descendants of the Oliver Cromwell Independents [during the seventeenth century]. They still had the Puritan tradition of no ritual. But they avoided the personal emotionalism which one found among the Methodists when I was a boy."[16]

Lawrence belonged to the great Nonconformist tradition of radical outsiders: Milton, Bunyan, Defoe, Blake, Burns and Browning. Milton, Defoe and Browning were Congregationalists, as was the hymn writer Isaac Watts—and Ernest Hemingway, whose parents were pillars of the Oak Park, Illinois, church. Congregationalism has traditionally occupied a central position between Presbyterianism and the more radical Protestants, like the liberal Baptists and the Quakers. It has characteristically stressed the right and responsibility of each congregation to make its own decisions, without submitting them to the judgment of a higher human authority. Its emphasis on freedom of conscience, on religious and civil liberty, evolved from its Protestant conviction about the sovereignty of God and the priesthood of all believers. It is consistently middle class in membership and ideology, democratic in organization, liberal in politics and individualistic in social conscience. Congregationalism places particular importance on preaching and the primacy of Scripture. It shared in the prosperity of the church in the Victorian era and played a prominent part in the cultural and educational life of provincial cities. In *The Lost Girl* (1920), Lawrence portrays the social and intellectual aspects of the church and writes of the heroine: "every Thursday evening she went to the subscription library to change the week's supply of books, and there again she met friends and acquaintances. It is hard to overestimate the value of church or chapel— but particularly chapel—as a *social* institution, in places like Woodhouse. The Congregational Chapel provided Alvina with a whole outer life, lacking which she would have been poor indeed."[17]

As a boy, on the Sabbath, Lawrence went to Sunday school as well as morning and evening service at the Congregational Chapel. The Scottish Reverend Robert Reid, a much admired friend of Mrs. Lawrence, was minister in Eastwood from 1897 to 1911. Even as an adult Lawrence was inspired by the inscription on the wall from I Chronicles 16:29: "Worship the Lord in the beauty of Holiness" and knew every word of all the verses of the Salvation Army tunes and the Moody and Sankey revival songs. "From early childhood," Lawrence wrote, "I have been familiar with Apocalyptic language and Apocalyptic image: not because I spent my time reading Revelation, but because I was sent to Sunday School and to Chapel, to the Band of Hope [a temperance union] and to Christian Endeavour [a youth movement that encouraged service in the local church], and was always having the Bible read at me or to me."[18]

By 1901, when he was sixteen, Lawrence had rejected the Christian dogma and reacted violently against religion. He felt that the meek and mild doctrines of Christianity had somehow emasculated the passive sons of Eastwood, and was intellectually repelled by the blood-soaked language of salvation, which he particularly associated with the Methodists:

From earliest years right into manhood, like any other nonconformist child I had the Bible poured every day into my helpless consciousness. . . . These "portions" of the Bible were *douched* over the mind and consciousness, till they became soaked in, they became an influence which affected all the processes of emotion and thought. . . .

The board-school, the Sunday-school, the Band of Hope and, above all, their mothers, got them under. Got them under, made them tame. . . .

Brought up a nonconformist as I was, I just was never able to understand the language of salvation. . . . Washed in the Blood of the Lamb! always seemed to me an extremely unpleasant suggestion. And when Jerome says: He who has once washed in the blood of Jesus need never wash again!—I feel like taking a hot bath at once, to wash off even the suggestion.[19]

The clergymen in his stories—Mr. Massy in "Daughters of the Vicar" and Arthur Saywell in *The Virgin and the Gipsy*—are uniformly loathsome. In "Fanny and Annie," he quotes a hymn and then satirizes its falsity:

> Come, ye thankful people, come,
> Raise the song of harvest-home.
> All is safely gathered in
> Ere the winter storms begin—.

"Even the hymn was a falsehood, as the season had been wet, and half the crops were still out, and in a poor way."

In *The Plumed Serpent* (1926), the Moody and Sankey hymn No. 499 is adopted for the barbaric Aztec rituals that replace Christianity in the lives of the regenerated Indians.

> Someone will enter the pearly gate,
>   By-and-by, by-and-by,
> Taste of the glories that there await.
>   Shall you? Shall I? . . .
> Someone will knock when the door is shut,
>   By-and-by, by-and-by,
> Hear a voice saying: I know you not.
>   Shall you? Shall I?

becomes, in Lawrence's pagan novel:

> Someone will enter between the gates,
>   Now, at this moment, Ay!
> See the light on the man that waits.
>   Shall you? Shall I? . . .
> Someone will knock when the door is shut.
>   Ay! in a moment, Ay!
> Hear a voice saying: I know you not!
>   Shall you! Shall I![20]

Yet the influence of Congregationalism on Lawrence was ultimately positive and encouraged his most characteristic qualities: individualism, enthusiasm, a sense of responsibility and a self-confident, didactic, prophetic and crusading spirit. In a valuable essay, Whigham Price summarized this profound influence as "a deeply-ingrained puritanism"; "an inheritance of intensity"; "a sturdy independence of conviction and action"; "a reiterated desire to collect round him a few like-minded friends and, with them, to form a little community which should order its life, both personal and corporate, on the basis of commonly-received insights"; "an idea of the 'gathered church,' whose members have been called 'out of the world' in order to bring salvation to it."[21]

The legacy of Lawrence's childhood was poor health, which led to a lifelong invalidism; a dominant mother, who crippled his emotional life; and an omnipresent chapel, which provoked strong hostility to religion. But poor health made him value time and use every moment of the day; his mother's love gave him enormous strength and self-confidence; and the chapel made him thoroughly familiar with the Bible, whose language and rhythms enriched his prose.

CHAPTER FOUR

Nottingham,
1898–1908

I N 1 8 9 8 , when he was nearly thirteen, Lawrence completed his education at the Beauvale Board School in Eastwood. Most of his classmates went into the mines. But he had been coached for a County Council scholarship by the irascible headmaster, W. W. Whitehead, and was the first boy from the school to win an annual grant of £12, which paid his tuition fees (three guineas a term) and railway fares to Nottingham High School. Lydia still had to scrimp to buy his clothes, boots and meals.

At the end of the nineteenth century Nottingham was a grim industrial town, dominated by the lace and hosiery factories that employed about half the working men, women and children. The city was also developing its new cultural centers, including the high school and the university. The largest library in the town was in the Mechanics Institute, which provided adult education for workers who wanted to improve their minds and advance their careers. The Castle housed the beginnings of a museum and art gallery. The principal local holiday was the Goose Fair, more for pleasure than trade, which took place in October, lasted nearly a week and offered clowns, hurdy-gurdy girls, dancing bears, theatrical groups, showmen and waxworks.[1]

Despite occasional diversions, Nottingham was a dreary place. It was intensely religious and had a rigid social hierarchy: landed gentry, mine and mill owners, professionals, tradesmen and a huge working class, who toiled long hours in the factories and lived in slums that horrified Lawrence. The people of Nottingham, like those in most provincial

Victorian cities, worked hard, went to bed early and did not have much money to spend. There was almost no leisure class; and social life took place in the local pub or chapel, rather than in the center of town. In 1922 T. E. Lawrence emphasized the sabbatarian nature of the city: "Nottingham is one of those 'Sunday' places—the market square deserted: dust and fog blowing unchecked along the empty streets. The crowds were going to a Wesleyan Mission."

Graham Greene, who worked there as a journalist in 1926, captured in *A Gun for Sale* (1936) the characteristic atmosphere—the coal miners awakened at dawn, the Bibles for sale in the shops, the dark, oppressive industrialism as well as the slow provinciality and pervasive seediness of the ugly Victorian city:

> The first tram crawled out of its shed and took the steel track down towards the market. An old piece of newspaper blew up against the door of the Royal Theatre and flattened out. In the streets on the outskirts of [town] nearest the pits an old man plodded by with a pole tapping at the windows. The stationer's window in the High Street was full of Prayer Books and Bibles.... Along the line a signal lamp winked green in the dark day and the lit carriages drew slowly in past the cemetery, the glue factory, over the wide tidy cement-lined river.... Nottwich went to bed early; the cinemas closed at ten-thirty and a quarter of an hour later everyone had left the middle of Nottwich by tram or bus. Nottwich's only tart hung round the market place, cold and blue under her umbrella, and one or two businessmen were having a last cigar in the hall of the Metropole.[2]

The headmaster of Nottingham High School, Reverend James Gow (1854–1923), was a distinguished scholar who had earned his degree at Trinity College, Cambridge and, after sixteen years in Nottingham, became headmaster of the famous Westminster School in London. Gow's son and Lawrence's classmate, Andrew, also had an impressive academic career. He left Nottingham for Rugby School in 1901—the year Lawrence graduated and Gow's father went to Westminster—took a degree at Trinity, became a master at Eton, where he taught George Orwell, and then a fellow of Trinity, where he was the close friend and biographer of A. E. Housman.

D. J. Peters has provided detailed information about Lawrence's teachers, curriculum and class standing. When Lawrence entered, in

1898, the buildings on Arboretum Street were only thirty years old, though the school had been founded as early as 1513. There were twenty masters (eight of them Cambridge men), including a music teacher and a drill sergeant. The 381 boys attended classes from 9:00 to 12:45 and from 2:30 to 4:15, except for Wednesday and Saturday half holidays. Lawrence joined Mr. Crofts' Lower Modern Fourth, which had thirty-nine middle-class Nottingham boys, many of whom went on to Oxford and Cambridge. Lawrence, the only coal miner's son, instinctively recoiled from the class of bourgeois boys. He had to commute by train from Eastwood, left home at seven in the morning and returned at seven at night, and had many lessons to prepare for the following day.

Lawrence did well in his first year and placed fifth in his form. He was third in English and drawing, fourth in German and tenth in French. That year he studied the Acts of the Apostles, Shakespeare's *Richard II*, English history from 1689 to 1783 and a d'Artagnan novel by Dumas. In his second year he read *As You Like It*, English history from James I to Charles II, Mérimée's *Colomba* and the German heroic sagas. He also took more practical subjects and learned shorthand, précis writing, bookkeeping, commercial geography and commercial correspondence. In his final year he studied the Gospel of St. Matthew, English history from the beginnings to 1702, the development of the English language and the medieval German poems of Walther von der Vogelweide. Clearly losing interest, motivation and perhaps self-confidence by the end of his school years, Lawrence finished fifteenth out of nineteen boys. Peters concluded that Lawrence's "stay there had been brief, his career had been quiet and undistinguished."[3] But, as his university scholarship examination and later career revealed, he had been taught well and had learned a great deal.

School was not easy for Lawrence. He had to work hard, and was often ill and exhausted from traveling. His friend George Neville noted that "even in those days Lawrence had that little, troublesome, hacking cough that used to bring his left hand sharply to his mouth." And Lawrence's nephew, who was nine years younger than his uncle, vividly recalled that when Lawrence felt tearful and despondent, Lydia would strengthen and encourage him:

When grandmother was coaching him, helping him with his home-work to take back to Nottingham High School, he used to cry and cry; he couldn't do it. "I can't do it, mother. I cannot do it." "Now Bertie, my dear boy, you can. Now you have some more of this grapefruit".... She used to prepare grapefruit, and the yolk of an egg—oh, he mustn't have the white, poor Bertie wasn't strong enough.... She carried him through; he got through his homework and she'd recite it with him. Without her help I doubt whether he'd have done it.[4]

When Lawrence finished high school he was sixteen years old, had no money to continue his education and was forced to seek menial employment. Advised by his experienced older brother, William Ernest, who was home for Goose Fair in Nottingham, Lawrence scanned the local newspapers for job advertisements and applied—in proper business language—to J. H. Haywood and Sons, founded in 1830, manufacturers of surgical appliances and artificial limbs.

In his first letter, possibly drafted or even written by William Ernest, the latter-day rebel claimed a knowledge of French, German, bookkeeping and mathematics; offered to furnish references of his character and ability from his teachers and his minister, Robert Reid; and closed with a formal promise: "Should you favour me with the appointment I would always endeavour to merit the confidence you place in me."[5] Accompanied by his mother and interviewed by Mr. Haywood, Lawrence secured the position at thirteen shillings a week, or less than £34 a year. He worked six days a week from eight in the morning until eight at night—excluding traveling time—with two hours less on Thursday and Friday evenings, and was rewarded for his labors with little more than tuppence an hour. This job fulfilled his mother's common, understandable but limited ambition for her working-class son: a safe, clean position—away from the factories and mines.

Haywood's was on a street in the industrial quarter of town, "gloomy and old-fashioned, having low dark shops and dark green house doors with brass knockers, and yellow-ochred doorsteps projecting on to the pavement; then another old shop whose small window looked like a cunning, half-shut eye." At Haywood's, which he portrayed as Jordan's in *Sons and Lovers*, Lawrence sorted the mail, carried new orders to the workshop, drew up invoices, tied parcels and copied letters (sometimes in French and German) below the drawings of elastic stockings and wooden legs on the company letterhead. "The employment of large numbers of females," noted a local historian, "endowed the women of the town with greater independence of spirit as well as economic freedom." The characteristically bawdy and aggressive mood of the spirited factory girls, deprived of male companionship and compensating for the

long, boring hours of repetitive work, provoked an extremely unpleasant and potentially humiliating incident. The girls—who probably resented Lawrence's clean hands and bit of French—attacked and
attempted to undress the priggish and sexually innocent young man:

> As he passed through [the warehouse], a number of girls rushed
> upon him, seized him, threw him down, and attempted to commit
> upon him the Great Indignity.
>
> I think those girls got the shock of their lives. They had the
> initial advantage of surprise, but I am certain that they would be
> utterly astonished when Lawrence got fairly started. Though only
> slim, he was tall and wiry, with very long arms and fingers, and in a
> rage he could be a very demon. I gathered that he had set about
> those girls with teeth, hoof and claw; that he had torn their dresses,
> bitten their fingers and arms, scratched their faces, kicked them,
> and finally driven them off, afraid of the fury they had aroused.[6]

Lawrence later used this incident in "Tickets, Please," when the tram
girls vengefully beat and symbolically rape the handsome but passive
inspector, John Thomas, who had played the field and broken their
hearts.

About two months after William Ernest's sudden death, while his
mother was still grieving for her older son, the younger came down with
a serious case of pneumonia that damaged his health for life. George
Neville linked this illness to the attack by the factory girls. Lawrence's
wife, Frieda, later reported "how desperately ill he had been at sixteen,
with inflammation of the lungs, how he was almost dead but fought his
way back to life with the fierce courage and vitality that was his."
Lawrence was nursed back to health by Lydia, who saved him as she had
failed to save William Ernest, and bound him even more closely to her.
In April 1902 Lawrence spent a month at a "select boarding house," run
by his maternal aunt, in Skegness on the Lincolnshire coast. Fifty years
later, his girlfriend Helen Corke remembered him saying: "If I wanted a
woman to fall in love with me I'd take her to Lincolnshire. The great
emptiness and loneliness must drive people together."[7]

After Lawrence and Lydia had decided he was not well enough to
return to the factory in Nottingham, he turned to teaching (her sometime profession), which in those days was the intelligent child's classic
escape route from manual labor. The Education Act of 1902, continuing
the achievements of the 1870 act, reorganized the English elementary

schools, expanded secondary education, and provided more training and jobs for new teachers. The pupil teacher system, which had started in 1846, provided small stipends for apprentices who taught in the lower forms and were themselves instructed by the head of the school.

After three and a half years of traveling to Nottingham, Lawrence assumed a position of both subservience (an apprentice teacher) and authority (the master of his class) in the grim atmosphere of his native village. Recommended by Reverend Reid, he became a pupil teacher at the British School in Eastwood, adjoining the Congregational Chapel, for four long academic years: October 1902 until July 1906. His sister Ada taught on the girls' side in the same school. In autobiographical notes written for a French publisher in 1928, Lawrence recalled his poor salary, his lack of ambition and his hatred of schoolteaching: "Taught in a rough & fierce elementary school of mining boys: salary, first year, £5 [one seventh of what he had earned at Haywood's]—second year £10— third year £15 (from age of 17 to 21). . . . You had to be clever & rise in the world, step by step.—D. H. however [unlike William Ernest] recoiled away from the world, hated its ladder, & refused to rise. . . . So he wrote for [Jessie Chambers]—still without any idea of becoming a literary man at all—looked on himself as just a school-teacher—& mostly hated school-teaching." A younger fellow pupil was rather more positive about Lawrence's enthusiasm and knowledge: "Lawrence never seemed to be cut out for a teacher at all. . . . He was very quick-tempered and erratic, and when he was annoyed with his class his face used to colour up very quickly. [But] as a teacher he was very good, seemed very well read, and knew something about everything."[8]

The young, idealistic, inexperienced Lawrence had a difficult time controlling the fifty savage children, disliked having to beat the blubbering boys and felt drained by the effort of forcing his pupils to learn. His portrayal of Ursula Brangwen teaching at St. Philip's School in chapter 13 of *The Rainbow* reflects his experiences at the British School. Ursula's school is a form of hell, and she is exhausted and overwhelmed by the claustrophobic atmosphere, by

the horrid feeling of being shut in a rigid, inflexible air, away from all feeling of the ordinary day. . . . The school squatted low within its railed, asphalt yard, that shone bleak with rain. The building was grimy, and horrible, dry plants were shadowily looking through the windows. . . . It made her sick. She felt that she must go out of this school, this torture-place. . . . The teaching hours were

too long, the tasks too heavy, and the disciplinary condition of the
school too unnatural for her. . . . It was agony to the impulsive,
bright girl of seventeen to become distant and official, having no
personal relationship with the children. . . . [And] the children
were simply awful. You've got to *make* them do everything. Everything, everything has got to come out of you. Whatever they learn,
you've got to force it into them—and that's how it is.[9]

During his third year at the British School, Lawrence also attended
the Pupil-Teacher Centre in Ilkeston, four miles south, across the
Erewash River, in Derbyshire. The principal, Thomas Beacroft, was the
model of the tyrannical Mr. Harby in *The Rainbow*, "a short, sturdy
man, with a fine head, and a heavy jowl. . . . There was something
insulting in the way he could be so actively unaware of another person,
so occupied." Lawrence's fellow pupils at the Centre included his sister
Ada and his closest friends: Jessie Chambers, George Neville and Louisa
Burrows. Other classmates found Lawrence unattractive, unhealthy
and impatient: "He wasn't a good-looking man. He was pale and worn
looking. . . . He wasn't very prepossessing in appearance. He looked
weedy. . . . He hadn't much patience at all, and if [the boys] defied him,
that did it. He couldn't stand that"[10]—and would lose his temper when
contradicted or opposed.

While teaching at Eastwood and studying at Ilkeston, Lawrence was
coached by Thomas Beacroft, and in December 1904 he took the examination for a King's Scholarship, which would pay his university tuition
fees. He did exceptionally well, placing in the First Division of the First
Class, among the first eleven candidates in the whole of England. Interviewed by the local newspaper on March 10, 1905, when the results were
announced, Lawrence listed his solitary recreations, which he pursued
throughout his life, as "reading, walking in the [nearby] country,
sketching, and painting."

Lawrence had earned a very low salary during his first three apprentice years at the British School and did not have enough money to pay his
university expenses. So he taught for one final year in Eastwood, pro-
gressed from pupil teacher to uncertified teacher and earned the considerably higher salary of £65 a year. Though he disliked teaching, he
worked hard and did as well in the classroom as in the examination.
When Lawrence left the school, he received an excellent reference from
his headmaster, George Holderness, who perspicaciously wrote: "I have
been in charge of these schools 28 years, and during that period we have

had many teachers, but in my opinion, none of greater promise than Mr. Lawrence."[11]

In September 1906 Lawrence entered the university and began a two-year course of study for a Teacher's Certificate, rather than a three-year course leading to a B.A., because he did not have the necessary qualification in Latin. In 1881, when University College, Nottingham, was founded, there were only nine other universities in England: Oxford, Cambridge, London, Durham, Manchester, Newcastle, Birmingham, Leeds and Bristol. The president of University College from 1903 to 1943, which included Lawrence's years as a student, was the sixth Duke of Portland, the half brother of Lady Ottoline Morrell, who later became Lawrence's close friend.

Lawrence's course in the Principles of Teaching included "elementary psychology; the elements of logic; the influence of school education on character; school organization; methods of teaching elementary school subjects; hygiene; and leading ideas and movements in elementary education in England since 1839." In English he studied Spenser's *The Faerie Queene,* Shakespeare's *A Midsummer Night's Dream* and *Macbeth,* Bacon's essays, Milton's "Comus," "Lycidas," "Arcades" and "Areopagitica," *The Memoirs of Colonel Hutchinson* (a historical work with strong local interest, written by Hutchinson's wife, Lucy, in about 1664 and first published in 1806), Macaulay's essays and Charles Kingsley's *Westward Ho!* (1855). He read Daudet, Loti, Balzac, Flaubert and Maupassant in French, and concentrated on English history from the reign of Henry VII (1485–1509) to Oliver Cromwell. His two favorite subjects were music, which was mostly singing, and botany, which "dealt with the structure and life-history of flowering plants, with special reference to reproduction, nutrition and adaptation to surroundings." At the end of his course, Lawrence won distinctions in mathematics, geography, history, French and botany, but not in education and English.[12]

Lawrence, who at twenty-one was several years older than most of the other students, was acutely disappointed in his teachers, disliked the petty restrictions and repressive atmosphere, resented the fact that the engineers looked down on the schoolteachers, and made no significant friendships. His attitude toward most of the college staff varied from amused mockery to cynical tolerance. Though he had published a story and was working on *The White Peacock,* his literary efforts were not well received. When he handed in his first English essay, on "Autumn," the teacher interpreted his striking opening as an impertinent attempt to attract attention, and "the essay was heavily scored in red ink with corrections, emendations and exhortations in the best manner of an elderly schoolmistress putting a forward youth in his place." He offered his early poem "Study" to the Nottingham University *Magazine,* but they rejected it. He also despised the fake heartiness and the mealy-mouthed puritan attitude toward sex, which he would oppose throughout his life and which was exemplified by Amos Henderson, the professor of education. Jessie Chambers overheard Lawrence maliciously telling her brother Alan "how this professor would go to no end of trouble to get the men students together away from the girls in order to talk to them 'as man to man.' Then all he could do was to stand up in front of them looking uncomfortable, making vague allusions, and beating about the bush, never succeeding in coming to his point." The one exception to Lawrence's contempt was Ernest Weekley, professor of modern languages. Lawrence admired his style and *savoir faire,* and became his prize pupil. "He's my favourite Prof.," Lawrence told Jessie. "He really *is* a gentleman. He's quite elegant. He leans back in his chair and points to the blackboard, too elegant to get on his feet. And he addresses us as 'gentlemen.' He's sarcastic, of course."[13]

Lawrence also disliked the curriculum and philosophy of his practice teaching in Nottingham, and anticipated Mellors' ideas in *Lady Chatterley's Lover* by telling Jessie: "It's vile, absolute ruin of their spontaneous expression.... What they ought to do is recreational work. Teach the adolescents to sing and dance and do gymnastics, and make things they enjoy making. It's a crime to expect lads to do sums at night after a day in the pit." Lawrence, by now more interested in his writing than his studies, felt the whole experience was a waste of time and told Jessie that "if he had known what College was like he would never have made the sacrifice of those two years and all the expense, but would have qualified in the same way that [she] did"[14]—by taking the external certificate examination.

In a letter of May 4, 1908, written just before he completed his course, he told Blanche Jennings, an ardent Socialist and suffragette who worked in the Liverpool post office, that the intellectually inferior university had diminished his respect for teachers and intensified his iconoclastic tendencies: "College gave me nothing, even nothing to do—I had a damnable time there, bitten so deep with disappointment that I have lost forever my sincere boyish reverence [absorbed from Lydia] for men in position. Professors and the rest of great men I found were quite small men." He was even more severe in *The Rainbow* when portraying

Ursula's sharp descent from naive idealism to harsh disillusionment with the pragmatic Midlands materialism of the university:

> She would not consider the professors as men, ordinary men who ate bacon, and pulled on their boots before coming to college. They were the black-gowned priests of knowledge, serving for ever in a remote, hushed temple.
>
> The life [soon] went out of her studies.... The whole thing seemed sham, spurious; spurious Gothic arches, spurious peace, spurious Latinity, spurious dignity of France, spurious naiveté of Chaucer. It was a second-hand dealer's shop, and one bought an equipment for an examination. This was only a little side-show to the factories of the town.... [There was] no perception of pure learning. It was a little apprentice-shop where one was further equipped for making money.[15]

Lawrence, who became an eternal wanderer and violently rejected the materialism, stability and social conventions of the middle class, always refused to acquire property, settle down and become respectable.

The historian of the university, A. C. Wood, regretfully summarized Lawrence's negative response to both students and teachers: "Lawrence himself was not kindly disposed towards his old college. He complained that there was nothing adult about life in it. The students, at least in the training department, were wrapped in an atmosphere of repression and treated like 'school kids.'... From his tutors he 'got nothing,' and made no real contact with any of them. [Amos] Henderson, his professor, he regarded as a well-meaning but timid ineffective individual.... Altogether the novelist's college career was a period of disappointment and disillusionment."

Despite his dissatisfaction, Lawrence performed as diligently in Nottingham as he had in Eastwood, and received a shrewd recommendation from the Teachers' Training Department:

> Well-read, scholarly and refined, Mr. Lawrence will make an excellent teacher if he gets into the right place. His work at present is uneven according to the ordinary standard owing to his lack of experience.... He would be quite unsuitable for a large class of boys in a rough district; he would not have sufficient persistence and enthusiasm but would become disgusted.... Like many intelligent teachers, Mr. Lawrence tends to teach the best pupils ex-

clusively.... He is emphatically a teacher of upper classes. Mr. Lawrence is fastidious in taste, and while working splendidly at anything that interests him would perhaps easily tire amid the tedium and discouragements of the average classroom.[16]

Despite the good advice in this recommendation Lawrence, unsuited to a large class of lower-form boys in a rough district, got into the wrong place and soon became disgusted with his new job in the south London suburb of Croydon.

Lawrence was eventually able to make his peace with Eastwood. In 1918 he wrote: "For the first time in my life I feel quite amiably towards it — I have always hated it. Now I don't." But he never revised his opinion of Nottingham. Two years later he was still fulminating against "cursed, cursed Nottingham, gutsless, spineless, brainless Nottingham, how I hate thee!"[17]

CHAPTER FIVE

Jessie,
1896–1910

IN 1896, when Lawrence was a student in Eastwood, he formed a close friendship with Jessie Chambers. This intimate and influential relationship, which lasted, through his high school and college years, until their traumatic break in 1910, was—with the death of his mother, the marriage to Frieda, the suppression of *The Rainbow,* the expulsion from Cornwall, the hemorrhage in Mexico and the publication of *Lady Chatterley's Lover*—one of the most significant experiences in his life.

Jessie, born in 1887 and two years younger than Lawrence, lived with her family at Haggs Farm, about four miles from Eastwood. She was the model for Emily in *The White Peacock* and Miriam in *Sons and Lovers.* Lawrence also formed an intense friendship with Jessie's older brother, Alan, the model for George Saxton in *The White Peacock.* And he was particularly fond of Jessie's father, Edmund, an idealized version of Lawrence's own father, "a man of considerable physical strength and of fearless courage, quick to answer a challenge." Lawrence later distanced himself from his family and wittily remarked: "I am really not 'our Bert.' Come to that, I never was." But late in life, when living in France, he got in touch with Jonathan Chambers, Jessie's younger brother, and wrote a moving letter about his still vivid memories of the idyllic family and farm that revitalized him and allowed him to escape from the domestic dissensions and pervasive ugliness of Eastwood:

Whatever I forget, I shall never forget the Haggs—I loved it so. I loved to come to you all, it really was a new life began in me there.

The water-pippin by the door—those maiden-blush roses that Flower would lean over and eat and trip floundering round.—And stewed figs for tea in winter, and in August green stewed apples. Do you still have them? Tell your mother I never forget, no matter where life carries us.—And does she still blush if somebody comes and finds her in a dirty white apron? Or doesn't she wear work-aprons any more? Oh, I'd love to be nineteen again, and coming up through the Warren and catching the first glimpse of the buildings. Then I'd sit on the sofa under the window, and we'd crowd round the little table to tea, in that tiny little kitchen I was so home in. . . .

I could never tell you in English how much it all meant to me, how I still feel about it.

If there is anything I can ever do for you, do tell me.—Because whatever else I am, I am somewhere still the same Bert who rushed with such joy to the Haggs.[1]

Jessie, attractive and vivacious like all Lawrence's girlfriends, had dark, curly hair and large eyes, a bold nose, wide mouth, firm chin and well-developed figure. Lawrence describes her appearance at the time they first met in *Sons and Lovers:* "She was about fourteen years old, had a rosy dark face, a bunch of short black curls, very fine and free, and dark eyes; shy, questioning, a little resentful of the strangers. . . . Her beauty—that of a shy, wild, quiveringly sensitive thing—seemed nothing to her." Helen Corke, who was also in love with Jessie, speaks of "the low tones of her voice, her reflective manner, and her dark, innate warmth."[2]

Lawrence was a frequent and always welcome visitor. He worked in the fields with the entire family, stimulated the father, helped the mother, befriended the brothers and educated Jessie. Mr. Chambers said: "Work goes like fun when Bert's there, it's no trouble at all to keep them going." Jonathan wrote that "he lit up our life at the Haggs with his own inextinguishable vitality." Jessie agreed that "no task seemed dull or monotonous to him. He brought such vitality to the doing that he transformed it into something creative." She praised Lawrence's sensitivity, charm, vulnerability and delicacy of spirit, and emphasized his quintessential traits—liveliness, understanding of nature, enthusiasm, spontaneity: "He was always to me a symbol of overflowing life . . . . With wild things . . . he was in primal sympathy—a living vibration passed between him and them. . . . In our home his name was a synonym for joy—radiant joy in simply being alive. He communicated that joy to all of us, and made us even happy with one another while he was there—no small achievement in a family like ours!"[3]

When Lawrence first met Jessie, who had been forced to leave school at the age of ten, she was humiliated by her lack of education and discontented with her role as family drudge. Jessie, the first of many people Lawrence taught, was, in contrast to the rough boys in his classes, a highly motivated and ideal recipient of his effective tuition in mathematics and French. Though he was sometimes short-tempered and even cruel, she was extremely grateful. Lawrence dreamed of communal life in an extended family—the earliest version of his plans for Rananim, his Utopian community—and told Jessie: "I should like to have a big house—you know there are some lovely old houses in the Park with gardens and terraces. Wouldn't it be fine if we could live in one of those houses, mother and all the people we like together? Wouldn't it be fine!"[4]

In October 1907, during his second year at university, Lawrence, who liked to collaborate on literary works, organized his first communal effort. He wrote three stories for the *Nottingham Guardian* Christmas competition and suggested that he, Jessie and Louie Burrows each submit one. Lawrence sent in "A Fragment of Stained Glass," Louie "The White Stocking" and Jessie the sentimental tale "A Prelude." The last story won the competition and was published in the newspaper under her name.

Lawrence had two problems with Jessie: their sexual relations and his mother. Both Lawrence and Jessie were brought up under a stern puritan code in which sex was anathema. Her mother used to shudder whenever that subject was mentioned. Jessie never showed any physical desire for Lawrence and was horrified by the idea of sleeping with him before marriage. Lawrence, equally afraid of sex and emotionally crippled by an abnormal attachment to his mother, was unable in youth to establish satisfactory relations with a woman. He therefore protected himself and masked his own insecurity by spiritualizing Jessie and refusing to permit or perceive the expression of her natural feelings. "I could feel at times the bitter struggle he had with himself to maintain his position of aloofness," Jessie wrote, and quoted his cruel criticism: "You have no sexual attraction at all, none whatever." "I was Psyche, I was the soul," she added, "and I had no other significance for him." It was impossible for the young girl, forced into this role by the social code and by Lawrence himself, to gainsay her mentor and proclaim her sexual passion. Lawrence's defensive denials allowed him not only to avoid potentially disastrous physical encounters, but also to blame Jessie for their failures. "I could not help feeling," she concluded, "that the whole question of sex had for him the fascination of horror, and also that in his repudiation of any possibility of a sex relation between us he felt that he had paid me a deep and subtle compliment."[5]

Lydia, who recognized that Jessie's intuitive understanding, girlish adoration and selfless love offered Lawrence even more than her own devotion could supply, felt jealous of and threatened by her younger rival. But Jessie's "spiritual" qualities had elevated her, as they had elevated Lydia, above commonplace carnality. To sleep with Jessie would be to desecrate his mother.

Lawrence had some understanding of this problem, but remained paralyzed by Lydia's emotional oppression. "You know," he told Jessie, "I've always loved mother. . . . I've *loved* her, like a lover. That's why I could never love you." And claiming the role of innocent victim, he confessed: "They tore me from [Jessie], the love of my life. . . . It was the slaughter of the foetus in the womb." Lawrence continued to resist Jessie's emotional claims, even after his mother's death, in December 1910. Jessie felt he was being strangled by a bond that had become more powerful and more morbid. Portraying his mother as a vengeful specter, Lawrence told Louie Burrows: "you know, my mother has been passionately fond of me, and fiercely jealous. She hated J.—and would have risen from the grave to prevent my marrying her."[6] If Lydia had helped to destroy Lawrence's relation with Jessie while she was alive, her death divided them permanently. Lawrence was devoted to her memory and could not defy her wishes.

Lawrence's sexual attitudes were ambivalent, his behavior contradictory. He wanted to sleep with Jessie but could not bring himself to do so, and he blamed her for his own denial of the body. In his first novel, *The White Peacock* (1911), he described his psychological conflicts and sexual ambivalence, and illuminated his attitude toward Jessie by writing of his ambivalent virginal heroines: "A woman is so ready to disclaim the body of a man's love; she yields him her own soft beauty with so much gentle patience and regret; she clings to his neck, to his head and his cheeks, fondling them for the soul's meaning that is there, and shrinking from his passionate limbs and his body." But late in life he shrewdly admitted: "when I was a very young man I was enraged when with a woman, if I was reminded of her sexual actuality. I only wanted to be aware of her personality, her mind and spirit. The other had to be fiercely shut out."[7]

Unable to resolve this crucial conflict, Lawrence first stifled Jessie's sexual feelings, then tried to arouse them. In a letter of January 1908, he rigidly categorized and bluntly rejected Jessie, who was then twenty years old: "you are a nun, I give you what I would give a holy nun. So you must let me marry a woman I can kiss and embrace and make the mother of my children." But two years later, assuming the role of sophisticated lover and writing from Croydon to Blanche Jennings, with whom he liked to discuss his volatile love affairs, he described his relations with Jessie: their mutual attraction, intuitive understanding, anguished separations, emotional upheavals and intimate embraces as well as her pathetic vulnerability and dependence:

> It is the old girl, who has been attached to me so long. . . . She knows me through and through, and I know her—and—the devil of it is, she's a hundred and fifty miles away. We have fine, mad little scenes now and again, she and I—so strange, after ten years, and I had hardly kissed her all that time. She has black hair, and wonderful eyes, big and very dark, and very vulnerable; she lifts up her face to me and clings to me, and the time goes like a falling star, swallowed up immediately.[8]

Lawrence's sexual impasse with Jessie was finally broken by an Eastwood radical, Alice Dax. Born in Liverpool in 1878, she worked in the post office with Blanche Jennings and shared her enthusiasm for militant socialism and suffragism. She married a pharmacist, Henry Dax, in 1905 and moved to Nottinghamshire, where she became a keen social reformer and took an active part in the local Nursing Association and the Congregational Literary Society. She was a close friend of Willie Hopkin's wife, Sallie, who introduced Alice, then estranged from her husband, to Lawrence. Sallie's daughter, Enid, recalled that Alice's defiance of social convention and espousal of radical ideas frightened her male contemporaries: "Alice Dax was one of the kindest persons I have ever met, but most of the men of her generation feared her. She represented a kind of ramrod, forcing the future into their present in an uncomfortable and uncomprehended manner." In a recent interview, Enid described Alice as a strange, brilliant and very peculiar-looking woman, with large hands and feet, and wispy, disordered blond hair. Her love affair with Lawrence was known about in Eastwood, and they probably did (as in *Sons and Lovers*) have sexual relations on the banks of the river Trent. Alice, who refused a lasting commitment to Lawrence, would neither marry nor elope with him. She knew he would be a great man and felt she could not live up to the role that was eventually assumed by Frieda. After the end of her affair with Lawrence, Alice returned—revitalized—to her husband.[9]

"I had a devil of a time getting a bit weaned from my mother, at the age of 22," Lawrence told Edward Garnett in 1913. "She suffered, and I suffered, and it seemed all for nothing, just waste, cruelty." In the first part of 1908, in his twenty-second year, Alice weaned the virginal Lawrence from Lydia and released his creative flow by sleeping with him. She told Sallie Hopkin, with simplistic exaggeration: "I gave Bert sex. I had to. He was over at our house, struggling with a poem he couldn't finish, so I took him upstairs and gave him sex. He came downstairs and finished the poem." After his death, Alice praised the potency of Lawrence (who must have been making up for a late start) and confided to a friend that he could "come back to a woman time after time." Alice's revelation substantiates the compliment that Johanna (based on Frieda) gives to Gilbert (based on Lawrence) in the autobiographical novel *Mr. Noon*. After their first sexual encounter Johanna, a sexual connoisseur, exclaims: "Do you know, I was rather frightened that you weren't a good lover. But it isn't every man who can love a woman three times in a quarter of an hour—so *well*—is it—?"[10]

According to Willie Hopkin, Alice hoped the child she later bore belonged to Lawrence, and after parting from him, "she never let another man touch her, not even her husband." Enid adds that after Alice gave him up, she "went through a hell of the sort we can barely imagine." Five years after Lawrence's death, when Frieda had published a memoir of their life together, Alice sent Frieda an extraordinary letter about her hatred of her father, her love affair with Lawrence (which had lasted from 1908 until he met Frieda, in the spring of 1912) and *Lawrence's* role in inciting a passion that led her to conceive a child with her husband:

When at last *knowledge* came to me, I loathed and detested my father (I had never been very fond of him); I swore vengeance on his sex when I should myself be married. . . .

I fear that [Lawrence] never even enjoyed morphia with me—always it carried an irritant—we were never, except for one short memorable hour, whole: it was from that one hour that I began to see the light of life. . . . The potential me would never have struggled to life but for his help and influence. . . .

My cup was bitter when he wrote from [Lake] Garda in the richness of fulfilment. How bitterly I envied you that day! How I resented his snobbery and his happiness whilst I was suffering in body and sick in soul, carrying an unwanted child which would never have been conceived but for an unendurable passion which only *he* had roused and my husband had slaked. So—life!

Lawrence writes of Clara's (i.e., Alice's) relations with her husband in *Sons and Lovers:* "With him, she was only half-alive; the rest was dormant, deadened. And the dormant woman was the *femme incompromise,* and she *had* to be awakened." Lawrence's friend and biographer, Richard Aldington, understood Alice's dormant and defiant character when he assured Edward Nehls, who had asked advice about how to describe Lawrence's sexual relations with Alice: "As to the married woman with whom L. had an affair—she'd probably be flattered."[11]

Alice not only seduced Lawrence, but also advised him to sleep with Jessie. In a crucial conversation in *Sons and Lovers,* Clara Dawes tells Paul Morel that he is ignorant of Miriam's feelings as well as of his own, and urges him to disentangle himself from his mother by despiritualizing his girlfriend:

> "[She] wants the soul out of my body. I can't help shrinking back from her."
> "And yet you love her!"
> "No, I don't love her. I never even kiss her."...
> "I suppose you're afraid," she said.
> "I'm not.... I know she wants a sort of soul union."
> "But how do you know what she wants?"
> "I've been with her for seven years."
> "And you haven't found out the very first thing about her."
> "What's that?"
> "That she doesn't want any of your soul communion. That's your own imagination. She wants you."[12]

As late as December 1908 Lawrence, implicitly contrasting his behavior with Alice and with Jessie, told his sympathetic and slightly older confidante, Blanche Jennings: "I have kissed dozens of girls—on the cheek—never on the mouth—I could not." But during the spring holiday of 1910, when he had returned from his teaching job in Croydon to Eastwood, Lawrence forced the sexual issue with Jessie and persuaded her to sleep with him. He then blamed her, rather than himself, when her reluctance—or frigidity—inevitably led to disappointment. In Jessie's account, his behavior seems as stiff and awkward as her own. "I could not conceal from myself a forced note in L's attitude, as if he was pushed forwards in his sensual desire—and a lack of spontaneity. The times of our coming together, under conditions both difficult and irksome, and with Lawrence's earnest injunction to me not to try to hold him, would not exhaust the fingers of one hand. . . . On this slight and inadequate experience he judged and condemned me, without stopping to inquire whether his own attitude was beyond reproach."[13]

Their sexual experience is fictionalized in *Sons and Lovers,* where Miriam—with her pleading gesture, resigned expression, unconvincing assent and passive gift of her body—is described, like the broken doll, Arabella, in chapter 4, as a sacrificial victim. Paul, nevertheless, moves from detumescence ("all his blood fell back") to arousal ("his blood beat back again"):

He never forgot seeing her as she lay on the bed, when he was unfastening his collar. First he saw only her beauty, and was blind with it. She had the most beautiful body he had ever imagined. He stood unable to move or speak, looking at her, his face half-smiling with wonder. And then he wanted her, but as he went forward to her, her hands lifted in a little pleading movement, and he looked at her face, and stopped. Her big brown eyes were watching him, still and resigned and loving; she lay as if she had given herself up to sacrifice: there was her body for him; but the look at the back of her eyes, like a creature awaiting immolation, arrested him, and all his blood fell back.

"You are sure you want me?" he asked, as if a cold shadow had come over him.

"Yes, quite sure."

She was very quiet, very calm. She only realised that she was doing something for him. He could hardly bear it. She lay to be sacrificed for him because she loved him so much. And he had to sacrifice her. For a second, he wished he were sexless or dead. Then he shut his eyes again to her, and his blood beat back again.[14]

But sexual relations divided the lovers instead of bringing them together. In the fall of 1910 Lydia, unaware of their intimacy, forced the issue by insisting that Lawrence was compromising Jessie. He then told her: "I've looked into my heart and I cannot find I love you as a husband should love his wife. Perhaps I shall, in time. If I ever find I do, I'll tell you. What about you? If you think you love me, tell me, and we'll be engaged." Jessie, bitterly hurt, "was conscious of a fierce pain, of the body as well as the spirit. I tried not to let him see my tears. . . . I could not have endured anyone to know the humiliation I had suffered, and the sense of irreparable loss."[15]

In August 1910, shortly before their break, Lawrence urged Jessie to read two novels by the successful Scottish writer J. M. Barrie. He was sexually impotent (though Lawrence did not yet know this), and was also a weak son, abnormally attached to his puritanical mother. Lawrence told Jessie that he was in exactly the same predicament as Barrie's fictional hero and that these books would help her to understand his dilemma—his sexual dysfunction with Jessie, though not with Alice. *Sentimental Tommy* (1896) concludes as Tommy Sandys rejects the adoring Grizel and confides to his sister: "You're the only one I love, and I care not a hair for Grizel." In *Tommy and Grizel* (1900), Barrie compensates in fiction for what he was unable to achieve in real life. Tommy tells a doctor, whom he has consulted about his problems with Grizel: "I can marry her, and I'm going to do it." But the doctor responds: "I was thinking how cruel to her if some day she came to her right mind and found herself tied for life to the man who had brought her to this pass." Nevertheless, at the end of the novel Tommy marries Grizel, to care for but not to sleep with her. And he attempts to justify his selfless and selfish behavior by confessing his infantile fixation on his mother: "He was a boy only. She knew that, despite all he had gone through, he was still a boy. And boys cannot love. Oh, who would be so cruel as to ask a boy to love?"[16]

Lawrence explained, rationalized, excused and defended his behavior in the unequal relationship with Jessie in letters to the poet Rachel Taylor and to Edward Garnett; and, when living in Italy, blamed Jessie, with some justification, for frustrating him and then regretting her debasing descent to the carnal: "It is true, [mother and I] have been great lovers. Then my betrothal of six years' standing I have just broken, and rather disgracefully. . . . [Jessie] is the girl I have broken with. She loves me to madness, and demands the soul of me. I had been cruel to her, and wronged her, but I did not know. Nobody can have the soul of me. My mother has had it, and nobody can have it again. . . . She bottled me up till I was going to burst. . . . She is bitterly ashamed of having had me— as if I had dragged her spiritual plumage in the mud."[17]

Lawrence later justified his marriage to Frieda by comparing her to

Jessie and explaining to Willie Hopkin—who knew the only three women with whom Lawrence had slept—"she is the one possible woman for me, for I must have opposition—something to fight or I shall go under. . . . It would have been a fatal step [to marry Jessie]. I should have had too easy a life, nearly everything my own way, and my genius would have been destroyed."[18] Lawrence was surely right about Jessie. In her memoir of Lawrence she portrays herself as shy, reserved, clinging, possessive, prudish and prosaic, and inadvertently justifies his rejection of her love. Sex with Alice made him realize that he could not feel sexually attracted to Jessie and that it would therefore be wrong to marry her. He had no money, and thought it would be impossible to escape from Eastwood and become a writer if he married a local girl and was condemned to the boredom of teaching.

Lawrence's understanding of his emotional problems with Jessie and his mother developed gradually, over a long period of time. His insight was limited during his actual love affair with Jessie, but intensified after he had pondered and acted on Alice's interpretation of that affair. He gained further insight after the death of his mother, after the composition of *Sons and Lovers,* after meeting Frieda (learning her Freudian ideas and discussing Jessie with her), after his revision of the novel (while living with Frieda in Italy) and after receiving Jessie's embittered response to it. Jessie, who felt Lawrence's description of her character and their relationship had been warped by his mother's hostile attitude, was devastated by the novel: "The shock of *Sons and Lovers* gave the death-blow to our friendship," she said. "I felt that I had suffered a terrible inner injury. It required all my effort to avoid a collapse."[19]

Lawrence's friendship with Jessie, despite its disastrous conclusion, had a powerful influence on the formation of his character. She provided his first experience with farm life—to which he would again be drawn in Cornwall and in New Mexico. She was the first woman to love him, the first to realize his genius and the first to make him aware of the emotional conflicts with his mother. She was the first reader of his novels, she participated in the publication of his first story, "A Prelude," and was the first to introduce his work to the London literary world. Most significantly, Jessie provided the inspiration for *Sons and Lovers,* his first major work of art.

CHAPTER SIX

Croydon,
1908–1912

I

THE CROYDON years were difficult and disturbing for Lawrence. Bored and exhausted by his teaching job, trying to write at night and on weekends, he frequently returned to Eastwood during the fall of 1910 to nurse his dying mother and was shattered by her death in December. He continued to see Jessie and Alice, and tried to compensate for the loss of his mother by looking for love with Helen Corke, Agnes Holt and Louie Burrows. Toward the end of 1911, he fell gravely ill with pneumonia and nearly died. Under these desperate conditions, Lawrence made his way into the literary world, met his two early mentors—Ford Madox Hueffer and Edward Garnett—and brought out his first two novels. In a cancelled Foreword to his *Collected Poems* (1928) he emphasized the almost mystical morbidity of that period of his life:

Then began . . . London, and school, a whole new world. Then starts the rupture with home, with Miriam [Jessie], away there in Nottinghamshire. And gradually the long illness, and then the death of my mother; and in the sick year after, the collapse of [his love for] Miriam, of Helen [Corke], and of the other woman [Louie], the woman of "Kisses in the Train" and "The Hands of the Betrothed."

Then, in that year, for me everything collapsed, save the mystery

of death, and the haunting of death in life. I was twenty-five, and
from the death of my mother, the world began to dissolve around
me, beautiful, iridescent, but passing away substanceless. Till I
almost dissolved away from myself, and was very ill: when I was
twenty-six.

Then slowly the world came back: or I myself returned: but to
another world.[1]

Many modern writers—Wells, Joyce, Eliot, Huxley, Orwell, Waugh,
Day Lewis, Betjeman, Auden—began their careers as schoolmasters.
But unlike all these other teacher-writers, only Lawrence was thoroughly trained for the profession. In October 1908 he left home for the
first time in his life and began teaching at the Davidson Road School in
Croydon, which had opened the previous year. He remained there, at an
annual salary of £95 (about the same as his father's average earnings),
for just over three years. Jessie recalled that when Lawrence "had to
leave us to take up his post in Croydon he looked like a man under
sentence of exile." Torn from his roots and the people who had loved him,
he felt alien, fearful and insecure. His first letter to her "was like a howl
of terror. People were kind, he said, but everything was strange, and how
could he live away from us all? He dreaded morning and school with the
anguish of a sick girl. Finally he said he felt afraid for himself; cut off
from us all he would grow into something black and ugly."

He lodged in Colworth Road, a fifteen-minute walk from Davidson
Road, with the family of John Jones, an attendance officer in the local
schools, who was seventeen years older than Lawrence. Lawrence was
very fond of Jones' daughters—the five-year-old Winifred and the new-
born infant Hilda—the first of a long series of children in whom Lawrence took a serious and sympathetic interest. He sometimes wrote with
the baby sitting on his knee, and often bathed the children, heard their
prayers and put them to bed. Though Lawrence had been fond of Jones,
he grew increasingly irritated by his character and habits. Toward the
end of his stay, in April 1911, he told Louie Burrows: "Mr. Jones has
shaved off his moustache, and I don't like him. He's got a small, thin
mouth, like a slit in a tight skin. It's quite strange. It shows up a part of
his character that I detest: the mean and prudent and nervous. I feel that
I really don't like him, and I rather liked him before."[2]

Helen Corke, a teacher in a nearby school, observed that Lawrence
did not get on well with his rather limited colleagues. In her novel about
Lawrence, *Neutral Ground* (1933), she described how they first pa-

tronized and then avoided him when they discovered his iconoclastic streak:

> He was avoided by the male members of the staff, a narrow-minded, extremely cautious set. He had failed signally to pass their tests of capacity both for sport and school discipline, so they first extended to him a contemptuous patronage; and later, when they had had some experience of his intellectual fearlessness and power of passionate argument, paid him a grudging respect and stayed out of his way. He puzzled and disturbed them by his ironic treatment of their accepted and unquestioned standards of work and living.

Lawrence's one close friend and colleague, with whom he corresponded for many years, was Arthur McLeod. Born the same year as Lawrence and sharing his enthusiasm for literature, McLeod had taken a degree in Greek from King's College, London University. He is portrayed as Howard Phillips in *Neutral Ground* and as Mr. MacWhirter in Lawrence's second novel, *The Trespasser.* Lawrence describes his extreme reserve, which provides a striking contrast to his own emotional frankness: "Mr. MacWhirter was tall, fair and stoutish; he was very quietly spoken, was humorous and amiable, yet extraordinarily learned. He never, by any chance, gave himself away, maintaining always an absolute reserve amid all his amiability. Therefore Frank would have done anything to win his esteem."[3]

McLeod felt Lawrence was fortunate in having as headmaster Philip F. T. Smith (born in 1866), a perceptive, enlightened and generous man who recognized Lawrence's ability and allowed him unusual freedom. But Lawrence's response to Smith was extremely negative. He felt the headmaster was weak and irresponsible, that his *laissez faire* attitude made it difficult to discipline the children: "The head is a weak kneed windy fool—he shifts every grain of responsibility off his own shoulders—he will not punish anybody; yourself, when you punish, you must send for the regulation cane and enter the minutest details of the punishment in the Pun. book—if you do. Discipline is consequently very slack and teaching is a struggle."

Smith's view of Lawrence, however, was quite favorable, and he often invited the young teacher to his house on Sunday evenings. Smith noted that "Lawrence was intolerant of authority. While imposing his own rule rigorously upon his pupils, he rebelled against any such process as being even suggested to himself." Lawrence doubtless was intolerant of author-

ity, a characteristic trait inherited from his father and his Congregational background. But Smith's criticism of Lawrence's inconsistency is
illogical. It was quite reasonable, indeed essential, for Lawrence to
control his students rigorously while, at the same time, to demand his
freedom as a teacher. In fact, Lawrence's teaching methods—especially
in botany, drawing, acting and singing—were innovative rather than
rigid, designed to encourage rather than repress the spontaneity of his
students. Smith noted another typically Lawrencean trait, which also
appeared in his letters to Blanche Jennings and to his various girlfriends (many of whom were quite intimate with each other): "He was
fond of recounting the [emotional rather than physical] conquests he
made among his lady friends and with some of his opinions on female
shortcomings my wife disagreed strongly."[4] The young Lawrence was
sufficiently cocky and self-confident to criticize women in front of his
headmaster's wife.

The big, new, finely appointed Davidson Road School contained an
unusually heterogeneous mixture: orphans of actors from a charity
home, lads with no boots who got free meals, and superior boys headed
for a good grammar school. In letters of October–November 1908 to
Blanche Jennings, and especially to Jessie and Louie, both of whom took
a professional as well as a personal interest in his work, Lawrence—
teaching forty-five boys in Standard IV of elementary school—
complained of the long hours, the fetid atmosphere, the tedious administrative rules, the lack of time and energy to write, the difficult and
rather stupid students, and particularly the great problem of corporal
punishment. (Ursula's excruciating encounter in chapter 15 of *The
Rainbow* with the devious, extortionate Mrs. Williams, whose son she
has beaten, suggests the sense of degradation as well as the moral
compromise Lawrence felt he had to make to maintain discipline.)

School is a conflict—mean and miserable—and I hate conflicts. I
was never born to command. I do not want to command. So the lads
and I have a fight, and I have a fight with my nature, and I am
always vanquished. . . .

The boss is nice, but very flabby; the kids are rough and insolent
as the devil. I had rather endure anything than this continual,
petty, debasing struggle [to dominate the boys with a cane]. . . .

I guess you never punish the wrong kid. As for me, I put up with
them until I can stand them no longer, then I land the nearest, and
as likely as not, he's innocent.[5]

Lawrence, who portrayed Ursula's botany class when Birkin inspects her school in chapter 3 of *Women in Love,* later recalled that "as a schoolmaster, the two things I liked teaching best were drawing and botany; and I had good classes in both. . . . It can be very bad; but I never had much trouble. The boys, I think, liked me. But even when a boy, I always felt there was something so mean in tormenting one's teacher." At least one of his pupils, who later became a journalist, recorded that Lawrence "was to his scholars a soft speaking, kindly, gentle, and sensitive man"[6]—precisely the sort to have trouble with unruly boys.

Lawrence's rather awkward poems about the school also express his bitterness and resentment:

> I will not waste my soul and my strength for this.
> What do I care for all that they do amiss!
> What is the point of this teaching of mine, and of this
> Learning of theirs? It all goes down the same abyss.

He made no secret of his intention to abandon teaching as a career and toward the end of his Croydon years hyperbolically exclaimed to McLeod:

> "I'll not go on. The Committee has had blood and tears out of me for a hundred a year. I'll not endure it. I'd rather work on a farm. I know a farmer at Eastwood [Edmund Chambers] who would take me on tomorrow. Nay, I'd rather be a tramp." Teaching was always a strain to him: he was always at tension; nevertheless he enjoyed much of his work, notably his nature-study lessons and his drawing periods when the whole class acquired his own free, vigorous style and painted boldly and with huge enjoyment.[7]

In one of his many essays on education, Lawrence reiterated his angry sentiments about the difficult and sometimes impossible role of the "mongrel" schoolteacher, who must uphold values which are not his own and in which he does not believe. He alluded to the sneers of the engineers at Nottingham University and to the degrading necessity of imposing one's own will on others: "The elementary school-teacher is in a vile and false position. Set up as representative of an ideal which is all toffee, invested in an authority which has absolutely no base except in the teacher's own isolate will, he is sneered at by the idealists above and jeered at by the materialists below, and ends by being a mongrel. . . . He is caught between the upper and nether millstones . . . and every shred of natural pride is ground out of him." When Lawrence renewed his correspondence with McLeod in 1927, sixteen years after he had left Croydon, he revealed his profound anxiety about teaching: "One of my troubled dreams, sleep-dreams, I mean, is that I'm teaching and that I've clean forgotten to mark the register, and the class has gone home! Why should I feel so worried about not having marked the register? But I do."[8]

II

In June 1909, after his first academic year at Croydon, Jessie urged Lawrence to try to publish his poetry. Fearful of rejection, Lawrence at first feigned indifference to the fate of his work, and then urged Jessie to send some of his poems to Ford Madox Hueffer, the editor of the *English Review*. When Lawrence returned from his holiday on the Isle of Wight (the setting of *The Trespasser*), Jessie said:

> "Oh, I've got a letter for you."
> He looked at me quickly, then his eyes narrowed.
> "From the *English?* About the poems. Show it me."
> I gave him the letter and his face became tense.
> "*You* are my luck," he murmured. Then he said with suppressed excitement, "Let me take it to show mother." And I never saw it again.[9]

Ford Madox Hueffer (who later changed his surname and is best known as Ford Madox Ford) was a tall, stout, warmhearted thirty-six-year-old man with fair hair, prominent blue eyes, gaping mouth, rabbit teeth and ragged lemon moustache. He was the grandson of a Pre-Raphaelite painter and the son of the German-born music critic of *The Times*. Ford had published his first book while still in his teens, was a brilliant novelist, a devoted collaborator with Conrad on *The Inheritors* (1901) and *Romance* (1903), and an influential figure in the literary world. In 1909 he discovered three geniuses—Lawrence, Wyndham Lewis and Ezra Pound—and published them all in the *English Review,* together with James, Conrad and Norman Douglas. According to a story that Ford told his assistant editor, Douglas Goldring, which illustrates the bohemian behavior in Ford's circle of friends, Wyndham Lewis entered the bathroom at 84 Holland Park Avenue and found Ford, like a pink egg, soaping himself in the tub:

> Disregarding any unconventionality in his surroundings, the "enemy" at once proceeded to business. After announcing in the most matter-of-fact way that he was a man of genius and that he had a manuscript for publication, he asked if he might read it. "Go ahead," Ford murmured, continuing to use his sponge. Lewis then unbuttoned his coat, produced "The Pole" and read it through. At the end Ford observed: "Well, that's all right. If you leave it behind, we'll certainly print it."

Ford expressed the editorial policy of the *English Review* in a high-minded circular: "The only qualification for admission to the pages of the Review will be ... either distinction of individuality or force of conviction, either literary gifts or earnestness of purpose, whatever that purpose may be—the criterion of inclusion being the clarity of diction, the force or illuminative value of the views expressed." The first issue of the *English Review* (December 1908)—which contained works by Tolstoy, Hardy, James, Conrad, Galsworthy, Hudson and Wells—immediately established it as the leading literary magazine in England.

Ford's commitment to the highest literary standards, combined with his total lack of business ability, led inevitably to financial disaster. In December 1909, after the *English Review* had lost £2,800, the financier Sir Alfred Mond bought the magazine at a nominal price and dismissed Ford as editor. The magazine then passed into the inadequate hands of Austin Harrison, who had been a reporter on the *Daily Mail*. According to Goldring, Harrison "knew nothing about literature, [and] proved rather an unfortunate choice on the part of the new proprietor."[10] Nevertheless, Lawrence remained faithful to the *English Review*, wrote for it from 1909 to 1923 and appeared in thirty-five issues.

In November 1909 Ford published four crisp, imagistic poems by Lawrence: "Still Afternoon," "Dreams Old and Nascent," "Baby Movements" and "Discipline." "He was very kind to me," Lawrence recalled, "and was the first man I ever met who had a real and a true feeling for literature. He introduced me to Edward Garnett, who, somehow, introduced me to the world." Ford was also extremely enthusiastic about *The White Peacock* and proclaimed, with a tinge of patronage: " 'It's got every fault that the English novel can have.... But,' shouted Hueffer in the 'bus, 'you've got GENIUS.' . . . In the early days they were always telling me I had got genius, as if to console me for not having their own incomparable advantages. But Hueffer didn't mean that. I always thought he had a bit of genius himself." Lawrence also said of his first editor: "Hueffer lives in a constant haze. He has talent, all kinds of it, but has everlastingly been a damn fool about his life. He's fine in a half a dozen lines of writing but won't stick to any one of them, and the critics can't stand that in a writer. . . . A bit of a fool, yes, but he gave me the first push and he was a kind man."[11]

In the fall of 1909 Lawrence took a major step from the provincial to the cosmopolitan world. Despite his working-class background, he was confident of his talent, quickly adjusted to the sophisticated salons and observed them with a critical eye. Ford, then living with but not married to the novelist Violet Hunt, invited Lawrence and Jessie to lunch. "Lawrence asked the servant who waited at table what knives he was expected to use with fish or asparagus," Ford wrote. "That being settled, he went on to talk and was completely at ease," impressing Ford with his extensive knowledge of literature. In a witty letter that satirized the weird dress and strange manners of his hostess, Violet Hunt (who was seven years older than Ford), Lawrence anticipated his later criticism of Lady Ottoline Morrell: "She was tremendous in a lace gown and a hat writhed with blue feathers as if with some python. Indeed she looked very handsome. She had on her best society manners. She is very dextrous: flips a bright question, lifts her eyebrows in deep concern, glances from the man on her right to the lady on her left, smiles, bows, and suddenly,—quick curtain—she is gone, and is utterly somebody else's, she who was altogether ours a brief second before."[12]

Ford later became much more critical of both Lawrence and his work. After Lawrence had rejected his patronage and their relations had soured, Ford characteristically exaggerated Lawrence's invalidism, weakness and dependence: "I cannot say that I liked Lawrence very much. He remained too disturbing even when I got to know him well. He had so much need of moral support to take the place of his mother's influence that he kept one—every one who at all came into contact with him—in a constant state of solicitude. He claimed moral support imperiously—and physical care too. . . . Although he was my 'discovery,' I'm not a hell of a lot in sympathy with him and find him difficult to re-read."[13]

Helen Corke, who gave Lawrence the idea for *The Trespasser,* said that Lawrence sent the novel to Ford. But Ford strongly disapproved of its romanticism and claimed it was too subjective and emotional. Writing to Louie Burrows in September 1910, Lawrence reported that Ford, unsympathetic to Lawrence's diversion from what he considered the mainstream of modern art, both praised and condemned the book: " 'It's a rotten work of genius, one fourth of which is the stuff of a masterpiece. . . . It has no construction or form—it is execrably bad art, being all variations on a theme. Also it is erotic—not that I, personally, mind that, but an erotic work *must* be good art, which this is not.' . . . He belongs to the opposite school of novelists to me [Lawrence said]: he says prose *must* be impersonal, like Turgenev and Flaubert. I say no." Two years later he remarked that Ford had criticized him for refusing to submit to the aesthetic conventions of the French novel: the ironic, detached narrator, the complex revelation of plot and the anguished striving for the *mot juste* that would exactly express the required shade of meaning. Ford stressed the technique of narration as much as the tale itself. "I suffered badly," Lawrence said, "from Hueffer re Flaubert and perfection."[14] Ford recognized Lawrence's extraordinary talent but disliked his passionate, subjective and intuitive form of expression.

In 1909 Ford introduced Lawrence to two important literary figures: H. G. Wells and Ezra Pound. Wells, the self-made son of a shopkeeper and a lady's maid, had already published *The War of the Worlds, Love and Mr. Lewisham* and *Kipps*. Lawrence satirically described Wells (who would appear in the south of France when Lawrence was on his deathbed) as "a funny little chap: his conversation is a continual squirting of thin little jets of weak acid: amusing, but not expansive."

The bearded, red-haired Pound affected a mode of bombastic behavior and outrageous dress, with *fin de siècle* velvet coat and turquoise earring. He was present at the lunch Ford and Violet Hunt gave for Lawrence and Jessie, who said (without naming Pound) that "he speared an apple with his knife, chopped it into quarters and gobbled it ostentatiously. I regarded him as an amiable buffoon." On another occasion, Lawrence missed the last train to Croydon and spent the night in Pound's London flat. And at the house of Ernest Rhys, who edited the popular Everyman series for Dent, he saw the childish and eccentric Pound, noticing that the dinner table was decorated with red tulips, seize the flowers and begin to eat them up in order to attract attention to himself.

Just after his first meeting with the wild poet, Lawrence emphasized the difference between Pound's aesthetic and his own realistic approach to literature. He was duly impressed by Pound's bohemian digs, aca-

demic qualifications, volumes of poetry and swaggering cosmopoli-
tanism (Pound had come to London from Venice in 1908 and would have
been at ease in Italian restaurants), as well as by his praise of Lawrence's
work. He also admired the outsider's ability to make his way in the
literary world:

> He is a well-known American poet—a good one. He is 24, like me,—
> but his god is beauty, mine, life. He is jolly nice: took me to supper
> at Pagnani's, and afterwards we went down to his room in Ken-
> sington. He lives in an attic, like a traditional poet—but the attic is
> a comfortable well furnished one. He is an American Master of
> Arts and a professor of the Provençal group of languages, and he
> lectures once a week on the minstrels at the London polytechnic.
> He is rather remarkable—a good bit of a genius, and with not the
> least self-consciousness.[15]

Pound (like Ford) was known for recognizing new talent and for his
generosity to fellow writers. In 1913 he told the American editor Harriet
Monroe, who later published Lawrence's work in her magazine *Poetry*,
that he disliked the priggish, provincial, didactic, self-conscious side of
Lawrence (whose Midlands sobriety contrasted with Pound's American
flamboyance) but admired his objective and original work:

> He is clever. . . . Detestable person but needs watching. I think he
> learned the proper treatment of modern subjects before I did. That
> was in some poems in *The Eng. Rev.* . . .
> Lawrence, as you know, gives me no particular pleasure. Never-
> theless we are lucky to get him. Hueffer, as you know, thinks highly
> of him. I *recognize* certain qualities in his work. If I were an editor
> I should probably accept his work without reading it. As a prose
> writer I grant him first place among the younger men.

In his review in *Poetry* of Lawrence's first book of verse, *Love Poems
and Others* (1913), Pound stated: "there is no English poet under forty
who can get within shot of him. . . . Mr. Lawrence has attempted realism
and attained it. . . . He has brought contemporary verse up to the level of
contemporary prose, and that is no mean achievement." But writing in
the *New Age* two years later, Pound felt Lawrence had not fulfilled his
early promise and suggested why he—like Ford—eventually rejected
Lawrence's erotic, highly charged work: "I have never envied Mr. Law-

rence, though I have often enjoyed him. I do not want to write, even good stories, in a loaded ornate style, heavy with sex, fruity with a certain sort of emotion."[16] Neither Pound nor Ford quite realized that Lawrence was using his early novels as emotional outlets for intense sexual feelings.

What difference would that have made to them?

III

While Lawrence was writing to Jessie and Louie about teaching in Croydon and meeting Ford and Pound, he was also courting two attractive young women—Agnes Holt and Helen Corke—who were a few years older than he was. Agnes, a fellow teacher in Croydon, was tall, with grey eyes and auburn hair. Jessie, who had met Agnes during her visit to London in November 1909, noted her rather awkward behavior with Lawrence, caused by the sexual strain between them. She seemed to patronize Lawrence and speak to him like an elder sister, while he masked his uneasiness with a curious air of bravado. Lawrence told Jessie he had thought of marrying Agnes, but by Christmas, when he had punctured her romantic illusions and she had repelled his sexual advances, he quickly changed his mind. As he explained to Blanche Jennings:

> She's so utterly ignorant and old-fashioned, really, though she has been to college and has taught in London some years. . . . She still judges by mid-Victorian standards, and covers herself with a woolly fluff of romance that the years will wear sickly. . . . She is all sham and superficial in her outlook, and I can't change her. She's frightened.
>
> Now I'm sick of her. She pretends to be very fond of me; she isn't really.[17]

Lawrence met Helen Corke—a small, reddish-haired woman— through her older friend and mentor, Agnes Mason, another teacher in the Davidson Road School. Helen shared Lawrence's interest in art, music and literature, and helped him make the final copy of *The White Peacock*. In the summer of 1910, during a holiday on the Isle of Wight, she had become the mistress of her violin teacher, Herbert MacCartney. Racked by guilt, galled by poverty, unhappily married and unable to commit himself to Helen, MacCartney returned to his nagging wife and children, and hanged himself at home. In her novel, *Neutral Ground*, Helen, who had been emotionally shattered by this experience, described how the immensely sympathetic character based on Lawrence "patiently and strenuously had worked to revive the zest of life in her, always hoping that, by and by, she would turn and see him, and love him with a wiser love than she had given [MacCartney]."[18]

Lawrence revived Helen's interest in life, but he did not become her lover. Though she was not virginal like his other girlfriends and had been MacCartney's mistress, she would not become his. She did not want to marry him or to bear his child, and could not "be 'woman' in the ordinary meaning of the term." "He might have been my lover," Helen sharply said, "but I shouldn't have been his lover." Traumatized by her destructive affair with MacCartney, she could not respond sexually to Lawrence.

Helen's description of Jessie's adoration of Lawrence provides a striking contrast to Jessie's account of his relations with Agnes Holt: "It wasn't just normal ordinary physical affection for a companion. She said to me once: 'David is one of the sons of God' [a favorite Lawrencean phrase, from Genesis 6:2]. She looked upon him as a completely superior being." Helen—who may have been a lesbian during and certainly became one after her affair with MacCartney—was more attracted to Jessie than to Lawrence and actually "fell in love with her."[19]

In a bitter letter to Helen in July 1911, Lawrence, tormented by his longing for sex before marriage, threatened to degrade himself with a prostitute (there is no evidence that he ever did so) and exclaimed that Helen (like Jessie) had pushed him to the breaking point: "I will never ask for sex relationship again, never, unless I can give the dirty coin of marriage: unless it be a prostitute, whom I can love because I'm sorry for her. I cannot stand the sex strain between us." The very titles of the love-hate poems that Lawrence wrote to Helen during this period—"Repulsed," "Coldness in Love"—express his bitter struggle with the cold, unresponsive woman:

How we hate one another to-night, hate, she and I
To numbness and nothingness; I dead, she refusing to die.
The female whose venom can more than kill, can numb and
    then nullify.[20]

IV

In August 1910—when Lawrence was deeply involved with Jessie, Helen and Louie—his mother, while visiting her sister Ada Krenkow in Leicestershire, discovered a cancerous tumor in her abdomen. Lawrence had witnessed Lydia's agony with William Ernest. Now it was his turn to suffer the same grief for her. He stayed with Lydia for the last three weeks of her life, trying to distract himself by reading and painting at her bedside.

Lawrence obtained an early bound copy of *The White Peacock,* which was due to be published in January 1911, so he could show it to his mother before the end. He described this anticlimactic presentation in a letter of December 1910 and an essay in 1925. In the former, Lydia looked at the book but was too exhausted to respond; in the latter, Lawrence intuited and expressed her silent disappointment:

> Mother just glanced at it. "It's yours, my dear," my sister [Ada] said to her. "Is it?" she murmured, and she closed her eyes. Then a little later, she said, "What does it say?"—and my sister read her the tiny inscription ["To my Mother, with love, D. H. Lawrence"] I had put in.

> The very first copy of *The White Peacock* that was ever sent out, I put into my mother's hands when she was dying. She looked at the outside, and then at the title-page, and then at me, with darkening eyes. And though she loved me so much, I think she doubted whether it could be much of a book, since no one more important than I had written it.[21]

Lydia suffered terribly during the last week of her life and died on December 9, 1910. In letters to Rachel Taylor and Louie Burrows, Lawrence set down his horror of the "many degrees of death" his mother had endured, his respect for her courage, his torment in parting from her, his sense that her agony was the culmination of a long, unhappy life: "She was very bad. The pains had been again. 'Oh my dear' I said, 'is it the pains?' 'Not pain now—Oh the weariness,' she moaned, so that I could hardly hear her. I wish she could die tonight." His mother's suffering seemed to concentrate all the misery and evil in the world. His own life was so closely bound up with his need of her love and approval that he wondered if he could survive without her: "She looks so grievous, pitiful this morning, still and grey and deathly, like a hieroglyph of woe. . . . While she dies, we seem not to be able to live."[22]

Two of Lawrence's poems on Lydia's death—"Suspense" and "Endless Agony"—express his guilty wish to put her out of her misery, both to end her suffering and to free himself from the overwhelming force of her love. It seems clear, from unpublished interviews, that Lawrence had both the means and the desire to end his mother's life:

Dr. [H. M.] Gillespie wouldn't give her more than an ordinary dose, but he gave her medicine and both Ada and Bert gave her extra doses to ease the pain. He said he couldn't bear to see his mother suffer.

It upset him so badly that he turned to Dr. Gillespie one day while I was there and said, "Can't you give her something to end it?" And Gillespie said, "I can't."

In 1914 Lawrence told Lina Waterfield, an Englishwoman he had met in Italy, that he had actually killed his mother, as Paul Morel does in Chapter 14 of *Sons and Lovers:* "You see *I* did it—I gave her the overdose of morphia and set her free." Lawrence realized that he had to kill Lydia in order to set *himself* free. He knew he could never love another woman while she was alive.

The last lines of the last poem on Lydia's death emphasized his own weakness:

> Spare me the strength to leave you
> Now you are dead.
> I must go, but my soul lies helpless
> Beside your bed.[23]

A man who has been the indisputable favorite of his mother keeps for life the feeling of a conqueror. But he also suffers more grievously when that bond is broken. After her death, Lawrence became increasingly bitter and caustic.

The contrasting characters of Lawrence's parents—the mother's silent but loving deprecation of her son, the father's incomprehension and sense of outrage—was revealed in his vivid accounts of Arthur's response to *The White Peacock:*

> After the funeral my father struggled through half a page, and it might as well have been Hottentot.
>
> "And what dun they gi'e thee for that lad?"
>
> "Fifty pounds, father."
>
> "Fifty pounds!" He was dumbfounded, and looked at me with shrewd eyes, as if I were a swindler. "Fifty pounds! And tha's niver done a day's hard work in thy life." I think to this day, he looks upon me as a sort of cleverish swindler, who gets money for nothing.

In a later version of the same incident, Arthur is shrewder and rather pleased by his son's "swindle": "I took my father a book and he said, 'What might you be getting for a wee bit book like that, David lad?' and I said 'Two hundred pounds, Father,' and he said that convinced him that not all the fools were dead in the world."[24]

Despite the sympathetic portrayal of his father in these anecdotes, Lawrence turned against him after the death of his mother. He prematurely called himself an orphan ("I've never had but one parent") and savagely blamed Arthur for Lydia's suffering: "[He is] disgusting, irritating, and selfish as a maggot. Yet I am sorry for him: he's old, and stupid, and very helpless and futile. . . . Let him eat a bit of the bread of humility. It is astonishing how hard and bitter I feel towards him." Lawrence's sister Emily, however, said "father got nicer as he grew older." And Emily's daughter Margaret remembered him as a pleasant rather than frightening old man, who lodged with a family (rather than living with one of his children) and spent a good deal of time swatting flies with a newspaper.[25] Lawrence seemed strangely unmoved when Arthur died, on September 10, 1924 (the day before Lawrence's birthday), and removed another barrier between himself and death.

V

Lawrence's break with Agnes Holt in 1908, with Jessie in 1910 and with Helen in 1911 propelled him toward the dark, attractive and apparently

passionate Louie Burrows. Born in Ilkeston, near Eastwood, in 1888, she
met Lawrence in about 1900, studied with him at the Ilkeston Pupil-
Teacher Centre and was a fellow pupil at Nottingham University.
Louie's father, Alfred, was a draftsman in a Nottingham lace factory and
a teacher of handicrafts; he had a passion for wood carving and architec-
ture, and was the model for Will Brangwen in *The Rainbow.*

While teaching at Croydon, Lawrence saw Louie mainly during the
school holidays. In early December 1910, depressed and emotionally
exhausted by his mother's impending death, his difficulties with Jessie
and Helen, his dissatisfaction with teaching, his anxiety about the
imminent appearance of his first novel and his intense sexual frustration, Lawrence—sparked by impulse and grasping at happiness amidst
the "crush of misery"—suddenly asked Louie to marry him. He described to Arthur McLeod his response to Louie's wistful looks and
subtle promptings in a train between Leicester and her home in Quorn:

> "And what do you think you'll do, Bert,—after Christmas?" said
> Louie. I said I didn't know. "What would you like to do?" she asked,
> and suddenly I thought she looked wistful. I said I didn't know—
> then added "Why, I should like to get married"—She hung her
> head. "Should *you?*" I asked. She was much embarrassed, and said
> *she* didn't know. "I should like to marry you" I said suddenly. . . .
>
> She is a glorious girl: about as tall as I, straight and strong as a
> caryatid . . . and swarthy and ruddy as a pomegranate, and bright
> and vital as a pitcher of wine. I'm jolly glad I asked her.

But the strict and proper Louie was not really like a caryatid, a
pomegranate or a jug of wine; and Lawrence, like any new fiancé, soon
had second thoughts. As he told Jessie, while attempting to strengthen
his resolve: "I was in the train with [Louie] on Saturday and I suddenly
asked her to marry me. I never meant to. But she accepted and I shall
stick to it." In his letter to Rachel Taylor—which described Lydia's
cancer, his parents' unhappy marriage and his abnormal attachment to
his mother—he defined the complicated psychological context of his
impulsive proposal but also revealed that he had misjudged Louie's
character and had imagined her as a promising alternative to as well as a
cruel betrayal of Jessie:

> I have been to Leicester today, and I have met a girl [Louie] who
> has always been warm for me—like a sunny happy day—and

I've gone and asked her to marry me: in the train, quite unpremeditated. . . .

She would never demand to drink me up and have me. She loves me—but it is a fine, warm, healthy, natural love—not like Jane Eyre, who is [Jessie]. . . . She will never plunge her hands through my blood and feel for my soul, and make me set my teeth and shiver and fight away. Ugh—I have done well—and cruelly [to Jessie]—tonight.[26]

Lawrence had told Rachel Taylor he wished he could marry Louie the day after Lydia's funeral. And he told Louie—three days after his proposal and three days before he mercy-killed his mother to free himself for Louie—"I must feel my mother's hand slip out of mine before I can really take yours. . . . This surcharge of grief makes me determine to be happy. . . . You will be the first woman to make the earth glad for me: mother, Jessie—all the rest, have been gates to a very sad world."

Though Louie was engaged to Lawrence for fourteen months, from December 1910 until February 1912, and inspired some of his best early love poems—"Snapdragon," "Kisses in the Train," "The Hands of the Betrothed"—she did not live up to his expectations. Lawrence hoped that Louie would give him a love relationship free from the torments he had experienced with Jessie and his other women, and would satisfy the physical side of his nature. She seemed to offer integrity, security and the prospect of sexual satisfaction. Though Louie shared his sexual feelings, his passion was constrained by her strict "code of manners." Lawrence suggested the conflict between emotion and restraint when he described Louie as "big, and swarthy, and passionate as a gypsy—but good, awfully good, churchy."[27] His inability to resolve the "but" finally led to his break with her.

Lawrence felt he needed an assured annual income of £150 and £100 in savings to marry on; and teaching, the only way to accumulate this money, was becoming increasingly distasteful to him. He also came to feel, several months before he broke their engagement, that Louie was not sufficiently mature and self-reliant, and might turn out to be as clinging and dependent as Jessie had been. On February 4, 1912, using the transparent excuses of poor health and lack of money, Lawrence broke his engagement to Louie: the doctors said "that I ought not to marry, at least for a long time, if ever. And I feel myself my health is so precarious, I wouldn't undertake the responsibility. Then, seeing I mustn't teach, I shall have a struggle to keep myself. I will not drag on an engagement—so I ask you to dismiss me. I am afraid we are not well suited."[28]

Lawrence, trapped by the sexual conflicts of Edwardian England, had a powerful effect on the well-educated professional women he had loved and left between 1908 and 1912. The mature, independent Alice Dax was willing to sleep with Lawrence, but would not commit herself to him. The others might have committed themselves, but were unwilling to sleep with him (though Jessie, who loved him the most, did so with extreme reluctance). All of them, to some extent, remained in love with him. Agnes destroyed all his letters. Helen never married and remained obsessed by Lawrence until her death, at the age of ninety-six. She wrote a memoir of Jessie and a novel, a book of poems, a critical book, a memoir and an autobiography about Lawrence; and she continued to discuss him in interviews and at conferences until the 1970s. Alice, who hoped to bear Lawrence's child, conceived a child with her husband through a passion that Lawrence had aroused. Jessie, deeply wounded and permanently embittered, married in 1915 and had no children. Louie (like Alice) suffered deeply after the break with Lawrence. She twice visited his grave in Vence in 1930, married in 1940, just before retiring from teaching, at the age of fifty-two, and (like Jessie) had no children.

VI

The White Peacock[29] (1911), which portrays Lawrence's sexual conflicts and search for a satisfying emotional relationship during the four years he was writing the novel, suggests a homosexual alternative to the frustrations of virginal love. In the novel, Cyril Beardsall (the narrator of the story) is based on Lawrence, Mr. Beardsall on a negative version of Lawrence's father, George and Emily Saxton on Alan and Jessie Chambers, and the personality of Leslie Tempest on the philanderer George Neville. Lawrence told Jessie that he was more interested in character than in plot and would follow George Eliot's plan of taking two couples and developing their relationships. The vain, life-denying heroine, Lettie, flirts with George Saxton while encouraging the attentions of Leslie Tempest, the son of the local squire. After Lettie represses her instinctive attraction to George and marries Leslie, George marries his cousin Meg, suffers a moral collapse and declines into *delirium tremens*.

On December 31, 1908, while composing the novel, Lawrence wrote an extremely enthusiastic letter about the aphrodisiac effects of seeing Maurice Greiffenhagen's *An Idyll* (1891). This popular Victorian painting represented to Lawrence a woman's swooning and seductive response to a man's ardent and dominating embrace. The woman, with half-closed eyes, turns away from him, but the man persists and gives fair promise to consummate his passion. Lawrence, who took five years to kiss Jessie, made four copies of *An Idyll*—a passionate ideal he could not openly express—and sent them to Arthur McLeod, his sister Ada, Agnes Holt and Louie Burrows.

In *An Idyll,* which plays an important symbolic role in the novel, a swarthy Pan figure, of great vigor and vitality, bare-chested and clothed in animal skins, seems rooted in a meadow, where grazing sheep and olive trees are lit up by a setting sun. He is lifting a pale, Pre-Raphaelite young woman off her feet, which are covered with bright poppies and daisies. He presses her half-naked bosom against his own body, entwines his fingers in the thick auburn hair cascading down her blue garment to her buttocks, and kisses her cheek as she turns away and swoons limply in his muscular arms, fearful of her feelings.

The painting represents an ideal of "splendid uninterrupted passion" that none of the characters in the novel—or the women in Lawrence's life—is able to achieve. The virile farmer, George Saxton, admires the painting, which arouses him sexually: "Wouldn't it be fine? . . . a girl like that—half afraid—and passion!"; but the response of the middle-class Lettie, who sees George as picturesque, is ironic and defensive: "She may well be half afraid, when the barbarian comes out in his glory, skins and all. . . . Make love to the next girl you meet, and . . . she'll have need to be more than half afraid." Yet when George hesitates and insists (in the subjunctive), "I don't know whether I should like any girl I know to—," Lettie mocks him and says he should have been a monk or martyr instead of a satyr. George, "breathlessly quivering under the new sensation of heavy, unappeased fire," glances at her breasts, shivers, and attempts to make small talk: "It was torture to each of them to look thus nakedly at the other, a dazzled, shrinking pain that they forced themselves to undergo for a moment, that they might the moment after tremble with a fierce sensation that filled their veins with fluid, fiery electricity."[30] The painting reveals emotions they cannot and dare not express.

This scene of barely restrained passion is repeated three times in *The White Peacock:* in the dance, the wood and the swim. Lawrence shows considerable skill in the presentation of the four scenes that express the conflict of class and the frustration of love, and lead to a homosexual consummation in the "Poem of Friendship." The plot of *The White Peacock* is similar to *Wuthering Heights,* where Catherine Earnshaw marries the stiff Linton instead of the passionate Heathcliff, for Lettie is afraid of sex with George but not with Leslie Tempest. When George and Lettie fail to find emotional fulfillment or sexual realization he marries the earthy Meg, who can satisfy his body but not his mind; and she weds Leslie, who provides mental but not physical satisfaction and who, in a fetishistic moment (the reverse of *An Idyll*), kneels down and rubs her cold feet while she touches his cheek and calls him "dear boy."

In the second scene of sublimated sexual passion, George's riotous dance with Lettie, the powerful prose rhythms approximate Dionysian music and end in the climactic exhaustion of a sexual orgasm. This scene also repeats, in a subtle way that becomes clear when we look at the painting, the sexual posture of *An Idyll:* the man's glowing look as he lifts and tightly clasps the woman, and the woman's loose hair, parted lips, trailing feet and attitude of fearful abandon.

Even after they are both engaged, George cannot give up Lettie, and in the wood that recalls the background of *An Idyll* he vainly pleads for her love and once again reenacts the emotions of the painting:

> "No, Lettie, don't go. What should I do with my life? Nobody would love you like I do—and what should I do with my love for you?—hate it and fear it, because it's too much for me?"
>
> She turned and kissed him gratefully. He then took her in a long, passionate embrace, mouth to mouth. In the end it had so wearied her, that she could only wait in his arms till he was too tired to hold her. He was trembling already.[31]

But their love cannot be resurrected, and their relationship does not progress beyond this embrace.

The swimming scene is the culmination of the novel, a synthesis not only of the idyll of the dance and the wood, but also of the story of the first marriage of the gamekeeper Annable, which predicts what the marriage of George and Lettie would have been like. When Annable, a malicious Pan whose physique, vigor and vitality, and swarthy, gloomy face recall the shepherd in *An Idyll,* was courting his first wife, he used to swim in the river and "dry myself on the bank full where she might see me. . . . I was Greek statues for her." Annable, like George, was a poor young man who suffered sexual humiliation. He openly expresses

George's more covert hostility to women. In Lawrence's novels frustrated passion and frustrating marriage lead inevitably to a moment of male love.

The swimming scene takes place immediately after Lettie's final rejection of George during the third idyll in the wood, and at the end of Cyril's tepid and unsuccessful courtship of George's sister, Emily. The sexual debilitation of Cyril suits him for the passive role of narrator-voyeur. He longs for someone to nestle against, and his strong attachment to George during the hay harvest culminates in the Whitmanesque chapter, "Poem of Friendship," where naked men roll in the grass and frolic in the pond, and the faithful dog chases away the intruding Emily. Cyril's physical attraction to the rugged masculinity of George and Annable is an attempt to break away from his possessive mother, who "hated my father before I was born," and to regain his lost father. Earlier in the novel George was sexually excited by looking at Cyril's reproductions of the homosexual Aubrey Beardsley's *Atalanta* and *Salome*. And at the pond, as Cyril admires George's naked body, George "laughed at me, telling me I was like one of Aubrey Beardsley's long, lean, ugly fellows. I referred him to many examples of slenderness," in the same way that Annable compared himself to Greek statues. As Cyril loses himself in contemplation of George's physical beauty he remembers the story of Annable. George

> saw I had forgotten to continue my rubbing, and laughing he took hold of me and began to rub me briskly, as if I were a child, or rather, a woman he loved and did not fear. I left myself quite limply in his hands, and, to get a better grip of me, he put his arm round me and pressed me against him, and the sweetness of the touch of our naked bodies one against the other was superb. It satisfied in some measure the vague, indecipherable yearning of my soul; and it was the same with him. When he had rubbed me all warm, he let me go, and we looked at each other with eyes of still laughter, and our love was perfect for a moment, more perfect than any love I have known since, either for man or woman.[32]

The rubbing is explicitly homosexual as Cyril replaces his tall and threatening sister, Lettie, and becomes "a woman he loved and did not fear" in this final representation of the limp, passive figure pressed against the powerful male in *An Idyll*. We are not told what George feels, but Cyril projects his own feelings onto his lover ("it was the same with him"). Cyril's final statement is a paraphrase of David's lament for Jonathan in II Samuel 1:26: "very pleasant hast thou been unto me: thy love to me was wonderful, passing the love of women."

The male characters in *The White Peacock* are either Lintons or Heathcliffs, and they form a symbolic representation of the descent of man from the overrefined to the barbarian—from Cyril and Leslie to George, Annable and the degraded and degenerate Mr. Beardsall—in which the cultured men lack passion and the passionate men renounce culture. Though these incomplete men are unable to establish a successful heterosexual relationship, their split is symbolically unified in the homosexual consummation of George and Cyril. In "Poem of Friendship" the Whitmanesque and the biblical motifs combine to form a satisfying male idyll that contrasts with and transcends unhappy marriage and frustrated love.

VII

The publication of *The White Peacock,* in January 1911, was associated in Lawrence's mind not only with the death of his mother and his complicated emotional relations with women and men, but also with the critical illness that overwhelmed him at the end of the "sick year." In "Return to Bestwood," written three years before his death, he recalled: "When I wrote my first book, and it was going to be published—sixteen years ago—and my mother was dying, a fairly well-known editor [Austin Harrison] wrote to my mother and said, of me: 'By the time he is forty, he will be riding in his carriage.' To which my mother is supposed to have said, sighing, 'Ay, if he lives to be forty!' . . . I was always weak in health, but my life was strong. Why had they all made up their minds that I was to die?"

Two weeks after his engagement to Louie, Lawrence emphasized the psychological basis of his physical illness and urged her: "always abuse me if I say I'm sick; I'm never ill unless I want to luxuriate in a little bath of sympathy."[33] Just as Lawrence's first serious illness, at the end of 1901, enabled him to escape from Haywood's surgical appliances factory, so his second bout of pneumonia, at the end of 1911, allowed him to escape from teaching in Croydon.

"The last fortnight I have felt really rotten," he told Edward Garnett in November 1911, "it is the dry heat of the pipes in school, and the strain—and a cold. I must leave school, really." He became gravely ill at the end of the month, was cared for in Croydon by Ada and by a professional nurse, and by mid-December had pronounced the dreaded word that he would scarcely mention for the rest of his life: "The doctor [William Addey, the Jones family physician] says I mustn't go to school again or I shall be consumptive."[34]

It is almost certain, as Dr. William Ober observed, that the pneumonia of 1911 "may very well have reactivated an arrested juvenile tuberculous infection," and that Lawrence suffered from this disease throughout his adult life. Dr. Addey's remark that returning to school would make him consumptive was probably a euphemistic way of saying that Lawrence already had tuberculosis, might infect the pupils and would not be permitted to return to teaching.

Ford Madox Ford, discussing the possibility of a disability pension, noted: "Had the school in which he taught been in the administrative County of London, he would have received substantial compensation," but the County of Kent school board "made no provision for disabled teachers." Far from receiving insurance or pension payments, Lawrence was actually penalized for his illness. In January 1912 he had £1.5.11 deducted from his salary "for absence occasioned by personal illness . . . more than the number of times allowed by the Standing Orders."[35]

However, James Smyth, clerk to the Education Committee at Croydon, and Philip F. T. Smith, Lawrence's headmaster, both gave him first-rate recommendations, which confirmed the praise from George Holderness of the British School in Eastwood and from the Teachers' Training Department of Nottingham University. James Smyth wrote: "Mr. Lawrence is an excellent teacher, resourceful and intelligent in his methods, a sympathetic and capable disciplinarian." Philip Smith agreed that as an instructor, "Mr. Lawrence is most successful. His methods are wholly modern, and have the great merit that they are particularly adapted to obtain results in the face of the limitations imposed by the elementary school curriculum."[36] Though Lawrence disliked schoolteaching, he was extremely idealistic, innovative, conscientious and hard-working. He took an intensely personal approach to the students and encouraged them to develop their individual potential. He wanted to do well in his job, mastered the requisite skills and overcame the difficulties of discipline. He was an excellent teacher and retained the didactic element in his life and work.

In January 1912 Lawrence convalesced in Bournemouth, on the south coast, as in April 1902 he had convalesced in Skegness, on the east coast. Pleased to be ambulatory and recuperating from his illness, he was at first extremely enthusiastic. "It's a jolly place—you would like it," he told Louie.

> I wish always you had come. There are 45 people in, all sorts. One gets up at 8.30, and breakfasts at nine—very prolific breakfasts— bacon and kidney and ham and eggs—what you like. I chatter in the smoke room till about 10.30—then work in my room where I have had a fire made—until 1.30, when we have lunch—which is a bigger meal, or as big as our usual dinners. In the afternoon I go out, or if it's wet, like today, I just stop in the recreation room and we play cards and games. After tea I went out with a man for a stroll, then gin and bitters, then dinner.

But only a month later, when he had observed conditions more carefully, he complained to Jessie that "the place exists for the sick. They hide the fact as far as possible, but it's like a huge hospital. At every turn you come across invalids being pushed or pulled along. . . . I shall be glad when I get away."[37] Lawrence also noted that Robert Louis Stevenson had been an invalid in Bournemouth in 1884.

In February 1912 Lawrence resigned from Croydon and broke his engagement with Louie. He seemed more introspective, anxious and morbid; he had rejected his old life, but was not quite ready for a new experience. "Illness changes me a good deal," he told Helen Corke, "like winter on the face of the earth." And Ada, who had nursed him, tried to console Louie by agreeing: "It's surprising how very much changed Bert is since his illness, and changed for the worse too, I think." His brush with death and the beginning of a lifelong invalidism—though he had many periods of remission—also intensified his mood of depression, negativity and isolation. Jessie, who saw him when he returned to Eastwood in February, reported that "below the surface was a hopelessness hardly to be distinguished from despair. . . . With all his gifts he was somehow cut off, unable to attain that complete participation in life that he craved for. . . . Utterly lonely, he looked as if life had turned to complete negation."[38]

Lawrence's recovery was not complete, and he continued to be troubled by ill health. In June 1913 David Garnett noticed that after a fit of coughing Lawrence's handkerchief was "spotted with bright arterial blood." Three months later, Lawrence bravely insisted that he was not tubercular and again emphasized the close connection between psychological stress and somatic disease: "my lungs are crocky, but I'm not consumptive—the type, as they say. I am not really afraid of consumption, I don't know why—I don't think I shall ever die of *that*. I am quite certain that when I have been ill, it has been sheer distress and nerve strain which have let go on my lungs."[39]

VIII

In the summer of 1911, between his mother's death and his own illness, Lawrence formed an important friendship with Edward Garnett (the father of David), who wrote to him soliciting a story for *Century* magazine in America and soon replaced Ford as mentor and father figure. The tall and mildly eccentric Edward, born in 1868, was the son of the Keeper of Printed Books in the British Museum and a boyhood friend of Ford. His wife, Constance, six years his senior, was a prolific and influential translator of Russian novels into English. She had won a scholarship to Newnham College, Cambridge, where she took a first-class degree in Greek, and had learned Russian from exiles in England and during a short visit to Russia, where she met Tolstoy. She maintained an adulterous liaison with the anarchist and assassin Sergei Stepniak, as Edward did with the painter Nellie Heath. Lawrence took Edward as a model of bohemian behavior and declared: "he is most beautifully free of the world's conventions." He first visited the Garnetts at The Cearne, their country house in Kent, in October 1911, and later told their son, David: "I always look on the Cearne as my jumping-off point into the world—and your father as my first backer."[40]

When they first met, Edward was an unsuccessful poet, playwright and novelist, and a brilliantly perceptive publisher's reader for Duckworth. He was the discoverer and close friend of Conrad and Galsworthy, and had also helped W. H. Hudson and H. E. Bates. Lawrence, echoing Ford's criticism and noting the faults of his own novel, had rashly told his editor at Heinemann that *The Trespasser* "is execrable bad art: it has no idea of progressive action, but arranges gorgeous tableaux-vivants which have not any connection one with the other." Despite these radical defects, Edward saw the artistic potential in Lawrence's worst novel and urged Duckworth to bring it out in May 1912.

The Trespasser, like *The White Peacock*, examines Lawrence's sexual conflicts and portrays the theme of cruel, destructive, "spiritual" women who "don't want [men]; they want the flowers of the spirit. . . . Therefore they destroy the natural man in us." Helena in the novel, like Helen Corke in Lawrence's poems, "has been rejecting the 'animal' in humanity, till now her dreams are abstract, and full of fantasy, and her blood runs in bondage, and her kindness is full of cruelty."[41] The theme of the cold woman who arouses and then rejects male passion was at the heart of Lawrence's first two, closely related novels.

The Trespasser is mannered, anxious, inert—and fashionably Wagnerian. It is a novel of dreamy, wildly fluctuating moods—a doom-laden *Liebestod.* It successfully portrays the natural seascapes and conveys the atmosphere of the Cowes Regatta of the Isle of Wight. But it is also terribly dull, the only Lawrence novel virtually devoid of literary interest. The main reason for these weaknesses is that, unlike his other works, it was adopted, secondhand, from Helen Corke's story and was not based on Lawrence's lived experience.

In the spring of 1912, the end of the Croydon years, Lawrence was cut off from his family and fiancée in the Midlands and from the teaching profession. After the death of his mother, he had suffered serious illness, developed tuberculosis and become a permanent invalid. But he had moved from Eastwood to London and had established himself in the literary world. He had met distinguished, bohemian men, who lived with women who were not their wives and carried on adulterous affairs. He craved complete participation in life and was ready, at last, for Frieda Weekley. She led him out of his sexual impasse and helped him realize his greatness as a man and as a writer.

CHAPTER SEVEN

Frieda,
1912

I

FRIEDA VON RICHTHOFEN WEEKLEY came from an aristocratic German family that no longer possessed vast estates or great wealth. The family included a distinguished explorer of Asia and a Prussian foreign secretary, as well as Frieda's cousin the "Red Baron," Manfred von Richthofen, the greatest German flier in World War I, who was finally shot down in April 1918 after eighty victories in the air. Another cousin, Wolfram von Richthofen, chief of staff under General Hugo von Sperrle when the Nazis bombed the Basque capital of Guernica in 1937, later commanded the Condor Legion in the Spanish Civil War.

The family had once owned twenty thousand acres of wheat, barley and sugar beet near Breslau in Upper Silesia (now Poland), where Frieda's father, Baron Friedrich, was born in 1845. He had fought in the Franco-Prussian War of 1870, been wounded in the right hand, which remained crippled, and been taken prisoner. His father's risky speculations and financial failure had deprived Friedrich of his ancestral inheritance, and his wound had suddenly ended his military career. Discharged from the army with the rank of lieutenant and an Iron Cross, he trained as an engineer, joined the civil administration of Metz—a garrison town in Lorraine, which Germany captured from

France in 1871 and lost in 1918—and was responsible for the canals around the city. He married Anna Marquier (born 1851), the daughter of a lawyer from Donaueschingen in the Black Forest. But when his wife discovered that the self-assertive but essentially weak man was a compulsive gambler and womanizer, she came to despise him, and their marriage soon deteriorated into an armed truce.

Friedrich and Anna had three exceptionally beautiful daughters. Else, born in 1874, was a pupil of the economist Max Weber and the mistress of his brother Alfred. She was one of the first women to earn a doctorate at Heidelberg, had been an inspector of factories in Karlsruhe and became professor of social economics at the university. In 1902 she married Edgar Jaffe, who in 1918–19 was finance minister in the short-lived revolutionary government of Bavaria. Else (like her mother) corresponded frequently with Lawrence and translated "The Fox" and *The Boy in the Bush* into German. Lawrence dedicated *The Rainbow* to her. Frieda, six years older than Lawrence, was born in Metz on August 11, 1879. Her younger sister, Johanna, born in 1882, was married to an officer on the German General Staff. She later divorced him and married a Berlin banker.[1] Frieda's family, though not wealthy or powerful, had made distinguished contributions to geography, diplomacy, military service, education and government. Frieda and her sisters were well-born, attractive and intelligent. And, like their father, they had unconventional sex lives.

Frieda was a German daughter of the regiment who attended balls at the Prussian court in Berlin in the late 1890s, the wife of an English university professor in Nottingham from 1899 to 1912, a wandering impoverished bohemian with Lawrence from 1912 to 1930 and a famous widow living with an Italian soldier in the Rockies from 1930 to 1956.

Her first husband, Ernest Weekley, fourteen years older than Frieda, had come from humble origins and had made his way in the world through hard work and intellectual ability. His father was a poorly paid official who distributed alms to the poor for the Hampstead Board of Guardians. Born in London, the second of nine children, Ernest became a schoolmaster at seventeen; he took a B.A. and an M.A. in French and German at London University and then a first-class degree in medieval and modern languages at Trinity College, Cambridge. He studied at Bern, Paris and Freiburg, where he was *Lektor* in English during 1897–98. In 1898 he became professor of French at University College, Nottingham. He met Frieda during a holiday in the Black Forest and married her in Freiburg, when she was just twenty, on August 29, 1899.[2]

According to Frieda, her wedding night with Weekley was a disaster. She was impulsive and playful; he was repressed and humorless. And she was shocked by the contrast between her idealistic expectations and the harsh reality of her first sexual experience. While he waited outside their hotel room in Lucerne, she undressed and impulsively climbed on top of a huge carved oak cupboard, with "the frills of her knickers flapping from her climbing legs. Triumphantly she reached the top, and sat there, wondering what he would do if he couldn't find her. . . . Two hours later, [after sleeping with Weekley] . . . she was in an unspeakable torment of soul. It had been so horrible, more than horrible. . . . She had expected unspeakable bliss and now she felt a degraded wretch."[3] Though they had three children (Montague, born 1900; Elsa, born 1902; Barbara, born 1904) and lived together for thirteen years, Frieda and Ernest could never resolve the essential differences in their temperaments, outlooks and expectations.

Her sister Else and daughter Barbara have explained Frieda's motives for marrying this conventional, cowardly and somewhat comical man, whom Aldous Huxley called "possibly the dullest Professor in the Western hemisphere." Else suggested that since she and her sisters had no fortune, they could not marry army officers. And since in Metz, the second-biggest garrison in Germany, they met almost no one but officers, their choice was extremely limited. Weekley seemed more profound, moral and earnest than Frieda's military suitors. She was genuinely fond of him and felt he would give her access to the academic world in England (of which she knew nothing).

Barbara believed that Frieda was impressed by "Ernst" (as she called him, for they spoke German at home). She thought him solemn but steady; he fell madly in love and worshipped her. She wanted to escape from a weak father who was a gambler, and from a silly mother who wished to get rid of her daughters and encouraged Weekley's courtship. Frieda's title impressed Nottingham, but she was too unconventional to help Weekley in his career. Frieda had considered marriage "a step somewhere," but she did not know what she was getting into and was in fact bored to death in Nottingham. "Ernst" always tried to repress her intellectually. When she offered to give French lessons, he said: "but the student is advanced."[4]

Weekley, a fanatical worker, wrote many textbooks and volumes on etymology, including the popular *The Romance of Words* (1912), *The Romance of Names* (1914) and *An Etymological Dictionary of Modern English* (1922). Stirred by his endless energy, even the indolent Frieda

joined the cottage industry and edited Schiller's *Ballads* (1902) and
Ludwig Bechstein's *Märchen* (1906) for Blackie's series of Little German Classics. But Frieda, a creature of emotion and impulse, soon
wearied of provincial academic life. Her son, Montague, retrospectively
observed that "it was a most incompatible marriage, hopeless from the
start. Looking back on it now, I see there was no prospect of its lasting. . . . My father had a crushing schoolmasterly manner and not much
tact; he couldn't resist putting her in her place."[5]

Frieda's first affair was with Will Dowson, a wealthy, married lace
manufacturer who owned one of the first private cars in Nottingham and
used it for their assignations. While visiting her family in Germany in
1907, Frieda became the mistress of Freud's brilliant pupil Otto Gross,
and then of Gross' disciple, the painter Ernst Frick. (Else also had an
affair with Otto Gross, and bore him a son in 1907.) Gross, who wanted
Frieda to leave Weekley and remain with him, later became a cocaine
addict and in 1920 died of undernourishment and exposure in a Berlin
sanatorium. In *Mr. Noon,* Johanna (Frieda) describes the virile
Eberhard (Gross) as a liberator and a Lawrencean precursor who
taught her about freedom and love: "He was a genius—a genius at love.
He understood so much. And then he made one feel so free. He was
almost the first psychoanalyst, you know—he was Viennese, too, and far,
far more brilliant than Freud. They were all friends. But Eberhard was
spiritual—he may have been demoniacal, but he was spiritual. . . . He
made me believe in love—in the sacredness of love. He made me see that
marriage and all those things are based on fear."[6] Gross taught Frieda
the elements of psychoanalysis and the principle of sexual freedom; he
taught her to recognize her desires and to have love affairs without
feeling guilty. Because of Gross' ideas, Frieda felt restricted by Weekley.
Yet Weekley remained naively unaware of Gross' influence and of
Frieda's infidelities, and was fond of calling her his "pure white lily."
When Lawrence became angry he would torment Frieda about this and
quote Shakespeare's sonnet to remind her: "Lilies that fester smell far
worse than weeds."

II

A Teutonic goddess, Frieda was a tall, strikingly handsome, golden-haired woman with a magnificent figure. Picturesque and arty, she favored peasant skirts and embroidered blouses. She had a deep, throaty voice, rolled her *r*'s and spoke with a distinct German accent. David Garnett, who accompanied the Lawrences on their honeymoon and walked across the Alps with them to Italy, described Frieda's forthright personality and luxurious catlike trances: "Her head and the whole carriage of her body were noble. Her eyes were green, with a lot of tawny yellow in them, the nose straight. She looked one dead in the eyes, fearlessly judging one and, at that moment, she was extraordinarily like a lioness: eyes and colouring, and the swift power of her lazy leap up from the hammock where she had been lying." Lady Ottoline Morrell, whose friendship with Lawrence aroused Frieda's jealousy, found her childish, violent and overwhelming:

> Frieda was indeed an extraordinary woman, very vital, robust and virile, a Prussian Brunhilde, who had educated herself on Nietzsche. She was clever in a way but too violent and had no wisdom. She combined timidity with violence, like a great, spoilt, self-willed ungovernable child, who, if she cannot get her own way, will sulk in peevish spiteful temper or steal round and get it another way and then be triumphant....
>
> Frieda is devilish, and she really is a wild beast, quite uncontrolled, cruel to Lawrence, and madly jealous if she thinks anyone esteems Lawrence more than her.[7] *Ottoline at Garsington*

Aldous Huxley met Frieda and Lawrence at Garsington, Ottoline's country house, became one of their closest friends during the last five years of Lawrence's life and portrayed Frieda as Katy Maartens in *The Genius and the Goddess* (1955). Unlike Ottoline, he stressed Frieda's unconventionality, self-assurance and tranquillity: "She had the most sovereign disregard for what people might think or say about her—a disregard based upon a certain native aristocracy, on the confidence of a very rich personality in its own essential rightness and excellence. This meant that she was never anxious, never apologetic, never tense or nervous." The aristocratic painter Dorothy Brett, who adored Lawrence and followed him to New Mexico in 1924, quarreled with Frieda and was banned from their household. But she recognized Frieda's best qualities and generously portrayed her rival as vital, responsive and robust: "she is a big, warm, bounding creature, eyes blue and free, mouth a broad grin, bodice and skirt colorful and glowing: rough, hearty, and undoubtedly handsome. . . . [Frieda's] immense, jolly, warm earthiness was so disarming. . . . [Her] laugh, her sparkling blue eyes, her zest for life were irresistible."8 And Mabel Luhan, who also struggled with Frieda for possession of Lawrence in New Mexico, admitted that Frieda was excellent company, had a gift of immediate intimacy and was the freest woman she had ever known.

Frieda was an attractive mixture of good and bad qualities. Spontaneous, generous and passionate, she was also indolent, selfish and amoral. Lawrence's acquaintances (who split into opposing camps over Frieda) admired her beauty, vitality, self-confidence and belief in Lawrence's genius, but condemned her aristocratic superiority, German chauvinism, infidelity and inability to care for her invalid husband. Lawrence admired Frieda's character and tried to accept, modify or balance the faults that seemed to derive from her nationality, background and class.

III

In March 1912, when Lawrence first met Frieda, he was twenty-six and she was thirty-two (a year younger than Alice Dax and nine years older than Louie Burrows). The descriptions of his appearance vary, according to the friend's point of view and relation to Lawrence, from the satiric to the idealistic. But they agree about essentials. According to the factual notations on his passport, Lawrence was five feet nine inches tall, had blue-grey eyes and light-brown hair. A Croydon acquaintance stressed the poor health of the spectral figure—his pale face, stooping shoulders, narrow chest, febrile hands and hollow cough—which led to pneumonia in November 1911.

David Garnett, whose description was biased by his quarrel with Lawrence in 1915, found him unattractive and emphasized his proletarian aspect:

Lawrence was slight in build, with a weak, narrow chest and shoulders, but he was a fair height and very light in his movements. This lightness gave him a sort of grace. His hair was of a colour, and grew in a particular way, which I have never seen except in English working men. It was bright mud-colour, with a streak of red in it, a thick mat, parted on one side. Somehow, it was incredibly plebeian, mongrel and underbred. His forehead was broad, but not high, his nose too short and lumpy, his face colourless, like a red-haired man's, his chin (he had not then grown a beard) altogether too large, and round like a hairpin . . . and the lower lip, rather red and moist, under a scrubby toothbrush moustache.

John Middleton Murry, Lawrence's closest male friend, agreed that he had an "irremediably plebeian nose, as if deficient in bone or cartilage." But Catherine Carswell, a loyal and adoring disciple, idealized his "deep-set jewel-like eyes, thick dust-coloured hair, pointed underlip of notable sweetness, fine hands, and rapid but never restless movements."[9]

Lawrence wore conventional clothes before the war. But in 1915 (influenced, no doubt, by Frieda) he adopted bohemian dress, parted his hair in the middle and grew a red beard— "behind which I shall take as much cover as I can"—in imitation of his father. Helen Thomas, widow of the poet Edward Thomas, who met Lawrence after his attack of influenza in 1919, found him tall and emaciated, delicate and deathly pale. Jonathan Chambers, Jessie's brother, noted that Lawrence, who loved to sing hymns and ballads, had a poor, squeaky voice. Frieda's daughter Barbara agreed that "he had a high-pitched voice, a slight Midlands accent, and a mocking but spirited and brilliant manner." (Barbara's brother said he had a strong accent; Lawrence's niece called it an educated Midlands accent.) And Rhys Davies, a Welsh writer who met Lawrence in Bandol in 1928, confirmed: "His voice became shrill as he was roused—and how easily he was roused to an extreme of intensity!"[10]

Earl Brewster, who met Lawrence in Capri in 1921 and became one of his closest companions during the last decade of his life, emphasized (like Catherine Carswell) his perception and vitality: "His face was pale; his hands long, narrow, capable; his eyes clear-seeing and blue; his brown hair and red beard glowing like flames from the intensity of his life; his voice was flexible, generally of medium pitch, with often a curious, plaintive note, sometimes in excitement rising high in key. He always appeared to be carelessly dressed."[11] The Danish painter Knud Merrild spent the winter of 1922 with Lawrence on the ranch above Taos and had ample opportunity to observe him closely. "We knew he wasn't so very strong," Merrild said, "but he didn't particularly strike us as a sick person." Yet the American author Carleton Beals, who met Lawrence in Mexico the following year, retrospectively described him as a sickly, post–*Lady Chatterley* satyr: "He was a thin man with a body that seemed about to fall to pieces; his face was pasty, expressionless, but his greenish eyes glared from out his pale beard with a curious satyr-like luster."[12]

Lawrence's fictional self-portraits are also perceptive. In *Sons and Lovers* he acknowledges his plebeian aspect but notes the vital, clear-seeing eyes: Paul Morel's "face was rough, with rough-hewn features, like the common people's; but his eyes under the deep brows were so full of life that they fascinated" Clara. And Hepburn's eyes, in "The Captain's Doll," had "that curious, bright, unseeing look that was more like second sight than direct human vision."[13]

IV

Lawrence had abandoned his position in Croydon and was still recovering from pneumonia. On about March 16, 1912, he went to the home of his favorite university teacher, Professor Ernest Weekley, to inquire about a job teaching English in Germany, where his intellectual uncle, Fritz Krenkow, was then living. Frieda remembered that Lawrence was very ill when she first met him, pale and thin but with a strange eagerness and intensity. He fiercely denounced the split between body and spirit in women (as he had done in his first two novels) and talked appropriately enough about Oedipus. Afterward he wrote to her: "You are the most wonderful woman in all England"—a rather cheeky thing for a coal miner's son to say to an older, married, aristocratic woman with three children.

Lawrence immediately and intuitively understood Frieda, penetrated her cheerful pose and perceived that she was unhappy in her marriage. A few days after their first meeting, they went for a walk in the country and he became absorbed in floating paper boats on a stream for Monty, Elsa and Barbie. Frieda vividly recalled: "crouched by the brook, playing there with the children, Lawrence forgot about me completely. Suddenly I knew I loved him." Moved by his tenderness, she boldly proposed they become lovers. Lawrence—who had waited in vain for such a warm response from Jessie, Agnes, Helen and Louie—wanted to begin properly and restrained himself with Frieda. He refused her offer on moral grounds, declared his love and insisted they elope: "No, I will not stay in your husband's house when he is away, but you must tell him the truth and we will go away together, because I love you."[14] Frieda wanted a love affair; Lawrence wanted marriage.

He was instantly enchanted by Frieda. The following month, before their elopement, he revealed his passion to Edward Garnett, a sympathetic and worldly bohemian, who understood Lawrence's feelings and behavior as well as his novels and poems. Lawrence praised Frieda's noble lineage and her intrinsic though nonconformist morality: "she is the daughter of Baron von Richthofen, of the ancient and famous house of Richthofen—but she's splendid, she is really.... Mrs. Weekley is perfectly unconventional, but really good—in the best sense.... She is the woman of a lifetime." Six weeks later, while living with Frieda in Germany, he added more personal details: "She's got a figure like a fine Rubens woman, but her face is almost Greek."[15]

Lawrence described, in two of his fictional works, his instant attraction to her sensuality and her *difference* from other women. In "Love Among the Haystacks," the German governess "was strange, foreign, different from the ordinary girls: the rousing, feminine quality seemed in her concentrated, brighter, more fascinating than in anyone he had known." And when Tom Brangwen first sees the foreign widow, Lydia Lensky, in *The Rainbow,* he reacts irrationally, impulsively: "'That's her,' he said involuntarily.... His eyes met hers. He looked quickly away, pressing back his head, a pain of joy running through him. He could not bear to think of anything."[16]

Unlike Lawrence's previous girlfriends, Frieda was not an English, virginal, intellectual, well-educated, professional teacher. The other women were red- or dark-haired; Frieda was blond. And with Frieda he did not need a secure job and a comfortable nest egg. When they left England for Germany in early May he had only £11. Agnes, Helen and Louie had refused to sleep with Lawrence; Jessie had unwillingly submitted; but Frieda responded with an unrestrained and exciting passion. Lawrence had told Louie: "my mother has been passionately fond of me, and fiercely jealous. She hated [Jessie]—and would have risen from the grave to prevent my marrying her."

Only Frieda was strong enough to conquer his mother—and then only after her death. "If my mother had lived I could never have loved you, she wouldn't have let me go," he confessed to Frieda. And she shrewdly perceived that "in his heart of hearts I think he always dreaded women, felt that they were in the end more powerful than men." Frieda was Lawrencean before Lawrence. She led him to Europe, to an expatriate existence, and to a defiant opposition to society. She satisfied his emotional and sexual needs and liberated him from the puritanism he had inherited from his mother. "One sits so tight on the crater of one's passions and emotions," Lawrence wrote, with a volcanic metaphor. "I am just learning—thanks to Frieda—to let go a bit."[17]

It is scarcely surprising that Lawrence fell in love with the beautiful baroness. But it is rather more difficult to understand why Frieda eloped with a penniless miner's son who had no job and few prospects. Ironically, she must have been influenced by Weekley's high opinion of one of his most promising students. Her son, Monty, remembered Frieda lying in bed (a characteristic Molly Bloom–like position) and devouring the early drafts of *Sons and Lovers*. And—like Jessie, Ford and Pound—she was struck by Lawrence's astonishing talent. Like Lawrence, she was attracted to the strangeness of someone from an entirely different background, and gave in to his imperious demands—even though it meant abandoning her children. She later ignored her initial indecision and suggested that she had always been committed to him: "That he came of the common people was a thrill to me. It gave him his candour, the wholesomeness of generations of hard work and hard living behind him, nothing sloppy, and lots of guts. . . . I had to be his wife if the skies fell, and they nearly did. The price I had to pay was almost more than I could afford, with all my strength."

Then there was Lawrence's respect for her, his insistent claim to her love, his absolute commitment, his life-and-death need for her as a wife. As Frieda wrote in her fictionalized third-person account: "In a sovereign way he took her for himself; she was his and he would never let her go again while he lived; he would kill her rather. She liked it. He wanted her, he needed her, and that was bliss. Nothing else mattered; all the misery of loneliness, of unconnectedness was gone." Finally, like Lawrence, she justified their behavior by a sentient morality that transcended all conventions. As she told Edward Garnett, who became her confidant as well as Lawrence's during the *Sturm und Drang* that followed their elopement: "He has taught me the feel and the understanding of things and people, that is morality, I think."[18] They had set each other free, and there were sufficient differences between them to provide endless dialogue and stimulation. But she was *déclassée* and outcast from the moment she left with him.

Though Lawrence boasted of his sexual performance in *Mr. Noon*, his
first night with Frieda—like Weekley's debut—was unsuccessful. In the
bravely honest poem "First Morning," Lawrence admits his own sexual
repression and sexual failure. He was plagued by thoughts of his past
loves and his dead mother, and Frieda, overcome with guilt about her
children, seemed—for all her eagerness—to reject him:

> In the darkness
>> with the pale dawn seething at the window
>> through the black frame
>> I could not be free,
>> not free myself from the past, those others—
>> and our love was a confusion,
>> there was a horror,
>> you recoiled away from me.[19]

V

Lawrence's scandalous elopement with Frieda on May 3, 1912, scarcely
six weeks after they first met, was the most radical decision of his entire
life. He permanently abandoned his teaching career and all hope of a
regular income, decided to live an expatriate life and planned to support
himself entirely as a writer. It was also a momentous step for Frieda.
Like Nora Barnacle, who had eloped with James Joyce in 1904, she
rejected received ideas about religion and morality and, soon after the
death of the writer's mother and their first meeting, ran away to the
Continent with this impoverished but confident young genius, who had
not yet become her husband.

Frieda often took trips from Nottingham to visit her family in Germany. The children, well cared for by their devoted nurse, Ida, were
always ecstatic when she returned. One day Frieda casually said: "Come
and say goodbye to me, Monty," and he failed to realize that this was her
final farewell. She took the two girls to their grandparents' house, at 40
Well Walk in Hampstead, and ran off with Lawrence. They thought she
had gone alone to Metz. After a few weeks, when they asked, "Where is
Mama?" Weekley turned pale and left the room. The grandparents said:
"don't disturb Father now, he's worried," and the children remained

bewildered by her absence. The Weekleys taught them to be bitter about Frieda. Like "She-who-was-Cynthia" in *The Virgin and the Gipsy* (1926), Frieda became an unperson; like the water closet, she was never mentioned. She had never expected to lose all contact with her children and hoped to have them and Lawrence as well.

After conversations in 1925 with Barbara Weekley, the model for the heroine in *The Virgin and the Gipsy,* Lawrence satirically portrayed the desolate atmosphere of the Weekley household after Frieda had left, right down to the addiction to crossword puzzles and the horribly obese grandmother:

> The rector was now forty-seven years old; he had displayed an intense and not very dignified grief after the flight of his wife. Sympathetic ladies had stayed him from suicide. His hair was almost white, and he had a wild-eyed, tragic look. You had only to look at him, to know how dreadful it all was, and how he had been wronged. . . .
>
> Out in the evil world, at the same time, there wandered a disreputable woman who had betrayed the rector and abandoned his little children. She was now yoked to a young and despicable man, who no doubt would bring her the degradation she deserved.[20]

If Lawrence had seemed the dominant partner in Nottingham, the balance of power shifted to Frieda when they left for Metz. During their first trip to Germany, Frieda was entirely at ease while visiting her family, speaking her own language, returning to her country and culture. Lawrence, traveling abroad for the first time, was an outsider and a foreigner, unfamiliar with the surroundings and barely articulate in German. He was completely committed to Frieda, much more in love with her than she was with him. He had very little money, was dependent on the goodwill of her family, submitted himself to their judgment and hoped to be accepted. He had to wait—first in Metz and then alone in the Rhineland—while Frieda made up her mind about whether to accept or reject him, whether to take a German lover (which she did) or to return to her family in England.

The first test occurred when Frieda, greeted at the Metz railroad station by her intellectual sister, Else, whispered to her: " 'I have brought someone with me. You must help me.' [Else then] met her with Lawrence in a little café on the Esplanade, with a fine view of the Moselle valley. He was a very young, sensitive, gentlemanly Englishman, quiet but not shy, who gave an impression of self-reliance." Lawrence passed the next test when he met Frieda and her elegant younger sister, Johanna, at a fair. When he suddenly appeared, looking odd in a cap and raincoat, Frieda was apprehensive about what her sister would think. But Johanna—as intuitive and impulsive as Frieda herself—surprised her by exclaiming: "You can go with him. You can trust him."[21]

Lawrence's presence in Metz became known to the old baron and baroness when, on his fifth day in the town and while dallying with Frieda on the fortifications, he was suspected of espionage and detained by the authorities: "I had to quit Metz because the damn fools wanted to arrest me as a spy. Mrs. Weekley and I were lying on the grass near some water—talking—and I was moving round an old emerald ring on her finger, when we heard a faint murmur in the rear—a German policeman. There was such a to-do. It needed all the fiery little Baron von Richthofen's influence—and he is rather influential in Metz—to rescue me. They vow I am an English officer."

Frieda's father was at that time celebrating the fiftieth anniversary of his entrance into the German army, and the family had gathered to honor him. Her contribution to the festivities was to tell the old soldier that she had left her respectable professor and three small children to run off with a younger, sickly, poor, unemployed, little-known English writer (the son of an illiterate coal miner), who had just been arrested as a spy.

The parents were naturally less enthusiastic about Lawrence than the sisters. The father, trying to boss but being rather nice, begged Frieda to come to her senses and resume her old life. The mother (who later became a great friend) thought Frieda was not suited to be Lawrence's wife and not unreasonably demanded: "Who was I, did I think, that a Baronesse should clean my boots and empty my slops: she, the daughter of a high-born and highly-cultured gentleman."[22] Nothing had been resolved when the police forced Lawrence to leave Metz.

VI

Lawrence, the greatest letter writer in English since Byron and Keats, wrote some of his best letters during his two-week separation from Frieda in mid-May 1912 and throughout the crisis with Weekley that year. They are marked by sympathy, energy, intellectual audacity and imaginative intensity. Though Lawrence and Frieda had committed adultery, they justified their behavior by the transcendent morality of love. Lawrence, who had refused to sleep with Frieda in Weekley's house, was determined to act honestly and openly, and contrasted his own forthright behavior with Weekley's desperate and disgraceful tantrums: "No more dishonour, no more lies," he declared, while still in Metz. "Let them do their—silliest—but no more subterfuge, lying, dirt, fear. I feel as if it would strangle me."

A week later, writing from his uncle Fritz's house in Waldbröl and bewildered by Frieda's uncertainty about whether to stay with Lawrence or return to her children, he shot off a series of questions about her plans (she was, at this point, holding the cards), tried to fortify her commitment and concluded with a nautical metaphor that stressed their precarious state:

> Quakiness and uncertainty are the death of us. See, tell me exactly what you are going to do. *Is* the divorce coming off?—*Are* you going to England at all? Are we going finally to pitch our camp in Munich? Are we going to have enough money to get along with? Have you settled anything definitely with Ernst?—One *must* be detached, impersonal, cold, and logical, when one is arranging *affairs*. We do not want another fleet of horrors attacking us when we are on a rather flimsy raft—lodging in a borrowed flat on borrowed money.

The following day his mood changed and he was calmer. In a letter that implicitly contrasted his real love for Frieda with his transient desire for previous girls, he compared himself to a medieval knight in a spiritual retreat. He emphasized the tremendous significance of their love and marriage (the fundamental basis of his thought and art) which had transcended passion and achieved tranquillity:

Like the old knights, I seem to want a certain time to prepare myself—a sort of vigil with myself. Because it is a great thing for me to marry you, not a quick, passionate coming together. I know in my heart "here's my marriage." . . .

It's a funny thing, to feel one's passion—sex desire—no longer a sort of wandering thing, but steady, and calm. I think, when one loves, one's very sex passion becomes calm, a steady sort of force, instead of a storm. Passion, that nearly drives one mad, is far away from real love.[23]

Lawrence, who had slept only with Alice and Jessie and would sleep with no other woman after he met Frieda, believed that "the instinct of fidelity is perhaps the deepest instinct in the great complex we call sex." Frieda, who was a virgin at her wedding but had had several affairs when she was married to Weekley, believed in the authority of impulse and in unrestrained sexual freedom. She took three lovers in her first four months with Lawrence (Udo von Henning, an anonymous woodcutter and Harold Hobson) and three others during their various marital crises (Cecil Gray in 1917, Middleton Murry in 1923 and Angelo Ravagli in 1926). In fact, Frieda had more lovers when she was with Lawrence than she had had when married to Weekley.

Immediately after his last quoted letter, on May 16 and 17, Lawrence responded to Frieda's challenge by mocking his current rival, von Henning (a German officer in Metz, later killed in Belgium in the first week of the war). He then, quite sincerely and with admirable disinterestedness, perceived her need to test her love and conceded her right to the same sexual freedom as a man. Weekley had wanted to tame her reckless spirit. Lawrence was willing to set it free and tolerate her infidelity until she was sure of his love and could commit herself completely to him:

You fling Henning in my teeth. . . . I think you're rather horrid to Henning. You make him more . . . baby-fied. Or shall you leave him more manly? . . . Where is the [sexually hungry] Henning to get his next feed?

If you want Henning, or anybody, have him. But I don't want anybody, till I see you. . . . I don't believe even *you* are at your best, when you are using Henning as a dose of morphia—he's not much else to you. . . . Only, my dear, because I love you, don't be sick, do will to be well and sane.[24]

According to David Garnett, when Frieda and Lawrence were living in Icking, near Munich, in the early summer of 1912, and after they had quarreled, Frieda, submitting to a sudden impulse, had gone down to the Isar River, "swum over to where a woodcutter was working, had made love to him and had swum back—just to show Lawrence she was free to do what she liked." This no doubt made the woodcutter's day. And Lawrence, who told Garnett about it, seems to have accepted the incident with reasonably good grace. Aldous Huxley, who added some Italian peasants to Frieda's list of lovers, commented with characteristic acuity on this aspect of their marriage. He suggested that Frieda's casual dalliances did not diminish her love for Lawrence and that he reluctantly accepted them because of his belief in her right to freedom and his great need of her: "Frieda and Lawrence had, undoubtedly, a profound and passionate love-life. But this did not prevent Frieda from having, every now and then, affairs with Prussian cavalry officers and Italian peasants, whom she loved for a season without in any way detracting from her love for Lawrence or from her intense devotion to his genius. Lawrence, for his part, was aware of these erotic excursions, got angry about them sometimes, but never made the least effort to break away from her; for he realized his own organic dependence upon her."[25]

A potentially more serious affair took place with Harold Hobson—the son of J. A. Hobson (the author of *Imperialism*), a friend of David Garnett and a consulting engineer—en route to Italy in August 1912. Lawrence described it in *Mr. Noon*—which portrays the turbulent first months with Frieda (May–September 1912) and complements her memoir, *Not I, But the Wind*—and his fictional portrayal is the only account we have of this incident.

The greatest moment in the book, which shows Lawrence's psychological penetration and artistic skill, occurs in the mountains when Johanna (Frieda) confesses that she has slept with one of the young Englishmen (based on Hobson) who had traveled with them for several days. This revelation is such a surprise for Noon (Lawrence) "that he did not know what to feel, or if he felt anything at all. It was such a complete and unexpected statement that it had not really any meaning for him." They walk for a time, and he suddenly says: "Never mind, my love. . . . We do things we don't know we are doing. And they don't signify. . . . I love you—and so what does it matter!" Though Lawrence was sufficiently tolerant of Hobson to have him as a guest at Lake Garda in December 1912, Frieda, who felt guilty and thought he should be angry, disliked his unmanly and humiliating Christian forgiveness: "He seemed to have put her more in the wrong, and assumed a further innocent glory himself."26

Apart from Frieda's infidelity during their first months together, they were troubled by the possibility of having their own children and by Frieda's attachment to the children she had left behind in England. Though he was nearly penniless, had an unstable relationship with Frieda and would not be able to marry her for some time, Lawrence did not believe in birth control. He was pleased at the idea of having a child and willing to undertake the responsibility. He told Frieda, who was alarmed by the prospect of pregnancy, that he was prepared to be a father and would regret not having children: "Never mind about the infant. If it should come, we will be glad, and stir ourselves to provide for it—and if it should not come, ever—I shall be sorry. I do not believe, when people love each other, in interfering there. It is wicked, according to my feeling. I want you to have children to me—I don't care how soon. I never thought I should have that definite desire." The unwanted child wanted children of his own.

But the children never came. In his destructive hagiography, *Son of Woman,* Middleton Murry called Lawrence a man incapable of begetting children and claimed that this caused Lawrence deep distress. Willie Hopkin noted that after his attack of pneumonia in 1901—which Lawrence said had "damaged his health for life"—"his voice grew high-pitched and light, almost like a girl's." Barbara Weekley confirmed Murry's statement, clarified Hopkin's implication and explained this crucial issue. When Lawrence was about sixteen (she said) he had a serious illness, rather like mumps. Though he and Frieda at first wanted to have children, they were unable to do so because the disease had made him sterile.27

VII

Lawrence's problems with the von Richthofen family and the German police, with Frieda's indecision and infidelity, with his sexual failure on the first night, with lack of money, lack of housing and lack of plans, were exacerbated by Ernest Weekley's behavior in Nottingham. The elegant and sarcastic philologist was a man of the world, who had studied at Cambridge and lived in Europe. But he adopted a tone of moral outrage

and then disintegrated into nervous collapse. He behaved with wild
inconsistency, veering from noble generosity to cruel vindictiveness, at
one moment wondering what the neighbors would think and at another
threatening pistols, murder and suicide. Finally, he hardened into self-
destructive bitterness.

On May 7, 1912, Lawrence wrote Weekley about his love for Frieda
and explained why they had gone away together. Weekley, then under
control, recovering from the shock and still hoping that Frieda might
change her mind, whined a little, did the decent thing and asked for a
divorce: "I had a letter from Lawrence this morning. I bear him no ill-
will and hope you will be happy with him. But have some pity on me. . . .
Let me know at once that you agree to a divorce. . . . You have loved me
once—help me now—but quickly." Only a few days later, however, he
appealed to Frieda's mother, emphasizing his shredded nerves and pathetic suffering:

> Dear Mama, please make her understand what a state I am in: I
> cannot see her hand-writing without trembling like an old
> cripple—to see her again would be my death. I would kill myself
> and the children too. . . . I have desperately to stretch every nerve
> in order not to cry out hysterically, and then I am weak as a child
> and can only lie there and think—if only for a quarter of an hour I
> could not think.

Lawrence fully understood Weekley's anger at his public shame and
humiliation (which continued, as Lawrence's fame grew, until his death
in 1954, at the age of ninety), as well as his passionate love for Frieda and
his use of every means to get her back. On April 29, a few days before
leaving for Germany, Lawrence had described Weekley's strange mixture of qualities—well-bred and brutish, pleasant and bitter—and the
ambivalent admiration and hatred the two men felt for each other: "He is
a middle class, gentlemanly man, in whom the brute can leap up. He is
forty six, and has been handsome, is usually ironic, pessimistic and
cynical, nice. I like him. He will hate me, but really he likes me at the
bottom. . . . He has had a bad illness a year or two back. He is getting
elderly, and a bit tired."[28]

In July, when they were living in a villa in Icking, lent by Frieda's
sister, the storm continued. Weekley, still madly in love with Frieda, was
tormented by her betrayal. He implored her to renounce her insane ideas
about free love and return, an obedient wife, to the bosom of her family.

When she received his letters, Frieda would fall on the floor, beating her head and groaning with misery, angry at Lawrence for not begging her to stay for *his* sake. He insisted that she had to decide for herself whether she wanted to live with him and share his poor prospects (*Sons and Lovers* had just been rejected by Heinemann) or return to her family and security. A week later, after yet another sudden shift in mood, Lawrence praised Weekley's love for Frieda and refusal to criticize her. Weekley now blamed Otto Gross for putting crazy ideas into her head. He even called Lawrence "honest" and conceded that he had a great literary future.

By December, when Lawrence and Frieda had moved to Lake Garda, in northern Italy, Weekley—betrayed, humiliated and wounded—had swung back to his violent and vindictive mood. When Lawrence wrote a letter to the children, Weekley threatened to come to Italy and kill them both. Then, playing his last and most potent card, he decided to punish Frieda through her children. He sent a photograph of them and said if she did not come home they would no longer have a mother and she would never see them again. Finally, he agreed that month to divorce Frieda if she promised to cut herself off completely from the family: "I have done with you, I want to forget you and you must be dead to the children. You know the law is on my side."

All this, as Weekley had intended, had a devastating effect on Lawrence and Frieda, and almost destroyed their love. Overwhelmed by the misery he had caused, Lawrence felt helpless, could not cope with her grief and shut himself off from her agony. In 1915, after Lawrence and Frieda had returned to England and married, Ottoline Morrell asked Weekley to allow Frieda to see the children. Writing with gratitude to Ottoline, Frieda explained how miserable she had been in 1912 when everyone—her parents, her children and Lawrence—had turned against her:

> It is so terrible to have hurt a man as I did, because after all he did his best according to his own lights, my first husband I mean and that everybody turned against me is only natural—but it has been so killing and desperate when I felt everybody against me, even Lawrence, who was always quite genuine, but could not bear it, when I was unhappy because of the children—Even they turned against me.... And now I am no longer alone in this battle, you have given me a generous helping hand and I am so grateful to you that I could sing.[29]

Frieda accepted the fact that Weekley hated her, but she could not forgive him for making the children suffer.

Weekley's attitude toward Frieda's desertion remained inflexible to the end. He sold his house, "Cowley," on Private Road in Nottingham. From 1912 he lived with his children and parents in Chiswick (west London) and commuted to the university. He did not mention Frieda for three years, but one day, sitting on a tombstone in a country churchyard, he asked Barbie: "Would you like to see Mama?" Yet when Frieda attempted to see them, he tried to protect the children from her malign influence. Defying these impediments, Frieda crept through the back entrance of their Chiswick house, entered the nursery and found the children at supper with the dreadful Granny and the maiden aunt Maude. She was soon driven out and the law invoked to restrain her. On another occasion, she simply entered the house and took Weekley by surprise. Goaded into fury, he tried to wound her and lapsed into snobbery: "Aren't you ashamed to show your face where you are known? Isn't the commonest prostitute better than you? . . . Do you want to drive me off the face of the earth, Woman? Is there no place where I can have peace? . . . *If you had to go away, why didn't you go away with a gentleman?*" The aristocratic lady attracted to an earthy, primitive, lower-class man would become one of the dominant themes in Lawrence's fiction.

Monty and Elsa, the older children, sided with their father. When they met Frieda as adults they told her: "we don't want to see you again." She seemed to accept this but went away crying. Barbie believed that Frieda "was right to act as she did. . . . But underneath some nasty resentment remained. A poison had seeped into my roots, and I felt an antagonism towards her."

Though Weekley had a few dalliances he was never serious about another woman. Once, when the children were grown up, Frieda came to the house, but they refused to let her meet him. He kept Frieda's letters and photographs in his desk, where they were found after his death. Weekley's obituary in the *Guardian* ignored Lawrence's momentous visit to his house in 1912 and stated, with unintentional irony, "As an old man well over eighty, he wrote: 'I find nothing more pleasantly stimulating than visits of old students.' . . . Domestic misfortune, which might have embittered or broken a lesser man, he accepted with reticent dignity."[30] Barbara believed, on the contrary, that he *was* embittered and broken, and that domestic misfortune had ruined his chance of getting a chair at Oxford or Cambridge.

VIII

The children remained a constant, agonizing, insoluble problem for Lawrence and Frieda. He had endured his mother's devouring love throughout his childhood and now had to suffer Frieda's love for her brood. She did not quarrel about the children when she was happy with Lawrence, but they became a great issue when his love failed to satisfy her. Though Lawrence accepted her lovers, he was fiercely jealous of her children.

Frieda thought Lawrence was unsympathetic and unaware of her misery. He thought there was an element of insincerity in her suffering, that she exaggerated her devotion in order to assuage her guilt. When he heard Frieda cry out in her loud voice (magnified for dramatic effect) that her womb hungered for her children, he would console her by quoting Isaiah, and then enrage her by declaring that she would not have abandoned her children if she had really loved them. " 'Don't be sad [he said]. I'll make a new heaven and earth for them, don't cry, you see if I don't.' I would be consoled yet he would be furious when I went on. 'You don't care a damn about those brats really and they don't care about you.' I cried and we quarrelled.... Over the children, I thought he was beastly; he hated me for being miserable, not a moment of misery did he put up with; he denied all the suffering and suffered all the more, like his mother before him; how we fought over this," Frieda wrote.[31]

Lawrence responded by exposing the irrationality of her behavior and condemning her feminine perversity: "Isn't it a funny thing, if a woman has got her children, she doesn't care about them, and if she has a man, she doesn't care about him, she only wants her children."[32] Lawrence refused to sympathize with Frieda's feelings for a number of complex, emotional reasons. He had experienced the destructive power of maternal love and he could not have children of his own. Since he wanted Frieda's undivided loyalty, he was unwilling to question her decision to leave her family or to confront the pain and suffering they had caused. He also found it difficult to justify her selfish behavior and to accept his own guilt-ridden responsibility.

Lawrence and Frieda came to terms with their adultery by identifying with and assuming the roles of Vronsky and Anna in Tolstoy's great

novel. "Frieda had carefully studied *Anna Karenin* in a sort of 'How to
be happy though livanted' [stolen away] spirit," he told Edward Garnett, and then ironically added: "She finds Anna very much like herself,
only inferior—Vronsky not much like me—too much my superior." In
fact, the comparison went deeper than Lawrence suggested. Like Alexei
Karenin, Weekley was cold, pompous, self-righteous, willing to forgive
his wife and take her back, reluctant to grant a divorce, vindictive in
alienating his children from the mother. Like Vronsky and Anna, Lawrence and Frieda caused a scandal, were disgraced in the eyes of their
families, were tainted by immorality, lost their place in society, led a
rootless life abroad and quarreled bitterly. When Lawrence wrote about
Anna Karenina in his essay "The Novel," he attacked Tolstoy's moral
condemnation of the lovers, which he felt ruined the book, and justified
his own defiance of society: "Nobody in the world is anything but
delighted when Vronsky gets Anna Karenin. Then what about the sin?—
Why, when you look at it, all the tragedy comes from Vronsky's and
Anna's fear of *society*. The monster was social, not phallic at all. They
couldn't live in the pride of their sincere passion, and spit in Mother
Grundy's eye. And that, that cowardice, was the real 'sin.' The novel
makes it obvious, and knocks all old Leo's teeth out."[33] Lawrence makes
the lovers' revolt a cornerstone of his attempt to change society. Tolstoy
seeks redemption in Christianity; Lawrence seeks salvation in love.

CHAPTER EIGHT

Italy,
1912–1913

I

THE IMPACT of Italy, in which he began a lifetime of exile and wandering, and his love for Frieda, who respected his intelligence and admired the power of his imagination, combined to make the seven months he spent in Gargnano the most intensely creative period in Lawrence's entire career. He completed two plays: *The Daughter-in-Law* and *The Fight for Barbara;* finished *Sons and Lovers;* and began *Look! We Have Come Through!*, *Twilight in Italy*, *The Rainbow* and *The Lost Girl*. *Sons and Lovers* clarified his relations with his parents and enabled him to come to terms with his past. *The Fight for Barbara* portrayed his successful struggle with Weekley. *Look! We Have Come Through!* celebrated the emotional riches of his love for Frieda. *Twilight in Italy*, despite its disturbing prophecies, explained why he chose to live mainly in Italy.

Life in Italy—which seemed inexpensive, exotic and adventurous—allowed Lawrence to escape from the class restrictions, familial torments and sexual frustrations of his life in England and Germany, and to devote all his time to writing. Lawrence and Frieda had very little money and very few friends, and spent virtually all their time in remote villages. But they lived in astonishingly beautiful, sunny and pristine settings—long before the invasion of tourists—at the edge of the lake

and the sea. They experienced the excitement of a new world where
everything—food, wine, language, customs—was different and fascinating. He soon sent scores of enthusiastic letters to friends about his
discoveries. They walked, swam, sat in the sun, painted, shopped in the
markets, cleaned and set up their flat. They talked to the peasants,
learned Italian and explored the region. They read the books sent by
Arthur McLeod and Edward Garnett, saw a visiting theatrical group
perform *Hamlet* in Italian. And Lawrence adopted the name Lorenzo.
They had occasional visitors from England, met some of the foreign
residents and—despite their quarrels, which kept them together by
reenacting their domestic drama—had their happiest year.

Both Lawrence and Frieda were extremely vital and responsive, and
derived great pleasure from ordinary things. "I believe the chief tie
between Lawrence and me was always the wonder of living," Frieda
wrote, "every little or big thing that happened carried its glamour with
it." Lawrence was delighted with the wonder of Frieda and wrote
ecstatically to Sallie Hopkin: "Whatever happens, I do love, and I am
loved. I have given and I have taken—and that is eternal. Oh, if people
could marry properly; I believe in marriage."[1]

Lawrence's first journey to Italy established the pattern of his later
travels. He was pleased to settle into a rented house after months of
wandering in Germany, he was enthusiastic about the landscape and
people, he sent eager invitations to friends to visit him. Then he became
bored and irritated by the local conditions. He was driven by a restless
desire for movement and change, and free to go wherever he wished but
uncertain of his desires, he altered his travel plans from day to day—and
then impulsively decamped for the north.

II

Lawrence's choice of Lake Garda as his first residence in Italy was
probably influenced by both Goethe and Pound. In his classic travel
book, *Italian Journey,* Goethe had rhapsodically described the revitalizing beauty of the lake and the landscape: "Lake Garda and the magnificent scenery along its shores ... [are] hemmed in by hills and
mountains, and glimmer with innumerable small villages.... The
beauty of the mirror-like water and the adjacent shore ... had refreshed

my whole being. Along the western shore, the mountains were no longer precipitous and the land steeped more gently down to the lake. . . . No words can describe the charm of this densely populated countryside."[2] And in June 1910, just back in London after a visit to Sirmione on Lake Garda—which had been praised by poets from Catullus to D'Annunzio—Pound told Lawrence it was "the earthly paradise."

Unlike many foreign writers in Italy, who were primarily concerned with Italian high culture—and with acquiring villas, furniture, antiques—Lawrence was seriously interested in folk art and the common people. In mid-September 1912 he rented, for the equivalent of sixty-six shillings a month, the first floor of the large Villa Igéa, whose windows overlooked the lake and had a good view of Monte Baldo. A few days later he wrote to Edward Garnett, praising the place and urging him to visit: "Gargnano is a rather tumble-downish place on the lake. You can only get there by steamer, because of the steep rocky mountainy hills at the back—no railway. You would come via Brescia I should think. There are vineyards and olive woods and lemon gardens on the hill at the back. There is a lovely little square, where the Italians gossip and the fishermen pull up their boats, just near."[3]

Lawrence had a gift for languages. He knew some German and could speak French, and he quickly learned Italian and Spanish. Writing to David Garnett in November, he mocked his first efforts in the new tongue: "Summoning up all my Italian, I say to him 'It's a late harvest.' '*Come?*' he says. I repeat—'A late harvest.' '*Signore*,' he grins. 'It's very early.' I feel like saying to him: 'Don't be a pig, I've done my best.'" He was immediately struck by the strong contrast to England; by the natural beauty, the cheap food and wine, the attractive, sympathetic people, the close family ties, the traditional life, the spontaneous, pagan, primitive element and the sense of freedom. "One must love Italy," he told Arthur McLeod, still stuck in dreary Croydon, "if one has lived there. It is so non-moral. It leaves the soul so free. Over these countries, Germany and England, like the grey skies, lies the gloom of the dark moral judgment and condemnation and reservation of the people. Italy does not judge."[4]

Lawrence and Frieda, who usually spent the hottest time of the year in northern Europe, visited England and Germany in the summer of 1913. They returned to Italy in the fall and settled in Fiascherino, near La Spezia, on the Ligurian coast, until June 1914. Lawrence was conscious of his place in the tradition of rebellious expatriate poets and lived only an hour's walk from San Terenzo, where Shelley had stayed.

Lawrence identified with Byron—a precursor and a kindred spirit—both in England and in Italy. On the last page of *John Thomas and Lady Jane*, the second version of *Lady Chatterley's Lover*, Connie and Parkin make love in "the old, old countryside where Byron walked so often," and he then promises: "We can go to Italy if you like." When a friend was visiting what Lawrence called "the country of my heart," Lawrence vividly recalled his native landscape and wrote from Italy: "How well I can see [the village] Hucknall Torkard and the miners! Didn't you go into the church to see the tablet, where Byron's heart is buried?"[5] Both writers came from Nottingham, were exiles, traveled continuously in the remote corners of Europe, rebelled against the prevailing social code, had a scandalous personal life and a notorious literary career. Like Byron, Lawrence was an expert in deracination and wrote some of his greatest works in Italy.

Once again, in Fiascherino, he found an isolated and inexpensive village (his rent for three small rooms and a kitchen was only fifty shillings a month), with a spectacular view, far from the cities where foreigners usually resided: "There is a little tiny bay half shut in by rocks, and smothered by olive woods that slope down swiftly. Then there is one pink, flat, fisherman's house. Then there is the villino of Ettore Gambrosier, a four-roomed pink cottage among a vine garden, just over the water, and under the olive woods. . . . You run out of the gate into the sea, which washes among the rocks at the mouth of the bay. The garden is all vines and fig trees, and great woods on the hills all round."

The peasants still led a traditional, almost ritualistic life, symbolized by the Good Friday procession in Tellaro, which aroused Lawrence's profound emotions about the meaning of religion and death: "a white, ghostly winding procession, with dark dressed villagers crowding behind. It was gone in a minute. And it made a fearful impression on me. It is the *mystery* that does it—it is Death itself, robbed of its horrors, and only Fear and Wonder going humbly behind."

The main event during his time in Fiascherino was the sudden appearance in that remote place of several Georgian poets, who accentuated the contrast between his life in England and in Italy:

The other day, suddenly descended upon us Lascelles Abercrombie and W. W. Gibson and [Robert] Trevelyan and a man called [Aubrey] Waterfield. We were at a peasant wedding at a house on the bay, dressed in our best clothes in honor of the bride, and having an awfully good time. . . . But it was so queer, to leave the feast and descend into the thin atmosphere of a little group of cultured Englishmen. At the upper room where the feast was spread were twenty-five people. There were nine fowls killed for the feast—and the next course was octopuses.... The wine was running very red—then suddenly we must descend to these English poets. It was like suddenly going into very rare air. One staggered and I quite lost my bearings. Yet they are folk I am awfully fond of.[6]

In Italy, Lawrence found he had escaped from the ugliness of the industrial north to a climate and culture that could provide new settings and characters for his fiction as well as teach him a new mode of consciousness. He tried to go back to the past, to discover a traditional peasant culture, even if the actual place could not satisfy his nostalgic longings or sustain the civilization he hoped to find there. During his first stay in Italy he saw the survival of pagan elements that seemed to revitalize his sense of the Christian religion. He also perceived the fundamental opposition between men and women in a society where labor was strictly divided and sexual roles were distinct. Here he formulated his faith in body and impulse, as opposed to mind and reason, and a justification for his elopement with Frieda: "My great religion is a belief in the blood, the flesh, as being wiser than the intellect. We can go wrong in our minds. But what our blood feels and believes and says, is always true."[7]

Lawrence's theory and practice of travel, his extraordinary sensitivity to foreign places, influenced his unusual approach to travel writing. Lawrence preferred a rough rather than a formal mode of travel, popular rather than high culture. Excited by change and movement, he wished to go to geographical extremes of temperature, altitude and distance. He sought a natural rather than a man-made world, was attracted to people who knew nothing about the machinery of modern civilization, and craved contact with a landscape that still retained its savagery. Travel for Lawrence was a relief from and an incitement to writing, a means of inner exploration and a source of immediate inspiration. Travel intensified his sense of being English at the same time as it removed him from England and allowed him to see his own country more clearly. Like Joyce, he was a regional novelist who became a good European.

Lawrence believed that "a new place brings out a new thing in man," and his lifelong credo became: "when in doubt, *move*." Like the aesthete

Gabriel Nash in James' *The Tragic Muse*, Lawrence was, from now on, always on his way "somewhere else" and could say: "I rove, drift, float." Like Alfred Brangwen in *The Rainbow*, he longed for an ideal place that would transform his inner life: "There seemed to him to be no root to his life, no place for him to get satisfied in. He dreamed of going abroad. . . . He wanted change, deep, vital change of living."[8] Lawrence felt that yearning for something absent or lost which is supposed to have driven Alexander the Great across the known world to India.

Lawrence thought it was his destiny to wander, try new places, know the world and search until he found something that gave him peace. But he was engagingly frank whenever he suffered backward and brutal people, boring journeys and self-created torments. Despite enthusiastic letters to friends, he was retrospectively forced to admit: "Travel seems to me a splendid lesson in disillusion—chiefly that." In his review of H. M. Tomlinson's *Gifts of Fortune*, Lawrence confirmed that though the pattern of his life—and travel books—moved from enchantment to disillusion, the quest itself was still valid: "We travel, perhaps, with a secret and absurd hope of setting foot on the Hesperides, of running our boat up a little creek and landing in the Garden of Eden. This hope is always defeated. There is no Garden of Eden, and the Hesperides never were. Yet, in our very search for them, we touch the coasts of illusion, and come into contact with other worlds."[9]

Lawrence had three main reasons for traveling. He moved because of poor health, he looked for locales that would stimulate his imagination by exposing him to new experiences, and he traveled to discover a place that was better than any place he had ever known. When setting out on his travels, Lawrence noted: "one suffers getting adjusted—but that is part of the adventure. . . . I love trying things and discovering how I hate them."[10] But he felt the excitement more than balanced the unpleasant aspects of the journey, willingly endured the incidental beastliness of travel and knew that the worst trips make the best reading. *Sea and Sardinia*, inspired by a powerful compulsion expressed in the opening sentence, "Comes over one an absolute necessity to move," revealed his psychology of travel and portrayed the traveler as victim.

Lawrence's first travel book, begun in Gargnano in January 1913, portrays his response to the country that became his principal home in the 1920s. *Twilight in Italy* (1916) is neither an account of a journey nor a description of Lawrence's life on Lake Garda, but rather a didactic argument about the religion, culture and society of rural Italy. The book is essentially about the opposition of the Christian and the sensual life, the conflict between the mechanical and the natural modes of existence. *Twilight in Italy* describes how these unresolved conflicts affect the emotional lives of the men and women in the village.

Lawrence argues that the greatest, most deeply rooted enemy of the intuitive and sensual life is Christianity. The regimented monks of the village express the deadening neutrality of the twilight that provides the dramatic title of the book: "The flesh neutralising the spirit, the spirit neutralising the flesh, the law of the average asserted, this was the monks as they paced backward and forward." In contrast to the sterile, solitary and mechanical monks, Lawrence believes in the possibility of unity and consummation between men and women, and attempts to achieve this ideal in his own marriage: "Where is the transcendent knowledge in our hearts, uniting sun and darkness, day and night, spirit and senses? Why do we now know that the two in consummation are one; that each is only a part; partial and alone for ever; but that the two in consummation are perfect, beyond the range of loneliness or solitude?"[11]

But none of the Italians has been able to achieve Lawrence's ideal. Nearly all the evidence presented in the book, and the whole disastrous tendency of modern Italy—with its materialism, money, emigration, machinery, factories, nationalism and war—opposes this fruitful and harmonious consummation of man and woman. Even Hamlet, whom Lawrence sees in the theater, becomes "the modern Italian, suspicious, isolated, self-nauseated, labouring in a sense of physical corruption," and personifies the true frenzy of unresolved polarities. The brief, doomed twilight, eclipsed by the powerful forces of the modern world, is destined to die into darkness: "This great mechanised society, being selfless, is pitiless. It works on mechanically and destroys us, it is our master and our God." It demolishes the old way of life and precipitates the deracinated peasants into unfamiliar chaos.

The anarchistic Italians in exile, who work in a raw Swiss factory and inhabit drab stone tenements, explain the reasons for the imminent extinction of the spinner, the lemon gardens and the traditional way of life: "They loved Italy passionately; but they would not go back."[12] They opposed government policy, refused to serve as soldiers in the colonial war against Turkey that led to the annexation of Libya, and were forced into permanent exile.

Twilight in Italy is a lament for a lost life; and its lyricism about a lovely, free and pagan Italy is radically undermined by its portrayal of "the hideous rawness of the world of men, the horrible, desolating harshness of the advance of the industrial world upon the world of nature. . . . It is as if the whole social form were breaking down, and the human element swarmed within the disintegration, like maggots in cheese."[13] Lawrence foresaw that Italy would become like industrialized England and fought unavailingly against this dehumanization.

III

While living in Gargnano, from September 1912 to March 1913, Lawrence adjusted to life with Frieda as well as to life in Italy. "We've had a hard time, Frieda and I," he told Sallie Hopkin. "It is not so easy for a woman to leave a man and children like that. And it's not so easy for a man and a woman to live alone together in a foreign country for six months, and dig out a love deeper and deeper."[14]

Lawrence's ideal was a tranquil and harmonious union: "The best thing I have known is the stillness of accomplished marriage, when one possesses one's own soul in silence, side by side with the amiable spouse." But he rarely achieved this peaceful state. Instead, he saw relations between men and women—the main subject of his books—as a necessary war, waged between people who love each other, leading to understanding and self-knowledge. For Lawrence, "sex-contact with another individual meant a whole meeting, contact between two alien natures, a grim rencontre, half battle and half delight always, and a sense of renewal and deeper being afterwards."[15] Lawrence hoped to win Frieda's submission without defeating her womanhood, but throughout their ceaseless struggle she was the dominant figure.

He had much to fear from Frieda, whose strengths seemed to match his own weaknesses. She was of noble birth, older, stronger, healthier than the sickly Lawrence; she was sexually experienced and sexually liberated. He resented his dependence on Frieda, was awed by her sexual sophistication and physical desire, was fiercely jealous of her longing for the children, hated her refusal to submit to his domination, and was alternately enraged, depressed and resigned to her flirtations and liaisons. Their conflicts led to an exciting but tense and violent struggle of wills, with the ostensible, though not actual, submission of the subtly powerful woman. Just as Lawrence's outbursts were directly related to his tubercular disease, so Frieda's domination—and his dependence— was closely connected to her overwhelming physical strength.

Lawrence's relationship with Frieda was based on a series of conflicting polarities: English and German, proletarian and aristocrat,
puritan and hedonist. Lawrence was used to doing things for himself;
Frieda had always had servants. He was tidy, she was slovenly; he was
exact, she was careless; he was energetic, she was lazy. He was restless,
disliked roots and "hanging curtains," wanted to be free from domestic
entanglements; she had a *Hausfrau* instinct, desperately wanted to settle
down and have a permanent home of her own. He was always busy; she
was usually idle. He was occupied with his writing, but accepted her
neglect of domestic duties and did most of the housework and cooking—
even when he was ill. Frieda had almost no work to do: she slept, lounged
about with a cigarette, read novels, sewed and embroidered.

The totally impractical Frieda, who had never done any housework
before she lived with Lawrence, recalled: "The first time I washed sheets
was a disaster. They were so large and wet, their wetness was overwhelming. The kitchen floor was flooded, the table drenched, I dripped from
hair to feet." Maria Huxley was quite right when she said: "Frieda is
silly. She is like a child, but Lawrence likes her *because* she is a child." He
was delighted to rescue Frieda from a watery fate and did the household
chores for her as he had once done them for his mother. Aldous Huxley
commented on his meticulous domestic ability: "He was able to absorb
himself completely in what he was doing at the moment; and he regarded
no task as too humble for him to undertake, nor so trivial that it was not
worth his while to do it well. He could cook, he could sew, he could darn a
stocking and milk a cow, he was an efficient wood-cutter and a good hand
at embroidery, fires always burned when he had laid them and a floor,
after Lawrence had scrubbed it, was thoroughly clean." Frieda confirmed this and explained that the contrast in their habits often
provoked his anger: "His movements were quick and yet precise. I don't
remember that he ever cut his finger or bumped himself. It infuriated
him more than the occasion seemed to call for when I did careless things.
'Woman, haven't you got your wits about you?' he would say."[16]

They were alone most of the time, living without company in isolated
places, and inevitably got on each other's nerves. And visits from Lawrence's friends (Frieda seemed to have none of her own) tended to
intensify their problems and lead to conflict. Frieda felt their quarrels
became notorious because they most often took place in public and were
reported by the people who had witnessed them.

He hated her superior attitude to the common people and her in-
grained emphasis on class distinction—even with members of his family.

She felt resentful when people disregarded or even despised her while admiring Lawrence. Sometimes his eruptions were merely a release from the tension of writing. When he was ill, he acted irrationally and seemed infuriated that she was well.

Their quarrels usually began with a trivial occurrence. Frieda might contradict one of his assertions or commands, or he would suddenly attack her for smoking or cutting her hair, for gluttony, ignorance or pretentiousness. Almost anything—from Frieda's defects in character to her chance remarks—would provoke his rage. He would then explode in one of his frequent and ungovernable furies. He would tongue-lash Frieda, as his mother had done to his father; and also try to dominate her physically, as his father had done to his mother. Frieda later said that though she never understood his terrifying changes of mood and temper, she managed to control or endure them: "We shall never understand L's hatred. It came like an impersonal, elemental thing out of nowhere and it frightened me, but a last scrap of me wasn't frightened and I think now I ought to have handled him better; but how can a poor woman handle a thunderstorm?"[17] She repaid his rages with violence and love affairs. In June 1913, after he had declared that women had no souls and could not love, she broke a plate over his head while he was washing the dishes and ran away for two days.

Lawrence's play *The Fight for Barbara* (i.e., Frieda), written in Gargnano in 1912, portrays their marital problems. Apart from differences in birth, background, character, temperament, habits, interests and tastes, their immediate difficulties were their poverty, their elopement and her children. They were poor and financially insecure; and though Lawrence was accustomed to this, it was much harder for Frieda to bear. She had made an abrupt transition from a comfortable and well-regulated existence with Weekley, where she had been the center of attention, to a precarious life with Lawrence, where she was subordinate to his books, the *raison d'être* of their existence. Instead of money and security, she now had intellectual fireworks and an intense emotional life. The fact that she endured the loss of her children and social status shows how deeply she loved Lawrence and how richly she was compensated for her sacrifice.

While struggling for the upper hand in their relationship, both felt isolated and cut off from their familiar world. They suffered from the scandal and shame, from parental disapproval and from guilt about the suffering they had caused. Weekley offered to take Frieda back, seemed unwilling to grant a divorce and feared the scandal would have a terrible effect on his career.[18]

Though Lawrence and Frieda's fights horrified and alienated many of their friends, the two of them seemed to enjoy these public combats and treated their guerrilla warfare as a kind of sexual foreplay. Though they seemed about to murder each other, they needed this violent release and forgot the battles as soon as they were over. Lawrence had told Willie Hopkin that Frieda "is the one possible woman for me, for I must have opposition—something to fight or I shall go under." Frieda also described her strategy and their almost orgasmic release: "What does it amount to that he hit out at me in a rage, when I exasperated him, or mostly when life around him drove him to the end of his patience? I didn't care very much. I hit back or waited until the storm in him subsided. We fought our battles outright to the bitter end. Then there was peace, such peace."[19]

Frieda had a profound influence on his art as well as on his life. She believed in his genius and was intensely responsive to his work; she explained women's feelings and helped him to imagine fictional scenes. She introduced him to Freud's ideas, which she had learned from Otto Gross and which were scarcely known in England at that time. These concepts helped Lawrence to clarify the mother-son relationship in *Sons and Lovers* and led to his residual sympathy for the loutish yet attractive father. But Frieda could also be critical and irreverent. When Lawrence was completing the revisions of *Sons and Lovers,* she got fed up with what she called the tragically doomed "House of Atreus feeling" and wrote a skit called "Paul Morel, or His Mother's Darling." Lawrence, wounded by her satire, lamely said: "This kind of thing isn't called a skit."

After expressing his ideas on love and sex, and portraying Frieda's faults, in the early draft of his next novel, *The Rainbow,* he felt that "it did me good to theorise myself out, and to depict Frieda's God Almightiness in all its glory." Yet when she asked him: "What do I give you, that you didn't get from the others?" he stressed her confidence in him as well as in herself, and replied: "You make me sure of myself, whole"— complete as a man and as an artist. He freely admitted that a woman's otherness, her sense of strangeness, was a vital stimulus for his art: "It is hopeless for me to try to do anything, without I have a woman at the back of me. . . . A woman that I love sort of keeps me in direct communication with the unknown."[20]

The more positive side of their marriage is portrayed in Lawrence's sequence of love poems *Look! We Have Come Through!,* which was mainly written in 1912 during his first months with Frieda in Germany and Italy, and published in 1917. In Europe, where the two lovers could approach each other on new territory, Lawrence was inspired to write about his passion. The poems are "an essential story, or history, or confession," as he wrote in the Foreword, "revealing the intrinsic experience of a man during the crisis of manhood, when he marries and comes into himself."[21] The title invites the reader to be both voyeur and participant in the most intimate of all Lawrence's writings, to share in the emotional convulsions and joyful consummation as he comes into a new awareness of himself—achieves self-knowledge and self-fulfillment—through his marriage to Frieda and life in Italy.

These love poems express what Lawrence called "pure passionate experience," a kind of emotion recollected in emotion that attempts to simulate and convey "the quality of life itself." In his essay "Poetry of the Present," his Introduction to the American edition of *New Poems* (1918), which "should have come as a preface to *Look!*," Lawrence exclaims: "This is the unrestful, ungraspable poetry of the sheer present, poetry whose very permanency lies in its wind-like transit. . . . Free verse is, or should be, direct utterance from the instant, whole man . . . the insurgent naked throb of the instant moment. . . . Free verse has its own *nature*, it is neither star nor pearl, but instantaneous like plasm."[22] Though Lawrence's essay suggests the dominant mood of the poems, they vary considerably in tone and feeling, and express much more than "pure passionate experience." The imagery is both mythical and biblical; and the style changes from the traditional forms of the early poems to loose, long-lined doctrinal assertions in the mode of Walt Whitman.

The "Argument" makes clear that the poems are a direct expression of Lawrence's own character, an intensely personal case history, "a biography of an emotional and inner life." Amy Lowell called the volume "a greater novel than *Sons and Lovers*." The themes are expressed through the characters and story, which describe his life after the break with Jessie Chambers: "After much struggling and loss in love and in the world of men, the protagonist throws in his lot with a woman who is already married. Together they go into another country, she perforce leaving her children behind. The conflict of love and hate goes on between the man and the woman, and between these two and the world around them, till it reaches some sort of conclusion, they transcend into some condition of blessedness."[23] Though Lawrence specifies Frieda's abandoned children (rather than inconstancy, jealousy and betrayal) as the major cause of their love-hate conflict, he is deliberately vague about the achievement and definition of their "condition of blessedness." But the poems show that the pain of his past struggles and loss in love all prepared him to respond fully to Frieda.

The lyrical core of the book—when Lawrence first achieves consummation—is signaled by "Green," the color of Frieda's eyes, reflected in the dawn sky and the moon, and continues in the series of five poems on roses. In the splendid "Gloire de Dijon," Frieda's glowing body—like that of a bathing woman in a painting by Renoir—is glorified by the sunlight:

> She drips herself with water, and her shoulders
> Glisten as silver, they crumple up
> Like wet and falling roses, and I listen
> For the sluicing of their rain-dishevelled petals.
> In the window full of sunlight
> Concentrates her golden shadow
> Fold on fold, until it glows as
> Mellow as the golden roses.

Lawrence's arrangement of the poems in *Look! We Have Come Through!* is careful and complex. Chronologically, the poems move from his mother's death, in December 1910, through his months in Germany (May–August 1912) and Italy (September 1912–April 1913), to his return to England, the outbreak of the war (another threat to love), his third anniversary with Frieda and his move to Cornwall in March 1916. Several poems—"Frohnleichnam," "Giorno dei Morti," "All Souls" and "New Year's Eve"—are connected to specific days in 1912. Geographically, the poems progress from Eastwood, Croydon and Bournemouth to the Rhineland, Bavaria, the Tyrol and Lake Garda, and then back to Kent, Sussex and Cornwall. The cosmic allusions (moon, sun, stars, sea) reflect the striving for transcendence. Lawrence feels pain in England, doubt in Germany and joy in Italy, where he achieves sexual fulfillment and "comes through" at Eastertide in "Spring Morning"—the last of the Italian cycle, written in San Gaudenzio, in the mountains above Gargnano, in April 1913.

Thematically, the poems follow a cycle from death to rebirth—in a reversal of its prototype, George Meredith's *Modern Love* (1862). Meredith describes the extinction, Lawrence the growth of love; Meredith the breaking, Lawrence the forging of the bond of marriage. Both Meredith and Lawrence deal with the agonies of modern love; but Meredith ends with suicide, Lawrence with rebirth.

The poems are unified by the two dominant themes: the natural conflict between men and women, and the striving for transcendence and consummation. He found the perfect expression of this sexual conflict in Italy, where "there is no comradeship between men and women, none whatsoever, but rather a condition of battle, reserve, hostility.... There is no synthetic love between men and women, there is only passion, and passion is fundamental hatred, the act of love is a fight." Lawrence developed this idea in "The Reality of Peace" (1916), where he asserted: "It is not of love that we are fulfilled, but of love in such intimate equipoise with hate that the transcendence takes place." For Lawrence, the physical union of man and woman, which symbolizes spiritual consummation and expresses the crucial mystery of human life, evolves directly from this love-hate polarity.

The imagery of the joyful "Song of the Man Who Is Loved," which was deleted from the original volume when the publisher objected to its frank sensuality, comes from the Song of Solomon 1:13: "A bundle of myrrh is my well-beloved unto me; he shall lie all night betwixt my breasts." Lawrence has discovered a tower of strength and a haven of peace in the sweet softness of Frieda's body:

> So I hope I shall spend eternity
> With my face down buried between her breasts;
> And my still heart full of security,
> And my still hands full of her breasts.[24]

But the element of infantile regression in Lawrence's search for passionless maternal security between the breasts and his attempt to resolve the conflict between his roles as son and lover embarrassed his readers. It was probably this "Song" (and the poems about swinging breasts and neck bites) that provoked Bertrand Russell's witty remark: "They may have come through, but I don't see why I should look"; Huxley's dry comment: "Reading these poems was like opening the wrong bedroom door"; and Auden's squeamish admission: "I must confess that I find Lawrence's love poems embarrassing because of their lack of reticence; they make me feel a Peeping Tom." Russell, Huxley and Auden, all highly intellectual and fastidious, were repelled by Lawrence's violation of English reticence and decorum, and by his frank treatment of sex and marriage. But his confessional tone and courageous self-exposure led to a radical change in taste, and taught contemporary readers to admire the raw sexual and psychological anguish in the poetry of Lowell and Plath and in Berryman's *Love Sonnets*. Lawrence had the last word on this sequence of poems when writing to Cecil Gray in November 1917: "Perhaps you are right to resent the impertinence of the 'Look!' None the less, we have come through."[25]

IV

Lawrence's way of writing—relying on impulse rather than on logic—was quite unusual for a novelist. He was a spontaneous, rapid writer as well as a critical reshaper of his works, and wrote *The Trespasser* twice, *The White Peacock* and *Sons and Lovers* three times. Lawrence had grown up with a large family in a small house, and so had developed great powers of concentration and the ability to write even when surrounded by noise and people. But he was inspired by close contact with the natural surroundings. In the mild Mediterranean climate, he preferred to go into the woods by himself and write with a pad on his knees and his back against a tree. "I find a forest such a strange stimulus," he said, "the trees are like living company, they seem to give off something dynamic and secret,—anti-human—or non-human." In *Lady Chatterley's Lover*, Connie, unhappy in her sterile life with Clifford in Wragby Hall, seeks refuge in the sexually alive woods and is revitalized in the same way as Lawrence was when writing: "Constance sat down with her back to a young pine-tree, that swayed against her with curious life, elastic, and powerful, rising up. The erect, alive thing, with its top in the sun!"[26]

Lawrence must have had some conception of the work in his mind, but never took notes or made outlines. When Dorothy Brett asked him if he planned his stories and had a clear vision of what he was going to write, he replied: "No. I never know when I sit down, just what I am going to write. I make no plan; it just comes, and I don't know where it comes from." He never forced himself to write, but poured out pages when he was in the mood. His writing was also seasonal, slacking off in the summer and picking up in the fall. He later advised the Australian writer Mollie Skinner, with whom he collaborated on *The Boy in the Bush*, to submit to the vital impulse and then refine the work with a careful eye: "Write when there comes a certain passion upon you, and revise in a later, warier, but still sympathetic mood." But he also believed that writing autobiographical works like *Sons and Lovers* could be therapeutic, like seeing the pattern and meaning of one's life in psychoanalysis. It could lead to self-knowledge and enable one to conquer the problems of the past: "One sheds one's sicknesses in books—repeats and presents again one's emotions, to be master of them."[27]

In a famous letter to Edward Garnett, written in November 1912, after the completion of *Sons and Lovers* (which was published by Duckworth in May 1913), Lawrence stated his intentions in the novel and also revealed how he diverged from them in significant ways:

> I want to defend it, quick. I wrote it again, pruning it and shaping it and filling it in. I tell you it has got form—*form:* haven't I made it patiently, out of sweat as well as blood. It follows this idea: a woman of character and refinement goes into the lower class, and has no satisfaction in her own life. She has had a passion for her husband, so the children are born of passion, and have heaps of vitality. But as her sons grow up she selects them as lovers—first the eldest, then the second. These sons are *urged* into life by their reciprocal love of their mother—urged on and on. But when they come to manhood, they can't love, because their mother is the strongest power in their lives, and holds them.... As soon as the young men come into contact with women, there's a split. William gives his sex to a fribble, and his mother holds his soul. But the split kills him, because he doesn't know where he is. The next son gets a woman who fights for his soul—fights his mother. The son loves the mother—all the sons hate and are jealous of the father. The battle goes on between the mother and the girl, with the son as object. The mother gradually proves stronger, because of the tie of blood. The son decides to leave his soul in his mother's hands, and, like his elder brother, go for passion. He gets passion. Then the split begins to tell again. But, almost unconsciously, the mother realises what is the matter, and begins to die. The son casts off his mistress, attends to his mother dying. He is left in the end naked of everything, with the drift towards death.[28]

In the letter, Paul's brother is killed by a split between sex and soul; in the novel, he dies, more realistically, of erysipelas. In the letter, Paul's mother realizes that the same fatal split is also affecting Paul and "begins to die." In the novel, she seems unaware of (or indifferent to) what she is doing to Paul, gets cancer and is poisoned by her son to end her misery. In the letter, Paul drifts towards death; the end of the novel is more positive as he turns away from home—and his mother's values—and "walked towards the faintly humming, glowing town, quickly."

In the unpublished Foreword to *Sons and Lovers,* Lawrence announced the dominant theme more abstractly and reiterated the fatal split when the man becomes the spiritual lover of his destructive mother, wastes away in the flesh and cannot fully give himself to his wife, who, in the next generation, seeks her own compensation in her sons:

> But the man who is the go-between from Woman to Production is the lover of that woman. And if that Woman be his mother, then he is her lover in part only; he carries for her, but is never received into her for his confirmation and renewal, and so wastes himself away in the flesh. The old son-lover was Oedipus. The name of the new one is legion. And if a son-lover take a wife, then she is not his wife, she is only his bed. And his life will be torn in twain, and his wife in her despair shall hope for sons, that she may have her lover in her hour.

The split in *Sons and Lovers*—as in *The White Peacock* and *The Trespasser*—is between spiritual and physical love. As he wrote in *Fantasia of the Unconscious:* "You will not easily get a man to believe that his carnal love for the woman he has made his wife is as high a love as that he felt for his mother."[29]

Sons and Lovers, then, is about the destructive power of love. All the righteousness is with the mother, but all the sympathy with the father. In fact, the mother—when not seen from Paul's point of view—is the villain of the novel, who destroys the lives of her husband, her son and Miriam. Though Paul loves Miriam, he manipulates her in order to protect himself and deflects his unconscious hostility toward his mother onto her. Fearful of sex, especially with someone who so closely shares his mother's finest qualities, Paul constantly insists that Miriam is all soul and no body: "In all our relations no body enters. I do not talk to you through the senses—rather through the spirit."[30] He first stifles Miriam's natural sexual feelings, then tries to arouse them. And when their sexual encounter fails, he blames her for his own inadequacy.

After abandoning Miriam, Paul resolves his conflict with his parents through his relations with the estranged couple, Baxter and Clara Dawes. Clara, a feminist and liberated woman who works with Paul in Jordan's factory, eventually becomes his mistress. The jealous Baxter takes revenge by surprising Paul on his way home from work and severely thrashing him. Because Dawes is so similar in speech and temperament to Walter Morel, his fight with Paul signifies Paul's need to be punished by his symbolic father for usurping his real father's role as lover and for unconsciously desiring sex with his mother. Walter and

Baxter each possess a woman whom Paul loves and steals from them. Though Paul repeats the offense against his father by robbing Dawes of his wife, he also atones for the wrong by reconciling Baxter and Clara at the end of the novel and restoring his ideal of family relations.

Clara resembles Paul's mother: both are superior, proud and strong, and they have the same kind of physical relationship with their husbands; and Clara concludes the erotic relationships Paul began with his mother and with Miriam. Paul adopts his father's dialect when intimate with Clara and hopes to prove with her that he is capable of awaking the same passion his father aroused in his mother. Paul seeks in the strong Clara what he is beginning to lose in his dying mother. But because of his erotic attachment to his mother, he must abandon both Miriam and Clara after having sexual relations with them.

Baxter and Clara Dawes resemble Walter and Gertrude Morel in significant ways. Paul uses Baxter to free himself from Clara, just as his late identification with Walter helps to liberate him from the influence of his mother. Through the Daweses, Paul works out the mixture of love, hate and guilt toward his parents. The Daweses learn too from their involvement with Paul, and become more receptive to each other: Baxter as patient, Clara as nurse.

Jessie Chambers (who felt her life was blighted by Lawrence's fictional portrait) complained to Helen Corke that Lawrence had distorted their love relation. Blinded by subjectivity, she could not appreciate the powerful effects he had achieved and angrily wrote: "The Miriam part of the novel is a slander, a fearful treachery. David has selected every point which sets off Miriam at a disadvantage, and he has interpreted her every word and action, and thought in the light of Mrs. Morel's hatred of her. . . . I am sick, sick to death of David and all that concerns him." Lawrence later took a different and more convincing view of the novel when he told Frieda: "I would write a different *Sons and Lovers* now; my mother was wrong, and I thought she was absolutely right."[31]

CHAPTER NINE

Literary London,
1913–1915

I

LAWRENCE —who grew up in the Midlands, lived during the war in
remote country villages and spent most of his writing life in Italy—
rarely met other writers except through introductions or their initiative.
His class feeling, diffidence and independence would have prevented
him from approaching literary figures even if he had wanted their
stimulation and help. Frieda was cut off from both her English family in
Nottingham and her German family in Metz, and knew almost no one—
apart from Weekley's family—in London.

Yet on their first trip back to England in the summer of 1913 (between
their stays in Gargnano and Fiascherino), to see Frieda's children and
Lawrence's family, and especially after their return to England and
their marriage in a London registry office on July 13, 1914, Lawrence
formed important, often lifelong friendships with an extraordinary and
diverse group of intellectuals, artists and aristocrats. At the same time,
Lawrence's first literary friends—Ford, Pound and the Garnetts—were
becoming unsympathetic to his work and less important in his life.

Lawrence's friends fell into two distinct but related groups: wealthy
and influential patrons, and poor literary bohemians who were struggling to establish their reputations. The well-born, well-educated and
well-connected figures in literary, academic and political dynasties

responded enthusiastically to Lawrence, recognized his genius and advanced his career. They had taste and discernment, were receptive to his radical ideas, strengthened his confidence and provided an ideal audience for his works. Lawrence's friendships reveal that even within the rigid class structure of prewar England it was possible for an artist to penetrate the highest circles of society and to be accepted by persons of rank and wealth.

Lawrence was an immensely attractive man, but lacked the traditional English aloofness and reserve. Spontaneous and volatile, he put a great strain on his personal relationships. He had an uncanny ability to pierce his friends' social façade, penetrate the essence of their character and reveal their inner core. He wanted to transform their lives, often a disturbing and unwelcome process, and the ability to withstand this onslaught was a prerequisite for retaining his friendship. Lawrence spoke and wrote to his friends with unusual — and even cruel — candor in order to destroy their defenses and revitalize their existence.

Lawrence had great insight into the characters of his friends, yet was intransigent about his prescriptions for their behavior. He could demonstrate, in long letters or personal harangues, his love for them and concern about their problems. But if they chose to ignore his advice, he felt wounded and betrayed, and harshly rejected them. This conflict accentuated his sense of isolation and self-righteousness, and gave him license to abuse them viciously.

Lawrence's friends provided an audience for his controversial theories about personality and his criticism of the modern world, and a stimulus to his own personal development. They were, before his popular success, his first, select readers. London friends, and those with country houses, inspired his fiction and appeared in his work. Lawrence did not join a literary circle, never felt entirely at home in England and always remained an outsider. As an expatriate, he saw more clearly than others the strains of society and the decay of civilization. Lawrence portrayed his friends with a searching, probing intuition, re-creating yet preserving their essential qualities, revealing their weaknesses and wounding their feelings. His art took priority over personal loyalty, and he endangered his friendships by satirizing his friends.

This rich, quickly expanding network of friendships — a cultural cross-section of the early Georgian era — usually developed when someone read and admired Lawrence's work, and sent him a letter suggesting a meeting or soliciting his literary contribution. In 1909 Jessie had sent Lawrence's poems to Ford, who then introduced him to his mistress,

Violet Hunt, to his assistant editors, Douglas Goldring and Norman
Douglas, and to Ezra Pound, a friend of Yeats, who was present at the
soirée when Pound munched the tulips. Edward Garnett's letter to
Lawrence had led to encouragement and support, friendship with his
wife, Constance, and his son, David, hospitality at the Cearne just before
Lawrence's elopement and again in June–July 1913, and to the publication by Duckworth of five of his books.

The invitation of Edward Marsh—private secretary to Winston
Churchill at the Admiralty and noted patron of the arts—to contribute
to his volume of *Georgian Poetry* led to a meeting with Rupert Brooke
(who, after his death in Skyros in 1915, left Lawrence a small legacy)
and to a close friendship with Lady Cynthia Asquith. Middleton Murry's letter to Gargnano soliciting a contribution to *Rhythm,* the little
magazine he edited with Katherine Mansfield, led to friendships with
the Irish barrister Gordon Campbell (later Lord Glenavy) and his wife,
Beatrice, with the novelist and actress Gilbert and Mary Cannan, with
the painter Mark Gertler and his fellow artist at the Slade School, the
Honourable Dorothy Brett. The minor novelist Ivy Low also wrote an
admiring letter and visited Lawrence and Frieda in Fiascherino in the
spring of 1914. Through Ivy Low they met the poet Viola Meynell, a
member of an important Catholic literary family, who lent Lawrence her
Sussex cottage during the war; the novelist Catherine Carswell, who
became another close friend; Dr. David Eder, a pioneering English
psychoanalyst; and the children's writer Eleanor Farjeon. Like Marsh
and Murry, the American poet Amy Lowell asked Lawrence to contribute to her Imagist anthology, and she introduced him to Richard Aldington and to Hilda Doolittle, who had been a college friend of Pound's
in Philadelphia. Lawrence met S. S. Koteliansky, a Russian law clerk, in
August 1914; and Kot became a close friend of Mansfield and Gertler.
After an admiring letter to Lawrence, Lady Ottoline Morrell drew him
into the brilliant circle of her country house at Garsington, which
included E. M. Forster, Aldous Huxley, Bertrand Russell, John Maynard Keynes, all the members of the Bloomsbury group, and lesser lights
like Philip Heseltine and Michael Arlen.[1]

II

Lawrence was drawn to lovely, lonely, titled and tragic ladies with artistic temperaments. These women accepted him as a didactic prophet and spiritual adviser who analyzed, interpreted and re-created their lives in his art.

In July 1913, while Lawrence and Frieda were on a seaside holiday at Broadstairs in Kent, Edward Marsh introduced them to Lady Cynthia Asquith, a "radiant *quattrocento* beauty" with perfect features and "heavy gold hair falling to her knees." Lawrence portrayed Cynthia as Lady Daphne in "The Ladybird," describing her elegance and refinement as well as the subtlety of her skin and hair: "Her face was lovely, fair, with a soft exotic white complexion and delicate pink cheeks. Her hair was soft and heavy, of a lovely pallid gold colour, ash-blond. Her hair, her complexion were so perfectly cared for."[2]

Cynthia, the daughter of the eleventh Earl of Wemyss, was born in a great country house in Wiltshire in 1887. She was educated at Cheltenham Ladies' College, presented at court, painted by John Singer Sargent and by Augustus John. In 1910 she had married Herbert Asquith, a barrister and the second son of the prime minister, who had been president of the Oxford Union and had once nourished political ambitions. They had two sons: John, born in 1911, and Michael, born in 1914. Herbert had practiced law unsuccessfully, then spent four years on active service in France and Flanders. He was badly shell-shocked in the war, found it difficult to live up to his father's name, tried to be a poet and man of letters, and worked for Hutchinson publishers. Unlike her sisters, Cynthia married a man with no money and received only a small dowry. Surrounded by the rich, she was always short of cash. During the war, when she had to live on Herbert's subaltern's pay, she became secretary, companion and confidante to the playwright Sir James Barrie. She worked for Barrie for twenty years and was left a considerable legacy when he died, in 1937.

Cynthia, an extremely sympathetic woman, was a lively though not mischievous gossip. She loved cultivating intimate but not sexual friendships with men as different as the literary critic Desmond MacCarthy and the distinguished New Zealand general, Bernard Freyberg.

According to her son Michael, Lawrence was a bit naive about the extent of her political power, for she was more a social chameleon or a "long, swaying water-weed" than a kingmaker. She did not have much influence on the prime minister and, in any case, would have been reluctant to use it.

Michael was critical, even resentful, of the glamorous yet elusive figure who, like many women of her class, neglected her children and was not a good mother. He felt she was too ambitious for her sons, made them part of her own aura and vanity, and forced them to follow the difficult and sometimes impossible plans she had made for them. Her love seemed conditional on their success; and Michael, always in and out of favor, resented having to play courtier. Her elder son, John, who was thought to be brain damaged by a forceps at birth but was actually an undiagnosed autistic, she considered a blemish. John was always disobedient and subject to violent outbursts; and they did not know enough about his illness at that time to be able to help him.[3]

Class differences—with Cynthia as with Frieda—made the friendship interesting on both sides. Lawrence was attracted to sympathetic upper-class women, Cynthia was drawn to Lawrence's literary genius, to his utter absorption in the task of the moment and to the extraordinary vitality of the man she called "half-faun, half-prophet." Illness was one common factor that drew them together (as it did Lawrence, Mansfield and Gertler), for in March 1913 (only four months before she met Lawrence) Cynthia had been diagnosed as tubercular. She spent three months in a sanatorium on the river Dee in Scotland and had just been released, apparently cured but still not free of suspicion.

An entry in Cynthia's diaries suggests the numerous reasons for her attraction to Lawrence. Unlike many of his friends—most notably Kot, Morrell, Russell and Brett—she liked Frieda, got along well with her and did not arouse her jealousy. She found Lawrence intellectually alive, mentally stimulating and personally acute, and compared being with him to the Christian festival that celebrates the descent of the Holy Ghost on the apostles:

I find them the most intoxicating company in the world. I never hoped to have such mental pleasure with anyone. It is so wonderful to be such a perfect *à trois*. I am so fond of her. She has spontaneousness and warm cleverness, and such adoration and understanding of him. He interests and attracts me quite enormously. His talk is so extraordinarily real and living—such humour and yet so much of the fierceness and resentment which my acquiescent nature loves and covets. He is a Pentecost to one, and has the gift of intimacy and such perceptiveness that he introduces one to oneself. I have never known such an X-ray psychologist.

Lawrence sometimes chided Cynthia for her superficiality and materialism. She was sufficiently perceptive to realize that "she had a detachment, a dislike of reality, a fatal lack of self-knowledge,"[4] and hoped to acquire new insight from her friend.

Always interested in and sympathetic to children, Lawrence was positively riveted by the freakishness of her son John. Throughout the war Lawrence tried to advise Cynthia (who had doubtless sought his help) about how to deal with the remote and deeply troubled child. He perceived the boy's resentment of her selfish demands (later articulated by Michael), believed John had been repressed, warped and even possessed by an evil spirit that also existed within his parents. (That Lawrence could state and Cynthia accept this cruel criticism says a good deal about the strength of their friendship.) He tried to encourage her and (using a mechanical metaphor) offered to look after, help and perhaps even cure the boy:

Your own soul is deficient, so it fights for the love of the child. . . . Put yourself aside with regard to him. You have no right to his love. Care only for his good and well-being: make *no* demands on him. . . .

He is a direct outcome of repression and falsification of the living spirit, in many generations of the Charterises [Cynthia's family] and Asquiths. He is possessed by an evil spirit that *you* have kept safely inside yourself, cynic and unbelieving. . . . John will come out all right. If ever there is an opportunity, I will help with him. . . . Perhaps, if we felt it might be any good, Frieda and I might have him with us for a time. I'm certain there is nothing primarily wrong—only something locked in the running.[5]

Lawrence's famous story "The Rocking-Horse Winner" (1926) was inspired by the desperate unhappiness in the Asquith family: by the parents' remoteness from each other (because of the war and its aftermath) as well as from the children, by Cynthia's obsession with money, by John's autistic frenzy and by the impossible demands she made on him. It portrays upper-class financial anxiety and social pretension, modern man's mad mechanical gallop for wealth and material goods, and the destruction of a family that chooses money above affection.

The opening paragraph, which echoes a fairy tale, describes the situation: "There was a woman who was beautiful, who started with all the advantages, yet she had no luck. . . . Everybody else said of her: 'She is such a good mother. She adores her children.' Only she herself, and her children themselves, knew it was not so. They read it in each other's eyes." The woman's anxiety and dissatisfaction are sexual as well as financial, and these two problems are linked. The wife seems sexually frigid. The anonymous and absent husband has no substance or significance and cannot give her what she wants. The parents' unhappiness encourages the boy's Oedipal urge to replace his father in his mother's affections. Despite her coldness and hard heart, the mother has ambivalent feelings about her children: she resents them and also has suppressed affection for them.

Paul's frantic riding on a toy horse becomes a substitute for maternal love—as money is for sexual love—and he makes a Faustian bargain with evil powers for forbidden knowledge. The extreme tension is gradually built up by the whispering house, estrangement of the children, financial troubles, anxiety about betting and Paul's frenzy on the toy horse. The rocking horse stands for real horses and actual races as well as for childish intuition and the instinctual rather than rational approach to experience. It also represents a self-induced, demonic and prophetic mania (analogous to John's illness) and the sexual act—or a child's imitation of the act—which goes and gets nowhere. Sex for Lawrence is the link between man and unknown powers. And Paul's orgasmic release enables him to divine and declare the winner of the race. Driven by his devouring mother, and by his desire to win her favor and redeem her love, Paul restores the family fortune by sacrificing his own wretched life.[6] "The Rocking-Horse Winner" is a brilliant example of how Lawrence, imagining the consequences of Cynthia's limitations, could transform his perception of a friend's life into fiction.

III

Catherine MacFarlane Jackson Carswell had a very different background from Cynthia Asquith's, but she too had a difficult marriage to a lawyer with literary ambitions, a tragedy with her child and similar though much more serious problems about money. Like Cynthia, she was a strikingly attractive but unhappy woman who aroused Lawrence's sympathy and inspired his fiction. Tall, fair and slender, Catherine had had a bizarre life before she met Lawrence.

She was born in Glasgow in 1879—the same year as Frieda and Lawrence's American patron, Mabel Luhan. Her father was a Scots Presbyterian businessman and, though fond of wine, a leader of the Temperance Society. After attending Glasgow University, she had visited relatives in Italy and studied piano for two years in the Frankfurt Conservatory. In 1904 she married Herbert Jackson, an artist who had fought in the Boer War and was the brother-in-law of Sir Walter Raleigh, her English professor at the university.

After their marriage Jackson, under the delusion that he was impotent, threatened her with a pistol when she told him she was pregnant, and was eventually declared insane. Their daughter, born in 1905, died of pneumonia in 1913. After a sensational trial in 1907, Catherine was granted an annulment of her marriage, based on Jackson's madness at the time of their wedding. Though her case was disputed by his family, who did not want the daughter to be declared illegitimate, Catherine won because Jackson was in a lunatic asylum and could not be produced in court.

Catherine then became the mistress of Maurice Grieffenhagen, a professor at the Glasgow School of Art and a married man seventeen years her senior. From 1907 to 1915, she was a literary critic on the *Glasgow Herald,* where she favorably reviewed *The White Peacock, The Trespasser* and *Sons and Lovers.* She must have been intrigued by Lawrence's reference in his first novel to Grieffenhagen's *An Idyll,* and he by her love affair with one of his favorite painters. She met Lawrence through her friend Ivy Low in 1914.

Both Lawrence and Catherine came from puritanical, conventional and smothering families. They had both lived abroad, read each other's novels in manuscript and shared a common interest in Robert Burns. Lawrence named his play *A Collier's Friday Night* (written in 1909) after Burns' poem "The Cotter's Saturday Night" and in December 1912 wrote one chapter of a novel based on Burns' life. Catherine later published a *Life of Robert Burns,* dedicated to Lawrence. Though she had a special kind of love and admiration for Lawrence, she did not make emotional demands on him or try to capture him. She admired his loyalty to Frieda and did not arouse Frieda's jealousy.

In 1915 Catherine married Donald Carswell, a quiet, scholarly, shy and impractical barrister who (like Herbert Asquith) was not suited to a career in law. Their son, John Patrick, was born in 1918. Donald had been a journalist with Catherine on the *Glasgow Herald,* and then on *The Times,* but he no longer had regular employment, was usually idle and earned very little money. He became depressed and alcoholic, would appear with a bottle in his pocket and talk incessantly. Catherine, by contrast, was an adventurous, determined and hard-working woman—as well as a warm and enthusiastic mother—but found it difficult to support the family. Her desperate poverty sometimes forced her to behave in a ruthless, opportunistic manner, and she could be unscrupulous about plagiarizing and even stealing jobs from friends in order to keep the household going.[7]

An incident that occurred during Catherine's visit to Lawrence in 1916 reveals that he had conventions of his own, that he could be a prude as well as a priest of love. Though he upset many people by refusing to make concessions to received ideas, he became upset when friends deviated from proper standards of behavior. Catherine recorded that

One night in Cornwall, after having just begun to undress for bed, I found I had left my book in the sitting-room where Lawrence and Frieda still were, and I returned to fetch it. I had brought no dressing-gown with me, but there seemed to me no impropriety in my costume—an ankle-length petticoat topped by a long-sleeved woollen vest! Lawrence, however, rebuked me. He disapproved, he said, of people appearing in their underclothes.[8]

IV

In 1914 Lawrence also formed important friendships with the actress Mary Cannan and the poet Amy Lowell. Though Lawrence was never close to Mary's husband, Gilbert, a popular novelist and playwright, he was drawn to her elegance, talent and wit. Mary's father had run a pub and her mother had kept a boardinghouse on the south coast. Lonely, neglected and poorly educated in her youth, she used her good looks and artistic inclinations to make her way in the theatrical world and got her first big part in James Barrie's play *Walker, London* (1892). She had been married for thirteen years to the sexually impotent Barrie, who still gave her a generous annual allowance on their wedding anniver-

sary. Quick-witted, determined and ambitious, Mary was "an inveterate
talker [who] liked to surround herself with those she found charming
and witty, to share if she could some of their vicissitudes. As a former
actress, she needed especially a defined role to play in life."

David Garnett described Mary as " 'wholesome, like rice pudding,'
impulsive, charming, chirpy and a little overwrought." When the Lawrences were living near and frequenting the Cannans in Chesham,
Buckinghamshire, from August 1914 to January 1915, Mary, then in her
mid-forties, "was desperately hanging on to the last shreds of her youth,
hair dyed a reddish-brown, thin mouth and fine features beautifully
made up."⁹

Mary's first husband was impotent, her second (like Carswell's first)
insane. By the spring of 1917 Gilbert's megalomania had become madness. He had suffered a mental breakdown, taken a mistress and impreg-
nated Mary's maid. After the dissolution of the Cannans' marriage,
Barrie continued to pay Mary's allowance. In 1917, therefore, two of
Lawrence's friends—Cynthia Asquith and Mary Cannan—were being
supported by James Barrie. Lawrence and Mary remained good friends
after Gilbert's confinement in a mental home. They corresponded frequently and traveled together to Malta in 1920.

Lawrence met Amy Lowell in England in the summer of 1914, and
they corresponded until her death in May 1925. The rich, influential,
cigar-smoking versifier was the sister of the president of Harvard and
belonged to the same poetic dynasty as James Russell Lowell. Amy
Lowell, the Gertrude Stein of Imagism, was obese, unattractive, wealthy,
well connected, ambitious, domineering, eccentric and emotionally deprived. Though good-natured, she combined execrable poetry with patronizing pomposity.

Lawrence's friendship with Lowell, unlike his others, was based on
mutual exploitation. The extreme individualist benefited from the
money and influence of his only personal contact in America, while the
crude careerist captured his poetic genius for her Amygistic antholo-
gies. She tried to collect royalties owed to Lawrence by the slippery
American publisher Mitchell Kennerley, and at Frieda's request sent
money during and after the war to the sick and penniless Lawrence.
Despite her generosity, Lowell sometimes exasperated Lawrence, who,
in March 1921, described the sinking lady as "trying to keep afloat on the
gas of her own importance: hard work, considering her bulk."¹⁰

V

The Honourable Dorothy Brett, daughter of the second Viscount Esher and sister of the Ranee of Sarawak, became Lawrence's most constant friend. Like Mary Cannan and Ottoline Morrell, she had an unhappy childhood. Her father, who had been a Liberal M.P., became secretary of the Office of Works and an influential figure in the courts of Victoria, Edward VII and George V. As a child, she had taken dancing lessons with the great-grandchildren of the old queen. Brett became deaf at an early age, which made her extremely sensitive and vulnerable. She was both ignored and humiliated by her father, a covert homosexual, who had married "when he would have preferred to live with another man. In fact, he almost always had some young man living in the house with them as secretary or chauffeur. He never showed any interest in his own daughters, and made them both feel quite stupid and unwanted."[11] Brett had been a student at the Slade School of Art with Mark Gertler, and met Lawrence through Gertler in November 1915. She was the only one of his friends to follow him on his second visit to New Mexico in 1924.

Unlike Ottoline, Brett did not seem to mind Lawrence's fictional portrayals of her, as Dollie Urquhart in "The Princess" and Hilda Blessington in *The Boy in the Bush*. In the Australian novel, he described the effect of her unhappy family background on her character:

> [She had] a rather tyrannous father who was fond of her in the wrong way, and brothers who had bullied her and jeered at her for her odd ways and appearance, and her slight deafness. [There was] the governess who had mis-educated her, the loneliness of the life in London, the aristocratic but rather vindictive society in England, which had persecuted her in a small way, because she was one of the odd border-line people who don't and *can't*, really belong. . . .
> The colour still was high in her young, delicate cheeks, but her odd, bright, round, dark-grey eyes were fearless above her fear. . . .
> There was something slightly uncanny about her, her quick, rabbit-like alertness and her quick, open defiance.

In *Lawrence and Brett* (1933), she portrayed herself as an extremely sensitive, timorous and vulnerable figure, easily embarrassed by sexual references, unconventional behavior and violent quarrels. Her deafness seemed to intensify her concentration on Lawrence. She tried to attune herself to his moods, was fearful of annoying him and, desperate to gain his approval, always took his side in the arguments with Frieda. She was invariably helpful and self-effacing, and did not mind when Lawrence criticized her or when he took the brush from her hand and altered her paintings.

Both Frieda and Ottoline were scornful of Brett's puffy cheeks, receding chin, prominent front teeth and rabbit-like appearance, and irritated by her clinging, almost parasitic adoration. Compton Mackenzie's wife, Faith, who knew Brett on Capri, described her as "the least exacting of [Lawrence's] satellites, the best behaved, perhaps the most unselfishly devoted, and certainly the least critical."[12]

VI

Kot, Gertler and Eder were Jewish friends—exiles, expatriates and outsiders. Lawrence shared the dogmatism of Kot, the passion of Gertler and the psychological perception of Dr. David Eder, who had been a ship's surgeon and doctor with revolutionary armies in Bolivia, and later became a medical attendant to Lawrence and to the Bolshevik colony in London, a Freudian propagandist in the *New Age* and a prominent Zionist. Lawrence subjected all three of them to his aggressive theorizing about the connection between Jewish and modern decadence.

In early August 1914, while on a walking tour of the Lake District with A. P. Lewis, a Vickers armaments engineer whom he had known in Italy, Lawrence met Samuel Solomonovitch Koteliansky, who was to become one of his closest male friends. Kot, a Russian Jew from a prosperous family, was born in the village of Ostropol in the Ukraine (about forty miles from Conrad's birthplace) in 1880. After enduring years of persecution and pogroms, he came to England on a scholarship from the University of Kiev in July 1911 and remained as a political refugee for the rest of his life.

In 1914 Kot was working at the Russian Law Bureau, a pretentious name for a law office run by his compatriot R. S. Slatkowsky, at 212 High Holborn. The hideous office, where the clerks liked to smoke hand-rolled cigarettes and drink Russian lemon tea in glasses, was dark, filled with dreary furniture, and incongruously decorated with pictures of kittens playing in a basket of flowers and Christ surrounded by little children. Despite Mark Gertler's claim that Kot's job was to black his boss' beard, he actually worked as a secretary and translator.

Kot collaborated on superb translations of Tolstoy, Dostoyevsky, Chekhov, Gorky, Bunin, Kuprin, Rozanov and Shestov with Mansfield, Murry, Gilbert Cannan, the Woolfs and Lawrence. With Kot, Lawrence renewed his interest in Russian literature, which had begun with Constance Garnett. Kot first made a literal translation in his own picturesque English, and his co-translators then corrected, polished and perfected his prose.

Gertler's portrait of Kot, painted in 1917, captures his unusual combination of hieratic integrity, moral authority and gentle benevolence. Murry wrote that Kot "looked like some Assyrian king ... with an impressive hooked Semitic nose, a fine head of coarse black curly hair, and massive features: very dark eyes with pince-nez." Dorothy Brett remembered him as "so broad-shouldered that he looks short, his black hair brushed straight up 'en brosse,' his dark eyes set perhaps a trifle too close to his nose, the nose a delicate well-made arch, gold eye-glasses pinched on to it. He had an air of distinction, of power, and also a tremendous capacity for fun and enjoyment."[13]

Lawrence modeled the physical description (but not the personality) of Ben Cooley, the Australian political leader in *Kangaroo* (1923), on Kot:

> His face was long and lean and pendulous, with eyes set close together behind his pince-nez: and his body was stout but firm. He was a man of forty or so, hard to tell, swarthy, with short-cropped dark hair and a smallish head carried rather forward on his large but sensitive, almost shy body. He leaned forward in his walk, and seemed as if his hands didn't quite belong to him. But he shook hands with a firm grip. He was really tall, but his way of dropping his head, and his sloping shoulders, took away from his height.[14]

Leonard Woolf provided the most thorough description of Kot's character and explained why Lawrence admired him:

> Kot's passionate approval of what he thought good, particularly in people; his intense hatred of what he thought bad; the directness

and vehemence of his speech; his inability to tell a lie—all this strongly appealed to Lawrence. When Kot approved of anyone, he accepted him absolutely; he could do no wrong and Kot summed it up always by saying of him: "He's a real person.". . . Lawrence liked this kind of thing in Kot, just as he liked Kot's ruthless condemnation of people like Murry. . . .

If you knew Kot well, you knew what a major Hebrew prophet must have been like 3,000 years ago. If Jeremiah had been born in a ghetto village in the Ukraine in 1882 [*sic*], he would have been Kot.[15]

Woolf said that Kot's vehement denunciation "It is hor-r-r-ible" was like the roll of thunder on Mount Sinai, and Katherine Mansfield liked to quote Kot's dreadful promise to deal with irritating people by "beating them, simply, but to death!" Kot, who later became a reader for the Cresset Press and worked on the *Adelphi* under Murry, would say in a deep, accented voice, "All men are scoundrels, but Murry is a *great* scoundrel." A bachelor, Kot was a close friend of Mark Gertler and Beatrice Glenavy, and fell in love with Katherine. He liked to give her cigarettes, chocolates, cakes and embroidered Russian shirts with high collars, and to perform his impressive trick of howling like a dog; his melancholy imitation was so penetrating and convincing that real dogs howled back from far away. Katherine respected him and trusted him absolutely.

Kot moved into Katherine's house in Acacia Road, St. John's Wood, when she left for the south of France in November 1915. Like Lawrence, he was scrupulously clean and handy at home: "His house was scrubbed and polished and dusted, with a special place for every cup, plate, book or piece of paper. He was an expert launderer and did all his own washing, even the blankets. He was also a good cook and enjoyed cooking little suppers for his friends.[16]

Kot heartily disliked Murry and Frieda as much as he adored and admired Katherine and Lawrence. In a letter to Gertler of August 1918, Kot described Frieda as annoying, ghoulish, quarrelsome, weepy and gluttonous, and said she had a disastrous effect on her husband:

The idea of Frieda coming here again irritates me and gives me a kind of stubborn muddle-headed anger. If she disappeared L. would be saved, because she is devouring him bit by bit, gradually, permanently. We had a few more quarrels and she shed profuse tears, but, I think, she weeps only to benefit her digestion. Tears to her seem to be a kind of purgative, after which she eats with increased appetite and gusto. . . . How I wish Frieda disappeared. Lawrence is most interesting and of the real few who matter.

Despite his few close friendships, Kot was a mysterious, somber and lonely man who found it difficult to form lasting relations. Poor but generous, he did many small favors for Lawrence: sent him books and small necessities, lent him money, and handled his business affairs when Lawrence was traveling and living abroad. And he was always a sympathetic listener to Lawrence's savage attacks on Frieda and Murry. Lawrence occasionally became irritated with Kot's Old Testament righteousness and rigidity, and once called him "a very bossy and overbearing Jew."[17] But Lawrence greatly admired him, wrote more letters to him than to any other friend and remained close to him until the end of his life. He constantly urged Kot to visit him in Italy, but Kot was reasonably content in London and, in any case, would not have been allowed to leave and reenter the country.[18]

VII

Mark Gertler—a friend of Brett, Kot and the Cannans—was born into a Jewish immigrant family in the East End of London in 1891, lived in Austrian Poland for four years and came back to England as a small child. He impressed everyone with his exuberant vitality, exotic beauty and artistic gifts. Aldous Huxley portrayed him as Gombauld in *Crome Yellow,* "a black-haired young corsair of thirty, with flashing teeth and luminous dark eyes." Roger Fry wrote, "he is most passionately an artist—a most rare and refreshing thing." To St. John Hutchinson, Gertler's friend and patron, "There has seldom been a more exciting personality than when he was young . . . with amazing gifts of draughtsmanship, amazing vitality and sense of humor and of mimicry unique to himself—a shock of hair, the vivid eyes of genius and consumption."[19]

Even these brief descriptions suggest important similarities between Gertler and Lawrence, who met in 1914 and remained friends until Lawrence's death. Both men had volatile and exciting personalities, a lack of self-control, and a tendency to be overbearing and possessive, to

dominate and to wound their friends. Both retained their regional
accents and remained working-class outsiders in society, were strongly
attached to their mothers and always resentful of and uneasy with rich
patrons. "I think poverty is a terrible tragedy!" Gertler wrote to Edward
Marsh. "How unfortunate I was to be born from the lower class—that is
to say without an income! A modern artist must have an income." And he
told his great love, Dora Carrington: "Yet you are the *Lady* and I am the
East End boy,"[20] which echoed Lawrence's feelings toward (and attraction to) Frieda. Both Gertler and Lawrence were in Ottoline Morrell's
circle of friends at Garsington, both took a pacifist stand, both suffered
from tuberculosis.

In 1916 Gilbert Cannan published *Mendel*, which was based on
Gertler's torturous relations with Carrington, and featured Lawrence
and Frieda as minor characters. Like most of Gertler's friends, Lawrence disliked and was angered by *Mendel*, and in 1916 he perversely
blamed Gertler for the novel and complained to Catherine Carswell:
"Gertler, Jew-like, has told every detail of his life to Gilbert." Lawrence
had a pronounced and unpleasant strain of anti-Semitism, activated by
his provincial background and by the prejudice of his fashionable
friends. His attitude is a curious compound of traditional hostility to
Jews and a belief that Jews were an ancient race with a depth of
experience, but in a state of decay. Lawrence seemed to reserve his
outbursts of anti-Semitism for Jewish friends like Gertler and Kot, who,
despite Lawrence's extremely offensive letters, either accepted or ignored his attacks and never quarreled with him.

In 1917 Lawrence gave the gentle and generous Kot this unwelcome
lecture:

> Why humanity has hated Jews, I have come to the conclusion, is
> that the Jews have always taken religion—since the great days,
> that is—and used it for their own personal and private gratifica-
> tion, as if it were a thing administered to their own importance and
> well-being and conceit. This is the slave trick of the Jews—they use
> the great religious consciousness as a trick of personal conceit. This
> is abominable.

And in a letter of the same year to another Jew, Waldo Frank, Lawrence
repeated: "The best of Jews is, that they *know* truth from untruth. The
worst of them is, that they are rather slave-like."[21] The letter to Kot stated
that the Jews were elitist and smug, while the letter to Frank suggested

that they were a cringing race, for their pride as the Chosen People both provoked and compensated for their persecution. This "slave trick" and "slave-like" quality seemed to be related in Lawrence's mind to Gertler's self-abasing revelations to Cannan and to Lawrence's scorn for Gertler, who could neither dominate the elusive and priggish Carrington nor abandon her for good.

Lawrence later made another anti-Semitic generalization that was consistent with his earlier views: "By virtue of not having a real core to him, he is eternal. . . that is the whole history of the Jew, from Moses to [the poetaster Louis] Untermeyer: and all by virtue of having a little pebble at the middle of him, instead of an alive core." Though this may have been true of Untermeyer, a poor stick to beat Moses and the "great days" of the Jews, it certainly does not apply to Gertler, whose vital core, intensified by failing lungs, was as lively as Lawrence's. But his letter of 1918 to Edith Eder, the Jewish wife of Lawrence's Jewish doctor, applied much more to Lawrence than to Gertler, for Lawrence, an outsider who was deeply critical of human weakness (especially during the war, when he opposed the mindless patriotism), identified himself with the vilified race of the Jews. Gibbon, Lawrence wrote, "says the Jews are the great *haters* of the human race—and the great *anti-social* principle.—Strikes me that is true—for the last 2,500 years, at least.—I feel such a profound hatred myself, of the human race, I almost know what it is to be a Jew."[22] Lawrence's tirades against Jews did not prevent him from having Jewish friends and publishers. And all of them, without exception, generously gave him money, houses, medical treatment, legal advice and professional support.[23]

VIII

Lawrence frequently quarreled with many of his closest friends and mocked their personal faults. Helen Thomas was shocked by his high-pitched, unpleasant laugh when recounting malicious stories about his acquaintances: "He spoke with derision and scorn of people I knew who had been most generous to him in many ways, and while telling my friend of some incident his high, steely voice rose into a mocking laugh." He also used insulting language in letters and arguments, and became angry when people resented it. But Lawrence quickly forgot his violent outbursts. He usually apologized to his friends and, after the eruption

had died down, resumed cordial relations. His caustic but sympathetic
friend Richard Aldington suggested that Lawrence's disease intensified
his irritation and anger: "It is so curious to me that both during DHL's
life and after people can't see that [his] wild accusations [against
friends] were nothing but the nervous exacerbation of a man whose
lungs were gone and who had a damnably rotten deal all round." Lawrence also tried to tell them how to conduct their lives. He recognized
and portrayed this fault in his autobiographical account of Birkin in
Women in Love: "There was his wonderful, desirable life-rapidity, the
rare quality of an utterly desirable man: and there was at the same time
this ridiculous, mean effacement into a Salvator Mundi and a Sunday-
school teacher, a prig of the stiffest type."[24]

Finally, like Wyndham Lewis and Ernest Hemingway, Lawrence
hated to be under an obligation, could not help caricaturing friends who
had helped him, and used his benefactors as satiric victims. He once
warned Mabel Luhan, who also had a sharp tongue and pen: "Remember,
other people can be utterly remorseless, if they think you've given them
away." But he himself was merciless in discerning and revealing the
weaknesses of his friends. When writing *The White Peacock,* he justified
his practice and boasted to Willie Hopkin that he would sacrifice friendship for art: "If I need any woman for my fictional purpose, I shall use
her. Why should I let any woman come between me and the flowering of
my genius."[25]

But Warren Roberts greatly exaggerates Lawrence's quarrels when he
asserts: "The Brewsters [whom Lawrence met in 1921] were among the
very few of Lawrence's friends who never turned on him or against whom
he never felt anger or disappointment."[26] Lawrence had many friends
with whom he never quarreled. He always remained on excellent terms
with his Eastwood friends Willie and Sallie Hopkin; Willie's daughter,
Enid Hilton; his childhood companions Gertie and Frances Cooper; his
Croydon colleague Arthur McLeod; his sister-in-law Else Jaffe; Cynthia
Asquith, Catherine Carswell, S. S. Koteliansky and Mark Gertler; the
South African painter Jan Juta, with whom he traveled in Sicily; and
Aldous Huxley, the closest friend during the last five years of his life.

Lawrence generated intense emotion wherever he went. He had the
power to change people, to arouse extreme love and hatred, to deepen his
friends' awareness of themselves and the world. He challenged them to
respond to him completely and to fulfill their own potential. His personality made a powerful impact on everyone he met. Friendship with
Lawrence, for many people, was the most significant event of their lives.

CHAPTER TEN

Mansfield and Murry,
1913–1916

I

LAWRENCE had a great deal in common with Katherine Mansfield, his most talented friend. Both were outsiders in English society: Lawrence because of his working-class background, Katherine because of her colonial origins. Though they left their birthplaces, they were strongly influenced by them and frequently re-created their native regions in their work. They spent many impoverished years on the Continent and maintained a European rather than an insular outlook, though Katherine was usually lonely and isolated abroad, while Lawrence— sustained by Frieda—traveled more widely and worked more productively. They experienced life with a feverish intensity, were passionately committed to their art and achieved a posthumous fame far greater than their contemporary reputations. Most important of all, they were physically sterile and seriously ill with tuberculosis for most of their adult lives, and wandered from country to country in search of a warm climate and good health. They were subject to sudden fits of rage, suffered the pain of disease and the threat of death.

Unlike his other friendships, Lawrence's relations with Katherine and Middleton Murry were based on the complex connections of two couples. Katherine and Lawrence were the creative poles of their marriages, and their genius was acknowledged by their partners. Both

couples had insoluble problems and frequent quarrels. But Katherine
and Murry, who were unable to marry until she finally secured a divorce
in 1919, had more serious conflicts, which sometimes led to extended
separations when each took a lover. Frieda's belief in Lawrence, which
kept him alive, was greater than Murry's belief in Katherine; and
Murry's weakness and betrayal led her to the mysticism of Gurdjieff and
hastened her death.

Both Lawrence and Frieda felt the Murrys were their most intimate
friends. They first corresponded about Lawrence's magazine articles,
then met and quickly established a friendship. Impelled by Lawrence's
desire for like-minded companions, they twice lived and worked in
neighboring houses. Both couples had fierce attractions and antago-
nisms toward one another. Lawrence and Frieda were physically attracted to Murry—a handsome, dreamy, weak and undependable man.
And Katherine and Murry were caught up in Lawrence's bitter quarrels
with Frieda.

Lawrence became more domineering as he became more alienated
from traditional society, and he constantly tried to persuade his friends
to conform to his ideals of sex and marriage. His temperamental extrem-
ism and his attempt to interfere with and manage his friends' lives
eventually forced Katherine and Murry to reject and withdraw from
him, with harsh letters and bitter recriminations on both sides. Katherine, who lived at close quarters with Lawrence, was much more
critical of him than were his other friends. She was attracted to his
vitality but repelled by his passionate enthusiasms and dogmatic obsessions, which intensified her natural inclination to retreat into her private world. Because their temperaments were radically different,
Katherine frequently appeared negative, cowardly and sickly to Lawrence, who blamed her for being ill; while to Katherine, Lawrence's
manic egoism seemed almost insane. But their bonds were strong and
they were always drawn back to each other. When they did not meet, they
read each other's books and kept in touch through letters and news from
their close mutual friends: Ottoline, Brett, Kot and Gertler. Katherine
recognized that Lawrence was a greater writer. When his work was
suppressed, he grew jealous of her success.

II

Katherine Mansfield (née Kathleen Beauchamp) was born in Wellington, New Zealand, in 1888, the daughter of a prosperous, philistine businessman who earned a knighthood as director and then chairman of the Bank of New Zealand. She was educated in Wellington and at Queen's College, London, returned to New Zealand for a year and then left permanently for London in August 1908. Within ten months of her arrival in England she had an unhappy love affair with one man, conceived his child, married a second man and left him the next day (after an unconsummated wedding night), endured a period of drug addiction, suffered a miscarriage and contracted venereal disease. She was a sexual extremist who both craved and repudiated men.

Katherine had fine features, intense dark eyes, clear skin, even white teeth, bobbed hair, a boyish body; she was colorful in her dress and quiet in her movements. She had been an actress and was fond of role playing, projecting contradictory selves and assuming a defensive mask-like persona. Lawrence captured her attractive, elusive character in his portrait of Gudrun Brangwen in *Women in Love:* she was "so *charming*, so infinitely charming, in her softness and her fine, exquisite richness of texture and delicacy of line. There was a certain playfulness about her too, such a piquancy of ironic suggestion, such an untouched reserve." And Dorothy Brett, who adored Katherine but was frequently the victim of her satire, mentioned her savage changes of mood and her cruel comments: "Her reputation of brilliancy, of a sort of ironic ruthlessness toward the small minds and less agile brains, simply terrified me.... She had daring, courage and a tremendous sense of humour. She was like a sparkling brook—like quicksilver. Her changes of mood were rapid and disconcerting; a laughing joyous moment would suddenly turn through some inadequate remark into biting anger.... Katherine had a tongue like a knife, she could cut the very heart out of one with it."[1]

John Middleton Murry, eighteen months younger than Katherine, was born in London in 1889, the son of a poor copy clerk at the War Office and a petty tyrant at home. Murry's biographer writes that his repressive childhood led to "an atrophy of the sensuous, a hypertrophy of the intellectual, from which he never recovered"; and Murry's aunt told his

son: "Your dad was never a *real* boy at all. He was just a little old man."
As late as 1919, when he was editor of the *Athenaeum,* Murry agreed
with this diagnosis and rather pathetically confessed: "I wish to God I
were a man. Somehow I seem to have grown up, gone bald even, without
ever becoming a man; and I find it terribly hard to master a situation."
Lawrence, who had a complex love-hate relationship with Murry and
was fond of diagnosing his weaknesses, agreed: "Spunk is what one
wants, not introspective sentiment. The last is your vice. You rot your
own manhood at the roots, with it."[2]

Murry's humble background and scholarly achievements resembled
Ernest Weekley's. His highly developed intellect won him scholarships
to Christ's Hospital and Brasenose College, Oxford, where he formed
friendships with the novelist Joyce Cary and the critic Michael Sadler.
Murry spent the Christmas vacation of 1910 in Paris, where he first
encountered Left Bank bohemianism and Fauvism, conceived the plan
for his avant-garde magazine, *Rhythm,* and had his first love affair, with
a Parisian *demi-mondaine,* Marguéritte.

Brett described Murry as an attractive and dreamy young man who
"rolls in with the gait of a sailor, his curly dark hair is getting a bit thin
on top. He is nervous, shy, a small man. The eyes are large and hazel, with
a strange unseeing look; the nose is curved one side and perfectly
straight the other, due to its having been broken. His lips are finely cut,
the mouth sensitive, the chin determined. A fine and beautiful head."
And Murry accurately characterized himself as "Part snob, part coward, part sentimentalist,"[3] as if the confession justified the faults.

Murry's fatal combination of indecision and self-deception, of intel-
lectuality and sentimentality, weakened his rational thought and made
him distrust his own feelings. This in turn led to a moral ambiguity, for
his intellectualism allowed him to escape from emotional dilemmas. He
was able to understand this flaw in himself and even condemn it, yet he
was disingenuous enough to believe that he could dispose of his defects
by acknowledging them and by attributing noble motives to selfish
actions. He believed he could be a great writer, but was primarily an
editor and a critic.

Katherine met Murry at a literary party in London in December
1911, when the "little Colonial" and the lower-middle-class undergradu-
ate were both *deraciné* outsiders in London and Oxford. After living
together in Gray's Inn Road in 1911–12, Katherine and Murry began
their itinerant life of poverty and squalor, and had nearly a dozen
addresses—in London, Bucks., Kent, Cornwall and Paris—during their

first two years together. Like Lawrence and Frieda, they suffered from poverty, illness and domestic discord; and began their life together without the conventional foundations of marriage, a supportive family, a secure home or a steady income. As Murry observed: we were "prey to a subtle sense of our own unreality, as though we were only a kind of dream-children."

Katherine's character was an odd mixture of the ethereal and the earthy; Murry was afraid of life and tended to withdraw from people. She was brave, he was cowardly; she was reserved, he wore his heart on his sleeve; and from the beginning she took the active role and he the passive one. Though Murry recognized that Katherine was his moral, artistic and intellectual superior, he was egotistic and self-absorbed. He constantly praised her genius, but she had to support him for many years, do the domestic chores and then write her stories with the little time that remained. Ottoline Morrell justly attributed Katherine's irritation to Murry's egoism and selfishness: "She seemed often as if she would like to shake him. She called him 'a little mole hung out on a string to dry.'"[4]

Virginia Woolf also treated her friends to a savage but accurate dissection of his character, which, she said, was "full of spite and backbiting and gush and highmindedness": "Middleton M[urry] is a posturing Byronic little man; pale; penetrating; with bad teeth; histrionic; an egoist; not, I think, very honest; but a good journalist, and works like a horse, and writes the poetry a very old hack might write. . . . He has a mania for confession. I suppose his instinct is to absolve himself in these bleatings and so get permission for more sins." Gerald Brenan spoke for most of Bloomsbury when he said: "Everyone detested Middleton Murry," and Bertrand Russell also "thought Murry *beastly.*"[5] People disliked Murry because he was a pretentious and ambitious self-made man who, though shy and diffident, conveyed an impression of condescension and learned superiority. He lived in a world of ideas rather than of people, and often adopted and then abandoned untenable beliefs.

III

In December 1912, after Lawrence (who was three years older than Katherine) had published *The White Peacock* and *The Trespasser,* and

Katherine *In a German Pension* (1911), he responded to Murry's request and asked Edward Garnett's advice about publishing his stories in *Rhythm*. The following month Katherine sent him a copy of *Rhythm* and again asked for a contribution. Lawrence replied from Gargnano on January 29, offering several stories, and in February he told a friend: "You should find some of my stuff in March *Rhythm*. It's a daft paper, but the folk seem rather nice." When the Lawrences returned to England in June 1913, they looked up Katherine and Murry and liked them immediately. The two men were extremely conscious of their humble origins, and when they discovered that neither couple was married and both women were waiting for a divorce, it seemed they were made for each other. Frieda felt "theirs was the only spontaneous and jolly friendship that we had. . . . Yes I like Katherine, there is something exquisite about her mind and body. . . . I fell for Katherine and Murry when I saw them quite unexpectedly on the top of a bus, making faces at each other and putting their tongues out." This was a charming but characteristically childish aspect of their relationship. Frieda was still estranged from her young children, and Katherine was far more understanding than Lawrence about Frieda's maternal feelings. Katherine visited the children and took them letters, and Frieda "loved her like a younger sister."[6] Later in the summer the two couples bathed on the deserted sands of Broadstairs, and Lawrence gave Katherine and Murry a copy of *Sons and Lovers*.

The Lawrences returned to Italy in September 1913, described their lonely life in Fiascherino as one long enchantment and urged Katherine and Murry to join them. Keenly interested in his friends' lives, Lawrence craved the stimulus he had enjoyed in London and was eager to establish his own intimate society. The great problem was lack of money. Murry's small income derived from reviewing in London. He did not want to give that up, nor did he want to live on Katherine's allowance of £100 a year (which was then being paid to the printers of their "daft paper" because a friend had gone into bankruptcy, leaving Murry responsible for his debts). Lawrence compared Murry's situation to his own, rightly seeing through some of Murry's excuses yet refusing to see that Murry was not a creative artist (despite his ambitions) but a man of letters in London: "When you say you won't take Katherine's money, it means you don't trust her love for you. When you say she needs little luxuries, and you couldn't bear to deprive her of them, it means you don't respect either yourself or her sufficiently to do it. . . . She must say, 'Could I live in a little place in Italy with Jack, and be lonely, have a rather bare life, but be happy.' If she could, then take her money. If she doesn't want to, don't try. But don't beat about the bush. In the way you go on, you are inevitably coming apart. She is perhaps beginning to be unsatisfied with you."[7]

Using his own marriage as a model, Lawrence discussed and dismissed this financial problem in a long letter to Murry written in November 1913. He also analyzed the essential defect in Murry's marriage and, unlike his later letters, was both shrewd and reasonable about how to improve relations with Katherine:

> It looks to me as if you two, far from growing nearer, are snapping the bonds that hold you together, one after another. I suppose you must both of you consult your own hearts, honestly. . . .
>
> You must rest, and you and Katherine must heal, and come together, before you do *any serious* work of any sort. It is the split in love that drains you. . . .
>
> If you want things to come right—if you are ill, and exhausted, then take her money to the last penny and let her do her own housework. Then she'll know you love her. You can't blame her if she's not satisfied with you. . . . But you fool, you squander yourself, not for *her*, but to provide her with petty luxuries she doesn't really want. You insult her. A woman unsatisfied must have luxuries. But a woman who loves a man would sleep on a board. . . .
>
> You've tried to satisfy Katherine with what you could earn for her, give her: and she will only be satisfied with what you *are*.

Lawrence saw that trust and love could overcome Murry's scruples about money, and that Katherine's "need" for luxuries was merely an excuse. Like Katherine, he also understood that a true marriage would strengthen her art. "I believe in marriage," she told a friend. "It seems to me the only possible relation that is really satisfying. And how else is one to have peace of mind to enjoy life and to do one's work?"[8]

Lawrence was clearly alluding to Frieda's sacrifice when he stated that "a woman who loves a man would sleep on a board." Murry, who could never satisfy Katherine's material or emotional needs, knew that she was *not* satisfied with what he was. But Murry's career was just as important to him as Katherine's. He did not love her enough to make this sacrifice, or have sufficient faith in his own talent to believe that he could write while living abroad and start afresh in London later on. Murry had a wife whom he had to support emotionally and intellectually. But since he was self-absorbed and had high, if unrealistic, literary ambitions, he was particularly unsuited to this sacrificial role.

Murry's weak character made it impossible for him to comply with Lawrence's commands. He had an endless capacity for self-deception and disguised his egocentricity as mock saintliness. Like Lawrence, Katherine had cruel insight and cutting humor; she loathed Murry's self-pity and accused him of being "just like a little dog whining outside a door." She impatiently exclaimed: "When you know you are a voice crying in the wilderness, *cry,* but don't say 'I am a voice crying in the wilderness.'" Katherine also condemned his high moral tone and pretentious philosophy, called him "a monk without a monastery" and said he "couldn't fry a sausage without thinking about God."[9]

Murry must have resented the invidious comparison between Lawrence's marriage and his own, as well as the attempt to direct his life, and he rejected Lawrence's argument as graciously as possible. Though Lawrence could rarely refrain from giving good, if tactless, advice, he understood Murry's feelings, was grateful for his forbearance and (echoing *Women in Love*) wrote rather apologetically in April 1914: "I thought that you and Katherine held me an interfering Sunday-school Superintendent sort of person who went too far in his superintending and became impossible:—stepped just too far, which is the crime of crimes. And I felt guilty. And I suppose I am guilty. But thanks be to God, one is often guilty without being damned."[10] But his impossible interference in their lives frequently *did* go too far and was a major cause of their most serious quarrels.

On July 13, 1914, when Lawrence and Frieda were married in London, with Murry and Katherine as witnesses, Frieda impulsively gave her friend her old wedding ring, which Katherine took to the grave. In one of their wedding photographs, Frieda and Murry are smiling, wearing light-colored clothing and looking quite smart. Lawrence, scowling, dressed in black and looking rather rough, appears much younger than Frieda and seems quite out of it—as if Frieda had just married Murry.

In October 1914, Katherine and Murry stayed with the Lawrences in Buckinghamshire for two weeks while they prepared Rose Tree Cottage, an hour's walk away, where they lived until February 1915. During this stay, Lawrence introduced them to Koteliansky and began to expound his plans for a Utopian community of like-minded friends, which he called Rananim. But Katherine proceeded to deflate his idealistic dreams. Catherine Carswell reported that "when Katherine, not without

realistic mischief, went and obtained a mass of detailed, difficult information about suitable islands, Lawrence fell sadly silent. . . . Hiding her
fun behind a solemn face, [Katherine] proved by time-tables and guide-
books that Rananim was impossible." Katherine could not "prove" that
Rananim was impossible. But, unlike the passive and dependent Murry,
she was too sceptical and individualistic to become a disciple of Lawrence. As Murry remarked, she had "a lightly mocking but ruthless way
of summing up various people over whom [Lawrence] was temporarily
enthusiastic, which made him smile rather crookedly. At such a moment,
he was a little afraid of her."[11]

Lawrence and Murry discussed their most intimate sexual problems
while living near each other in the fall of 1914. An entry from Murry's
November journal suggests that he sympathized with Lawrence's sexual
difficulties and found Frieda extremely irritating:

> There is no high degree of physical satisfaction for him. That is all
> wrong between them. F. accuses him of taking her "as a dog does a
> bitch," and last night he explained his belief that even now we have
> to undergo a dual "mortification" by saying that very often when he
> wants F. she does not want him at all. . . . And the idea that she
> should have been allowed to tyrannize over him with her damnably
> false "love" for her children is utterly repulsive to me. I have all my
> work cut out to prevent myself from being actively insolent to her.
> She is stupid in any case, and stupid assertiveness is hard enough to
> bear.[12]

Lawrence inevitably had his turn analyzing the defects of Murry's
rather rudimentary sexual performance, of which his biographer has
said: "There were no caresses, no preliminaries, their love-making (such
as it was) was a climax without crescendo." In March 1915, after Lawrence had pondered and then criticized some of Murry's intimate revelations, Murry naively told Katherine—alluding more to his own
ineptitude than to any imaginative perversions—Lawrence "says that it
gave him quite a shock to discover how crude I was physically, apparently as between you and me. . . . I haven't the least idea of what he was
driving at."[13]

Lawrence and Frieda, who helped them clean and paint Rose Tree
Cottage, saw Katherine and Murry every day. They sang folk songs,
talked of Rananim and exposed the Murrys to their ferocious quarrels.
Katherine and Murry, caught up in the Lawrences' emotions, tried to

find a way to make peace without taking sides or expressing their horror. Katherine's *Journal* entries for January 1915 in Buckinghamshire suggest the difficulties of living close to the exciting yet exasperating Lawrences, and the extreme variation of her attitude toward them:

> In the evening Lawrence and Koteliansky. They talked plans; but I felt *very* antagonistic to the whole affair. (January 9)

> In the morning, Frieda suddenly. She had had a row with Lawrence. She tired me to death. . . . [At night:] L. was nice, very nice, sitting with a piece of string in his hand, on true sex. (January 10)

> In the evening we went to the Lawrences'. Frieda was rather nice. (January 15)

> Walked to the Lawrences'! They were horrible and witless and dull. (January 16)

> Lawrence arrived cross, but he gradually worked round to me. (January 19)

After a quarrel about her children, a few months after their marriage, Frieda sent Katherine to threaten Lawrence that she would not come back. " 'Damn the woman,'" shouted Lawrence in a fury, " 'tell her I never want to see her again.'"[14] Katherine's relations with Murry were exacerbated by their living near the Lawrences. In February 1915 she left him for her more sophisticated lover Francis Carco, a French writer whom she had met through Murry in Paris. Warm, high-spirited and self-confident, Carco was then in the French army near Besançon, behind enemy lines.

Katherine's absence allowed Lawrence to establish a new intimacy with Murry. The abandoned husband came to see Lawrence, who had moved to Greatham in Sussex, and during the long walk from the station his cold turned to influenza. Lawrence devoted himself to nursing Murry and enjoyed the opportunity to give strength and comfort to his ailing friend, an episode that inspired the passage in *Aaron's Rod* when Lilly nurses the sickly Aaron back to health. Murry's letters to Katherine about his visit to Lawrence were extremely dull, and unless he was trying to hide his feelings, the experience apparently meant much more to Lawrence than to Murry. Lawrence's new bond of intimacy with Murry alienated him from Katherine, who spent most of that spring in France, disillusioned with and wounded by the selfishness of Carco (who had not met her expectations) and the indifference of Murry. In May, after Katherine had stayed briefly with the Lawrences at Greatham, Lawrence wrote to Kot: "Does Katherine depress you. Her letters are as jarring as the sound of a saw."[15]

In September, when Lawrence was living in Hampstead and Katherine and Murry in nearby St. John's Wood, the three writers started a new little magazine, *Signature,* which had a brown cover and octavo format. They published Lawrence's "The Crown," Katherine's "The Wind Blows" and "The Little Governess" and a story by Murry. Lawrence recalled that the group held weekly meetings near Red Lion Square "up a narrow stair-case over a green-grocer's shop.... We scrubbed the room and colour-washed the walls and got a long table and some windsor chairs from the Caledonian market. And we used to make a good warm fire: it was dark autumn, in that unknown bit of London. Then on Thursday nights, we had meetings: about a dozen people," during October and November 1915.[16] *Signature* was printed in the East End by I. Narodiczky, who had a Hebrew sign on his shop front in the Mile End Road and had printed Isaac Rosenberg's first book of poems in 1912. But no one had much time for or interest in the little magazine during those momentous days of the war, and *Signature* died after only three issues.

Lawrence and Katherine were drawn together in the autumn of 1915 by a tragic event. Her younger brother, Leslie, had come from New Zealand to England for training en route to the battlefields of France, and they had spent some happy days together recollecting and idealizing their childhood. In October, a week after Leslie reached the front, he was killed. "Do not be sad," Lawrence wrote with an optimistic compassion that anticipates his poem "The Ship of Death": "It is one life which is passing away from us, one 'I' is dying; but there is another coming into being, which is the happy, creative you. I knew you would have to die with your brother; you also, go down into death and be extinguished. But for us there is a rising from the grave, there is a resurrection, and a clean life to begin from the start, new, and happy. Don't be afraid, don't doubt it, it is so. . . . Get better soon, and come back, and let us all try to be happy *together,* in unanimity, not in hostility, creating, not destroying."[17] Lawrence believed that a community of idealistic artists was really possible, and that his friendship and understanding could help Katherine over her grief.

After Leslie's death Katherine and Murry moved to Bandol, near Marseilles. By this time, her illness made it impossible for her to spend the winter in London. Murry saw Lawrence on a brief trip to England, when Lawrence took the opportunity to give him some good but gratuitous advice. Lawrence emphasized the psychological basis of Katherine's illness and insisted that if the Murrys achieved happiness, she would get well. "Lawrence went for me, about you, terribly," Murry wrote to Katherine. "He said that it was all my fault, that I was a coward, that I never offered you a new life, that I would not break with my past, that your illness was all due to your misery and that I had made you miserable, by always whining & never making a decision; that I should never have left you there." By December, Lawrence had revived his plans for Rananim and wrote about his hopes for a harmonious and purposeful life: "My dear Katherine, you know that in this we are your sincere friends, and what we want is to create a new, good, common life, the germ of a new social life together."[18]

IV

In February 1916, after Lawrence had moved from London to Cornwall, he intensified his campaign, begun in Fiascherino, to persuade his friends to live with him. Writing to them in the guise of a courting lover, he said: "I've waited for you for two years now, and am far more constant to you than ever you are to me—or ever will be." And in March he pleaded: "Really, you must have the other place. I keep looking at it. I call it already Katherine's house, Katherine's tower. There is something *very* attractive about it. It is very old, native to the earth." Though Katherine was strongly opposed to Cornwall and distrusted the very idea of a community, she and Murry allowed themselves to be seduced by Lawrence's desperate pleas: "No good trying to run away from the fact that we are fond of each other. We count on you two as our only two *tried* friends, real and permanent and truly blood kin." Lawrence had great faith in his own curative powers: he believed that Katherine would get well and the Murrys would achieve happiness, as he had achieved it with Frieda, if they lived close to him and allowed him to guide their lives.

Dubious about the plan to rejoin the Lawrences after the *débâcle* in Buckinghamshire, Katherine wrote an ironic letter to Ottoline Morrell and accurately predicted that their stay would be short: "We are going to stay with the Lawrences for ever and ever as perhaps you know; I daresay eternity will last the whole of the summer."[19] The relations of the two couples in Cornwall were described in minute detail in many letters from Lawrence and Katherine to their mutual friends: Kot and Beatrice Campbell as well as Ottoline.

The Lawrences were overjoyed at their arrival in April. "I see Katherine Mansfield and Murry arriving sitting on a cart," Frieda later remembered, "high up on all the goods and chattels, coming down the lane to Tregerthen." And Lawrence, who loved to do manual work, wrote enthusiastically to Ottoline: "The Murrys have come and we are very busy getting their cottage ready: colouring the walls and painting and working furiously. I like it, and we all enjoy ourselves. The Murrys are happy with each other now. But they neither of them seem very well in health."[20] Though the couples were irresistibly drawn to each other, they could not live together; their second communal experience, like the first, ended in failure.

Though Lawrence yearned for a starlike "equilibrium, a pure balance of two single beings," Frieda recognized that what he really wanted was a satellite, a woman submissive to his absolute will. Frieda always fought this, and the conflict was invigorating to both of them. As he later explained to Katherine: "I do think a woman must yield some sort of precedence to a man, and he must take this precedence. I do think men must go ahead absolutely in front of their women, without turning round to ask for permission or approval from their women. Consequently the women must follow as it were unquestioning. I can't help it, I believe this. Frieda doesn't. Hence our fight." Another problem, as Katherine caustically explained to Beatrice Campbell, was Lawrence's obsession with man's animal nature and with sexual symbolism: "I cannot discuss blood affinity to beasts for instance if I have to keep ducking to avoid the flat irons and the saucepans. And I shall *never* see sex in trees, sex in the running brooks, sex in stones & sex in everything. The number of things that are really phallic from fountain pen fillers onwards! . . . I suggested to Lawrence that he should call his cottage The Phallus & Frieda thought it was a very good idea."[21]

Though Lawrence was struggling—and failing—to dominate Frieda, their marriage was basically secure. Katherine and Murry's relationship, though outwardly calm, was more vulnerable and insecure. Though more creative than Murry, Katherine tried to fulfill the conventional wifely role. But Murry was too narcissistic to respond to her needs. Lawrence saw the weakness in their marriage and wanted to help them. At the same time, Lawrence himself was attracted to Murry.

Lawrence devised a plan that would revive his friends' marriage and give him a new and closer connection to Murry. As Murry wrote in *Between Two Worlds:*

> Lawrence believed, or tried to believe, that the relation between Katherine and me was false and deadly; and that the relation between Frieda and himself was real and life-giving; but that his relation with Frieda needed to be completed by a new relation between himself and me, which I evaded. . . . By virtue of this "mystical" relation with Lawrence, I participate in this pre-mental reality, the "dark sources" of my being come alive. From this changed personality, I, in turn, enter a new relation with Katherine. . . .
>
> He appeared to think that we, simply because we had nothing to correspond with his intense and agonizing sexual experiences, were flippant about sex. . . . It struck us as quite exorbitant that Katherine should be regarded as a butterfly and I as a child, merely because our sex-relation was exempt from agony.

The emotional yet abstract language does not explain precisely why Lawrence needed a completion he could not get from Frieda nor how Katherine and Murry could recharge themselves on Lawrence's marital battery. But it is not difficult to see how Lawrence's attempt to make Murry more like himself (though he never equated sexual pleasure with agony) offended Katherine, who naturally resented Lawrence's assaults on Murry. Their friendship inevitably degenerated as Katherine reacted against Lawrence's powerful influence on Murry and his attempt to revitalize their existence through a passionate attachment to her lover. When Murry turned toward Lawrence, Katherine felt completely isolated. "I am very much alone here," she wrote to Kot in May 1916, after a few gloomy weeks in Cornwall. "It is not a really nice place. It is so full of huge stones. . . . I don't belong to anybody here. In fact, I have no being, but I am making preparations for changing everything."[22]

Katherine's phrase "ducking to avoid the flat irons and the saucepans" alluded to Lawrence's violent battles with Frieda and his humiliating dependence upon her, which astounded and repelled the rather reserved Katherine far more than the bleak and rocky landscape, and soon drove her away. She described her reaction in a letter to Kot: "I don't know which disgusts one worse—when they are loving and playing with each other, or when they are roaring at each other and he is pulling out

Frieda's hair and saying 'I'll cut your bloody throat, you bitch.'" She gave a vivid and dramatic account of one explosion that took place in Cornwall in May 1916.

Frieda said Shelley's Ode to a Skylark was false. Lawrence said: "you are showing off; you don't know anything about it." Then she began. "*Now* I have had enough. Out of my house—you little God Almighty you. I've had enough of you. Are you going to keep your mouth shut or aren't you." Said Lawrence: "I'll give you a dab on the cheek to quiet you, you dirty hussy." Etc. Etc. So I left the house. At dinner time Frieda appeared. "I have finally done with him. It's all over for ever." She then went out of the kitchen & began to walk round and round the house in the dark. Suddenly Lawrence appeared and made a kind of horrible blind rush at her and they began to scream and scuffle. He beat her—he beat her to death— her head and face and breast and pulled out her hair. All the while she screamed for Murry to help her. Finally they dashed into the kitchen and round and round the table. I shall never forget how L. looked. He was so white—almost green and he just hit—thumped the big soft woman. Then he fell into one chair and she into another. No one said a word. A silence fell except for Frieda's sobs and sniffs. In a way I felt almost glad that the tension between them was over for ever—and that they had made an end of their "intimacy." L. sat staring at the floor, biting his nails. Frieda sobbed.... And the next day, whipped himself, and far more thoroughly than he had ever beaten Frieda, he was running about taking her up her break- fast to her bed and trimming her a hat.[23]

Despite the passion and violence, their operatic playlet contains an element of slapstick and self-parody. The first act begins with Law- rence's destruction of Frieda's aesthetic judgment, leads to her verbal abuse of his assumed omniscience, and ends with his colloquial threat of punishment and Katherine's exit. The second act opens with Frieda's absolute pronouncement ("It's all over for ever"), which is absolutely unconvincing, and leads to her exit and Lawrence's sudden reap- pearance as an avenging Fury. But the brutality of his attack is allevi- ated by the burlesque chase around the table and softened by the description of a green Lawrence thumping a pillow-like Frieda. The curtain falls on this act as both protagonists collapse with physical exhaustion, sobbing and biting nails, and as Katherine, acting as

Chorus, makes another absolute pronouncement ("the tension ... was over for ever"). The third act reveals a comic reversal of sexual roles, with the defeated male aggressor serving and wooing his lady love.

In May, Katherine gave Beatrice Campbell another precise and lively description of Lawrence's rages, which excited her emotions, exhausted her and made it impossible to concentrate and to work: "Once you start talking I cannot describe the frenzy that comes over him. He simply *raves,* roars, beats the table, abuses everybody.—But that's not such great matter. What makes these attacks insupportable is the feeling one has at the back of one's mind that he is completely out of control— swallowed up in an acute *insane* irritation. After one of these attacks he's ill with fever, haggard and broken. It is impossible to be anything to him but a kind of playful acquaintance."

And in a letter to Ottoline, Katherine emphasized Lawrence's madness, which could only be controlled by friends or cured by laughter, and (like Ottoline and Kot) blamed Frieda, who had him "completely in her power," for his irrational behavior: "Left to himself Lawrence goes mad. When he is with people he expands to the warmth and the light in them, he is a darling and often very wonderful, but left to himself he is [like Cornwall] cold and dark and desolate. Of course Frieda is at the bottom of it. He has chosen Frieda and when he is with real people he knows how fatal that choice is. . . . I am *sure* there is only one way to answer him. It is very cruel, but it's the only weapon to prick his sensitive pride. It is to laugh at him—to make fun of him—to make him realise that he has made a fool of himself." In other letters to Ottoline, Katherine continued to condemn Frieda as a malign influence who weakened Lawrence by provoking his rages. She believed Frieda deified—without understanding—the Nietzschean influence on Lawrence's ideas[24] and claimed that she had defeated him. Frieda tried to brutalize and bury Lawrence, and then took masochistic pleasure in being beaten:

> Sooner or later all Frieda's friends are bound to pop their heads out of the window and see her grinding it before their door—smoking a cigarette with one hand on her hip and a coloured picture of Lorenzo and Nietzsche dancing together "symbolically" on the front of the barrel organ. . . .
>
> It is really over for now—our relationship with L. The "dear man" in him whom we all loved is hidden away, absorbed, completely lost, like a little gold ring in that immense German Christmas pudding which is Frieda. . . .

Though I was dreadfully sorry for L. I didn't feel an atom of sympathy for Frieda. . . .

I think it's horribly tragic, for they had degraded each other and brutalized each other beyond Words, but—all the same—I never did imagine anyone so thrive upon a beating as Frieda seemed to thrive. I shall never be persuaded that she did not take some Awful Relish in it. . . . Lawrence has definitely chosen to sin against himself and Frieda is triumphant.

Katherine was frightened by the insane quality of Lawrence's outbursts, and felt that she had to humor him if she wanted to avoid the rages that had such a disastrous effect on his health. Though these eruptions were embarrassing and unpleasant, Katherine was most disturbed by the fact that they closely resembled the kind of behavior she hated and feared in *herself:*

A funny feature about this sort of illness is one's temper. I get so irritable, so nervous that I want to *scream*, & if many people start talking I just lose my puff and feel my blood getting black. . . . My fits of temper are really terrifying. I had one this . . . morning and tore up a page of the book I was reading—and absolutely lost my head. Very significant. When it was over J[ack] came in and stared. "What is the matter? What have you done?" "Why?" "You look *all dark*." He drew back the curtains and called it an effect of light, but when I came into my studio to dress I saw it was not that. I was a deep earthy colour, *with pinched eyes.* I was *green*. Strangely enough these fits are Lawrence and Frieda all over again. I am more like L. than anybody. We are *unthinkably* alike, in fact.[25]

In a few brief weeks, Lawrence's dream of a new, harmonious colony was ended. Frieda refused to be dominated, Katherine was aloof and unhappy, Murry could not respond to Lawrence's overtures. When, in a fit of rage, Lawrence screamed at Murry: "I hate your love, I *hate it*. You're an obscene bug, sucking my life away," the break between the couples was inevitable. A man with a horse and cart carried away the Murrys' possessions, and Murry, who felt this separation was final, wrote: "It would have been unlike Lawrence, even at such a moment, not to have lent a hand: and he did. But our hearts were sore. When the last rope was tied, I said good-bye and hoped they would come over to see us.

Frieda, who took such incidents lightly, said they would; but Lawrence did not answer. I wheeled my bicycle to the road and pedalled off, with the feeling that I had said good-bye to him forever."[26]

After Katherine and Murry had left in mid-June, Lawrence wrote defensively to Ottoline, blamed the barrenness of Cornwall for the failure with his friends and ironically suggested the proper setting for their unrealistic child-love: "Unfortunately the Murrys do not like the country—it is too rocky and bleak for them. They should have a soft valley, with leaves and the ring-dove cooing." Soon after, Lawrence visited them in Mylor, on the south coast of Cornwall, and Katherine wrote of him affectionately to Ottoline: "Lawrence has gone home again. We walked with him as far as the ferry and away he sailed in a little open boat pulled by an old, old man. Lawrence wore a broad white linen hat and he carried a ruck sack on his back." But in July, after having subjected the Murrys to his intense scrutiny, Lawrence sent Kot his usual depressing diagnosis: "I think—well, she and Jack are not very happy—they make some sort of contract whereby each of them is free. . . . Really, I think she and Jack have worn out anything that was between them.—I like her better than him. He was rather horrid when he was here."[27]

Lawrence re-created his intimate relations with Katherine and Murry in Buckinghamshire and Cornwall in his greatest novel, *Women in Love*. Murry said that when he read and reviewed the novel in 1921 he did not see any biographical similarities and "was really astonished when, one day, Frieda told me that I was Gerald Crich." Katherine, who shared Murry's hostility and is supposed to have called it a "filthy rotten book," criticized the egoistic exaggeration in the novel and denied the biographical resemblances. As she wrote to Ottoline, another angry victim of Lawrence's fiction: "It is so absurd that one can't say anything; it is after all almost purely pathological, as they say. But it's sad to think what might have been. Wasn't it Santayana who said: Every artist holds a lunatic in leash. That explains L. to me. You know I am Gudrun? Oh, what rubbish it all is."[28]

In *Women in Love*, which he was writing while living with Katherine and Murry in 1916, Lawrence uses Katherine as an inspiration rather than as a precise model for Gudrun, expresses his resentment about the failure of their friendship and triumphs over his friends in the novel in a way that he never did in actual life. Gudrun and Gerald's intense struggle of wills reflects the extreme violence of Lawrence's own marriage, and represents his very subjective conception of Katherine's mistress-love relationship with Murry: the violent, destructive and disintegrating "union of ecstasy and death" which provides a powerful contrast to the healthy and vital marriage of Ursula and Birkin.

Gudrun really represents Lawrence's gross exaggeration of the negative aspects of Katherine's character: her self-destructive quest for experience and the bitterness of her *early* work, for she had published only the satiric *In a German Pension* before Lawrence completed his novel in 1916. In *Women in Love,* Lawrence transforms Katherine's delicate art into attenuated preciosity, her satire into corrosion, her reserve into negation, her resistance to his demands into arrogance and insolence, her insecurity and loneliness into infantile dependence, her quest for love into destructive sterility, her restless search for health into a rootless outcast life, her illness into evil.

CHAPTER ELEVEN.

War,
1914–1915

I

"THE TRAGEDY of the First World War," writes John Keegan, a leading military historian, "was that the waging of siege warfare and the proliferation of rapid-firing weapons had suddenly coincided." The result was squalid battles for a few hundred yards of mud, in which tens of thousands died in a single afternoon. In the first battle of Ypres (April 1914) the French sacrificed 64,000 men in a hopeless assault on the St. Mihiel salient. The second attack on Verdun (July 1, 1916) was the most disastrous day in British military history: 20,000 men were killed, 40,000 wounded; the slaughter continued for four and a half months, until the casualties reached half a million. In the course of that battle the front was pushed forward to a maximum of six miles.

Despite two years of horrific trench warfare, the strategy of massive frontal assault continued. "Nothing had been learnt from previous failures," writes A.J.P. Taylor, "except how to repeat them on a larger scale." The Somme offensive (July–August 1916), which followed Verdun, was an unredeemed defeat. During the most bitterly fought battle in France, 23,000 men were expended to gain, after six weeks, one mile of ground. By November the Allies had lost 600,000 men (two thirds of them British) and the Germans 615,000. At Passchendaele (summer 1917), once again, "a heavy price was paid for nought." Keegan concludes that "by 1917 the infantry units of all armies that had fought at the front since 1914 had, if wounded are counted with killed, suffered 100 per cent casualties, and by the end some units and formations would have suffered over 200 per cent casualties. . . . No armies ever before, not even in the worst passages of siege warfare, sustained courage or casualties with the suicidal relentlessness of those on the Western Front."[1] By the end of the war the British Empire had suffered a casualty rate of 36 percent, with 908,000 killed and more than two million wounded. The total number of war deaths on all sides was ten million.

Lawrence was acutely aware of this carnage. He had described German militarism in stories like "The Thorn in the Flesh" and "The Prussian Officer" (both 1914). In the latter, the destructive power of Germany is expressed in terms of sadistic homosexuality that ends in murder and self-destruction. But (like almost everyone else) Lawrence had ignored the menace of war in the Balkans. In November 1912, while living in Gargnano, he naively wrote: "The Italian papers are full of Servia and Turkey—but what had England got to do with it?" As soon as war began—and while political and military leaders encouraged and justified the senseless slaughter to which they had committed the country (any generals who questioned the strategy ran the risk of dismissal)—Lawrence became visibly changed and intensely distressed by the cruel stupidity that drove nations to destroy one another. His anger became more violent, his ideas more extreme. He became a preacher, a prophet, a denouncer of evil, and had to give vent to his fury or be destroyed by it. He later identified with the fierce anger of St. John of Patmos, the author of the Book of Revelation, and exclaimed: "John's passionate and mystic hatred of the civilization of his day, a hatred so intense only because he knew that the living realities of men's being were displaced by it, is something to which the soul answers now."[2]

Lawrence's reaction to the war was very different from Henry James' passive disillusionment with the idea of progress, Leonard Woolf's tragic acquiescence in the horrors of the modern world or the war poets' initial idealism and profound disenchantment with the lies that had sustained the conflict. On August 5, 1914, the day after Britain entered the war, the aged Henry James, referring to the German Kaiser and the Austrian Emperor, realized the hollowness of the concept of amelioration that had dominated European thought since the Renaissance. Instead of civilized progress, James felt, there was only meaningless destruction: "The plunge of civilisation into this abyss of blood and darkness by the wanton feat of those two infamous autocrats is a thing that so gives away the whole long age during which we have supposed the world to be, with whatever abatement, gradually bettering, that to have to take it all now for what the treacherous years were all the while really making for and meaning is too tragic for any words." Woolf emphasized the stark contrast between the prewar and postwar point of view: "In 1914 in the background of one's life and one's mind there were light and hope; by 1918 one had unconsciously accepted a perpetual public menace and darkness and had admitted in the privacy of one's mind or soul an iron fatalistic acquiescence in insecurity and barbarism."[3]

Wyndham Lewis, Robert Graves, Siegfried Sassoon, Ford Madox Ford and Richard Aldington, who were tested in combat and wrote about the war, had a deep sympathy with French art and culture, and felt obliged to defend civilization against German barbarism. They thought the crucible of war would be valuable to a writer, believed they had a patriotic obligation to help their country and companions in time of crisis. These writers—as well as the mass of ordinary men—were at first idealistic, eager to join the army and test themselves in war before the anticipated victory came at Christmas. Five hundred thousand men volunteered in the first month; and over one hundred thousand a month joined during the next year and a half. These writers, like the other volunteers, adopted a more realistic and embittered view only *after* they had been in combat.

Lawrence—from the beginning and without firsthand experience— had greater intuition into and historical understanding of the meaning and effects of war. He was cynical about the chauvinism, angry about the slaughter and outspoken about the war when nearly everyone else in England enthusiastically supported it. And he was determined to proclaim what Wilfred Owen in "Strange Meeting" called the "truth untold."

Lawrence's opposition to the war was influenced by his Nonconformist heritage, which taught him to think independently and, if necessary, to oppose the prevailing mode of thought; by his German wife, who made him sympathize with both sides instead of becoming a blind chauvinist; and by his prewar travels and residence in Italy, which also encouraged a European rather than a purely insular point of view and led him to believe that both sides would be badly damaged by the war— no matter who won the final, and inevitably Pyrrhic, victory.

Most of Lawrence's friends—apart from Ford, Aldington and Herbert Asquith—were not involved in the war, and the tragedy did not touch him directly. Pound and Kot were foreigners, Marsh and Forster homosexuals, Russell and Garnett pacifists, Gertler and Murry in poor health—and all were excused from military service. Unlike the war poets, Lawrence did not feel that the experience of combat would be valuable to him as an artist. (He was perhaps mistaken about this, for he excelled in portraying violence: the mob scenes in *Aaron's Rod*, the political riots in *Kangaroo* and the attack of the rebels in *The Plumed Serpent*.) And it is difficult to imagine Lawrence, in full military regalia, hurling himself over the top against the soldiers of Frieda's fatherland.

Lawrence was intensely dissatisfied with the decaying spirit of England and the collapse of the traditional values of European civilization. His description of wartime London as a barren inferno anticipates, by seven years, the mood and imagery of Eliot's *Waste Land*: "The traffic flows through the rigid grey streets like the rivers of Hell through their banks of dry, rocky ash." In November 1915—between the Allies' success in the battle of Loos and the replacement of John French by Douglas Haig as British commander in chief—Lawrence wrote an exceptionally moving letter to Cynthia Asquith (whose father-in-law was directing the wartime government). He evoked the gracious beauty of Garsington and the familiar Oxfordshire countryside, linked them to decline, decay and death, and anticipated the great opening sentences of *Lady Chatterley's Lover*:

When I drive across this country, with the autumn falling and rustling to pieces, I am so sad, for my country, for this great wave of civilisation, 2000 years, which is now collapsing, that it is hard to live. So much beauty and pathos of old things passing away and no new things coming: this house of the Ottolines—It is England—my God, it breaks my soul—this England, these shafted windows, the elm-trees, the blue distance—the past, the great past, crumbling down, breaking down, not under the force of the coming buds, but under the weight of many exhausted, lovely yellow leaves, that drift over the lawn and over the pond, like the soldiers, passing away, into winter and the darkness of winter—no, I can't bear it. For the winter stretches ahead, where all vision is lost and all memory dies out.[4]

Lawrence perceived the war as the pure suicide of humanity, a collective desire for death; as senseless destruction, caused by some hidden morbidity in European civilization, lacking any positive purpose or constructive ideal. In September 1914 he predicted that men "will receive such a blow from the ghastliness and mechanical, obsolete, hideous stupidity of war." As an antidote to this destructive process Lawrence—resembling his father, who "liked non-human things best," and possessing extraordinary powers of perception—wanted "to realise the tremendous *non-human* quality of life—it is wonderful. It is not the emotions, nor the personal feelings and attachments, that matter. They are all only expressive, and expression has become mechanical. Behind us all are the tremendous unknown [natural] forces of life, coming unseen and unperceived." Two years later, after the battle of the Somme, he was suffering intensely and told Cynthia Asquith: "for *me* the war is utterly wrong, stupid, monstrous and contemptible. . . . War cannot be thought of, for me, without the utmost repulsion and desecration of one's being."[5]

Freud, like Lawrence, believed that war expressed mankind's aggressive urge for power, corrupt sensation and self-destruction—for the triumph of dissolution and death. Discussing the war in *Civilization and Its Discontents* (1930), Freud observed: "In consequence of this primary mutual hostility of human beings, civilized society is perpetually threatened with disintegration. . . . Instinctual passions are stronger than reasonable interests."

Lawrence was a pugnacious man but would not fight in the war. He adopted a pacifist position, not on religious and moral grounds (which would have exempted him from military service, if he had passed the medical examinations), but on commonsensical opposition to meaningless death (which did not satisfy the authorities and inevitably led to conflict and persecution). "Kill a man by order that has never done me any harm?" Frieda remembered him saying. "No, I couldn't do it. They can kill me first. But I'll watch it that they don't." In 1914, when Lawrence was very badly off, the playwright Alfred Sutro had given him £10 and helped him obtain another £50 from the Royal Literary Fund. In an unpublished letter of September 10 to Sutro, Lawrence, who feared he would be drafted, imagined a scenario in which he received an "honourable little paper" from the army that stated: "It is certified that D. H. Lawrence presented himself for enlistment at the Aylesbury [Bucks.] barracks, but could not be sworn in owing to weakness of chest."[6]

II

In early 1915, a few months after the war broke out, Lawrence met and formed intense friendships with Lady Ottoline Morrell, E. M. Forster and Bertrand Russell, all of whom were associated with what came to be called the Bloomsbury group. Ottoline—daughter of Lieutenant General Arthur Cavendish-Bentinck, half sister of the sixth Duke of Portland and wife of a liberal M.P.—was born in 1873 and had a lonely, neglected childhood in Welbeck Abbey, twenty-five miles north of Nottingham. She married Philip Morrell, an old Etonian and a lawyer, in 1902. Though she was neither affectionate with nor fond of children, she had a daughter, Julian, whose twin brother died in infancy. During her marriage she had affairs with the painters Augustus John and Henry Lamb, the art critic Roger Fry and the philosopher Bertrand Russell, who became a pacifist ally of Philip Morrell during the war.

Ottoline was described by Osbert Sitwell as an "over-size Infanta of Spain."[7] She was extremely tall and striking, with dyed red hair and jutting jaw, nasal voice and neighing laugh, and wore extravagant costumes that resembled the plumage of an exotic bird. A baroque, flamboyant, eccentric and even grotesque personality, she had a malicious sense of humor and an exalted though indiscriminate devotion to the arts. Though not herself a good conversationalist, she was an encouraging patron and generous hostess who provided a stimulating atmosphere, comfortable surroundings, little drink but good food. She allowed her guests to work quietly all day and enjoy brilliant conversation in the evenings and on weekends, which were characterized by high spirits and high-mindedness, pacifism, poetry and all that was ultramodern in the arts.

Ottoline wrote Lawrence an admiring letter about his work, and they met first at her house at 44 Bedford Square and then, according to her guest book, at her country home near Oxford on June 16, November 6 and November 29, 1915. Garsington, an Elizabethan manor house with mullioned windows and a steep-pitched roof, was built on the slope of a hill and surrounded by an estate of five hundred acres. Dons and undergraduates, artists and writers, poets and young bohemians, aristocrats and distinguished politicians gathered in the luxurious mansion and magnificent gardens, embellished with a swimming pool and pea-cocks. The interior of the house—which Lytton Strachey described as "very remarkable, very impressive, patched, gilded and preposterous"—was sumptuously decorated with silk curtains and Persian carpets, precious knickknacks and strange scents; the large, oak-paneled rooms were painted in bright colors and adorned with works by Stanley Spencer, Mark Gertler and Augustus John. "Is the sunlight ever normal at Garsington?" Virginia Woolf once asked. "No, I think even the sky is done up in pale yellow silk, and certainly the cabbages are scented."[8]

Ottoline's hospitality to novelists was sometimes accepted with in-gratitude and repaid with ridicule. She was satirized as Priscilla Wim-bush in Huxley's *Crome Yellow* (1921), as Lady Septuagesima Goodley in Osbert Sitwell's "Triple Fugue" (1924) and as Hermione Roddice in *Women in Love* (1920). Huxley delineated her strange features and peculiar coloring: "Her voice, her laughter, were deep and masculine. Everything about her was manly. She had a large, square, middle-aged face, with a massive projecting nose and little greenish eyes, the whole surmounted by a lofty and elaborate coiffure of a curiously improbable shade of orange." Sitwell portrayed her giraffish stature and prominent features: "Of impressive height—a height that was over life-size for a woman, so that without looking a giantess she might yet seem an animated public monument—Lady Septuagesima had an almost masculine face, deep-set flowerlike eyes, with a golden calyx, a long definite nose, and cut-out chin; strong animal-like teeth, which showed when she laughed, a mass of red-brown hair, cut short but not cropped."

Lawrence also described the extraordinary effect of her hypnotic bearing, peculiar movement and chromatic clothing:

> She drifted forward as if scarcely conscious, her long, blenched face lifted up, not to see the world. She was rich. She wore a dress of silky, frail velvet, of pale yellow colour, and she carried a lot of small rose-coloured cyclamens. Her shoes and stockings were of brownish grey, like the feathers on her hat, her hair was heavy, she drifted along with a peculiar fixity of the hips, a strange unwilling motion. She was impressive, in her lovely pale-yellow and brownish-rose, yet macabre, something repulsive.... Her long, pale face, that she carried lifted up, somewhat in the Rossetti fashion, seemed almost drugged, as if a strange mass of thoughts coiled in the darkness within her.[9]

Much grander than Cynthia Asquith and Dorothy Brett, Ottoline was an absolute aristocrat who despised the values of her class. She was interested in art and culture rather than in animals and sport, had the courage to oppose the conventions of the time, and wanted to be considered a woman of imagination and taste. Despite their differences, Lawrence and Ottoline found common ground in their Nottinghamshire origins. Her family owned considerable parts of the coalfields where Lawrence's father worked as a miner (two mines in the area are still named Bentinck and Welbeck). The Duke of Portland "took an unusual interest in the welfare of the miners and the development of the model villages." And Lawrence, who used to know some of her family servants, told Ottoline that "the Portlands were well-regarded and even revered" by the miners. He used to amuse Ottoline by speaking the local dialect; and coming from Nottinghamshire, she felt she understood him better than his other friends did.[10]

Ottoline, who wanted a guru, was impressed by Lawrence's character as well as by his works. Quite independently, she agreed with Cynthia Asquith about his intensity, sympathy and penetration, as well as his ability to renew and transform his friends:

Lawrence's vitality and presence seemed to make every moment of the day throb with its own intense life, so that whatever one did with him was right and perfect to do. . . .

Lawrence identifies himself completely with people he meets and for a time seems to enter into their skins and sympathetically lives their lives. This is upsetting to them for he can seldom leave them as they are, his interest penetrates and envelops them, encouraging, stimulating, inspiring, but after a time he begins to strip them bare of their reserve and he penetrates into their secret life and then starts to recreate them into beings after his own heart.[11]

There were inevitably problems about Lawrence's distressing desire to change people as well as about his public quarrels with Frieda. Another difficulty was Frieda's jealousy of Ottoline and Ottoline's belief (shared by Kot) that Frieda provoked Lawrence's offensive behavior and was responsible for his obsessive ideas about sex. Frieda disingenuously told Ottoline (as she would later tell Brett) that she could tolerate Lawrence's straightforward sexual relations but loathed his more menacing spiritual unions: "I would not mind if you and he had an ordinary love-affair—what I hate is this 'soul-mush.'"[12]

Ottoline's adoration of art, her beautiful house and her social power meant a great deal to Lawrence. After his first visit to Garsington, he praised "that wonderful lawn, under the ilex trees, with the old house and its exquisite old front—it is *so* remote, so perfectly a small world to itself." Though he admired the traditional aspects of Garsington, a model for Breadalby in *Women in Love,* he became critical of its artificiality, which often made him feel ill at ease. In November 1915, when Europe was disintegrating, he wrote from Garsington to Edward Marsh: "Here one feels the real England—this old house, this countryside—so poignantly." But in February 1921 he warned Mark Gertler, who was ill with tuberculosis: "I should beware of Garsington. I believe there is something exhaustive in the air there, not so very restful."[13]

Ottoline had been generous to Lawrence, and he seemed to have responded to her friendship. But when she read the manuscript of *Women in Love,* in November 1916, she was deeply shocked by Lawrence's ingratitude and wounded by what she felt was a contemptuous portrait:

Lawrence, to whom we had given so much and had stood by him in his hard times, derides and distorts and caricatures me, making me publicly a pornographic image of his own mind. . . .

I read it and found myself going pale with horror, for nothing could have been more vile and obviously spiteful and contemptuous than the portrait of me that I found there. It was a great shock, for his letters all this time had been quite friendly, and I had no idea that he disliked me or had any feeling against me. I was called every name from an "old hag," obsessed by sex-mania, to a corrupt Sapphist. . . . My dresses were dirty; I was rude and insolent to my guests. . . . The hurt that he had done me made a very great mark on my life.[14]

Ottoline, who may have recognized the element of truth in Lawrence's caricature, made matters worse for herself by returning the manuscript with a foolish reply that revealed how deeply she had been hurt. Lawrence was estranged from Ottoline for twelve years; but in May 1928, when he heard she was seriously ill, he called her "a queen, among the mass of women" and wrote her a charming letter emphasizing the character and generosity that had inspired so many artists: "You've been an important influence in lots of lives, as you have in mine: through being fundamentally generous, and through being Ottoline. After all, there's only one Ottoline. And she has moved one's imagination."[15] They were finally reconciled, but never met again.

III

The novelist E. M. Forster, born into a middle-class suburban family in 1879, met Lawrence at a dinner party at Ottoline's house in Bedford Square in January 1915. He had been to Cambridge, had already published his first four novels, including *Howards End* (1910), and was working on *A Passage to India*. The two writers, who knew each other's work, took to each other immediately; two days later Forster described him in a letter as passionate and extraordinarily nice. In mid-February, when Forster spent a weekend at Lawrence's cottage in Greatham, Sussex, things began well, became passionately personal and ended disastrously.

The correspondence of Forster and Lawrence allows us to follow their personal reactions from day to day. On February 11 Forster, an intensely repressed, private and virginal homosexual, mentioned Lawrence's characteristic self-revelation and response to nature: "The Lawrences I like—especially him. We have had a two hours walk in the glorious country between here and Arundel, and he told me all about his people—drunken father, sister [Ada] who married a tailor: most gay and friendly, with breaks to look at birds, catkins."

Lawrence's letters of the same and the next day to the analyst Barbara Low and to Forster's close friend Bertrand Russell suggest the imminent danger of conflict as he began to strip Forster bare and penetrate his secret life. But his diagnosis of what was wrong with Forster and his remedies for a cure seemed to miss or ignore the fact that Forster was homosexual: "Forster is here. He is very nice. I wonder if the grip has gone out of him. I get a feeling of acute misery from him—not that he does anything—but you know the acute, exquisite pain of cramps—I somehow feel that. . . . Why can't he act? Why can't he take a woman and fight clear to his own basic, primal being? Because he knows that self-realisation is not his ultimate desire." Two weeks later, writing to Mary Cannan, he seemed surprised that Forster (who did not believe a woman was the way to his primal being) had been offended by his acute but brutal analysis and failed to appreciate that Lawrence was trying to help him: "We had E. M. Forster here for a day or two. I liked him, but his life is so ridiculously inane, the man is dying of inanition. He was very angry with me for telling him about himself."

Forster was deeply offended and thought Lawrence irrational and disloyal. He did not know enough about Lawrence to realize that he was criticizing not only Forster's homosexual tendencies but also his own. On February 12, immediately after leaving Greatham, Forster broke off their friendship. But he found it easier to deliver a blast against Lawrence's heterosexual prescriptions in writing than in person:

> I like Mrs. Lawrence, and I like the Lawrence who talks to Hilda and sees birds and is physically restful and wrote *The White Peacock,* he doesn't know why; but I do not like the deaf imperci-pient fanatic who has nosed over his own little sexual round until he believes that there is no other path for others to take, he some-times interests & sometimes frightens & angers me, but in the end he will bore [me] merely, I know."[16]

IV

In February 1915 Lawrence met Bertrand Russell—grandson of a prime minister, brother of an earl and lecturer at Trinity College—through Ottoline Morrell. Lawrence saw Russell as a powerful ally in his opposition to the war. Russell, frequently accused of being a slave to reason, felt he would be given a beneficial dose of the irrational by a man who rejected the methods and products of scientific thought. Lawrence believed, instead, in the power of touch and "the dark loins of man," and held that greater freedom for instinct and intuition would help solve the problems that had led to war.

Soon after the first meeting, Ottoline noted that Russell, like Lawrence's other friends, fell immediately under his spell: "Bertie had a great admiration for the fiery prophet. He thought of him as a second Ezekiel, and had a belief in his vision." Russell confirmed Ottoline's observation and wrote: "I liked Lawrence's fire, I liked the energy and passion of his feelings, I liked his belief that something very fundamen-tal was needed to put the world right." Lawrence strengthened Russell's conviction that "social history had to be based on a psychology which was not afraid of the instincts." Lawrence satisfied Russell's desire for "some form of mystical insight" and shared his utopian hopes for the future.[17]

In early February, Lawrence sent Russell a passionate, though simplistic, plan for a socialist welfare state in England. The revolution "shall begin by the nationalising of all industries and means of communication, and of the land—in one fell blow. Then a man shall have his wages whether he is sick or well or old. . . . Which practically solves the whole economic question for the present." Russell, sympathetic and unusually tolerant, told Ottoline (who often received confidences from both men): "I love him more & more. I wouldn't dream of discouraging his socialist revolution. He has real faith in it, & it absorbs his vital force—he must go through with it. He talks so well about it that he almost makes me believe in it."[18]

After Russell had invited him to spend the weekend of March 6–8 at Trinity, Cambridge (Weekley's old college), Lawrence wrote that he felt coming to Cambridge would be a momentous occasion for him, that he feared he would be unwillingly impressed and intimidated. But the weekend with Russell, like the one with Forster the previous month, was a disaster. Lawrence was horrified and repelled by the deadness, snobbishness and superiority of the college, and, most especially, by the homosexual atmosphere. He told David Garnett that his irrational revulsion was aroused by the sudden appearance of the economist John Maynard Keynes, blinking from sleep and standing in pajamas: "as he stood there gradually a knowledge passed into me, which has been like a little madness to me ever since. And it was carried along with the most dreadful sense of repulsiveness—something like carrion—a vulture gives me the same feeling. I begin to feel mad as I think of it—insane." "It is true Cambridge made me very black and down," he wrote, with characteristic frankness, to Russell. "I cannot bear its smell of rottenness, marsh-stagnancy. I get a melancholic malaria. How can so sick people rise up? They must die first."

The following month David Garnett visited Lawrence with a homosexual friend, Francis Birrell. Lawrence—in a well-intentioned but typically tactless letter—warned Garnett (a member of the Bloomsbury circle, but not homosexual) to sever all relations with that corrupt group of inverts and (as he had told Forster) to try to love a woman:

It is like a blow of triumphant decay, when I meet Birrell or the others. I simply can't bear it. It is so wrong, it is unbearable. It makes a form of inward corruption which truly makes me scarce able to live. Why is there this horrible sense of frowstiness, so repulsive, as if it came from deep inward dirt—a sort of sewer—deep in men like Keynes and Birrell and Duncan Grant. It is something almost unbearable to me. . . . Never bring B. to see me any more. There is something nasty about him, like black-beetles. He is horrible and unclean. I feel as if I should go mad, if I think of your set, D.G. and K. and B. It makes me dream of beetles. In Cambridge I had a similar dream. Somehow, I can't bear it. It is wrong beyond all bounds of wrongness.

Lawrence's extremely emotional reaction to Keynes and Birrell influenced his portrayal of homosexuality in *Women in Love*.

Garnett, like Forster, severed relations with Lawrence—instead of with his homosexual friends—because he felt that Lawrence wanted disciples and was trying to direct his life.[19] But Russell, and even Keynes himself, actually sympathized with Lawrence's point of view. Just after the visit to Cambridge, Russell praised Lawrence's insight, agreed with his views on inversion and wrote to Ottoline: "Lawrence has quick, sensitive impressions which I don't understand, tho' they would seem quite natural to you. I love him more and more. . . . Lawrence has the same feeling against sodomy that I have; you had nearly made me believe there is no harm in it, but I have reverted; and all the examples I know confirm me in thinking it is sterilizing."

Keynes, writing twenty years later on "My Early Beliefs," admitted the element of truth in Lawrence's manic reaction, though he was discreetly silent about the homosexuality that had provoked it. Though hostile to Lawrence, Keynes contrasted Lawrence's passion, morality and seriousness to the emphasis on reason, homosexuality and sceptical irreverence that prevailed at Cambridge:

If I imagine us as coming under the observation of Lawrence's ignorant, jealous, irritable, hostile eyes, what a combination of qualities we offered to arouse his passionate distaste; this thin rationalism skipping on the crust of the lava, ignoring both the reality and the value of the vulgar passions, joined to the libertinism and comprehensive irreverence, too clever by half for such an earthy character as Bunny [David Garnett], seducing with its intellectual *chic* such a portent as Ottoline. . . . But that is why I say there may have been just a grain of truth when Lawrence said in 1914 that we were "done for."[20]

On June 19 and 20 Russell visited Lawrence in Greatham, about forty miles southwest of London. Though temperamental and intellectual opposites (the intuitive, mystical Lawrence believed in "blood-consciousness," the analytic, sceptical Russell in "mind-knowledge"), both thought that psychology could not be divorced from politics; they wanted to reorganize society along Socialist lines and planned to give a series of joint public lectures—Russell on ethics, Lawrence on immortality—expressing their opposition to the war. With this end in view, Russell, in early July, sent Lawrence the lecture notes that became the basis of his first popular book, *Principles of Social Reconstruction* (1916). In it, Russell wrote, "I suggested a philosophy of politics based upon the belief that impulse has more effect than conscious purpose in moulding men's lives." Russell vaguely concluded that life must be made whole "by freedom for impulse of growth and creation, by freedom to love. [This is] to be achieved by new standards, [by] less belief in material goods, by unity in freedom through new political institutions."21

Lawrence had once been "mortified at being treated 'like a school-kid'" when his university English mistress corrected his essay on "Autumn" in red ink. But he now crossed out and corrected Russell's work. Lawrence violently objected to Russell's statement that man is "moral" (by which, Lawrence thought, he merely meant "well-behaved") in order to win the esteem of others and "because action against the desires of others makes him disliked, which is disagreeable." And he wrote "NO! NO! NO! NO! NO!" and "This is *not good*" directly across the typescript, as if he were an impatient schoolmaster dealing with a backward boy instead of a younger colleague responding to one of the great minds of the time.

Their fundamental disagreement, as Lawrence explained in three letters of mid and late July, was that the earl's son believed in democracy, the miner's son in aristocracy. The war intensified the expression of Lawrence's anti-rational, primitivistic and autocratic ideas, based on blood consciousness and a powerful leader. To Lawrence, who wanted radical change, Russell's remedy seemed feeble, ineffectual and negative: "*this* which you say is *all social criticism;* it isn't social reconstruction.... [Truth is] ... the *most fundamental* passion in man, for Wholeness of Movement, Unanimity of Purpose, Oneness in Construction. *This is the principle of Construction.* The rest is all criticism, destruction."

Lawrence, whose views were closer to Lenin's than to Russell's, wanted to overthrow the government. He thought the masses had elected

weak leaders, who had brought the country into the disastrous war; that
democratic society had to be abolished rather than reconstructed; that a
new elite, based on wisdom rather than votes, had to replace the present
moribund leaders. The essential choice, Lawrence felt, was between
dictatorship and democracy. Russell believed authority belonged to the
people and that power invested in leaders should be strictly limited.
Lawrence insisted:

> You must drop all your democracy. You must not believe in "the
> people." . . . There must be an aristocracy of people who have
> wisdom, and there must be a Ruler: a Kaiser. . . .
>
> In your lecture on the State, you must criticise the extant
> *democracy.* . . . There must be a body of chosen patricians. . . . The
> whole must culminate in an absolute *Dictator.* . . . Can't you see the
> whole state is collapsing. . . . It will be a ghastly chaos of
> destruction. . . .
>
> I rather hated your letter, and am terrified of what you are
> putting into your lectures. I don't want tyrants. But I don't believe
> in democratic control. . . . The thing must culminate in one real
> head, as every organic thing must—no foolish republics with
> foolish presidents, but an elected King, something like Julius
> Caesar. . . . There must be an elected aristocracy.[22]

Lawrence never specified, however, who would be dictator, how he would
be chosen and how his autocratic system would work.

This was strong stuff, and not very subtly expressed. But on September
14, after Russell had sent him his essay on "The Danger to Civilization," which stressed the perils of a long war but ignored the social
factors that had caused it, Lawrence launched into an even more personal and devastating attack, declaring that Russell's pacifism was
actually rooted in and perverted by blood lust:

> Your basic desire is the maximum desire of war, you are really the
> super-war-spirit. What you want is to jab and strike, like the
> soldier with the bayonet, only you are sublimated into words. . . .
>
> You are simply *full* of repressed desires, which have become
> savage and anti-social. And they come out in this sheep's clothing of
> peace propaganda. . . .
>
> Your will is false and cruel. You are too full of devilish repres-
> sions to be anything but lustful and cruel. I would rather have the

German soldiers with rapine and cruelty, than you with your words of goodness. It is the falsity I can't bear. . . . The enemy of all mankind, you are, full of the lust of enmity. . . . It is a perverted, mental blood-lust. Why don't you own it. Let us become strangers again, I think it is better.

There was no rational basis to this letter, which attributed to Russell his own "repressed desires" and scorn for mankind. Lawrence probably wrote it because Russell disagreed with him about the proper mode of political action and still supported, in a modified form, the dying democratic system, which Lawrence believed had been discredited by the outbreak of the war. When he received this devastating letter Russell, overwhelmed by the force of Lawrence's personality, was at first convinced that Lawrence had preternatural insight into unconscious motives that Russell's own intellect could not perceive. "For twenty-four hours," Russell later noted, "I thought that I was not fit to live and contemplated committing suicide."[23] But he soon recovered his balance and severed relations with Lawrence.

Lawrence, guided by passion rather than by reason (a fact that particularly troubled Russell), had no coherent views or clear system of thought. His ideas were transformed by external circumstances, and fluctuated wildly when he suffered fits of exasperation and rage. He was both passionately committed to his ideas and willing to abandon them when he changed his mind. His hopes for social revolution were grandiose and naive; he assumed a prophetic stance but had no understanding of political reality. During the half year that he was involved with Russell, Lawrence shifted from a fervent belief in Socialism in February to a contempt for democracy and an advocacy of a powerful leader in July. His views were shaped by his reading as well as by the war: by Heraclitus' concept of a struggle in which the strong man establishes power over the weak; by Plato's elite, hierarchical, slave-based Republic; by Hegel's dialectical conflict of good and evil; by Carlyle's concept of the hero and Nietzsche's exaltation of the superman; and by Shelley's notion that poets are the unacknowledged legislators of mankind. Paul Delany perceptively notes that "One can account for Lawrence's sudden enthusiasm for dictatorship in various ways: the influence of Heraclitus, the impact of outside political events, and so forth. But all such explanations seem inadequate to the radical shift in his ideas. His conversion to a belief in 'a Kaiser' was just one of a series of intellectual somersaults . . . [one of] a gratuitous sequence of obsessions." Lawrence complained:

"They say I can't think," and Ottoline told Russell: "He is quite unbalanced."[24]

Lawrence responded to his failure with Russell by turning to Katherine and Murry and founding the *Signature*, which published his long and boring essay "The Crown." In this work Lawrence argued that the true self "could be created only after the individual had fulfilled the possibilities of the warring extremes of his own nature." When this essay was reprinted in a book in 1925 Lawrence, remembering his quarrel with Russell, regretfully wrote that there was no point in superficial remedies—the only hope was revolutionary change: "I knew then, and I know now, that it is no use trying to do anything—I speak only for myself—publicly. It is no use merely trying to modify present forms. The whole great form of our era will have to go."[25]

But Lawrence could not remain a stranger to Russell. He calmed down after his explosions and saw Russell at Garsington at the end of November. *The Rainbow* had been suppressed that month, and Lawrence was particularly eager for influential allies. On December 8 he sent an important letter expressing his fundamental beliefs, which he knew Russell would dislike. Echoing his letter of January 1913 ("My great religion is a belief in the blood"), he reaffirmed his idea, based on anthropology texts, that feeling should dominate mind; that blood-consciousness, achieved through sexual intercourse and experienced by coal miners and primitive people, was superior to mere rationality:

> I have been reading Frazer's *Golden Bough* and *Totemism and Exogamy*. Now I am convinced of what I believed when I was about twenty—that there is another seat of consciousness than the brain and the nerve system: there is a blood-consciousness which exists in us independently of the ordinary mental consciousness, which depends on the eye as its source or connector. There is the blood-consciousness, with its sexual connection, holding the same relation as the eye, in seeing, holds to the mental consciousness. One lives, knows, and has one's being in the blood, without any reference to nerves and brain. This is one half of life, belonging to the darkness.

After this exposition of mystical physiology, Lawrence even had the cheek—or self-confidence—to ask Russell (who eventually outlived him by forty years) to leave him something in his will.

After their quarrel, Lawrence parodied Russell's stale and familiar philosophy, and satirized him in *Women in Love* as Sir Joshua Matheson, "a learned, dry Baronet of fifty, who was always making witticisms and laughing at them heartily in a harsh, horse laugh. . . . [He] was talking in his . . . rather mincing voice, endlessly, endlessly, always with a strong mentality working, always interesting, and yet always known, everything he said known beforehand."

Russell retaliated for the satire in his chapter on Lawrence (1953) in *Portraits from Memory*, reprinted in the second volume of his *Autobiography* (1968). He used his immense prestige as a thinker to buttress his absurd but extremely damaging attack on Lawrence, who wrote "I don't want tyrants," as a proto-Nazi. He falsely accused Lawrence of passionately hating mankind, of being a positive force for evil (thus reversing Lawrence's charges against Russell) and of believing "that when a dictatorship was established he would be the Julius Caesar." He claimed that Lawrence anticipated "the whole philosophy of fascism before the politicians had thought of it" and (more reasonably) condemned Lawrence's belief in blood-consciousness as "frankly rubbish." He then abandoned all logic, appealed to emotion and drew a wild inference: "I did not then know that it led straight to Auschwitz."[26]

Russell, who had been dismissed from his position at Trinity, had his library seized, had (like Lawrence) been refused a passport for America and had been imprisoned for four months in 1918, felt he had suffered far more than Lawrence for his opposition to the war. But, as Richard Aldington perceived: "This association with Russell made DHL a marked man for the authorities, and he hadn't aristocrat birth and friends to shield him" from persecution and punishment.[27]

Russell was at first stimulated by Lawrence because his view of man included and valued the power of feeling, which Russell, an icy rationalist, basically feared. Lawrence saw war as a betrayal of man's true feelings; Russell saw war as irrational and therefore bad. Russell, who had the last word, chose to identify Lawrence (as Lawrence did Russell) with the irrational evil of war, and later said that he found Lawrence's views repellent. Their bitter quarrel and mutual hatred had three different elements. On the personal level, Russell was hurt and enraged by Lawrence's criticism of his repressed personality and his obvious emotional defects, and by Lawrence's ability to destroy his composure. He regretted his early enthusiasm for Lawrence ("he sees everything and is always right")[28] and overreacted by grotesquely exaggerating his influence on Nazi ideology. On the political level, Russell advocated a characteristically English modification of existing democracy, while Lawrence demanded nothing less than a cataclysmic revolution leading to an authoritarian regime. On the philosophical level, they had radically different ideas about the nature and potential of man. Russell believed man could be led toward the good, Lawrence felt he must be restrained from evil. Though their friendship, inspired by Ottoline, seemed full of promise, it was actually doomed from the start.

V

The war impelled Lawrence not only to advocate an autocratic dictator who would control and transform corrupt society, but also to plan an idealistic community that would escape this corruption and form the nucleus of a new society. The idea of Rananim had its roots in his boyhood dream of a great house in Nottingham Park for his mother and all the people he liked, and lingered on in his late dream of escaping to sea with a few friends in his own boat—a floating Utopia. Lawrence never saw most of the places—the orange groves of Florida, the east slope of the Andes, the South Sea islands, the isles of Greece—in which, at various times, he hoped to settle.

The name came from the Hebrew words *ranenu rananim* of Psalm 33—"Rejoice in the Lord, O ye righteous"—which Kot loved to chant. The literary models for Rananim went back to the Brook Farm of Nathaniel Hawthorne and Margaret Fuller in the 1840s and to the communal Pantisocracy that Coleridge and Southey planned to realize on the banks of the Susquehanna. As Coleridge wrote of his disappointed ambitions in *The Friend* in October 1809: "What I dared not expect from constitutions of Governments and whole Nations I hoped from Religion and a small Company of chosen Individuals, and formed a plan, as harmless as it was extravagant, of trying the experiment of human Perfectibility on the banks of the Susquehannah; where our little Society . . . was to have combined the innocence of the patriarchal Age with the knowledge of and general refinements of European culture."

Most of Lawrence's friends (including Russell) were co-opted as candidates for the community at one time or another; and Lawrence, like Noah, planned to lead the elect—those whose goodness opposed contemporary evil—to salvation. As he wrote to Willie Hopkin in January 1915:

I want to gather together about twenty souls and sail away from this world of war and squalor and found a little colony where there shall be no money but a sort of communism as far as necessaries of life go, and some real decency. It is to be a colony built up on the real decency which is in each member of the Community—a community which is established upon the assumption of goodness in the members, instead of the assumption of badness.[29]

Lawrence was distressed not only by the difficulty of implementing his visionary plan, but also by his conflicting desires for the stimulation of society and the solitude he needed for his work. Later on, he regretted his lifelong isolation and said: "I should love to be connected with something, with some few people, in something. As far as anything *matters,* I have always been very much alone, and regretted it." But in *Aaron's Rod* (1922), he declared himself "Alone, choosing to be alone, because by one's nature one is alone." And, disillusioned by his putative followers at the end of the war, he told Mark Gertler that he longed to resume his old rootless, solitary life: "I don't want to act in concert with any body of people. I want to go by myself—or with Frieda—something in the manner of a gipsy, and be houseless and placeless and homeless and landless, just move apart."[30] Frieda (for once) did not oppose his colony—because she never believed it would become a reality.

Lawrence's attempts to live with Katherine and Murry, and (later on) with Mabel Luhan, suggest that Rananim would have turned out disastrously. There would have been many practical problems, and no means of earning sufficient money to support the enterprise. He would have tried to impose his will on others and would have quarreled with his followers. The disciples would inevitably have become disaffected and would have left Lawrence disillusioned and embittered.

VI

When adults failed to respond to his ideas during the war, Lawrence turned to the more tangible rewards of teaching children. He had extraordinary insight about the thoughts and feelings of boys and girls, and would have made a good father. He was kind and sensitive to children, admired their spontaneity and intuition, charmed them and portrayed them brilliantly in his work: the young Ursula in *The Rainbow,* Winnie Crich in *Women in Love,* Paul in "The Rocking-Horse Winner" and Joyce in "England, My England." He had spent a good deal of time playing with and caring for Hilda and Winifred Jones in Croydon. He was fascinated by Cynthia Asquith's autistic son, John, as well as by his brother, Michael; and was fond of and genuinely interested in his other friends' children: John Patrick Carswell, Julian Morrell and Harwood Brewster (all of whom remember him with affection). Helen Thomas' small daughter was attracted to the delightful stranger and climbed into bed with him. Lawrence also befriended and tutored Mary Saleeby at Greatham in 1915 and Hilda Brown at the Hermitage in 1918.

From late January until late July 1915 Lawrence and Frieda lived in a renovated cowshed, a long narrow cottage with a kitchen, sitting room and two bedrooms, borrowed from the poet and novelist Viola Meynell. Viola's parents, Wilfred and Alice Meynell—who owned and edited a Catholic monthly, *Merrie England*—had built cottages for each of their children near their country home in Greatham, Sussex. Partly out of genuine interest and partly out of a desire to repay his benefactor, Lawrence spent three and a half hours each day, from mid-May till late July, giving lessons to Viola's rather wild ten-year-old niece, Mary Saleeby, in order to prepare her for entry into St. Paul's Girls School.

Because of her parents' separation and her mother's nervous breakdown, Mary had had no formal schooling. A combination of her need and Lawrence's willingness to help led to the private tutorials. At that time, Mary could scarcely read and had terrible handwriting. She enjoyed being tutored at the long oak refectory table in the cottage, for Lawrence was a good teacher whose patience and enthusiasm inspired her own keenness to learn. She took dictation from Viola's novels and improved her handwriting. She still remembers the words to the song that Lawrence taught her about the assassination of President McKinley. In the fall of 1915, she entered St. Paul's at the proper grade for her age. Elsa and Barbara Weekley were also at the school, and Mary rather naughtily told them: "I know your mother."

Mary said that she "got on very well at school, so the tuition must have been good—particularly as the pupil was so *very* uncouth and unpromising!"[31] After finishing St. Paul's, Mary first took an agricultural degree at Reading University, then studied medicine at Newnham College, Cambridge, and at University College Hospital in London, and qualified as a doctor in 1930. She was the only child to be extensively tutored by Lawrence, and was his most brilliant and successful pupil.

The Meynell family and their country home provided the inspiration for one of Lawrence's finest stories, "England, My England." Percy Lucas, the model for Egbert, came from a Quaker background. Born in 1879, he was married to Mary's Aunt Madeleine and lived at Rackham Cottage, a mile away, at the end of the Meynells' property. Percy was very gentle and quiet; Madeleine, by contrast, was forceful and "got on with things." Though delightful, Percy was just the sort of aesthete, dilettante and rentier who irritated Lawrence and provoked his anger. According to his niece: "He was a charming person, a little feckless perhaps, but always sweet-tempered. By profession a genealogist, his ruling passion in life was Morris dancing, and his hobby he pursued all round England. He was so unwarlike by temperament, so preoccupied with peaceful, pleasant matters, that his action of enlisting immediately war broke out was rather surprising."

Viola Meynell gives precise details about the terrible accident that happened to Percy's daughter (and Mary's cousin) Sylvia, born in 1908, which Lawrence used—and crucially transformed—in his story: "In 1913 Sylvia had an accident, cutting her leg with a knife with such disastrous consequences that even her life was in danger. For months her desperate illness and suffering, at the age of five, when she seemed too small to be so much hurt, and did not even know the words with which to describe her own distress, were a terrible experience to the family."[32]

Thus, in reality, Sylvia's accident had occurred two years before Lawrence arrived in Greatham (though its consequences were still visible in the crippled child); Percy had enlisted in 1914, was abroad at the time, and had *not* caused the accident. Robert Nelson, a close friend of the family and a weekend visitor, had carelessly left the tool hidden in the tall grass. Sylvia fell on it and suffered a deep wound, which, before the era of antibiotics, led to septicemia of the bone. Her inept medical treatment was accurately described in the story. She was badly treated by the local G.P., then seen by Dr. Maitland Radford, who sent her to a London hospital, Sts. John and Elizabeth, which was run by Catholic nuns. She was in hospital for a long time, nearly lost her leg and almost died, but was stoical and courageous during her illness.[33]

Viola's unintentionally ironic memorial of her brother-in-law, Percy, assumes a grotesque meaning in light of his daughter's accident, his rather precious character and his subsequent death in the war:

He was indifferent. . . . He was exclusive. . . . He became a Catholic [convert]. . . . His masterful but gentle hands . . . had a way of

shepherding his little world of children. . . . Nothing in his cottage,
or elsewhere, carries a hint of reproach to his memory. . . . No risks
checked him. . . . I do not know when he made up his mind to enter
the army, but I think it was in his mind from the first day of the
war. . . . I think he was testing the alternative, the home task, to see
if it sufficed. . . . Once the test failed him, he decided to enlist.

The title of Lawrence's story "England, My England" comes from a
patriotic poem by William Ernest Henley, "For England's Sake" (1900),
and laments the fate of England in the war. The theme of the story is the
triumph of the death wish over the impulse to new life. The numerous
biblical references heighten the prophetic mood and subtly suggest the
themes of menace, evil, sacrifice, mourning, outcasts and apocalyptic
doom.[34]

In this story Egbert, an epicurean hermit who has retreated from the
world into the depths of the countryside and lives on the income of his
wife, Winifred, has managed to create a precious if precarious Eden.
But when he carelessly leaves a fag-hook—a half-moon-shaped, wooden-
handled sickle used to cut grass—in the garden, his young daughter,
Joyce, gashes her leg, suffers incompetent medical treatment and becomes permanently crippled. The accident reveals the weakness in Egbert's character, mode of life and marriage, and leads to an emotional
and sexual estrangement from Winifred. His wife and father-in-law
punish him by urging him to enlist when the war breaks out. Though
thoroughly unsuited to military life, Egbert accepts his guilt and sacri-
fices himself.

Both Egbert's wife and his daughter have Oedipal relationships with
their fathers, and in both cases the bond between father and daughter is
stronger than that between husband and wife. Winifred's sexual with-
drawal from Egbert and alliance with her strong father impel Egbert to
leave his daughter, join the army, assuage his guilt and satisfy his death
wish. He is encouraged to enlist by his father-in-law, who takes command
of the desperate medical situation, sends Joyce to a London specialist
and saves her life. He wants to free Winifred from a weak husband and
repossess his daughter, as well as to punish Egbert and make a man of
him. The only point of agreement between Egbert, Winifred and her
father is that Egbert must sacrifice himself in the war.

Lawrence's attitude toward Egbert, who enlists because he feels responsible for his daughter's wound and lameness, is ambiguous. Like
Lawrence himself, he refuses to worship the money god, retreats into the

lovely countryside and instinctively opposes the war. But unlike Lawrence, he is weak and null, and joins the army in a futile gesture that leads to pointless death. "England, My England," like *Women in Love,* which Lawrence was writing at the same time, portrays the effect of the war mentality on civilian life.

Lawrence's prophetic story was published in the *English Review* in October 1915; Percy was killed in the Somme offensive, at Fricourt, on July 9, 1916. A week later, when Lawrence heard the news, he sent an ambivalent letter to Catherine Carswell, expressing regret, which was unusual for him, that he had written the story. He stated one of its major themes, discussed the Meynell family, called Percy a spiritual coward for sacrificing himself, said he was sorry that he had ever gone to Greatham, feared that Percy's widow would be terribly hurt—and yet justified the story because it was "true":

> It upsets me very much to hear of Percy Lucas. I did not know he was dead. I wish that story at the bottom of the sea, before ever it had been printed. Yet, it seems to me, man must find a new expression, give a new value to his life, or his women will reject him, and he must die. I liked Madeleine Lucas best of the Meynells really. She was the one who was capable of honest love: she and [her sister] Monica. Lucas was, somehow, a spiritual coward. But who isn't? I ought never, never to have gone to live at Greatham. Perhaps Madeleine won't be hurt by that wretched story—that is all that matters. If it was a true story, it shouldn't really damage.

Lawrence's fears were well founded. The Lucas family had suffered first from Sylvia's accident and then from Percy's death. They felt victimized and betrayed by Lawrence's deadly portrayal of Percy's character and coincidental depiction of his death, and thought Lawrence had been both ungrateful and cruel.[35]

VII

In March 1915 Lawrence was living with the Meynells, tutoring Mary Saleeby and preparing to write "England, My England." While he was away for the weekend of March 6–7, seeing Russell in Cambridge, Ford

Madox Ford, who had published Lawrence's early work in the *English Review,* visited Greatham with Violet Hunt and Mrs. H. G. Wells. Since this visit had momentous consequences for Lawrence, Ford's motives and the conflicting accounts of what happened merit careful consideration.

In 1910 Ford, whose father was German, had moved to Germany and unsuccessfully attempted to establish German citizenship and obtain a German divorce in order to marry Violet Hunt. *The Desirable Alien,* written with Hunt and published in 1913, was filled with extravagant expressions of love for Germany and stated their desire to make it their homeland. In the Preface to the book, Ford called Germany "my beloved country" and spoke of the Kaiser as "my august sovereign." In conversation, Ford might recall "his year's service in an aristocratic German regiment," or begin an anecdote with "When I was last with the Kaiser," talking voluble German and remarking, "Of course, you English . . ." During the first years of the war, when these sentiments seemed embarrassing and even dangerous, Ford made a determined effort to reject the German in himself. After 1914 he "discovered that he was and always had been a patriotic English gentleman." He later changed his surname from Hueffer to Ford, wrote propaganda books to support the war and (though he was over forty) joined the British army. He also suffered recurrent attacks of neurasthenia, which lasted into 1915.

Violet Hunt, Ford and Frieda each left an account of the March 1915 visit. According to Hunt, Ford had just published his patriotic poem *Antwerp* (January 1915), and they both felt that Frieda's country had been responsible for the plight of the hundred thousand Belgian refugees who had fled to England. She wrote that when this subject was mentioned, Frieda exclaimed, "Dirty Belgians! Who cares for them!" and, as she quarreled with Frieda, that Ford disappeared to avoid getting involved in the argument.

Ford had been sent down to Greatham by the government to report on (rather than to assist) Lawrence and to suggest what should be done about him, and he retreated when the argument broke out between the women. Ford wrote:

The last time I saw [Lawrence] was during the War when, of course, he was pro-German and was supposed to be a good deal persecuted. That is to say, Authority—in the shape of the Minister of Information [Ford's close friend C. F. G. Masterman, who was director of the Propaganda Department during 1914–18 and had a seat in the cabinet]—was afraid that he was being persecuted and I was sent down to see what could be done for him.... As Mrs. Lawrence saw fit to address, on the side, unfavourable remarks to the uniform I was wearing, I thought it was better—because I *was* there to make a report to Authority—to retire to an outhouse and await the close of the discussion. So the last image I have is of Lawrence standing there.[36]

Frieda gave her version of the incident three times, over a period of thirty years. During Kyle Crichton's interview with Lawrence in 1925, Frieda incorrectly recalled that David Garnett was present and said that when she (vaguely) mentioned Germany, Ford, who had recently been a vociferous German chauvinist, suddenly claimed he was Dutch: "Do you remember the time he came with Garnett at the first of the war and Mrs. Wells was there? ... I mentioned something about Germany and he puffed up right away and started talking about his Dutch relatives. Before he had always kept German servants and blasted the British Empire and said he wasn't a subject of the King and spoke German at the table—and now he was Dutch." Two years later, in a letter to Mabel Luhan, Frieda omitted Garnett, implied that Lawrence was absent, specified her reference to Germany and said that Hunt claimed Russian (rather than Dutch) nationality for Ford: "[I] remember that Ford Madox Hueffer and [Violet Hunt] and Mrs. Wells came to see me and when I said to him, 'We are both German, aren't we?' she said, unhappily, 'No, no, Russian.' Now he is Ford Madox Ford."

Frieda gave her fullest and final account in a letter of January 1955 to Lawrence's biographer Harry Moore, and directly contradicted Ford's memoir, which had been published in 1937. She omitted Mrs. Wells, gave the words she spoke to Ford in German, emphasized his discomfort, emphatically denied that she had said "Dirty Belgians!" and refuted the details of Ford's version:

The Hueffers coming: this is *my* story. When they came, he and Violet Hunt, I said to him: "*Wir sind auch Deutsch?*" That made him squirm and he hummed and hawed. It was wartime. So I did not think much of him. I never said: those "dirty Belgians," I never felt like that! Lawrence was not there, there was no outhouse Ford could have retired to, I made no tirade, he wore no uniform, just dislike of me, which I returned, or rather despised them.[37]

The late letters of two of Lawrence's close friends, David Garnett and Richard Aldington, shed additional light on this episode. In 1957 Gar-

nett told Edward Nehls that Ford was desperate to prove that he was not
German and that in another anti-German propaganda book, *When
Blood Is Their Argument* (1915), he spoke of his quite imaginary
Russian ancestors. Three years later, Harry Moore told Aldington that
Garnett "believes that Ford warned the government in 1915 that the
Lawrences were pro-German, and that all their troubles during the rest
of the war stemmed from Ford's report."

Aldington—in letters to Lawrence Durrell and to Moore—said that
Ford probably reported to the Foreign Office, which had hired him to
write war propaganda, that he had to exculpate himself for his German
background and adoration of Germany, and that he had a powerful
friend (actually in the Ministry of Information and Propaganda) who
probably had sent him on the mission to Greatham:

> [David Garnett says that Lawrence] would have been forgiven
> [for his working-class genius], but Ford Hueffer made an adverse
> report in 1915 on the loyalty of DHL and Frieda, either to the
> W[ar] O[ffice] or the F[oreign] O[ffice]—I should think the F.O.,
> as Ford was hired by them to traduce his native land (Germany) at
> 50 quid a book. Ford is such a liar that I discounted the boast in his
> memoirs that he had been sent to report officially on the Law-
> rences, and that they were so anti-English he (Fordie) had to hide
> in a barn because he could not endure those insults to the King's
> uniform he was wearing. . . . I'd hate to think that fat Fordie had
> been so goddam mean as to put in an unfavourable official report
> on the civisme [good citizenship] of Lorenzo and Frieda. If he did,
> what a bastard. Of course, he needed to whitewash himself—he
> looked as much a Hun as Hindenburg—and, it is true, that he was
> friends with the Minister of Education [i.e., Minister of Informa-
> tion and Propaganda], C. F. G. Masterman.[38]

Ford's memoir takes on a new meaning in the light of Aldington's
confirmation of Garnett's testimony. In March 1915 Ford, recovering
from three years of neurasthenia, was undoubtedly trying to compensate
for his German ancestry and appearance, and for his Germanophile
views, by changing his name, writing propaganda for Masterman and
enlisting in the army—where he was later gassed, shell-shocked and
invalided home. The old soldier may have resented Lawrence's pacifism
(as well as his unwillingness to continue as Ford's protégé).

There is no mention, by Hunt or by Frieda, of the avowed purpose of

Ford's visit: to rescue Lawrence from persecution. Ford wrongly assumed that Lawrence, absent that weekend, was pro-German. To ease his guilt and assert his patriotism, Ford projected his recently rejected pro-German views onto Lawrence. He antedated Lawrence's persecution to explain his visit to Greatham and confirmed, rather than investigated, the rumor that Lawrence was disloyal to England. Ford, whom Lawrence would be inclined to trust, *was* in fact sent by the authorities to report on the Lawrences. But he invented evidence ("Dirty Belgians!") to incriminate Lawrence by association with Frieda. Because she was German, she had been suspected by the villagers of flashing lights to zeppelins and had been questioned about this by the police.[39] Twenty-two years later, Ford justified his treachery by claiming he had gone to Greatham to help Lawrence instead of to betray him.

Ford's secret, semi-official report to Masterman on the Lawrences' opposition to the war and supposedly suspicious behavior in Greatham—combined with Lawrence's damaging association with Russell's pacifist activities and his powerful anti-war story, "England, My England"—encouraged the authorities to suppress *The Rainbow* in November 1915 and, because Lawrence remained under government surveillance, to expel him from Cornwall in October 1917.

CHAPTER TWELVE

The Suppression of The Rainbow, 1915

I

LAWRENCE made astonishing technical and thematic progress in his fiction between *The White Peacock* in 1911 and *The Rainbow,* published in 1915, when he was thirty years old. *Sons and Lovers* had developed the themes of *The White Peacock* and *The Trespasser;* it was written in a realistic mode and was his first masterpiece. But *The Rainbow,* Lawrence's first symbolic work, surpassed the considerable achievement of his autobiographical novel.

Lawrence's abstract, metaphorical letter of June 1914 to Edward Garnett, describing his intentions in *The Rainbow* and distinguishing it from the conventional form of *Sons and Lovers* as well as from the tradition of the English novel, anticipates his wartime interest in the non-human (as opposed to the mechanical) and his letter to Bertrand Russell about blood (as opposed to mental) consciousness. In this letter Lawrence uses the metaphor of coal, deep-rooted in his family, childhood and native village, to represent and reveal the profoundest elements of human character:

That which is physic—non-human, in humanity, is more interesting to me than the old-fashioned human element—which causes one

to conceive a character in a certain moral scheme and make him
consistent. . . .

I only care about what the woman *is*—what she *is*—inhumanly,
physiologically, materially. . . . You mustn't look in my novel for the
old stable ego of the character. There is another ego, according to
whose action the individual is unrecognisable, and passes through,
as it were, allotropic states which it needs a deeper sense than any
[sense] we've been used to exercise, to discover are states of the
same single radically-unchanged element. (Like as diamond and
coal are the same pure single element of carbon. The ordinary novel
would trace the history of the diamond—but I say "diamond, what!
This is carbon." And my diamond might be coal or soot, and my
theme is carbon.)

Lawrence now rejects the stable and consistent creation of character
in fiction and replaces it with the more elemental concepts of being and
consciousness. He seeks to analyze the instinctual and irrational psychological forces that surge beneath the surface, that determine the complex
motivation and behavior of men and women. As Mark Schorer explained: "He will now create more *essential* beings, will be concerned
first of all not with the 'ego' that interests the traditional novelist, but
with the 'primal forces' that are prior to 'character.'"[1] Lawrence offered
a radically new conception of character, revealed the deepest sexual
drives (which had been suggested but not described by previous writers) and transformed the moral scheme of the novel.

Between March 1913 and March 1915 Lawrence wrote four versions of
the novel. He first called it *The Sisters*, then *The Wedding Ring,* and
finally *The Rainbow.* In 1915 he split it into two works, and the sequel
(completed in 1916) became *Women in Love.*

The Rainbow, which introduced sexual life into the family-chronicle
novel, portrays a visionary quest for love by three generations of men
and women. Each generation becomes successively weaker in character
and spirit after the Industrial Revolution has destroyed their communal
sense. The main characters of the first generation, Tom and Lydia
Brangwen, have a strong family bond, a close relation to the eternal
round of the seasons and a connection to the landscape, which seems—as
in Hardy's novels—to exist as an independent force. The opening section
reveals that the Brangwen women are traditionally distinguished from
the men by their longing for something above and beyond themselves.
While the men face inward, the women want "to enlarge their own scope
and range and freedom," and achieve a higher mode of being. Tom

Brangwen's experience establishes a recurrent pattern of consummation in love, alternating with emotional isolation, that is inherited by succeeding generations.

As the Brangwens become more ambitious and seek a widening circle of experience, they find it more difficult to achieve this consummation and fulfillment. Lydia finds satisfaction in her husband, Anna in her children, and Ursula seeks it in her teaching career; Tom in the land, Will in art and Anton Skrebensky (Ursula's lover) in war. If the second and third generations suffer a decline from the heroic standard of Tom and Lydia, they are not so easily satisfied and do succeed in extending their range and freedom.

Ursula's judgment of Anton is ultimately, and justly, negative. She must experience and "come through" (in the Lawrencean sense) a sequence of failures before she can become illuminated by the hopeful light and color of the rainbow. These bitter but enriching failures—her narrow-minded school, her materialistically-oriented university, her corrupt lesbian love with her teacher Winifred Inger, her unhappy affair with the mechanical and dominating soldier Anton (which foreshadows her mercurial and unstable love for Rupert Birkin in the sequel), even her miscarriage of Anton's baby (a strong contrast to Anna's swarm of children)—prepare her for the natural promise of the final rainbow:

> The arc bended and strengthened itself till it arched indomitable, making great architecture of light and colour and the space of heaven, its pedestals luminous in the corruption of new houses on the low hill, its arch the top of heaven.
>
> And the rainbow stood on the earth . . . [and promised] that new, clean, naked bodies would issue to a new germination, to a new growth, rising to the light and the wind and the clean rain of heaven.[2]

The architectural metaphor of the rainbow connects the first judgment of Noah in Genesis with the Last Judgment of Christ in Revelation. The rainbow is not a logical conclusion to the events in the novel, but a regenerative symbol that opposes Ursula's negative experiences and promises the sexual fulfillment and emotional salvation she eventually achieves in *Women in Love*.

The Rainbow opposed both literary and social conventions. Sexual explicitness had previously been confined to overtly erotic or pornographic works, and Lawrence's sexual passages were assumed to be shocking and obscene. Critics and police believed it was a "dirty book," and in the weeks following publication Lawrence was betrayed by his publisher, who allowed stocks of the novel to be destroyed.

The authorities specifically mentioned two objectionable passages in the novel. The first passage, from the "Shame" chapter, describes Ursula's lesbian bathing with Winifred Inger:

> And the elder held the younger close against her, close, as they went down, and by the side of the water, she put her arms round her, and kissed her. And she lifted her in her arms, close, saying, softly,
> "I shall carry you into the water."
> *Ursula lay still in her mistress's arms, her forehead against the beloved, maddening breast.*
> *"I shall put you in," said Winifred.*
> *But Ursula twined her body about her mistress.*
> After a while the rain came down on their flushed, hot limbs, startling, delicious.

The reviewers, court and Home Office all ignored the fact that Lawrence condemns this lesbianism and uses sexuality to enhance the themes of the novel. When Ursula, in an attempt to free herself from Winifred's perversion, takes her to meet her uncle, Tom Brangwen, the manager of a colliery, he detects in Winifred "a kinship with his own dark corruption." Tom's marriage to Winifred unites sexual with industrial corruption.

The second passage, from "The Bitterness of Ecstasy" chapter (also about destructive sexual love), describes Ursula's love-making with Anton Skrebensky near the water and then on land. In this scene, Ursula initiates the sexual encounter, expresses powerful sexual feelings and forces Anton into the passive role that is usually ascribed to the woman. A sexually independent woman (a vivid contrast to the Victorian sexual victim) was particularly threatening when the men were away at war:

> Then there in the great flare of light, she clinched hold of him, hard, as if suddenly she had the strength of destruction, she fastened her arms round him and tightened him in her grip, whilst her mouth sought his in a hard, rending, ever-increasing kiss, till his body was powerless in her grip, his heart melted in fear from the fierce, beaked, harpy's kiss. The water washed again over their feet, but she took no notice. She seemed unaware, she seemed to be pressing

in her beaked mouth till she had the heart of him. Then, at last, she drew away and looked at him—looked at him. He knew what she wanted. He took her by the hand and led her across the foreshore back to the sandhills. She went silently. He felt as if the ordeal of proof was upon him, for life or death. He led her to a dark hollow.

"No, here," she said, going out to the slope full under the moonshine. She lay motionless, with wide-open eyes looking at the moon. He came direct to her, without preliminaries. She held him pinned down at the chest, awful. The fight, the struggle for consummation was terrible. It lasted till it was agony to his soul, till he succumbed, till he gave way as if dead, and lay with his face buried, partly in her hair, partly in the sand, motionless, as if he would be motionless now for ever, hidden away in the dark, buried, only buried, he only wanted to be buried in the goodly darkness, only that, and no more.[3]

But the authorities, on the lookout for salacious passages, did *not* object to a scene that strongly hints of sodomy between Will and Anna Brangwen—either because they failed to notice it or because the suggestion was too awful to contemplate:

> All the *shameful,* natural and *unnatural* acts of sensual voluptuousness which he and the woman partook of together, created together, they had their heavy beauty and their delight. . . . The secret, shameful things are most terribly beautiful. . . . They accepted shame, and were one with it in their most unlicensed pleasures. . . . It was a bud that blossomed into beauty and heavy, *fundamental* gratification.

There is no evidence for Lawrence's assertion in a letter of 1920 to his publisher Martin Secker that "the scene to which exception was *particularly* taken was the one where Anna dances naked, when she is with child." In this scene, the pregnant Anna, admiring the story of King David, who danced before the Lord and uncovered himself exultingly (II Samuel 6:14–16), decides that she will dance Will's "nullification" and dance to her unseen Lord. Like David's wife, Michal, Will reacts angrily to this naked dance before the fire, which exalts "Anna Victrix" and excludes him. Since only the "Shame" chapter was specifically mentioned in court, Lawrence remained vague about exactly what was considered objectionable in the novel. In the first American edition of *The Rainbow,* published by Huebsch in 1922, he retained the sodomy and naked dancing scenes as well as Ursula and Anton's amphibious love-making.[4]

II

In 1915, twenty years after the trial of Oscar Wilde, the prevailing attitudes about sexual morality and sexual expression were essentially those of the Victorian period; and they were compounded with a patriotic self-righteousness that attempted to justify the war. Unlike most authors of his time, Lawrence refused to be oblique in his discussion of sex. He insisted on frankness about lesbianism and the sexual desires of women when even an acknowledgment of these subjects was considered offensive. He adopted a prophetic stance, propounded a new morality based on feeling and brought sexual emotions to the forefront of the novel. He opposed contemporary attitudes toward both sex and war, and was made to suffer for expressing his views. Though several influential writers—Arnold Bennett, John Drinkwater, Hugh Walpole and Clive Bell—supported Lawrence and opposed censorship, many established literary figures—James, Wells and Galsworthy (as well as Ezra Pound)—agreed with the authorities that he had gone too far. By publishing *The Rainbow*—which was sensual in subject and style—Methuen moved outside the security of its normal list and into the uncertain territory of the *avant-garde.*

Lawrence was closely associated, during the suppression of *The Rainbow,* with J. B. Pinker, who became his literary agent in 1914. Born in 1863, Pinker had very little formal education. He had worked as a journalist in Constantinople, married a wealthy woman and returned to England in 1891. He became assistant editor of an illustrated weekly, *Black and White,* read for a publishing house and briefly edited the popular *Pearson's Magazine.* In 1896 he became a literary agent, with offices in Granville House, Arundel Street; and his early clients included Wilde, Crane, Bennett, Wells, James and Conrad. Pinker helped to support the impoverished Conrad for many years; and in 1904 the grateful author testified to his generosity: "[Pinker] has stepped gallantly into the breach left open by the collapse of my bank; and not only gallantly, but successfully as well. He has treated not only my moods but even my fancies with the greatest consideration."

Lawrence anticipated difficulties with *The Rainbow* when he submitted it to the publisher in April 1915, and he told Pinker: "I'm afraid there are parts of it Methuen won't want to publish. He must. I will take out sentences and phrases, but I won't take out paragraphs or pages." When, in July, the publisher duly objected, Lawrence cut out all the objectionable phrases. But he maintained there was nothing offensive in the longer passages and refused to alter them. On November 16, 1915, three days after the novel was suppressed, Pinker wrote to the pedestrian and ineffectual G. H. Thring of the Society of Authors, who considered and then rejected the idea of defending Lawrence. Pinker summarized the history of Lawrence's reasonable response to and satisfaction of the publisher's objections:

> When the MS. was delivered the publishers told me that their reader reported it as impossible for publication in its existing form. I told Mr. Lawrence of the criticism, and asked him to reconsider the MS. and Mr. Lawrence not only reconsidered it but decided that he would rewrite the novel. This he did and the new version was delivered to Messrs. Methuen. They considered it still too frank in places, and I asked them to indicate the particular passages in order that I might ask Mr. Lawrence to modify them. This Mr. Lawrence did. He only left unchanged, I think, one passage of which they complained.[5]

Though Methuen was sufficiently confident to publish the novel in an edition of 2,500 on September 30, 1915, it was attacked by moralistic critics who had no conception of Lawrence's astonishing achievement. In the *Sphere* of October 23, three weeks after publication, Clement Shorter condemned the book absolutely: "There is no form of viciousness, of suggestiveness, that is not reflected in these pages." He assumed a threatening tone, held up "family fiction" as the ideal standard and particularly criticized Lawrence's *negative* description of Ursula's physical infatuation with Winifred Inger in the chapter called "Shame": "unless [the publishers] hold the view that Lesbianism is a fit subject for family fiction I imagine they will regret this venture."

In the *Star* of the previous day, James Douglas, an equally undistinguished man of letters, was even more severe than Shorter. His review combined—and equated—moralism and patriotism. Douglas savaged Lawrence's "eloquent lubricity" and (with a hint at Oscar Wilde) his "unnameable and unthinkable ugliness," and claimed Lawrence's subtlety "is used to express the unspeakable and to hint at the unutterable." More menacingly, he exclaimed: "A thing like *The Rainbow* has no right to exist in the wind of war. . . . The young men who are dying for liberty are moral beings. They are the living repudiation of such impious denials of life as in *The Rainbow*. The life they lay down is a lofty thing. It is not the thing that creeps and crawls in this novel."[6]

The courts, provoked by the reviews of Shorter and Douglas, and by the complaints of the National Purity League[7] (whose counsel, Herbert Muskett, K.C., appeared for the Commissioner of Police), proceeded against the novel under the Obscene Publications Act of 1857. The original intention of this act was to prevent the sale of pornography in London. According to that antiquated, mid-Victorian statute, the mere complaint of indecency by an ordinary citizen could be sufficient to suppress a book:

> A police magistrate or any two justices, on complaint being made by oath, may issue a warrant to search any premises in which it is alleged that obscene books are kept for publication or sale, and if such books are seized on the execution of the warrant the occupier of the premises may be summoned to show cause why such books should not be destroyed, and the justices, if satisfied that the books are of the character stated in the warrant, may order them to be destroyed.

Though Methuen had surrendered all its copies of *The Rainbow* on November 3—ten days before the trial—Lawrence was never notified. He knew nothing about the seizure of his books until after the proceedings were concluded, when he was notified by the novelist and critic Walter Lionel George—a French Jew and a friend of Katherine Mansfield, "small, black moustached, brisk, and opinionated"[8]—who had rung up Methuen to ask why it had stopped advertising the book.

Herbert Muskett, prosecuting the book and quoting the reviews by Shorter and Douglas in court on November 13, described it—with a philistine sneer—as "a mass of obscenity of thought, idea, and action throughout, wrapped up in language which he supposed would be regarded in some quarters as an artistic and intellectual effort." The sixty-seven-year-old judge, Sir John Dickinson, whose son had recently been killed in the war, agreed that "he had never read anything more disgusting than this book. . . . It was utter filth; nothing else would describe it." Many reporters were in the courtroom and publicized the case. The

Daily Telegraph dryly noted, in reporting the proceedings, that two members of the firm had read the "Shame" chapter, to which particular exception was taken, "without conceiving the [lesbian] suggestion it contained."[9] Neither Methuen nor Lawrence was represented in court.

Algernon Methuen, who tried to protect the good name of his firm and escape with the lightest possible penalty, apologized abjectly and acquiesced in the suppression of *The Rainbow*. He made no attempt to defend the novel or protect the interest of the author, and expressed regret that he had published it. Sir John Dickinson ordered the 1,011 remaining copies to be destroyed and the defendants to pay costs of ten guineas. Lawrence later recalled, with some exaggeration: "Methuen published that book, and he almost wept before the magistrate, when he was summoned for bringing out a piece of indecent literature. He said he did not know the dirty thing he had been handling, he had not read the work, his reader had misadvised him—and Peccavi! Peccavi! [I have sinned!] wept the now be-knighted gentleman." But *The Rainbow* was not legally banned. The publisher voluntarily surrendered its copies of the book to the police, who, acting on complaints about the "Shame" chapter, destroyed all these copies. Algernon Methuen's gentlemanly contrition paid off, for he avoided a fine and placed all the blame on Lawrence. The following year, he was made a baronet.

Lawrence's sometime friend Ezra Pound, whose poem had been blacked out in Wyndham Lewis' *BLAST* (July 1914), wrote to friends in May 1916 that the suppression of *The Rainbow* had led to a panic among printers and created an oppressive wave of censorship. Even the tolerant Pound thought Lawrence's novel was too sexually frank and believed, quite mistakenly, that Lawrence had exploited the sexual scenes for commercial gain. Pound, quoting J. B. Pinker, also suggested that the novel would not have been suppressed if Methuen—or Lawrence himself—had defended it, since the Home Office had decided not to prosecute the book:

The printers have gone quite mad since the Lawrence fuss. . . . Something has got to be done or we'll all of us be suppressed, à la counter-reformation, dead and done for. . . .

It was a novel sexually overloaded, a sort of post-Wellsian barrocco and it depended for its sale precisely on its sexual overloading. . . . [Pinker] put the whole blame on Methuen. Some crank went to a magistrate and said the book was immoral. Methuen admitted it. Then the magistrate gave various orders, *in excess of his powers*. If Methuen had declined to obey, or if they had denied that the book was immoral, NOTHING could have been done until the Home Office moved. The Home Office had inspected the book (Mr. [Augustine] Birrell being asked for an opinion said the book was too dull to bother about) and decided that they would do nothing.[10]

Lawrence was naturally outraged by Methuen's betrayal, by the unfairness of the proceedings that had condemned him without a hearing and by the suffering it had caused him. In one of his prophetic denunciations, he cursed "them all, body and soul, root, branch and leaf, to eternal damnation."[11] He had been offered a cottage in the orange groves of Florida—a possible site for Rananim—by the composer Frederick Delius, had obtained passports and booked his voyage to America. He now saw that country as his future audience. But in the middle of November he made the fateful decision to defer his departure and await further developments in his case.

There were several possible ways to oppose the suppression. The Society of Authors or influential writers might help him. He could bring a libel case against Clement Shorter and James Douglas. He could arrange to have another copy of *The Rainbow* seized and then defend the book in court. Or friends could raise questions in the House of Commons about the justice of the proceedings.

The most important person Lawrence's family had ever known was the Congregational minister in Eastwood. But now, in his moment of crisis and only a few years after leaving home, Lawrence could confidently solicit the assistance of titled friends, members of Parliament, powerful figures in the government like Edward Marsh and Gordon Campbell, and the daughter-in-law of the prime minister. Lady Ottoline Morrell noted the cynicism behind the prevailing morality: "Philip did all he could in the House of Commons to get the ban removed, but without success. We lent our copy to [the home secretary] Sir John Simon and other influential men, who read it with eyes that greedily swept the pages for indecent passages."

Philip Morrell and his allies made some telling points in Parliament about the unfairness of the trial, but they were deftly handled by the legalistic mind of the home secretary:

MR. MORRELL asked the Home Secretary . . . whether the author of the book had any opportunity of replying to the charge made against him? . . .

SIR JOHN SIMON. The publishers, and not the author, were the defendants, and they had the customary opportunity to produce such evidence as they considered necessary to their defence. . . . So far from resisting the proceedings [Methuen] said they thought it right that the order should be issued. . . .

COMMANDER WEDGWOOD. Is it not monstrous that a man should have this charge levelled against him and have no opportunity of defending himself? . . .

SIR JOHN SIMON. I imagine it will be possible, if the author thinks he has been wrongly treated, for another copy to be seized by arrangement, in order that he might defend the book.[12]

Morrell's eccentric minority view had few supporters in the House, and the questions raised in Parliament did no good. His defense of Lawrence's novel confirmed suspicions in the House of Commons that pacifism and sexual immorality were closely connected.

III

Unpublished papers of the Bow Street Police Court and of the Home Office in both 1915 and 1930 illuminate the details of the trial, the answers to Morrell's questions in Parliament, the objectionable passages in *The Rainbow* and the reconsideration of the case just after Lawrence's death. Though no transcripts were made of summary trials, all notebooks for the period have been destroyed and no detailed case papers have survived, the brief but revealing manuscript entries in the court register still exist in the Greater London Record Office. The court register explicitly mentions the right to appeal, and records the suppression of one of the greatest novels of the century amidst cases of assault, drunkenness and urinating in public:

Complainant: Inspector Draper, CID [Criminal Investigation Department].

Defendant: Methuen.

Nature of Offence: For order to destroy 245 Bound copies and 766 Unbound copies of a book entitled *The Rainbow* seized [on their premises] at 36 Essex Street, Strand.

Date of Offence: 3 and 5 November 1915 [the dates the copies were seized].

Adjudication: Order to be destroyed at expiration of 7 days (in the interim to be impounded) if no appeal. £10-10-0. costs.[13]

The Home Office papers, under the heading "Publications (including indecent)," contain several revealing notes on the "Proceedings taken by the police for the suppression of *The Rainbow* by D. H. Lawrence." A reference to "a Mrs. Weekley living at address of D. H. Lawrence" suggests that they planned, if necessary, to condemn Lawrence for his adulterous relationship with Frieda, though he had been married to her for eighteen months. A statement that "the author is not accused, nor is he any party to the case" disingenuously implies that Lawrence had no connection whatsoever with the book. Sir Edward Troup, the permanent under-secretary, concedes that Sir John Simon's proposed reply "is correct but rather avoids answering the questions" put by Philip Morrell. And a note next to a clipping of *The Times'* report of the trial alludes to *Macbeth* (5.3.40) and states that "the author dwells on the sexual feelings of a number of people in a way which suggests a diseased mind."

The climate of opinion changed dramatically in England after the war. When Martin Secker republished *The Rainbow* in February 1926, using the sheets of the expurgated American edition, no one protested and the authorities took no action of any kind. On March 10, 1930—eight days after Lawrence's death—Sir Sidney Harris, an assistant secretary in the Home Office, who had not read the novel, noticed that it had been reissued by Secker. He noted the suppression of the book in 1915 and the radical change of attitude toward obscenity in the last fifteen years. But he recommended (though the novel had been in print in England since 1926), that the police intervene:

The Rainbow is included among D. H. Lawrence's published works but in 1915 proceedings were successfully taken by the Police for the destruction of this book. I have not seen *The Rainbow* but there is no doubt, according to the press report, of its obscenity according to the standard of fifteen years ago, though in recent years opinion has moved very rapidly away from anything like a conventional standard. I think the attention of the Police should be called to the matter.

Eleven days later, an official of the Prosecutions Branch of the Metropolitan Police noted (as Herbert Muskett had hinted in court) that "although the 1915 proceedings were taken in the [Police] Commis-

sioner's name, they were practically initiated by the late Sir Charles
Matthews," who had been director of public prosecutions in 1915. The
official disagreed with Harris' suggestion and added: "I have gone
through the book again. There are a few passages that would still be
adjudged obscene by some Courts; but I feel quite clear that proceedings
would be unwise."

Harris, the perfect bureaucrat, who had just recommended suppression, immediately changed his mind to conform to higher authority and
now conceded, with a properly Pecksniffian tone:

> It would certainly be unwise to give the works of Lawrence any
> further advertisement or to appear to be attacking a writer after
> his death. If all the critics were to write as plainly and boldly as the
> author of the paragraph from the *Daily Telegraph* of the 4th March
> (see within) we should have no further cause for anxiety.

The sneering obituary of Lawrence in the *Daily Telegraph* of March 4,
1930, which was included in the Home Office file and gave Harris moral
reassurance, misrepresented the proceedings against *The Rainbow* and
repeated the description of Lawrence as a "diseased mind" that had
appeared in *The Times'* report of the trial on November 15, 1915: "His
later books and poems were rightly banned [*sic*] by the Censor. . . .
Lawrence's case calls not so much for censure as for pity. The man was ill,
the mind diseased."[14]

IV

The extraordinary travesty of British justice in the trial of *The Rainbow*
engendered an atmosphere of repression and was, as Lawrence and his
friends realized, caused by something more than the objectionable sexual passages in the novel. The reviews by Shorter and Douglas were
unusually vicious and ignored the context and meaning of the passages
they condemned. Douglas specifically stated that the book had "no right
to exist in the wind of war." The real complainant, probably the National
Purity League, was never named. Its counsel, Herbert Muskett, prosecuted for the commissioner of police and hinted in court that he had the
powerful backing of the director of public prosecutions. Muskett cited

the potentially libelous reviews by Shorter and Douglas as if they were objective truth, and the judge agreed with him completely. Because Methuen, desperate to avoid bad publicity, had made no attempt to defend the book, appeal the decision, or inform Lawrence or Pinker until after the trial was over, Lawrence was effectively robbed of the opportunity to defend himself and never knew precisely which passages were objectionable. The Society of Authors refused to act on Lawrence's behalf, and the few writers who tried to support him were ineffectual. Lawrence did not have the funds for a costly appeal in court and was discouraged by the virulent hostility to his work. In any case, it seemed too late to do anything about the destruction of the books. The critical questions raised in the House of Commons by Philip Morrell were easily evaded by the home secretary, who (as his colleague noted) did not actually answer them.

Lawrence was known to have a German wife and to have lived adulterously with her until their marriage in July 1914. In the spring of 1915, he was threatened with bankruptcy by Weekley's lawyers for his inability or unwillingness to pay the costs of the divorce. (He eventually made some arrangement for payment over a period of years.) Lawrence's German dedication to his German sister-in-law—*"Zu Else"*—which he originally wanted to print in thick black Gothic letters, may also have provoked the authorities. Lawrence had been associated with Russell's pacifist protests (considered treasonable in some quarters), had been officially reported by Ford in March 1915 as pro-German and politically unreliable, and had published anti-war sentiments in "England, My England" in the *English Review* of October 1915. Even Cynthia Asquith, whose help he solicited, was torn between loyalty to Lawrence and disapproval of his ideas. As she wrote in her diary of his criticism of the war in the *Signature* during October–November 1915: "I am not sure that technically it doesn't amount to treason."[15]

The war was going badly for the Allies at the end of 1915. Britain had suffered damaging zeppelin raids as well as a military disaster at Gallipoli. The British believed they were fighting for great moral principles and that their opponents—both Germans and pacifists—were immoral. *The Rainbow,* read through the eyes of James Douglas, confirmed the sexual immorality of those who opposed the war. Lawrence criticized the role of Anton (a professional soldier) in the Boer War, which Ursula compares to hell: "The idea of war altogether made her feel uneasy, uneasy. When men began organised fighting with each other it seemed to her as if the poles of the universe were cracking, and the whole might go

tumbling into the bottomless pit. A horrible bottomless feeling she had."
Richard Aldington stated that Lawrence's opposition to war was mentioned during the trial, when "the prosecution skilfully obscured the
issue by pointing to some criticisms of the Boer War, which were ab-
surdly maintained to be hindering recruiting."[16] All this evidence sup-
ports Aldington's assertion that he knew in his bones "the real reason for
the attack was that [Lawrence] denounced War"; he had heard this
stated as a fact both by Lawrence and by such sympathizers as the author
May Sinclair.

Aldington summarized the disastrous consequences of the affair:
Lawrence "lost all chance of earning anything [in England] for three
years of work . . . he was publicly stigmatised as 'obscene'; and his name
was made so notorious that publishers and periodicals for a long time
avoided using his work."[17] After November 1915, only one story—
"Samson and Delilah," in the *English Review* of March 1917—was
published in England until the conclusion of the war. Though Lawrence
completed *Women in Love* in 1916, he was unable to publish it until
November 1920—and then only privately and in New York.

The suppression of the novel made Lawrence desperately poor. He
remained trapped in England (when subsequent requests for passports
were denied) and persecuted during the rest of the war. He was determined to leave the country as soon as the war was over and to live as an
expatriate for the rest of his life. He abandoned all hope of achieving
popular success in England and turned to America as his potential
audience.

CHAPTER THIRTEEN

Cornwall,
1916–1918

L A W R E N C E and Frieda remained in Hampstead (where they had been living since August 1915) until late December, attempting to enlist support for the vindication of *The Rainbow*. He spent Christmas with his sister Ada in Derbyshire; and moved with Frieda to a cottage borrowed from the writer J. D. Beresford, near Padstow, on the north coast of Cornwall, during January and February 1916. Pressed for money and craving isolation, he then rented a little cottage for £5 a year in Higher Tregerthen, a remote village in west Cornwall, on the shaggy moors above the surging sea.

Lawrence was in a desperate financial position, for the unsavory content of his polemical works and his reputation as an obscene novelist made it almost impossible to place his work in England. Though Frieda shared Lawrence's belief in his creative work, she disapproved of (but was often blamed for) his prophetic denunciations and mocked his failure to find an audience: "'There you are Lorenzo, they've all come back again! Your writings are all philosophy and bosh and nobody wants them!'" Frieda would say. "And into the fire they went."

Lawrence's poor health and the constant rejection of his work placed additional strains on his marriage. He had always fought with Frieda about emotional and intellectual issues. Now they endured not only extreme poverty, his poor health and army medical examinations, but also constant harassment from their neighbors and the police, culminating in their expulsion from Cornwall in October 1917.

During this period Lawrence and Frieda were often estranged and sometimes separated. Their sexual life may have become less satisfactory because of his poor health and nervous stress, and each sought love from another source. Lawrence developed intimate attachments with an American journalist, Esther Andrews, and with a Cornish farmer, William Henry Hocking. Frieda, deeply hurt by these new emotional ties, found comfort with the composer Cecil Gray. Throughout these years of physical and emotional strain Lawrence was writing his greatest novel, *Women in Love,* which portrayed his sexual conflicts and expressed his homosexual ideas.

I

Until his first commercial success, with the privately printed *Lady Chatterley's Lover,* in 1928, Lawrence, like most of his contemporaries of genius—Ford, Conrad, Joyce, Lewis, Pound and Eliot—was trapped by poverty. During 1913–14 he had earned between £450 and £500; during 1917–18 his annual income was reduced by eighty percent, and he made considerably less than £100. Yet he willingly abandoned the pretense of middle-class respectability and chirpily wrote that poverty "isn't any such awful thing, if you don't care about keeping up appearances. There is no cure for this craven terror of poverty save in human courage and insouciance." Though he would sometimes have to swallow his pride and borrow money, he maintained his independence by reducing his standard of living and cutting down to the barest necessities. Looking back on his life, without regrets, he observed in 1929: "I have never starved, and never even felt poor, though my [uncertain] income for the first ten years was no better, and often worse, than it would have been if I had remained an elementary school-teacher."[1]

Yet Lawrence often had to sail very close to the wind. In July 1916, after five months in Cornwall, he told Pinker he had only £6 and asked for an advance on future earnings. A year and a half later, he had just under £7, with not a penny due, and felt he had exhausted his financial resources. Despite a grant of £50 from the Royal Literary Fund in July 1918, he reached the depths of pessimism three months afterward and wrote to Mark Gertler: "it is hopeless to go on [as a writer] any longer, with no money and no hope." Two years later, writing to Amy Lowell, he said he could not earn enough to live on, despite the prodigious amount of work he had completed, and complained of his perennial role as the "charity boy of literature." Though he was forced to ask for money, his appeals during the war were generously met by many friends: Amy Lowell, Ada, Kot, Catherine Carswell, Cynthia Asquith, Ottoline Morrell, Edward Marsh, J. B. Pinker, J. D. Beresford and the barrister Montague Shearman, as well as by prominent literary figures: Charles Whibley, Arnold Bennett and Bernard Shaw. Though Lawrence had very little money, he was, as even hostile witnesses confirmed, extremely economical, punctilious about repaying his smallest debts and always ready to give part of his savings to friends whose need (he felt) was greater than his own.

Frieda, who had none of Lawrence's scruples and reticence about money, once tried to land a patron on her own. When Cynthia Asquith introduced her to a successful but very shy writer, Frieda bungled his title and took the approach direct. "How do you do, Sir Barrie," she said to the benefactor of Mary Cannan and Lady Cynthia. "I hear you make an income of fifty thousand a year. . . . Why shouldn't you give Lorenzo enough money to pay our passage to Australia [i.e., America]?"—at which her host shrank silently back into his shell.[2]

II

After the quarrel with Katherine and Murry and their departure in June 1916, after only two months in Higher Tregerthen, Lawrence became intimately involved with a young American, Esther Andrews— who was introduced by her lover, Robert Mountsier. Mountsier came from a French Protestant family (the name derived from "monsieur") and was born in Charleroi, south of Pittsburgh, in 1888. He graduated from the University of Michigan in 1909 and the following year joined the staff of the *New York Sun* as a reporter and book review editor. He began but did not finish work on a doctorate at Columbia University in New York. Mountsier met Lawrence in England in 1915; he visited him (with Esther Andrews) in Cornwall in November and December 1916; in Baden-Baden, Germany, and Zell-am-See, Austria, in July 1921; and in Taos (with Lawrence's American publishers, Thomas and Adele Seltzer) in December–January 1922–23. During 1917–18 he worked in Europe as a captain in the American Red Cross; after the war, he served under Herbert Hoover in the American Relief Commission. He was Lawrence's American agent from 1920 to 1923; and published his own book, *Eleven Billion Dollars: Europe's Debt to the United States,* with Seltzer in 1922. Mountsier lived in Greenwich Village and, as aviation editor of the *New York Sun,* traveled throughout the world. Though always attracted to women and with many lady friends, he never married.

Mountsier was "a tall, well-built man with fine features, a high forehead, brown eyes, and light brown hair. He was modest and self-effacing, and at times seemed shy." One great-nephew characterized him as "a very exacting person, frugal, well mannered, well spoken, well read—a gentleman. He was quiet but not retiring. Sure of himself and his capabilities. Forthright and upright and of strong opinions."[3]

In November 1916 Lawrence said Mountsier was "very nice and gentle and decent in every way, a man one likes to know," and described the Americans as "a queer, gentle couple, so old-old, that they are more innocent than children." In the "Nightmare" chapter of his Australian novel, *Kangaroo* (1923), Lawrence portrays his Christmas Eve celebration with Mountsier and Andrews, which was interrupted when the police knocked on the door and demanded Mountsier's documents. This scene reveals that when Lawrence was under surveillance in Cornwall, his friends were also suspected, persecuted and actually jailed:

[It was] a pouring black wet night outside. Nowhere can it be so black as on the edge of a Cornish moor, above the western sea, near the rocks where the ancient worshippers used to sacrifice. . . . The American woman friend was crouching at the fire making fudge, the man was away in his room, when [there was] a thundering knock at the door. . . .

Somers fetched the American friend, and he was asked to produce papers, and give information. He gave it, being an honourable citizen and a well-bred American, with complete *sang-froid.* . . .

[But] when Monsell got back to London he was arrested, and conveyed to Scotland Yard: there examined, stripped naked, his clothes taken away. Then he was kept for a night in a cell.[4]

Like Katherine and Murry, Andrews and Mountsier were an unmarried couple, slightly younger than Lawrence, living together as man and wife. Lawrence, isolated and lonely in Cornwall, was pleased to form a friendship with his temperamental opposite. He was especially eager to develop an American audience, and Mountsier was a perfect representative in the United States for an author whose latest novel had been suppressed for obscenity. He was respectable, practical and efficient; willing to work as a literary agent when Lawrence could not place his books and had no prospects of earning much money. In June 1921, at the height of their friendship, Lawrence encouraged Mountsier to buy a ship in which a small group of like-minded companions could sail around the eastern Mediterranean.

In March 1921, writing to Mountsier about Seltzer, Lawrence exclaimed: "I hate Jews and want to learn to be more *wary* of them all." But in November of that year, after Mountsier's visit to Baden-Baden, Lawrence told Kot that he was annoyed by Mountsier's equally irrational prejudice: "He is one of those irritating people who have generalised detestations: his particular one being Jews, Germans, and Bolshevists. So unoriginal. He got on my nerves badly in Germany."

Mountsier's visit to Taos with the Russian-Jewish Seltzer finished off their friendship. In February 1923, after Seltzer had complained that he could no longer do business with Mountsier, Lawrence terminated relations with his agent. Lawrence's feeling that Mountsier had lost faith in him and his work, and was inwardly antagonistic, is confirmed by his great-nephew's statement that Mountsier "thought Lawrence was brilliant, but felt he was misdirected in his [attempts] to reach the American public. Robert apparently felt that the language used by DHL was not necessary to get across the intent of his writing. They had a number of confrontations on this point."[5]

Much less is known about the significant but shadowy figure of Esther Andrews than about Robert Mountsier. She quarreled with him before he left Cornwall for London, after Christmas 1916, stayed on alone with the Lawrences until mid-January, and returned for a second visit, after Mountsier had sailed to New York without her, from mid-April to mid-May 1917.

Lawrence called Andrews, who was writing a never completed book on women's work in the war, Hadaffah. The word, a variant of the Hebrew Hadassah, means "myrtle" and is an alternative name for Esther (see Esther 2:7). Lawrence's fondness for the youthful Esther, expressed in letters to his confidantes Cynthia Asquith and Catherine Carswell, aroused the hostility of Frieda, who was growing increasingly matronly and stout. During Esther's second visit, one of Frieda's rare illnesses—ptomaine poisoning and colitis—allowed Lawrence and his guest to spend an unusual amount of time together. "We liked her very much," Lawrence told his friends, "she is not really a journalist: very understanding.... Esther Andrews is still here. She makes me feel that America is really the next move.... I try my best to bring them both to reason—Frieda and Hadaf—but in vain. It is a duel without pistols for all of us."

While Lawrence was emotionally and perhaps even sexually involved with Esther, he admitted the negative aspects of his messy entanglements with adoring women in a letter to his neighbor Cecil Gray. But he also defended them, in his role as prophet and social innovator, as a brave attempt (like *The Rainbow*) to discover a new mode of instinctual perception: "the pure understanding between the Magdalen and Jesus went deeper than the understanding between the disciples and Jesus.... My 'women,' Esther Andrews, Hilda Aldington, etc., represent, in an impure and unproud, subservient, cringing, bad fashion, I admit,—but represent none the less the threshold of a new world, or underworld, of knowledge and being.... My 'women' want an ecstatic subtly-intellectual underworld, like the Greeks."[6] Catherine Carswell, who had also visited the Lawrences in Cornwall and discussed Esther with them, shed some light on her attraction to Lawrence and rivalry with Frieda: "The Lawrences already had a guest—a woman. She was unhappy [with Mountsier], and in the strength of her unhappiness could not resist attaching herself to Lawrence and trying to match her strength against Frieda's—disastrously to herself. Yet she took away with her, when she left later that summer [i.e., May], an enduring admiration" for Lawrence's intellectual and imaginative powers.[7]

Born in Des Moines, Iowa, in about 1885, Esther moved to Brooklyn and then to Connecticut with her parents and two older sisters. She was witty, always amusing and a vivid contrast to her respectable family. Her nephew described her as "glamorous, slim, fairly tall, around 5'7", and usually dressed in slacks and a shirt of painter's colors. Her voice was somewhat husky but clearly articulated, in a sort of international accent clearly influenced by her dramatic training." She attended both the Yale Art School and the Yale Drama School in the early 1900s. Defying family resistance, she went on the stage in about 1910 and toured widely in stock companies before the war. When the Great War broke out, long before American involvement, Esther enlisted in the Red Cross and also worked with the Quakers to help those suffering in France.

It is not clear whether Esther and Lawrence were ever lovers. "It would have been in the cards, but may also have been only mutual friendship and admiration. Esther was reticent about her private life, though I often heard her speak of Lawrence's electric personality." The one surviving letter from Lawrence to Esther "was interesting about Lawrence, but not very personal. There was an account of their life in Cornwall, the suspicions of the government and their neighbors, and visiting among their coterie of friends and sympathizers."

Esther disappeared from Lawrence's life in mid-1917. But she surfaced in New York in the 1920s, met Mabel Dodge Sterne and sent her a long description of "one of the most fascinating men I ever met." According to Mabel, an unreliable and at times malicious witness, Frieda (who did *not* visit her mother in Germany during the war) confided that Lawrence had betrayed her with both Esther and William Henry Hocking:

Frieda told me about the two times Lawrence had evaded her. One time was with the American girl in Cornwall when she was absent for a visit to her mother, I think. She had returned to the little house and found a feeling in the air that she had not left there. She forced Lawrence to tell her about it and then showed the girl the door. It had, or at least so he told her, been a miserable failure, anyway. The other one had been a young farmer, also in Cornwall.

"Was there really a *thing* between them?" I asked.

"I think so. I was dreadfully unhappy," she answered.[8]

After attaching herself to Lawrence during the war, Esther became a friend of John Dos Passos (as well as an acquaintance of Hemingway and Edmund Wilson) in New York. In his autobiography, *The Best Times,* Dos Passos portrays Esther as arty, stylish, rebellious and generous. As an admirer of famous writers, Esther apparently would have been quite willing to sleep with Lawrence if he had wished her to:

Esther had been one of many attractive women who pour into New York from the Middle West, learn diction at a drama school and yearn for the illdefined glamor of a stage career. When that didn't work Esther took a job with *Women's Wear Daily.* She had ability and a natural flair for clothes and was pretty well paid but she elevated her scorn and hatred of the women's clothing business into a religion. . . . She had taken up with a nicelooking young man of Quaker extraction named Canby Chambers, who was somewhat younger than she was. Children, family, matrimony were old-fashioned notions. She utterly repudiated the idea of marriage.

Esther was a born hostess. In spite of her scorn of conventional values ... she was an attractive and warm-hearted woman.[9]

Esther and Mountsier had a significant impact on Lawrence's life. They encouraged his interest in American literature, which led, through Melville, to his visit to the South Seas and to his seminal work *Studies in Classic American Literature* (1923). Mountsier, acting as Lawrence's agent, placed Lawrence's literary work, negotiated with Thomas Seltzer and helped attract an American audience. The attractive, bohemian and impressionable Esther represented "a new world of knowledge and being." She adored Lawrence, became his disciple and provided valuable emotional support when he was having serious difficulties with his marriage, his work and the police. The Lawrences had hoped to go to America with Esther in the spring of 1917; but they could not leave the country, except for some purpose in the national interest, and were refused passports in February of that year. Nevertheless, when Esther returned to New York she aroused Mabel Dodge Sterne's interest in Lawrence and was partly responsible for Lawrence's invitation to Taos in 1922.

III

Lawrence's involvement with Esther Andrews was closely connected to his problems with Frieda. They had survived the divorce proceedings and regularized their union in July 1914, and during the war she had occasionally been able to see her children. But this was also a difficult time for Frieda. As a naturalized British citizen, she was torn between loyalty to her native and her adopted country. She was extremely Germanic in appearance and accent, and inevitably experienced a certain amount of hostility. She too suffered from Lawrence's reputation as an obscene author and disloyal Englishman; she endured his bitter rages and shared his humiliating poverty. The passage "you never satisfy me now," deleted by Lawrence from the American edition of *The Rainbow,* may have referred to his own sexual difficulties.

Ottoline's lively diaries reveal how at Garsington Frieda provoked Lawrence's anger, assumed a haughty attitude and, despite his abusive threats, dominated him by superior strength and force of will:

Time after time when with Lawrence I have heard Frieda with great zest and gaiety mock and deride whatever she thought was sacred to him, thus goading him into fury. . . .

He [would say], "Come off that, lass, or I'll hit thee in the mouth. You've gone too far this time." . . .

When they were quarreling, [Frieda] would sometimes draw herself up and say, "Do not forget, Lorenzo, I am a baroness!" . . .

He is very weak with her, although he abuses her to us and indeed often to her face he shouts abusive things, yet she will always win if she wants to; for she had ten times the physical vitality and force that he has, and always really dominates him, however much he may rebel and complain.

Ernest Jones, the disciple of Freud whom Lawrence met through Dr. David Eder in about 1916 (when he was having the fierce quarrels with Frieda that Katherine Mansfield described), confirmed Ottoline's diaries, though he may have exaggerated the Lawrences' rows. The psychoanalyst believed that they were temperamentally antagonistic and that Frieda often went out of her way to provoke Lawrence's rages: "Jones wrote of Mr. and Mrs. Lawrence that they were 'impelled by mischievous demons to goad each other into frenzy.' . . . Late one night a panic-stricken Frieda Lawrence burst into Jones' [London] flat and begged for refuge since her husband was about to murder her. To her complete surprise Jones snapped at her 'From the way you treat him I wonder he has not done so long ago.'"[10]

Lawrence alluded to his sexual problems with Frieda in several of his works: the failure of their first night together in *Look! We Have Come Through!* and *Mr. Noon*, the anxiety about being unable to satisfy her in *The Rainbow*, and the fear of overpowering women from *Sons and Lovers* to *Lady Chatterley's Lover*. Lawrence and Frieda undoubtedly had, as Huxley observed, a profound and passionate love life. But Lawrence also feared domination by women and, according to the novelist Compton Mackenzie (who patronized Lawrence and attempted to diagnose his sexual difficulties), was deeply troubled in 1920 by one aspect of his relations with Frieda: "What worried him particularly was his inability to attain consummation simultaneously with his wife, which according to him must mean that their marriage was still imperfect in spite of all they had both gone through. . . . He became more and more depressed about what *he* insisted was the only evidence of a perfect union." In Mackenzie's account, Lawrence emphasized the physical basis of marriage and rather naively equated marital perfection with simultaneous orgasm. When he failed to achieve this perfection, he tried to transcend the limitations of the physical through the "higher" love of man. "I believe the nearest I've ever come to perfect love," he told Mackenzie, alluding to Alan Chambers, "was with a young coal miner [i.e., farmer] when I was about sixteen." And Cecil Gray—who had been satirized by Lawrence as the unpleasant nonentity Cyril Scott in *Aaron's Rod* and by Huxley as Mr. Mercaptan in *Antic Hay* ("a sleek, comfortable young man" with "a rather gross, snouty look")— categorically stated: "It might not be true to say that Lawrence was literally and absolutely impotent . . . but I am certain that he was not very far removed from it."[11] The basis of Gray's "certainty" is not explained, but it is clear that Lawrence was not impotent if he experienced orgasms.

Gray—a caddish composer and music critic, born in 1895—had been exempted from military service because of a defective heart. In 1917 he rented Bosigran Castle (which was nothing more than an ordinary cottage) near the Lawrences' house in Cornwall. Frieda, frequently neglected and left alone during the summer of 1917 while Lawrence worked in the fields with William Henry and visited the Hockings in the evenings, spent a great deal of time with Gray at Bosigran. For the fourth (but not last) time in her marriage, she sought the consolation of another man.

The main evidence for Frieda's affair with Gray (apart from her history of infidelity and her concurrent difficulties with Lawrence) is the *roman à clef Bid Me to Live* (1960), by Hilda Doolittle. Frigid and bisexual, H.D. was Pound's fiancée, Aldington's wife (from 1913), Lawrence's friend and Freud's patient. Lawrence met her in 1914; and after his expulsion from Cornwall he and Frieda lived in her flat at 44 Mecklenburgh Square from October 20 until December 1, 1917. The novel suggests that Frieda encouraged Lawrence to have an affair with H.D., when he visited London in April 1917, so she herself would be free to sleep with Gray while he was absent. In fact, H.D. had an affair with Gray, who in 1919 became the father of her child. Lawrence, who disliked Gray and was angry that H.D. had left Aldington, told her: "I hope never to see you again." In a passage omitted from a published letter of June 1926, Lawrence expressed sympathy for Aldington and confirmed his disapproval of H.D. and Gray: "Arabella [Dorothy Yorke] had been living with Richard [Aldington] ever since we knew them [in 1914]. They want to get married but Hilda Aldington is a cat, and won't give them a divorce, though she herself went off with Gray."[12] Though the details of these sexual entanglements are vague, it is likely that Frieda had an affair with Gray.

IV

In Cornwall, Lawrence explored the possibilities—theoretical, symbolic, fictional and perhaps even actual—of male love. He was more interested in William Henry Hocking than in Esther Andrews, and his relations with the Cornish farmer can best be understood in the context of his attitude to homosexuality.

F. D. Chambers, a member of Jessie's family, said, "Lawrence was a woman in a man's skin and only women had much sympathy with him. He disliked male company from his earliest years." Lawrence himself believed his intrinsic sexual nature was dual and not entirely male, that his male and female elements were in conflict, not in balance. "Every man comprises male and female in his being," he wrote in "Study of Thomas Hardy," "the male always struggling for predominance."[13]

Lawrence's affinity for women was a considerable advantage to a creative writer. But his inner conflicts led him to see sexual relationships in terms of struggle rather than harmony, and to a fear of merging rather than a confidence in union. His novels describe a number of cruel and mutually destructive conflicts between men and women as well as an alternative search for satisfying relationships between men.

Lawrence's conflicting attitudes about the possibility of male love are expressed throughout his works, where his life erupts into art, and most specifically in four overt homosexual scenes: the swimming idyll in *The White Peacock*, the wrestling match in *Women in Love*, the nursing episode in *Aaron's Rod* and the initiation ceremony in *The Plumed Serpent*. Each of these scenes was inspired by Lawrence's intimate friendships with men: *The White Peacock* by Alan Chambers, *Women in Love* and *Aaron's Rod* by Middleton Murry, *The Plumed Serpent* by a fantasy about the submission of the men he loved.

These scenes portray a recurrent theme in the novels and share three common characteristics. First, they are modeled on the biblical friendship of David and Jonathan and not, as in works by practicing and more reticent homosexuals, on the Greek ideal of male love (Lawrence has other uses for *The Symposium*). The clearest example of Lawrence's version of this male friendship appears in his play about his namesake, *David* (1926), where the two heroes (again based on Lawrence and Murry) swear a divine and eternal agreement that binds them together, body and soul:

> JONATHAN: We have sworn a covenant, is it not between us? Wilt thou not swear with me, that our souls shall be as brothers, closer even than the blood? O David, my heart hath no peace save all be well between thy soul and mine, and thy blood and mine.
>
> DAVID: As the Lord liveth, the soul of Jonathan is dearer to me than a brother's. — O brother, if I were but come out of this pass, and we might live before the Lord, together!

Second, in each of these scenes homosexuality is seen as an alternative to heterosexual love and invariably occurs after a frustrating humiliation with a woman. The failure of the male to achieve dominance over the female, especially the female will, leads directly to a triumph of the female element within man. Third, Lawrence's inner struggle with repressed homosexual desires results in an ambiguity of presentation, for none of his heroes can commit himself completely to homosexuality although it is portrayed as a "higher" form of sexual love that transcends the merely physical. Though this ambiguity has an artistic function — it deflects attention from the realistic to the symbolic aspects of the scene — it also exposes Lawrence's moral and personal doubts about the corruption and sterility of sexual relations with men. Homosexual lovers like the Prussian officer, Banford in "The Fox," Winifred Inger in *The Rainbow* and Loerke in *Women in Love* are portrayed as perverse and corrupt. Yet the homosexuality in the four fictional scenes is described as nourishing and life-enhancing. For Lawrence, men were less emotional and possessive than women, and their bodies were more beautiful.

In letters and conversations with friends, in his nonfiction, especially his essays on Whitman, and in his poetry, Lawrence attempted to clarify his ambiguous position and to resolve the conflict between homosexual feelings and a moral sense of guilt. In December 1913, while living with Frieda in Fiascherino, he wrote to the man of letters Henry Savage:

> I should like to know why nearly every man that approaches greatness tends to homosexuality, whether he admits it or not: so that he loves the *body* of a man better than the body of a woman — as

> I believe the Greeks did, sculptors and all, by far. . . . He can always
> get satisfaction from a man, but it is the hardest thing in life to get
> one's soul and body satisfied from a woman, so that one is free for
> oneself. And one is kept by all tradition and instinct from loving
> men, or a man.[14]

Lawrence, himself "approaching greatness" as a writer, characteristically uses ambiguous language ("tends to homosexuality, whether he
admits it or not"). The first sentence asserts as a general rule that *every*
young man in his position finds a man's body more attractive than a
woman's; the second affirms the superior satisfaction of male love, which
allows rather than inhibits individual freedom; and the third places
tradition *with* instinct as obstacles to male love, although in his case
instinct opposed tradition.

In a letter of March 1920 Lawrence seems to have found an answer in
Whitman, who, with his English disciple Edward Carpenter, was the
greatest public apologist for homosexuality. For Lawrence could say,
like Gerard Manley Hopkins, "I always knew in my heart Walt Whitman's mind to be more like my own than any other man's living."

> You are a great admirer of Whitman. So am I. But I find in his
> Calamus, and Comrades one of the clues to a real solution—the new
> adjustment. I believe in what he calls "manly love," the real im-
> plicit reliance of one man on another: as sacred a union as mar-
> riage: only it must be deeper, more ultimate than emotion and
> personality, cool separateness and yet the ultimate reliance.

These ideas are close to the ones he had expressed in *Women in Love,*
completed a few years earlier, in 1916. Because Lawrence valued individuality and felt sexual relations with women threatened his physical
and spiritual integrity, male love seemed a "real solution" to the struggle
for dominance and conflict of wills in heterosexual love, and comradeship seemed justified as being more profound than and just as sacred as
marriage. In *Studies in Classic American Literature,* he could not shed
his repugnance for the physical aspects of inversion. But Lawrence
writes of Whitman, a practicing homosexual:

> He found, as all men find, that you can't really merge in a woman,
> though you may go a long way. You can't manage the last bit. So you
> have to give it up, and try elsewhere if you *insist* on merging. . . .

> For the great mergers, woman at last becomes inadequate. For
> those who love to extremes. Woman is inadequate for the last
> merging. So the next step is the merging of man-for-man love. And
> this is on the brink of death. It slides over into death. David and
> Jonathan. And the death of Jonathan.[15]

The paradox of Whitman's real solution is that the merging of men goes
beyond women—but into a sexual dead end, into masturbation and
sterility.

During his stay in New Mexico in 1922–23, Lawrence again tried to
clarify this problem:

> All my life I have wanted friendship with a man—real friendship,
> in my sense of what I mean by that word. What is this sense? Do I
> want friendliness? I should like to see anybody being "friendly"
> with me. Intellectual equals? Or rather equals in being non-
> intellectual? I see your joke. Not something homosexual, surely?
> Indeed you have misunderstood me—besides this term is so imbed-
> ded in its own period. I do not belong to a world where that word
> has meaning. Comradeship perhaps? No, not that—too much love
> about it—no, not even in the Calamus sense, not comradeship—not
> manly love. Then what Nietzsche describes—the friend in whom
> the world standeth complete, a capsule of the good—the creating
> friend, who hath always a complete world to bestow? Well, in a way.
> That means in my words, choose as your friend the man who has
> centre.

Though Lawrence rejected intimacy, equality and Wildean inversion, he
still longed for homosexuality. "I do believe in friendship," he told
Katherine Mansfield. "I believe tremendously in friendship between
man and man, a pledging of men to each other inviolably [like David
and Jonathan]. But I have never met or formed such a friendship."[16]
Though his inexperience with homosexuality allowed him to idealize it,
his deep residue of puritanical repression as well as certain intellectual
scruples inhibited the physical culmination of this kind of friendship.
Like most artists, Lawrence had many homosexual friends: Marsh
and Forster in England; the novelist Norman Douglas, the bookseller
Pino Orioli, the friend of Wilde, Reggie Turner, and the confidence man
Maurice Magnus in Florence; the poet Witter Bynner, his lover Spud
Johnson, and Mabel's follower Clarence Thompson in New Mexico. De-

spite his predisposition toward inversion and his numerous homosexual friends, he wrote (as we have seen) a manic and minatory letter to David Garnett about the horrible and unclean black-beetle corruption of Keynes, Birrell and Grant. In a letter to Kot of April 1915, shortly after Garnett's visit to Greatham, he emphasized the symbol of corruption in *Women in Love:* "I like David, but Birrell I have come to detest. These horrible little frowsty [smelly] people, men lovers of men, they give me such a sense of corruption, almost putrescence, that I dream of beetles. It is abominable." There was always a vast, unbridgeable difference for Lawrence between the ideal concept and the actual practice of homosexuality.

The insect metaphor recurs in Lawrence's wartime letters and connects the corruption of inverts to soldiers, to his enemies and to all mankind. His fascinating letter to Ottoline of April 1915, which quotes Dostoyevsky's *The Brothers Karamazov* and compares soldiers to obscenely mounted insects, suggests his ambivalent desire for and fear of homosexuality, and anticipates his hysterical reaction when forced to spread his buttocks and expose his anus during his medical examinations:

> Yesterday, at Worthing [in Sussex], there were many soldiers. Can I ever tell you how ugly they were: "to insects—sensual lust." I like sensual lust—but insectwise, no—it is obscene. I like men to be beasts—but insects—one insect mounted on another—oh God! The soldiers are like that—they remind me of lice or bugs.[17]

As his views grew even more extreme during the war years, and as the destruction of men continued in wartime Europe, Lawrence expressed a godlike or demonic desire to exterminate mankind. Human beings did not seem to justify their existence or deserve to live. He wanted to cleanse the earth of evil and start a new world: "Oh, if one could but have a great box of insect powder, and shake it over them, in the heavens, and exterminate them. Only to clear and cleanse and purify the beautiful earth, to give room for some truth and pure living. . . . To learn plainly to hate mankind, to detest the spawning human-being, that is the only cleanliness now." In *Women in Love,* Birkin expresses this essential idea in a milder form when he longs for clean nature to replace human evil: "don't you find it a beautiful clean thought, a world empty of people, just uninterrupted grass, and a hare sitting up?" Lawrence's namesake and contemporary, T. E. Lawrence, expressed a similar idea but in far more misanthropic terms: "had the world been mine I'd have left out animal life upon it." Revolted by sex, he imagined a Nietzschean elimination and eugenic replacement of ordinary, unclean human beings: "What is wanted is a new master species—birth control for us, to end the human race in 50 years—and then a clear field for some cleaner mammal."[18]

Though Lawrence condemned inversion, he would not, because of the homosexual element within himself, allow the validity and fulfillment of heterosexual love, at least as it was practiced by middle- or upper-class Anglo-Saxons. In February 1915 he told Bertrand Russell that sex among the English was not a mystical as well as physical union, based on a profound knowledge of women, but merely disguised perversion: "That is what nearly *all* English people now do. When a man takes a woman, he is *merely* repeating a known reaction upon himself, not seeking a new reaction, a discovery. And this is like self-abuse or masturbation. The ordinary Englishman of the educated class goes to a woman now to masturbate himself. . . . When this condition arrives, there is always Sodomy."

In a late, bitter poem in *Pansies,* he projected his own fears about homosexuality onto the egoistic class he had come to hate:

Ronald you know, is like most Englishmen,
by instinct he's a sodomist
but he's frightened to know it
so he takes it out on women.

Oh come! said I. That Don Juan of a Ronald!—
Exactly, she said. Don Juan was another of them, in love with
    himself
and taking it out on women—

Even that isn't sodomitical, said I
But if a man is in love with himself, isn't that the meanest form
    of homosexuality? she said.[19]

V

After his disappointment with Murry, the departure of Esther Andrews and his estrangement from Frieda, Lawrence became emotionally attached to William Henry Hocking. A striking contemporary photograph of the Cornish farmer—born in 1883 and two years older than Lawrence—reveals a handsome, square-jawed fellow, holding a menacing scythe and wearing a broad-brimmed black hat, white blouse, thick patched breeches tied by a cord and high black boots. Lawrence's "Mr. W. H.," the "onlie begetter" of "Goats and Compasses," was the oldest of seven children, forced to leave school at thirteen and tied—by tradition and the war—to the land. He had a pleasant temperament, was well liked, was curious about the world and fond of reading. In 1916, dissatisfaction with his limited life and lack of prospects made him a responsive candidate for the Andean Rananim. He knew but was afraid to reveal that Lawrence was under surveillance by the neighbors and the authorities; and as Lawrence's friend he came under suspicion himself. Lawrence's expulsion from Cornwall ended their relationship. Though Lawrence wrote to him, fear and caution prevented William Henry from answering his letters. He married in 1918, when he was thirty-five, and had at least two children.[20]

Lawrence's attraction to William Henry, his attachment to the Hocking family and his joy in working with the men in the fields during the summers of 1916 and 1917 inevitably brought back memories of his youth in Eastwood and the idyllic days at Haggs Farm. He taught French to both Jessie Chambers and William Henry, and was physically drawn to both Alan Chambers and the Cornish farmer. Jessie's younger brother David Chambers said that when the young Lawrence "came into the hayfield . . . work went with an unaccustomed swing"; Lawrence (though in much poorer health in Cornwall) said work "went like steam" when he labored outdoors with the Hockings. F. D. Chambers believed Lawrence "was a woman in a man's skin"; Stanley Hocking, William Henry's brother, agreed that he was "rather effeminate. His was a feminine disposition on the whole . . . he was so tall and thin and delicate."[21]

Lawrence said that William Henry, in contrast to Murry, had "a high *sensuous* development." Lawrence praised his thoughtfulness and virility, mentioned his idealistic hopes and believed he embodied the Celtic mysteries of Cornwall: "He has thought deeply and bitterly. 'I have always dreamed,' he says, 'of a new order of life.—But I am afraid now I shall never see it'. . . . There is something manly and independent about him—and something truly *Celtic* and unknown—something non-christian, non-European, but strangely beautiful and fair in spirit, unselfish." In the suppressed Prologue to *Women in Love,* which expresses the homosexual themes more strongly than in the novel, Lawrence attributes to Birkin his own overwhelming physical desire to devour, absorb and satisfy himself on the handsome animal-like body of the Cornish type embodied in William Henry:

> There would come into a restaurant a strange Cornish type of man, with dark eyes like holes in his head, or like the eyes of a rat, and with dark, fine, rather stiff hair, and full, heavy, softly-strong limbs. Then again Birkin would feel the desire spring up in him, the desire to know this man, to have him, as it were to eat him, take the very substance of him. And watching the strange, rather furtive, rabbit-like way in which the strong, softly-built man ate, Birkin would feel the rousedness burning in his own breast, as if this were what he wanted, as if the satisfaction of his desire lay in the body of the young, strong man opposite.[22]

William Henry believed that "Lawrence was homosexual. . . . [He] used to come down to the farm and talk to him about it a lot." But according to Frieda, Lawrence did more than talk about it: he actually had, with the sensuous, uneducated and adoring William Henry, the physical relationship he had been unable to have with the repressed, intellectual and critical Middleton Murry.

Frieda told Mabel there really was "a thing" between Lawrence and William Henry that made her "dreadfully unhappy." In October–November 1917, while staying at H.D.'s flat, Frieda said: "Lawrence cared only for men, that H.D. had no idea what he was *really* like." These secondhand reports from admittedly unreliable sources would remain unconvincing unless substantiated by more persuasive evidence. But they were confirmed both by Frieda herself and by her daughter Barbara. In a letter of April 1949 to H.D.'s former husband, Richard Aldington, Frieda described Lawrence's love relations with William Henry in the same way she had described his relations with Esther Andrews: "in his bewilderment he had a passionate attachment for a cornish farmer, but of course it was a failure." And Barbara Weekley Barr, who confirmed what Frieda told Mabel, H.D. and Aldington, provides the conclusive evidence: "Yes, there was of course a kind of irregular relationship for a short time between D.H.L. and the young Hocking, which the latter may wish forgotten: his daughter spoke of it to me when I first met her in London a few years ago."[23]

VI

Lawrence wrote two overtly homosexual works while influenced by his love for William Henry: "Goats and Compasses" and the suppressed Prologue to *Women in Love*. The first work was destroyed by Lawrence; the second survived and illuminates the homosexual themes in the novel. Lawrence sometimes circulated his unpublished or unpublishable works among his friends; and two of them, Ottoline Morrell and Cecil Gray, left negative accounts of "Goats and Compasses." Their reports indicate that its turgid style may have resembled that of his wartime tract, "The Crown" (1915), and that its title probably suggested the conflict between Pan-like passion and scientific rationalism.

Ottoline usually admired Lawrence's works—unless they were satires on herself. But she said this wordy and illogical outburst expressed Lawrence's wartime rage, and attributed his bizarre ideas to Frieda: "It seems to me deplorable tosh, a volume of words, reiteration, perverted and self-contradictory. A gospel of hate and violent individualism. He attacks the will, love and sympathy. Indeed, the only thing that he doesn't revile and condemn is love between men and women. . . . I feel very depressed that he has filled himself with these 'evening' ideas. They are, I am sure, the outcome of Frieda." Gray, usually caustic about Lawrence, agreed with Ottoline about the style and suggested that Lawrence was quite sympathetic to homosexuality:

> Lawrence at his very worst: a bombastic, pseudo-mystical psycho-philosophical treatise dealing largely with homosexuality—a subject, by the way, in which Lawrence displayed a suspiciously lively interest at that time. There were two typescript copies of the book. Lawrence himself destroyed the one, while the other, which Philip [Heseltine] had in his possession, was gradually consumed by him some years later, leaf by leaf, in the discharge of a lowly but none the less highly appropriate function.

Though the disposal of the typescript seems shocking as well as unfortunate, Frieda reported that Lawrence himself used the manuscript of *Sea and Sardinia* for the same purpose at their house in Sicily in 1922. In the

"Nightmare" chapter of *Kangaroo,* Lawrence says that he destroyed the "Goats and Compasses" typescript, just after he received the order to leave Cornwall, in "a great fire of all his old manuscripts."[24] He probably feared this incriminating document might be seized by the police.

Lawrence himself suppressed the Prologue to *Women in Love,* which was not published until 1963, because of the trouble he had had with *The Rainbow.* The Prologue illuminates three aspects of the novel. It portrays the destructive relationship of Rupert Birkin (the autobiographical hero) and Hermione Roddice (based on Ottoline), which explains her potentially lethal attempt, in the novel, to crush his skull with a piece of lapis lazuli after his rejection of Hermione for Ursula. It describes the Tyrolean journey as well as the friendship, attraction and intimacy of Birkin and Gerald Crich (based partly on Murry), which clarifies Birkin's lament after Crich's snowy death in the Austrian mountains: "He should have loved me. I offered him. . . . I wanted eternal union with a man too: another kind of love." And it expresses the conflict between Birkin's love of women and his deeper — but repressed — passion for men, which illuminates Birkin's strong attraction to Crich:

> His fundamental desire was, to be able to love completely, in one and the same act: both body and soul at once, struck into a complete oneness in contact with a complete woman. . . .
>
> Although he was always drawn to women, feeling more at home with a woman than with a man, yet it was for men that he felt the hot, flushing, roused attraction which a man is supposed to feel for the other sex. . . .
>
> In his mind was a small gallery of such men: men whom he had never spoken to, but who had flashed themselves upon his senses unforgettably, men whom he apprehended intoxicatingly in his blood. . . .
>
> So he went on, month after month, year after year, divided against himself, striving for the day when the beauty of men should not be so acutely attractive to him, when the beauty of woman should move him instead.[25]

VII

Lawrence's experience with dominating and possessive women taught him to see heterosexual love as an endless struggle of clashing wills in which man either maintains a precarious dominance or is overcome by humiliating defeat. He inevitably found sexual relations more painful than pleasurable:

> The cross,
> The wheel on which our silence first is broken,
> Sex, which breaks up our integrity, our single inviolability, our
>   deep silence,
> Tearing a cry from us.[26]

Murry believed that Lawrence sought "to escape to a man from the misery of his own failure with a woman,[27] and Knud Merrild, who spent the winter of 1922–23 with the Lawrences in New Mexico, wrote:

> When he spoke of his beloved idea of starting a new life and forming a colony, he never included women. He always conceived of realizing it with men alone, in the beginning at least. . . . Only at times he added, "I suppose eventually the men shall want to take women unto themselves!". . .
>
> There is no use blinking the fact that Lawrence included the possibility of homosexuality in the scheme of modern existence, that he offered it as a tentative relief from an antagonism between the sexes, a symptom of a disease that had spread over Europe.[28]

Lawrence's marriage suffered three major crises: in Cornwall in 1916 during the composition of *Women in Love*, in New York in 1923 and in Spotorno in 1926. The plot of *Women in Love* dramatizes Lawrence's struggle with Frieda in 1916, his despair and sense of failure, and his attempt to achieve an emotional and physical bond with Murry. The novel focuses not only on the love relations of two couples—Ursula Brangwen and the school inspector Rupert Birkin (based on Frieda and Lawrence), Gudrun Brangwen and the mine owner Gerald Crich (based

on Katherine and Murry) —but also on the sexual attraction of the two
men. Ursula and Birkin, despite their problems, eventually marry.
After Gudrun becomes involved with Loerke, a corrupt bisexual artist
whom they meet in the Tyrolean Alps, Gerald fulfills his death wish by
committing suicide in that icy wasteland. The novel ends as Birkin
laments the death of his friend.

Birkin is threatened not only by the bullying, clutching, powerful
will of his first mistress, Hermione Roddice, but also by Ursula's asser-
tive "lust for possession, a greed for self-importance in love." The violent
hostility between men and women erupts throughout the novel: in Hermione's relations with Birkin and Gudrun's with Gerald. Even when
Birkin and Ursula's love is relatively successful, Birkin fears the loss of
his sexual identity in submergence and "horrible fusion":

> On the whole, he hated sex, it was such a limitation. It was sex that
> turned a man into a broken half of a couple, the woman into the
> other broken half. And he wanted to be single in himself, the woman
> single in herself. He wanted sex to revert to the level of the other
> appetites, to be regarded as a functional process, not as a
> fulfilment. . . .
> Why should we consider ourselves, men and women, as broken
> fragments of one whole? . . .
> In the old age, before sex was, we were mixed, each one a
> mixture. The process of singling into individuality resulted in the
> great polarisation of sex. The womanly drew to one side, the manly
> to the other. But the separation was imperfect even then.[29]

This is Lawrence's interpretation of the Platonic theory of physical
love. In *The Symposium,* Aristophanes explains love by supposing that
"the primeval man ["In the old age, before sex was"] was round, his back
and sides forming a circle; and he had four hands and four feet, one head
with two faces," and was subsequently divided in two. After the division,
the two parts of man, each desiring the other half, came together and
threw their arms about one another, eager to grow into one. Plato's
theory is appealing because it explains the attraction of the sexes and
shows that the union of masculine and feminine complements is a return
to an original wholeness. But in Lawrence's version the polarized broken
half, frightened of merging and domination, wants to remain single and
never experiences the Platonic fulfillment with women. Birkin professes
to believe that a man and a woman ought to achieve "a pure balance of
single beings," but Ursula, like Frieda, recognizes that Birkin really

wants a woman submissive to his will. When she refuses to submit, Birkin rejects the torments of marriage and attempts to forge a "bond of pure trust and love with the other man," Gerald Crich.

Right after his confession that he hates sex, Birkin realizes what was apparent in the Prologue: that "he had been loving Gerald all along, and all along denying it." So he proposes a *Blutbrüderschaft* to Crich, who, doomed and limited, denies his animal self and begs to "leave it till I understand it better." Just as Birkin's primeval proposal comes from dissatisfaction with Ursula, so, as Murry wrote in an illuminating comment on this scene, Lawrence's "relation with Frieda left room, and perhaps need, for a relation with a man of something of the kind and quality of my relation with Katherine; and he wanted this relation with me. It was possible only if it left my relation with Katherine intact." But Lawrence threatened Murry's relation with Katherine. He wanted to control his body and dominate his mind:

> So at this critical moment, I began to withdraw towards Katherine. And as he felt my withdrawal, Lawrence became more urgent to bind me with him. He talked of the blood-brotherhood between us, and hinted at the need of some inviolable sacrament between us—some pre-Christian blood-rite in keeping with the primeval [Cornish] rocks about us. . . .
>
> No doubt the queer wrestling match between the two [Birkin and Crich] is more or less what he meant by the "blood-sacrament" between us.

Murry, as we have seen, could not respond to Lawrence's offer of a mystical relation, based on blood-consciousness, in which the dark sources of his being would come alive. His biographer noted that a homosexual incident in his childhood made him react with "repugnance to anything of this sort." Frieda later told an inquisitive correspondent: "Murry and he had no 'love affair.' But Lawrence did not disbelieve in homosexuality"—which suggests that Lawrence would have wanted an affair if Murry had acquiesced. Referring, toward the end of her life, to the Cornwall period, Frieda told Murry that she had rescued Lawrence from his homosexual impulses, that Lawrence wanted from Murry a sensual connection that would go beyond ordinary friendship and transcend the merely physical: "I think the homosexuality in him was a short phase out of [the war] misery—I fought him and won—and that he wanted a deeper thing from you."[30]

After Birkin's marriage proposal to Ursula ends in a comic fiasco, he again turns to Crich for consolation and makes another proposal: "let us strip, and do it properly." Birkin's confession that he used to wrestle with a Japanese is his metaphorical revelation of homosexual experience. He explains that [Japanese] "repel and attract, both. They are very repulsive when they are cold. . . . But when they are hot and roused, there is a definite attraction." The two men begin to struggle together, and the scene, which begins with an energetic renewal, ends with an orgasmic swoon:

> They seemed to drive their white flesh deeper and deeper against each other, as if they would break into a oneness. . . . It was as if Birkin's whole physical intelligence interpenetrated into Gerald's body, as if his fine, sublimated energy entered into the flesh of the fuller man, like some potency. . . . Now and again came a sharp gasp of breath, or a sound like a sigh, then the rapid thudding of movement on the thickly-carpeted floor, then the strange sound of flesh escaping under flesh. . . . The physical junction of two bodies clinched into oneness. . . .
>
> At length Gerald lay back inert on the carpet, his breast rising in great slow panting, whilst Birkin kneeled over him, almost unconscious. Birkin was much more exhausted. He caught little, short breaths, he could scarcely breathe any more. The earth seemed to tilt and sway, and a complete darkness was coming over his mind. . . . The world was sliding, everything was sliding off into the darkness. And he was sliding, endlessly, endlessly away.

Birkin and Crich, by penetrating and entering the flesh and experiencing mutual excitement, achieve a Platonic oneness that they fail to achieve in heterosexual love. Birkin tells Crich, "you are beautiful," and Crich confesses: "I don't believe I've ever felt as much *love* for a woman, as I have for you—not *love*."[31] This scene—with its emphasis on physical intelligence, sublimated energy and healthy bodies—is Lawrence's imaginative construction, his glamorized dream, of the ecstasy of physical contact.

Despite their complete satisfaction, neither Crich nor Birkin can commit himself entirely to homosexuality. Crich chooses a love with Gudrun that is doomed to disaster by his mechanical will; Birkin again demands Ursula's total submission, while she accuses him of perverse and obscene sex with Hermione. The sexual solution to Birkin's conflicting desires for male friendship and woman's love, as far as the novel admits of one, comes in "Excurse."

Lawrence presents the sexual transfiguration of Birkin and Ursula in biblical terms in order to disguise and ennoble unacceptable acts, and to include them in a tradition of revealed truth. At the country inn, Birkin and Ursula reach the fundamental

> source of the deepest life-force, the darkest, deepest, strangest life-source of the human body, at the back and base of the loins. . . . From the smitten rock of the man's body, from the strange marvellous flanks and thighs, deeper, further in mystery than the phallic source, came the floods of ineffable darkness and ineffable riches.

In this crucial passage Lawrence compares sodomy (the back and base of the loins, beyond the phallic source) to the Sons of God taking the fair daughters of men (Genesis 6:2) and to Moses smiting the rock in Horeb with his rod so "there shall come water out of it, that the people may drink" (Exodus 17:6), and equates anal intercourse with the deepest life source. Later in the novel Ursula remembers the freedom achieved through her degrading, bestial and shameful experiences with Birkin. By contrast, Lawrence describes the heterosexual intercourse of Gudrun and Crich as "the terrible frictional violence of death." Lawrence had come a very long way, imaginatively, in eight years, from his virginal statement of 1908: "I have kissed dozens of girls—on the cheek—never on the mouth—I could not."

By denying Ursula's female integrity and sexuality, and by penetrating her anus, Birkin uses Ursula as a sexual substitute for Crich and does to the woman what he wants to do to the man. But Birkin's own actions belie his assertion that if Crich "pledged himself with the man he would later be able to pledge himself with the woman: not merely in legal marriage, but in absolute mystic marriage,"[32] for Birkin never actually abandons homosexuality. The novel enacts a curious accommodation between Lawrence's homosexual yearnings and his belief that his marriage with Frieda would endure. His heightened language both disguises and reveals the homosexual themes, and expresses his characteristic desire to extend the boundaries of what was socially, or even imaginatively, permissible.

VIII

In *Women in Love,* the emotional and sexual lives of the characters are crippled by the effects of the war. Its central theme is the decadence of modern English society, dominated by industrial machinery and destructive technology. Like Yeats in "The Second Coming," Pound in "Hugh Selwyn Mauberley" and Eliot in *The Waste Land,* Lawrence, in *Women in Love,* recognized that the rational tradition of thought in the West had ended in a war that had destroyed the values of civilized society.

Though Lawrence raged against the war in his yet unpublished novel, he was—despite recurrent illnesses and isolation in Cornwall—still subject to its malign influence. The passing of the Second Military Service Bill in May 1916 made conscription compulsory for all able-bodied men between the ages of eighteen and forty-one. It cancelled all forms of exemption and recalled for examination all men who had previously been rejected.

The austerity, poverty and emotional anxiety of the war years—as well as the harsh, damp English winters—brought back the serious illnesses that had plagued Lawrence before he moved to Italy with Frieda. He had influenza in March 1915, and in November Philip Heseltine remarked: "He is, I am afraid, rather far gone with consumption." He was seriously ill in January and February 1916 while living in north Cornwall. Dr. Maitland Radford, the son of Lawrence's friend Dollie Radford, examined him in February and—according to Lawrence, who almost never mentioned his real illness—said "the stress on the nerves sets up a referred inflammation in all the internal linings" of the lungs.[33] At the end of April 1917 he collapsed in London with a combination of flu and diarrhea. In February 1919 Lawrence fell victim to the epidemic of Spanish influenza then ravaging postwar Europe; and in March the doctor feared he might not survive.

Despite his medical history and recent illnesses, Lawrence was ordered to three different army medical examinations, in June 1916, June 1917 and September 1918. As the military authorities became increasingly desperate for new conscripts, the medical boards lowered the standards of acceptable health. The first two examinations took place at

Bodmin, in Cornwall. Lawrence found none of the intimate camaraderie among the soldiers that he had sensed in his youth among the miners. In 1916 he spent the night in the barracks, like a criminal, and felt degraded by the loss of individuality and the merging with the mass of Cornishmen. But the doctors said he had tuberculosis and gave him a complete exemption. At the second examination at Bodmin, he was classified C-3—unfit for military service—urged to find another way to serve his country and left alone for another fifteen months.

The third examination, also described in "Nightmare," was far more traumatic. Lawrence found the barracks at Derby "full of an indescribable tone of jeering, gibing shamelessness." The "poor, bare, forked animal" was ashamed of his ridiculously thin legs and feared they would cut off his beard. When the sneering, sceptical doctors handled his genitals and peered up his anus, his residual puritanism and repressed homosexuality led to a manic rage and biblical malediction: "Because they had handled his private parts, and looked into them, their eyes should burst and their hands should wither and their hearts should rot. So he cursed them in his blood, with an unremitting curse."[34]

It is difficult to sympathize with his solipsistic self-pity when thousands of men were being sacrificed for a mile of mud, and Europe from the Channel to the Alps and beyond was suffering slaughter and devastation that would last for four long years. Yet Lawrence's independent, almost solitary stand against the monstrous machinery of war and his lucid, penetrating vision of the rotten spirit of mankind was courageous and impressive. He was one of the very few, sane people who realized, at that time, how futile and horrible the war was, how long it would last, how profound would be the consequences, how radically it would destroy the culture of Europe.

Lawrence told the doctors he had had pneumonia three times (while working at Haywood's in 1901, teaching in Croydon in 1911 and possibly when seriously ill in north Cornwall in 1916) and been threatened with consumption. They classified him as C-2—fit for military service—but the war ended two months later, before he could be conscripted.

IX

The author of *The Prussian Officer* (1914) was suspected of being an English spy in Germany and a German spy in England. And he was persecuted under two different British governments. *The Rainbow* was suppressed in 1915 when Herbert Asquith was prime minister, and Lawrence was expelled from Cornwall in 1917 during the administration of Lloyd George. After March 1915, he was placed under police surveillance for the duration of the war. David Garnett, for example, had "to interview three different sets of detectives after Lawrence and Frieda had stayed late one night to dinner [early] in 1915."[35]

Lawrence knew that he was suspect, but behaved recklessly rather than cautiously in Cornwall. To his neighbors, he seemed healthy and worked long hours in the fields, yet had not been called for military service. He wrote books, wore a beard and had an obviously German wife. Frieda wore Bavarian dress and boasted of her baronial background. His strange sexual entanglements were also incriminating. His friends—Katherine and Murry, Esther Andrews and Robert Mountsier—lived together but were not married. The close and constant scrutiny by the neighbors (who were encouraged by the authorities to do their patriotic duty) would certainly have revealed Lawrence's apparent involvement with Esther and Frieda's with Gray. And Lawrence proselytized for homosexuality while maintaining an unusually warm interest in the innocent native son William Henry.

Lawrence did not seem to realize the terrible impression he made on the local folk. He was outspoken in his opposition to the war and exposed to the Cornish farmers the patriotic "lies" in the newspapers. He sang German and Hebridean folk songs (many of which came from Percy Buck's *Oxford Song Book*, 1916), and both seemed equally suspicious to the neighbors. Richard Aldington believed that his rudeness to the local police and soldiers, who had to investigate his behavior, was a significant factor in his expulsion. According to Cecil Gray, the Cornish, "under a disarmingly affable exterior, conceal a deep hatred of the intruder, the *foreigner* (as any visitor is regarded by them)."[36]

Almost everything the Lawrences did seemed to arouse official distrust. Even he realized this when Frieda, intoxicated one day by the air and the sun, jumped and ran and allowed her long white scarf to blow in the wind. "'Stop it, stop it, you fool, you fool!' Lawrence cried. 'Can't you see that they'll think you are signalling to the enemy!'" On another occasion coastguards suddenly pounced on them from behind a hedge, accused them of hiding a camera and were disappointed when it turned out to be a loaf of bread. More seriously, when the Lawrences were spending a weekend with Gray, the police knocked on the door, said Gray had a light burning in a window facing the sea and later severely fined him £20. When the Lawrences were away from home, the day before their expulsion, the police ransacked their house.

External conditions also contributed to their difficulties. The war was going badly in the fall of 1917. There were huge casualties but no significant gains in Flanders. Austria was successful on the Italian front. And Russia withdrew from the war following the Bolshevik Revolution. Just after the Lawrences moved into the coastal village, German submarines began sinking English ships. The suspicious Cornishmen, hitherto isolated from the war and aroused by Lawrence's peculiar behavior, believed: "The Germans are getting ready to invade us. They have their spies out.... They could have a secret code for signalling to the German submarines and giving the position of our ships." In December 1917, two months after he had been forced to leave the village, Lawrence told Cynthia Asquith that their enemies in Higher Tregerthen made certain that their persecution continued in London: "It is quite evident that somebody from Cornwall—somebody we don't know, probably—is writing to these various [government] departments—and we are followed everywhere by the persecution."[37]

Lawrence and Frieda did not attend church (itself suspicious in that region) and enraged the vicar by blasphemously mocking one of the fundamental concepts of Christianity. Lawrence told Stanley Hocking, who sang in the choir: "You sing that you believe in the resurrection of the body and life everlasting, and any intelligent being knows that dead bodies do not rise again. It would be a terrible thing if they did! What would happen if all the graves were to open and the dead came trooping back? Wouldn't it be horrible? Their own friends and family wouldn't want to see them. What would we do with them?" Lawrence's principal enemies were the vicar of Zennor, David Rechab Vaughan,[38] and his daughter, who distrusted and hated him and "may well have contacted the police in London."

Lawrence was suspected not only of signaling the German submarines with white scarves and night lights, but also of supplying them with secret stores of food and petrol. Frieda reported that on the morning after their house had been ransacked,

> there appeared a captain, two detectives, and my friend the policeman. The captain read us a paper that we must leave the county of Cornwall in three days. Lawrence, who lost his temper so easily, was quite calm.
>
> "And what is the reason," he asked.
>
> "You know better than I do," answered the captain.
>
> "I don't know," said Lawrence.
>
> Then the two awful detectives went through all our cupboards, clothes, beds, etc., while I, like a fool, burst into a rage.

As soon as he reached London and settled in H.D.'s flat, Lawrence—who had no idea of how provocative he had been—appealed to Cynthia Asquith to help him find out why he was being persecuted. Like Josef K. in Kafka's *The Trial*, Lawrence knew the punishment but could not discover the crime. Though the loyal Cynthia agreed to assist Lawrence, she felt the order was a reasonable precaution in time of war. She noted in her journal that the expulsion had a bad effect on Lawrence's desperate finances and delicate health, and intensified his wartime misanthropy:

> I promised to do what I could in the matter, but doubt whether it will be much—after all, the woman *is* a German and [the banning order] doesn't seem unreasonable....
>
> It is hard for him. In Cornwall he lived so cheaply and healthily, and he will have to go on paying for the house there. His health doesn't allow of his living in London and all the money he has in the world is the *prospect* of eighteen pounds for the publication of some poems [*Look! We Have Come Through!*, published November 1917]....
>
> He described his hatreds for people and said there were certainly not more than eight people in the whole world with whom he could bear to spend two hours—all the rest made him ill.[39]

Richard Aldington, more sympathetic to his friend, diminished Lawrence's responsibility and emphasized the consequences of his expulsion: "The 'intellectuals' let him down as badly as anybody. From 1916 to about 1921 Lawrence felt, and indeed almost was, a pariah." The expulsion inevitably reinforced Lawrence's authoritarian ideas. "No man who has really consciously lived through this [persecution]," he wrote in

Kangaroo, "can believe again absolutely in democracy."[40] In April 1919, a year and a half after the banning order and five months after the Armistice, Lawrence was informed that the Cornwall order against him had been revoked.

X

The police surveillance, which followed the Lawrences from London to Cornwall and back to London, continued at Chapel Farm Cottage, near Newbury, in Berkshire. They lived there from December 1917 until May 1918, and returned (after spending a year in a cottage rented by Ada in Derbyshire) from April to July and from August to September 1919. David Garnett had been questioned and Robert Mountsier arrested because of their association with Lawrence. His sister Emily reported that the butcher in Berkshire would not supply them with meat because Frieda was German. Frieda recalled: "Suspicion was ever present. Even when we were gathering blackberries in the nearby hedges a policeman popped up behind a bush and wanted to know who we were."[41] When the Lawrences were not in residence, the police frequently questioned the neighbors about their behavior.

During their stay in Berkshire, the Lawrences were near neighbors of two spinsters—Cecily Lambert and her cousin Violet Monk—who became the models for March and Banford in "The Fox" (1922). Lambert, who had an observant eye, vividly described the puritanism, abusiveness, conflict and servility that characterized Lawrence's relations with Frieda:

> I can see her now on that evening, sitting back on a low arm chair, purring away like a lazy cat and shewing a great deal of plump leg above the knee encased in calico bloomers probably made by D.H. himself. She was not permitted to wear silk or dainties. . . . He appeared to love an opportunity to humiliate her—whether from jealousy or extreme exasperation one could never tell. I was only surprised that she listened to his abuse or obeyed his orders. . . .
>
> They occupied two bedrooms . . . and when I suggested to Frieda that it would ease things if they shared one, her reply was that she did not wish to be too much married. . . .
>
> [Yet she remembered] Frieda saying . . . how welcome a child of D.H.L. would be. . . .

[Frieda] started her visit to us by succumbing to bed ... and expected to be waited on. Most of this fell to D.H. ... I can see D.H. in a raging temper, carrying a brimming chamber pot down to the front garden and emptying it over our flower beds.

Lambert also clarified the background of "The Fox"—the character of her neurasthenic, dominant and manly cousin, her brother's attitude toward the cousin, the hunt of the fox and the felling of the tree—which provided the reality that Lawrence transformed into fiction:

Miss Violet Monk, my cousin, who was helping on the farm, was not at all socially inclined and tended to be belligerent, resenting the intrusion of strangers. ... An unfortunate love affair had broken up her health, and before going to the Farm she had suffered a severe nervous breakdown. ... On the Farm she dressed in Land Girl uniform [jodhpurs, high boots, man's shirt and tie]. ... Towards me she was possessive and jealous which caused friction. ... We were desperately poor, being complete novices at the farm game. ... At this time also a brother of mine was home on sick leave from the East Africa War Zone. ... But far from having any amorous feelings toward the lady (my cousin), he actively disliked her. ... I believe between them they did mutilate a tree. ... I do remember we were infested with foxes. ... [They borrowed a gun but] never succeeded in making a kill.

"The Fox" is closely connected to Lawrence's ideas about homosexuality. In his bitter poem "Ego-Bound Women," he exclaims that lesbianism is the "most appalling" of the passions: "a frenzy of tortured possession/and a million frenzies of tortured jealousy."[42] In the story, two inexperienced lesbian women, Banford and March, are running a farm just after the war—and making a bad job of it. Their cattle and hens are unable to reproduce, and a demonic fox carries off the fowl. March, the more masculine but less dominant woman, tries to shoot the fox but cannot do so when the animal stares her down in mystical eye-to-eye combat: "she lowered her eyes and suddenly saw the fox. He was looking up at her. His chin was pressed down, and his eyes were looking up. They met her eyes. And he knew her. She was spell-bound—she knew he knew her. So he looked into her eyes, and her soul failed her."

Into this ménage comes a spellbinding, foxy-looking Cornish soldier, Henry Grenfel, who had enlisted in Canada and has just arrived from

Salonika. He declares, "there wants a man about the place," moves in and makes himself useful. The fox, meanwhile, continues to dominate March's unconscious, to represent and reveal her sexual desires. The night Henry arrives she dreams that the fox "bit her wrist, and at the same instant, as she drew back, the fox, turning round to bound away, whisked his [phallic] brush across her face, and it seemed his brush was on fire, for it seared and burned her mouth with a great pain."

Henry then decides to marry March and to recapture the vital spirit of the farm, which had once belonged to his grandfather. He enters into a subtle battle both to wrest the male role from March and to win her from Banford. Twice he is sexually aroused by hearing March comfort the jealous, sobbing Banford and by realizing he is winning the struggle against her. He kills the fox, absorbs its feral power and hangs the pelt upside down. Like the scene with the rabbit Bismarck in *Women in Love,* the lovers come together and experience excitement through the sexual power of the animal: "She passed her hand down [its belly]. And his wonderful black-glinted brush was full and frictional, wonderful. She passed her hand down this also, and quivered. Time after time she took the full fur of that thick tail between her hand, and passed her hand slowly downwards." Later that day Henry nails the fox, as if crucified, to a board.

When Henry departs to complete his military service, March writes that she cannot marry him after all. So he gets leave, returns to the farm and fells a dead tree—the symbol of the lesbian relationship—so that it falls on Banford and kills her. Henry marries March, but their sexual struggle continues. He wants her to give herself completely to him and become submerged in him. When she refuses to do so—for she is still bound by the memory of her lesbian connection to Banford—Henry bitterly thinks "that he ought to have left her. He ought never to have killed Banford. He should have left Banford and March to kill one another."[43] The memory of the dead lover seems more powerful than that of the dead fox, and has a greater effect on March than her physical ties to her husband.

XI

While living in Berkshire in February 1918—nine months before the end of the war—Lawrence told Gertler what he had previously told Russell: "I feel that nothing but a quite bloody, merciless, almost anarchistic revolution will be any good for this country, a fearful chaos of smashing up." On Armistice Day, November 11, 1918, Lawrence's enemy Lloyd George expressed the banal, naive and mindless sentiments that seemed appropriate to the occasion and had no more basis in reality than the rabid patriotism that since 1914 had been used to justify the war: "I hope we may say that thus, this fateful morning, came an end to all wars." That evening Lawrence went to a party given by the barrister Montague Shearman. As the guests were celebrating the beginning of the long-hoped-for peace, Lawrence, who had opposed the war from the very start, assumed his prophetic voice and accurately predicted the terrible fate that would inevitably overwhelm Europe: "I suppose you think the war is over and that we shall go back to the kind of world you lived in before it. But the war isn't over. The hate and evil is greater now than ever. Very soon war will break out again and overwhelm you."[44]

CHAPTER FOURTEEN

Capri and Taormina, 1919–1922

LAWRENCE was finally allowed to leave England in November 1919. He was critical of his country, determined to be an expatriate, eager to return to Italy. He had lived there cheaply and contentedly before the war, and it seemed to provide a freer atmosphere and a secure refuge after his humiliating persecutions at home. (During the last decade of his life he made only four trips to England, and spent less than five months in his own country.) Lawrence did not return to the familiar places on Lake Garda or the Gulf of Spezia in northern Italy. After three weeks in Florence, ten days in the Abruzzi and two months in Capri, he sought a more traditional way of life, first in Sicily and then on a ten-day visit in January 1921 to the primitive island of Sardinia.

Italy provided the stimulus of travel and of new friendships as well as the isolation necessary for writing. Released from the restrictions of England, he soon regained his imaginative powers and poured out a series of novels, stories, poems, travel books, memoirs and translations. His impressions of Italy, just before the Fascists seized power, and his encounters with Maurice Magnus, Norman Douglas, Compton Mackenzie and Earl and Achsah Brewster were immediately expressed in his books.

I

Lawrence spent his first two nights near Turin, as the guest of Walter Becker, a wealthy shipowner who had founded a hospital for British soldiers during the war and had recently been knighted. Lawrence described the Beckers as parvenus, living in great luxury but "rather nice people really," and clashed with his host about essential values: "The old knight and I had a sincere half-mocking argument, he for security and bank-balance and power, I for naked liberty. . . . We hated each other—but with respect."

Lawrence spent the next three weeks in the alien but fascinating homosexual ambience of Florence, where he looked up Norman Douglas (who had been assistant editor of the *English Review* under Ford), and met Maurice Magnus and Reggie Turner. In Florence he saw the sleazy side of expatriate life: the pederasts, inverts and frauds who had fled the puritanism of England and lived in a tolerant, inexpensive world as rentiers, writers and con men. Lawrence himself, though scrupulously honest, also lived on the fringe of respectable society and liked the contrast between their homosexual hedonism and his own commitment to work.

The handsome, leonine Douglas—a well-bred cad—was a lover of Italy and a lover of boys. But he was also a linguist and a diplomat, who had begun a promising career in St. Petersburg; a strange alloy of savage and scientist, who wrote specialized monographs on zoology and geology; a traveler and travel writer; the author of *South Wind* (1917), a hedonistic and amoral novel of Capri; and, with Pino Orioli in Florence, the successful publisher of his own works. Douglas' deepest conviction: "Do what you want to do, and be damned to everybody else," and his frank acknowledgment of the pleasures of homosexual pursuit appealed to Lawrence's desire for "naked liberty," though not to his sense of morality. Douglas' life was haphazardly ordered by the pragmatic necessity to "hop it" across the frontier whenever his liaisons became dangerous. "Burn your boats!" he declared. "This has ever been my system in times of stress."[1]

Lawrence had asked Douglas, who "never left [him] in the lurch," to find him a room in a cheerful hotel. He met Douglas at the Pensione

Balestri in the Piazza Mentana, where he was paying ten lire (about twenty-two pence) per day. The grandiose but courtly Douglas "was decidedly shabby and a gentleman, with his wicked red face and tufted eyebrows." Douglas never opened the windows of his dreadful room, and the queer smell was something new to Lawrence: "But I didn't care. One had got away from the war." When they had eaten dinner, Douglas made the waiter measure the remaining half liter of wine and deduct it from the bill.

Lawrence's sketch of Douglas in his Introduction to Magnus' *Memoirs* complements his satiric portrait of him as James Argyle in *Aaron's Rod* (1922). Argyle admits: "I'm a shady bird, in all senses of the word," and asks, "what is life but a search for a friend?" Though attractive in his day, "now his face was all red and softened and inflamed, his eyes had gone small and wicked under his bushy grey brows." He is extremely cynical about men's claim to heterosexuality and women's to purity. While in his cups he insists: "Impotence set up the praise of chastity.... They can't do it, and so they make a virtue of not doing it." Aaron's attitude toward Argyle foreshadows Lawrence's view of Magnus: "He had never met a man like Argyle before—and he could not help being charmed."[2]

Lawrence was clearly intrigued by the paradoxical Maurice Magnus, whom he met through Norman Douglas. Magnus resembled a common actor-manager down on his luck and was "just the kind of man [he] had never met": "He looked a man of about forty, spruce and youngish in his deportment, very pink-faced, and very clean, very natty, very alert ... little smart man of the shabby world.... His voice was precise and a little mincing, and it had an odd high squeak." Lawrence portrayed Magnus' fussy and finicky character through his possessions as well as his person, for he acted like a little pontiff, surrounded by essences, pomades and powders in cut-glass silver-topped bottles. He wore a blue silk dressing gown, had affected manners and speech, insisted on his status as a gentleman and was a rabid woman-hater.

Lawrence could never quite make up his mind about the elusive Magnus. Born in 1876, the illegitimate grandson of a German Kaiser, he was a Catholic convert who had been Isadora Duncan's manager, had edited the *Roman Review,* which began and ended in 1914, had translated Barbier's libretto for *Tales of Hoffmann* into English and Gordon Craig's pamphlet *The Art of the Theatre* into German. He joined the French Foreign Legion during the war and deserted after it. Lawrence felt that Magnus was common yet sensitive as a woman, a bounder yet delicate and tender, pompous and superior yet unusually intelligent.

The son of Gordon Craig—the actor, designer and producer—provided a vivid account of Magnus' background, snobbism, name dropping, accent, manners and lack of scruples in Berlin in 1905–06:

He was born in New York; his mother was separated by only one generation from the royal blood of the Hohenzollerns. . . . He had an insatiable desire to collect celebrities, the more illustrious the better, so he had left New York and come to his motherland, where, although he could not boast openly of his connection with the Kaiser, he could at least feel that he was *near* the Court. He knew how to conjure with great names, for he actually believed in their power and the spells they cast. . . .

Magnus was charming, dignified, and intelligent. . . . Although he was American, he spoke English without a trace of an accent. He seemed to know everyone in Berlin. Craig was fascinated by his manner, for he appeared to regard all things as possible— "only one has to know the right people." . . .

At the house of Mendelssohn, the banker and music lover, they paused for a moment in the hall; in a flash, Magnus looked over the visiting cards that were lying on a magnificent silver salver on the hall table, and selecting a couple, pocketed them. Craig looked on, amazed. Said Magnus: "You can never tell—might be useful one day—names mean such a lot, you know."

Reggie Turner, also illegitimate, was the son of one of the Lawsons who owned the London *Daily Chronicle*. A wealthy Jewish homosexual and a loyal friend of Oscar Wilde, he wrote minor novels and belonged to the English set in Florence. He was "large-nosed and small-headed, with eyelids that blinked accidentally as well as deliberately. He was also excellent company, given to mimicry of sermons and the repartee that Wilde favored."[3] Turner was the model for Algy Constable in *Aaron's Rod* and Magnus for Mr. May in *The Lost Girl* (1920).

After three weeks with his rakish friends in Florence, Lawrence spent ten days in Picinisco, in the wild, mountainous Abruzzi in central Italy. He went there to do a friend a favor and to explore an unknown region. In July 1919, four months before leaving England, he had spent a weekend at Pangbourne in Berkshire as the guest of Rosalind Baynes, whom he had first met through David Garnett in 1912. Garnett rapturously described her as "a lovely creature—russeted apple in face, delicate and critical in spirit," whose "beauty was cool and flower-like."

Rosalind was the daughter of the sculptor Sir Hamo Thorneycroft, whose former model, Orazio Cervi, had returned to his rude home in Picinisco. Rosalind, estranged from her husband, was planning to take her children to live there. Lawrence, himself seeking an isolated and inexpensive place to live, offered to visit the village and tell Rosalind if it was suitable.

As usual, the approach to the village was difficult, the domestic comforts minimal. As he explained to Rosalind: "Rome being vile, we came on here. It is a bit staggeringly primitive. You cross a great stony river bed, then an icy river on a plank, then climb unfootable paths, while the ass struggles behind with your luggage. The house contains a rather cave-like kitchen downstairs—the other rooms are a wine-press and a wine-storing place and corn bin: upstairs are three bedrooms, and a semi-barn for maize and cobs: beds and bare floor."[4]

But Picinisco was too remote, icy and mountainous—even for Lawrence. After ten torturous days he moved to the milder climate of Capri and took a small flat above Morgano's restaurant, looking across the bay to Naples. "The depravity of Tiberius, or the salacity of Suetonius," writes Anthony Burgess, "had left its mark on an island all sodomy, lesbianism, scandal, and cosmopolitan artiness." The natural beauty as well as the scandal had attracted many writers. In the nineteenth and early twentieth centuries August von Platen, Hans Christian Andersen, Ivan Turgenev, Tristan Corbière, Joseph Conrad, Axel Munthe, Gerhart Hauptmann, Norman Douglas, Maxim Gorky, Booth Tarkington, Ivan Bunin and Rainer Maria Rilke had visited and often written about the island. Conrad, who visited Capri in 1905, said the air was too stimulating for consumptives and complained of the hot winds, violent contrasts and sexual scandals: "Too much ozone they say: too exciting and that's why no lung patients are allowed to come here. . . . This place here, this climate, this sirocco, this transmontana, these flat roofs, these sheer rocks, this blue sea—are impossible. . . . The scandals of Capri—atrocious, unspeakable, amusing, scandals international, cosmopolitan and biblical."[5]

Lawrence met three wealthy and respectable friends who were living on Capri: Mary Cannan, Compton Mackenzie and Francis Brett Young. Mackenzie, whom he had known since 1914, was a good-looking and extremely successful Scottish novelist. He was published by Martin Secker, who brought out Lawrence's works in England from 1918. The author of *Carnival* (1912) and *Sinister Street* (1913), Mackenzie owned two luxurious houses on the island. Lawrence noted the novelist's wealth and objected to his precious style: "He seems quite rich and does himself quite well, and makes a sort of aesthetic figure . . . walking in a pale blue suit to match his eyes, and a large woman's brown velour hat to match his hair." Lawrence, who had been nauseated by Maynard Keynes' sleeping garments, told Mackenzie, "I hate those damn silk pajamas you wear," and satirized his materialism and patronizing manner in "The Man Who Loved Islands" (1927). Mackenzie retaliated, after Lawrence's death, with waspish revelations about Lawrence's unsatisfactory orgasms and Frieda's puritanical undergarments, which contrasted with his own silky style. " 'But why won't Lorenzo let me have lace on my underclothes, Mackenzie?' she once asked. 'Look at what he makes me wear.' And pulling up her skirt above her knees she displayed the austere calico drawers on which Lawrence insisted."6

Francis Brett Young—a doctor, prolific minor novelist and friend of Mackenzie—had served in the East African campaign and described his experiences in *Marching on Tanga* (1917). Lawrence complained that Young wearied him and likened him to "a fretful and pragmatical and dictatorial infant: always uttering final and ex cathedra judgments in the tone of a petulant little boy."7 After two months on Capri, Lawrence felt intensely irritated by the spiteful scandal of the English residents. At the end of February 1920 he left Capri for Taormina, at the foot of Mount Etna in Sicily, where he lived for eighteen months during 1920–22.

II

While living on Capri—angered by the atmosphere of luxury, hedonism and malice—Lawrence provoked a bitter quarrel with Katherine Mansfield and Middleton Murry. Ever since the failure of their communal life in Cornwall, Lawrence had resented Katherine's rejection of his attempts at quadrilateral intimacy, her unwillingness to allow his participation in her emotional life with Murry, her caustic ridicule of Lawrence's most cherished ideas and her hatred of his violent quarrels with Frieda. Now he criticized the defects of her character, envied her literary success and was irrationally enraged by her attitude toward her potentially fatal disease. This ugly episode can only be understood in the context of his fluctuating relations with Katherine and Murry since their unhappy departure from Cornwall in June 1916.

Katherine had shown her friendship for Lawrence by defending him in the Café Royal in Piccadilly in September 1916. She was sitting with Kot and Gertler, when she heard the novelist Michael Arlen and an Indian called Suhrawardy, both of whom had been friendly with Lawrence, maliciously reading and publicly ridiculing his new volume of poems, *Amores.* Though Katherine was still feeling hostile to Lawrence, she was nevertheless loyal to his work and outraged that it should be mocked by the *canaille.* So she snatched the volume from their hands, bore it triumphantly out of the café and rescued her friend from their scorn—exactly as Gudrun does in "Gudrun at the Pompadour," a chapter that was added to *Women in Love* just before Lawrence completed it in October 1916. Katherine also used this incident in her story "Marriage à la Mode" (1921). When William, whose wife has abandoned him for a corrupt set of bohemian admirers, returns to the city, he sends his wife a love letter to set things right. But Isabel reads it aloud to her friends, who mock the letter and become hysterical with laughter.

Katherine's gallant gesture at the Café Royal did not prevent relations with Lawrence from deteriorating once again, perhaps because Lawrence had found out more about her reasons for leaving Cornwall. In November he wrote angrily to Kot: "I have done with the Murries, both, for ever—so help me God." But Lawrence, fascinated by the Murrys, could neither break with them nor forget them. In letters of December 1916 and January 1917 to Murry's friend Gordon Campbell, he dismissed Murry as a clever but not original or creative writer, and synthesized in a sentence his complex mixture of attraction and repulsion: "Murry fills me with loathing: still, somewhere, I am fond of him"— fond of his good looks, lively mind and (sometimes) sympathetic character.

In February 1917 Lawrence voiced his first direct, if ambiguous, criticism of Katherine and told Kot, who was her staunchest friend and must have resented Lawrence's attack: "Only for poor Katherine and her lies I feel rather sorry. They are such self-responsible lies." And he later repeated this charge, but much more vehemently, in a letter to Mary Cannan: "The *Nation* said K's book [*Bliss*] was the best short story book that could be or had been written. Spit on her for me when you see her, she's a liar out and out. . . . Vermin, the pair of 'em. And beware."[8]

Katherine had published only a few stories between 1916 and 1920, and *Bliss* was her first book in nine years and her first important collection. Lawrence's *Rainbow* had been suppressed in 1915 and *Women in Love* (though completed in 1916) was not published until 1920. He thought Katherine had only a minor talent, and was angry to see his own novels attacked and rejected while her stories received enthusiastic reviews in the leading weeklies.

Lawrence's criticism of Katherine's work suggests what he meant by her lies. He told Catherine Carswell that "the author of *Prelude* would come in time to find a certain essential falseness so closely entwined with the charm in her literary fabric that she would herself condemn even the charm and write nothing further until she had disentangled herself from the falseness." In *Women in Love,* Lawrence also condemned Gudrun's criticism of Birkin as a lie: "Gudrun would draw two lines under him and cross him out like an account that is settled. There he was, summed up, paid for, settled, done with. And it was such a lie. This finality of Gudrun's, this dispatching of people and things in a sentence, it was all such a lie."[9] Lawrence thought that the defects in Katherine's character—her ruthless mockery, subtle malevolence, cynicism and negativism—were related to the faults of her work; that the idealization of her unhappy childhood and the sentimental portrayal of "innocent" heroines in her stories falsified her art.

Despite Lawrence's criticism in February 1917, he was certainly not done with Katherine forever. He still believed in her fundamental integrity. Their friendship revived once again, in April and August 1917, when Katherine, using one of Kot's favorite phrases, "real people," referred to Lawrence in the past tense and suggested she liked him better at a distance than in person: "Lawrence was one of the few real people— one cannot help loving the memory of him." And she told Murry: "I have read a long letter from Lawrence. He has begun to write to me again and quite in the old way. . . . I am so fond of him for many things. I cannot shut my heart against him and I never shall."

But in early October 1918—when Lawrence, desperate for money, had the unrealistic notion of obtaining an office job—the prospect of Lawrence appearing in the flesh reminded Katherine of his overwhelming personality during their disturbing proximity in Higher Tregerthen. Writing to Ottoline, she caustically characterized Lawrence in his prophetic mood:

The Lawrences are coming to live in London indefinitely. This really horrifies me. I am sure they will turn up here. . . . I have a terrible idea [Lawrence and Murry] will fight—and it will be hideous and lacerating. L. has come to look for work in an office— which of course he'll *never* do for more than three days. But altogether, I feel they are better as many miles away as there *are*

1. (ABOVE) During hard times, when laid off or on strike, the
miners would scavenge for usable coal among the slag heaps.
In the background, the refuse burned like the pits of hell.
2. (BELOW) In this family portrait of c.1893, Lydia Lawrence looks much older and frailer than her vigorous,
bearded husband, Arthur. Ada, seated on the far left, gapes
at the unfamiliar camera while Emily tilts toward the center.
Young Lawrence, in an Eton collar, is surrounded by the
good-looking George and by the slightly simian Ernest.

3. Jessie Chambers, 1909. "She has black hair, and wonderful eyes, big and very dark, and very vulnerable."

4. Louie Burrows, c.1910. "She is a glorious girl: about as tall as I, straight and strong as a caryatid ...swarthy and ruddy as a pomegranate."

5. Alice Dax and her daughter, c.1916: "a strange, brilliant and very peculiar-looking woman, with large hands and feet, and wispy, disordered blond hair."

6. Lawrence, Nottingham, 1908, when he graduated from the university and was about to start teaching in Croydon. "His face was rough, with rough-hewn features, like the common people's; but his eyes under the deep brows were full of life."

7. (ABOVE) Ford
Madox Ford, c.1909,
with gaping mouth,
rabbit teeth and a
ragged lemon
moustache.
8. (RIGHT) Edward
Garnett, c.1908. The
bespectacled Edward,
with hair and chin
parted in the middle,
wears a heavy wool
suit and a dreamy
expression.

9. (LEFT) Frieda Weekley with her son, Montague, 1901: a tall, strikingly handsome, golden-haired woman with a magnificent figure.   10. (BELOW) Lady Cynthia Asquith, c.1915. "Her face was lovely, fair, with a soft exotic white complexion and delicate pink cheeks. Her hair was soft and heavy, of a lovely pallid gold colour, ash-blond."

11. (ABOVE) Lawrence, Katherine Mansfield, Frieda and Middleton Murry, London, July 13, 1914, the Lawrences' wedding day. The group looks unusually somber, despite their summer apparel, and only Murry (books under his arm) attempts a smile. 12. (RIGHT) Catherine Carswell, c.1914: a strikingly attractive but unhappy woman who aroused Lawrence's sympathy and inspired his fiction.

13. S. S. Koteliansky, c.1910.
Kot "looked like some
Assyrian king . . . with an
impressive hooked Semitic
nose, a fine head of coarse
black curly hair, massive
features and very dark eyes."

14. Mary Cannan, c.1910:
"hair dyed a reddish-brown,
thin mouth and fine features
beautifully made up."

15. Lady Ottoline Morrell, 1903. "Her long, pale face, that she carried lifted up, somewhat in the Rossetti fashion, seemed almost drugged, as if a strange mass of thoughts coiled in the darkness within her."

16. Dorothy Brett, self-portrait, 1922. "The colour still was high in her young, delicate cheeks, but her odd, bright, round, dark-grey eyes were fearless above her fear."

17. Percy Lucas, center, seated on the ground, posing with a cricket team before the Great War. "He was tall and slim and agile, like an English archer with his long supple legs and fine movements."

18. Lawrence, c.1917. The bearded prophet, in a defiant mood.

19. (ABOVE) Mansfield and
Murry, 1918. Katherine's gaunt
expression and deep-set eyes
reveal the illness that killed
her in 1923. Murry seems
nervous and concerned.
20. (RIGHT) Robert Mountsier,
1918, in a Red Cross uniform.

21. (LEFT) Esther Andrews,
c.1910. In this stage photo, she
wears bobbed hair, a seductive
expression and a kimono-like
dress. To Lawrence, she
represented "a new world of
knowledge and being."

22. (BELOW) William Henry
Hocking: a handsome, square-
jawed fellow, holding a
menacing scythe and wearing a
broad-brimmed black hat,
white blouse, thick patched
breeches tied by a cord and
high black boots.

23. Maurice Magnus, 1915. "He looked a man of about forty, spruce and youngish in his deportment, very pink-faced, and very clean, very natty, very alert."

24. Achsah, Harwood and Earl Brewster, Capri, c.1921: gentle American expatriate painters, with a precocious daughter, looking uncommonly severe.

25. (ABOVE) Frieda and Lawrence, Chapala, Mexico, 1923. Frieda, though heavy, is still attractive. Lawrence is lined and lean.   26. (BELOW) Mabel and Tony Luhan, New Mexico. Mabel "had a small, square, determined body, bright grey eyes, and a soft melodious voice." Tony was a bold-featured, bronze-skinned, black-braided Taos Pueblo Indian.

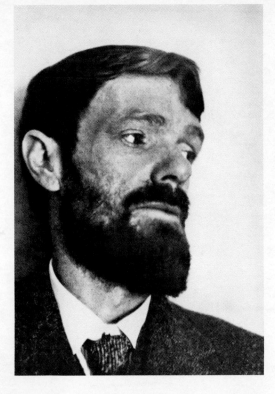

27. (LEFT) Lawrence, Mexico
City, November 1924,
photograph by Edward
Weston. "His face was pale;
his hands long, narrow,
capable; his eyes clear-seeing
and blue; his brown hair and
red beard glowing like flames
from the intensity of his life."
28. (BELOW) Aldous Huxley
and Lawrence, seated on the
ground and smiling, at the
Villa Mirenda, near Florence,
October 1926.

29. Lawrence, in Florence, 1928, photograph by Robert Davis. "The beard, tending to Van Dyke, was soft and silken. His hair was ample and glossy, falling around a splendid forehead . . . . The eyes were clear as crystal, with a touch of brilliancy."

30. Richard Aldington, with cigarette and natty sweater, 1929, the year he published his finest novel, *Death of a Hero*.

31. (RIGHT) Lawrence, *Fauns and Nymphs*, 1928. A bearded, bronze-skinned Lawrence, with a lecherous grimace, embraces a large-breasted Frieda figure.
32. (BELOW) Lawrence, "The Ship of Death," 1929, the clearly written manuscript of one of his greatest poems.

Already our bodies are fallen, bruised, badly bruised,
already our souls are oozing through the exit
of the cruel bruise.

Already the dark and endless ocean of the end
is washing in through the breaches of our wounds,
already the flood is upon us.

Ye build your ship of death, your little ark
and furnish it with food, with little cakes, and wine
for the dark flight down oblivion.

II.
Piecemeal the body dies, and the timid soul
has her footing washed away, as the dark flood rises.

We are dying, we are dying, we are all of us dying
and nothing will stay the death-flood rising within us
and soon it will rise on the world, on the outside world.

We are dying, we are dying, piecemeal our bodies are dying,
and our strength leaves us,
and our soul cowers naked in the dark rain over the flood,
cowering in the last branches of the tree of our life.

VII.
We are dying, we are dying, so all we can do
is now to be willing to die, and to build the ship
of death to carry the soul on the longest journey.

A little ship, with oars and food
and little dishes, and all accoutrements
fitting and ready for the departing soul.

Now launch the small ship, now as the body dies
and life departs, launch out, the fragile soul
in the fragile ship of courage, the ark of faith
with its store of food and little cooking pans
and change of clothes,
upon the flood's black waste
upon the waters of the end
upon the sea of death, where still we sail
darkly, for we cannot steer, and have no port.

There is no port, there is nowhere to go
only the deepening blackness darkening still
blacker upon the soundless, ungurgling flood
darkness at one with darkness, up and down
and sideways utterly dark, so there is no direction any
more.

miles. Everytime the bell goes I hear Frieda's "*Well* Katherina—
here we are!" and I turn cold with horror. . . .

Perhaps his whole trouble is that he has not a real sense of
humour. He takes himself dreadfully seriously now-a-days; I mean
he sees himself as a symbolic figure—a prophet—the voice in the
wilderness crying "*woe*."[10]

In late October 1918, when Lawrence came down to London from the
Midlands and saw Katherine for the last time, they forgot their quarrels
and remembered their love for each other. Like Cynthia Asquith, she
referred to Lawrence in spiritual terms; and like Forster, she thought he
was at his best when responding to the natural world: "For me, at least,
the dove brooded over him too. I loved him. He was just his old merry,
rich self, laughing, describing things, giving you pictures, full of enthusiasm and joy in a future where we were all 'vagabonds.' We simply did
not talk about people. We kept to things like nuts and cowslips and fires
in woods and his black self *was* not. Oh, there is something so loveable
about him—and his eagerness, his passionate eagerness for life—that is
what one loves so."

But Lawrence persisted in comparing himself to his friends and
analyzing their defects, and kept the discussion alive in voluminous
correspondence. The following month he sent Katherine a book by Jung
and analyzed their marriages in terms of its mother-incest idea: "At
certain periods the man has a desire and a tendency to return unto the
woman, make her his goal and end, find his justification in her. In this
way he casts himself as it were into her womb, and she, the Magna Mater,
receives him with gratification. This is a kind of incest. It seems to me it
is what Jack does to you, and what repels and fascinates you. I have done
it, and now struggle [with] all my might to get out."[11] Lawrence recognized that Katherine was both repelled and fascinated by Murry's
passive dependence because he himself had some of Murry's tendencies.

In January 1919 Murry was named editor of the *Athenaeum,* a well-
established and widely read journal, which instantly made him a power
in the literary world. Though justifiably nervous about Lawrence's
vitriolic prose—for Lawrence was still furious at England and likely to
shock Murry's respectable readers—Murry loyally asked Lawrence to
contribute. He published Lawrence's first article, "Whistling of Birds."
But in March, when he rejected Lawrence's "Adolf," a charming autobiographical essay about his pet rabbit, the impoverished Lawrence
became angry and embittered about Murry's betrayal. As he told Kot: "I

heard from Murry, very editorial—he sort of 'declines with thanks' the things I did for him. He will publish one essay next week—too late to ask for it back—and that is the first and last word of mine that will ever appear in the *Athenaeum*. Good-bye Jacky, I knew thee beforehand."

In April Katherine attempted to make a joke of the quarrel and told Kot: "F[rieda] writes me that there is a 'rumpus' between me and—them, I suppose.... But I refuse to have anything to do with it. I have not the room now-a-days for rumpuses." The quarrel was between Lawrence and Murry, and Katherine had no wish to join in. In a letter to Virginia Woolf, who had been thinking of renting the house Lawrence had been forced to abandon, Katherine remembered the magic of Cornwall with fond nostalgia: "Perhaps the house itself is very imperfect in many ways but there is a ... something ... which makes one long for it. Immediately you get there—you are *free,* free as air.... I mustn't talk about it. It bewitched me."12

Writing from Derbyshire in March 1919, Lawrence also revealed that Katherine, and her illness, was on his mind. He acknowledged that he had offended her and seemed to indicate that she now meant more to him than Murry. He reaffirmed his belief that they would all be harmoniously united, said the stormy months in Cornwall had brought him *closer* to her and told her of his dream parable about her disease:

> Frieda said you were cross with me, that I *repulsed* you. I'm sure I didn't. The complication of getting Jack and you and F. and me into a square seems great—especially Jack. But you I am sure of—I was ever since Cornwall, save for Jack—and if you must go his way, and if he will *never* really come our way—well!—But things will resolve themselves.
>
> I dreamed such a vivid little dream of you last night. I dreamed you came to Cromford [near Lawrence's cottage in Derbyshire], and stayed there. You were not coming on here because you weren't well enough. You were quite clear from the consumption—quite, you told me. But there was still something that made you feel that you couldn't come up the hill here.

Katherine had her first hemorrhage in February 1918, and was warned the following October that she would die in a few years if she did not submit to the discipline of a sanatorium. In Lawrence's dream she is cured of consumption, but is not well enough to come up the hill to him. They do meet, however, go outside together to look at the brilliant sky, and are momentarily pierced and possessed by a "star that blazed for a second on one's soul." The blazing star unifies their souls in a moment that transcends the common battle of their bodies against consumption. Two weeks before Lawrence told Katherine his encouraging dream, he wrote sympathetically to Kot: "Poor Katherine—I'm afraid she is only just on the verge of existence."[13]

Nearly a year later, in February 1920, Lawrence's attitude toward Katherine suddenly shifted from sympathy to hostility. His quarrel with Murry had persisted, and in January he told him: "you are a dirty little worm, and you take the ways of a dirty little worm." He resented Murry's status and role as an editor, as he had previously resented Katherine's success with *Bliss,* and now allowed his anger with Murry to affect his attitude toward Katherine. As she became seriously sick, he irrationally blamed the patient for the disease, and sent Katherine what Murry rightly called a "monstrously" and "inhumanly" cruel letter.

When Katherine received it, she was separated from Murry, desperately unhappy in Menton, in extremely bad health, and emotionally dependent on letters from her husband and friends. On February 4 she recorded in her *Journal:* "Horrible day. I lay all day and *half* slept in this new way—hearing voices," and the following day she noted: "Couldn't work: slept again. Dreadful pain in joints. . . . Fearfully *noisy* house!" When Lawrence sent the letter, he was still smoldering about the article Murry had rejected for the *Athenaeum,* living in Capri near Compton Mackenzie and becoming entangled in the affairs of Maurice Magnus. He was very much the "black self" that Katherine so dreaded. On February 5 Lawrence wrote to Catherine Carswell: "I am very sick of Capri: it is a stewpot of semi-literary cats. . . . I can't stand this island. I shall have to risk expense and everything, and clear out: to Sicily, I think."[14] In early February, then, Katherine was extremely vulnerable and Lawrence extremely angry.

Katherine, deeply wounded and embittered about the betrayal of their friendship, complained to Murry on February 7: "Lawrence sent me a letter today. He spat in my face and threw filth at me and said: 'I loathe you. You revolt me stewing in your consumption. . . . The Italians were quite right to have nothing to do with you' and a great deal more." According to Murry, Lawrence also said: "You are a loathsome reptile—I hope you will die." On February 10 Katherine, horrified by Lawrence's saurian metaphor and by his allusion to the fact that she had recently been forced to leave a hotel in San Remo because of her disease,[15] told Murry: "I wrote to Lawrence: 'I detest you for having dragged this disgusting reptile across all that has been.' When I got his letter I *saw* a reptile, *felt* a reptile—and the desire to hit him was so dreadful that I knew if I ever met him I must go away *at once*. I could not be in the same room or house, he is somehow filthy. I never had such a feeling about a human being." Murry told Lawrence that "he had committed the unforgivable crime," and wrote to Katherine with unusual ferocity: "may God do so unto me & more also if I ever enter into any communication whatever with him. If I ever see him, no matter when or where, the first thing I shall do is to hit him as hard as I can across the mouth." But Katherine, knowing the depths of their friendship, correctly doubted Murry's resolve. At the end of March, she asked him: "Will you one day forget and forgive Lawrence—smile—give him your hand?"[16]

Lawrence's terrible letter was intimately connected with his refusal to recognize his own illness and his dream vision of Katherine "clear from the consumption." Like Katherine, Lawrence suffered the pain of disease and the threat of death. He admitted that he was seedy, sick, inflamed; had colds, coughs and bronchitis; and he defensively joked about his death. But he would never admit that he had tuberculosis—even after his near-fatal hemorrhage in Mexico in February 1925—and would rarely accept treatment for the disease (there was no cure) until he was forced to, in Bandol and Vence, at the very end of his life. Despite, or because of, his disease, he restlessly drove himself about the world and, like Katherine, would not enter a soul-destroying clinic.

In 1920 Lawrence was not, like Katherine, in the terminal phase of tuberculosis, and he never truly believed in her illness any more than he did in his own. He preferred to ignore the disease and pretend it would vanish, and his amazing vitality allowed him to do so until the last five years of his life. But by 1920 Katherine, who complained about her disease (while Lawrence remained stoical), had admitted her tuberculosis and feared she might die: "Life is—getting a new breath: nothing else counts." Lawrence felt threatened by Katherine's admission, was terrified that the same thing would happen to him (just as Katherine had been terrified by—and identified with—his "black rages"), and he irrationally lashed out at what he considered to be Katherine's weakness. She had praised his "passionate eagerness for life"; he felt she had a "death urge."[17] His savage remark about Katherine stewing in her consumption expressed his *own* fear of death, for as she had observed: "I am more like L. than anybody. We are *unthinkably* alike."

In March 1921, a year after this letter, Lawrence again refused to face the reality of Katherine's disease. He characterized her as a hypocritical

Camille and told Kot: "I hear [Murry] is—or was—on the Riviera with K.—who is doing the last gasp touch, in order to impose on people—on Mary Cannan, that is." And in November, after Murry had published a volume of soppy poems and Katherine two stories in the *Sphere* of August 1921, he wrote: "I see Murry and the long-dying blossom Katherine have put forth new literary buds. Let 'em." It is ironic that at the end of her life, after many unsuccessful medical treatments, Katherine (like Lawrence) denied her disease and pretended it was nonexistent. Neither Lawrence nor Katherine could give up freedom and endure (as she wrote) "being alone, cut off, ill with the other ill."[18] This refusal to submit to the regime of a sanatorium may have hastened their deaths.

Katherine's final judgment of Lawrence was positive: "He is the only writer living whom I really profoundly care for," she wrote Kot in July 1922. "It seems to me whatever he writes, no matter how much one may 'disagree,' is important. And after all even what one objects to is a *sign of life* in him. He is a living man." In August 1922 she also emphasized their intuitive understanding, despite some differences in their ideas: "I do not go all the way with Lawrence. His ideas of sex mean nothing to me. But I feel nearer L. than anyone else. All these months I have thought as he does about many things."[19] The influence of his beliefs is apparent in Katherine's journal and letters of 1921–22, where many of the entries sound more like Lawrence than Katherine. Though Katherine was strongly affected by Murry, her editor, A. R. Orage, and her guru, George Gurdjieff, Lawrence had the most positive influence on her ideas.

A passage from Katherine's letter to Murry in January 1922 quotes Lawrence's concept of friendship, which he felt was as solemn as marriage. Though Katherine found this idea fanatical when Lawrence had expounded it, first in Cornwall and then in a letter of November 1918, she now recognized the importance and the truth of his belief: "I remember once talking it over with Lawrence and he said 'We must swear a solemn pact of friendship. Friendship is as binding, as solemn as marriage. We take each other for life, through everything—for ever. But it's not enough to say we will do it. We must *swear.*' At the time I was impatient with him. I thought it extravagant—fanatic. But when one considers what this world is like I understand perfectly why L. (especially being L.) made such claims." In a second passage, written in December 1922, Katherine explained her mystical reaction against intellectual life in purely Lawrencean terms: "I can see no hope of escape except by learning to live in our emotional and instinctual being as well, and to balance all there."[20]

The last contact between Lawrence and Katherine took place in the spring and summer of 1922, when he traveled to Australia and New Zealand. In May he told Kot: "If you were here you would understand Katherine so much better. She is *very* Australian—or New Zealand. Wonder how she is." Katherine realized that Lawrence's rather frenetic travels resembled her own and were closely related to his disease. As she told Kot, who rarely left London, in August: "It is a pity that Lawrence is driven so far. I am sure that Western Australia will not help. The desire to travel is a great, real temptation. But does it do any good? It seems to me to correspond to the feelings of a sick man who thinks always 'if only I can get away from here I shall be better.'" That same month Katherine left Lawrence a book in her will, as a token of remembrance, forgiveness and love; and Lawrence, who had not written to her since the cruel letter of February 1920, pleased her very much by sending a postcard from Wellington with just one word: "*Ricordi*" (Memories). "Yes, I care for Lawrence," Katherine told Murry in October. "I have thought of writing to him and trying to arrange a meeting after I leave Paris—suggesting that I join them [in New Mexico] until the spring." And the following month she asked Murry: "Do you ever feel inclined to get in touch with Lawrence again, I wonder? I should very much like to know what he intends to do—how he intends to live now his *Wanderjahre* are over."[21]

But Katherine's desperate wanderings ended seven years before Lawrence's. When in February 1923 they heard of her death in Gurdjieff's Institute for the Harmonious Development of Man, Frieda recalled her beauty and wit: "It grieved us both deeply—She was such an exquisite creature and we had real fun with them." And Lawrence wrote Murry one of his most moving letters: "Yes, it is something gone out of our lives. We thought of her, I can tell you, at Wellington. Did Ottoline ever send on the card to Katherine I posted from there for her? Yes, I always knew a bond in my heart. Feel a fear where the bond is broken now. Feel as if the old moorings were breaking all. . . . [I] asked Seltzer to send you *Fantasia of the Unconscious*. I wanted Katherine to read it. She'll know, though. The dead don't die. They look on and help."[22]

Murry and Katherine played a significant role not only in *Women in Love* but also in Lawrence's satiric short stories. "The Border Line" (1924), "Jimmy and the Desperate Woman" (1924) and "The Last Laugh" (1928) concern his jealousy and posthumous revenge for Murry's affair with Frieda in 1923. "Smile" (1926) portrays Murry after the death of Katherine, who "had always wanted her own will. She had loved him, and grown obstinate, and left him, and grown wistful, or contemp-

tuous, or angry, a dozen times, and a dozen times come back to him."
They also appear in *John Thomas and Lady Jane*, the second version of
Lady Chatterley's Lover, as Jack and Olive Strangeways, who have a
stimulating but sado-masochistic marriage: "Olive was always saying
deadly things about her husband, 'the good-looking boy.' . . . She picked
up a lover [like Francis Carco] where she could. But invariably she
found him terribly unsatisfactory, and invariably she returned to her
tension with Jack. . . . A great deal of it was mutual torment! And that
was the most real thing she had in her life."

Katherine made her last appearance in Lawrence's late story "Mother
and Daughter" (1929), an allegory of her seduction by the mysticism of
George Gurdjieff. Lawrence hated Gurdjieff's ideas, blamed him for
Katherine's death and told Mabel Luhan: "I have heard enough about
that place at Fontainebleau where Katherine Mansfield died, to know it
is a rotten, false, self-conscious place of people playing a sickly stunt."[23]
Virginia Bodoin, the heroine of the story, expresses Lawrence's feelings
about Katherine's personality, her work, her relationship with Murry
and her illness. Virginia's decision to exchange her deadly existence with
her mother for a kind of death-in-life with the horrible yet attractive
suitor, Arnault, symbolizes Katherine's fatal submission to Gurdjieff.
After Katherine had died and was no longer a literary rival and disappointing friend, Lawrence became more sympathetic about her unhappy
marriage and hopeless disease.

III

Lawrence moved from Capri to Taormina in late February 1920, and
liked Sicily even more than Gargnano and Fiascherino. The triangular,
mountainous island, lying between the Ionian and Tyrrhenian seas, is
one hundred miles north of Africa. It had been, at various times in
history, invaded and settled by Phoenicians, Carthaginians, Greeks,
Romans, Byzantines, Arabs, Normans, Germans, French, Spanish and
Italians. In a rhapsodic and lyrical passage from "The Professor and the
Siren," Tomasi di Lampedusa stressed the timeless and unchanging
character of Sicily:

So we spoke about eternal Sicily, nature's Sicily; about the scent of
rosemary on the Nèbrodi hills, the taste of Melilli honey, the

waving corn seen from Enna on a windy day in May, of the solitudes around Syracuse, the gusts of scent from orange and lemon
groves pouring over Palermo, it's said, during some sunsets in
June. We talked of the enchantment of certain summer nights
within sight of Castellammare bay, where stars are mirrored in the
sleeping sea and the spirit of anyone lying back amid the lentisks is
lost in a vortex of sky, while the body is tense and alert, fearing the
approach of demons.[24]

Taormina was a lovely old town, with a mild climate, strung along the
spine of a hill overlooking the sparkling sea, a few miles below, and
dominated by a Dominican monastery. In his house, Fontana Vecchia,
named after the old fountain in the garden, Lawrence enjoyed the
sensation of being "on-the-brink," able at any moment to hop out of
Europe, across the sea to North Africa or to the ends of the earth: "We
have quite a lovely villa on the green slope high above the sea, looking
east over the blueness, with the hills and the snowy, shallow crest of
Calabria on the left across the sea, where the straits [of Messina] begin to
close in.—The ancient fountain still runs, in a sort of little cave-place
down the garden."

But Lawrence soon became critical as well as enthusiastic about the
island. In the Introduction to his translation of Giovanni Verga's novel *Mastro-don Gesualdo,* he noted the powerful distinction—as in
Eastwood—between the exhilarating landscape and the depressing
peasant life. "Sicily, the beautiful, that which goes deepest into the blood.
It is so clear, so beautiful, so like the physical beauty of the Greek. Yet the
lives of the people all seem so squalid, so pottering, so despicable: like a
crawling of beetles. And then, the moment you get outside the grey and
squalid walls of the village, how wonderful in the sun, with the land
lying apart."[25]

In the 1920s Lawrence continued the pattern of travel in Europe that
he had established before the war. He would live for about nine months in
Italy and, when the weather got hot and the country began to get on his
nerves, would go to Baden-Baden to visit Frieda's mother (her father
had died in 1915) and travel a bit in the cooler, cleaner, more orderly
atmosphere of northern Europe. While in Sicily he sometimes yearned
for the cool pine trees, green grass and wet flowers of Germany, where
the children did not beg and the life was never sordid or degrading.

Just after he arrived in Taormina, in March 1920, Lawrence met a
young South African painter, Jan Juta. The straight-backed, blue-eyed

son of a successful attorney general who had served in Cecil Rhodes' cabinet, Juta had studied at the Slade School in London and was then at the British School in Rome. In *Sea and Sardinia*, which Juta illustrated with rather stodgy woodcuts, Lawrence described him as "very tall and alert and elegant, looking as if he expected us to appear out of the air for his convenience." Juta, who had been brought up in great luxury, found Fontana Vecchia "very stark." He called Lawrence "D.H." and said the restless and rootless novelist "did not belong anywhere, really." Soon after their meeting, Juta painted a powerful portrait of the intense, bold-featured, red-bearded Lawrence.

In April 1920 Lawrence visited the Honourable Alexander Nelson Hood—a descendant of Admiral Horatio Nelson and honored as Duca di Brontë in Sicily—at his feudal estate at Maniaci, in the mountains beyond Etna. Lawrence found it a "rather wonderful place" and—more impressed by his host's title than by the conditions around him—had a "jolly time" at tea with the Duca. But the Italian novelist Carlo Levi, making the same contrast that Lawrence had made about Sicily, reported that even after World War II Maniaci offered "a spectacle of the utmost peasant misery, unexpected in this paradisal stretch of country.... The struggle for land is fiercer than ever: one of the many anachronistic examples of the survival of a vanished world of feudalism ... and of the stubborn attempts of the peasants to exist as human beings.... They feel wretched and abandoned, surrounded by hostile powers and maneuverings."[26] Lawrence saw that the peasants were in a desperate state, but he did not think the Duca was in any way responsible.

IV

Lawrence, like most writers of his generation, came to political awareness after 1914. But he was never concerned with social justice for its own sake. His political ideas in the three novels of power—*Aaron's Rod*, *Kangaroo* and *The Plumed Serpent*—influenced by the war in Europe, his persecution in England and his direct experience with the rise of Fascism in Italy, focused on the question of how a mass society should be organized and governed.

After the war Italy had grave problems: a huge national debt, rising inflation, high unemployment, economic collapse, a mass of dissatisfied veterans. These conditions caused serious riots, and in 1919 there were many Communist risings and counter-revolutionary reprisals. In September 1919 Gabriele D'Annunzio captured Fiume, which had been awarded to Yugoslavia by the Paris Peace Conference, and was driven out by the Italian navy, which bombarded the Adriatic city in December 1920. The harvest failed in 1920, and agrarian strikes continued throughout the year.

During 1920–22 a civil war raged in Italy between the Fascists and the Socialists; three hundred of the former and three thousand of the latter were killed in riots. After a no-confidence vote, the nation had no government for several weeks in July 1922. When a general strike was declared the following month, the Fascists aligned themselves with the police and public opinion, which called for authoritarian rule. The successive governments—weak, confused, paralyzed—could not control the economic chaos or the civil war, and took no action when the Fascists mobilized their cohorts. Mussolini's March on Rome in October 1922 was neither a revolution nor a *coup d'état*. Denis Mack Smith writes that it was actually "a comfortable train ride, followed by a petty demonstration, and all in response to an express invitation from the monarch," Victor Emmanuel III.

Mussolini, born two years before Lawrence, in 1883, and named after the Mexican revolutionary Benito Juárez, had emigrated to Switzerland in 1902 to avoid the draft—like the exiled workers described in *Twilight in Italy*. Mussolini, whose supporters were particularly brutal in Tuscany, believed that a violent minority insurrection could achieve authoritarian rule. "Under the pretense of saving the country from bolshevism, the fascists were thus able to attack governmental authority and create anarchic conditions which would make people long for authoritarian government."

Fascism claimed to be a movement, not a doctrine; its program was always changing and inconsistent. An article in the *Enciclopedia italiana* of 1931 vaguely proclaimed: "The fascist conception of the state is all embracing, and outside of the state no human or spiritual values can exist, let alone be desirable." Despite or perhaps because of this, Mussolini, who had only seven percent of the deputies in November 1922, gained sixty-five percent of the votes in the last free election, in April 1924. He was supported by such notable Italians as D'Annunzio, Pirandello, Marinetti, Puccini, Marconi and Croce (who later recanted), and by Englishmen like Churchill and Shaw. The dictatorship—which became increasingly tasteless, inefficient and corrupt—was absolute by January 1925, and by 1926 the anti-Fascist movement had disappeared. Mack Smith concludes: "The success of Fascism in 1919–22 was due less to any interior logic or merit of its own than to the vacuum left by the failure of other parties."

Lawrence lived in Italy from November 1919, when he left England, until February 1922, when he sailed for Ceylon; and he remained outside Italy for three and a half years. Thus, he was there during the postwar breakdown of government authority and the civil war between Socialists and Fascists, when there was a real need for strong rule. But he was away during the March on Rome (October 1922), the brutal consolidation of Fascist power (1922–24) and the murder of the Socialist deputy Giacomo Matteotti (June 1924). By the time he returned, in November 1925, the opposition had been destroyed, the dictatorship was absolute and civil order had been restored.

Lawrence's letters from postwar Italy reflect his fear of violence (particularly disturbing to a foreign resident who desires stability and is not especially concerned with the kind of government that provides it), and mention the prospect of revolution and the need for absolute authority. The threat of revolution prompted him to restate the anti-democratic ideas he had first formulated during the war: "I don't believe either in liberty or democracy. I believe in actual, sacred, inspired authority: divine right of natural kings: I believe in the divine right of natural aristocracy, the right, the sacred duty to wield undisputed authority."[27] But Lawrence was still vague about precisely who the natural kings were and how they would rule. The opposition of the aristocracy and the masses, the emphasis on unity, leaders, heroism, will, responsibility, authority, rule and power, frequently recur in the works written in postwar Italy: *Fantasia of the Unconscious* and *Aaron's Rod*.

V

On January 3, 1921, Lawrence and Frieda moved from a cold spell in Sicily to a much colder climate in Sardinia, where they spent ten days. They got up at dawn, took a long train ride along the coast to Palermo, sailed to Cagliari on the southern tip of Sardinia, and traveled north through the poor, mountainous country, by train and bus, to Terranova on the northeast coast. They then sailed from Sardinia to Civitavecchia, near Rome, and completed the circle by taking the train south to Taormina.

Only the powerful compulsion to travel, to go anywhere, enabled Lawrence to endure the tedious vicissitudes of Sardinia. Unlike most of his predecessors in the travel-writing tradition, who romanticized and glorified their experience, Lawrence was frank about the torments of his trip and his own self-created discomfort. Economic necessity determined his mode of travel. He could not afford luxury—or even comfort—and had to accept crude transport and lodging. As soon as he had devoured the good English bacon and tea he had brought from Taormina, his food became horrible.

Lawrence had unusual and irrational motives for traveling to Sardinia. He took Ulysses as his model and wanted "to be free of all the hemmed-in life—the horror of human tension, the absolute insanity of machine persistence." He hoped a change of place would lead to a change of mind. He had a prewar nostalgia for a lost past and was attracted to a remote place—free of cultural associations—which he could penetrate in a "fascinating act of self-discovery—back, back down the old ways of time." Sardinia, which (Lawrence claimed) "has no history, no date, no race, no offering," lay outside the circuit of civilization. There the strange, sinister and diverse spirit of the place still prevailed against the grey, mechanical sameness of modern life.

Lawrence also wanted to escape from the intensely irritating Sicilians, whom he lumped with the Italians. In *Sea and Sardinia,* they are portrayed as shamelessly intimate, physically all over one another, infatuated with ill-mannered children, vain, mercenary, prying, ignorant, insolent, indiscreet, callous, restless, slovenly and extortionate. The Sardinians provided a welcome contrast: "There was a certain pleasant, natural robustness of spirit, and something of a feudal free-and-easiness"—without constraint or presumption.[28] The solitary, self-contained men did not idealize their women, and were courteous, hospitable and unselfconscious.

Though Lawrence was pleased with the people, he was misinformed about conditions on the island and disappointed when the coarse reality failed to match his fascinating expectations. In Sicily, Messina was dismal and horrible; Palermo windy and desolate. The ship was late, the cabin smelly, the food disgusting. Trapani, which looked so lovely from the distance, was filthy and crude. Cagliari, in Sardinia, was "rather bare, rather stark, rather cold and yellow," with a hideous cathedral that "oozed out baroque and sausagey." The southern sea plain was malarial; Mandas freezing cold, with nothing to do: "one goes to bed when it's dark, like a chicken." The waiter in Sorgono, a dreary hole, was disgustingly dirty and outraged Lawrence by his maculate shirt breast. The proud inhabitants gathered in groups to relieve themselves in the shit-filled streets.

By the time Lawrence got to Nuoro, where, of course, there was nothing to see, he began to make a virtue of necessity: "sights are an irritating bore. Thank heaven there isn't a bit of Perugino or anything Pisan in the place: that I know of. Happy is the town that has nothing to show. What a lot of stunts and affectations it saves!" But it was also an affectation for Lawrence to pretend that he was a complete philistine. As he continued northward, he found Orosei a dilapidated, godforsaken hell; Siniscola "just a narrow, crude, stony place, hot in the sun, cold in the shade." Even Civitavecchia, on the Italian mainland, was scrubby and desolate.

Lawrence portrayed himself as critical, impatient, irascible; and Frieda, the "queen-bee" dislodged from her hive and accompanied by an ineffectual drone, as foolish, irrational, officious. They traveled *déclassé*, were furious that the Italians rejoiced when conveying bad news, were besieged by tourist touts and parasites. They were often cold, hungry and acutely uncomfortable, but were accused of being mercenary exploiters.

Sea and Sardinia is an essay in the psychology of travel, in which the traveler is a victim. His suffering validates his experience and adds a heroic element to the pestiferous journey. When Lawrence returned to Taormina he told Rosalind Baynes: "We went to Sardinia—it was an exciting little trip—but one couldn't live there—one would be weary-dreary."[29]

VI

While stopping briefly in Capri en route to Baden-Baden in April 1921, Lawrence met two American expatriate painters, Earl and Achsah Brewster. With Aldous Huxley, they became his closest friends in the 1920s. Earl was born in Ohio in 1878, briefly attended Oberlin College, studied painting in Cleveland and New York, and visited Sicily with his

grandmother in 1908, at the time of the Messina earthquake. The poet
Vachel Lindsay introduced Earl to Achsah (a biblical name, from
Joshua 15:16). Born in 1878, she grew up in New Haven and graduated
from Smith College in 1902. They married in 1910, went immediately to
Sicily and, by chance, inhabited Fontana Vecchia ten years before Law-
rence arrived there. As restless as Lawrence, they also lived in Paris,
Portofino, San Filippo (near Rome), Ravello and Florence, where they
worked in an Italian hospital during the war. After the war, they lived in
Athens, Sorrento and Capri.

The Brewsters had no gift for languages and spoke Italian and
French badly; Earl would shout to make himself understood. Achsah
had a small income; Earl worried about money all his life but never
spoke openly about it. They managed to live by occasionally selling their
paintings and by gifts from their families. A maiden aunt helped pay the
school fees of their daughter, Harwood; after Lawrence had urged the
Brewsters to break their close ties and send her away to school, she
became a student at Dartington Hall in Devon in 1929. Earl had been
interested in Theosophy since the age of nineteen. They became Bud-
dhists, studied Pali scriptures and lived in Ceylon, where Lawrence
visited them in 1922.[30] Earl published a life of Buddha in 1926. The
following year he took a walking tour with Lawrence through the
Etruscan towns of central Italy, and in a shop window in Grosseto saw a
toy rooster coming out of an egg, which suggested the title for Lawrence's novella *The Escaped Cock*. The Brewsters were philosophically
inclined, ethereal, gentle, formal, rather old-fashioned; and they were
deeply devoted to Lawrence. They moved to India in 1935, and remained
there until the end of their lives.

Brett described Earl as small, with "gray hair, almost white, a sharp,
pointed nose, and dark, dark eyes with a strange hidden look." Lawrence
liked to poke fun at Earl's vegetarianism and Yoga exercises, "which
make him hold his breath till his brain goes silly." He mentioned their
straitened circumstances, and mildly criticized their rather idle and
self-indulgent way of life: "People who don't work and who live in
comfortable hotels, shouldn't have money problems." Lawrence, by contrast, was always austere and anti-materialistic. "I don't want to own a
house," he maintained, "nor land, nor a motor-car, nor shares in anything. I don't want a fortune—not even an assured income. . . . There is
deep inside one a revolt against the fixed thing, fixed society, fixed
money, fixed homes, even fixed love."[31]

Though Lawrence was fond of the Brewsters, he could not resist satirizing them in "Things" (1928). In this story, a New England Buddhist expatriate couple with a comfortable income live in France and Italy, collect art "things" and become burdened by their material possessions. They return to America, store their things and hate life there. So they go back to Europe and find they hate that life as well. Finally, the husband accepts an academic position in Cleveland, where he can house and exhibit the things that have dominated and destroyed his character and very existence.

The Brewsters, calm and philosophical, were not (like most friends who had been satirized by Lawrence) seriously upset. The story, in fact, was not a true portrait of them. Lawrence used the Brewsters as expatriate types and then invented the details of their life. Their only possessions were boxes of books (which they liked to read aloud to each other), they did not have the means to collect furniture and antiques, and they always lived in furnished houses. They never stored their things or paid to view them while in storage. Lawrence, an impulsive man and writer, felt he could honestly criticize close friends. The Brewsters accepted this and the story never threatened their friendship with Lawrence, which continued to the end of his life.[32]

VII

It became more difficult for Lawrence, while living in Italy, traveling in Europe and writing prolifically, to manage his increasingly complicated business affairs with publishers and editors. Yet in January of 1920, the year Robert Mountsier began to act as his American agent, he severed relations with J. B. Pinker, who had handled his precarious affairs in England since 1914. Lawrence felt he had become, from Pinker's point of view, an unsatisfactory bother, and that Pinker had lost faith in his prospects for success as a writer. He was also weary of Pinker's complacency and vagueness. He decided in future to act for himself—and make his own mess.

By 1921, however, he had come to an agreement with Pinker's rival, Curtis Brown, who took over Lawrence's American affairs after he had parted from Mountsier in 1923 and handled world rights until two years after Lawrence's death. Brown was born in New York State in 1866, spent fourteen years as a journalist in Buffalo and New York City, and worked in London from 1898 until 1915 as the English representative of several American newspapers. The following year he became a literary agent in London, and soon built up a large and prosperous business.

Lawrence had been treated badly by his two American publishers, Mitchell Kennerley (who brought out *Sons and Lovers*) and Ben Huebsch (who brought out *The Rainbow*). Just after the war Douglas Goldring, Ford's assistant editor on the *English Review,* sent a type-script of *Women in Love* to the American publisher Thomas Seltzer, who would bring out twenty works by Lawrence between 1920 and 1925. Seltzer, a tiny man, was born in Russia in 1875 and came to America with his family when he was twelve years old. He graduated from the Univer-sity of Pennsylvania in 1897, married in 1906, and lived mainly as a translator from Russian and German. He was the uncle of Albert and Charles Boni, and joined the publishing firm of Boni and Liveright in 1917. Both Thomas and his wife, Adele, adored Lawrence and admired his works. Adele, who noted Thomas' fetishistic tendencies toward Law-rence, thought Lawrence was "Chaucer, Piers Ploughman, John Bun-yan, Fielding, Shakespeare, Goethe, Schopenhauer and Nietzsche rolled into one, modernized and added to. . . . [Thomas] carefully, most tidily, most scrupulously keeps L's letters in a locked drawer in the office. I have come upon him unawares, when he has opened the drawer and is tenderly fingering the piles. He won't let me touch a letter unless I have just washed my hands." Thomas simply could not "get over the wonder that we are the publishers of this greatest genius of our age."

Lawrence liked and trusted Seltzer, who visited him in Taos in De-cember 1922, and took Seltzer's side when he quarreled with Mountsier. The great problem, from Lawrence's point of view, was that Seltzer, unbusinesslike and always late, made his own unsettled life even more precarious. Seltzer tottered on the edge of bankruptcy and finally could not pay his authors. Lawrence became justifiably nervous in 1925 when the "two little Seltzers" seemed dangling by a single thread and still owed him five thousand dollars. In April 1925 Lawrence moved from Seltzer to Alfred Knopf, who brought out *St. Mawr* in June of that year and published nine other titles between 1925 and 1930, as well as books by Mabel and Frieda. A hitherto unknown letter from the young novel-ist Storm Jameson, who was Knopf's English editorial representative, reveals that Knopf had heard about Lawrence's troubles with Seltzer and was interested in taking over his rights as early as 1923. On Decem-ber 4 of that year, Jameson sent a letter to Lawrence (who was sailing from Vera Cruz to London) in care of Murry and appealed to Murry to help with Lawrence's all too genial agent and forbidding publisher: "Knopf declares that Mr. Lawrence is leaving Seltzer. Curtis Brown says 'D. H. Lawrence is in my hands,' and C. B. is too affable to be true. Martin Secker, who presumably knows all, so frightens me that I'd do anything rather than deal with him." When Lawrence finally changed publishers he contrasted Knopf's stability, prosperity and energy with Seltzer's rather hopeless way of operating: "I've got a new publisher over here: Knopf—a Jew again—but *rich* and enterprising—seems very nice. Seltzer is staggering, staggering. . . . The new publishers, the Knopfs, are set up in great style, in their offices on Fifth Avenue. . . . The Knopfs seem really sound and reliable."[33] Knopf remained Lawrence's American publisher until Frieda, after his death, sold the rights of his books to Viking.

VIII

Lawrence was as stimulated by the release from England and the life in Italy in the early 1920s as he had been before the war, and published sixteen books during 1920–23. The works that most significantly reflected his life in Italy during this period were *Sea and Sardinia, The Lost Girl* and *Aaron's Rod,* as well as his Introduction to Maurice Magnus' *Memoirs* (1924) and his translations of Giovanni Verga (1923 and 1925).

The Lost Girl (1920) was started in 1913, interrupted by the war and finished in May 1920. Lawrence began the novel as "The Insurrection of Miss Houghton" in Gargnano in 1913, when he wrote about two hundred pages; he revived it after his journey to Italy in November 1919 and concluded it while living in Taormina. The original manuscript has not survived; and the extant novel, entirely rewritten between March and May 1920, is probably a very different kind of book from the 1913 version.

The Lost Girl raises two questions that are central in Lawrence's work: "What is one's own real self?" and "How does one realize one's true nature?" Lawrence insists that "extraordinary people [have] extraordinary fates" and that Alvina Houghton "*was* her own fate." At the very end of the novel, as she urges her husband, Ciccio, to come back from the war, she exclaims: "We have our fate in our hands."[34]

Alvina's impressive ability to determine her own fate resolves the novel's secularized paradox, expressed in Matthew 10:39: "He that loseth his life for my sake shall find it." At various times in the novel Alvina is mentally, morally, physically and geographically lost. She loses her parents, her friends, her fiancés, her social position, her career, her inheritance, her self-respect, her virginity, her reputation, her security, her language and her country. She is "lost to Woodhouse, to Lancaster, to England ... cut off from everything she belonged to." Ciccio feels he cannot bear to lose her; she fears she will lose him—in the war, or afterward. She finds salvation not of the soul, but of the flesh.

Each phase and major experience of Alvina's life prefigures Ciccio and prepares her for Italy. She comes from an ugly, provincial, class-constricted mining town; from a family declining in both health and fortune. Her mother is a professional invalid; her father a frantic failure; the governess, Miss Frost, and the manageress, Miss Pinnegar, are rather cold and bitter examples of spinsterhood. The lives of the women in the household provide a grim warning about Alvina's future just as their deaths release her from a repressive life. She has nothing to gain by remaining buried alive in Woodhouse, and almost any other mode of existence appears more appealing. She escapes from Woodhouse (Lawrence's Eastwood) to become a nurse in London and to join the wandering troupe of "American Indian" entertainers in Sheffield. She runs away from the troupe to meditate in Scarborough, becomes a nurse in Lancaster, escapes from her enforced engagement to Dr. Mitchell, lives with Ciccio in London and leaves with him for Italy.

Internal evidence suggests that the first five chapters—which have an intrusive narrator and a racy, satiric style—were originally written before the war, for Mr. May, based on Maurice Magnus, whom Lawrence met in November 1919, first appears in chapter 6. The plump and perky Mr. May, who manages the Houghtons' theater in Woodhouse, is not as brilliantly drawn as the real Magnus in Lawrence's Introduction to his *Memoirs,* but he is still the liveliest character in the book. Like Magnus, Mr. May is an American Catholic who attended a German school and wears expensive clothes: smart overcoat, velour hat, blue silk underwear. He is afraid of being stranded without cash, but stays at the best hotel; is married, but hates women and prefers mental to physical friendship. He appears as a tempter, "whose pink, fat face and light-blue eyes had a loud look," and convinces James Houghton to start a cinema that eventually ruins him. He is blatant, "but fastidiously so," a "disconsolate bird pecking at the crumbs of Alvina's sympathy." Yet Alvina (the emotional touchstone of the novel) likes him and suggests the reasons for Lawrence's attraction to Magnus, a smart but shady personage.

Lawrence's landlord in Taormina was Francesco "Ciccio" Cacopardo; Alvina Houghton's lover, Francesco "Ciccio" Marasca, is introduced in chapter 7. At the beginning of chapter 11 Lawrence describes the malicious spying on the traveling troupe of entertainers that recalls his wartime persecution in Cornwall: "[There was] all the repulsive secrecy, and all the absolute power of the police authorities. The sense of a great malevolent power which had them all the time in its grip, and was watching, feeling, waiting to strike the morbid blow: the sense of the utter helplessness of individuals who were not even accused, only watched and enmeshed!"

The last three chapters, which describe Lawrence's journey to Picinisco in the Abruzzi, could only have been composed after the war. Though Lawrence spent only ten days in the Abruzzi, Picinisco provided a shock of inspiration. "This is what is so attractive about the remote places," Lawrence wrote in *Sea and Sardinia*, "the Abruzzi, for example. Life is so primitive, so pagan, so strangely heathen and half-savage."[35] Both Alvina and Ciccio decline in Italy. The wild and savage landscape and the new mode of life reflect the difficulties of Alvina's marriage and force her to examine her innermost self.

The novel describes Alvina's inability to find a man who has both passion and intellect, and her willingness to choose the former if she cannot have both. Lawrence creates three types of characters in his fiction: the sensitive intellectual (Paul Morel, Rupert Birkin, Richard Somers in *Kangaroo*), the passionate animal (Annable, Ciccio, Mellors in *Lady Chatterley's Lover*) and the strong leader (Rawdon Lilly, Ben Cooley, Ramón Carrasco in the novels of power). But the ideal hero, who combines all these qualities, is never realized in his work. In December 1921 *The Lost Girl* won the only honor Lawrence ever received in his life: the James Tait Black prize of £100.

IX

Aaron's Rod (1922), which begins in England on December 24, 1919 and ends in Florence a year later, in November 1920, reflects Lawrence's first postwar journey to Italy in November 1919, his brief stay at Sir Walter

Becker's villa near Turin and his three weeks in Florence, during November and December, when he renewed his friendship with Norman Douglas and met Maurice Magnus. Like Alvina in *The Lost Girl*, Aaron leaves his family in a Midlands mining village, takes a different job in another town, has sexual relations with a hot-blooded foreigner and journeys to a new life in Italy. Most of the English scenes take place at night, but the Italian scenes are suffused with brilliant sunshine.

The fourth sentence of the novel—"A man felt the violence of the nightmare [of war] released now into the general air"—expresses the dominant theme, symbolized by the splashing explosion of the blue ball of glass at the beginning of the novel, which foreshadows the detonation of the bomb at the end. The release of violence also threatens to lead to civil war and revolution in Italy. The revolutionary struggle in the background of the novel is analogous to the fight for power between men and women. Rawdon Lilly announces to Aaron Sisson: "there are only two great dynamic urges in *life:* love and power," and the novel attempts to work out the complex relation between them.

In London, Aaron works as a flutist in the opera house and becomes involved with a group of bohemians. He is sexually pursued by Josephine Ford and at first refuses to kiss her. But he eventually succumbs to her demands and collapses immediately afterward in front of Lilly's Covent Garden flat. Aaron, who has always kept to himself, attributes his physical breakdown not to the influenza epidemic of 1919, but to his affair with Josephine. "I gave in to her," he explains to Lilly, as if he had contracted venereal and not viral disease, "and that's what did it. I should have been all right if I hadn't given in to her."[36] Aaron is terrified when Lilly wants to call Lottie, Aaron's wife; he gets into his friend's pajamas and "goes rotten" in his soul. Aaron expresses Lawrence's fear of dominating women and longing for a man; Lilly is Lawrence's female self longing for a male.

In order to "rouse Aaron up," Lilly says, "I'm going to rub you with oil. I'm going to rub you as mothers do their babies whose bowels don't work," although Aaron is not constipated and massaging his genitals would not cure him if he were:

Quickly he uncovered the blond lower body of his patient, and began to rub the abdomen with oil, using a slow, rhythmic, circulating motion, a sort of massage. For a long time he rubbed finely and steadily, then went over the whole of the lower body, mindless, as if in a sort of incantation. He rubbed every speck of the man's lower body—the abdomen, the buttocks, the thighs and knees, down to the feet, rubbed it all warm and glowing with camphorated oil, every bit of it, chafing the toes swiftly, till he was almost exhausted. Then Aaron was covered up again, and Lilly sat down in fatigue to look at his patient.

He saw a change. The spark had come back into the sick eyes, and the faint trace of a smile, faintly luminous, into the face. Aaron was regaining himself. But Lilly said nothing. He watched his patient fall into a proper sleep.[37]

The rhythmic, incantatory, metaphoric and repetitive (the whole, every speck, every bit) quality of this passage should not distract from the literal meaning, especially since Lilly darns Aaron's socks, talks like a woman and serves him like a housemaid. And in a violent fit of revulsion against his wife Tanny's refusal to submit to him (as Aaron has just passively submitted to the rubdown), Lilly joins his revived friend in a corrosive condemnation of women.

The intimacy and physical contact of the crucial nursing scene was based on a significant moment in Lawrence's friendship with Murry. In February 1915 Murry arrived in Greatham to visit Lawrence. During the long walk from the station Murry's cold turned to influenza and Lawrence devoted himself to nursing his friend. The opportunity to give strength and comfort to the ailing Murry afforded Lawrence a gratifying reversal of his weak and passive role, for he and Katherine were tubercular, just as Frieda and Murry were usually healthy. According to Murry, Lilly's rubbing of Aaron provided the "crucial physical contact which was, for Lawrence, a necessary and essential part of a relation between man and man." Just as Lawrence sought a homosexual union with Murry "because he finds it impossible to achieve sexual fulfilment in marriage,"[38] so Lilly (Lawrence) desires a homosexual relation with Aaron (Murry) to complete his marriage to Tanny.

Aaron's Rod has many components of a homosexual novel: three unhappy marriages and two unsuccessful love affairs; an intense hatred and fear of women, who are characterized in two male gatherings as threatening, frightening and repulsive; a symbolically castrated hero who is afraid to let himself go in heterosexual love and runs away from his three women (which suggests a fear of impotence); and a doctrinaire appeal for homosexuality on a theoretical if not actual basis. In the novel Aaron reaches a sexual dead end: he will not give himself to women and cannot submit himself to men.

X

Lawrence's meeting with Maurice Magnus in Florence in November 1919 began an unpleasant, protracted relationship, which Lawrence described in his long and little-known Introduction to Magnus' *Memoirs of the Foreign Legion* (1924), written in Taormina in January 1922. He declared this essay to be "the best single piece of writing, *as writing,* that he had ever done." The Introduction is geographically structured by Lawrence's restless movements around Italy, as the scene shifts six times, from Florence (November) to Capri and Montecassino (February), Taormina (April), Syracuse and Malta (May 1920). Each place evokes a distinctive mood; all are linked by a recurrent pattern of emotional encounters and financial demands, by Lawrence's search for a postwar haven and Magnus' desperate quest for cash. Lawrence found Magnus deceitful, resourceful, repellent and fascinating. In their strange friendship, Magnus was the exploitive leech, while the impoverished Lawrence became (for Magnus) the man with money and security.

Magnus was an unctuous Catholic who talked of becoming a monk and was a constant guest at Montecassino, south of Rome. This monastery, the oldest in Western Europe and the parent house of Western monasticism, was founded by St. Benedict in 529, educated St. Thomas Aquinas and was still an active center of arts and learning. Lawrence left Florence in December and, after ten days in the Abruzzi, moved to Capri. But when he became sick of its tawdry atmosphere, he wrote to Magnus at Montecassino, reminding him that Magnus had said Lawrence might visit him there. In his reply, Magnus hinted that he needed money. Since Lawrence had just received an unexpected £20 from Amy Lowell in America, he sent £5 to Magnus. Grateful that Lawrence had intuitively "saved his life," Magnus asked him to come to the monastery.

When Lawrence arrived alone at the fortress-palace in mid-February, Magnus looked seductively into his eyes "with that wistful, watchful tenderness rather like a woman who isn't quite sure of her lover." Lawrence then assumed a passive role and was treated by Magnus with the same wheedling affection he had previously lavished on Norman Douglas. Douglas' remark that Magnus was "one of those people who are never happy, never quite happy, unless they are obliging others,"[39] was particularly ironic in view of Magnus' ruthless parasitism. Magnus, a worldly, sybaritic, swindling would-be monk, who had offended the Benedictine brothers by his dishonesty and pompous manner, was actually hiding in Montecassino from the police.

When Lawrence's visit ended, he returned to Capri and then moved to Sicily. Magnus, who had paid a hotel bill in Rome with a worthless check, was no longer safe in Montecassino. As the police climbed up to the monastery in April to search for him, his friend, the monk Don Bernardo, gave him some money and urged him to flee down the hill. He spent an agonizing time hiding in the toilet of the train until he reached Naples. Assuming Lawrence would be responsible for his welfare, he came straight to Taormina for help.

Magnus praised Lawrence's house and wanted to reestablish their intimacy—and Lawrence's responsibility—by moving in with him. Lawrence refused, and Magnus, to save money, rented a room in a local house. When he failed to pay this bill, the Italian landlord complained to Lawrence of Magnus' behavior. Lawrence (made intensely aware of his absurd relationship with Magnus) sorted matters out by advancing Magnus seven guineas in return for a supposedly misplaced check that had been sent to Magnus as payment for an article. In May, Magnus promised to leave Taormina for Malta, where he had friends and his prospects seemed more promising.

Freed—it appeared—from Magnus' clutches, Lawrence and Frieda accepted an invitation from Mary Cannan to come to Malta as her guests. When Lawrence (traveling second class) boarded the ship for Valetta and breathed free for the first time since leaving the monastery, he spotted Magnus smoking a cigar and chatting with the captain on the first-class deck—his ticket paid for, of course, with Lawrence's money.

In Valetta, Lawrence inevitably ran into Magnus, who introduced him to Michael Borg and Walter Salomone, Maltese friends of Don Bernardo, and they all went for a drive in a car. Magnus loved Malta, which had been a strategic center in the fight against Moslem power in the eastern Mediterranean and was controlled by the British. Lawrence, by contrast, found the place dreadful, "a bit of stony desert by the sea, with unhappy villas and a sordid, scrap-iron front . . . a bone-dry, bone-bare, hideous landscape." He left Malta feeling secure in the knowledge that he had finally rid himself of his incubus and Magnus was "safely shut up in that beastly island."

The tragic climax occurred six months later, in November 1920, exactly a year after the two men had first met. The Italian police finally caught up with Magnus and were about to extradite him for defrauding a hotel in Rome. Magnus, seriously contemplating suicide, had prepared for this possibility by hiding poison in his room. When the police waited outside for him to change his clothes, he swallowed prussic acid—thus damning himself in the eyes of the church. In his will Magnus left all his literary property to Douglas and characteristically demanded: "I want to be buried first class, my wife will pay." Magnus, having survived the extreme hardships of the French Foreign Legion, killed himself over a hotel bill.

Lawrence's disturbing portrait of Magnus bears a close resemblance to the character of Frederick Rolfe, the self-styled Baron Corvo. It reveals Magnus as a would-be artist in the Decadent tradition of the 1890s—a tradition that Lawrence disliked and also found intriguing. Both Corvo and Magnus were overt homosexuals, masochists, pornographers, aesthetes, snobs, parasites, petty criminals, shady con men operating (to the embarrassment of their respectable friends) in Italy. (Both men died there in middle age.) Both were escapists and escape artists who suffered from delusions of grandeur and a persecution complex. Both were bogus aristocrats, Catholic converts and spoiled priests, who sought refuge in the Church and had ecclesiastical fantasies. Both endured, as Graham Greene wrote of Corvo, "the long purgatories in foreign *pensions*, the counted coppers, the keeping up of appearances."

With Magnus, Lawrence was passive, helpless, uncomfortable, susceptible to his wheedling ways, unable to refuse his exacting demands. Magnus behaved as if he had honored Lawrence by coming to Taormina and as if Lawrence had betrayed him there. He appealed for protection to the masculine side of Lawrence's nature and for sympathy to the feminine side. Lawrence, who had associated Whitman's man-for-man love with death, felt he was right to let Magnus die so that Lawrence could kill his own fearful homosexuality: "I would let him go over into death. He shall and should die, and so should all his sort."[40] Lawrence's Introduction is not only a memoir, memorial, critique, confession and apologia, but also an exorcism.

A recent edition of Magnus' *Memoirs* includes several passages deleted by Martin Secker from the *Memoirs* and from Lawrence's Introduction, which illuminate Lawrence's attitude toward Magnus. In one excised passage from the *Memoirs,* Magnus frankly refers to the effects of sodomy when he overhears a soldier asking: "Can't you walk? Did he hurt you last night?" He also self-righteously recounts how, in a bathhouse, "as I leaned down to wash my lower extremities, he deliberately tried to assault me in the face." In an excised passage from Lawrence's Introduction, Lawrence criticizes Magnus for his hypocrisy about homosexuality, since Magnus himself paid for and practiced inversion. "To me, the blood-passions are sacred, and sex is sacred," Lawrence writes, and attacks prostitution as "the modern form of vampirism, sucking the blood from hot living individuals into those white-blooded 'superior' individuals like Magnus."[41]

The death of Magnus did not end his controversial connection to Lawrence, whom he continued to plague from beyond the grave. After his death, two of his Maltese creditors, Borg and Salomone, sent Lawrence the manuscript about Magnus' life in the Foreign Legion, then called *Dregs*, in the hope of publishing it to recover the money Magnus owed them. Though Lawrence wrote the Introduction a year later, it took two more years to get the book in print. Seltzer offered to bring out Lawrence's Introduction without Magnus' book. Murry rejected the book as a serial in the *Adelphi*. Martin Secker had refused the book shortly before Magnus' death, but Lawrence persuaded Secker to change his mind, and the book appeared, with the Introduction, in October 1924.

Douglas responded to the Introduction in a long pamphlet, *D. H. Lawrence and Maurice Magnus: A Plea for Better Manners*. It was privately published by Douglas in Florence in December 1924 and twice reprinted in 1925. Douglas, who adopted a charming, chatty, familiar, roguish and worldly persona that confirmed Lawrence's portraits, softened his criticism by calling Lawrence's Introduction a wrongheaded "masterpiece of unconscious misrepresentation." As Magnus' sometime collaborator and literary executor, he claimed that he should have been consulted about the publication of the *Memoirs* and had a right to half the profits. Lawrence, who appropriated the manuscript, "has now recouped himself many times over by the sale of these Memoirs." He concluded his criticism of Lawrence by angrily declaring that the novelist's touch was "hitting below the belt, and a damnably vulgar proceeding"[42]—a snobbish swipe at Lawrence's working-class origins.

Douglas' pamphlet was provoked not only by Lawrence's penetrating dissection of Magnus' character in his Introduction, which was meant to present his posthumous work to the public, but also by his fictional satire in *Aaron's Rod* of Douglas' gentlemanly upper-class pretensions. Douglas—who maintained a respectable front but was often in trouble with the Italian police—was really infuriated by Lawrence's potentially dangerous suggestions about his homosexual relationship with Magnus.

Lawrence, who had moved to New Mexico in September 1922, was willing to tolerate Douglas' carelessly printed Italian pamphlet. But when Douglas included this polemic in *Experiments* (1925), Lawrence was roused to defend himself publicly. He first worked out the strategy of his counterattack in two letters to his agent, Curtis Brown, in April 1925, soon after the pamphlet appeared. He stated that he had acted more generously toward Magnus than Douglas did, received *carte blanche* from Douglas to deal with the *Memoirs* as he wished, written the Introduction only to repay Magnus' creditors, and refused offers to publish it separately (though this entailed financial sacrifice). He felt that he deserved fifty percent of the royalties since he had composed nearly half the book himself and was entirely responsible for its publication. He also denied the importance of Douglas' supposed collaboration:

> I hear Norman Douglas attacks me on behalf of Magnus. Rather disgusting, when one knows what N.D. is: and how he treated M., wouldn't give him a sou: and when I have a letter from Douglas telling me to do what I liked and say what I liked about that MS: and when one knows how bitter Magnus was about Douglas, at the end. And when one knows how much worse the *whole* facts were, than those I give. . . .
>
> I bothered about that MS. only for the sake of those two Maltese [creditors]. From 1921 to 1924 I tried to get the thing published. The New York publisher [Seltzer] wanted to publish my introduction, alone, as an essay, without the *Legion* MS. I refused, and waited. Having written half the book surely half the proceeds are due to me.
>
> As for Douglas' co-writing—it's a literary turn. Besides, Magnus re-wrote the *whole* thing, after I talked with him at Montecassino. I really sweated to get that fellow money, and Douglas wouldn't give him a cent. . . .
>
> He only thinks I am hard on M.M. But in *life*, Douglas was much harder on him—very much.

Lawrence elaborated these arguments in an extremely strong and effective letter that appeared in the *New Statesman* on February 20, 1926, soon after a review of *Experiments*. Lawrence's most devastating weapon, which decisively won the argument, was the letter from Douglas that gave Lawrence permission to act as he wished and hinted at his own immorality:

> By all means do what you like with the MS. As to M. himself, I may do some kind of memoir of him later on—independent of *Foreign Legions*. Put me into your introduction, if you like.

Pocket all the cash yourself. [Borg] seems to be such a fool that he doesn't deserve any.

I'm out of it and, *for once in my life,* with a clean conscience.[43]

Lawrence added that after Magnus' death, Borg, who never met Douglas and knew of him mainly through Magnus, said he "would never put anything in the hands of Douglas." (Douglas admitted that he applied for, but failed to obtain, Magnus' papers.) Borg eventually received half the royalties, and the £55 he had lent to Magnus were repaid in full.

Despite the acrimonious quarrel, Lawrence and Douglas were reconciled by Pino Orioli in his bookstore on the Lungarno during the winter of 1926–27. Though Douglas disliked certain aspects of Lawrence's character, he admired his gifts. According to Aldington, when Douglas met Lawrence in the bookshop he courteously offered his snuffbox and said: "'Have a pinch of snuff, dearie.' Lawrence took it. 'Isn't it curious'—sniff—'only Norman and my father'—sniff—'ever gave me snuff?'" This symbolic gesture renewed their friendship, if not their old intimacy. In April 1927 Virginia Woolf, traveling through Italy, wrote to her sister: "Looking out of the carriage window at Civita Vecchia, whom should we see, sitting side by side on a bench, but D. H. Lawrence and Norman Douglas—unmistakable: Lawrence pierced and penetrated; Douglas hog-like and brindled."[44]

XI

When Lawrence settled in Sicily in 1920 he reread Giovanni Verga, the preeminent novelist of that region, and became absorbed in his work: "He exercises quite a fascination on me, and makes me feel quite sick at the end. But perhaps that is only if one knows Sicily.—Do you know if he is translated into English?—*I Malavoglia* or *Mastro-don Gesualdo*—or *Novelle Rusticane,* or the other stories." He was fascinated by Verga's spare and concentrated language, which tried to express the workings of unsophisticated minds and, as Thomas Bergin has observed, "to arrange good Tuscan words in Sicilian word order and to make the reader aware of the rhythm of dialect under the Italian sentence."

Lawrence's "sickness" was caused by Verga's emphasis on the squalid and depressing aspects of peasant life. But Lawrence's fascination with

Verga's brutal details showed that he was determined to penetrate below the surface and discover the truth about primitive existence. He saw that Verga had used the realistic techniques of the modern European novel to capture the essence of peasant life, believed there was a similarity between the Sicilian and Midlands dialects, and felt an instinctive affinity with Verga that made him an ideal translator of his work. Lawrence stated his principle of capturing the essence rather than the exactness of the original in an unpublished letter to his German translator: "I don't care about little mistakes and mistranslations, if only the *spirit* of the original can be preserved. . . . Frau Jaffe [Frieda's sister, who had rendered *The Rainbow* into German] understands me very well, yet she has not the peculiar *mastery* a translator needs, to give a work its own life in a new language."[45]

The main reason for Lawrence's attraction to Verga was undoubtedly the raw power and emotional extremes of the characters, driven by brute force and blind fate. The lives of Verga's peasants, like those of Lawrence's miners, are dominated by toil and poverty but redeemed by spontaneous vitality. Lawrence also identified with aspects of Verga's character. As he wrote in the self-reflective Preface to *Cavalleria Rusticana:* "His nature was proud and unmixable. At the same time, he had the southern passionate yearning for tenderness and generosity. . . . [He was] by instinct haughty and reserved: because, partly, he was passionate and emotional, and did not choose to give himself away." Lawrence shared Verga's anti-clericalism and political conservatism, his belief that the masses were corrupt and the aristocracy defunct. Inspired by imaginative insight, Lawrence's translations of Verga were both re-creations of a sympathetic spirit and expressions of the major themes of his own art.

Lawrence did half his translation of *Mastro-don Gesualdo* in Taormina, worked on it while sailing from Naples to Colombo on the *Osterley*—between finishing *Aaron's Rod* and beginning *Kangaroo*—and completed it in Kandy, Ceylon, in March 1922. He started work on the *Little Novels of Sicily* soon afterward and continued the translation on the *Orsova* en route from Ceylon to Australia. Achsah Brewster provided a detailed picture of her friend translating Verga in Ceylon: "Lawrence sat curled up with a schoolboy's copy-book in his hand, writing away. He was translating Giovanni Verga's short stories from the Sicilian [i.e., Italian]. Across the pages of the copy-book his hand moved rhythmically, steadily, unhesitatingly, leaving a trail of exquisite, small writing as legible as print. No blots, no scratchings marred its beauty. When the book was finished, he wrapped and tied it up, sending it off to the publisher."[46]

After eighteen months in Taormina, Lawrence, whose motto was "When in doubt—move," was seized by his habitual dissatisfaction and restlessness. The prewar idyll was irrevocably lost. Everything had become expensive, and Italy now cost about the same as England. The inefficiency was often exasperating. And he began to mistrust and dislike the people: "The Italians are really rather low-bred swine nowadays: so different from what they were. . . . The Taorminisi natives are as mean and creeping as ever—really begin to feel . . . that one must have done with Italy." The south seemed so torpid and lifeless (though it "cured one of caring") and began to go rancid in his mouth: "I have been hating Taormina—but one hates everywhere in fits and starts." As riots and strikes increased and the Fascists prepared for their coup of October 1922, Lawrence felt he had to leave: "The country is sickening, and such a muddle ever increasing. I am tired of it. There are not many forestieri [foreigners] here, all afraid of strikes and railway smashes."[47]

In February 1922 Lawrence was offered hospitality and summoned to New Mexico by Mabel Luhan, who had read his books and heard about him from Esther Andrews. "We sit ready to travel," he told his mother-in-law, "4 trunks, one household trunk, one book trunk, Frieda's and mine—and then two valises, hat-box, and the two quite small pieces." These, and the gaily painted panel of a Sicilian cart, which he carried round the world, were the sum of their worldly possessions.

They left Italy by way of Ceylon, Australia and the South Seas. His ultimate plan, he told Earl Brewster, was "to get a little farm somewhere by myself, in Mexico, New Mexico, Rocky Mountains, or British Columbia. The desire to be away from the body of mankind—to be a bit of a hermit—is paramount." But Italy would not release him from its emotional hold, and he soon longed to return: "We saw our Etna, like a white queen, or a white witch standing there in the sky: so magically beautiful, but I think wicked. She said to me 'Come back here'—I only said no, but wept inside with pain—pain of parting." Several months later he wrote from Taos: "My heart still turns most readily to Italy. . . . My spirit always wants to go south."[48]

CHAPTER FIFTEEN

Ceylon and Australia,
1922

I

DURING THE WAR, when his movements were severely restricted, Lawrence had dreamed of escaping to the farthest corners of the earth: "I wish I were going to Thibet—or Kamschatka—or Tahiti—to the Ultima, ultima, ultima Thule. I feel sometimes, I shall go mad, because there is nowhere to go, no 'new world.' One of these days, unless I watch myself, I shall be departing in some rash fashion, to some foolish place."[1] Though Lawrence never reached Tibet or Kamchatka, he did visit Tahiti en route to the New World.

After the war, Lawrence's travels were marked by restlessness and indecision. In January 1922, when he had finally decided to cross the Atlantic and travel from the East Coast to Taos, he suddenly changed plans and wanted to avoid the harsh climate and unpleasant atmosphere of New York. He felt it was his destiny to know the entire world, so he visited the Brewsters in Ceylon and approached New Mexico from the west. Lawrence's great problem was that he always longed to be in *another* place: he yearned for Europe in America and wished he were in America as soon as he returned to Europe.

In the early 1920s, when more money and better health allowed him to roam the earth, Lawrence contemplated visits to Greenland, Russia, China and India. When he was unhappy in Mexico, he thought: "perhaps

I've no business trying to bury myself in out-of-the-way places." But as soon as he was back in Europe, the Mediterranean inspired him to wander like Ulysses. From Italy he planned trips to Ragusa, Dalmatia, Crete, Cyprus, Constantinople, Damascus, Jerusalem, Jaffa, Egypt, Tunisia and Morocco. "Anything, anything to shake off this stupor and have a bit of fun in life," he said. "I'd even go to Hell, en route." When his health deteriorated, he inevitably realized: "As one gets older, one's choice in life gets limited—one is not free to choose any more." But only three months before his death, he was still thankful to escape a permanent way of life and told Maria Huxley: "I sort of wish I could go to the moon."[2]

Travel provided a relief from writing, changed the pattern of his daily life and introduced him to new people and stimulating experiences. He planned to write a novel about each continent, but died before he could capture Asia, Africa and America. Yet he did write distinctively on an enormous range of subjects: literature, history, art, religion, philosophy, psychology, anthropology and education. His visits to Ceylon and Australia inspired his poem "Elephant" and his novel *Kangaroo*.

II

The Lawrences sailed from Naples on the *Osterley* on February 26, 1922, passed through the Suez Canal and entered the Red Sea, where he saw "Mount Sinai like a vengeful dagger that was dipped in blood many ages ago, so sharp and defined and old pink-red in colour." He translated Verga aboard ship and reached Colombo in mid-March.

Kandy—a hill town in the center of Ceylon, about fifty miles northeast of Colombo—is one of the most beautiful places in Asia. The views are magnificent, the foliage luxuriant; the town has a large lake in the center and is dominated by an exotic temple that is said to hold a tooth of the Buddha. Leonard Woolf, who served as a colonial official in Ceylon and visited Kandy fifteen years before Lawrence arrived, remarked that the town had thirty thousand inhabitants and was full of white men. And he was extremely enthusiastic about the atmosphere, the scenery and the early-morning climate: "Everything in Kandy sparkles, including the air; it is wonderfully soft and cool before the sun gets up high overhead. . . . In 1907 Kandy and its surroundings were entrancingly beautiful. It was half-way between the low country and the high mountains and enjoyed the best of every climate and every world. The great lake, which was the centre of the European part of town, lay in a hollow with the hills gently rising up all round it."

The Brewsters had leased an old bungalow, with a broad veranda and many servants, about a mile and a half from the center of town. It was isolated in the midst of the jungle, stood on top of a high hill, and overlooked Kandy Lake and the Great Elephant River. There was no strife with the gentle Brewsters. Lawrence walked through the jungle, watched the animals, boated on the river, looked at precious jewels and visited the temples in this holy center of southern Buddhism. He wrote for four hours in the morning, and in the afternoon read the work aloud to his friends.[3]

The outstanding event of his visit was the Perahera ceremony. Buddha's sacred tooth was taken out of the temple, placed on the back of an elephant and carried in a colorful procession before the great crowds of people who had swarmed into Kandy for the festival. The young Prince of Wales (later Edward VIII and Duke of Windsor), on an official visit to Ceylon, was guest of honor. But he seemed, Lawrence told his sister Emily, exhausted and frightened, and nearly slept through the ceremony:

We were down at the Perahera at night—were just opposite the Prince. Poor devil, he is so thin and nervy: all twitchy: and seems worn out and disheartened. No wonder, badgered about like a doll among a mob of children. A woman threw a bouquet, and he nearly jumped out of his skin.

But the Perahera was wonderful: it was night, and flaming torches of cocoanut blazing, and the great elephants in their trappings, about a hundred, and the dancers with tomtoms and bagpipes, and half naked and jewelled, then the Kandyan chiefs in their costumes, and more dancers, and more elephants, and more chiefs, and more dancers, so wild and strange and perfectly fascinating, heaving along by the flame of torches in the hot, still, starry night. Afterwards fireworks over the lake, and thousands and thousands of natives, so that it looked like some queer dream when the fire flared up and showed their thousands of dark faces and white wraps packed on the banks.

Lawrence also expressed his excitement about the dazzling midnight procession under the tropical stars in his long, incantatory satiric poem, "Elephant." His theme is power: its transformation and expression. The poem begins as he goes down to the river, past paddy fields where water buffalo are idling and half-naked men are threshing rice, and meets a working elephant carrying a heavy log. Elephants reappear that night in the Perahera and provide a strong contrast to the wispy, diffident Prince of Wales. His ironic, mock-modest motto is "*Ich dien*" (I serve), and he seems a feeble representative of imperial rule. Lawrence describes the hot dark blood of the devil dancers, whose energy, like the elephant's, contrasts to the prince's lassitude. As Lawrence dodges "under the hanging, hairy pigs' tails / And the flat, flaccid mountains of the elephants' standing haunches," he feels dejected and frustrated by the pale, nervous royal boy. The prince also disappoints the Ceylonese, who expect and deserve an impressive show of power. The poem urges the prince to reject his unworthy motto and his weary irony, be truthful about his power, and adopt the natural might and dignity of the elephant. The prince should tell the people: "*Serve me, I am meet to be served. / Being royal of the gods*," and should tell the great beasts: "*A Prince has come back to you, / Blood-mountains. / Crook the knee and be glad.*" "Elephant" expresses the same authoritarian ideas as the novels of power.

Lawrence had had his usual winter fortnight of flu in January 1922, shortly before leaving Sicily, and the extreme heat and steamy humidity of Ceylon, which a healthy man might not have noticed, affected him badly. It was the antithesis of the dry Alpine air recommended for lung disease. He hated the debilitating climate, found it difficult to breathe and could scarcely drag himself about. Achsah Brewster explained that "as the rainy season continued we felt as mildewed as our garments in the recesses of the rooms where there was waged a continual battle against mould. Lawrence sat disconsolately, his voice reduced to a minor key, reiterating that he felt his 'heart's blood oozing away, but literally ebbing out drop by drop.'"[4] He later told Earl that he hated much of his time in Ceylon and had never felt so sick in his entire life. Though Lawrence did not know it at the time, he had contracted malaria in Kandy.

Lawrence shifted, quite dramatically and characteristically, from fascination with the spectacular beauty to disenchantment with the teeming masses of Ceylon. Only two weeks after the Perahera he was (like George Orwell, then serving in Burma) repelled by the "barbaric substratum of Buddhism" as well as by the overpowering heat, the oleaginous people, the sickening smells, the claustrophobic jungle, the screeching of birds and animals, the nastiness of the monks and tawdriness of the temples:

Here the heat is terrific — and I hate the tropics. It is beautiful, in a lush, tangled, towsled, lousy sort of way. The natives too are quite good-looking, dark-skinned and erect. But something about it all just makes me sick. . . . My inside has never hurt me so much in all my 36 years as in these three weeks.—I'm going away. . . .

The East doesn't get me at all. Its boneless suavity, and the thick, choky feel of tropical forest, and the metallic sense of palms and the horrific noises of the birds and creatures, who hammer and clang and rattle and cackle and explode all the livelong day, and run little machines all the livelong night: and the scents that make me feel sick, the perpetual nauseous overtone of cocoanut and co-coanut fibre and oil, the sort of tropical sweetness which to me suggests an undertang of blood, hot blood, and thin sweat; the undertaste of blood and sweat in the nauseous tropical fruits; the nasty faces and yellow robes of the Buddhist monks, the little vulgar dens of temples: all this makes up Ceylon to me, and all this I cannot bear.

As usual, he blamed his illness on the climate, told Earl, "My being requires a different physical and psychic environment: the white man is not for this region," and was glad to have seen that corner of the East so he would have no more illusions about it. It is a great pity that Lawrence did not stay a bit longer and write, as Orwell did of Burma, a caustic novel of the English in Ceylon.

Ceylon, nevertheless, had a powerful effect on his imagination and recurred several times in his writings and conversations of the 1920s. He compared the religious feeling of the devil dancers in the Perahera to that of the Pueblo Indians in his essay "New Mexico," and drew on Buddhist sounds and ceremonies when describing Mexican customs and religion in *The Plumed Serpent:* "In Ceylon the natives tiptoe in to the little temples and lay one flower on the table at the foot of the big Buddha statues. And the tables of offering are all covered with these flowers, all put so neatly. The natives have that delicate oriental way of putting things down. . . . It was the sound of drums, of tom-toms rapidly beaten. The same sound . . . heard in the distance, in the tropical dusk of Ceylon, from the temples at sunset." And in 1928, when living in Port-Cros in France, he again recalled the menacing jungle of Ceylon and told Brigit Patmore: "The nights were black, oh black. The jungle was just outside the bungalow and it seemed to step closer and bend over us when the darkness came. Sounds boomed, some animal shot a cry at you."[5] In Ceylon, cut off for the first time in his life from Western culture, Lawrence felt physically and psychologically uncomfortable. On April

24, 1922, he sailed for Perth in Western Australia and, living for a time in a coal-mining town near Sydney, recaptured the familiar atmosphere of his youth.

III

The Lawrences reached Perth on May 4 and stayed for two days. Following the advice of Australians they had met on the ship, they then moved sixteen miles inland to Darlington and spent two weeks in a guest house and nursing home run by Mollie Skinner. Born in Perth in 1876, she was the daughter of an English captain in the Royal Irish Regiment. She had spent her childhood in various parts of Great Britain, completed her nurse's training before returning to Australia in 1900, and served as a nurse in India and Burma during World War I. In 1922, when Lawrence met her, she was "a middle-aged Quaker spinster of fairly Victorian standards." In his Preface to her novel *Black Swans* (1925), Lawrence recalled: "There was Miss Skinner, in the house on the hills at the edge of the bush, in Western Australia, darting about rather vaguely in her white nurse's dress, with the nurse's white band over her head, looking after her convalescents."

Lawrence had been given a copy of Skinner's book about her nursing experiences, *Letters of a V.A.D.* (Voluntary Aid Detachment), published in 1918, and was impressed by its originality and freshness. He encouraged her writing and said: "You have been given the divine spark and you would bury it in a napkin." He became her collaborator, revised the novel, changed the title from *The House of Ellis* to *The Boy in the Bush* (which echoed the title of Henry Lawson's Australian novel *The Children of the Bush*, 1902). He also wrote the last two chapters, in which Dorothy Brett appears as Hilda Blessington, and persuaded Secker to publish it (with Lawrence as co-author) in 1924.

Lawrence had always liked artistic collaboration, especially with less artistically experienced women. He considered Louie Burrows the co-author of his early story "Goose Fair" and worked briefly with Catherine Carswell on an unfinished novel about Robert Burns. " 'I like that story of yours so much, Catherine,' he said, 'that I've written out a little sketch of how I think it might go. Then, if you like the idea, we might collaborate in the novel. You do the beginning and get the woman character going, and let me have it, and I'll go on and fill in the man.'"[6] He helped Mary Cannan revise her book about pet dogs, began to write a novel with Mabel Luhan (until Frieda put a stop to it), rewrote Kot's literal translations of Ivan Bunin and Leo Shestov, and offered to write up Frederick Carter's notes on the Book of Revelation. And Lawrence, a talented amateur painter, boldly touched up and even repainted not only the work of Barbara Weekley but also that of young professionals like Knud Merrild and Dorothy Brett. These artistic collaborations released him from the writer's solitude and allowed him to indulge his passion for teaching.

Lawrence received some attention from the tiny literary circle in Perth (where he found a copy of *The Rainbow*), and one writer became so excited by the prospect of meeting him that she gave birth prematurely. Frieda, angry with a fellow guest at Darlington who disliked *The White Peacock*, tactlessly exclaimed: "But how stupid you people are! You do not know my husband. He is the genius Lawrence."

In a letter to Kot of May 20, written when sailing from Perth to Sydney, Lawrence praised the natural landscape and described the intellectual limitations of the provincial Australians: "We stayed two weeks in Western Australia: weird land, marvellous blue sky, clear air, pure and untouched. Then the endless hoary grey 'bush'—which is gum trees, rather thinly scattered, like a thin wood, with a healthy sort of undergrowth: like a moor with trees. People very friendly, but slow and as if unwilling to take the next step: as if everything was a bit too much for them."[7]

The Lawrences reached Sydney on May 27, stayed only two days, and then found a comfortable, attractive bungalow called "Wyewurk" in Thirroul, a mining village on the south coast, about fifty miles from the city. They lived an isolated life for two and a half months, swimming, walking on the vast beach and seeing almost no one. Lawrence immediately began to write *Kangaroo* and finished the long novel in only six weeks.

Lawrence, in his authoritarian phase, disliked the quintessential Australian (and also American) characteristics: aggressive familiarity, offhand manner, rejection of class distinctions and contempt for authority. In a letter of mid-June to his sister-in-law Else, he described the rather ramshackle town and condemned the prevailing political attitudes:

The township is just a scatter of bungalows, mostly of wood with corrugated iron roofs, and with some quite good shops: "stores." It lies back from the sea. Nobody wants to be too near the sea here: only we are on the brink. About two miles inland there is a great long hill like a wall, facing the sea and running all down the coast. This is dark greyish with gum trees, and it has little coal-mines worked into it. The men are mostly coal-miners, so I feel quite at home. The township itself—they never say *village* here—is all haphazard and new, the streets unpaved, the church built of wood. That part is pleasant—the newness. It feels so free. And though it is midwinter, and the shortest day next week, still every day is as sunny as our summer, and the sun is almost as hot as our June. But the nights are cold. . . .

This is the most democratic place I have *ever* been in. And the more I see of democracy the more I dislike it. It just brings everything down to the mere vulgar level of wages and prices, electric light and water closets, and nothing else. You *never* knew anything so nothing . . . as the life here.[8]

In *Kangaroo,* Lawrence portrayed a society solidly based on Western materialism, but isolated from the intellectual traditions of Europe.

IV

In *Kangaroo* (1923), Lawrence imagines the Australian political system falling prey to the kind of organized Fascist movement he had seen in Italy. He contrasts Fascism to the distasteful democracy and uses the resulting chaos to symbolize the frightful emptiness of the uprooted people and their wild landscape. An Englishman, Richard Lovat Somers, the autobiographical hero of the novel, and his wife, Harriet, are visitors to Australia. Through their neighbors, the Callcotts, Somers becomes involved with a militant organization of World War I veterans, the Diggers. Their leader is Ben Cooley, or Kangaroo, but their fascistic principles are more accurately represented by the ex-officer Jack Callcott. He explains their military make-up, their revolutionary aims and their ambition to seize political power, while the thunderous ocean nearly drowns out his words. Jack insists that authority, discipline and obedience are needed to oppose the rotten politicians and the exploded ideal of democratic liberty. The old soldiers, returned from the war, "chaps with some guts in them," are secretly sworn to keep silent, obey the leaders and wait for the moment to strike. The well-equipped Diggers' Clubs practice martial sports, have regular military training and are indoctrinated with nationalistic ideology. There is a strong emphasis on intimate comradeship — "Men fight better when they've got a mate" — modeled on David and Jonathan, which had always been Lawrence's cherished ideal.

The model for the Diggers, the Returned Servicemen's League, represented almost everything that Lawrence disliked about Australia. It was militaristic, philistine, bigoted, brutal, crude, conformist, democratic and nationalistic, and had considerable influence in shaping the values of modern Australia:

> The Returned Servicemen's League did a great deal to make the values associated with Anzac Day and the "old digger" dominant in the Australian community. Along with the virtues ascribed to the idealised digger — courage, loyalty, mateship and democratic levelling — went other less admirable characteristics. The stereotyped figure exhibited also tough, sardonic contempt for coloured people and foreigners generally, for minority views, for art, literature, culture and learning; and something not far from contempt — patronage disguised as chivalrous protectiveness — for "good" women and brutal disdain for "bad" ones. He magnified "male" virtues like decisiveness, directness, physical strength, and despised "female" ones like thoughtfulness, gentleness, subtlety. The tone of most of the writing in the *Bulletin* or *Smith's Weekly* at this period exactly mirrors the prevailing ethos — levelling values, rough manners and philistine tastes as the outer form; conformity, conservatism and unquestioning Anglo-Australian patriotism as the inner content.

Kangaroo is the first of Lawrence's tyrant heroes who try to impose their will on the masses. When Somers meets Kangaroo he is struck by the unusual mixture of essential Jewish kindness and "shrewd fiendish subtlety of will" — though we never see anything of the latter. Unlike the ferocious Jack, Kangaroo favors benevolent tyranny, with humane laws and wise authority. But Kangaroo is also a charismatic and sexually attractive figure. Though Somers rejects his party and his ideas, he is drawn to the ugly, shapeless leader. Somers has to restrain his desire to touch Kangaroo's body, which emits a "magnetic effusion." He thrills to his voice and thinks: "the man is like a god, I love him." But when Kangaroo presses Somers' slight body against his own big breast, squeezes him so he can hardly breathe and passionately declares: "I love you so. I love you so," Somers rejects this love and wishes that Kangaroo were dead. Lawrence portrays the attraction to Fascist power as a frightening homosexual force.

There are a number of serious contradictions in Lawrence's portrayal of the Diggers, which undermine the credibility of the political theme in the novel. First, there is no motive for revolution in Australia and no real reason for the Diggers to exist, for unlike Italy, political affairs are running quite well. Somers feels that the real enemy is boredom (not democracy) and that the returned war heroes "were doing it all just in order to have something to do, to put a spoke in the wheel of the bosses, to make a change." Jack's colleague Jaz admits: "You can die in Australia if you don't get a bit of excitement."

Second, there is an illogical gap between the violent methods of Jack and the idealistic love of his leader, Kangaroo; between Jack's anti-Semitic fulminations—"I hate the thought of being bossed . . . by Jew capitalists and bankers"[9]—and his fanatical allegiance to the "physically warm love" of the orderly, clever Jewish intellectual and savior with the not very Jewish-sounding name, Ben Cooley. Third, Kangaroo's naive, high-minded and idealistic politics of love, which is much closer to Woodrow Wilson (whom Lawrence scorned) than to Mussolini, makes him an extremely ineffectual leader. During the Socialist riots, the defenseless Kangaroo bellows at the wild crowd while a gunman shoots him in the guts.

Jaz, who is aware of Kangaroo's defects as a political leader and has a greater grasp of *Realpolitik,* wants to start the revolution by having the Diggers join their enemies and by inciting the Communists to act in Australia as they did in Russia: "Couldn't we get [Kangaroo] to use all his men to back Red Labour in this country, and blow a cleavage through the old system. . . . These Diggers' Clubs, they've got all the army men, dying for another scrap. And then a sort of secret organisation has ten times the hold over men than just a Labour Party, or a Trades Union. He's damned clever, he's got a wonderful scheme ready. But he'll spoil it, because he'll want it all to happen without hurting anybody." When Somers puts this proposal to Kangaroo, the leader calls Jaz a traitor, rejects Somers and orders him to leave Australia.

Somers fares no better in his talk with the Labour leader, Willie Struthers. For Struthers, like his ideological adversary, wants to base his political movement on Whitman's democratic-homosexual love of man for man: "He wanted this love, this mate-trust called into consciousness and highest honour. He wanted to set it where Whitman tried to set his Love of Comrades. It was to be the new tie between men, in the new democracy. It was to be the new passional bond in the new society." Somers reacts to Struthers as he did to Kangaroo, on the physical level ("I don't like him physically—something thin and hairy and spiderish"[10]), and rejects his offer to edit a Socialist newspaper because he is repelled more by his person than by his ideas.

After the complementary interviews with Struthers and Kangaroo, the action of the novel is interrupted and the climax delayed by the most lively and interesting part of the book. The retrospective and autobiographical "Nightmare" chapter describes Somers' three humiliating medical examinations, his persecution by the military authorities who ransacked his house and accused him of spying, and his expulsion from his cottage on the Cornish coast. Though Graham Hough declares that "Nightmare" is "almost wholly irrelevant to the progress of the narrative," this chapter is, in fact, crucial to the structure and meaning of the novel.

"Nightmare," which seems to provide a contrast between England and Australia, actually reveals the fundamental similarities between the two countries. The chapter shows the evils of mass rule in the army, which tried to compel Somers to serve a dead ideal, and in Australia, where he felt a similar dread of the democratic mob. In *Mornings in Mexico,* Lawrence compares himself to his servant Rosalino, who refused to join the army and has "a horror of serving in a mass of men, or even of being mixed up with a mass of men." This fear of the army and the mob explains Somers' refusal to join the militaristic, authoritarian, violent and fascistic Diggers, who helped to create in Australia the kind of world he has just escaped in England. Somers, who had been falsely accused of spying in both Germany and England, is again called a spy by Jack Callcott in Australia.

Somers' dearest friend in Cornwall, John Thomas Buryan, is based on William Henry Hocking. The passionate friendship with Buryan, whom Somers connects with the Cornishman Jaz, explains why Somers is so strongly attracted to male comradeship in the political movements of *Kangaroo.* Finally, the "Nightmare" chapter reveals why Somers left his own country: "England had lost its meaning for him. The free England had died, this England of the peace was like a corpse."[11] It also explains why he came to Australia in search of a new mode of life and why he had to leave Australia when its oppressive politics reminded him of the morbid atmosphere in England.

The climax of the novel occurs when Willie Struthers makes a speech to a packed Canberra Hall on the solidarity of labor, a group of Diggers shout him down and annihilate him "by their moral unison," and an anarchist bomb explodes. The chaotic mass, "struggling with the Diggers, in real blood-murder passion," inspires Somers with a blind but vague urge to kill: "small as he was, [he] felt a great frenzy on him, a great longing to let go. But since he didn't *really* know whom he wanted to let go at, he was not quite carried away." Guns are fired, Kangaroo is shot and Somers escapes to a remote Diggers' Club. There he meets Jack, who gleefully describes how, with an iron bar, he bashed out the brains of the man who shot Kangaroo. He then makes a crude analogy between sex and power: "there's *nothing* bucks you up sometimes like killing a man — *nothing*. You feel a perfect *angel* after it. . . . Having a woman's something, isn't it? But it's a flea-bite, nothing, compared to killing your man when your blood comes up" — as in an erection. The newspaper accounts of the riot, in which three people were killed, blame the Labour incendiaries and cautiously praise Jack Callcott, who is neither tried nor punished for murdering two men.

When Somers visits the dying Kangaroo, who emits a sickening smell, the leader ironically claims "Perfect love casteth out fear" (I John 4:18) and begs Somers to save him from death, by love. Somers, who willed Kangaroo's death during their previous interview, once again rejects the Christian doctrine of love and "kills" Kangaroo: "I don't love him — I detest him. He can die. I'm glad he is dying."[12] Somers' words on Kangaroo's death are strikingly similar to Lawrence's words on Magnus' death: "He shall and should die, and so should all his sort."

Somers had always insisted: "I never take part in politics at all. They aren't my affair." Though he longs for a smash-up of the social-industrial world, which has led to war and the postwar chaos, he considers love and benevolence to be as dangerous and unreal as riots and revolutions. He loathes both the politicians and the working class, holds himself back from both Jack and Jaz, denies the appeals of Struthers and Kangaroo, and remains "the most forlorn and isolated creature in the world, without even a dog to his command." Somers resolves the conflict between artistic and political commitment by firmly rejecting both Fascism and Socialism. At the end of the novel, his vague and rather irrelevant commitment to the greater mystery of the dark gods — "This dark, passionate religiousness and inward sense of an indwelling magnificence,

direct flow from the unknowable God"—undermines the significance of
the political themes and prepares the way for *The Plumed Serpent*.

Jack and Victoria Callcott have tempted Somers with power and love,
threatened his marriage with political and sexual involvement. But he
finally chooses individuality within marriage. His wife, Harriet, criticizes his vain attempts to succeed in the world of men, and he inevitably
returns to the protective security of the love of woman: "It only angered
her when he thought these other things—revolutions or governments or
whatnot—higher than their essential marriage. But then he would come
to himself and acknowledge that his marriage *was* the centre of his life,
the core, the root."[13] *Kangaroo* expresses Lawrence's attraction to political movements, to the idea of the brotherhood of man and to homosexual
comradeship. But for Somers, as for Lawrence, political activity is
ultimately meaningless.

V

On August 11, about three weeks after completing *Kangaroo,* the Lawrences returned to Sydney and sailed for San Francisco on the *Tahiti.*
Lawrence had told Earl Brewster, with perverse satisfaction, that he
actually courted disappointment in the South Pacific: "I'm determined
to *try* the South Sea Isles. Don't expect to catch on there either. But I love
trying things and discovering how I hate them." He stopped at Wellington (where he sent Katherine the postcard with *"Ricordi"*), in
Rarotonga in the Cook Islands, and in Tahiti, but these islands could no
longer sustain the legend of an exotic paradise that had been established
by Melville, Gauguin and Stevenson. Lawrence found the tropics as
rancid and revolting as Ceylon and thought the people were "ugly, false,
spoiled and diseased": "Papeete is a poor sort of place, mostly Chinese,
natives in European clothes, and fat. . . . I never want to *stay* in the
tropics. There is a sort of sickliness about them, smell of cocoa-nut oil and
sort of palm-tree, reptile nausea. . . . These are supposed to be the earthly
paradises: these South Sea Isles. You can have 'em."

While living in Taormina, Lawrence had told Compton Mackenzie
that he was drawn to the South Seas by Stevenson's writings: "I read
some of Stevenson. Idiot to go to Samoa just to dream and get thrilled
about Scotch bogs and mosses. No wonder he died. If I go to Samoa, it

will be to forget, not to remember." Yet Lawrence's attitudes were very similar to Stevenson's, whose savage pilgrimage anticipated, in many significant ways, Lawrence's own way of life and mode of travels.

Both Stevenson and Lawrence were archetypal expatriate writers whose cultural identities and artistic insights were strengthened by residence in foreign lands. Both rejected their family background but retained a strong sense of their native place. Both had adulterous affairs with and then married older, foreign, impractical women who had children from their previous marriages. Both remained childless themselves. Both were spontaneous, enthusiastic, generous men who inspired the adoration of possessive friends, despite their volatile temperaments and furious rages during sickness. Both wanted to live the life they wrote about, willingly endured the "incidental beastliness of travel," and sought a simple and even spartan existence. Both were oppressed by civilization and hoped to create an ideal community. Both were brought up in puritan households but believed, as Stevenson told his cousin Bob, that man should "honour sex more religiously. THE DAMNED THING of our education is that Christianity does not recognise and hallow sex."[14]

There are also striking similarities between Stevenson in Silverado and Lorenzo in Taos. Both became interested in America through Whitman and American literature, and were drawn to the continent by an older, divorced woman (Fanny Osbourne and Mabel Luhan). Both established a private and isolated life in a remote, rustic mountain cabin, near canyons and pinewoods, eagles, lions and bears. Both lived with their wives and with a painter as guest and companion, repaired and improved a dilapidated house, drew water, cut wood, practiced carpentry, fetched milk from a neighboring ranch, gave lessons in their household, bathed in medicinal springs. Both admired the Indians, defined their own identity and revalued civilization in relation to a primitive society.

Though Stevenson's style was more constrained and self-conscious, he and Lawrence shared a similar aesthetic of travel: a preference for a rough and relaxed rather than a comfortable and formal journey, popular rather than high culture, colloquial rather than mandarin style. Both *An Inland Voyage* (1878) and *Sea and Sardinia* end with a description of a marionette theater and return to their starting point in a final chapter, called "Back to the World" and "Back."

Unlike most men, whose lives are narrow and restricted, Stevenson and Lawrence had an infinite number of possibilities (especially in the days when the Empire and the pound were strong) and wanted to explore many of them before they finally decided where to live. Both wished to go to geographical as well as emotional extremes of temperature, height and distance. They were always excited by change and movement, by the exhilaration of departure and recourse to flight, by the opportunity to avoid people and mail, to clear out and be free. In *Travels with a Donkey* (1879), Stevenson wrote: "I travel not to go anywhere, but to go. I travel for travel's sake. The great affair is to move."[15] Lawrence opened *Sea and Sardinia* by exclaiming: "Comes over one an absolute necessity to move."

For both men travel was a method of inner exploration and a source of immediate inspiration. It intensified their sense of being British at the same time that it removed them from Britain and allowed them to see it more clearly. Both searched for a wild landscape and people who would reflect their own mood. "The frame of mind was the great exploit of our voyage," Stevenson observed. "It was the farthest piece of travel accomplished." Both felt the excitement more than balanced the discomfort of travel, that hardship intensified experience and made it more real. Stevenson declared: "Discomfort, when it is honestly uncomfortable and makes no nauseous pretensions to the contrary, is a vastly humorous business. . . . Six weeks in one unpleasant country-side had done more, it seemed, to quicken and educate my sensibilities than many years in places that jumped more nearly with my inclination."[16]

The initials of Richard Lovat Somers, wanderer in the antipodes and hero of *Kangaroo*, are doubtless a subtle acknowledgment of Stevenson's pervasive influence. For in 1923, the year that novel was published, Lawrence expressed a desire to travel exactly as Stevenson had done: "I think I shall go to California, and either pack with a donkey in the mountains, or get some sailing ship to the islands."[17]

CHAPTER SIXTEEN

To the New World,
1922–1923

I

AFTER READING *Sea and Sardinia* and some of the poems later collected in *Birds, Beasts and Flowers,* Mabel Dodge Sterne had realized that Lawrence was "the only one who can really *see* this Taos country and the Indians, and who can describe it so that it is as much alive between the covers of a book as it is in reality." She had written to Lawrence about the Indians, the town and the clear air of the Sangre de Cristo Mountains, offered to lend him a comfortable adobe guest house, sent Frieda a necklace that "carried some Indian magic" and *willed* them to come to Taos. In his first, cautious response to her letter, Lawrence asked some practical questions and inquired if Taos was the same sort of dreadful sub-arty colony that had driven him from Capri in February 1920. But he soon warmed to the idea. He wanted to connect himself to "the last dark strand from the previous, pre-white era" and liked the sound of Taos, which reminded him of Taormina.[1]

Weary of the political chaos in Italy, eager to visit the Brewsters in Ceylon and keen to see the New World, Lawrence responded to Mabel's enthusiastic invitation for three reasons. He wanted to write about American subjects, to develop an American audience and to put himself in touch with the primitive and regenerative powers of the Indians. "The Indian mode had sunk so far into forgetfulness," he told Catherine

Carswell, "so far beyond the confident prying of the intellect, that it was almost one with nature and therefore ready to re-nourish human life." Yet even before he reached Australia and America he expressed, in a letter to Mabel, his well-founded fears about the puritanism, material-ism and mass freedom that were the antithesis of the values he sought in the Indians: "I wish I could come to America without meeting the awful 'cultured' Americans with their limited self-righteous ideals and their mechanical love-motion and their bullying, detestable negative creed of liberty and democracy. I don't believe either in liberty or democracy."[2]

The Lawrences took the train from San Francisco to Lamy, New Mexico, where they were met by Mabel and her Indian chauffeur-lover, Tony Luhan. After they had driven for a while the car suddenly stopped. Tony looked under the hood but knew nothing about motors. Frieda urged Lawrence to have a look, but he knew even less than Tony. When Tony tried the car again and it started, he blamed the mechanical failure on the evil emanations of a nearby snake.

Since they could not reach Taos that night (the eve of Lawrence's thirty-seventh birthday), they stopped in Santa Fe, sixteen miles north of Lamy, where Mabel arranged for the Lawrences to stay with the poet Witter Bynner. Lawrence got out of the car, holding the painted panel of the Sicilian cart they had hauled all the way from Taormina. As he rested one end of it on the ground, Tony backed up the car, the panel buckled and split, and Lawrence exploded: "It's your fault, Frieda! You've made me carry that vile thing round the world, but I'm done with it. Take it, Mr. Bynner, keep it, it's yours!"

Mabel Ganson Evans Dodge Sterne Luhan, the daughter of a wealthy banker and of a mother who had had three husbands, was born in Buffalo in 1879 and was the same age as Frieda. In 1900 she married Karl Evans, the son of a prominent Buffalo family. He was killed in a hunting accident in 1903, the year after their son, John, was born. She married the Boston architect Edwin Dodge in 1903 and lived in a palazzo near Florence from 1905 until 1912, when she divorced him. In Italy she had befriended Eleonora Duse, Gertrude Stein and Bernard Berenson, and had tried suicide by laudanum. During the next four years she lived at 23 Fifth Avenue, near Greenwich Village, in New York. Her salon included the well-known journalists Lincoln Steffens and Walter Lipp-mann, and the sculptor Jo Davidson. She took many lovers, had a well-publicized affair with the revolutionary John Reed, was intimately involved with Max Eastman and began her twenty-year psychoanalysis with Freud's American translator, A. A. Brill. In 1916 she married the

Russian-Jewish painter and sculptor Maurice Sterne; and divorced him in 1922 during her menopause. She had always been frigid and could not enjoy sex with anyone for more than a short time. Her first three marriages were unhappy.[3]

Mabel, the last in a series of possessive women in Lawrence's life, had a great deal in common with Ottoline Morrell. Aristocratic, wealthy, imperious and irritating, Mabel was a bohemian patron of the arts and had had several famous lovers. She disliked Frieda, had tempestuous relations with Lawrence and was satirized in his works. Georgia O'Keeffe, who met Mabel a few years after Lawrence's stay in Taos, said she "had a small, square, determined body, bright gray eyes, and a soft melodious voice; she wore her thick chestnut hair in bangs, squaw style, often with a girlish ribbon." Enid Hilton found Mabel attractive: "Not pretty, but lively and powerful."[4]

Mabel was precisely the sort of woman Lawrence disliked, condemned, tried to avoid—and never could. By her own account, she was arrogant, egoistic, vain, petty, jealous and malicious: an overbearing and overwhelming woman. She was passionate about the Taos Indians; had a mystical streak and a weakness for Gurdjieff and Jung; led a meaningless existence; was often overcome by a dreadful sense of boredom and futility. The vital and amusing Lawrence made her life seem worthwhile, and she admitted: "I had tried to seduce his spirit so I could make it work for me instead of doing all the work for myself." Mabel constantly irritated and provoked Lawrence and made him feel as H. G. Wells felt about his mistress Elizabeth Russell (Bertrand's sister-in-law and Katherine Mansfield's cousin): "When you've had her for a week you want to bash her head through the wall."[5]

Yet with all her faults, and there were many, Mabel could be kind-hearted and generous in her way. She helped "discover" Taos in 1917, supported the local hospital, did a good deal for the welfare of the six hundred sun-worshipping Indians, took a serious interest in their cultural life and in their cubist, multitiered, flat-roofed, brown adobe Pueblo (just outside town). She recognized the importance of Lawrence, Robinson Jeffers and the photographer Edward Weston. Tony and Mabel introduced Lawrence to the Indian dances and rituals of the neighboring tribes. Mabel's invitation made possible the literary work that followed from Lawrence's journey to Taos: "Eagle in New Mexico," "Mountain Lion," "The Princess," *Mornings in Mexico, The Plumed Serpent* and two works that condemned her: "The Woman Who Rode Away" and *St. Mawr.*

Mabel's consort, Tony Luhan, was a tall, good-looking, heavily built, bold-featured, bronze-skinned, black-haired, pig-tailed Taos Pueblo Indian. He was illiterate and had only limited English, but was "intelligent in an Indian way: very aware of people and things." He would sit in a corner of Mabel's grand house, wrapped in a blanket and beating a drum. Tony, a carpenter, had supervised the Indian workers who built Mabel's house. When her marriage to Maurice Sterne broke up in 1922, she caused a scandal by seducing Tony and by marrying him the following year. The painter Knud Merrild told Lawrence: "The Indians don't like the marriage, and the Taos people don't, but they have something to talk about and that they *do* like." After Tony left his Indian wife, he was excluded from tribal ceremonies, and Mabel had to pay Candelaria thirty-five dollars a month for life in exchange for not interfering with them. Tony then began to wear expensive boots and tailored pants, which were forbidden on the reservation. He drove Mabel's guests around in her Cadillac, had several mistresses (including Candelaria) and gave Mabel syphilis. (Twelve percent of the Taos Indians suffered from this disease.) Yet Tony and Mabel got on well, were happy together and remained married until her death, in 1962. "Tony developed my latent feeling," Mabel explained, "and made me learn to love for the first time in my life, but he had no need to talk to me or have me talk to him."[6]

Lawrence took Mabel seriously, admired her energy, taught her to scrub floors and dress more modestly, tried to write a novel with her and remained a loyal friend—from a distance. In a letter to Frieda's mother, written two months after arriving in Taos, he sketched Mabel's background and noted the radical defects in her character:

Mabel Dodge: American—rich—only child—from Buffalo, on Lake Erie—bankers—42 years old—short, stout—looks young—has had three husbands—an Evans (dead), a Dodge (divorced), and a Maurice Sterne (Jew, Russian painter, young) (also divorced). Has now an Indian, Tony, a fat fellow. Has lived much in Europe—Paris, Nice, Florence—is rather famous in New York, and little loved—very clever for a female—another culture-bearer—likes to play the "patroness"—hates the white world, and loves the Indians out of hate—is very "noble," wants to be very "good," and is very wicked—has a terrible will to power.

Mabel confessed that she wanted to seduce Lawrence, in the spiritual if not the physical sense, and to subject him to her oppressive will: "I wanted to seduce his spirit so I could make him carry out certain things.... I did not want, particularly, to touch him. There was no natural, physical pleasure in contact with him. He was, somehow, too dry, not sensuous enough, and really not attractive to me physically." She also admitted that Lawrence considered her "the prototype of that greatest living abomination, the dominating American woman."[7]

Lawrence and Frieda found it difficult to distinguish between Mabel's spiritual and physical desires. They felt, despite Mabel's denials, that she *did* want to seduce him, and serious conflicts soon broke out with her. They could not bear, especially while living as dependents in Mabel's guest house, her patronizing manner, her hostility to Frieda and her attempts to destroy their marriage. In November, Lawrence defended his marriage and bluntly condemned her pernicious behavior: "I believe that, at its best, the central relation between Frieda and me is the best thing in my life, and, as far as I go, the best thing in life. You are *antagonistic* to the *living* relation of a man and his wife: because you only understand a sort of bullying: viz. Tony, John Evans [her son] and the rest.—So, I count you antagonistic to the living relation between Frieda and me."

Mabel undoubtedly exacerbated the conflicts between Lawrence and Frieda—the Indians called the Lawrences Red Fox and Angry Winter—and reported with great relish their guerrilla warfare and winter offensives. On one occasion, she wrote, he shook his finger in Frieda's face and screamed: "Take that dirty cigarette out of your mouth! And stop sticking out that fat belly of yours." To which Frieda replied, threatening to expose some horrible intimacies that only a wife could reveal: "You'd better stop that talk or I'll tell about *your* things." When they bathed naked in the local hot springs, Mabel noticed great bruises on Frieda's fair skin, and she sometimes saw her eyes red and swollen from weeping. According to Mabel, Frieda could not bear Lawrence's violent changes of mood: "I cannot stand it. He tears me to pieces. Last night he was so loving and so tender with me, and this morning he hates me. He hit me—and said he would not be any woman's servant. Sometimes I believe he is mad.... You don't know what it's like—living with him. Sometimes I think I'll leave him." But when Mabel told Frieda she was not the right woman for Lawrence, she angrily replied: try living with a genius and see how easy it is, and challenged Mabel to "take him if you can." In 1922 Frieda echoed Lawrence's judgment by attacking Mabel's will to power and predatory predisposition: "You never cared a rap about me, you don't want a *relationship* with either Lawrence or me, you only want people in your *power*—the game you play with him *bores* me in both of you.... I despise it—it's the same man-hunt, the female on the hunt." After Lawrence's death, Frieda's perceptive letter to Mabel summarized the crucial defect in her character: "You never cared for anybody and you never will, that is your tragedy."[8]

Mabel's repellent egoism forced the Lawrences to leave her protective custody in Taos after two and a half months and move into the mountains. And when Mabel continued to provoke him from a distance, Lawrence exclaimed: "I feel I could kill and that I should enjoy doing it.... I will kill Mabel first.... I will use a knife! ... *I will cut her throat!*" In *The Plumed Serpent* (1926), Kate's degrading relations with Cipriano are based on Lawrence's perception of Mabel's marriage to Tony. In *St. Mawr* (1925), Lawrence portrays her as Mrs. Witt, who exemplifies the radical problem in Lawrence's willful women. She destroyed all the men she met, but secretly wanted to be dominated by a strong male will: "Examining herself, she had long ago decided that her nature was a destructive force. But then, she justified herself, she had only destroyed that which was destructible. If she could have found something indestructible, especially in men, though she would have fought against it, she would have been glad at last to be defeated by it. That was the point. She really wanted to be defeated, in her own eyes. And nobody had ever defeated her." Lawrence described Mabel's corruption of Tony, who traded old customs for new Cadillacs, when he wrote of the Indian Phoenix, whom Mrs. Witt wants to marry: "he was ready to trade his sex, which, in his opinion, every white woman was secretly pining for, for the white woman's money and social privileges."[9]

The heroine of Lawrence's story "The Woman Who Rode Away" (1925) is also based on Mabel. The American woman—living in the wilds of Mexico, bored with her jealous, materialistic husband and dead inside—rides off on horseback to discover the savage customs and old religion of the Indians. While living among them and experiencing their rituals (including a vivid experience with drugs), she submits to their power and offers herself as a human sacrifice to bring back the dark gods. At the winter solstice, when a shaft of ice symbolically penetrates the sacred cave, the high priest attempts to restore the tribe's power by giving her heart to the sun. In this apocalyptic story about the end of the old order, the woman experiences a rebirth through new awareness and a return to an original state of primitive purity. But the woman's cruel fate (which reflects Lawrence's desire to kill Mabel) and her worship of death (an expression of Mabel's malign will) do not seem a convincing way to cure the ills of modern civilization.

II

On December 1, 1922, the Lawrences finally escaped from "Mabeltown." When she raised difficulties about their living on her mountain ranch, they rented from the Hawk family two cabins on the Del Monte ranch, in the mountains, seventeen miles from Taos. Lawrence always felt the contrast between Taos and the isolated ranch. In the town, the main square and the adobe houses of the local artists, malicious gossip was rampant. And the white man, who had transformed Taos into a bohemian dude ranch and playground, was corrupting the intense animistic religion of the Indians: "It is all rather like comic opera played with solemn intensity. All the wildness and woolliness and westernity and motor-cars and art and sage and savage are so mixed up, so incongruous, that it is a farce, and everybody knows it. . . . And the Indian, with his long hair and his bits of pottery and blankets and clumsy home-made trinkets, [is] a wonderful live toy to play with. More fun than keeping rabbits, and just as harmless."[10]

The Del Monte ranch was surrounded by the silver gray of the sagebrush, the quick, clear water of the irrigation ditches, the heavy green of the alfalfa and the high trails where the shy deer jumped. Lawrence's old five-room log cabin had been built at the turn of the century among the pine trees at the foot of the Rockies, about 8,500 feet high, with spectacular views of the desert and the range of distant peaks. Lawrence found a great deal of satisfaction in living independently in the untouched country—with its silence and space, its clear skies and starry nights—that still retained its aboriginal quality.

Lawrence's tuberculosis and his recent disease in Ceylon made it impossible for him to do all the heavy chores (Frieda remained idle and impractical) during the long winter months in the high Rockies. In Taos he met two adventurous Danish painters, Knud Merrild and Kai Götzsche, who had arrived in America in 1921 and driven across the country in a rattletrap Model-T Ford. He liked the Danes and invited them to share the work and spend the winter of 1922–23 as his guests—and as a buffer between himself and Frieda—on the Del Monte ranch.

The Danes made the strenuous horseback ride to Taos whenever necessary, brought supplies, mail and gossip from the town, provided company and conversation, and owned a car that (weather permitting) would take Lawrence wherever he wished to go. (On one perilous trip they were forced off the road by a Mexican wagon and nearly fell over a cliff.) Merrild wrote, with defensive modesty: "We did not possess the brilliance of his mind nor the abundance of his knowledge; we had only horse sense, and knew people and the world by experience. . . . We did not play up to him, and were not afraid of voicing our opinions, whether they were contrary to his or not. We did not hesitate to side with Frieda, either, when we thought him wrong."[11]

The modest and unpretentious Danes were honored by their friend-ship with Lawrence, respectful of Frieda and (after being snubbed as inconsequential by Mabel) delighted that Lawrence preferred their company to hers. Merrild explained that despite their different back-grounds, they had many things in common with Lawrence: "We had served apprenticeships as workers and lived among the working-classes. We had had academic training, and then as artists had had access to the highest circles of society. Then too, we had travelled far and wide."

Though Merrild was then twenty-eight years old and Götzsche thirty-six (only a year younger than Lawrence), they seemed quite boyish and developed a filial relationship with the Lawrences. Frieda took motherly care of them, made sure they had enough to eat and inspired their profound affection. Lawrence, who also felt responsible for their welfare and commissioned them to do dust jackets for several of his books, constantly played the benefactor and schoolmaster. He taught them riding, cooking and Spanish, commented on their music and art, and endlessly expounded his ideas. Their great virtues were loyalty to Lawrence and willingness to help when they were needed.

On the ranch, Lawrence utilized the experience he had gained on the farms of the Chamberses and the Hockings. He was as adept as ever at household chores. Bynner noticed, the morning after Lawrence had been his guest in Santa Fe, that Lawrence had got up early, made his bed, washed the dinner dishes, laid the table and cooked an ample breakfast. On the ranch he would paint and write, sit for portraits by the Danes, go fishing, pick wild berries, sing songs, play charades, look through the Montgomery Ward catalogue for Christmas presents and drink a bit of moonshine whiskey. He would bake bread, cook the simple meals, chop wood, mend fences, repair the house, clean the irrigation ditches and feed the horses. While living at Del Monte he was visited by Seltzer and Mountsier, and heard about the death of Katherine Mansfield. He also wrote several poems, revised the Verga translations and *Kangaroo,* and completed his influential critical book, *Studies in Classic American Literature.*

Lawrence's greatest joy was exploring the countryside on horseback. Mabel, usually hostile to Lawrence, reported that with no training or experience he was absolutely fearless, never fell off a horse, and always had courage and will. But Rachel Hawk criticized Lawrence's riding. She thought he was selfish, rode too fast and had no consideration for the horse's legs when going downhill. He should have been thrown and taught a lesson, but never was.[12]

Though they lived in proximity, Lawrence got on as well with the Danes as he had with the Brewsters. But they had ample opportunity to observe his idiosyncrasies, and there were inevitably some moments of tension. Götzsche described how "he bends his head far down, till his beard is resting on his chest and he says (not laughing) 'Hee, hee, hee' every time one talks to him. A cold stream always runs down my spine when he does that. I feel it is something insane about him." One day Meta Lehmann, a friend of the Danes, hitchhiked and walked up to their cabin to discuss an exhibition she had arranged for them at the Santa Fe Museum. It was impossible for her to return to Taos that night. She did not want to impose on the Hawks (whom she did not know). Lawrence refused to allow her to sleep in his cabin. And he vehemently objected to her staying alone with the Danes. Meta was "a lost soul, but attractive to men. . . . [She] was a little 'gone' on the Indians, in fact had an Indian lover." Lawrence thought Meta had a dubious reputation. He fussed about like a maiden aunt, worried about the virginity of the Danes, and was seriously concerned about the gossip and scandal she might cause. The Danes ignored his fulminations and made a bed for Meta on their couch: "Since the door between the two rooms could not be locked, we advised Meta to barricade it so that we couldn't come in and rape her during the night. She laughed and said we were the ones who had to look out for the lecherous witch." Despite Lawrence's scandalous adultery with Frieda and the powerful sexual themes in his work, he always retained his deep-rooted puritanism. He objected to the Danes' over-night guest as he had objected to Catherine Carswell appearing in her modest sleeping garments in Cornwall, and reacted to their visitor exactly as his mother would have done.

A second "sexual" incident also provoked Lawrence's irrational rage. When his little black snub-nosed French bull terrier, Pips, went into heat and became "sex-alive," she ignored Lawrence's commands and ran off with a big Airedale. Lawrence thought she had "appropriated" his emotions, felt betrayed and was horrified by her indiscriminate love-making. He finally found the dog resting on Götzsche's lap, cursed her and screamed: "So there you are you dirty, false little bitch," struck her with all his might and knocked her to the floor. Pips ran out of the cabin and into the snow, but Lawrence caught up with her. She refused his orders to come home; he kicked her and hurled her to the ground. Merrild prevented him from doing more harm to the dog, and they almost came to blows. The next day, though Lawrence did not apologize, he brought the Danes a peace offering of freshly baked bread and cakes.

Lawrence was affronted by the dog's open expression of sexual desire. She was the first living creature that had belonged to him since the rabbits of his childhood, and he took her "infidelity" personally. He may even have associated it with Frieda's past behavior. Lawrence expressed his possessive, self-righteous feelings about the dog's natural impulses in his poem "Bibbles":

> Then when I dust you with a bit of juniper twig
> You run straight away to live with somebody else,
> Fawn before them, and love them as if they were the ones you
>   had *really* loved all along.
> And they're taken in.
> They feel quite tender over you, till you play the same trick
>   on them, dirty bitch.
>
> Fidelity! Loyalty! Attachment!
> Oh, these are abstractions to your nasty little belly.
> You must always be a-waggle with LOVE. . . .
>
> All right, my little bitch.
> You learn loyalty rather than loving,
> And I'll protect you.[13]

Lawrence was also fond of and on excellent terms with the young, educated Hawks, who had a dairy farm on the Del Monte ranch. Rachel was born in Pennsylvania in 1898, William in Oklahoma in 1891. Her mother and his father, who were tubercular, had come to New Mexico for their health. William's sisters attended the same school in Pennsylvania as Rachel, and she met William there when he was on his way back from World War I. They married after the war and had two children, Walton and Shirley. Rachel, who had Swedish ancestors, was a beautiful woman, with curly blond hair and a fine complexion. Dorothy Brett wrote that "her bobbed, wavy, golden hair curls round her head; the eyes are bright hazel; the nose short and straight. She smiles at you: her teeth are white and even. There is strength in her movements, in the slim, upright figure; a boyish hardness about her whole appearance." But Rachel could be cold and was sometimes cruel to Brett. Since William was congenial but lazy, Rachel did most of the work on the ranch.[14]

Rachel was not surprised when Lawrence wanted to rent the two cabins. The thin mountain air was healthy, and it was common for invalids to spend the winter in New Mexico. Rachel found him a "skinny little man," sickly part of the time but never coughing and spitting. She did not think he had tuberculosis and (like the Brewsters) did not fear her children would be infected by his disease. Lawrence was independent and managed quite well on the ranch without their help or advice. He knew how to do the chores and milk the cow. He cooked for his guests and could prepare a good steak-and-potatoes dinner.

Rachel found Lawrence a selfish and short-tempered man, and was astonished by his public fights with his wife. Frieda would slowly say, "Oh mmmyyy!" and try to ignore his frequent explosions. But he was fascinating when he described natural scenery and his travel experiences. Though Frieda never did much work, she kept the house clean and (in contrast to Lawrence) was always in a good mood. Since Rachel was extremely busy with her family and farm, and felt "people should be left alone," she had neither the desire nor the time to see Lawrence—or anyone else. She knew nothing of his reputation as a writer and never read any of his books. She disliked some aspects of his character and thought him an unimpressive man.

Lawrence spent twenty-two months in New Mexico—broken by three trips to Mexico—between September 1922 and September 1925. The pristine beauty of mountains and desert and the traditional life of the Indians epitomized for him the best aspects of the New World and seemed to offer a hopeful alternative to the mechanical civilization of Europe and America:

> I think New Mexico was the greatest experience from the outside world that I have ever had. It certainly changed me for ever. . . . The moment I saw the brilliant, proud morning shine high up over the deserts of Santa Fe, something stood still in my soul, and I started to attend. . . . In the magnificent fierce morning of New Mexico one sprang awake, a new part of the soul woke up suddenly, and the old world gave way to the new.[15]

III

On March 18 the Lawrences left Taos, traveled south by train through Santa Fe and El Paso, reached Mexico City a week later and settled into the small, modest Hotel Monte Carlo, run by an Italian family. (The American writer Carleton Beals called it "a smelly Italian hostelry.") Lawrence's first impressions of Mexico were favorable. The climate was pleasantly warm, the atmosphere was like Naples, free and easy, the people were human instead of mechanical. But he also sensed in the gruesome Aztec carvings the cruel, ghastly spirit of the country. Mexico City, a mongrel town, combined American modernism with urban slums. The countryside was more attractive, but disfigured by houses and haciendas that had been damaged by the recent revolutions. Nevertheless, he felt Mexico might be a promising subject and a good place to work. He decided to look for a house and to live there for a while.

During his month in the capital Lawrence visited the cathedral and the vast open market, planned to meet the minister of education (who enraged Lawrence when he was forced to cancel the appointment at the last moment), went to a bullfight, inspected the frescoes by Rivera and Orozco, and traveled to the nearby towns. Lawrence said that he ran away from the terrible bullfight on April 1 after only ten minutes, but he was sufficiently interested in the spectacle to see another bullfight six months later, in Tepic, in October 1923.

Lawrence gives a detailed description of the *corrida* in the opening chapter of his Mexican novel, *The Plumed Serpent*. At the bullfight, the spectators are searched for firearms because the outgoing president (Álvaro Obregón) plans to attend. The *corrida* immediately establishes the revolutionary atmosphere and symbolizes to the Irish heroine, Kate Leslie, the violence and corruption of the country. She is so revolted by the disemboweled horse that she leaves (like Lawrence) before the first kill.[16] The fat, cowardly *matadores* seem to represent the exploitive upper class; the bull signifies the army; and the sacrificial horse of the *picador,* the victimized peons. Lawrence's account of the bullfight is factually inaccurate, for he was more interested in conveying the mood than in presenting it correctly. He writes that seven bulls were killed by four *toreros,* but there is always the same number of bulls for each *matador,* so that the risk is equal. Lawrence's disgusted description of the *corrida* provides a striking contrast to the portrayal by the *aficionado* Hemingway in chapter 18 of *The Sun Also Rises,* also published in 1926. Lawrence portrays his response to Diego Rivera's frescoes at the university in chapter 3 of the novel: "the impulse was the impulse of the artist's hate. In the many frescoes of the Indians, there was sympathy with the Indian, but always from the ideal, social point of view. Never the spontaneous answer of the blood. These flat Indians were symbols in the great script of modern socialism, they were figures of the pathos of the victims of modern industry and capitalism." And he finds the frescoes by José Clemente Orozco (not named in the novel) even more repellent: "They are ugly and vulgar. Strident caricatures of the Capitalist, and the Church, and of the Rich Woman and of Mammon painted life-size and as violently as possible."

In April, Lawrence took short trips to neighboring towns— Cuernavaca, Puebla, Tehuacán and Orizaba—where he first experienced the violence of Mexico. The revolutions that had taken place between 1911 and 1920 had achieved social progress, especially in land reform, and had weakened the old feudal system, but the results of the long civil wars were disastrous. As Lawrence wrote in the novel: "the last census of Porfirio Díaz gave seventeen million people in Mexico, and the census of last year [c.1923] gave only thirteen millions." The profoundly depressing effects of the Mexican Revolution and the almost indistinguishably unstable and corrupt regimes of Francisco Madero, Adolfo de la Huerta, Venustiano Carranza, Álvaro Obregón and Plutarco Calles were later summarized by the Mexican novelist Carlos Fuentes: "the men who believed the Revolution's purpose was to liberate the people have been eliminated. The purpose today is to glorify leaders. . . . We have allowed ourselves to be divided and controlled by the ruthless, the ambitious and the mediocre. Those who [like Pancho Villa and Emiliano Zapata] wanted a true revolution, radical and uncompromising, are unfortunately ignorant and bloody men."[17]

Lawrence observed the chaotic course of the revolution during three visits in two years. The Lawrences first visited Mexico with Witter Bynner from March to July 1923, when Lawrence completed the first draft of his novel. He went back with Kai Götzsche from September to November 1923. And the Lawrences returned with Brett from October 1924 until March 1925, when he rewrote and finished the novel. His personal reaction to the violence, expressed in his letters as well as his novel, was fear, tempered by a fascination with primitive power.

In April 1923, Lawrence noted a disturbing combination of vitality and morbidity, beauty and destruction: "We were in Cuernavaca— where Zapata held out so long. Dead, dead, beautiful cathedrals—dead Spain—dead!—but underneath, live peons.—Soldiers everywhere— riding on roof of trains to guard them—soldiers, soldiers—And ruins! Nearly all the big haciendas and big houses are ruins, shells. A great deal of waste country. . . . You can't live even one mile outside the village or town: you will probably be robbed or murdered by roving bandits and scoundrels who still call themselves revolutionaries." Two months later he wrote Merrild with ironic bravado: "now they are expecting more revolution, and it is so risky. . . . If I can't stand Europe we'll come back to Mexico and spit on our hands and stick knives and revolvers in our belts—one really has to—and have a place here."[18]

In May the Lawrences rented a house on Lake Chapala, about thirty miles from Guadalajara, and lived there until early July. The long, low villa had its own little garden with flowers and bananas, a family of servants who obliged them to speak Spanish, and a young man armed with a pistol, who slept on the terrace outside their door. Lawrence said the cloudy lake—forty miles long, twenty miles wide, surrounded by low mountains and dry country—had "sperm-like water." In late June he took a three-day boat trip on the lake with Witter Bynner and a group of American friends.

Witter Bynner (four years older than Lawrence) and his young lover, Willard "Spud" Johnson, traveled with Lawrence in Mexico and lived near him in Chapala. Bynner was born in New York, had graduated from Harvard in 1902, traveled extensively in China and was extremely wealthy. Johnson was a sweet, quiet, faintly poetic soul. They were satirized as the thrill-seeking Owen Rhys and the bland Bud Villiers in *The Plumed Serpent*. Though Kate Leslie is fond of Owen, she cannot respect him: he is "so empty, and waiting for circumstance to fill him up. Swept with an American despair of having lived in vain, or of not having *really* lived. Having missed something. Which fearful misgiving would make him rush like mechanical steel filings to a magnet, towards any crowd in the street. And then, all his poetry and philosophy [would be] gone with the cigarette-end he threw away."

Bynner, a bald poet, with limited talent and waspish tongue, mocked Lawrence's embarrassment about his pale, skinny body. Lawrence had written many descriptions of fictional characters running, rolling, dancing, swimming and love-making naked in a natural setting. But he "never joined us in the lake. . . . [He] was acutely sensitive concerning his bony, pinched, pigeon-breasted, clay-white body, and I believe he was a touch jealous when Frieda would gaily join us." In the "Nightmare" chapter of *Kangaroo,* Lawrence confirms Bynner's assessment and describes Somers' "ridiculously thin legs" when he strips for his medical examination. Yet after his quarrel with Bertrand Russell in 1915, Lawrence, forgetting his own physical limitations, criticized the philosopher for having the same defect. When a friend told Lawrence that Russell had insisted, "Lawrence has no mind," "Lawrence 'sniffed' and said: 'Have you seen him in a bathing dress? Poor Bertie Russell! He is all Disembodied Mind!'"[19]

Lawrence's attitude toward Mexico remained ambivalent: he loved it and detested it, planned to buy his ticket back to Europe and then changed his mind. He thought the country was half civilized, half wild; the people gentle and honest, yet strange and savage underneath. And he penetrated to the somber, torpid essence of the place in two perceptive sentences: "Mexico altogether is terribly heavy, as if it had hardly the energy to get up and live. . . . The soul of the country sulks, and won't look up." He felt, at times, that it was wrong to live in such a remote place, that he ought to take another trip around the world and write a novel in India or China.

IV

The violence in Mexico seemed to release the violence in Lawrence and intensify his conflicts with Frieda. Bynner reported that their arguments about her children continued, like a running sore, until well after the children had grown up. When Frieda proudly showed photographs of her brood, Lawrence, attempting to bind her more closely to himself by cutting her off from his rivals, reacted with irrational rage: "Lawrence was out of his chair like a rattler. 'You sniffling bitch!' . . . He snatched the pictures from Frieda, tore each one across the face twice, flung the first one, then the other on the floor, treading on each in turn. 'That's better,' he yelped, 'much better. Now you can't be a fool over them any more.'"

If Frieda called an idea "hellish," Lawrence would abuse her for being vulgar and, at the same time, call the same idea "shit and nonsense." Bynner also reported that Lawrence would criticize Frieda for her smoking and slovenly demeanor, condemn her past behavior and even throw wine in her face:

> "Take that thing out of your mouth!" She gazed at him, wide eyed, without answering. "Take it out, I say, you sniffling bitch! . . . There you sit with that thing in your mouth and your legs open to every man in the room! And you wonder why no decent woman in England would have anything to do with you!" Flinging the remaining drops of Chianti at her, he darted past the other tables into the lobby.

Frederick Leighton, an acquaintance who supervised the teaching of English in Mexican schools, failed to perceive that the Lawrences liked high tension and public displays of emotion. He was astonished by their mutual vilification in public: "Never before or since have I heard a human being, in educated society, repeatedly release such a flow of obscene vile abuse on his wife (or on anyone) in the presence of comparative strangers as Lawrence did on Frieda; nor, I must admit, have I heard such apparently uninhibited response."[20] At the Fontana Vecchia in Taormina, Lawrence had once tried to choke her and screamed in his rage: "I am the master, I am the master!" Frieda, gasping for air, remained remarkably cool and conceded: "Is that all? I don't care, you can be the master as much as you like."[21]

In July 1923, just after Lawrence had completed the first draft of *The Plumed Serpent,* they traveled from Chapala to New York with the intention of returning to Europe. His rootlessness, isolation, financial problems with Seltzer and confusion about the future as well as Frieda's longing for a settled home and for her mother and children (whom she had not seen for four years), exacerbated their eternal conflicts about dominance and submission, and precipitated the most serious crisis of their marriage.

The Lawrences, staying for a month at the Seltzers' country cottage in New Jersey, had planned to see the Brewsters in New Haven on their way to visit the generous but irritating Amy Lowell in Boston. But they were now too distracted and angry to do so. Lawrence's uneasy *de haut en bas* relations with Amy surfaced when he wrote: "Not having a secretary to [type and] sign my letter I sign it myself," and when he gave his Sicilian landlord, coming to work in Boston, a letter of introduction. Amy, who could not conceive of a connection with a cook, replied: "I will look up your Sicilian, although I cannot see what good it will do as I am not by way of being able to employ him." Amy had, at first, defended her literary territory and discouraged Lawrence's visit to America and to Boston. Then she relented, and invited him for three days. But Lawrence, using the excuse of Frieda's urgent dental appointment in New York, decided not to go.

Frieda was determined to return to Europe. But Lawrence, for reasons unclear even to himself, kept postponing the sailing date. He originally planned to leave as early as July 18, but the thought of England made him melancholy, and he could not bear the idea of chasing after the Weekley children. On August 18 he took Frieda to the ship; she begged him to leave with her and he refused. "When they parted," wrote Catherine Carswell, "it was in such anger that both of them felt it might be for always."[22]

New York revolted Lawrence and made him want to journey to the ends of the earth. He decided to recross the country alone, stopping in Buffalo to meet Mabel's family and to see Niagara Falls; and reached Los Angeles, where the Danes were then living, at the end of August. Tired of the solid world, he revived the idea of finding a ship and sailing to the South Seas, though he had intensely disliked the islands when he was there in the summer of 1922. But he always planned to return to Europe or to meet Frieda in America. There was no reference in letters to friends of an explosive quarrel and no suggestion of a permanent separation.

V

When Lawrence reached Los Angeles, the Danes noticed that he was gloomy and restless without Frieda. He stayed there for a month, and then slowly wandered down the hot west coast of Mexico—wilder, emptier and more hopeless than Chapala—with Kai Götzsche. In Navojoa, about halfway between the border and Mazatlán, he wrote Bynner a vivid letter about the climate, the landscape and the strange atmosphere of the town:

There is a blazing sun, a vast hot sky, big lonely inhuman green hills and mountains, a flat blazing littoral with a few palms, sometimes a dark blue sea which is not quite of this earth—then little towns that seem to be slipping down an abyss—and the door of life shut on it all, only the sun burning, the clouds of birds passing, the zopilotes [buzzards] like flies, the lost lonely palm-trees, the deep dust of the roads, the donkeys moving in a gold-dust-cloud. In the mountains, lost, motionless silver-mines. Alamos a once lovely little town, lost, and slipping down the gulf in the mountains, forty miles up the awfullest road I've ever been bruised along. But somehow or other, you get there. And more wonderful, you get *out* again.—There seems a sentence of extinction written over it all.— In the middle of the little covered market at Alamos, between the meat and the vegetables, a dead dog lay stretched as if asleep. The meat vendor said to the vegetable man: You'd better throw it out. The veg-man looked at the dead dog and saw no reason for throwing it out. So no doubt it still lies there.

The dead dog lying in the marketplace reappears on the first page of "The Woman Who Rode Away" to represent the "deadness within deadness" of the little town forgotten among the mountains, from which the woman escapes to her cruel regeneration and death.

At Tepic, about two hundred miles south of Mazatlán, Lawrence turned inland. He rode a mule on a rocky path over the mountains and down the ravines, slept in a shed, rose at dawn, got more mules and rode for six more hours, until he reached the railway. He then spent a month in Guadalajara and revisited Chapala. The lake was still beautiful, but he could not recapture the past. Something was gone, and Chapala now seemed raw and alien. Yet Mexico still fascinated him: "It seems to me as if the gods were here." He felt that England, to come fully alive, needed a transfusion of the "dark volcanic blood" of the Mexican people. On All Souls Day in Guadalajara, the great feast of the dead, he saw this spirit represented in the local artifacts that were sold at the fair:

[They] sell toys of skeleton men on skeleton horses, skeletons in coffins, skeletons like jack-in-the-boxes—skeletons of marzipan— skeletons on bulls, skeleton bull-fighters fighting skeleton bulls.— Bones! And they seem fascinated. They all buy little toys. Galeana St. is crowded—like a sort of Arabian Nights, booths, awnings, water-carriers, balloons, big hats, serapes, candles, lanterns. Quite amusing.[23]

Frieda refused to come to Mexico and cabled Lawrence to return to England. Their fight continued and he submitted (as usual) to her will.

But as he weakened, he complained to his mother-in-law about Frieda's expression (in her letters) of her love: "It's stupidity. . . . The man does not need, does not ask for love from his wife, but strength, strength, strength"—which he would certainly need in the years to come.

On November 22, after two months in Mexico, Lawrence sailed with Götzsche from Vera Cruz, stopping in Havana and Vigo, and arrived in Plymouth on December 12. Frieda, remembering her infidelity and the treacherous "Last Supper" that took place in London after Lawrence's arrival, later admitted that he had been right in not wanting to return to England: "[The children] didn't want me any more, they were living their own lives. I felt lost without him. . . . I should have gone to meet him in Mexico, he should not have come to Europe; these are the mistakes we make, sometimes irreparable."[24]

CHAPTER SEVENTEEN

London, Taos
and Oaxaca,
1923–1925

I

LAWRENCE'S troubled relations with Murry reached a crisis when
he returned to London from Mexico in December 1923. Although Murry
had rejected Lawrence's offer of a deeper intimacy, he continued to
express his devotion in letters. In 1917 an exasperated Lawrence had
criticized his hypocritical effusions: "You shouldn't say you love me. You
disliked me intensely when you were here, and also at Mylor," in south
Cornwall. Murry's admiration for Lawrence was always compounded
with rivalry and envy. He later confessed in his journal that "he had
been 'a fool, a jealous fool' in those early days, when each man saw himself
as the Novelist of the Age."[1]

In February 1920 Lawrence sent his cruel letter to Katherine, "stewing in her consumption"; and Murry's treacherous reviews of Lawrence's
books, rejection of his work and intimacy with Frieda may have been a
deliberate or unconscious attempt at revenge. Murry promised to follow
Lawrence to Fiascherino in 1913, to Taos in 1923 and to Spotorno in
1925; but he broke his word and disappointed Lawrence on all three
occasions.

Murry's influential review of *The Lost Girl* in the *Athenaeum* of December 17, 1920, entitled "The Decay of Mr. Lawrence," claimed not only that the novel revealed "a very obvious loss of imaginative power" but also that "Lawrence had lost some power of immediate contact with human beings." Murry, who was to become after Katherine's death much more mystical than Lawrence ever was, concluded with words that inevitably recalled the earlier condemnations of *The Rainbow:* "Life, as Mr. Lawrence shows it to us, is not worth living; it is mysteriously degraded by a corrupt mysticism. Mr. Lawrence would have us back to the slime from which we rose." His review in the *Nation and Athenaeum* of August 13, 1921, of *Women in Love,* the novel that portrayed aspects of Katherine's and Murry's characters in Gudrun and Gerald, was even more negative and obtuse. He insisted that Lawrence—in what is now considered his greatest novel—had "sacrificed his gifts, his vision, his delicacy, and his eloquence . . . [in] wave after wave of turgid, exasperated writing," "that he is an artist no longer . . . [but] deliberately, incessantly, and passionately obscene." Murry expressed his repulsion and weariness with the novel and, repeating his viscous metaphor, pronounced it "sub-human and bestial, a thing that our forefathers had rejected when they began to rise from the slime." Murry's reviews suggest that he both lacked critical insight and was jealous of Lawrence's gifts.

In 1919 with the *Athenaeum* and again in 1923 with the *Adelphi,* Murry first solicited and then rejected Lawrence's work. As Lawrence told his disciple Rolf Gardiner in August 1924: "Murry said to me last year: 'Come, only come, and do what you like with the *Adelphi.*' I came in December. He went green at my first article ["On Coming Home"], and—wouldn't print it. *No Lorenzo, you'll only make enemies.*—As if that weren't what I want."[2] At the same time that he denigrated and rejected Lawrence's work, Murry was inflating the reputation and establishing the cult of Katherine Mansfield.

Murry's guilt about his selfish and irresponsible treatment of Katherine, whom he had abandoned to Gurdjieff at the end of her life, led directly to the egoistic enshrinement of his wife. As high priest of Katherine's cult, Murry glorified his own role, image and importance. He exploited her tragic death, created an idealized portrait that falsified her achievement, and made a good deal of money by publishing her posthumous works.

Aldous Huxley, who was Murry's editorial assistant on the *Athenaeum* in 1919, characterized him as Burlap in *Point Counter Point*

(1928) and exposed the spurious self-projection that Katherine had also condemned when she wrote: "His very frankness is a falsity. In fact it seems falser than his insincerity."

> When Susan died Burlap exploited the grief he felt, or at any rate loudly said he felt, in a more than usually painful series of those always painfully personal articles which were the secret of his success as a journalist ... pages of a rather hysterical lyricism about the dead child-woman. ...
>
> At the end of some few days of incessant spiritual masturbation, he had been rewarded by a mystical realization of his own unique and incomparable piteousness. ... Frail, squeamish, less than fully alive and therefore less than adult, permanently under-aged, [Susan] adored him as a superior and almost holy lover ... [who would] roll at her feet in an ecstasy of incestuous adoration for the imaginary mother-baby of a wife with whom he had chosen to identify the corporeal Susan.

Huxley perceived not only the falseness of the cult and Murry's exploitation of his grief, but also his emotional immaturity and childish role playing with Katherine. And he described the destructive aspect of Murry's "mystical" love in the metaphor of sexual perversion.

Lawrence's story "Smile" (1926), also based on Murry's response to Katherine's death, emphasized Murry's passivity and confusion. He portrayed the selfish reaction of a man who sees his dead wife's body in a French convent (Katherine had died in Gurdjieff's "Priory" at Fontainebleau) and feels an ambiguous mixture of guilt, self-pity, indifference and lust for a young nun: "He did not weep: he just gazed without meaning. Only, on his face deepened the look. I knew this martyrdom was in store for me! She was so pretty, so childlike, so clever, so obstinate, so worn—and so dead! He felt so blank about it all!"[3]

In September 1923, nine months after Katherine's death, Murry brought out twenty-one of her stories (of which fifteen were unfinished) in *The Dove's Nest*. Lawrence thought it outrageous to ask readers to buy that wastepaper basket. Six years later, commenting on Murry's cult in an unpublished letter to his German translator, Lawrence wrote: "Poor Katherine Mansfield! ... She belongs to her day and will fade. I know her too well, though, to accept her as a saint." He expressed his disgust at Murry's commercialization of Katherine and, accurately predicting the future, told Bynner: "Katherine Mansfield was worth a thousand Murrys! But he drove her sick, neglected her, wandered away from her till she died, and then prowled back like a hyena to make a meal of her! He'll do the same to me!"[4]

II

Lawrence had inadvertently encouraged Murry by telling him in August 1923: "Frieda intends to come to England. . . . I wish you'd look after her a bit: would it be a nuisance? She will be all alone." The following month, after Frieda had quarreled with Lawrence, left America without him and been rejected by her children, who were leading their own lives and no longer needed their mother, she turned to Murry. He was a serious threat to the Lawrences' marriage, both in 1916, when Lawrence was attracted to him, and in 1923, when Frieda was. Murry wrote that Frieda arrived in England completely out of love with her husband, and he justified her infidelity: "She had had enough of Lawrence in his Mexican 'moods,' and in fact she had left him. She felt— rightly enough—no more loyalty to him."

Since Katherine had died in January and Lawrence was in America, Frieda and Murry decided to travel together to Germany (as she had traveled with Lawrence to Metz in 1912). According to Murry's cliché-ridden, unconvincing account, they fell in love and—though Frieda had left Lawrence and rightly felt no loyalty to him—restrained themselves and did not become lovers: "On the journey we declared our love to each other. She was sweet and lovely, altogether adorable, and she wanted us to stay together in Freiburg [where she had first met Ernest Weekley] for a few days anyhow, and I wanted it terribly. The idea of our sleeping together, waking in each other's arms, seemed like heaven on earth. I was worn out with the long strain of Katherine's illness, and Frieda's love was the promise of renewal. And Lawrence had been horrible to her in Mexico—something really had snapped between them. So I felt free to take Frieda, or thought I did; but when it came to the point, I didn't. . . . 'No, my darling, I mustn't let Lorenzo down—I can't.'"[5]

Murry's profession of loyalty is not persuasive. Frieda was then trapped in her marriage to Lawrence. She had become alienated from her children, refused to be a burden on her family in Germany and was unable to earn her own living. She turned to Murry, demanding solace and satisfaction. He was a weak man who had frequently "let Lorenzo down." He had been easily seduced by Katherine in 1912; and, in his confusion of grief and love, would not have been able to resist the passionate, impulsive and strong-willed Frieda.

Though Murry slept with Frieda, he did not try to "take" her away from Lawrence. Kot, passionately loyal to Lawrence, was furious about Frieda's adulterous journey with Murry. When she came back to England, Kot quarreled bitterly with her, and he vented his anger when Lawrence arrived in December. Lawrence knew instinctively what had happened. As Catherine Carswell wrote, the sight of "Murry and Frieda waiting for him so chummily together [at Waterloo Station] was enough to turn him greenish pale all over." Lawrence's fictionalized description of Murry in "The Border Line" (1924) shows that he knew why Frieda was also attracted to him: "This look of knowing in his dark eyes, and the feeling of secrecy that went with his dark little body, made him interesting to women. Another thing he could do was to give off a great sense of warmth and offering, like a dog when it loves you. . . . And Katherine [Frieda], after feeling cool about him and rather despising him for years, at last fell under the spell of the dark, insidious fellow."

Murry's affair with Frieda had a bizarre impact on Lawrence's "Last Supper," at which Murry played Judas to Lawrence's Jesus, at the Café Royal. The Lawrences hired an ornate, gilded, red-plush room and invited to dinner seven of their closest friends: Murry, Kot, Gertler, Brett, Mary Cannan and the Carswells. The emotional connections between hosts and guests were intense and complex. Murry, Kot and Gertler had been in love with the dead Katherine. Murry's affair with Frieda had ended his liaison with Brett. Kot, Brett and Catherine Carswell competed for Lawrence's friendship and love. Frieda and Catherine Carswell were jealous of Mary Cannan's beauty, elegance and wealth. And, wrote John Carswell, "Everyone present . . . had drawn the obvious inference from Frieda's trip with Murry to Germany."[6]

Lawrence ordered port, though he could not tolerate that drink. Kot, who hated Frieda and Murry, expressed his love for Lawrence, shattering a number of wineglasses to emphasize his feelings. Lawrence then asked the five unmarried and two married friends if they would follow him back to New Mexico. His intensely personal plea suggested, to Catherine Carswell, "his overwhelming loneliness" and desire for the devotion of his friends.

The emotional climax of the evening occurred when Lawrence appealed directly to Murry and revealed his suspicions of the affair. This crucial episode has been variously reported. Murry's biographer, F. A. Lea, quotes Murry's distortion of what was said:

> Lawrence, drunk and despairing, appealed to Murry not to "betray" him: and he, drunk too but "clairvoyant," spoke the celebrated words, "I love you, Lorenzo, but I won't promise not to betray you." They meant, as [Murry] explained later on, "I am full of affection for you and pity for what you are suffering; but I won't promise to conceal my knowledge of why you are suffering."

Frieda's friend and editor, E. W. Tedlock, more perceptively suggested that "Murry confessed rather vaguely to a betrayer's role, and thereby increased Lawrence's scorn." Catherine Carswell's eyewitness version portrayed Murry as Judas and made his confession quite explicit:

> Murry again embraced Lawrence, who sat perfectly still and unresponsive, with a dead-white face in which the eyes alone were alive. "I *have* betrayed you, old chap, I confess it," continued Murry. "In the past I *have* betrayed you. But never again. I call you to witness, never again." . . .
>
> It must have been almost immediately after the strange episode with Murry that Lawrence, without uttering a sound, fell forward with his head on the table, was deadly sick, and became at once unconscious.[7]

Lawrence felt he had made a fool of himself by vomiting in the restaurant. He associated this humiliation not only with the port he had drunk, but also with Frieda's affair and Murry's cowardly confession. In the years that followed, he maintained his relationship with Murry but continued to criticize him directly and in letters to friends. Murry's pathological identification with Judas (he called him "the brokenhearted lover" and believed he was "the only one of the disciples who understood Jesus; and Jesus knew that he was the only one who understood") reinforced Lawrence's belief that Murry would, at the same time, both blame and excuse his own faults. In a letter about the "Last Supper," Lawrence urged Murry to face the truth about himself and "wipe off all that Judas-Jesus slime. Remember, you have betrayed everything and everybody up to now." Later in 1925, he criticized Murry's self-reflective *Life of Jesus* and told Brett that Murry "got Jesus badly, and nastily." And in 1929, he parodied Murry in a brief squib:

"*Life of JMM* by J[esus] C[hrist]. John Middleton was born in the year of the Lord 1891. It happened also to be the most lying year of the most lying century since time began."[8]

Lawrence could never quite sever his attachment to Murry and had more sympathy for him than the contemporaries who considered Murry "the best-hated man of letters in the country." Eliot thought him "a man of weak character and great vanity" and did not trust him. Virginia Woolf condemned his reviews of Lawrence and called him "that bald necked blood dripping vulture. . . . The one vile man I have ever known." And Frieda "loyally" vilified Murry and attributed to personal vindictiveness his bitter attack on Lawrence in *Son of Woman* (1931): "L[awrence] had seen through M[urry] years ago as an unreliable & treacherous friend. He had dismissed the little 'twister,' did no longer answer his loving letters [after 1926] except once or twice ferociously. . . . So Murry wrote this book out of revenge."[9] It is ironic, considering Murry's treatment of Mansfield and Lawrence, that he is no longer remembered for his writing, but for his association with them.

III

During his two and a half months in Europe, from mid-December to early March 1924, Lawrence saw his sisters in Nottingham and Derbyshire, went to Shropshire to visit Frederick Carter, with whom he had corresponded about the Book of Revelation, stopped in Paris and traveled to Baden to see Frieda's mother. The Lawrences spent a final week in London at Garland's Hotel on Suffolk Street, off the Haymarket. They sailed with Brett (the only friend who followed him to New Mexico) from Southampton on March 5 and arrived in America a week later. He disliked New York as much as ever; found it stiff, man-made and unnatural; but it was still more stimulating than Europe.

The Lawrences reached Taos on March 22 and (despite all the difficulties they had had with Mabel in 1923) stayed with her until early May. When Mabel arrived at the end of March, the Lawrences moved into the guest house and Brett into the studio, and they all took meals in the main house. Mabel at first seemed very mild. But by August she had antagonized nearly everyone and was also having serious problems with Tony. "Artists and 'live people,'" Lawrence wrote from Taos to a friend in Mexico, "are usually most lively hating one another."

In April, Mabel gave Frieda (since Lawrence disliked ownership and possessions) her mountain ranch, two miles above Del Monte and a good deal wilder, in exchange for the manuscript of *Sons and Lovers.* Mabel called it the Flying Heart; Lawrence changed the name first to Lobo (wolf), from Lobo mountain, and then to Kiowa (an Indian tribe). Mabel had paid twelve hundred dollars in 1918 for the 160-acre ranch, with log cabins and pine trees, and had let it go to ruin. Though Lawrence loved the ranch and never regretted the exchange, he was later told by appraisers that the dilapidated property was valued at only a thousand dollars, while the manuscript was worth three or four thousand.[10]

Lawrence hired three Indians and a Mexican carpenter, rebuilt the collapsing three-room cabin and made a chimney of sun-dried bricks. He kept the two-room cabin for Mabel's infrequent visits and gave Brett the tiny one-roomer, which scarcely had space for a small bed and a stove. He bought saddles and five horses—Contentos, Chiquita, Poppy, Azul and Bessie—and felt well set up. He liked the solitude and independence, and was deeply moved by the primeval spirit of the wilderness:

> There is something savage, unbreakable in the spirit of the place out here—the Indians drumming and yelling at our camp-fire at evening....
>
> I am glad to be out here in the south-west of America—there is the pristine something, unbroken, unbreakable....
>
> It [is] good to be alone and responsible. But also it is very *hard* living up against these savage Rockies.

Toward the end of August he traveled by car with Mabel and Tony through the spectacular landscapes of New Mexico and Arizona. They saw the snake dances of the Hopis—"priests dancing with live rattle snakes in their mouths"—and the religious prayers, chants and ceremonies that seemed to permeate and vitalize the life of the Navajos. He described them first in his letters and then in *Mornings in Mexico,* which begins with an account of his life in Oaxaca and ends (achronologically) in America: "The trip to the Hopi Country was interesting, but tiring, so far in a motor-car. The Navajo Country is very attractive—all wild, with great red cliffs bluffing up. Good country to ride through, one day. The Navajos themselves real wild nomads: alas, they speak practically no English, and no Spanish. But strange, the intense religious life they keep up in those round huts. This animistic religion is the only live one[;] ours is a corpse of a religion."[11]

The following month Lawrence heard that his father had died on September 10, his son's birthday, at the age of seventy-eight. Remembering the agonizing experience of his mother's death in 1910, and fearing his own, he was glad to have missed the funeral. When Ada sent their father's photograph, Lawrence saw in it a good deal of himself. But he had not yet forgiven Arthur for his harsh treatment of Lydia, had severed emotional ties with his father and did not show much feeling about the old man's death.

Frieda was also delighted with the ranch, the first "home" they had ever owned. But her conflict with Lawrence, though not as intense as it had been earlier, remained a constant feature of their life. Like Mabel and Bynner, Brett took malicious delight in recording their rows. When Frieda got on a horse and into one of her Lawrencean moods, he was quick to deflate her pretensions:

> "Oh, it's wonderful [Frieda exclaims]; wonderful to feel his great thighs moving, to feel his powerful legs!"
>
> "Rubbish, Frieda!" [Lawrence] calls back. "Don't talk like that. You have been reading my books: you don't feel anything of the sort!"

But Frieda always gave as good as she got. When Lawrence warned her: "Not so much intensity, Frieda," she replied: "If I want to be intense I'll be intense, and you go to hell!"

Frieda would lash out at Lawrence for trying to be superior and making a god of himself; would insist she was just as important as he was and—reminding him of her preeminence in the Weekley household— claim she had always played first fiddle at home. When she attacked, contradicted and denounced Lawrence, he replied with threats, with violence—and with complaints: " 'Beware, Frieda! If you ever talk to me like that again [and of course she did], it will not be the tea things I smash, but your head. Oh, yes, [he said, repeating his threat about Mabel], I'll kill you. So beware!' And down comes the poker on the teapot." Later he lamented: "You have no idea, Brett, how humiliating it is to beat a woman; afterwards one feels simply humiliated."[12]

IV

Brett, brought to America as a buffer—like the Danes—complicated the Lawrence-Frieda-Mabel triangle. And she soon replaced Mabel as the major—and more intimate—irritant in the Lawrences' marriage. Brett closely watched Lawrence's moods, served him with an eager though clumsy devotion and balanced Frieda's mockery with blind adoration. Though Frieda offered her half a crown if she would but once contradict Lawrence, she never took up the offer.

Mabel, who barely tolerated Brett and considered her an annoying appendage to Lawrence, described her as a tall, oldish girl with "pretty, pink, round cheeks and a childish expression. Her long, thin shanks ended in large feet that turned out abruptly. . . . She was an amusing and an attractive grotesque, and her eyes were both hostile and questioning." Brett, often Mabel's victim, retaliated with a Lawrencean analysis of her destructive behavior: "Mabel was born bored. She had an insatiable appetite for tasting life in all its aspects. She tasted and spat it out. She was unsentimental: she sized up a situation between two people and proceeded to break it to pieces as soon as possible. Whatever was wilting, she aided and abetted to wilt. In that way she was dangerous and cruel."[13]

Brett (in 1933) and Mabel (in 1932) have left conflicting accounts of two episodes—an evening of dancing and an occasion when Brett cut Mabel's hair—that reveal the hostile, hothouse atmosphere of Mabel's house in Taos and the intense rivalry of the two women for Lawrence's attention. The first incident involved Mabel's young, arty protégé and parasite, Clarence Thompson. Born in Connecticut in 1898, he graduated from Exeter and spent two years at Harvard. He later became a free-lance writer of magazine articles and "cheap 'B' pictures" in Hollywood, and called himself "a Republican and reactionary." One Taos writer characterized Clarence as an unpleasant homosexual: "gentle, effeminate, weighted down with Indian silver—a delicate face but an inner black ruin. . . . He longed for Lawrence in his strange effeminate way. He was tall and blond and vainly arrogant."[14]

In Brett's version, Lawrence, Frieda, Brett, Mabel and Clarence gathered to dance in Mabel's big studio. Lawrence brought a bottle of brandy and Brett got very drunk. She asked Lawrence to dance, he reluctantly agreed, and she ecstatically wrote: "I feel you *warm;* I can feel the stream of quick life in you; it is like dancing with a faun, with some wild, woodland spirit: fierce, flickering, a gliding, leaping run. Wild, elfish humor seizes you: as we pass Mabel and Clarence, decorously dancing the American dance, we bump into them, you with a wicked laugh, until Clarence, furious, rushes out of the studio. Frieda follows him—and Mabel vanishes, too. Then suddenly you tire."

Mabel's account is equally egoistic, less "Lawrencean," more sexual, conspiratorial and ominous. They all gathered in the studio. Lawrence and Clarence disappeared for a mysterious half hour and returned with a bottle of moonshine. Frieda begged Lawrence to dance, but he sharply refused. Frieda and Clarence then danced ecstatically; Lawrence unexpectedly agreed to dance (awkwardly, not faunishly) with Mabel; and Brett, holding her brass ear trumpet, danced alone:

> Lawrence and I flew, circling the room, bumping into [Frieda and Clarence] as hard as we could at every round! We gathered speed and momentum as we went, and each bump was heavier than the last. Brett, not quite catching on to what it was all for, spun around too, and endeavored to crash into *me,* and at the same time to avoid shattering Lorenzo.... Lorenzo kicked Frieda as often as he could.... I was having a grand time, for there I was, clutched by Lorenzo, united at last, one will, one effort, to break, to crush, to shatter if we could, the ease and beauty of those two others.... Although that was the end of the dancing, it was not the end of the evening. Frieda and Clarence, whispering to each other, melted out of the wide door and disappeared into the night.[15]

In Brett's version of the second incident, she cut Lawrence's hair and Mabel wanted her hair cut too. But when she unexpectedly moved, Brett accidentally cut Mabel's ear, wrapped it up (Van Gogh–like) in toilet paper and felt a bit sick:

> Then I start snipping round Mabel's Florentine boyish bob. "Keep quiet," I warn, "because of your ears." She turns her head suddenly; I feel the scissors bite into something soft—there is a jet of blood.
>
> "You *have* cut my ear," says Mabel in an amazed voice. "You *have* cut it!" I stare at the dripping blood helplessly. How could so much blood come out of an ear!

In Mabel's psychoanalytic interpretation, Brett is sadistic, Lawrence sympathetic. Mabel longed to have Lawrence cut her hair, but Brett offered to do it instead, claiming she had always cut Katherine Mansfield's hair. As Lawrence directed her, Brett slashed at Mabel's hair, taking pleasure in the compensatory mutilation. Mabel found *her* compensation by appealing to Lawrence's sympathy:

> I could hear her panting a little. She slashed and slashed and suddenly cut the end of my ear off!
>
> The blood ran down and Lawrence palely offered me his handkerchief. I looked at Brett in amazement and, I must admit, in some admiration! She was half snuffling, with tears in her eyes, and laughing too.
>
> "Why, you cut my ear off!" I exclaimed. I couldn't get over it. She hated me, and she was deaf, and she tried to mutilate my ear! That seemed so interesting that I forgot to be indignant. However, I didn't forget to make a good deal of it to the tender-hearted Lorenzo.[16]

Lawrence was central to the emotional dynamics of both incidents, for the aggression of the dance-bumping and the bloodletting of the haircut both expressed the overt hostility of the women fighting for his favor.

Lawrence appreciated Brett's help with the chores and the typing, and considered her rather simple but harmless. Frieda, however, thought she was a more clinging and dangerous rival than Mabel. She had no emotional life of her own and seemed to feed on Lawrence. Things reached a breaking point in Oaxaca in January 1925, when Frieda, unable to stand Brett any longer, forced Lawrence to send her back to the ranch alone. When they returned to Kiowa, she banished Brett to the Del Monte ranch; but Brett retaliated by spying on them with binoculars and turning up whenever interesting guests arrived.

Frieda accused Brett, by letter, of acting with Lawrence like a spinster with a curate. Frieda resented the fact that they did not make love to each other (as she herself had done with various lovers), but also insisted—wounding Brett and justifying her own substantial and ever-increasing bulk—that "Lawrence says he could not possibly be in love with a woman like you—an asparagus stick!"

On January 9 in Oaxaca, Lawrence wrote to Brett with some difficulty, since he had invited her to accompany them to Mexico and felt responsible for her welfare: "You, Frieda and I don't make a happy combination now. The best is that we should prepare to separate: that you should go your own way. I am not angry: except that I hate 'situations,' and feel humiliated by them. . . . Believe me, there will be no more ease between the three of us. Better you take your own way in life. Not this closeness, which causes a strain."

Two weeks later, when Brett had returned to the ranch, he bluntly attacked her (since she had ignored his more subtle suggestions to disengage) both for dragging sex into their friendship and for having sex in the head instead of the loins: "Your friendship for Murry was spiritual—you dragged sex in—and he hated you. . . . The halfness of your friendship I also hate, and between you and me there is no sensual correspondence. . . . You like the excitation of sex in the eye, sex in the head. It is an evil and destructive thing. . . . Your 'friendship' for me betrays the essential man and male that I am, and makes me ill. . . . I am so much better now you have gone." Three months later, when he had returned from Oaxaca to the ranch, he completed the attack by calling Brett a "born separator," who set people against one another and turned everyone into an enemy.

Rejected by Lawrence, Brett had an affair with Trinidad, a married Indian who worked on the ranch and whom Lawrence naively called "chaste as a girl."[17] When he discovered their liaison, he dismissed Trinidad, and portrayed Brett and the Indian in "The Princess" (1925). In this story she appears as an aristocratic, repressed spinster who has always denied her sexual feelings. She recklessly rides on horseback with a hot-blooded Mexican into the wilderness of virgin forests, blood-red leaves and crouching animals, which represent her unconscious desire for sex and death. Her brain goes numb as her body awakens; she dreams of being buried alive in a cold, sexless, deathly existence; and, despite her ambivalence about sex, unequivocally agrees when the Mexican offers to "make her warm." He pants with desire; she pants with relief when it is over. And when he asks: "Don't you like last night?" she wounds his manly pride with a cold denial. He retaliates by breaking the frozen ice (a symbol of her virginity) and throwing her clothes into the lake. When the white men come looking for her a few days later, they kill the Mexican for sleeping with her. She then mentally reconstitutes her virginity and marries an undemanding elderly man, who replaces her dead father. Though the reluctant white woman must learn the dark man's sexual lesson, she cannot respond to his brutality and violence. In "The Princess," Lawrence anatomized Brett's rather pathetic attempt to achieve sexual fulfillment with a primitive man.

Brett outlived everyone, had the last word on Lawrence and died in Taos at the age of ninety-four. Abandoning the roles of adolescent schoolgirl, chummy sister and maiden aunt, Brett claimed at the very end of her life that in Ravello in March 1926, after he had quarreled with and separated from Frieda, Lawrence entered Brett's hotel room and said: "I do not believe in a relationship unless there is a physical relationship as well"—though Brett was the only woman to claim that Lawrence made this a condition of their friendship.

> I was frightened as well as excited. He got into my bed, turned, and kissed me. I can still feel the softness of his beard, still feel the tension, still feel the overwhelming desire to be adequate. I was passionately eager to be successful, but [despite her affairs with Murry and with Trinidad] I had no idea of what to do. Nothing happened. Suddenly Lawrence got up. "It's no good," he said, and stalked out of the room. I was devastated, helpless, bewildered.

According to Brett, after their second, "hopeless horrible failure" to have sex, Lawrence said either "Your boobs are all wrong" or "Your pubes are wrong"[18] and again stalked out of the room. Immediately afterward, he ordered Brett to leave Ravello and never saw her again.

Lawrence's behavior in Brett's bizarre anecdote is completely out of character. He was never promiscuous or unfaithful to Frieda after their marriage. He was not at all attracted to Brett, had told her they had "no sensual correspondence" and exclaimed: "I can't stand it when she clings too tight."[19] He would not, in any case, have wanted to reveal the sexual difficulties that had developed as a consequence of his disease. He disliked vulgar speech and would never have used the expressions "boobs" or "pubes," which were clearly based on American slang acquired by Brett during her long years in New Mexico and retroactively attributed to Lawrence in 1926. Faith Mackenzie noted that it was heavenly for Brett to have Lawrence, estranged from Frieda, all to herself for a brief time in Italy. Three of Brett's close friends—Lady Juliette Huxley, Julian Morrell Vinogradoff and Harwood Brewster— have confirmed in recent interviews that Brett's late story was certainly a fantasy. It expressed her "Princess"-like fears of sexual inadequacy and made Lawrence assume Murry's role as her lover in order to compensate for his blunt rejection of her love in Oaxaca and Taos in 1924–25.

V

Lawrence, with Frieda and Brett, left the ranch in mid-October 1924 on his third trip to Mexico and reached the capital on the twentieth. This time he found Mexico City shabby, depressed and unpleasant. During his two weeks there he showed Brett the sights, was photographed by Edward Weston, dined with the PEN writers' club, lunched with Zelia Nuttall, an American archaeologist, whose books were a source for *The Plumed Serpent* (he described this "ghastly" luncheon party in the second chapter of the novel), and met Somerset Maugham, who was also in Mexico in search of fictional material.

Lawrence considered the homosexual Maugham a superficial, commercial writer who catered to the establishment that had suppressed *The Rainbow*. Maugham considered Lawrence "a pathological case." Given Lawrence's touchy temperament, the stage was set for misunderstanding and hostility. Frieda wrote that Lawrence made the first overture: "One day William Somerset Maugham was expected in Mexico City; so Lawrence wrote to him if they could meet." But Maugham's secretary [i.e., lover] answered for him, proposing that since they were all going to lunch together with Zelia Nuttall, who lived in the rather distant suburb of Coyoacán, they should share a taxi. "Lawrence was angry that Maugham had answered through his secretary [as he had been annoyed by Amy Lowell's use of a secretary] and wrote back: 'No, I won't share a car.'" Lawrence was as quick to take offense with Maugham as he had been with José Vasconcelos, the Mexican minister of education, when he unavoidably broke an appointment at the last minute. He did not realize that Maugham had used his secretary as an intermediary because his stutter was especially bad with strangers and on the telephone.

Predictably enough, Lawrence disliked Maugham and described him to Bynner as joyless, opportunistic and repressed: "Somerset Maugham left for Cuernavaca the day we got in, but apparently he too is no loss. Disagreeable, with no fun left in him, and terrified for fear he won't be able to do his next great book, with a vivid Mexican background, before Christmas.—A narrow-gutted 'artist' with a stutter." When Lawrence reviewed Maugham's spy tales, *Ashenden,* in July 1928, he criticized them as bogus in much the same way as he had previously criticized Maugham's character: "These stories, being 'serious,' are faked.... It would be hard to find a bunch of more ill-humoured stories, in which the humour has gone more rancid."[20]

In mid-November, Lawrence moved south to Oaxaca, which then had a population of thirty thousand. He was at first enthusiastic about the town (the most attractive in Mexico), but by the end of his stay he cursed both Oaxaca and Mexico for ruining his health. In November he described the ambience of the town, and its inhabitants, rivers and market:

> Oaxaca is a very quiet little town.... It is very peaceful, and has a remote beauty of its own. The Hotel Francia *very* pleasant—such good amusing food—4 pesos a day for everything. We want to go out to [the ruins at] Mitla and Tule and Ejutla.... There are two rivers, but I've only seen one, with naked Indians soaping their heads in mid-stream. I shall bathe.... The Indians go about in white cotton—they don't make them wear proper trousers as in most towns—. I think we shall move into a house with a patio,—stay here ten days or so more—and Miss Brett stay in the hotel....
>
> Every day is perfectly sunny, a bit too hot at midday. The natives are mostly Zapotec Indians, small, but very straight and alert and alive: really very nice. There is a big market humming like a beehive, where one can buy anything, from roses to horse-shoes.... The governor is an Indian from the hills. I called on him in the palace!!![21]

By the end of the month the Lawrences had rented a house from Father Eduardo Rickards, a Mexican-born Englishman and Catholic parish priest, who lived in the adjoining wing. The sparely furnished villa had large rooms, a veranda and an enclosed garden with coffee plants and tropical flowers. But Lawrence still felt uneasy about the bad vibrations of the "malevolent continent" and reported that a local resident had been shot in the leg when playing tennis.

VI

While living in Oaxaca, Lawrence wrote the first four chapters of *Mornings in Mexico* (1927), which he dedicated to Mabel, and completed the second version of *The Plumed Serpent*. Wyndham Lewis, in his polemical *Paleface* (first published in his magazine, the *Enemy,* in September 1927 and issued as a book in 1929), defended the sovereignty of the mind against what he took to be Lawrence's exaltation of the emotions and (with characteristic exaggeration) concentrated his fire on the celebration of Indian primitivism in Lawrence's minor but representative travel book. In a twenty-page onslaught—perhaps the most serious and damaging attack on Lawrence in his lifetime—Lewis attempted to show that Lawrence had completely fallen under the spell of the Henri Bergson–Oswald Spengler school of "evolutionist, emotional, non-human, 'mindless' philosophy: and how thoroughly he reads it into and applies it to the manifestations of the Indian 'consciousness'. . . . Mr. Lawrence is repeatedly telling his White readers that they are poor specimens compared to his energetic and 'mysterious' Indians," who manifest a "visceral consciousness." "If we followed Mr. Lawrence to the ultimate conclusion of his romantic teaching," Lewis wrote, "we should allow our 'consciousness' to be overpowered by the alien 'consciousness' of the Indian."

Though Lawrence did celebrate the "experience of the blood-stream" over that of the mind, he clearly believed that there was a radical discontinuity and mutual negation between the modern and primitive ways of experiencing the world: "The Indian way of consciousness is different from and fatal to our way of consciousness." And he did not, as Lewis claimed, want to surrender his European to an archaic consciousness. As he wrote in his Introduction to Frederick Carter's book on Revelation: "We can never recover an old vision, once it has been supplanted."²²

On June 8, 1914, while staying with Gordon Campbell in south Kensington, Lawrence had laconically reported that Wyndham Lewis, who had just published BLAST, "came in, and there was a heated and vivid discussion." Nothing is known about the substance of this meeting, but given the personalities of the two figures, it was bound to have been turbulent and contentious. Like Lawrence, whom he resembled in a number of significant ways, Lewis was a dogmatic and didactic crusader against cant and hypocrisy, a volatile and temperamentally intolerant man who felt driven to condemn the evils of the world and to proclaim his own authoritarian views. And like Lawrence, Lewis could not refrain from attacking and alienating even his closest friends in his attempt to impose his vision and values upon society. After his own books were suppressed in 1932, Lewis optimistically told his publisher that he too might receive the kind of useful notoriety that had eventually helped Lawrence's sales after the ban of *The Rainbow* and *Lady Chatterley's Lover.* He also praised Lawrence's fight against repressive modes of thought: "Half the popular success of D. H. Lawrence it is obvious was due to the constant banning of his books, and the exhilarating spectacle of his battle with antiquated and unreal prejudices of the puritan conscience." Though Lewis admired Lawrence's intellectual courage, he criticized his emphasis on the child, his glorification of the feminine principle and his Freudian stress on the unconscious. He also, while attacking *Mornings in Mexico,* grossly distorted and underestimated two of Lawrence's finest novels: "With *Sons and Lovers,* his first [i.e., third] book, he was at once hot-foot upon the fashionable trail of incest; the book is an eloquent wallowing mass of Mother-love and Sex-idolatry. His *Women in Love* is again the same thick, sentimental, luscious stew."[23]

Lawrence responded angrily to *Paleface* in *Lady Chatterley's Lover* (1928) and in his Introduction to Edward Dahlberg's *Bottom Dogs* (1929). Though David Garnett claimed that Duncan Forbes in Lawrence's novel was based on Duncan Grant, the paintings by the "fellow with straight black hair and a weird Celtic conceit of himself" are far more violent and abstract than Grant's tepid Post-Impressionist pictures and resemble those of Lewis' Vorticist period: "His art was all tubes and valves and spirals and strange colours, ultra modern, yet with a certain power, even a certain purity of form and tone: only Mellors thought it cruel and repellent." The last two adjectives might possibly be applied to Lewis' art, which Lawrence associated with the machine civilization he attacked in *Lady Chatterley's Lover.* But the *ad hominem* pronouncement of Mellors, whose strong point is not art criticism and who advocates a kind of William Morris *ashram* to rejuvenate mankind, was both arrogant and ill-informed: "I think all these tubes and corrugated vibrations are stupid enough for anything, and pretty sentimental. They show a lot of self-pity and an awful lot of nervous self-opinion,

seems to me." In the Dahlberg Introduction, Lawrence, who was intellectually and aesthetically antithetical to Lewis, violently condemned his
hostile response to human emotions: "Wyndham Lewis gives a display of
the utterly repulsive effect people have on him, but he retreats into the
intellect to make his display. It is a question of manner and manners. The
effect is the same. It is the same exclamation: They stink! My God, they
stink!"[24]

Lawrence's crude condemnation was a fascinating mixture of moral
judgment, personal bias and self-criticism. He was perceptive about
Lewis' habitual mode of suppressing his emotions, which he mistrusted
and feared, beneath an intellectual carapace; and he reasonably rejected
Lewis' combative technique and unpleasant tone ("manner and manners"). Lawrence was undoubtedly provoked by *Paleface* and may have
recognized in himself the same faults that he condemned in Lewis.

Provoked this time by Lawrence, Lewis continued to attack his enraged exoticism, "his fetish of promiscuity and hysterical paeans to all
that is 'dark and strange,'" in *Hitler* (1931). He mocked and parodied
the super-sexed Zarathustran in the "Sol Invictus—Bull Unsexed" section of *Snooty Baronet* (1932). And in *The Roaring Queen* (1936), Baby
Bucktrout reads Lawrence's notorious novel as an antidote to that
Edwardian devil, sexual inversion: "I am compelled to read *Lady Chatterley's Lover*, if you please, and such books as that, in order to prevent
myself from falling back into the vices upon which I was nurtured."[25]
Both Lewis and Lawrence, who represent two strongly contrasting
modes of modern thought, accused each other of sentimentality and
could not recognize the merits of their rival's books. Both—goaded by
personal attacks—isolated the elements they disliked and ignored the
greatness of the work that remained. Lewis was much more emotional,
Lawrence far more intellectual, than either of them cared to admit.

VII

Lawrence was thoroughly familiar with the contemporary political
situation—the revolutions and civil wars that had raged in Mexico
during the decade before he visited the country—and *The Plumed
Serpent* (1926) is based on a political reality that the mythology attempts to transcend and redeem. Pancho Villa had raided Columbus,

New Mexico, in March 1916; and was murdered in July 1923, during Lawrence's first visit to Mexico. Plutarco Calles became president in 1924; and in 1925 the church and the state began a violent struggle that led to the Cristero religious wars during 1926–29. "The Calles administration survived on the brink of catastrophe and in the midst of a profound inner stress that threatened to snap at any time. That the country survived these four fateful years [1924–28] will remain . . . evidence of inner vitality."

The Plumed Serpent, Lawrence's most important political novel, attacks the violent horrors of Mexican socialism and constructs an imaginary religious aristocracy in its place. He hated and feared the ideology that was associated with the two dynamic generals, Pancho Villa and Emiliano Zapata; portrayed political events from the viewpoint of the *hacendados,* the conservative landowners who were violently overthrown by their impoverished peons; and expressed a powerful longing for the peace of pre-revolutionary days. Calles is said to have created a central bank and stabilized the fiscal system; carried on road construction and irrigation projects; enacted a petroleum law protecting oil rights; codified the power industry; founded the Bank of Agricultural Credit; professionalized and reduced the army.[26] Yet for Lawrence, writing to Murry from Oaxaca in November 1924, things seemed very unstable: "The country is always unsettled. They've spread such an absurd sort of Socialism everywhere—and these little Zapotec Indians are quite fierce. . . . Everything is so shaky and really so confused. . . . 70% of these people are real savages, quite as much as they were 300 years ago. The Spanish-Mexican population just rots on top of the black savage mass. And Socialism here is a farce of farces: except very dangerous."

Lawrence's reaction to Socialism and revolution was twofold: he desired to keep the Indian masses in the purity of their primitive innocence, and wished for a powerful and physically attractive leader who would tame the revolution and maintain the *status quo.* In order to suppress dangerous agitators like Benito Juárez, Lawrence believed that the masses must unite "round one great chosen figure, some hero who can lead a great war, as well as administer a wide peace. . . . Men have got to choose their leaders, and obey them to the death. And it must be a system of culminating aristocracy, society tapering like a pyramid to the supreme leader."[27]

In his Mexican novel, Lawrence glorified power (in the right hands) and proposed a revitalizing religion. The success of the fantastic

Quetzalcoatl movement, a rebellion from the right and against the right, was realistically based on the long and powerful anti-clerical tradition in Mexico, on the ecclesiastical depredations during the revolution and on the moribund state of the Church in the 1920s. As Lawrence told Bynner: "The Church is foreign here. [The peasants] need their own religion, which used to let them kill."[28] In the novel, under Ramón's regime, drums sound instead of bells, and the plumed serpent, Quetzalcoatl, replaces the cross. But Lawrence was unable to create a credible society or religious alternative to the frightening revolutionary reality that he knew so well. He had often praised authoritarian control in his theoretical writings, but the leaders in *The Plumed Serpent* are bloodthirsty and brutal. Unlike Conrad or Orwell, Lawrence could not conceive the political destiny of a nation.

The Plumed Serpent has personal as well as political and religious themes. Frieda's affair with Murry intensified Lawrence's desire for male friendship as well as his need to dominate, even obliterate, the sexual power of women. The characters in the novel represent the wider political struggle: Kate Leslie is controlled by Cipriano as the Mexican masses are dominated by Ramón. Kate craves strong and despises weak men (the foreign-educated Mexican leaders, Cipriano and Ramón, provide a powerful contrast to her American homosexual friends, Bud and Owen). And she unconsciously associates the Quetzalcoatl movement with her dead husband, Joachim, a sacrificial leader in the fight for Irish independence. The deification of personal terror and sexual slavery near the "sperm-like" lake (which symbolizes the release of sexual energy and gigantic ejaculation of semen) destroys Kate's sexual identity, and betrays both her personal and her political ideals. Kate's role in the Quetzalcoatl pantheon is never made clear, but her abject deference to Cipriano—she kisses his feet and abandons the pleasure of orgasm— leads to a loss of her individuality. With Cipriano she regresses to a state of "virginity," which effectively eliminates her two husbands and two children, and satisfies her overweening ego. Kate's marriage to Cipriano thus parallels the sultan-slave marriage of Ramón and Carlota (whom he calls a "stale virgin") and of Ramón with his second wife, Teresa, who loves him "with a wild, virgin loyalty."

The novel charts the degeneration of Kate from a woman who is revolted by the cruelty of the bullfight to one who is indifferent to Cipriano's bloody executions; from the wife of Joachim Leslie, who "*can only love a man who is fighting to *change* the world, to make it freer, more alive,*" to one who marries Cipriano, a sinister, almost repellent general, who suppresses rebellions to preserve the interests of the conservative landowners; from "a modern woman and a woman in her own right," who states, "I'm not going to submit. . . . Why should one give in," to one who believes that "Without Cipriano to touch me and limit me and submerge my will, I shall become a horrible, elderly female. I ought to *want* to be limited. I ought to be *glad* if a man will limit me with a strong will." Kate's sexual apotheosis is merely her sexual degradation.

The execution scene, a savage regression to the elaborate ritual of death when "the Aztecs raised their deities to heights of horror and vindictiveness," is related to Cipriano's subjugation of Kate. When Cipriano plunges his knife into a helpless victim, he experiences "the clutching throb of [sexual] gratification as the knife strikes in and the blood spurts out!"[29] Cipriano's "dark and powerful instinct" is actually a cruel desire to dominate Kate and make her submit to his will—the triumph of unnatural authority, of power over love. The violent events of the novel are the political manifestation of Cipriano's struggle for sexual domination, and he suppresses the rebellions of the peons as well as that of Kate.

Lawrence managed to complete *The Plumed Serpent,* at tremendous cost to himself, on about February 2, 1925. That very day, he was stricken, "as if shot in the intestines," with malaria, influenza and typhoid. Though he never mentioned it to any of his friends, he also had his first, and nearly fatal, tubercular hemorrhage.

CHAPTER EIGHTEEN

Tuberculosis,
1925

I

LAWRENCE had bronchitis when he was two weeks old and remained thin, frail and sickly throughout his boyhood. Two serious attacks of pneumonia, an inflammation of the lungs, in 1901 and again in 1911, permanently damaged his health and led to chronic tuberculosis (with periods of remission) throughout his adult life. He spat blood in Kent in June 1913; and two and a half years later a friend reported, with some exaggeration, that he was "far gone with consumption." Long winters, especially in England, and hot summers in Italy were the worst times for Lawrence. He was seriously ill early in 1916, was rejected for military service in June, and in July actually admitted (which was unusual) that he had tuberculosis. He suffered from influenza during the postwar epidemic in February–March 1919 and was extremely ill with malaria in Ceylon in April 1922. The high altitude and thin cold air of the ranch seemed good for his lungs. But during his second stay, in early August 1924, two months before leaving for Oaxaca, he spat out splashes of bright-red blood. His chest was sore, his throat ached and he remained in bed, feeling limp as a rag.

In pulmonary tuberculosis, the lungs are damaged by the multiplication of bacilli in infected tissues. As bacteria attack and destroy body tissues, small rounded nodules or tubercles form, which contain bacteria and white blood cells. The bacteria cause lesions in the lung tissue, and the germs enter the sputum. The wasting disease slowly progresses from tuberculous lesions, necrosis and formation of cavities to erosion of blood vessels and bleeding into the lungs, which, if massive, may cause drowning in one's own blood. In *The Magic Mountain* (1924), Thomas Mann described this pathological process, and its usually fatal resolution, as "the formation of nodules, the manifestation of soluble toxins and their narcotic effect upon the system; the breaking-down of the tissues, caseation, and the question of whether the disease would be arrested by a chalky petrifaction and heal by means of fibrosis, or [more likely] whether it would extend the area, create still larger cavities, and destroy the organ."

Lawrence's life and character were strongly influenced by the progress of his disease. He had (at various times) all the symptoms of consumption, which intensified toward the end of his life. He suffered from irregular appetite, loss of weight, emaciation, facial pallor, flushed cheeks, unstable pulse rates, fever, night sweats, shortness of breath, wheezing, chest pains, frequent colds, severe coughing, spitting of blood, extreme irritability and sexual impotence. The toxemia of Lawrence's lungs influenced the state of his mind and provoked febrile rages. As John Keats had told Fanny Brawne, emphasizing the gulf between the sick and the well: "A person in health as you are can have no conception of the horrors that nerves and a temper like mine go through." Witter Bynner wrote of Lawrence's stoic attitude but uncontrollable anger: "He had never given me any evidence of his illness by complaint in words or faltering in spirit but only by bursts and acts of temper."[1]

Until Selman Waksman discovered streptomycin in 1944, there was no effective treatment of tuberculosis. Doctors, who ranged from the patently deceptive to the brutally honest, could palliate but not prevent or cure the disease. In the 1920s patients followed the regimen described in *The Magic Mountain,* which consisted of rest cure, proper diet, open air and lung-collapse therapy (the latter usually did more harm than good). X-rays were not widely used for diagnosis until the thirties; advanced techniques in pulmonary surgery and antibiotics were not employed until the late forties. The expensive sanatoria prevented many patients from infecting other people, taught them hygienic discipline, decreased their mental and physical strain, and allowed the disease to be studied by doctors. But, as an authority on tuberculosis has stated, the regimen was futile: "The importance attributed to prolonged rest, to a change in climate, or to special diets is no longer warranted.... No

locality or climate specifically prevented the development of tuberculosis or caused its cure." A recent study reported that it was healthier,
in 1921, to stay out of the hospital: "a damaging survey of sanatoria,
home and untreated patients found that 54 per cent of non-sanatoria
stage I cases were 'cured' at four years after diagnosis, compared with 31
per cent of sanatoria cases."[2] In 1934, 36,000 people died of tuberculosis
in Britain.

Given the dubious treatment for tuberculosis, many patients instinctively rejected both a climatic cure and the strict regimen of a
sanatorium, and were determined to continue as far as possible their
normal existence. Aubrey Beardsley sceptically wrote: "It is bad enough
to be an invalid, but to be a slave to one's lungs and to be found wintering
in some unearthly place and sniffing sea-breezes or pine-breezes, with
the mistaken idea that it will prolong one's existence, seems to me utter
foolishness." Katherine Mansfield could not tolerate the exclusive company of consumptives and believed a sanatorium would extinguish her
creative inspiration: "any institutional existence would kill me—or
being alone, cut off, ill with the other ill." In her review of R. D. Prowse's
A Gift of the Dusk (1920), a fictionalized account of life in a sanatorium,
which Murry sent Katherine in the terminal phase of her illness, she self-
reflectively wrote that the tubercular patient clings pathetically and
hopelessly to the customs of ordinary life: "The peculiar tragedy of the
consumptive is that, although he is so seriously ill, he is—in most cases—
not ill enough to give up the precious habits of health. . . . Thus the small
stricken company, living its impersonal life together among the immense mountains, is forever mocked by the nearness of those things
which are forever out of reach."[3]

Katherine wrote detailed descriptions of her illness and suffering in
her diaries and letters as well as in stories like "The Man Without a
Temperament" (1920), which portrays Murry's callous reaction to her
consumption. Since she and Lawrence were, in their disease and their
temperament, "unthinkably alike," her writings on this subject illuminate his thoughts and feelings. Katherine had proof of her physical
decay in her own being. Each day the microscopic organisms gnawed
through her tissue and destroyed a tiny bit more of her lung. As she grew
weaker, she found it increasingly difficult to walk and to breathe: "I
cough and cough and at each breath a dragging, boiling, bubbling sound
is heard. I feel that my whole chest is boiling. I sip water, spit, sip, spit. I
feel I must break my heart. And I can't expand my chest [because the
lung tissue was destroyed]; it's as though the chest had collapsed. Life

is—getting a new breath: nothing else counts." In July 1918 she wrote
with pathos to Ottoline Morrell about the antagonism of body and spirit,
and her longing for "a body that isn't an enemy—a body that isn't
fiendishly engaged in the old, old 'necessary' torture of—breaking one's
spirit."[4]

Though Lawrence hated the shameful subjugation to doctors,[5] he was
examined by a great number of physicians, some of them (David Eder,
Maitland Radford, Max Mohr) trusted personal friends. But he knew
there was no cure for consumption and was extremely sceptical about the
treatment. Lawrence advised his childhood friend Gertie Cooper, who
was in a tuberculosis sanatorium and had been urged to have an operation, to rely on her own instinct: "Listen to the doctors carefully, when
they advise you. But when it comes to deciding finally, decide out of your
own real self." And he told Earl Brewster that even the concept of a
healthy climate was merely a matter of trial and error: "All that doctors
can do for me is to say—You might *try* this or that climate—they don't
know—it's just a matter of experiment."

Yet his search for a salubrious climate accounts, more than anything
else, for his restless, frenetic movements to—and constant dissatisfaction with—north and south, mountains and flatlands, mainlands and
islands, hill towns and coastal regions, during the last five years of his
life. In the late 1920s, he tried to spend winters in the sun and summers
in the mountains. But as tuberculosis took hold and began to extinguish
his vitality, he desperately denied the disease and blamed it on the
climate, on the country and even on the malign spirit of the continent.
Huxley, always perceptive about Lawrence and very close to him at the
end, observed of Lawrence's self-deception: "Like a great many tubercular people, he was convinced that climate had a great effect on him—not
only the temperature, but the direction of the wind, and all sorts of
atmospheric conditions. He had invented a whole mythology of
climate."[6]

The psychological effects of Lawrence's chronic illness and progressive deterioration were, to an artist, almost as important as the
physical symptoms; and his mental health determined, to a great extent,
his will to live and ability to survive. He sometimes found it difficult to
concentrate on his work, for in the uneasiness of sleep and the panic of
waking his imagination dwelt on death. He often felt like a repulsive
pariah, cut off from the healthy, betrayed by his body and trapped in the
world of the ill. Tuberculosis undoubtedly sharpened his sense of imminent extinction but also heightened—in his late works on the resurrec-

tion theme—his appreciation of physical sensations and the beauty of
the body. Most important of all, his awareness of doom gave him a
terrible sense of urgency, which intensified his feelings and his powers of
expression. When Catherine Carswell lamented how unproductive her
life seemed compared to his, Lawrence replied: "Ah, but you have so
much longer than I to do things in!"[7]

II

Lawrence, chest and throat still sore from spitting blood in August, was
eager, as winter approached the ranch in October, to go south to Mexico.
In late January 1925 in Oaxaca, nearly at the end of *The Plumed
Serpent,* he was run down, exhausted and "seedy." Frieda felt that their
friction with Brett was exacerbating his illness and forced him to send
Brett back to the ranch—just when she could have been vitally helpful in
nursing Lawrence. Like Merrild, Götzsche, the Brewsters and the
Hawks, Frieda did not realize, until confronted with dramatic evidence,
that Lawrence actually had a highly infectious and incurable disease.
She seemed persuaded by his calm denials and refusal to face the truth.
Healthy herself, she was not afraid of contracting his illness, though
spouses exposed to tuberculosis have a great risk of infection.

On about February 2, the day he completed the Mexican novel,
Lawrence had his first, and nearly fatal, tubercular hemorrhage. He
suddenly gasped for breath and put up his hand to stop the flow as the
bright flame of blood gushed fiercely through the cavities in his lungs,
poured out of his mouth and oozed through his fingers. Anton Chekhov,
with astonishing aesthetic objectivity, had remarked of his own hemorrhage: "There is something ominous in blood running from the mouth;
it's like the reflection of a fire." Keats, trained as an apothecary, recognized that his hemorrhage would recur and prove fatal: "I know the
colour of that blood—it is arterial blood—I cannot be deceived in that
colour; that drop is my death warrant. I must die."[8]

Frieda summoned the local Mexican doctor, but he was afraid to deal
with the emaciated foreigner and would not come. Lawrence, more
seriously ill than Frieda realized, knew the gravity of his own disease
and thought she would have to bury him in the ugly Oaxaca cemetery.
Sensing his near end, he affirmed his love and acknowledged her inspira-

tion: "But if I die, nothing has mattered but you, nothing at all." Frieda helped him get better by putting hot sandbags on his tortured chest and abdomen. While he was sick, there was a violent thunderstorm and a small earthquake (not recorded in the local newspapers), which shifted the beams of the roof.

On February 25, with Lawrence still weak but determined to escape the malarial region, they traveled north to Mexico City, stopping in Tehuacán. There Frieda, having survived the crisis, broke under the strain of his illness and cried all night. She thought: "He will never be quite well again, he is ill, he is doomed. All my love, all my strength, will never make him whole again." In the capital, he was examined by Dr. Sidney Uhlfelder, head of surgery at the American hospital. In Lawrence's presence, perhaps to emphasize the gravity of his condition, the doctor rather brutally pronounced: "Mr. Lawrence has tuberculosis. . . . Take him to the ranch; it's his only chance. He has T.B. in the third [most severe] degree. A year or two at the most."[9]

Three other diseases complicated Lawrence's tuberculosis. He repeatedly told friends that he also had malarial fever and nausea, influenza in his chest and typhoid fever (endemic to the region), which caused severe intestinal pain. He said Oaxaca was full of malaria, that he had become infected by mosquitoes from a nearby river and that he was being treated by another doctor, José Larumbe (an educated Indian), with large injections of quinine. The doctors in Mexico City confirmed this diagnosis and at first advised him to recuperate for a few months at sea level. But they soon changed their minds, forbade a sea voyage from Vera Cruz to England and—though Lawrence said the "malaria comes back in very hot sun, or any malaria conditions"—advised him to either remain in the Mexican sun or return to the ranch. Ross Parmenter claimed that "because Oaxaca City is too high for the mosquito that transmits the disease, the malarial element in his illness was likely a recurrence of his Ceylon infection." But according to the standard medical authority on this subject, malaria is prevalent below 2,000–2,500 meters in tropical countries. Since Oaxaca is 1,555 meters high, mosquitoes *could* exist there. Lawrence most likely contracted malaria from anopheles mosquitoes, which either transmitted the disease directly or had bitten the malarial patients brought up from the plains and then infected Lawrence with the disease.[10] Considering the severity of his illness and the quality of the treatment in that remote region (hot sandbags, quinine and calomel), it is amazing that Lawrence survived.

Since Lawrence blamed his disease on Mexico, he was determined, after resting for three weeks in the capital, to drag himself back to the ranch. But he still had one more difficult obstacle to overcome. United States law prohibits foreigners with tuberculosis from entering the country. Immigrants must produce a recent X-ray to prove their lungs are healthy and if there is any doubt about this must submit to an examination by a doctor at the frontier. Lawrence, deathly pale and obviously suffering from consumption, rouged his face and tried to bluff his way past the "terrible doctor" at El Paso.

As he told friends, with considerable anger and bitterness (for the ordeal at the border must have reminded him of the traumatic army medical examinations during 1916–18), they treated him as an illegal immigrant and nearly killed him a second time: "The Emigration people in El Paso—the Americans—were most insulting and hateful. Before you grumble at the Mexicans, as the worst ever, try this sort of American. *Canaille* of the most bottom-doggy order, and filthy with insolence." Lawrence finally succeeded in crossing the border, with the help of Stuart Grummon, secretary of the American Embassy in Mexico City, who convinced the border officials to bypass the regulations and treat Lawrence as a special case.[11]

When Lawrence reached the ranch in late March, Brett observed that he tottered down the stairs, was pale green in color and piteously frail. Lawrence noted that Frieda, who seemed to expand as he withered, was twenty pounds heavier than he was. He swore he would never return to Mexico, and he never forgave Oaxaca for having done him in. After Oaxaca, he was never completely well. Another attack of bleeding could lead to sudden death.

Lawrence's hemorrhage and constant awareness of his disease made him desperately concerned about friends who had tuberculosis. Cynthia Asquith had been in a sanatorium in 1913. Hilda Shaw, a friend of Louie Burrows and Lawrence's contemporary at Nottingham University, and Frances Cooper, a childhood friend, had died of consumption in 1913 and in 1918; and Katherine had died in 1923. The popular novelist Michael Arlen and Murry's second wife, Violet Le Maistre, also had the disease. The painter Mark Gertler and Frances' sister, Gertie, who lived with Ada's family, were during 1925–26 being treated at the Mundesley Sanatorium in Norfolk.

Through Kot, their mutual friend, Lawrence kept a close watch on Gertler. Lawrence was pleased by his progress and encouraged Gertie Cooper to use the same doctors and hospital. During her long months in Mundesley, Lawrence gave Gertie the advice, sympathy and moral support that only an old friend and fellow sufferer could provide. He told her to follow the strict regulations, eat well and get fat; he agreed that it was awful to be in hospital but good that she could be cured; and he mentioned that his own temperature, like hers, was always up and down. Most important, he roused her spirit and — expressing his deepest beliefs — urged her to fight for her life: "I do hope you don't feel very strange and dismal. . . . Make friends if you can, and don't be too shy. The great thing is to have the courage of life. Have the courage to live, and live well."

Lawrence clearly identified Gertie's fate with his own. When her case became more serious, he dropped his cheerful tone and confided to Ada: "I know her left lung is much worse than we had thought — I suspected it all the time. . . . Your letter from Mundesley, and the news about the operation for Gertie, does rather take the wind out of one's sails. I doubt if *I* should have the operation, if it was me."[12]

III

Lawrence, though sterile, had always enjoyed healthy physical relations with Frieda. But toward the end of 1926, as Frieda later revealed, his sexual capacity suffered as a result of tuberculosis. As the pathologist William Ober noted: "A man suffering from far advanced pulmonary tuberculosis would be sufficiently debilitated to be unable to respond to sexual stimuli and unable to perform as satisfactorily or as frequently as before."

In an intensely personal passage that erupts from "The Reality of Peace," Lawrence acknowledged the Pauline belief in the corruption of the body and responded to it with a spiritual affirmation: "We, ourselves, are the living stream of seething corruption . . . as well as the bright river of life." In his late poems and fiction, he expressed for the first time his feelings about his own impotence, illness and impending death. Three short poems in *Pansies* (1929) — "Man Reaches a Point," "Grasshopper Is a Burden" and "Basta!" — use the phrase "and desire shall fail" from Ecclesiastes 12:5 to reveal Lawrence's stoical response to loneliness and a numb heart:

> When a man can love no more
> and feel no more

and desire has failed
and the heart is numb

then all he can do
is to say: It is so!
I've got to put up with it
and wait.[13]

Lawrence's unfinished narrative "The Flying Fish," which he began after his hemorrhage in Oaxaca, frankly portrays his illness, evokes the spirit of the place, describes the tedious train trip up to Mexico City and the sea voyage back to England (based on his journey with Götzsche in November–December 1923):

He lay in his bed in the hot October evening, still sick with malaria. In the flush of fever he saw yet the parched, stark mountains of the south. . . .
    He was as yet too ill to go. He lay in the nausea of the tropics, and let the days pass over him. . . .
    His body was sick with the poison that lurks in all tropical air. . . . He wanted to get out, to get out of this ghastly tropical void into which he had fallen.

Later on, when the Brewsters urged him to finish the story, he replied that it would be too painful to relive the experience. It had been "written so near the borderline of death, that I have never been able to carry it through, in the cold light of day."[14]

The leading male characters in *Lady Chatterley's Lover* (1928) reveal two aspects of Lawrence's illness: Clifford Chatterley is sexually incapacitated (a war injury has paralyzed him from the waist down) and his gamekeeper, Oliver Mellors, has had tuberculosis. During military service Mellors caught pneumonia, which left him ill and coughing, with a weak heart and lungs. Lawrence portrays his own disease in Mellors' narrow escape from death, damaged health and extreme exhaustion (after Clifford orders him to push his broken wheelchair up a hill) as well as in his unwillingness to kiss Connie on the lips.

Lawrence often came close to death, both in Mexico and later in Italy, and his near-fatal experiences gave him great insight about suffering and a tremendous desire to live. The most moving expression of his morbid fears and feelings occurs in *The Man Who Died* (1929). The

crucified Christ, waking and aching in the tomb, comes back to life and
(like Lawrence) nearly lapses into death:

> He woke numb and cold. . . . Through all the long sleep his body had
> been full of hurt, and it was still full of hurt. He did not open his
> eyes. Yet he knew that he was awake, and numb, and cold, and rigid,
> and full of hurt. . . .
>
> He could move if he wanted: he knew that. But he had no want.
> Who would want to come back from the dead? A deep, deep nausea
> stirred in him, at the premonition of movement. . . .
>
> [His hands] fell again, cold, heavy, numb, and sick with having
> moved even so much, unspeakably unwilling to move further. . . .
>
> He lapsed again, and lay dead, resting on the cold nullity of
> being dead. It was the most desirable. And almost, he had it
> complete: the utter cold nullity of being outside.

Lawrence told Earl Brewster, with a Christ-like resignation and courage, that if pain could not be avoided, it had to be borne: you "should *not*
pass beyond suffering: but you can find the power to endure."[15]

IV

Lawrence regained his strength at the ranch, made astonishing progress
and, within a month, was riding his beloved horses. In April he supervised the workmen as they finished the corral, reroofed the barn, and
directed the precious water from Gallina Canyon round the hills and
into his irrigation ditch. In the summer he tended his garden, chopped
wood and shot the huge porcupine, all his bristles up, that had lanced
quills into the noses of his squealing horse and dog (Lawrence had to
pull them out with pliers, one by one).

He also milked the obstreperous runaway cow, Susan. "Sounds idyllic," he told Martin Secker, but the ranch sometimes resembled the
disastrous farm he had described in "The Fox": "The cow escapes into
the mountains, we hunt her on horseback and curse her blacker than she
is: an eagle strikes one of the best hens: a skunk fetches the eggs: the half
wild cows break in on the pasture, that is drying up as dry as pepper—no
rain, no rain, no rain. It's tough country." Rachel Hawk added that

though Lawrence liked to complain about Susan the cow and exaggerate the trouble she caused, he always knew where to find her.[16]

In mid-May, Frieda's twenty-two-year-old nephew, Friedel Jaffe, visited the ranch for two months. Though he helped with the chores, he was no substitute for the companionable Danes and was scarcely mentioned in Lawrence's letters. He had come from Germany as an exchange student, studied at St. John's in Annapolis and at Johns Hopkins, and hated his time in the East. Friedel later recalled that Lawrence was uncommunicative with him and would become "combative" if the conversation turned to literature. Lawrence, still not very well, was trying to "prove himself" by getting up before everyone else and doing his share of the work. His illness extinguished his gentleness and made him "bitter and perhaps near desperate. He locked himself away with *The Plumed Serpent* manuscript and emerged only to milk blackeyed Susan and mend the beastly barbed-wire fences. . . . I liked him so much. He was so perceptive. You could tell he felt and understood your inner workings. He was dearer than in his writings." Though Friedel liked Lawrence, it seems clear, from Lawrence's behavior, that he avoided and ignored the arrogant and unpleasant young German.[17]

Apart from his illness, another constant problem during 1924–25 — when he did less work and had expensive medical bills — was the difficulty in collecting the long-overdue royalties on published books, a substantial part of his income, from his former admirer and publisher, Thomas Seltzer. In March 1924 Seltzer told Lawrence that he had lost $7,000 the previous year, had no money in the bank and could not pay him. But in September, with the help of Robert Mountsier — who was still Lawrence's agent for previously contracted books and who (as Lawrence admitted) had been right to warn him about Seltzer's impending collapse — Lawrence had been able to collect $3,000. "If I can get it like this, bit by bit, I don't mind at all," he told Ada. "My fear is that he may go bankrupt."

In 1925, when he was being published by Alfred Knopf, Lawrence still had to live partly on the small doles that could be squeezed out of Seltzer. Things came to a crisis in September, when the Lawrences left the ranch for the last time and stopped in New York — "so nerve-jumpy, and steamy hot" — en route to England. Frieda, much more aggressive than Lawrence about money, told Brett that the publishers became angry and defensive about their unpayable debt: "Seltzers horrid and finished. — I went to lunch with them taking the attitude they would pay us if they *could,* but no, she almost hit me in the eye. — We are a lot of money grubbers." At the end of the year, scarcely managing to survive, the Seltzers still owed Lawrence $5,000. Despite all his disappointments with them, Lawrence, unlike Frieda, was more sympathetic than angry: "Seltzer is hopeless, he ought to go bankrupt and have done with it. But his creditors won't *make* him bankrupt hoping to squeeze him bit by bit.—I wish he'd never existed, poor devil."[18]

The Lawrences left New York aboard the *Resolute* on September 21. Though he always hoped to return to America, he lacked the energy for the exhausting journey and arduous life in the Rockies. He never forgot his ordeal at El Paso and feared that his tuberculosis or the scandalous reputation of *Lady Chatterley's Lover* would prevent his readmission to America.

CHAPTER NINETEEN

Spotorno and Scandicci,
1926–1928

I

LAWRENCE returned to Europe in poor health and without a permanent home. During the next five years he continued his restless quest for
a congenial climate and an attractive place to stay. He lived mostly in
small villages in Italy, first in Spotorno, on the Ligurian coast west of
Genoa, and then in Scandicci, seven miles southwest of Florence. He
made his last journey to England in the summer of 1926. In the spring of
1927 he went on a walking tour of the Etruscan places, and spent the
early fall in Austria and Germany. In 1928 he divided his time between
Tuscany, the Swiss Alps and an island off the south coast of France. His
quarrels with Frieda were as violent as ever, and his tuberculosis became
increasingly grave.

Lawrence found England in October 1925 dark, dismal and depressing. The rain, bad economic conditions and general gloom made it seem
"almost gruesome," even worse than his previous visit, in December
1923. "There's no *kick* in the people," he complained, "they're about as
active as seaweed." During his month in England he visited his two
sisters. Emily was "a fair, stolid-looking Midlands type"; Ada, "a handsome, dark version of Lawrence, had a rather unhappy adoration for
him," and he could not fully reciprocate her feelings. He met for the first
time the novelist William Gerhardie, who noted the gravity of his illness:

Lawrence's "satanic look was absent. In the sunlight his red-bearded face looked harrowed and full of suffering, almost Christ-like."[1] He saw Cynthia Asquith; and when he met Murry for the last time, attacked his soppy Christianity.

He also stopped briefly in Buckinghamshire, first with Martin Secker and then with Catherine Carswell. Secker, three years older than Lawrence, was "round-headed, fresh-complexioned, with jet-black hair, short and slim; he spoke with an almost imperceptible drawl, and laughed heartily but not very often." He had worked as a reader for Eveleigh Nash, founded his own firm in 1910 and had offices at 5 John Street, just off the Strand, near Charing Cross. Secker's first great success was Compton Mackenzie's novel *The Passionate Elopement* (1911). He also published Frank Swinnerton, Hugh Walpole, James Elroy Flecker, Francis Brett Young and Norman Douglas as well as Mann's *Buddenbrooks* and Kafka's *The Castle*. He became Lawrence's publisher in 1918. Fredric Warburg, who took over the firm when it collapsed in 1935, felt Secker lacked energy and ambition. Lawrence called him "quite nice, really, and perfectly unassuming—shy."[2]

Catherine Carswell thought that in 1925 (as in 1923) Lawrence seemed very solitary. He "did not speak of his health, and, as usual, there was nothing of the invalid about him; but under his big-brimmed Mexican hat his face looked pinched and small, and one easily guessed that he could not face London in the winter." After a walk in the country, an unexpected visitor appeared. This was Yvonne Kapp, a friend of Catherine and an aspiring author, whose husband, Edmond, had in 1923 done a pencil drawing of Lawrence. Yvonne found Lawrence extremely sympathetic and later recalled: "He treated me with what I can only call tender respect, talking to me as though I were a fellow-writer, in all seriousness. I feel immensely grateful and fond of him." Yvonne noted the striking contrast between Lawrence's wasted appearance and Frieda's bulky figure. They reminded her of those species who mate by the tiny male fastening onto the back of the enormous female.[3]

Summarizing his depressing and disappointing visits to family and friends in England, Lawrence told Brett that he had coughed like the devil in the filthy air of the Midlands, could not bear to see the gloomy Kot, felt he had lost his old intimacy with Cynthia, had nothing in common with the self-absorbed Murry and was sorry for Catherine's poverty.

In 1921 Secker had married Rina Capellero, who came from Spotorno, a village he recommended to Lawrence. Though Lawrence was not

especially fond of the Riviera and preferred to live farther south, in
Capri or Sicily, they compromised because Frieda wanted a place that
would be more accessible to her children and their friends. Lawrence
rented the Villa Bernarda from mid-November until April 1926. The
four-story villa, with a peasant living in the cellar, was perched on a hill
overlooking the village and the sea. Sitting on the balcony and writing
in the sun, Lawrence told friends that he liked the clear air and the mild
Mediterranean winter, though the rough winds often confined him to the
damp and chilly house:

> But the house is on the hill above the roofs, just under the castle,
> and the sea goes in and out of its bays, and glitters very bright.
> There is something forever cheerful and happy about the Mediter-
> ranean: I feel at home beside it. We've got a big garden of vines and
> almond trees, and an old peasant Giovanni.

Ten days after settling into the villa, Lawrence, who had expressed his
weariness with travel while in England, was already making plans for
the spring and consoling himself for being an invalid by fantasizing
about travel. He had started to learn Russian, still longed to visit the
isles of Greece and sail through the Bosporus—though Rananim "had
sunk out of sight." He wanted to see the coasts and islands of Spain,
Sicily, North Africa and Yugoslavia. He had published ten important
novels as well as many volumes of poems, plays, travel books and essays,
but had very little cash with which to realize his dreams:

> Now then, let's do something [he told Earl Brewster]. The Ship for
> preference. Or Spain in March—Balearic Isles, Majorca and
> Minorca—or central Sicily, that place, is it Castelvetrano, in the
> centre, where the flowers are really a wonder, in March. It's where
> Persephone rose from hell, each spring. Or Calabria—though most
> people get typhoid there, with the filthy water. Or Tunis, and to
> Kairowan, to the edge of the desert. Or across Italy to Dalmatia,
> Spalato and Ragusa, very lovely; and Montenegro. But with the
> ship we could do all that to a marvel. I could put £100 sterling to the
> ship.[4]

Though Lawrence could not bear the conventional chirpiness and
conceit of Frieda's daughters (then in their early twenties), he was,
despite his fierce temper, very kind when the long-legged Barbara

arrived on her first visit in December. Lawrence had tutored adults—
Jessie Chambers, William Henry and Stanley Hocking, Knud Merrild
and Kai Götzsche—as well as children. He was also curious about
Barbara Weekley, took a friendly and fatherly interest in her, taught her
Italian, helped with her painting, gave advice and affection, cunningly
roused her resentment against her mother and enlisted her sympathy
during his battles with Frieda. He was pleased when the peasants in the
village thought Barbara was his child and told him: "Your daughter is
tall like her father."

Lawrence knew that one day he would be considered a great writer
and in "The Border Line" had autobiographically written: "Alan had
had a weird innate conviction that he was beyond ordinary judgment."
He told Barbara that when Frieda had been childishly terrified during a
storm at sea, he calmed her by asserting: "No boat that I'm on will ever go
down."[5]

Sensing a potential ally in Barbara, Lawrence attacked Frieda for
smoking too many cigarettes, eating too many pastries, bobbing her hair,
acting like an aristocrat, expressing muddled thoughts, trying to be
intellectual and imitating his ideas. Huxley captured a characteristic
exchange in *Point Counter Point*:

"Oh, for god's sake shut up!" said Rampion.

"But isn't that what you say?"

"What I say is what *I* say. It becomes quite different when you
say it."

Frieda recorded that one evening at dinner, Lawrence, jealously
enraged, exaggerated Frieda's egoism and emotional defects, and told
Barbara:

"Don't you imagine your mother loves you; she doesn't love
anybody, look at her false face." And he flung half a glass of red
wine in my face [as he had done in Mexico]. Barby, who besides my
mother and myself was the only one not to be scared of him, sprang
up. "My mother is too good for you," she blazed at him, "much too
good; it's like pearls thrown to the swine." Then we both began to
cry. I went to my room offended.

"What happened after I went?" I asked Barby later on.

"I said to him: 'Do you care for her?' 'It's indecent to ask,' he
answered; 'haven't I just helped her with her rotten painting?'"

Ada's appearance in this emotional maelstrom in February 1926 provoked a bitter, three-sided quarrel and a separation that was as serious as the crisis in New York in August 1923, when Frieda had returned to England without him. Ada was possessive, Frieda hostile, Lawrence ill. He complained bitterly about his wife to his sister. Ada, who may have noticed Frieda's interest in their Italian landlord, assumed her mother's dominating role and felt Frieda was bullying Lawrence when he was ill. She lost control and shrieked at Frieda: "I hate you from the bottom of my heart." When Frieda went to Lawrence's room, she found it locked against her and discovered that Ada had taken the key and excluded her from nursing Lawrence. It was "the only time he had really hurt [her]." So she hardened her heart and thought: "Now I don't care."

In a tactical retreat, Frieda moved into a hotel with her daughters. After a fortnight Ada returned to England, Lawrence wandered around central Italy for six weeks and Frieda returned to the villa. He visited the Brewsters in Capri; inspired Brett's sexual fantasy in Ravello; and then took a little *giro* with two older women painters—Millicent Beveridge and Mabel Harrison, whom he had known in Sicily in 1921—to Rome, Assisi, Perugia, Florence and Ravenna. Frieda relented and wrote more mildly; but she still irritated Lawrence by justifying herself and laying down the law. He sent her a drawing of Jonah about to be devoured by the whale, with the minatory inscription: "Who is going to swallow whom?"[6]

Frieda's daughters urged reconciliation. When Lawrence returned to Spotorno on April 3, the three women were dressed festively to greet him. "For the moment I am the Easter Lamb," he told his mother-in-law. "When I went away, I was very cross. But really one has to forget a lot, and to live on." After living for a few weeks with their mother, Barbara and Elsa's childhood resentment resurfaced. They began to sympathize with Lawrence, and he came to admire—and even envy—their technique of handling their mother: "Frieda's children are very fierce with her, and fall on her tooth and nail. They simply won't stand her egotism for a minute: she is furious, then becomes almost humble with us all. I think *they've* taught her a lesson. Being her own family, they can go for her exactly in her own way, and pretty well silence her. It makes me die with laughing. She's caught more than she bargained for, in her own offspring. Makes her really appreciative of me."

Frieda—the daughter of a Prussian officer, brought up in a garrison town—had always admired soldiers and uniforms. In September 1914 she told Edward Marsh: "I used to think war so glorious, my father such a hero with his iron cross and his hand that a bullet had torn." Eleven years later, she wrote Brett that she was attracted to their landlord in Spotorno: "We have a nice little Bersaglieri [elite corps] officer to whom the villa belongs. I am thrilled by his cockfeathers; he is almost as nice as the feathers!"[7]

Angelo Ravagli, twelve years younger than Frieda, was born in Florence in 1891. He entered the war as a corporal; was wounded twice and decorated three times, promoted to lieutenant and captured by the Austrians in October 1917. Frieda's biographer described Angelo's appearance, background and sexual affairs:

> He was smaller than Frieda, but well-proportioned, and his movements were graceful. His virile, open features betrayed his peasant origin, but were otherwise in no way remarkable. It was the face of a man who had worked himself up from below and who set great store on outward appearances. He did not allow the fact that he was married and had three children to stand in the way of his erotic adventures: his wife, a schoolteacher, lived far away [from his army posts] in Savona.

Barbara, who disliked Angelo, called him an ordinary chap: practical and capable, but limited, dull and rather too pleased with himself.[8]

On her honeymoon in 1912 Frieda had slept with Udo von Henning, Harold Hobson and a German woodcutter in order to show her freedom and independence; in Cornwall in 1917 she had had a liaison with Cecil Gray to compensate for Lawrence's infatuation with William Henry Hocking. Richard Aldington remarked, with some exaggeration and hostile intent, that in 1926 "Frieda used to go about complaining that [Lawrence] had become impotent"—no doubt to justify her own behavior. Frieda—who had hardened her heart against Lawrence and thought: "Now I don't care"—probably began her affair with Angelo after her quarrel with and separation from Lawrence in February 1926, just as she had revenged herself with Murry under similar circumstances in the fall of 1923. Barbara and Juliette Huxley both thought Lawrence knew about Frieda's affair. But he was determined to maintain his marriage. He understood Frieda's nature and expected her to have a life of her own. He tolerated her selfishness and underestimated the seriousness of her attachment to Angelo. Though he must have found it sad and painful to have to share Frieda's love at the end of his life, he rarely became jealous or upset about Ravagli.[9]

II

In April 1926, when the lease expired on the Villa Bernarda, Lawrence moved south to Florence, partly perhaps to avoid Angelo's visits. There he met Arthur Wilkinson, a conscientious objector and a Socialist, who had a wild red beard, wore sandals and carried a knapsack. He painted, played the guitar, made puppets and wrote puppet plays, which he performed while touring in a caravan around the villages of England. Wilkinson lived with his wife and two children in Scandicci, a few miles from Florence in the Tuscan hills, and told Lawrence about the nearby Villa Mirenda, which became his last home in Italy.

The house belonged to Raul Mirenda, an army officer passionately devoted to history and literature. Close to the city, where Lawrence had several old friends, it was also secluded, restful and well suited to his work. It was a mile and a half from the terminus at Scandicci, where a half hour's tram ride took one to the Duomo in the center of town. The large, square, white-stone farm villa, which dated from the days of the Medici, stood in unspoiled country near the church of San Paolo Mosciano. Perched on a hill overlooking gardens, fields, vineyards and olive trees, it had a picturesque and paintable view of the woods and meadows of the Val d'Arno. The rooms had red-brick floors and were big and bare; there was little furniture and no kitchen utensils or linens. The Lawrences rented the top floor and garden for 3,000 lire (about £70) a year and lived there, off and on, until June 1928. Frieda seemed to be happiest at the Mirenda, the most settled home they ever had.

Pino Orioli, the Florentine bookseller, called Mirenda "a distant and dilapidated place," and Lawrence was not exaggerating when he said it had no comforts. It lacked electricity and running water, and the cooking had to be done on a charcoal fire. Lawrence reported that there was "no light, rainwater to be pumped up, sanitary arrangements primitive, the whole thing very rough—linen just calico, beds hard." It was too hot in high summer, too cold in midwinter, and not the best place for an invalid.

Yet in June and July Lawrence painted an idyllic picture of the place. The fireflies were thick in the garden, the cicadas rattled away in the sun, the church bells rang, the girls sang while cutting the wheat and corn.

The peasants, who worked the land and gave half the produce to the landlord, brought in huge baskets of ripe cherries, apricots, figs, peaches and plums, and the big white oxen walked slowly home past the olive trees. Lawrence's country life was completely different from the lives of most foreigners, who lived in cities, went to the museums and bought antiques: "There is something eternal about it: apart, of course, from villas and furniture and antichità and aesthetics. But we see few people, and live rough, which is what I prefer." Lawrence retained his independence by living economically and spending only £300 a year. He felt he had undermined his health with *The Plumed Serpent* and did very little work in hot weather. Despite relative idleness, the days passed quickly. He read, did the household chores, walked in the surrounding hills, talked to the Wilkinsons and observed the life of the peasants.

In June, Lawrence visited Sir George and Lady Sitwell, the parents of the poets, who owned a strange and rather disheartening castle some fourteen miles outside Florence, and whose eccentric existence was antithetical to his own. He mischievously explained that "Sir G. collects *beds* . . . as if he were providing for all the dead . . . those four-poster golden Venetian monsters that look like Mexican high-altars. Room after room, and nothing but bed after bed. I said 'but do you put your guests in them?'—Oh! he said. They're not to sleep in. They're museum pieces. Also gilt and wiggly-carved chairs. I sat on one. Oh! he said. Those chairs are not to sit in!—So I wiggled on the seat in the hopes that it would come to pieces."[10]

After settling into the Villa Mirenda, the Lawrences traveled north from mid-July to late September in order to escape the intense heat of summer. As the Mediterranean expatriate Norman Douglas wrote: "Anything for fresh air; anything to escape from the pitiless blaze of the South, and from those stifling nights when your bedroom grows into a furnace, its walls exuding inwardly all the fiery beams they have sucked up during the endless hours of noon!" Travel for Lawrence was at times a struggle for existence, a pilgrimage from country to country in search of warm climate and good health. Both Taormina and Taos had extreme summer and winter temperatures, which forced him to leave for part of the year. He often blamed the place for his illness and felt he had to abandon houses in which he had been gravely sick.

In Baden-Baden, which reminded Lawrence of Holbein's *Dance of Death,* the aged and infirm, clutching at life, seemed proud to be still alive. Later on, Lawrence, conscious of his approaching death, prophetically wrote from there: "Truly old and elderly women are ghastly,

ghastly, eating up all life with hoggish greed, to keep themselves alive. They don't mind who else dies. I know my mother-in-law would secretly gloat, if I died at 43 and she lived on at 78."

Lawrence's last, two-month trip to Britain during the General Strike of 1926 inspired his grim portrayal of industrial England in *Lady Chatterley's Lover.* He visited the cold and showery Scottish Highlands and Isle of Skye with the lively painter Millicent Beveridge, driving to the various lakes and picnicking around a damp wood fire. Though Lawrence was not one to go banging at the birds, he wittily told Brett that "Grouse shooting began day before yesterday—an event for those that shoot, and a still bigger one for those that get shot."[11] He spent a few days on the sweeping sands of the "bracing and tonicky" Lincolnshire coast, where he had taken holidays as a boy. After visiting his sisters in the Midlands (he never saw his older brother, George) and taking a last walk around "the country of my heart" with Willie Hopkin, he saw a few friends in London before returning to the Villa Mirenda in early October.

Lawrence found Weimar Germany freer and more pleasant than Italy. Fascism had driven Italy into a state of nervous tension and spread the blight of authoritarian boredom. Mussolini urged his countrymen to live dangerously, but enacted hundreds of repressive laws to protect the power of the state. As Lawrence conclusively told his disciple Rolf Gardiner, who admired totalitarian governments: "One can ignore Fascism in Italy for a time. But after a while, the sense of false power forced against life is very depressing."[12]

It is scarcely surprising that Lawrence finally broke with another would-be follower, Middleton Murry, in the spring of 1926. He could not stand Murry's sentimental self-exposure in the *Adelphi* or his repulsive mixture of ingratiating impudence. In January, Murry wrote spitefully to Lawrence about *Reflections on the Death of a Porcupine* (1925) and then, Lawrence said, "adds insult to injury, asking if I will allow him to print the essay on power ["Blessed Are the Powerful"], gratis, and various other things, gratis, in his *Adelphi;* 'as the gift of one man to another.' To which I can only say; 'as one writer to another, I will give you nothing, paid for or unpaid for.' He is an incorrigible worm." Murry retaliated by continuing to condemn Lawrence's major works in the *Adelphi.* According to Murry, *The Plumed Serpent* showed that Lawrence had "lost faith in his own imagination"; the *Collected Poems* contained a "hard, bleak quality of dogmatic asseveration"; and *Lady Chatterley's Lover* was "a deeply depressing book."[13]

In the fall of 1926 Aldous Huxley, who was also living in Italy and seeing a good deal of Lawrence, replaced Murry as Lawrence's closest friend. Tall, thin and bespectacled, nine years younger than Lawrence, Aldous was the grandson of the eminent Victorian scientist Thomas Huxley. Educated at Eton (where he later taught George Orwell) and at Balliol, he had overcome a period of blindness, been Murry's assistant on the *Athenaeum* and published several witty, stylish and intelligent novels, including *Crome Yellow* (1921) and *Antic Hay* (1923). In 1919 he had married the gentle Maria Nys, a Belgian refugee who had entered the Garsington circle and become a protégée of Ottoline Morrell.

Lawrence, the intuitive mystic, and Huxley, the scientific rationalist (who later had a mystical phase), had originally met at Garsington in 1915. Ottoline noted then that the rather reserved Huxley, like Forster and Russell, was alarmed by Lawrence's personal, penetrating analyses: "I think he was puzzled and rather overcome, and perhaps scared, at Lawrence's quick and immediate approach, brushing away all preliminaries—vetting him in fact, putting him under his X-ray." But their friendship developed swiftly in Italy, where they exchanged visits and took holidays together. Huxley was attracted by his temperamental opposite; Lawrence by Huxley's gentleness, incisiveness and formidable intelligence, by his dependability and devotion. In a letter of July 1927 to his father, Huxley praised Lawrence's genius and remarked that his temper had been tamed by illness: "He is a very extraordinary man, for whom I have a great admiration and liking—but difficult to get on with, passionate, queer, violent. However, age is improving him and now his illness has cured him of his violences and left him touchingly gentle." After Lawrence's death, Huxley defended him against his detractors and called him "the most extraordinary and impressive human being" he had ever known, "a being, somehow, of another order, more sensitive, more highly conscious, more capable of feeling than even the most gifted of common men."[14]

III

Though weak, Lawrence seemed to be slowly recovering from his first serious hemorrhage. But in Spotorno in February 1926, he had a second hemorrhage (which he called "bronchial" rather than "tubercular").

Toward the end of 1926 and throughout the following spring, while he lived at the Villa Mirenda, Lawrence's health seemed to deteriorate. In his letters, he frequently mentioned his sore chest, bronchial trouble, pneumonia, influenza and a recurrence of the malaria that had begun in Ceylon and continued in Mexico. At Eastertime, anticipating the mood of *The Man Who Died,* he seemed to be losing his grip on life and drifting toward death: "I'm just simply suffering from a change of life, and a queer sort of recoil, as if one's whole soul were drawing back from connection with everything. This is the day they put Jesus in the tomb — and really, those three days in the tomb begin to have a terrible significance and reality to me."

On a hot afternoon in early July, after gathering peaches in the garden, Lawrence went inside to rest. Frieda wrote that he suddenly

called from his room in a strange, gurgling voice; I ran and found him lying on his bed; he looked at me with shocked eyes while a slow stream of blood came from his mouth. "Be quiet, be still," I said. I held his head, but slowly and terribly the blood flowed from his mouth. I could do nothing but hold him and try to make him still and calm and send for Doctor Giglioli. . . . In this great heat of July nursing was difficult—Giulia, all the peasants—helped in every possible way. The signor was so ill—Giulia got down to Scandicci at four in the morning and brought ice in sawdust in a big handkerchief, and milk, but this, even boiled straightaway, would be sour by midday. . . . I nursed him alone night and day for six weeks, till he was strong enough to take the night train to the Tyrol.

Lawrence bravely wrote, in a note to Pino Orioli: "early this morning the hemorrhage came again. Frieda wept, and I felt like all the martyrs in one. But it doesn't seem bad, and I shall get up again tomorrow—deo volente [God willing]."[15]

Dr. Giglioli could give little more than a coagulant and feeble reassurance. As Lawrence optimistically explained to Mark Gertler, who had recently been treated in a sanatorium: "It's chronic bronchial congestion—and it brought me on a series of bronchial hemorrhages this time. I've had little ones before. It would be serious if they didn't stop, he says: but they do stop: so it's nothing to worry about. . . . These hemorrhages are rather shattering—but perhaps they take some bad blood out of the system." The real problem, as Lawrence admitted to the Brewsters, was that he needed "a new breathing apparatus."

In August, Lawrence recovered sufficiently to spend two and a half months in Villach, Austria; at his sister-in-law's villa in Irschenhausen, Bavaria (where he had lived in the summer of 1913); and in Baden-Baden. In Bavaria he was examined by two German doctor-writers: Max Mohr and Hans Carossa. Carossa gave a comforting diagnosis and warned him against a pernicious treatment: "He listened to my lung passages, he could not hear my lungs, thinks they must be healed, only the bronchi, and the doctors are not interested in bronchi. But he says not to take more inhalations with hot air: it might bring the hemorrhage back."

The truth, however, was quite different. And Lawrence, who had two and a half years to live, was probably not deluded. For Carossa told the literary editor Franz Schoenberner, with devastating accuracy: "An average man with those lungs would have died long ago. But with a real artist no prognosis is ever sure. There are other [psychological] forces involved. Maybe Lawrence can live two or even three years more. But no medical treatment can really save him." Huxley confirmed Lawrence's will to live when he wrote: "by all the rules of medicine, he should have been dead. For the last two years he was like a flame burning on in miraculous disregard of the fact that there was no more fuel to justify its existence."[16]

In mid-October, Lawrence returned to the Villa Mirenda, which had lost its charm and now reminded him of his serious illness in July. He was depressed by his lack of money and of energy, his inability to work, his physical deterioration and his proximity to death. "I'm not very happy here," he told Kot, "and I don't know where else to go, and have not much money to go anywhere with—I feel I don't want to work—don't want to do a thing—all the life gone out of me. Yet how can I sit in this empty place and see nobody and do nothing. . . . I do think this is the low-water mark of existence. I never felt so near the brink of the abyss."

In January–February 1928, desperately in search of a remission if not a cure, the Lawrences rented a house near the Huxleys in Diablerets, Switzerland, and near the tuberculosis sanatoria of the Alps. The doctors said the altitude, thin air and snow would be good for him, but he actually felt worse than in Tuscany. He coughed, panted and could not walk uphill.

They spent the spring months at the Villa Mirenda, and then left the house forever. Signora Mirenda later recalled Lawrence's friendship with the peasant families, his illness and his painting:

He was very thin with a red beard and looked like Jesus. They often quarreled, shut in their rooms, he often shouted at his wife. They

loved our peasants: the Pini, Orsini, Bandelli. On Christmas they
used to [decorate a tree and] arrange a great feast for more than
twenty people, and there were many presents for the children. He
suffered from tuberculosis and when he had a hemorrhage, he was
helped by Giulia, a girl of twelve, daughter of the Pini. We were so
worried for her, for the danger she was suffering by nursing a
patient like that. Then, when he started writing *Lady Chatterley's
Lover,* he used to paint strange paintings, shameful ones, and even
painted Pini while ploughing, naked.[17]

In mid-June the Lawrences met the Brewsters in the French Alps,
where an unpleasant incident occurred. They settled into a charming
inn at St. Nizier, in the mountains above Grenoble. The next morning the
owner knocked on Earl's door and complained about the coughing that
had lasted through the night: "He was sorry not to be able to keep
Lawrence, but there was no choice, since the law on that plateau pro-
hibited his having guests with affected lungs. Monsieur would have to
go." According to their daughter, Harwood, the Brewsters took no
precautions against his disease and even used the same utensils as
Lawrence. And Lawrence continued to maintain that his coughing
resulted from an annoying irritation of his bronchials. But this was the
first time he had been evicted from a hotel, and the episode must have
jolted the Brewsters into acknowledging the seriousness of his illness.

The Brewsters and Frieda decided not to tell Lawrence what had
happened. They pretended they disliked the place and wanted to leave,
obtained his agreement and never knew if he suspected what had occurred. But Lawrence, remembering his humiliating encounter with the
American officials at El Paso, knew perfectly well what had transpired.
A few days later, he wrote Pino Orioli: "That St. Nizier place was very
rough—and the insolent French people actually asked us to go away
because I coughed. . . . I felt very mad."[18]

The Lawrences, once again without a fixed place to live, spent July to
mid-September in Gsteig, Switzerland, where his sister Emily and her
daughter Margaret visited him. In Margaret's photograph Lawrence,
looking tense and sitting on a bench outside the villa, has wasted away
and wears a loose, baggy suit that seems much too large for him.

In October he stayed at Port-Cros with Richard Aldington, who was
then having affairs with the American Dorothy Yorke and the Irish
Brigit Patmore, both of whom Lawrence had met during the war. He
sent the Brewsters a lively description of the island, an old coastguard
fort off the coast of Toulon:

The Vigie isn't a castle but a top of a hill with a moat and low fort wall enclosing a bare space, about 2 acres, where the wild lavender and the heather grow. The rooms are sort of cabins under the walls—windows facing the inner space, loop-holes looking out to sea—a nice large sitting room—a bedroom each—then across, a great room where we throw the logs, and a kitchen, pantry and little dining-room. It's very nice, rather rough, but not really uncomfortable—and plenty of wood to burn in the open fireplaces.

But the grim reality was entirely different. Lawrence was clearly dying and, according to Aldington, became embittered when Frieda returned from a tryst with Ravagli and infected him with her cold:

He had to spend his days in bed or in a deck-chair, so weak that he could pass the drawbridge only for a few yards, and was almost too weak to climb to the glassed-in look-out. Most unfortunately, Frieda came back with one of her usual heavy colds, which Lawrence instantly caught, and this ended up in a hemorrhage. . . . Night after night I listened to his deep hollow cough. . . . Only then did I realise how frail and ill he was, how bitterly he suffered, what frightening envy and hatred of ordinary healthy humanity sometimes possessed him, how his old wit had become bitter malice, how lonely he was, how utterly lonely he was, how utterly he depended on Frieda, how insanely jealous of her he had become.

At the end of November, Lawrence felt a change of continent and the clean air of the Rockies might do him good. But he told Brett that he dared not risk the trip: "At present I feel America rather hostile to me and they might do something mean to one, if one came over. . . . They hate you so if you cough—particularly on ships—and cough I do."[19]

IV

In early April 1927, after a year in the Villa Mirenda and during the last period of relatively good health before his serious hemorrhage in July, Lawrence took a two-week walking tour with Earl Brewster to the Etruscan towns of central Italy. In the three summers before the war, Lawrence and Frieda had crossed the Alps on foot, and he had met Kot

on a walking tour of the Lake District in August 1914. But he would soon
lose the remnant of strength he still possessed; and the long walk to
Cerveteri, Tarquinia, Volci and Volterra was the last he would ever take.

Lawrence's last travel book, *Etruscan Places* (serialized in *Travel* in
1927–28), is a synthesis of history and direct experience. It combines
description and interpretation with social criticism and political com-
mentary, and concerns both the past and the present of Italy. The central
paradox of the book is that the Etruscans, though destroyed by the
Romans, still live in their art and are more vital than their conquerors:
"the carved figure of the dead rears up as if alive, from the lid of the
tomb. . . . The underworld of the Etruscans becomes more real than the
above day of the afternoon."[20]

Though Lawrence relies heavily on Etruscan scholars like George
Dennis, Pericles Ducati and Fritz Weege for factual information, he
instinctively opposes their negative interpretation of the people. He also
condemns their efforts to tear Etruscan art from its customary setting
in the rough hillside, where the guide kneels to light his lamp and the
travelers quite naturally dive down into the little one-room tombs "just
like rabbits popping down a hole."

The vague and mysterious quality of the Etruscans, who half emerge
from the dim background of time, allows and even encourages Lawrence
to construct an imaginative but entirely convincing picture of their
vanished life, to re-create them in his own image. He laments that "We
have lost the art of living" and believes that the Etruscans, who express
the qualities he admires, can by their still vivid example restore their
precious gifts to modern man.

Lawrence announces, on the opening page, that he is instinctively
attracted to the Etruscans, who have captured his imagination. He
makes specific connections between the characteristics of the ancient
Etruscans and the modern Italian peasants. According to Lawrence,
Etruscan places have a stillness and repose. The Etruscans were connected to a primitive and prehistoric Mediterranean world, were in
touch with the gods, and had a phallic as opposed to the present-day
mental and spiritual consciousness. They possessed a delicacy, sensitivity and spontaneity, and saw death as a pleasant continuance of life, with
wine, flutes and dance. Their religion, which preceded the Roman gods,
was expressed in terms of ritual, gesture and symbol; their ship of death
represented "the mystery of the journey out of life." Everything they
made was ephemeral, conveyed a sense of everlasting wonder and provided immediate pleasure. Their confederacy of loosely linked, indepen-

dent city-states expressed the Italian political instinct and resembled modern Italy before unification in 1861—and even afterward. In a magnificent passage that proclaims his vitalism in the face of death, Lawrence writes:

> To the Etruscan all was alive; the whole universe lived; and the business of man was himself to live amid it all. He had to draw life into himself, out of the wandering huge vitalities of the world. The cosmos was alive, like a vast creature. The whole thing breathed and stirred. . . . Every man, every creature and tree and lake and mountain and stream, was animate, had its own peculiar consciousness.
>
> And it has to-day.
>
> The active religious idea was that man, by vivid attention and subtlety and exerting all his strength, could draw more life into himself, more life, more and more glistening vitality, till he became shining like the morning, blazing like a god.

In Lawrence's view, the brutal, imperial Romans were antithetical to the Etruscans. The Romans dominated and eventually destroyed their charming neighbors, who held out against overwhelming mechanical force for more than a hundred years. The historical justification for the destruction of Etruria was that the people were vicious. Lawrence stoutly defends them against the charge of cruelty and convincingly refutes the traditional "picture of a gloomy, hellish, serpent-writhing, vicious Etruscan people who were quite rightly stamped out by the noble Romans."

Lawrence associates the ancient Romans with the modern Fascists just as he equates the Etruscans with the peasants. He thus gives a satiric twist to the nationalistic propaganda of the Italian conquerors, who revived the Roman salute, spoke of the Mediterranean as *mare nostrum* and were inspired by imperial ambitions to invade Africa. But Lawrence notes, with considerable perspicacity, that Fascist (like Roman) power is doomed because the party members do not trust their leaders: the Nietzschean "will-to-power is a secondary thing in an Italian, reflected onto him from the Germanic races that have almost engulfed him. . . . Brute force and overbearing may make a terrific effect. But in the end, that which lives lives by delicate sensitiveness."[21]

CHAPTER TWENTY

Lady Chatterley's Lover
and the Paintings,
1928–1929

I

AFTER HIS ILLNESSES in Oaxaca and Florence, and during the last five years of his life, Lawrence became seriously concerned with the theme of resurrection. His last, positive works, which balanced the despair of the war years, were his personal response to and artistic preparation for the imminent threat of death. After his nearly fatal hemorrhage, Lawrence abandoned his faith in a strong leader ("fake power forced against life") and his hope for a political solution to the postwar chaos, which he had explored in the novels of power during 1921–25. He returned to his prewar belief in the regeneration of society through the personal relations of men and women—an early title of *Lady Chatterley's Lover* was *Tenderness*—and portrayed characters who defied disease and experienced rebirth in *this* life.

The resurrection theme originated in Lawrence's early experience with evangelical Christianity and its imagery of holiness, salvation and rebirth. It was complicated by his simultaneous identification with and rejection of Christ: his view of himself as prophet and redeemer, martyr and messiah of a decaying civilization, and his hostility to what he considered the repressive and life-denying elements of Christianity: its renunciation of the present, guilt about the body, emphasis on death. Lawrence's relation to Christianity was essentially negative, but he used its imagery in an attempt to lead society back to a pre-Christian, pagan awareness of vital possibilities. As Lawrence approached his own death, he preached the radical limitations of Christ—the lack of vitality and the death wish—to his own disciple, Dorothy Brett: "I think Christ was profoundly, disastrously wrong. . . . Jesus becomes more unsympatisch to me, the longer I live: crosses and nails and tears and all that stuff! I think he showed us into a nice cul de sac. . . . He never *experienced* life as the old Pagan Gods did. . . . He never knew animals, or women, from a child—never. He held forth in the temple and never *lived*. He was out to die, that's what makes his preaching disastrous."

In his essays Lawrence condemned, even more forcefully, the Christian split between body and spirit: "The history of our era is the nauseating and repulsive history of the crucifixion of the procreative body for the glorification of the spirit, the mental consciousness." And in his last work, *Apocalypse,* he maintained:

What man most passionately wants is his living wholeness and his living unison. . . . Man wants his physical fulfilment first and foremost, since now, once and once only, he is in the flesh and potent. For man, the vast marvel is to be alive. For man, as for flower and beast and bird, the supreme triumph is to be most vividly, most perfectly alive. Whatever the unborn and the dead may know, they cannot know the beauty, the marvel of being alive in the flesh. The dead may look after the afterwards. But the magnificent here and now of life in the flesh is ours, and ours alone, and ours only for a time. We ought to dance with rapture that we should be alive and in the flesh, and part of the living, incarnate cosmos.[1]

To the dying Lawrence, the survival of the spirit was not enough; there also had to be a sensual cure and recognition of the needs of the body in *this* life. He was determined to transform the Christian myth— maintaining its images but abandoning its renunciation—and to achieve the promise of salvation while on earth.

The three works of 1926–28 that most clearly express the theme that dominated the last phase of his career were the story "Sun" and the novel *Lady Chatterley's Lover*—both of which revealed the characteristic movement from illness to health, from an arty society at the beginning of the work to a sensual cure at the end—and the novella *The Man Who Died*. Finally, Lawrence's greatest poem, "The Ship of Death," directly inspired by his vision of the Etruscan tombs, transformed the theme of rebirth into pagan terms and expressed his acceptance of death.

Juliet, the heroine of "Sun," surrenders her naked self to the personified, penetrating Sicilian sun, which connects with and flows into her body, and "*knew* her, in the cosmic carnal [sun-woman] sense of the word." Her little boy, who rolls a sun-like orange across the red tiles of the terrace, also becomes acclimatized and transformed from his grey father's to his golden mother's son. Like Juliet, he no longer fears the sun, sheds his civilized tension and accepts even the poisonous gold-brown snakes as a natural part of the harmonious environment.

Juliet's ritual is shattered by the unexpected appearance of her grey-faced husband, who contaminates her Eden with the lifeless world of urban America. The monastic husband, "dazed with admiration, but also, at a deadly loss," is frightened by Juliet's hostility and does not know how to respond to her strange behavior. Juliet immediately places the burden of responsibility for their future life on him and vaguely demands: "What are you going to do about it, Maurice?" Maurice, grey from earning money to support his narcissistic wife and child, finds it difficult to follow her example and impossible to compete sexually with the sun. Apparently defeated, he submits to her wishes to remain in Sicily and allows her complete freedom.

Juliet, who walks through the fields completely naked, then focuses on the local peasant who has been aroused by the spectacle of her body. His animal vitality, quick blood and *farouche* shyness provide a striking—if unfair—contrast to her lifeless husband. Her bold thought: "Why shouldn't I meet this man for an hour, and bear his child?" anticipates Connie Chatterley's feeling about Mellors.

But this parable, unlike most of Lawrence's works, ends in bitter irony, for Juliet's sensual cure is still incomplete—she has experienced peasant life and a physical but not a mental change. She acts dishonestly by submitting to her husband, who has remained indifferent to the Sicilian sun and "smelled of the world, and all its fetters and its mongrel cowering. . . . Her next child would be Maurice's. The fatal chain of continuity would cause it."

The unexpurgated ending of "Sun" was more explicit and more crude in its contrasts. Lawrence explained that Juliet "had not enough courage, she was not free enough," though she felt "the rousing of [the peasant's] big penis against his body—for her, surging for her." But she submits to the etiolated body of her city-branded husband, who "would possess her, and his little frantic penis would beget another child in her."[2] In both versions of the story the fiery sun-soaked peasant, who has no children of his own, rouses the lust that is slaked by the feeble husband.

The unexpurgated edition of "Sun" was published in Paris by Harry Crosby's Black Sun Press in 1928 and magnificently paid for with the Queen of Naples' snuffbox and five twenty-dollar pieces of gold. Crosby took this treasure to the Gare de l'Est in Paris, went to the Rome express, looked for an honest man (who turned out to be the Duke of Argyll) and asked him to deliver the gold to Lawrence in Italy.

Crosby—a handsome, arty, egoistic, manic playboy—was the nephew of J. P. Morgan. When Lawrence visited him outside Paris in March 1928, Crosby ignored Lawrence's genius, adopted a patronizing attitude about his humble background and unhealthy appearance, and noted in his diary: "He is commonplace. I am not. He is unthoroughbred. I am thoroughbred. He was 'seedy' looking." Crosby could have added: He has genius. I lack talent.

Lawrence, alert to the morbid element in Crosby's character, sensed the futility of his sensual and alcoholic distractions: "Harry's loves— just like his whiskies, to excite his head and die away dead! Nothing!" When Crosby shot his mistress and himself in a New York apartment nine months after meeting Lawrence, Achsah Brewster reported that Lawrence "looked utterly miserable and sorrowfully reiterated: 'That's all he could do with life, throw it away. How could he betray the great privilege of life?'" Observing that Crosby had killed himself while he himself was desperately struggling to stay alive, Lawrence called Crosby's violent death "the last sort of cocktail excitement" and told Orioli: "He had always been *too* rich and spoilt: nothing to do but commit suicide."[3]

II

Lawrence's last visit to Nottingham and Derbyshire, in September 1926, and his confrontation with the poverty, despair and class warfare inspired by the impending collapse of the miners' strike, influenced the creation of his last and boldest novel. The British General Strike, the most severe of the century, began on May 3, and within a week four million workers had left their jobs. The miners were locked out for seven months, the railroad network was paralyzed and British industry came to a halt. But the strike ultimately failed, and the defeated miners voted to go back to work on November 19.

Lawrence, who had become more conservative since his anarchic days during World War I, feared the strike would incite class hatred and destroy the traditional social order:

> Coal was the making of England, and it looks as if coal were to be the breaking of her too. . . .
>
> It seems, for the first time as far as I know it, to have made the miners really class conscious, and full of resentment. . . .
>
> This strike has done a lot of damage—and there is a lot of misery—families living on bread and margarine and potatoes—nothing more. The women have turned into fierce communists—you would hardly believe your eyes. It feels a different place: not pleasant at all.

In earlier novels, like *Women in Love,* the miners were idealized and sensual: their broad dialect "seemed to envelop Gudrun in a laborer's caress, there was in the whole atmosphere a resonance of physical men, a glamorous thickness of labour and maleness, surcharged in the air." In *Lady Chatterley's Lover,* the miners have become mechanical and degraded: "the grey, gritty hopeless . . . England of today . . . was producing a new race of mankind, overconscious in the money and social and political side, on the spontaneous, intuitive side dead, but dead. Half-corpses, all of them. . . . The iron and coal had eaten deep into the bodies and souls of the men."[4]

Lawrence wrote three different versions of *Lady Chatterley's Lover,* while living at the Villa Mirenda, between October 1926 and March 1928.[5] He sometimes wrote in the tower of the house, sometimes on the sunny balcony, and most often in the nearby pinewoods, with an exercise book on his knees and his back against the trunk of a living tree.

The ambitious and innovative novel focuses on the relation of Lady Chatterley and her husband's gamekeeper, and achieved notoriety by its acknowledgment of Connie's sexual desires, approval of her adultery with a social inferior and explicit sexual descriptions. But it also goes beyond their love to consider the effects of the war, the horrors of industrialism, the decayed state of English civilization, the rigidity of the class structure. It proposes the possibility of vital connections between men and women, the need for a radical change in consciousness, the self-affirmation and triumph of life in opposition to the destructive and sterilizing forces of the modern world.

Many aspects of Mellors' life are autobiographical. Like the young Lawrence, Mellors was a clever lad who had learned French and won a scholarship to an urban grammar school. The photograph of Mellors taken when he was married at twenty-one, which he destroys to show his loyalty to Connie, reveals him for what he was: "a young curate" and a "prig." Lawrence said that his own photograph, taken at the age of twenty-one, portrays him as a "clean-shaven, bright young prig in a high collar like a curate." Mellors' description of his early love affairs is clearly based on Lawrence's relations with Jessie Chambers, Louie Burrows and Helen Corke, just as his "bringin' her breakfast in bed" refers to his habit of serving Frieda. Connie's first, unsuccessful sexual encounter with Mellors recalls Lawrence's wedding night with Frieda, described in his poem "First Morning." Mellors' loathsome and messy divorce—"I hate those things like death, officials and courts and judges. . . . Couldn't one go right away, to the far ends of the earth, and be free from it all?"[6]— reflects Lawrence's squeamish response to Frieda's divorce. Mellors' disease is like Lawrence's, just as Connie's infidelity reflects Frieda's affair with Angelo Ravagli.

Mellors' programmatic plea for men who could sing, swagger and wear bright red trousers as a way to replace money with manhood may seem an absurd residue of *The Plumed Serpent*. But this scheme for rebirth has deep roots in the regenerative idealism of John Ruskin and William Morris as well as in Lawrence's youthful ideas about encouraging spontaneity in miners' schools.

Lawrence adapted the vital theme first expressed in the Proverbs of Blake's *Marriage of Heaven and Hell* (1790) — "the nakedness of woman is the work of God"—and in *Ecce Homo* (1888), where Nietzsche proclaimed: "Every kind of contempt for sex, every impurification of it by means of the concept 'impure,' is the crime *par excellence* against life—is the real sin against the holy spirit of life." In "A Propos of *Lady Chatterley's Lover*," Lawrence explained that he hoped to regenerate a sexless England by recapturing "the warm blood-sex that establishes the living and revitalizing connection between man and woman." He also expressed the idea that provided both the thematic and the structural unity of a work that begins in autumn and follows the seasonal cycle to spring, moves from morbidity to vitality and ends (like *The Rainbow,*

The Lost Girl, "Sun" and *The Man Who Died*) with a hopeful pregnancy: "The greatest need of man is the renewal forever of the complete rhythm of life and death, the rhythm of the sun's year, the body's year."[7]

Lawrence attacks the upper-class, intellectual, materialistic and mechanical civilization that thwarts this potential regeneration. It is embodied not only in the paralyzed Clifford Chatterley but also in Connie's lover, the "street-rat" Michaelis, "the last word in what was caddish and bounderish," who was based on Michael Arlen. Born Dikran Kouyoumdjian in Bulgaria, Arlen remarked that he suffered from "pernicious Armenia" and was "every other inch a gentleman." Ottoline said that he seemed to pollute the atmosphere and described him as "fat, dark-blooded, tight-skinned. . . . He has a certain vulgar sexual force, but he is very coarse-grained and conceited." Arlen was one of the two men whom Katherine Mansfield had seen mocking Lawrence's *Amores* in the Café Royal in 1916. After his quarrel with Lawrence he published in Orage's *New Age* "a most scathing and amusing satire on a 'brilliant young author, whose work [*Women in Love*] was too good to be published' discovering his subconscious self in the middle of the night!"[8]

Connie's dislike of the intellectualism and smart talk about sex at the beginning of the novel prepares her to respond to the inarticulate animalism of Mellors, the Boy in the Bush. Her sexual rebirth develops with her maternal longing. And she rejects Clifford's belief, expressed when he urges her to have a child and heir by another man, that emotion and procreation can somehow be separated. Lawrence evokes the maternal theme in the superb scene where Connie feeds the pheasant chicks — who are destined to be slaughtered (like the soldiers in the war) as soon as they reach maturity. Like Miriam in *Sons and Lovers,* Connie is afraid of the fierce pecks of the protective mother hen and draws back, startled and frightened. Then Mellors, in a subtle mixture of sexual exploration and midwifery, "slowly, softly, with sure gentle fingers, felt among the old bird's feathers and drew out a faintly-peeping chick in his closed hand." As Connie holds the soft baby bird and begins to weep about the tragedy of her life, the maternal is linked to the sexual theme. Mellors comes to life and is suddenly "aware of the old flame shooting and leaping up in his loins, that he had hoped was quiescent forever."[9] He caresses Connie, establishes his authority by commanding her to lie down and makes love to her for the first time as sex transcends class through the "democracy of touch."

As in his conversation with Compton Mackenzie on Capri, Lawrence emphasizes the importance of simultaneous orgasm and carefully shows how Connie progresses from a kind of clitoral masturbation with her prewar German lover and again with Michaelis, to early sex with Mellors where only he is satisfied, to vaginal and simultaneous climax. Her sexual relations change from secular, adulterous and contraceptive to sacramental, marital and procreative with Mellors.

Connie and Mellors, attracted by their difference of class and drawn together by threats of scandal and separation, oppose with their bodies and their love the catastrophic results of the war, which Lawrence described in Spenglerian terms in the great opening sentences of the novel: "Ours is essentially a tragic age, so we refuse to take it tragically. The cataclysm has happened, we are among the ruins." As W. B. Yeats observed: "Those two lovers, the gamekeeper and his employer's wife, each separated from their class by their love, and by fate, are poignant in their loneliness, and the coarse language of the one, accepted by both, becomes a forlorn poetry uniting their solitudes, something ancient, humble and terrible."[10]

III

Radclyffe Hall's lesbian novel, *The Well of Loneliness,* was banned in 1928, and Lawrence knew his novel would also be considered improper when judged by the prevailing standards of taste and morality. Though it could not be printed as he wrote it, in England or America, he absolutely refused to cut it. Dylan Thomas has said: "there are only three vocabularies at your disposal when you talk of sex: the vocabulary of the clinic, of the gutter and of the moralist." Lawrence attempted to transform the language of the gutter into the language of the moralist, and to treat sex honestly, sincerely and reverently.

Though Secker and Knopf were the best publishers he'd ever had, he was exasperated by their inefficient ways. As he told a friend in April 1927: "Either a publisher is so dilatory, you think he's dead: or in such a hurry, you think he's taken salts."[11] So he decided, *faute de mieux,* to bring out the book himself.

In the eighteenth century, Alexander Pope had made enormous profits by selling his translations of Homer in advance and by subscription. More recently, in 1922, James Joyce had published *Ulysses* with Sylvia Beach, who owned the Shakespeare & Company bookstore in

Paris. And Norman Douglas, who printed his books privately with Pino Orioli in Florence, also stimulated Lawrence to follow his profitable example. By risking his own money on the publication of the book, Lawrence could earn the publisher's ninety percent of the profits and his agent's fee of ten percent, and also avoid payment of English taxes.

Orioli, a year older than Lawrence, was born near Bologna, the child of a sausage-maker. He had worked as a barber during his teens and had served in the army during 1904–07. He then moved to England, gave Italian lessons, learned the book trade in London and opened his own shop on Museum Street in Bloomsbury. He claimed to have met Lawrence in Cornwall, though Lawrence did not live there until Orioli had returned to Italy to serve in the war. A short, chubby man with lively eyes behind owlish spectacles, Orioli was "warm and alive, vividly amusing, spirited, generous and refreshing," with a scurrilous tongue, a Rabelaisian turn of mind and (like Douglas) a predilection for young men.

In April 1928, just after completing the novel, Lawrence was buying paper, correcting proofs and designing his personal symbol, a phoenix rising from its nest in flames, which he had printed on his *Way of All Flesh*. The first edition, of a thousand copies, was published in July at a cost of £300 in "a nice little printing shop, all working away by hand— cosy and bit by bit, real Florentine manner—and the printer doesn't know a word of English—nobody on the place knows a word—where ignorance is bliss! Where the serpent is invisible! They will print on a nice hand-made Italian paper—should be an attractive book. I do hope I'll sell my 1000 copies—or most of 'em—or I'll be broke. I want to post them direct to purchasers." Unlike the English, the Italians accepted sex as a natural part of ordinary life. The Florentine printer, when told about certain words in the novel, replied: "Oh! *ma!* but we do it every day!"[12] The book did well, and a second edition, of two hundred copies, was brought out in November.

The notorious novel was stopped by the American customs officials almost immediately. Though there was a fortunate delay in obstruction by the English authorities, Lawrence reported in February 1929: "Lately they have been making a great fuss over *Lady C*. Scotland Yard holding it up—visiting my agents—sort of threatening criminal proceedings—and holding up my mail—and actually confiscating two copies, MS. copies of my poems, *Pansies*. . . . [They are] putting me to a lot of trouble. I don't mind when I'm well, but one gets run down."[13]

The home secretary was then William Joynson-Hicks (later Lord

Brentford), who had strong religious beliefs and had been president of
the Church League in 1921. In 1929 he expressed the prevailing repressive attitude and followed Lawrence's *Pornography and Obscenity* in the
Criterion Miscellany Series with *Do We Need a Censor?* Though he
makes no direct reference to Lawrence, he mentions "the storm which
broke over my head ... in regard to the censorship of books" and
concludes with the purifying hope that "by the spread of education and
the extension of religion in the hearts of the people they will themselves
learn to reject all unpleasant conduct, literature, art—and beyond all,
personal thought." Evelyn Waugh's *Vile Bodies* (1930) alludes to both
Joynson-Hicks and the illegal importation of *Lady Chatterley's Lover*
when a customs official says: "Particularly against books the Home
Secretary is. If we can't stamp out literature in the country, we can at
least stop its being brought in from outside. That's what he said the other
day in Parliament."[14]

Lawrence knew his novel and paintings would have a hostile recep-
tion, but he had a profound belief in the truth of his own convictions and
great moral courage in opposing puritanical views about how sexual
relations should be represented in art. He was outraged to find that
though he loathed promiscuous sex, he was considered by the public to be
a lurid specialist in sexuality. In a letter to Ottoline, with whom he had
had a reconciliation, he explained the crucial difference between ad-
vocating complete sexual freedom and urging people to bring sexual
thought and sexual acts into healthy harmony. Thinking, no doubt, of
himself and Frieda, he also made the important distinction between
youthful and senescent sex:

> About *Lady C.*—you mustn't think I advocate perpetual sex. Far
> from it. Nothing nauseates me more than perpetual sex in and out
> of season. But I want, with *Lady C.*, to make an *adjustment in
> consciousness* to the basic physical realities. ... God forbid that I
> should be taken as urging loose sex activity. There is a brief time for
> sex, and a long time when sex is out of place. But when it is out of
> place as an activity there still should be the large and quiet space in
> the consciousness where it lives quiescent. Old people can have a
> lovely quiescent sort of sex, like apples, leaving the young quite
> free for *their* sort.[15]

The common reaction to the novel—including that of his rather
proper sisters—was "superior disapproval, or slightly mingy, narrow-

gutted condescension." Though Lawrence might have expected a more enlightened response from the author of *Ulysses,* who shared his sexual frankness, Joyce harshly criticized both the style and the inverted puritanism of the novel. He insisted: "That man really writes very badly" and, adopting a patronizing tone, told Harriet Weaver, the editor of the *Egoist:* "I read the first 2 pages of the usual sloppy English and Stuart Gilbert [Joyce's translator, critic and editor] read me a lyrical bit about nudism in the wood and the end which is a piece of propaganda in favour of something which, outside D.H.L.'s country at any rate, makes all the propaganda for itself."

Lawrence had reciprocal feelings about *Ulysses.* He thought Joyce lacked warmth and spontaneity, fussed about with trivial details, sought sensation and (as Lawrence had said of Wyndham Lewis) was physically repelled by human flesh. Lawrence was also revolted by the content of *Ulysses,* which, in a strange way, inspired him to write what Joyce called *Lady Chatterbox's Lover:* "The last part of it is the dirtiest, most indecent, obscene thing ever written. Yes it is, Frieda. It is filthy. . . . This *Ulysses* muck is more disgusting than Casanova. I *must* show that it can be done without muck." When Harry Crosby tried to introduce Joyce to Lawrence in the spring of 1929, Joyce was unwilling to confront his preeminent English rival: he "didn't want to meet Lawrence—said his eye hurt him—he is very timid."[16]

The reviews of *Lady Chatterley's Lover* were predictably hostile. *John Bull*'s characteristic review employed chauvinistic rhetoric and stigmatized Lawrence with the Shakespearean tag that had been applied during the suppression of *The Rainbow:* it is "the most evil outpouring that has ever besmirched the literature of our country. The sewers of French pornography would be dragged in vain to find a parallel in beastliness. . . . Unfortunately for literature as for himself, Mr. Lawrence has a diseased mind." The *London Chronicle,* like other contemporary newspapers, opportunistically pretended moral outrage in order to crucify Lawrence, generate publicity and increase sales: "In *Lady Chatterley's Lover* he had delivered himself to us in our newspaper office; and in a newspaper office there is little mercy. . . . This was our chance to come out with a bang for an attack and a demand for banning."[17]

Huxley, foreseeing Lawrence's profound influence on contemporary culture, observed how his ideas had been (and would be) distorted by his disciples: "Lawrence's doctrine is constantly invoked by people, of whom Lawrence himself would passionately have disapproved, in defence of a behaviour, which he would have found deplorable or even revolting."[18]

IV

Lawrence's attack on Christianity in *The Man Who Died,* 1929 (which echoed the title of Edwin Arlington Robinson's *The Man Who Died Twice,* 1924), was specifically directed against St. Paul's emphasis on the division of body and spirit, and his belief that the flesh is the source of corruption: "For we know that the law is spiritual: but I am carnal, sold under sin" (Romans 7:14). The most powerful modern onslaught against Paul's deviation from the Gospels was Nietzsche's *The Antichrist* (1888), which condemned, with the passionate rhetoric that Lawrence would later adopt, the degeneration of God into a force that opposed human life:

> The Christian conception of God—God as god of the sick, God as a spider, God as spirit—is one of the most corrupt conceptions of the divine ever attained on earth. It may even represent the low-water mark in the descending development of divine types. God degenerated into the *contradiction* of life instead of being its transfiguration and eternal Yes!
>
> God as the declaration of war against life, against nature, against the will to live! God—the formula for every slander against "this world," for every lie about the "beyond"! God—the deification of nothingness, the will to nothingness pronounced holy!

Lawrence found the germ of his story in Gabriele D'Annunzio's *Le Vergini delle rocce* (1895)—which he read before December 1916—for that Nietzschean sensualist wrote: "Perhaps the Jew, had his enemies not killed him in the flower of his years, would have finally shaken off the weight of his sadness, and finding a new taste in the ripe fruits of his Galilee, would have shown to his band another happiness."[19] As early as March 1911 (after first reading Nietzsche in Croydon) Lawrence told Ada: "Don't meddle with religion: I would leave all that alone, if I were you, and try to occupy myself full in the present." In *The Rainbow,* Ursula expressed Lawrence's resentment of evangelical teaching. She felt "there was something unclean and degrading about this humble side of Christianity" and was overwhelmed by horror when urged to eat the dead body of "Jesus with holes in His hands and feet." In Lawrence's essay on Walt Whitman, written toward the end of the war, he echoed Nietzsche and announced the theme of his Christ story: "The Christians, phase by phase, set out actually to *annihilate* the sensual being in man."[20] And in his letters and his late essay "The Risen Lord," he discussed the relation of the resurrection in the flesh to the resurgence of nature in the spring:

> Church doctrine teaches the resurrection of the body; and if that doesn't mean the whole man, what does it mean? And if man is whole without a woman then I'm damned. . . .
>
> He rose to become at one with life, to live the great life of the flesh and the soul together, as peonies or foxes do, in their lesser way. If Jesus rose as a full man, in full flesh and soul, then He rose to take a woman to Himself, to live with her, and to know the tenderness and blossoming of the twoness with her.

Lawrence's description of the novella shifts from the slangy and blasphemous to the vital and responsive: "I wrote a story of the Resurrection, where Jesus gets up and feels very sick about everything, and can't stand the old crowd any more — so cuts out — and as he heals up, he begins to find what an astonishing place the phenomenal world is, far more marvellous than any salvation or heaven — and thanks his stars that he needn't have a 'mission' any more."[21]

The Man Who Died combines the "sun" and "tenderness" themes, which merge when the Man first becomes attracted to the priestess of Isis. And the novella, like "Sun" and *Lady Chatterley's Lover,* moves — through a reawakening of the senses — from a Christian to a pagan world and follows the cycle of the seasons through winter to triumphant spring.

The morbid stirring of the Man in the tomb was clearly connected to Lawrence's tuberculosis and gave personal poignancy to the theme of rebirth. As in the biblical account of the raising of Lazarus (John 11:44), there is no attempt to describe how it felt to be dead. The crowing of the cock, which awakens the Man and draws him to the peasant's house, alludes to Peter's denial — and, indirectly, to Judas' betrayal — of Christ in the Gospels (Matthew 26:34); and signifies the transformation, in Lawrence's tale, of cock into phoenix. The Man regrets his sacrificial mission and admits: "I brought betrayal on myself. And I know I wronged Judas. . . . But Judas and the high priests saved me from my own salvation. . . . If I had kissed Judas with live love, perhaps he would never have kissed me with death." Like Christ in Dostoyevsky's "The Grand Inquisitor," the crucified Man realizes: "if they discover me, they will do it all over again."[22]

The story progresses through a series of symbolic sensual temptations, which parallel Satan's temptation of Christ (Matthew 4:1–11), turn the Man away from his redemptive mission on earth and lead him to a regenerative sexual experience with the priestess of Isis. When he sees the cock pounce on his favorite hen, "the destiny of life seemed more fierce and compulsive to him even than the destiny of death." He twice denies Mary Madeleine and his mother; and does not respond to the peasant's wife, who desires him, "though he felt gently towards her soft, crouching, humble body." These experiences prepare him to respond to the priestess when she "was touched on the quick at the sight of a man, as if the tip of a fine flame of living had touched her."[23] Though the resurrection is complete, the Man must escape from the Romans who have come to arrest him. He slips away in the night, following the current along the coast; and abandons the priestess, pregnant like so many women at the end of Lawrence's fiction, to a hopeful but uncertain fate.

The Man Who Died is an exemplary fable in which Christ, a man of the flesh rather than the spirit, moves from death to life. "The Ship of Death," Lawrence's noble contribution to the *ars moriendi* and the literature of salvation, moves from life to death. As in the novella, the poem—Lawrence's last word on his own extinction—attempts to reconcile body and soul in an "act of self-mourning." The images of drowning in "the soundless, ungurgling flood" and "the cruel dawn of coming back to life" suggest the ravages of his disease and the imminence of death. The poem, like most of Lawrence's late works, combines pagan and Christian elements. It was inspired by the tomb in Cerveteri that suggested Egypt and was described in *Etruscan Places*: "Facing the door goes the stone bed on which was laid, presumably, the Lucumo [nobleman] and the sacred treasures of the dead, the little bronze ship of death that should bear him over to the other world."

The central metaphor portrays death as a journey from physical life to spiritual peace. The ship is a way of accepting death, not in the modern mode of fear and trembling, though there is no religious consolation, but with a calm and stoical resolution. The poem opens in the late autumn of 1929, as Lawrence expires and "death is on the air like a smell of ashes!" The falling apples are bruised (like his pain-racked body) as they strike the frost-hardened earth and "exit from themselves." He rejects the idea of suicide: violence will not provide the requisite release of a heart at peace. And he is psychologically prepared, as the flood rises, for the ship that carries the body on the journey "between the old self and the new."[24]

The turning point occurs when "the ark of faith" departs with its store of food and cooking pans. The process of dying is then completed; the body is gone and oblivion is reached. A thread leads out of the darkness and into the dawn, the flood subsides, the frail soul steps out of the ship and the heart is renewed. The unerring ship, Lawrence's consummate symbol of the resurrection, is both a *memento mori* and a means to achieve the peace of death.

V

While living in the Villa Mirenda in October 1926, a single imaginative impulse inspired Lawrence to begin *Lady Chatterley's Lover* and to start painting. In "Making Pictures" (1929) he recalled: "If Maria Huxley hadn't come rolling up to our house near Florence with four rather large canvases, one of which she had busted, and presented them to me because they had been abandoned in her house, I might never have started on a real picture in my life." Lawrence's paintings were a visual representation of the themes he simultaneously expressed in his writing: the resurrection of the flesh and triumph of pagan over Christian values. His painting *Lizard* is analogous to "Sun" just as *Resurrection* is to *The Man Who Died* and *Boccaccio Story* to *Lady Chatterley's Lover.*

Lawrence responded immediately to the empty canvases and found: "It's rather fun, discovering one can paint one's own ideas and one's own feelings—and a change from writing. . . . I like to paint rather wet, with oil, so the colour slips about and doesn't look like dried bone." It was also a complementary means of expression. When writing, he waited for the moment of inspiration and sometimes dashed off long novels in a matter of months. When painting, he made no preliminary studies or sketches. He believed the creation of a painting was similar to writing and "comes clean out of instinct, intuition and sheer physical action. . . . The picture itself comes in the first rush, or not at all. It is only when the picture has come into being that one can struggle and make it *grow* to completion. . . . [There must be] concentration of delight or exaltation of visual discovery."[25]

The most direct and powerful influences on Lawrence's paintings are not Cézanne and the Post-Impressionists, but the tomb paintings of the ancient Etruscans. Though Lawrence did not visit the Etruscan towns until April 1927, he had seen their art in the Villa Giulia in Rome and described the "sensitive-footed, subtly-smiling Etruscans" in his poem "Cypresses," written in Tuscany in 1920. Like the Etruscan painters of the dancing *Masker* and of the birds and fish in the fresco of *Four Men Fishing,* Lawrence loved dance and ritual, and delighted in natural creatures. Both Lawrence and the Etruscans emphasized the sexual organs of their highly stylized rust-colored figures. He praised "the subtlety of Etruscan painting . . . [which] lies in the wonderfully suggestive *edge* of the figures. It is not outlined. It is not what we call 'drawing.' It is the flowing contour where the body suddenly leaves off, upon the atmosphere."

Etruscan paintings like *Wrestlers,* which foreshadows Lawrence's *Renascence of Men,* and the lively *Red-Figured Stamnos* (Vase), whose brilliant color prefigures *Red Willow Trees,* portray the kind of dramatic action that Lawrence admired and re-created in his own art. The obliteration of many Etruscan paintings made the remnants seem even more precious: "Fragments of people at banquets, limbs that dance without dancers, birds that fly in nowhere, lions whose devouring heads are devoured away! Once it was all bright and dancing: the delight of the underworld; honouring the dead with wine, and flutes playing for a dance, and limbs whirling and pressing. And it was deep and sincere honour rendered to the dead and to the mysteries."[26] Like Lawrence's late works, the Etruscans' obsessive concern for the final fate of man made their art a constant meditation on the nature and end of death.

Lawrence believed painting must hit deep in the senses and, like Van Gogh's landscapes, make a violent assault on the emotions. He admired a picture that expressed passion, appealed to the sensual self, had "a meaning of its own, and concerted action." As Herbert Read observed, "Lawrence was an Expressionist, an extreme example of that type of artist who seeks a direct correspondence between feeling and representation, to the neglect of the more sophisticated values of proportion and harmony."[27]

The most striking aspect of Lawrence's paintings, and of *Lady Chatterley's Lover,* was the desire to provoke, to shock, to teach, to challenge the repressive attitude toward sex and to release the holiness of pagan life from the deadly stranglehold of Christianity. He announced his aesthetic credo to Earl Brewster: "I put a phallus, a lingam you call it, in each one of my pictures somewhere. And I paint no picture that won't shock people's castrated social spirituality. I do this out of positive belief, that the phallus is a great sacred image: it represents a deep, deep life which has been denied in us, and still is denied." Yet Lawrence recognized the powerful opposition and hostility to his art, and told Secker that his friends the Wilkinsons could not bear to see it: "I've painted a nice big picture that our vegetarian neighbours the Wilkinsons are afraid to look at, it's too 'suggestive.' Why do vegetarians always behave as if the world was vegetably propagated?"[28]

The exhibition of the twenty-five pictures that Lawrence painted between 1926 and 1928 opened at the Warren Gallery on Maddox Street in London on June 14, 1929, when he was living in Italy. Lawrence had first met Dorothy Warren, the niece of Philip Morrell, at Garsington in November 1915. She had been educated at Queen's College (Katherine Mansfield's old school), became an interior decorator and designer, and in 1928 married Philip Trotter, who ran the business side of the gallery. Dorothy was a tall, thin, rather grand upper-class eccentric. Her cousin described her as an attractive, amusing, kind bohemian type. Barbara Weekley had exhibited at her gallery. And the young Henry Moore, who had been strongly influenced by Lawrence, remembered her as "a woman of great flair, energy and courage." Moore had his first one-man show at the Warren Gallery in January 1928.[29]

Enid Hilton, who had hidden copies of *Lady Chatterley's Lover* in her long knickers and smuggled them into England, brought the paintings—rolled up and secreted in a suitcase—from Italy to London. The most potentially shocking painting, *Dandelions,* which showed a man pissing, was withheld from the exhibition. Lawrence put a very high price on the paintings. He had become fond of them as they hung in the Mirenda and did not really want to sell them. To coincide with the exhibition, *The Paintings of D. H. Lawrence* was privately printed for subscribers only by the Mandrake Press. P. R. Stephensen, Mandrake's founder, was then co-editing with Jack Lindsay the mildly pornographic *London Aphrodite,* which gave a dubious reputation to his firm and to Lawrence's book.

Lawrence's "Introduction to These Paintings" contained what Sir Kenneth Clark called "the best criticism ever written on Cézanne." Lawrence perceived Cézanne's revolutionary struggle, achievement and influence, and wrote: "Cézanne's apples are a real attempt to let the apple exist in its own separate entity, without transfusing it with personal emotion. Cézanne's great effort was, as it were, to shove the apple away from him, and let it live of itself. It seems a small thing to do: yet it is the first real sign that man has made for several thousands of years that he is willing to admit that matter *actually* exists."

The reviews of the exhibition, like those of the novel, were extremely negative, and Lawrence was persecuted for his paintings—which seemed to illustrate the novel—as he had been for his political and sexual ideas. Critics wrote of the "repellent and distorted nudes" that "compel most spectators to recoil in horror." The bad notices and the fact that Lawrence had again become notorious, after the confiscation in England of privately printed copies of *Lady Chatterley's Lover,* attracted thirteen thousand spectators to the paintings. But the combination of blasphemy and indecency was too provocative. On July 5 the gallery was raided by the police, who politely waited to carry out their orders until the Aga Khan had finished viewing the pictures.

"You have heard of the catastrophe of course," Lawrence wrote to Maria Huxley, "13 pictures seized and in gaol—yours among them—and threatened to be burnt—*auto-da-fe.*"[30] *Boccaccio Story* and *Fight with an Amazon* precipitated the crisis, and every painting with pubic hair was instantly seized. The fact that a copy of Blake's *Pencil Drawings* was impounded on the same charge did not soften the blow.

Hitherto unknown documents in the Public Record Office reveal that the official raid on the gallery—like the suppression of *The Rainbow* in 1915—was prompted first by a private complaint and then by self-serving attacks by the London press. The complaint was made on June 27, 1929, in a letter to the superintendent of the Bow Street police station by the publisher Grant Richards. A personal friend of Martin Secker, Richards was the publisher of A. E. Housman's *The Shropshire Lad* and founder of the World's Classics. In the prewar years he had put Joyce through agonies about the publication of *Dubliners* and had rejected *A Portrait of the Artist.* In 1922 he had offered to buy English rights of Magnus' *Memoirs of the Foreign Legion.*

With Victorian self-righteousness, Richards directed the attention of the police to Lawrence's paintings and book (neither of which he had seen), and casuistically implicated the government in the exhibition:

> Not as a joke but with a due sense of responsibility, I suggest that you should pay a visit to the Warren Gallery, 39A Maddox Street, and examine the pictures by D. H. Lawrence there exhibited. And it may perhaps also be worth while, in the circumstances, looking at the books there that appear to be on sale. One large one, which I did not myself examine, would hardly, I think, bear investigation.
>
> The fact that the catalogue has, properly cancelled, the Excise Revenue twopenny stamp may give ignorant people the impression

that Mr. Lawrence's paintings have already received the approval
of the Government.

On June 30 Detective Inspector Gordon Hester, who had received
Richards' letter, wrote to the superintendent of police about the need to
act on the complaint. Three days later the police commissioner took
Lawrence's file to the Home Office and urged Sir John Anderson, the
permanent under-secretary, to take action. But Sir John stressed that
the government did not wish to interfere. That same day, July 3, the
Evening Standard forced the issue by condemning the paintings, reporting that complaints had been made and quoting a condemnatory review
by Paul Konody in the *Observer* of June 16, 1929:

> Repeated protests have been made that many of the pictures were
> not suitable for public display. It is understood that representa-
> tions have now been made to the Home Office, and that the matter is
> being officially considered. Complaint is made of 15 out of the 25
> pictures exhibited. Among recent comments on the exhibition was
> that of a well-known art critic who wrote: "This author-artist,
> weary perhaps of the easier task of being subtly misbehaved in
> print, has elected to come straight to the point, and is frankly
> disgusting in paint."

The following day Sir Ernley Blackwell, a senior legal official in the
Home Office, rang up the police commissioner to say that in view of the
article in the *Evening Standard,* action would have to be taken.

On July 9 Detective Inspector Hester reported to the superintendent
of police his conversation with Philip Trotter during the raid of July 5:

> I said, "Do you accept responsibility for this exhibition and its
> conduct?" Mr. Trotter replied, "My wife and I are responsible. It is
> our exhibition; we are the occupiers of the premises and reside on
> the top floor." I then said, "I am directed by the Commissioner of
> Police to inform you that unless this exhibition is closed forthwith
> proceedings will be taken against you." Mr. Trotter said, "On what
> grounds?" I said, "On the grounds that a number of the pictures
> exhibited are of an obscene nature."[31]

The warrant to seize the paintings was issued under the antiquated
Obscene Publications Act of 1857, which had previously condemned *The*

Rainbow, and the prosecutor was the same Herbert Muskett who had appeared for the police during the suppression of the novel. Repeating the familiar ritual, he now charged that Lawrence's paintings were "gross, coarse, hideous, unlovely, and obscene." At the trial, the eighty-two-year-old magistrate, Frederick Meade, said: "I would destroy these pictures, as I would destroy wild beasts."[32]

Dorothy Warren had wanted to fight the case, and eminent artists like Augustus John, Sir William Orpen and Glyn Philpot were willing to testify that Lawrence's paintings had artistic value. But Lawrence, who had witnessed the destruction of a thousand copies of *The Rainbow* in 1915 and was under attack for *Lady Chatterley's Lover,* was weary of the martyr's role. He was now an older, a wiser—and a dying—man. He feared another disaster, wanted above all to rescue his paintings and urged Warren to accept the authorities' offer to give back the pictures in return for a promise that they would never again be exhibited in England:

> I think it's a mistake to want to go to High Court. What to do? prove that the pictures are not obscene? but they are not, so how prove it? And if they go against you there, then more is lost than will be got back in years. No, no, I want you to accept the compromise. I do not want my pictures to be burned, under any circumstances or for any cause. The law, of course, must be altered—it is blatantly obvious. Why burn my pictures to prove it? There is something sacred to me about my pictures, and I will not have them burnt.

On August 10, two days after the court hearing at Great Marlborough Street, Lawrence told Orioli that the volumes of reproductions that accompanied the exhibition were going to be destroyed: "I had telegrams to say: Pictures to be returned, books to be burned. Let them burn their own balls, the fools. This has given me a great sickness of England. . . . It leaves me feeling depressed and nauseated—so many insults, such silly extravagance of insults, and a meek or gloating public." Lawrence expressed his outrage in three poems—"13,000 People," "Innocent England" and "Give Me a Sponge"—which were published in his satiric *Nettles,* just after his death in 1930:

> But it can't be so, for they behaved
> like lunatics looking, they bubbled and raved

or gloated or peeped at the simple spot
where the fig-leaf might have been, but was not. . . .

Virginal, pure policemen came
and hid their faces for very shame,

while they carried the shameless things away
to gaol, to be hid from the light of day. . . .

Ah, my nice pictures, they are fouled, they are dirtied,
not by time, but by unclean breath and eyes
of all the sordid people that have stared at them uncleanly
looking dirt on them, and breathing on them lies.

The solicitors for the Warren Gallery had a long correspondence with
Wontner & Sons, acting for the police commissioner, about damage done
to *Boccaccio Story*. But the police, who maintained that "this particular
picture was one of the most obscene," denied all responsibility for the
damage.[33]

Lawrence's paintings are interesting both in themselves and as the
work of a literary genius. The aim of all his art was to change people's
way of thinking and feeling, and to make the "dirty" seem holy. But his
long residence abroad had put him out of touch with the morality of
contemporary England; and after the hostile response to his Florentine
novel, it was naive to imagine that his provocative paintings would be
well received. Lawrence, determined to shock the English public with
pubic hair and genitalia, was surprised when the disaster took place. As
Frieda wrote, with passionate indignation:

When I think that nobody wanted Lawrence's amazing genius, how
he was jeered at, suppressed, turned into nothing, patronized at
best, the stupidity of our civilization comes home to me. How
necessary he was! How badly needed! . . . Critics indeed! Had they
been able to *take* instead of criticizing, how much richer their own
lives might have been![34]

Bandol and Vence,
1929–1930

I

DURING THE LAST fifteen months of his life Lawrence maintained his desperate and often frantic search for a climate that would restore his failing lungs. But in France, Spain, Italy and Germany, his health continued to deteriorate. He spent the winters of 1928 and 1929 in Bandol, a charming fishing village on the French coast, between Toulon and Marseilles, living first at the Hôtel Beau Rivage and then at the Villa Beau Soleil. Despite his weakness, he still had sufficient energy in 1929 to seek distractions and to travel to Paris (to visit Harry Crosby and the Huxleys) in March, to Majorca in April-June, to Forte dei Marmi, Florence and Baden-Baden in July, and to Rottach, Bavaria, in August-September, before returning for his second sojourn in Bandol. But neither the north nor the south seemed to suit him. In 1929 he told Frieda that he hated Italy like poison and was sure it would kill him; he told Else that he thought Germany would also kill him if he lived there for long.

Lady Chatterley's Lover was not protected by copyright, and pirated editions, capitalizing on its notoriety, drained away his royalties. The police raid on his paintings in July 1929 also caused severe emotional strain, weakened Lawrence and undoubtedly contributed to his death. But he continued to write until the very end, producing two-thousand-word articles at £25 each for London newspapers (collected in *Assorted Articles*) as well as *Pornography and Obscenity, Apocalypse,* the satiric verse in *Pansies* and *Nettles,* and his two greatest poems: "Bavarian Gentians" and "The Ship of Death."

After his illness in Port-Cros and a rough crossing to the French mainland in November 1928, Lawrence could not travel very far. So he settled in Bandol, where Katherine and Murry had been so happy before joining the Lawrences in Cornwall in the spring of 1916, and at the Hôtel Beau Rivage, where in February 1918 Katherine had had her first hemorrhage. A tiny port with carefree people, Bandol had mild Mediterranean weather and was very quiet. It seemed more cheerful, less oppressive, than Fascist Italy. Lawrence had a number of visitors that winter: Rhys Davies, a Welsh writer; Barbara Weekley; Brewster Ghiselin, a young American poet; the Huxleys; and his sister Ada. As usual, Lawrence kept up a brave front, tried to disguise the gravity of his disease and felt a certain morbid comfort from the association with Katherine. As he told Murry, who was concerned about Lawrence's health: "I'm pretty well, but a scratchy chest and cough as ever—sickening—but pretty well in spite of it all. I believe Katherine once stayed here, so perhaps you know the place."

In April 1929, stimulated by his usual wanderlust, a desire to visit Spain and Frieda's pining for more islands (they had already been to Capri, Sicily, Sardinia, Ceylon, Tahiti, Rarotonga and Port-Cros), the Lawrences traveled from Bandol to Paris and then to Palma de Majorca, off the coast of Barcelona. He found it quite pleasant and Mediterranean, not terribly exciting but comfortably restful. "This island—Majorca—is rather like Sicily," he told Pino Orioli, "but not as beautiful, and much more asleep. But it has that southern sea quality, out of the world, in another world. I like that—and the sleep is good for me." An attack of malaria, which made his teeth chatter, prevented him from making long-term plans and renting a house on the island or from traveling to Madrid and the cities of southern Spain.

Mark Gertler, writing to Kot in April 1929, alluded to Lawrence's brief trip to the Huxleys at Suresnes, a suburb west of Paris, in mid-March and remembered Lawrence's concern when Gertler had been in a tuberculosis sanatorium. He was disheartened not only by the gravity of Lawrence's disease but also by his fatalistic attitude and his unwillingness (abetted by Frieda) to accept medical treatment: "The news of Lawrence is very depressing. He seems to be ill in mind and body. The picture [the Huxleys] gave us was gruesome and preyed on my mind all night. While Frieda was away they managed to get him to see a doctor, who pronounced his lungs to be in a bad state and his general condition serious, but he would not believe it and won't allow himself to be X-rayed."[1]

Lawrence's strife with Frieda inevitably diminished and turned into relative calm after the hemorrhage of July 1927 had weakened him and the affair with Ravagli had provided her with a gratifying distraction. Despite the strain of their quarrels and her infidelity, all their friends agreed that as his illness increased he became even more dependent on Frieda, whose courage matched his own, that she strengthened him and satisfied his deepest emotional needs. The spiky Richard Aldington admired Lawrence's writing but contrasted his character to Frieda's: "They were made for each other. Only a woman such as Frieda, with her health, strength, good looks, vitality and self-confidence could have endured life with a 'genius' which included so much exasperation, frayed nerves, cocksure assertiveness, profound self-mistrust, and downright perversity." Huxley defined their intense bond in physiological terms and emphasized Frieda's uncanny power to revitalize the dying man: "Lawrence was, in some strange way dependent on her presence, physically dependent, as one is dependent on the liver in one's belly, or one's spinal marrow. I have seen him on two occasions rise from what I thought was his death bed, when Frieda, who had been away, came back after a short absence. The mysteries of human relationships are impenetrably obscure."[2]

On August 20, 1923, two days after their serious quarrel in New York had sent Frieda back to England (and to Murry) without him, Lawrence gave a rare newspaper interview. Contrasting his volatile personality to Frieda's passive indolence, he emphasized the salutary and stabilizing restraint of women: "If men were left to themselves, they would rush off . . . into destruction. But women keep life back at its own center. They pull the men back. Women have enormous passive strength, the strength of inertia."[3]

II

In early July, while Frieda was at the Warren Gallery exhibition in London, Lawrence visited the Huxleys at Forte dei Marmi, on the

Italian coast. He then returned to Florence, repeated the terrible experience of July 1927 and, in Orioli's flat, had his fifth hemorrhage.
Terrified at seeing Lawrence's head and arms hanging over the side of
his bed, as if he were dead, Orioli called the doctor and telegraphed for
Frieda. When he asked Lawrence: "What will Frieda say when she
arrives?" Lawrence answered: "Do you see those peaches in the bowl? She
will say, 'What lovely peaches,' and she will devour them." And she did.

In a long letter of July 13 to his brother, Julian, Huxley described Dr.
Giglioli's diagnosis and Lawrence's deterioration; his futile wanderings,
sickly state and unusual listlessness as well as Frieda's acquiescence in
Lawrence's fatal self-delusion:

> The Dr. told M[aria] that, from just sounding him he could hear
> that one lung was practically gone and the other affected. He
> doubted whether very much cd be done.... He doesn't *want* to
> know how ill he is.... He just wanders about, very tired and at
> bottom wretched, from one place to another, imagining that the
> next place will make him feel better and, when he gets to the next
> place, regretting the one before and looking back on it as a para-
> dise. But of course no place will make him feel any better than any
> other now that he's as ill as he is. He's a great deal worse than he was
> when you saw him at Diablerets [early 1928]—coughs more,
> breathes very quickly and shallowly, has no energy. (It's pathetic to
> see the way he just sits and does nothing. He hasn't written a
> line or painted a stroke in the last 3 months. Just lack of vital
> strength.) ...
> Frieda is worse than he is. We've told her that she's a fool and a
> criminal; but it has no more effect than telling an elephant. So it's
> hopeless. Short of handcuffing him and taking him to a sanatorium
> by force, there's nothing to be done.

Lawrence believed in intuition and insisted that scientific truth was
an illusion. Though he wanted to live, he realized he was dying, knew
that he could not be helped by doctors and courageously accepted his
fate. Frieda shared his belief that the depressing routine of a clinic
would stifle his creative powers. She felt that her own marvelous energy
could resurrect and cure—or at least strengthen and revive—the man
who had nearly died. Aware of her therapeutic effect, Frieda told Kot:
"Christ rose only once but Lawrence has done the trick many times."[4]

After recovering from his hemorrhage in Florence, Lawrence traveled first to Baden-Baden, where a doctor tried to comfort him and

seemed "content with his lung." He then spent a month in Rottach, south of Munich in the Bavarian Alps, at the edge of the Tergensee and near the farmhouse of the German doctor-writer Max Mohr, who had examined him in September 1927.[5] After Lawrence, who felt a wreck, had been in bed for a week, other doctors put him on a quack cure of phosphorus and arsenic. Not surprisingly, considering the toxic effects of arsenic, he became much worse, felt he was being poisoned and, in late September, managed to crawl back to Bandol.

During their second season on the French coast, the Lawrences rented the rather gaudy Villa Beau Soleil, which had originally been built as the setting for an illicit love affair. It was considerably more comfortable if less attractive than their previous dwellings: "The house is just an ugly six-room bungalow, but it has [a sunken marble] bath and water and central heating, a big terrace, a wilderness garden, and stands in a rather lovely position on the sea, so let's hope the gods will be good to us and I shall get strong and Frieda will be happy having a new place to play with."

In the fall of 1929—in bed with linseed poultices (similar to the hot sandbags that had comforted him in Oaxaca)—Lawrence continued to emphasize his bronchials and asthma, instead of his lungs. But he admitted that his bronchials were beginning to affect his heart, that his condition was serious and that he would be forced to enter a sanatorium if he did not improve. On October 29, echoing Katherine's agonizing letter to Ottoline of July 1918, he described his disease as a devil that was alien and inimical to his body: "There is this beastly torturing chest superimposed on me, and it's as if there was a demon lived there, triumphing, and extraneous to me."[6]

The Brewsters rented a house in Bandol to be close to Lawrence. Earl massaged him with coconut oil; and they accompanied him on car trips to the surrounding villages, helped him correct proofs and shared the Christmas hamper brought from England by Harwood. In November 1929 the painter and writer Frederick Carter, with whom Lawrence had corresponded about the Book of Revelation and visited in Shropshire in January 1924, came to Bandol. Carter, disgusted by Lawrence's invalid habits, gave a vivid description of his physical state: "Most difficult of all to pass over without alarm and even horror was his incessant spitting, that in itself gave an atmosphere of fear and threat. He didn't cough loudly, but simply and carefully spat into an envelope. . . . These he had about everywhere from his ample correspondence, and they were kept to expectorate into."

Two months later Barbara Weekley arrived. Lawrence confided to her that his illness sometimes made him feel suicidal: "The nights are so awful," he told her. "At two in the morning, if I had a pistol I would shoot myself." He thought that Frieda no longer had the power to revive him, and felt acutely isolated. Sometimes he walked feebly outside and lay on a chaise longue. Covered with rugs, and lying in the garden with a grey, drawn expression on his face, he said: "Your mother is repelled by the death in me."[7]

In late January 1930 Andrew Morland—Gertler's physician, future head of the Department of Chest Diseases at University College Hospital in London and last in the long series of Lawrence's doctors[8]—was sent by Kot and Gertler to examine Lawrence in Bandol. Morland made his grim diagnosis and warned that if Lawrence did not enter a sanatorium, he would be dead in three months:

> Lawrence had obviously been suffering from pulmonary tuberculosis for a very long time—probably 10 or 15 years. . . .
>
> There was very extensive scarring but only one tiny cavity. . . .
>
> Both lungs appear to be affected with moderate severity but it is his general condition which is causing the greatest amount of anxiety; his appetite is poor and he does not seem to be responding to treatment. . . .
>
> His resistance to the disease must have been remarkable to have enabled him to survive so long while doing all the wrong things. . . .
>
> I am afraid a really long period of strict-rest is the only possible treatment now and it will not be easy to get him to submit to it.[9]

Lawrence had wasted away to ninety-seven pounds and was still losing weight. Morland insisted that he go into the Ad Astra sanatorium in Vence, a lovely old town in the Maritime Alps, a few miles above Cannes. Lawrence moved to Ad Astra, which did not have a strict regime and resembled a private hotel with nursing facilities, on February 6. He adjusted reasonably well to the new conditions and felt less "looked after" than in the Beau Soleil. But he soon felt worse and thought the place did not suit him. He lost more weight, lost faith in the doctors and the treatment, and believed that he would be better off in Bandol.

The moving letters that Lawrence wrote during the last months of his life describe his brave but hopeless fight against tuberculosis. Always reluctant to face the reality of his illness, he had, at first, blamed the harsh climate and decaying atmosphere: "This winter makes me know I shall just die if I linger on like this in Europe any more; and what's the good of my dying! And anyhow it's so wearying and painful, being ill. . . . I do want to do something about my health, for I feel my life leaving me, and I believe it's this old moribund Europe just killing me." In February 1930, when he weighed only ninety pounds, he emphasized the disease of the bronchials, belly and liver, and still refused to recognize the immediate danger of death: "The lung has moved very little since Mexico, in five years. But the broncs are awful, and they have inflamed my lower man, the *ventre* and the liver. I suppose that's why I've gone so thin—I daren't tell my weight—but I've lost a lot this winter, can't understand why. . . . The lung trouble is slight, but the bronchial-asthma condition very bad, it uses up my strength—and I've lost my appetite. . . . I'm not in any sudden danger—but in slow danger. . . . Time is the best healer, when it isn't a killer." After two weeks in Ad Astra, he finally admitted his terrible suffering: "I am rather worse here—such bad nights, and cough, and heart, and pain decidedly worse here—and miserable. Seems to me like *grippe,* but they say not. It's not a good place—shan't stay long—I'm better in a house—I'm miserable." Lawrence's coughing provided no physical relief; it was just a feeble, dreadful welling up of the juices of organic dissolution. After his death, Dr. Morland realized the futility of the treatment, regretted his decision and told Kot: "I wish now that I had never urged him to go to Vence as I am afraid my efforts only made his last weeks more unhappy."[10]

Lawrence's final week was astonishingly eventful. On February 24 H. G. Wells, whom Lawrence had met through Ford in 1909, paid a visit. The Huxleys came from Cannes to help look after Lawrence on the twenty-fifth and twenty-eighth. On about the twenty-sixth the American sculptor Jo Davidson made a clay head that captured Lawrence's sharp beard, sunken cheeks, deep-set eyes and Christ-like expression of pain and suffering. On the twenty-seventh, the Aga Khan, who had admired Lawrence's paintings at the Warren Gallery, came to pay homage to the artist. And Lawrence continued to work on his review of Eric Gill's *Art Nonsense and Other Essays* until a few days before his death.

III

On the first of March—which Aubrey Beardsley had called "a fiendish month and must settle scores of people"—Lawrence moved from Ad

Astra to a private house, the Villa Robermond, in Vence. He had told
Gertie Cooper: "While we live, we must be game. And when we come to
die, we'll die game too"—and he kept his word. He never entirely gave up
hope that he would recover and told Frieda: " 'Come when the sun rises,'
and when I came he was glad, so very glad, as if he would say: 'See,
another day is given me.'" Like his namesake King David, who took the
young Abishag to warm him in his deathbed (I Kings 1:2), one night
near the end Lawrence asked Frieda to sleep with him: "All night I was
aware of his aching inflexible chest, and all night he must have been so
sadly aware of my healthy body beside him . . . always before, when I
slept by the side of him, I could comfort and ease him . . . now no more. . . .
He was falling away from life and me, and with all my strength I was
helpless."[11]

Lawrence began to have hallucinations of detachment from his own
body—or premonitions of death—and exclaimed: "I see my body over
there on the table!" On his final visit, Huxley told his brother, Julian,
with clinical sympathy:

> [We] found him very weak and suffering much pain and strangely
> *égaré* [bewildered], feeling he wasn't there—that he was two peo-
> ple at once. We got the doctor up at nine, who stuck some morphia
> into him, and he settled off to sleep. . . . The heart had begun to go
> and the intestines were badly affected—general intoxication, I
> suppose—and he seemed to have hardly any lungs left to breathe
> with. It had been most distressing, the two or three times we saw
> him during the past week—he was such a miserable wreck of
> himself and suffering so much pain.

Moreover, the illness has reduced him to an appalling state of emaciation. The poet Robert Nichols, who was also with Lawrence at the end,
said: "Lawrence went very quickly. He refused oxygen saying it made
him worse. I fear he suffered frightfully. Just before they gave him
morphia ('I think I'll have a little morphia now!'—he had refused it for a
long while) he ordered Frieda's bed to be moved across the foot of his
own."[12]

Lawrence begged Frieda: "Hold me, hold me, I don't know where I
am, I don't know where my hands are . . . where am I?" His last words
were: "I am better now"—and in a sense, he was. As he lay dying, Frieda
held his ankles in her hands. She believed his last, unfinished poem,
"Prayer," "refers to this, as if he had *known* beforehand":

O let my ankles be bathed in the moonlight, that I may go
Sure and moon-shod, cool and bright-footed
towards my goal.[13]

At 10:15 p.m. on March 2, 1930, Lawrence died of pulmonary tuberculosis, at the age of forty-four.

Though they had worried about his health for years, his death came as
a terrible shock to Lawrence's sisters. Similarly, Harwood Brewster, who
had seen Lawrence for the last time in December 1929, thought he
seemed thin, pale, sickly and weak. But he had been that way for a long
time, and neither Harwood nor Earl, who had left for India a week
before Lawrence's death, believed he was in serious danger.

On March 4, the day of the funeral, as Barbara Weekley opened the
door to take flowers into Lawrence's room, Robert Nichols got a glimpse
of the corpse. He "saw Lawrence's nose 'sharp as a pen' and his little
Greek satyr's beard sticking up (his feet covered by a sheet were towards
me)."[14] At four in the afternoon a rickety old hearse drawn by a single
horse set out for the cemetery in Vence, accompanied by a group of
ancient gravediggers dressed in dark clothes. No friends were able to
come from England, and only ten people followed the hearse to the
grave: Frieda and Barbara, Aldous and Maria Huxley, Achsah Brewster and Robert Nichols, Ida Rauh (a beautiful actress whom Lawrence
had known in Taos), the di Chiaras (an American wife and Italian
husband from the days in Capri) and Thys (the Paris publisher of *Lady
Chatterley's Lover*). No words were spoken, no service read. Achsah
thought it odd that Frieda wore a red dress.

Just after the funeral, Frieda described, in letters to Mabel and to
Forster, Lawrence's unflinching attitude toward death and legacy of
love:

The courage, the courage with which he fought. I am so full of admiration that I can hardly feel much else. . . .

Lawrence died so splendidly—Inch by inch he fought and life
with him never lost its glamour, not right to the end, when he asked
for morphine and died without pain or struggle—He looked uncon-
quered and fulfilled when he was dead, all the suffering smoothed
out—If England ever produced a perfect rose, he was it, thorns and
perfume and splendour—He has left me his love without a grudge,
we had our grudges out; and from that other side, that I did not know
before his death, he gives me his strength and his love for life.[15]

Epilogue

THE ENGLISH obituaries of Lawrence were generally hostile. They emphasized his perversity and the scandal attached to his works, and portrayed him, as Catherine Carswell complained, as a "morose, frustrated, tortured, even sinister failure." E. M. Forster opposed the prevailing attitude and defended his friend and adversary against his detractors. Despite their personal quarrel, which precluded further meetings, Forster and Lawrence had retained respect for each other's work. Writing from Egypt (where he was working for the Red Cross) in 1917, Forster had distinguished the artist from the man and defined the major weakness in Lawrence's writing: "I am a great admirer of D. H. Lawrence, especially of his early work, before he became so didactic and theoretical. I know him a bit—most alarming and explosive but I like him." Seven years later, when *A Passage to India* appeared, Lawrence praised the novel and called Forster the best of his English contemporaries. In his generous obituary of Lawrence in the *Listener*, Forster recalled their meetings, remembered the best aspects of Lawrence's character and mentioned his plans for Rananim, formulated during the Great War: "In the spring of 1915 I met him three or four times. I did not know him well, or meet him again subsequently, but he leaves a vivid impression—so quick with his fingers and alive in his spirit, so radiant and sensitive, so sure that if we all set out at once for one of the South Sea islands we should found a perfect community there which would regenerate the world." Forster synthesized his view of Lawrence by boldly asserting: "he was the greatest imaginative novelist of our generation."[1]

Shortly after Lawrence's death, Frieda's life became desperately complicated by emotional, medical and legal problems. She had another affair with Murry and resumed relations with Angelo Ravagli. Barbara contracted tuberculosis and had a nervous breakdown. Frieda's mother died. And Frieda became involved in a dispute with Lawrence's brother and sisters about his lost will.

Murry's biographer reports, without a trace of irony, that in March 1930 Murry "sped to the South of France to pay his last respects to Lawrence." In fact, Murry gratified his morbid compulsion to sleep with Frieda after Lawrence's death in 1930 as he had after Katherine's death in 1923. The guilt-ridden *Reminiscences of D. H. Lawrence* (1933), which Murry began to write and publish in the spring of 1930, expressed the remorse he inevitably experienced when he returned to his second wife, Violet Le Maistre, who was dying of tuberculosis. Murry's intensely personal attack on Lawrence's character and ideas in *Son of Woman* (1931) not only attempted to exorcise Lawrence and justify himself, but also reflected his attraction and hostility to Frieda, who had rejected him (as Lawrence had done) and chosen to live with Ravagli.

Huxley, who knew the full story of Frieda's affair with Murry, was disgusted by *Son of Woman* and condemned both the book and the author. As he told a friend: "Murry's vindictive hagiography was pretty slimy—the slug's-eye view of poor L: and if you knew the intimate history of his relations with L and Mrs. L, you'd really shudder. One day it really ought to be published. Some of the details are quite fantastically ghoulish and foul." In his surprisingly mild review of Murry's book, Wyndham Lewis, who had met Lawrence in 1914 and criticized him in *Paleface,* found Murry's attack distasteful, praised Lawrence's character and perceptively attributed the defects of his work to his disease: "I have no inclination myself *to judge* so near to the death of Mr. Lawrence, at a time when many people must be mourning sincerely the vanishing of such a gifted and, it would seem, attractive man. Again, the terrible disease that at last accounted for him, and which hunted him through life . . . was responsible (so it seems to me) for a good deal that was most hysterical and feeble in his work."[2]

In mid-March, Barbara contracted tuberculosis of the bone and had to have her back put in plaster. In July she had a mental breakdown, ran past the room in the Villa Robermond where Lawrence had died and cried in a terrible voice: "There's nothing, nothing, nothing anymore. . . . My poor mother, her child is dead." Barbara had spent her childhood listening to the Weekleys revile Frieda's character. Now, in her fits of delirium, she screamed out her suppressed resentment and violent hatred of her mother. Frieda, desperate and convinced of the restorative power of sex, persuaded Barbara to spend several nights with a young Italian peasant called Nicola. When Barbara's doctor discovered this, he stopped the sexual therapy. Frieda's sisters and Ottoline Morrell were as horrified as Lawrence would have been by Frieda's bizarre experiment. Barbara's former son-in-law, Alfred Alvarez, believes that her breakdown was partly caused by Frieda's immediate "betrayal" of Lawrence with Murry and then with Ravagli, which reminded her of Frieda's betrayal of Ernest Weekley when Barbara was a child.[3]

Lawrence died just as his books were beginning to earn money. His works continued to appear after his death and to increase the value of his literary estate.[4] Though he did not leave a will, in September 1929 he told his sister Emily that after his death his manuscripts and paintings would have to be sold to provide an income for Frieda. He had earned more than £1,000 on *Lady Chatterley's Lover* and £500 on *Pansies,* and left an estate of £4,000.[5] The bitterness behind Frieda's dispute with Lawrence's family, who felt they had first claim on his estate, went back to their disapproval of her elopement with Lawrence in May 1912, to her fierce quarrel with Ada in Spotorno in February 1926 and to the family's belief that his "pornographic" works had been inspired by Frieda.

Since Lawrence had died intestate, Huxley urged Frieda not to go to court and criticized her behavior in a letter to a friend: "The stupid woman is embarking on enormously expensive legal proceedings. . . . Her diplomatic methods consist in calling everyone a liar, a swine and a lousy swindler, and then in the next letter being charming—then she's surprised that people don't succumb to the charm. Since L is no longer there to keep her in order, she plunges about in the most hopeless way. I like her very much; but she's in many ways quite impossible."

The hearing about Lawrence's will took place in London on November 3, 1932, with the decisive evidence provided by Murry. He testified that at Cholesbury, Buckinghamshire, on November 9, 1914, he and Lawrence had made and witnessed each other's wills, and had left everything to their wives. Though Lawrence's will had been lost, Murry convinced the court by producing his own nearly identical document. It is quite possible that Murry, who had recently been Frieda's lover and knew that Lawrence had intended to leave everything to her, lied in court about the existence of the will. Witter Bynner amusingly exaggerated the events in court and reported that when Frieda's lawyer described her intensely harmonious marriage, she impulsively cried out: "Oh, but no! That's not true! We fought like hell!"[6] The judge pronounced in favor of the will. Ada, irritated by Frieda's "blackening" remarks about the Lawrence family, was bitterly angry when she lost the case. Frieda acted generously by giving £500 each to George, Emily and Ada.

In 1931, when Frieda was fifty-two, she told a friend: "[Angelo] is so human and nice with me and *real,* no high falute, but such a genuine warmth for me—I shall be allright. . . . We have been fond of each other for years and that an old bird like me is still capable of real passion and can inspire it too, seems a miracle." The victory in court allowed Frieda to buy Ravagli out of the Italian army and make a financial settlement with his wife in 1933. In an ironic parallel to her own behavior with Weekley in 1912, Ravagli left his wife and three children. He was an officer like her father and, like Lawrence, came from a lower-class background. Angelo and Frieda moved to the ranch in 1933, married in 1950 and remained together until her death in 1956. In Taos, Ravagli occupied himself with farming and building, amateur painting and ceramics, and took care of the business connected with Lawrence's estate. Though Frieda sometimes regretted Ravagli's intellectual limitations, she was undoubtedly happy with him.

Frieda's friends in Taos were shocked at first by the strange personality who had replaced Lawrence in her life. He seemed rather crude, though warm and helpful. Rachel Hawk said that Ravagli was strong, energetic and capable; more thoughtful and much kinder to Frieda than Lawrence ever was. Barbara disliked Ravagli and thought he had married Frieda for money. But Huxley, while visiting Frieda in 1937, told his brother: "The Capitano turns out to be a very decent sort of [by now] middle-class Italian—rather naif, at the same time intelligent and active. As far as one can judge he doesn't exploit Frieda: on the contrary, manages her affairs very efficiently."[7]

The western writer Frank Waters, a Taos friend, mentioned that Ravagli, much younger than Frieda and a great womanizer, was as unfaithful to her as she had been to Lawrence:

Angie was all Italian. Emotional, sensual, practical. An excellent workman, builder and potter. I don't believe he ever read a book. He took good care of Frieda up at the ranch but was delighted to leave its isolation and move down to Taos where there was more company. Everybody liked him, but thought little of him. For Frieda, getting old, liked to stay home or visit old friends. Angie was a woman chaser, picking up every new promising woman arrival, taking them to dance and to bed. Frieda knew this but it did not seem to worry her.

Brett, who lived near her old friend in Taos, remarked that Frieda "became a much nicer woman when married to Angie. Her frustration of *not* being the magnet . . . was appeased when *she* became the magnet." Waters believed that Frieda was completely dedicated to, though objective about, Lawrence and did everything possible to increase his posthumous fame.

The painter Georgia O'Keeffe, who met Frieda in 1934, provided a vivid picture of her surprising appearance and character: "Georgia was astonished to discover that Frieda was a chunky, gold-toothed, gutturalvoiced woman who looked more like a German hausfrau than the mate of the mythic Lawrence. 'I can remember clearly the first time I ever saw her, standing in a doorway, with her hair all frizzed out, wearing a cheap red calico dress that looked as though she had just wiped out the frying pan with it. She was not thin, not young, but there was something radiant and wonderful about her.'"[8] After Frieda's death, Ravagli sold their Los Pinos ranch in Taos as well as Lawrence's manuscripts and paintings. He then returned to the Villa Bernarda in Spotorno, to the patient wife who had waited twenty-five years for his return, and lived there until his death in 1976.

Lawrence, so restless during his lifetime, continued to move around after his death. Eventually he returned to his beloved New Mexico. In 1935 Frieda sent Ravagli to Europe to arrange to have Lawrence's body disinterred from the cemetery in Vence and cremated in Marseilles. With great difficulty, he got the urn past the customs officials and into America. The ashes of the phoenix were lost and recovered at the railroad station in Lamy, lost and recovered at Tinka Fechin's studio in Taos, and then nearly stolen by Mabel before her sinister plot was discovered. Finally, Lawrence was cemented into place and enshrined in the gaudy chapel that Ravagli had devotedly built for him on the ranch.

If Lawrence had recovered from his illness, lived for another thirty years and completed a normal term of life, he would have continued the phase of calm with Frieda and enjoyed the relative wealth he had earned from *Lady Chatterley's Lover*. He might have realized with younger disciples his vision of Rananim, returned to the ranch, achieved his dream of chartering a boat and sailing around the Mediterranean to places he had always wanted to visit: southern Spain, Yugoslavia, Greece, Cyprus, Turkey and North Africa. He might have taken another trip around the world: to Russia, India and China; fulfilled his ambition of writing novels about the remaining continents: Asia, Africa and America; completed his unfinished books and continued to publish them privately with Orioli: the novel about Burns, "The Flying Fish" and the last half of *Etruscan Places*.

As early as 1912 Lawrence prophetically wrote: "I think the new generation is rather different from the old. I think they will read me more gratefully." Lawrence's social impact—especially after the trial of *Lady Chatterley's Lover* in 1960 and the first unexpurgated English edition of the novel (1960), which sold 3,225,000 copies in the first eight months—influenced the abolition of state censorship, freedom of language and sexual permissiveness as well as the acceptance of homosexuality and the salvation of touch.

Lawrence's belief that "the greatest virtue in life is real courage, that knows how to face facts and live beyond them," enabled him to defy social, political and literary conventions by eloping with Frieda, opposing the war and publishing *Lady Chatterley's Lover,* and to overcome, for five years and with consummate bravery, his agonizing illness. Catherine Carswell, one of his oldest friends and staunchest defenders, has attested to his freedom, taste, imaginative power, truthfulness and fidelity:

He did nothing that he did not really want to do, and all that he most wanted to do he did. He went all over the world, he owned a ranch, he lived in the most beautiful corners of Europe.... He painted and made things, and sang and rode. He wrote something like three dozen books, of which even the worst page dances with life that could be mistaken for no other man's, while the best are admitted, even by those who hate him, to be unsurpassed. [He was] without vices, with most human virtues, the husband of one wife, scrupulously honest.[9]

Appendix
A History of Illness

2 weeks old: bronchitis; a puny, fragile infant

grammar school: a thin, pale, weakly lad, seldom without a cold

high school: troublesome hacking cough

late 1901: pneumonia in Eastwood. April 1902: convalescence at Skegness

November–December 1911: pneumonia in Croydon. Examined by William Addey.

January 1912: convalescence at Bournemouth

March 1912: ill, pale and thin when he first meets Frieda in Nottingham

June 1913: spits blood in Kent

c. April 1915: examined by David Eder

November 1915: "far gone with consumption" in Hampstead

January–February 1916: seriously ill in north Cornwall. Examined by Maitland Radford

June 1916: diagnosed as tubercular and rejected for military service

July 1916: admits consumption in a letter from west Cornwall

February–March 1919: influenza in Ripley, Notts. Examined by Mullan-Feroze

April 1922: extremely ill with malaria in Kandy, Ceylon

August 1924: spits blood in Taos. Examined by Dr. Martin

February 1925: 1st hemorrhage, in Oaxaca. Examined by José Larumbe. Sidney Uhlfeder, in Mexico City, diagnoses TB and gives him a year or two to live

February 1926: 2nd hemorrhage, in Spotorno

July 1927: 3rd hemorrhage, in Scandicci

September 1927: examined by Hans Carossa and Max Mohr in Irschenhausen

June 1928: forced to leave hotel in St. Nizier, France, because of TB

October–November 1928: 4th hemorrhage, in Port-Cros

July 1929: 5th hemorrhage, in Florence. Examined by Professor Giglioli and in September 1929 by Max Mohr in Rottach, Germany

September 1929: extremely ill from disastrous arsenic and phosphorus "cure" in Baden-Baden

January 1930: examined in Bandol by Andrew Morland, who gives him three months to live, without a sanatorium

February 1930: losing weight in Bandol; enters Ad Astra sanatorium in Vence

March 2, 1930: dies in Villa Robermond, Vence

Notes

CHAPTER ONE: EASTWOOD: A MINING VILLAGE

1. D. H. Lawrence, "Nottingham and the Mining Countryside," *Phoenix*, ed. Edward McDonald (London, 1936), p. 135.
2. Sigmund Freud, *Dora: An Analysis of a Case of Hysteria*, trans. Alix and James Strachey (New York, 1963), p. 27.
3. *Collected Letters of D. H. Lawrence*, ed. Harry Moore (New York, 1962), p. 852.
4. Lawrence, "Nottingham and the Mining Countryside," *Phoenix*, p. 133.
5. S. G. Checkland, *The Rise of Industrial Society in England, 1815–1885* (New York, 1964), pp. 162–163.
6. George Orwell, *The Road to Wigan Pier* (London, 1937), pp. 21, 23–25.

   In July 1988, wearing a battery lamp and carrying a gas mask, I went 964 meters down a mine and, after riding on a conveyor belt and tramcar, walked a final 300 meters underground to the coal face in Haworth, north Nottinghamshire. The winding gear at the pithead still resembled Lawrence's drawing for the dust wrapper of *The Rainbow*, the miners still used a modern form of the Davy lamp and — though the butty system had been abolished and the pit ponies were gone — it was still extremely hot, dusty and dangerous. There are now showers at the pitheads so the miners can go home clean, but a stern sign warned the men not to piss in the baths.

7. Checkland, *Rise of Industrial Society,* pp. 164–165.

8. J. E. Williams, *The Derbyshire Miners: A Study in Industrial and Social History* (London, 1962), pp. 64–65.

9. Cecil Day Lewis, *The Buried Day* (London, 1960), p. 145.

10. Michael Flinn and David Stoker, *The History of the British Coal Industry. Volume 2: 1700–1830* (Oxford, 1984), p. 434.

11. Day Lewis, *The Buried Day,* p. 130.

12. Jessie Chambers, *D. H. Lawrence: A Personal Record* (1935), 2nd edition, ed. Jonathan Chambers (London, 1965), p. 58; Jessie Chambers, "The Collected Letters of Jessie Chambers," ed. George Zytaruk, *D. H. Lawrence Review,* 12 (1979), 81.

13. W. H. Auden and Louis MacNeice, *Letters from Iceland* (1937; London, 1967), p. 49.

14. D. H. Lawrence, *Sons and Lovers* (New York, 1967), p. 320. In Joseph Conrad's *Victory* (New York, 1957), p. 140, Schomberg sends three villains to destroy Heyst, who has been living in isolation on the island of Samburan and attempting to mine coal for steamships. Schomberg directs them by exclaiming: "What do you think of a pillar of smoke by day and a loom of fire at night? There's a volcano in full blast near that island."

15. Interview with Enid Hopkin Hilton, Ukiah, California, May 7, 1988; Lawrence, "Return to Bestwood," *Phoenix II,* ed. Warren Roberts and Harry Moore (New York, 1970), pp. 263–264; Lawrence, "Nottingham and the Mining Countryside," *Phoenix,* pp. 135–136.

16. Lawrence, "Men Must Work and Women as Well," *Phoenix II,* p. 586; Lawrence, "Return to Bestwood," *Phoenix II,* p. 262; Lawrence, "Autobiographical Fragment," *Phoenix,* p. 823.

17. D. H. Lawrence, *Lady Chatterley's Lover* (New York, 1962), pp. 13, 142; Catherine Carswell, *The Savage Pilgrimage* (New York, 1932), p. 104. Jessie Chambers, *Personal Record,* p. 209, recalls "youths coming home from the pit with bunches of violets and celandines."

18. John Benson, *The British Coalminer in the Nineteenth Century: A Social History* (New York, 1980), p. 125. I have also used the following books for this chapter: Alan Griffin, *The Miners of Nottinghamshire. Volume 1: 1881–1914* (Nottingham, 1956); A. R. Griffin and C. P. Griffin, "The Role of the Coal-Owners Associations in the East Midlands in the Nineteenth Century," *Renaissance and Modern Studies,* 17 (1973), 95–121; C. P. Griffin, "The Social Origins of D. H. Lawrence: Some Further Evidence," *Literature and History,* 7 (1981), 223–227; M. W. Kirby, *The British Coalmining Industry,*

1870–1946: A Political and Economic History (London, 1977); J. U. Nef, *The Rise of the British Coal Industry,* Volume 2 (London, 1932); Ronald Storer, *Some Aspects of the Brinsley Colliery and the Lawrence Connection* (Selston, Notts., 1985); Robert Waller, *The Dukeries Transformed: The Social and Political Development of a Twentieth Century Coalfield* (Oxford, 1983); G. C. H. Whitelock, *250 Years in Coal: The History of the Barber Walker Company* (Derby, 1955).

19. Quoted in George Neville, *A Memoir of D. H. Lawrence,* ed. Carl Baron (Cambridge, England, 1981), pp. 200–201 n12.

CHAPTER TWO: A DISASTROUS MARRIAGE

1. Lawrence, "Nottingham and the Mining Countryside," *Phoenix,* p. 133.
2. Roy Spencer, *D. H. Lawrence Country* (London, 1980), p. 29.
3. May Chambers, in Edward Nehls, *D. H. Lawrence: A Composite Biography* (Madison, 1957–59), 3.554; Lawrence, *Sons and Lovers,* p. 9.
4. Lawrence, "Autobiographical Sketch," *Phoenix II,* p. 592; Ada Lawrence and Stuart Gelder, *Young Lorenzo* (London, 1931), p. 9.

   Martin Green, *The Von Richthofen Sisters* (New York, 1974), p. 106, echoes the standard line, probably invented by Lydia herself, that "Mrs. Lawrence's father had been an engineer and a friend and rival of both General Booth of the Salvation Army and Jesse Boot of the great chemists' chain-stores." Though George Beardsall may have quarreled with Jesse Boot, he is not mentioned in the standard two-volume life of the revivalist. See Harold Begbie, *The Life of General William Booth: The Founder of the Salvation Army* (New York, 1920).
5. Spencer, *D. H. Lawrence Country,* pp. 73, 63.
6. Ada Lawrence, *Young Lorenzo,* p. 21; Jessie Chambers, *Personal Record,* pp. 24, 36, 54, 138.
7. Interview with Enid Hilton; Taped interview with William Ernest Lawrence, Nottingham County Library, pp. 2, 12.
8. Lawrence, "Return to Bestwood," *Phoenix II,* pp. 259–260.
9. Interview with Lawrence's niece Margaret King Needham, Shipley, Derbyshire, July 22, 1988.
10. J. D. Chambers, "Memories of D. H. Lawrence," *Renaissance and*

Modern Studies, 16 (1972), 7–8; Ada Lawrence, *Young Lorenzo,* p. 24; Taped interview with William Ernest Lawrence, p. 5.

11. William Hopkin, in Nehls, *Composite Biography,* 1.22; William Hopkin, quoted in A. L. Rowse, "D. H. Lawrence at Eastwood," *The English Past* (London, 1951), p. 231.

12. J. D. Chambers, "Memories of D. H. Lawrence," p. 8.

13. Taped interview with Mrs. Bircumshaw, pp. 1, 8, Nottingham County Library.

14. D. H. Lawrence, "Jimmy and the Desperate Woman," *Complete Short Stories* (New York, 1963), 3.621; Jessie Chambers, *Personal Record,* p. 35.

15. D. H. Lawrence, "That Women Know Best," Bancroft Library, University of California, Berkeley.

16. Ada Lawrence, *Young Lorenzo,* p. 25; D. H. Lawrence, *Etruscan Places,* in *D. H. Lawrence and Italy* (New York, 1972), p. 115.

17. Neville, *Memoir of D. H. Lawrence,* p. 51; *Letters of D. H. Lawrence, Volume I: 1901–1912,* ed. James Boulton (Cambridge, England, 1979), pp. 190–191. I have, whenever possible, used the excellent Cambridge edition of Lawrence's letters and works.

18. Lawrence, "Enslaved by Civilisation," *Phoenix II,* p. 580; Lawrence, "Autobiographical Sketch," *Phoenix II,* p. 592.

19. Rhys Davies, *Print of a Hare's Foot* (New York, 1969), p. 141; Earl and Achsah Brewster, *D. H. Lawrence: Reminiscences and Correspondence* (London, 1934), pp. 254–255.

20. Emile Delavenay, *D. H. Lawrence: The Man and His Work,* trans. Katherine Delavenay (London, 1972), p. 8.

CHAPTER THREE: CHILDHOOD AND CHAPEL

1. *The Letters of D. H. Lawrence. Volume III: 1916–1921,* ed. James Boulton and Andrew Robertson (Cambridge, England, 1984), p. 333; A. R. and C. P. Griffin, "A Social and Economic History of Eastwood and the Nottinghamshire Mining Country," *A D. H. Lawrence Handbook,* ed. Keith Sagar (Manchester, 1982), p. 139.

2. William Hopkin, in Nehls, *Composite Biography,* 1.21; Lawrence, "Autobiographical Sketch," *Phoenix II,* p. 593; George Arthur Lawrence, in Nehls, *Composite Biography,* 1.17.

3. Frieda Lawrence, Untitled manuscript relating to Lawrence's will, c.1930, Bancroft Library, University of California, Berkeley.

4. Quoted in David Newmarch, "Death of a Young Man in London: Ernest Lawrence and William Morel in *Sons and Lovers,*" *Durham University Journal,* 76 (December 1973), 78.

5. Interview with Margaret King Needham.

6. Jonathan Chambers, Introduction to Jessie Chambers, *Personal Record,* p. xv.

7. Lawrence, "Nottingham and the Mining Countryside," *Phoenix,* pp. 134, 138; Jessie Chambers, *Personal Record,* p. 55.

8. Neville, *Memoir of D. H. Lawrence,* p. 38; Albert Limb, in Nehls, *Composite Biography,* 1.32.

9. Quoted in Neville, *Memoir of D. H. Lawrence,* p. 186 n14; Lawrence, "Enslaved by Civilization," *Phoenix II,* p. 581.

10. Mabel Thurlby Collishaw, in Nehls, *Composite Biography,* 1.31.

11. D. H. Lawrence, *Mr. Noon,* ed. Lindeth Vasey (Cambridge, England, 1984), p. 4; Interview with Enid Hopkin Hilton.

In Nehls, *Composite Biography,* 1.134–135, Enid Hilton states that Philip Snowdon, Ramsay MacDonald and other Socialist leaders "visited us frequently" and that "Keir Hardie stayed with us." Since there is no reference to Willie Hopkin in David Marquand's *Ramsay MacDonald* (London, 1977) or Kenneth Morgan's *Keir Hardie* (London, 1975), the friendships could not have been very close.

12. Quoted in Newmarch, "Death of a Young Man," *Durham University Journal,* p. 78.

13. Sigmund Freud, *Leonardo da Vinci,* trans. A. A. Brill (New York, 1961), p. 88; May Chambers, in Nehls, *Composite Biography,* 3.592.

14. *Letters:* Cambridge, 1.190.

15. Ada Lawrence, *Young Lorenzo,* p. 59; Jessie Chambers, *Personal Record,* p. 88; May Chambers, in Nehls, *Composite Biography,* 3.578.

16. Lawrence, "Hymns in a Man's Life," *Phoenix II,* p. 600.

17. D. H. Lawrence, *The Lost Girl,* ed. John Worthen (Cambridge, England, 1981), pp. 20–21. For works on Congregationalism, see A. W. W. Dale, ed., *History of English Congregationalism* (London, 1907); Donald Davie, *A Gathered Church* (Oxford, 1978); Daniel Jenkins, *Congregationalism: A Restatement* (London, 1954).

18. Lawrence, "Introduction to *The Dragon of the Apocalypse* by Frederick Carter," *Phoenix,* p. 302.

19. *Apocalypse,* ed. Mara Kalnins (Cambridge, England, 1980), p. 59; Lawrence, "Autobiographical Fragment," *Phoenix,* p. 817; Lawrence, "Introduction to These Paintings," *Phoenix,* pp. 566–567.

20. Lawrence, "Fanny and Annie," *Complete Short Stories,* 2.465; Roger

Dattaler, "Eastwood in Taos," *Adelphi,* 28:4 (1952), 675–676. This hymn appears in *The Plumed Serpent,* ed. L. D. Clark (Cambridge, England, 1987), p. 195.

21. A. Whigham Price, "D. H. Lawrence and Congregationalism," *Congregational Quarterly,* 34 (July–October 1956), 326, 322, 324, 330, 331.

CHAPTER FOUR: NOTTINGHAM

1. See Roy Church, *Economic and Social Change in a Midland Town: Victorian Nottingham, 1815–1900* (New York, 1966), pp. 232, 355, 213.

2. *T. E. Lawrence: The Selected Letters,* ed. Malcolm Brown (New York, 1989), p. 300; Graham Greene, *A Gun for Sale* (1936; Harmondsworth, 1963), pp. 40–41, 69.

3. D. J. Peters, *Nottingham Guardian Journal,* March 22, 1972. For background on English education, see J. S. Hurt, *Elementary Schooling and the Working Classes: 1860–1918* (Oxford, 1979); P. S. Musgrave, *Society and Education in England Since 1800* (London, 1968); John Roach, *A History of Secondary Education in England: 1800–1870* (London, 1986); David Wardle, *English Popular Education: 1780–1975* (Cambridge, England, 1976).

4. Neville, *Memoir of D. H. Lawrence,* p. 40; Taped interview with William Ernest Lawrence, p. 2.

5. *Letters:* Cambridge, 1.21.

6. Church, *Economic and Social Change,* p. 208; Neville, *Memoir of D. H. Lawrence,* p. 90; Lawrence, *Sons and Lovers,* p. 93.

7. Frieda Lawrence, *Not I, But the Wind* (New York, 1934), p. 44; Letter from Helen Corke to Edward Nehls, February 20, 1952, Humanities Research Center, University of Texas, Austin.

8. Lawrence, "Autobiography," in Nehls, *Composite Biography,* 3.232–233; W. R. Parkinson, in Nehls, *Composite Biography,* 1.42.

9. D. H. Lawrence, *The Rainbow* (New York, 1964), pp. 372, 369, 388, 408, 393, 382.

10. *Ibid.,* p. 373; Taped interviews with W. H. King (p. 1), Mrs. Cotterel (pp. 1–2), and George Arthur Lawrence (p. 4), Nottingham County Library.

11. Quoted in Spencer, *D. H. Lawrence Country,* p. 43; Letter from George Holderness, July 18, 1908, University of Nottingham.

12. Delavenay, *The Man and His Work,* pp. 38–39.

13. Jessie Chambers, *Personal Record,* pp. 78, 77, 76.

14. *Ibid.,* pp. 80, 81.

15. *Letters:* Cambridge, 1.49; Lawrence, *The Rainbow,* pp. 431, 434–435.

16. A. C. Wood, *A History of University College, Nottingham, 1881–1948* (Oxford, 1953), p. 64; Quoted in Nehls, *Composite Biography,* 1.75.

17. *Letters:* Cambridge, 3.250, 3.509–510.

CHAPTER FIVE: JESSIE

1. J. D. Chambers, in Nehls, *Composite Biography,* 3.534; Quoted in Harry Moore, *The Priest of Love* (Harmondsworth, 1976), p. 569; *The Letters of D. H. Lawrence,* ed. Aldous Huxley (New York, 1932), pp. 769–770.

2. Lawrence, *Sons and Lovers,* pp. 124–125, 143; Helen Corke, *D. H. Lawrence: The Croydon Years* (Austin, 1965), p. 14.

3. Jessie Chambers, *Personal Record,* pp. 31, xvi, 222–223; Jessie Chambers, "Collected Letters," *D. H. Lawrence Review,* p. 58.

4. Jessie Chambers, *Personal Record,* p. 49.

5. *Ibid.,* pp. 133, 160, 153.

6. *Ibid.,* pp. 184, 186; *Letters:* Cambridge, 1.197.

7. D. H. Lawrence, *The White Peacock,* ed. Andrew Robertson (Cambridge, England, 1983), pp. 277–278; Lawrence, "The State of Funk," *Phoenix II,* p. 568.

8. *Letters:* Cambridge, 1.43; 1.154.

9. Enid Hopkin Hilton, in Nehls, *Composite Biography,* 1.135–136; Interview with Enid Hopkin Hilton.

10. *Letters:* Cambridge, 1.527; Quoted in Moore, *Priest of Love,* p. 149; Quoted in Delavenay, *The Man and His Work,* p. 155; Lawrence, *Mr. Noon,* pp. 145–146.

11. Quoted in Moore, *Priest of Love,* p. 149; Frieda Lawrence, *The Memoirs and Correspondence,* ed. E. W. Tedlock (New York, 1964), pp. 247–248; Lawrence, *Sons and Lovers,* p. 317; Letter from Richard Aldington to Edward Nehls, November 17, 1953, University of Texas.

12. Lawrence, *Sons and Lovers,* pp. 277–278.

13. *Letters:* Cambridge, 1.99; Quoted in Moore, *Priest of Love,* p. 76.

14. Lawrence, *Sons and Lovers,* pp. 289–290.

15. Jessie Chambers, *Personal Record,* pp. 66, 69.

16. J. M. Barrie, *Sentimental Tommy* (New York, 1896), p. 478; J. M. Barrie, *Tommy and Grizel* (New York, 1900), pp. 448, 466.

17. *Letters:* Cambridge, 1.187, 1.190–191, 1.545.

18. William Hopkin, in Nehls, *Composite Biography,* 1.71.

19. Jessie Chambers, *Personal Record,* pp. 202–203, 216.

CHAPTER SIX: CROYDON

1. Lawrence, "Foreword to *The Collected Poems,*" *Phoenix,* p. 253.

2. Jessie Chambers, *Personal Record,* pp. 149, 151; *Letters:* Cambridge, 1.263.

3. Helen Corke, *Neutral Ground* (London, 1933), p. 193; D. H. Lawrence, *The Trespasser,* ed. Elizabeth Mansfield (Cambridge, England, 1981), p. 218.

4. *Letters:* Cambridge, 1.84; Quoted in Moore, *Priest of Love,* pp. 124, 128.

5. *Letters:* Cambridge, 1.85, 1.93, 1.87.

6. Dorothy Brett, *Lawrence and Brett* (Philadelphia, 1933), p. 277; Frank Turner, in Nehls, *Composite Biography,* 1.91.

7. "Last Lesson of the Afternoon," *The Complete Poems of D. H. Lawrence,* ed. Vivian de Sola Pinto and Warren Roberts (New York, 1964), p. 74; Quoted in Moore, *Priest of Love,* p. 122.

8. D. H. Lawrence, "Education of the People," *Reflections on the Death of a Porcupine and Other Essays,* ed. Michael Herbert (Cambridge, England, 1988), pp. 89–90; *Letters:* Moore, p. 966.

9. Jessie Chambers, *Personal Record,* p. 159.

10. Douglas Goldring, *South Lodge* (London, 1943), pp. 40, 24; Douglas Goldring, *Privileged Persons* (London, 1955), p. 127.

11. Lawrence, "Foreword to *The Collected Poems,*" *Phoenix,* p. 253; Lawrence, "Autobiographical Sketch," *Phoenix II,* pp. 593–594; Quoted by Kyle Crichton, in Nehls, *Composite Biography,* 2.412–413. See Robert Lowell, "Ford Madox Ford," *Life Studies* (New York, 1964), p. 50: "Ford, / you were a kind man and you died in want."

12. Ford Madox Ford, *Return to Yesterday* (1933; New York, 1972), p. 376; *Letters:* Cambridge, 1.170.

13. Ford Madox Ford, *Portraits from Life* (1936; Chicago, 1960), p. 113; *Letters of Ford Madox Ford,* ed. Richard Ludwig (Princeton, 1965), p. 247.

14. *Letters:* Cambridge, 1.178, 1.339, 1.417.

15. *Ibid.,* 1.144; Jessie Chambers, *Personal Record,* p. 172; *Letters:* Cambridge, 1.145.

16. Ezra Pound, *Selected Letters, 1907–1941,* ed. D. D. Paige (New York,

1950), pp. 17, 22; Pound, Review of *Love Poems and Others, Poetry,* 2 (July 1913), 149, 151; Pound, "The Non-Existence of Ireland," *New Age,* February 15, 1915, p. 452.

17. *Letters:* Cambridge, 1.153.

18. Corke, *Neutral Ground,* p. 274.

19. Corke, *Croydon Years,* p. 13; Malcolm Muggeridge, "The Dreaming Woman—Helen Corke, in Conversation with Malcolm Muggeridge, Tells of Her Relationship with D. H. Lawrence," *Listener,* 80 (July 25, 1968), 105–106.

20. *Letters:* Cambridge, 1.286; Lawrence, *Complete Poems,* p. 98.

21. *Letters:* Cambridge, 1.194; Lawrence, "Introduction to Edward McDonald's *A Bibliography of D. H. Lawrence,*" *Phoenix,* p. 232.

22. *Letters:* Cambridge, 1.194, 1.189, 1.195.

23. Taped interviews with Alice Holditch (a friend of Lawrence's youth and teacher at the British School in Eastwood), (p. 7), and with his brother, George Lawrence, (p. 5), Nottingham County Library; Lina Waterfield, *Castle in Italy* (London, 1961), p. 139; Lawrence, *Complete Poems,* p. 102.

24. Lawrence, "Introduction to McDonald's *Bibliography,*" *Phoenix,* p. 232; Quoted by Kyle Crichton, in Nehls, *Composite Biography,* 2.417–418. Lawrence did not receive an advance of £200 for any of his early books. He got £50 each for *The White Peacock* and *The Trespasser,* £100 for *Sons and Lovers* and £300 for *The Rainbow.*

25. *Letters:* Cambridge, 1.181, 1.220, 1.230; Interview with Margaret King Needham.

26. *Letters:* Cambridge, 1.193; Jessie Chambers, *Personal Record,* p. 183; *Letters:* Cambridge, 1.190–191.

27. *Letters:* Cambridge, 1.195; 1.343.

28. *Ibid.,* 1.361.

29. Lawrence had considerable difficulty with titles, and the original names of many of his works were changed when the books were published. *Letitia* and *Nethermere* were changed to *The White Peacock; The Saga of Siegmund* was changed to *The Trespasser; Paul Morel* to *Sons and Lovers; Honour and Arms* to *The Prussian Officer; The Sisters* and *The Wedding Ring* to *The Rainbow* and *Women in Love; Italian Sketches* to *Twilight in Italy; The Insurrection of Miss Houghton* and *A Mixed Marriage* to *The Lost Girl; The House of Elois* to *The Boy in the Bush; Quetzalcoatl* to *The Plumed Serpent; The Escaped Cock* to *The Man Who Died; Tenderness* and *John Thomas and Lady Jane* to *Lady Chatterley's Lover.*

30. Lawrence, *The White Peacock,* pp. 29–30.

31. *Ibid.,* p. 215.

32. *Ibid.,* pp. 222–223. Greiffenhagen's *An Idyll* is reproduced in Jeffrey Meyers, *Painting and the Novel* (Manchester, 1975), p. 47.

33. Lawrence, "Return to Bestwood," *Phoenix II,* p. 260; *Letters:* Cambridge, 1.206–207.

34. *Letters:* Cambridge, 1.323; 1.337.

35. William Ober, "Lady Chatterley's *What?,*" *Boswell's Clap and Other Essays* (Carbondale, Illinois, 1979), p. 90; Ford, *Return to Yesterday,* p. 376; *Letters:* Cambridge, 1.368n.

36. Quoted in Ada Lawrence, *Young Lorenzo,* p. 98; Philip F. T. Smith, in Nehls, *Composite Biography,* 1.150.

37. *Letters:* Cambridge, 1.347; Jessie Chambers, *Personal Record,* p. 194.

38. *Letters:* Cambridge, 1.360; 1.361n; Jessie Chambers, *Personal Record,* pp. 199, 213.

39. David Garnett, *The Golden Echo* (London, 1953), p. 254; *The Letters of D. H. Lawrence, Volume II: 1913–1916,* ed. George Zytaruk and James Boulton (Cambridge, England, 1981), pp. 72–73.

40. *Letters:* Cambridge, 1.362; *Letters:* Moore, p. 1080. See George Jefferson, *Edward Garnett: A Life in Literature* (London, 1982).

41. *Letters:* Cambridge, 1.229; Lawrence, *The Trespasser,* pp. 112, 64.

CHAPTER SEVEN: FRIEDA

1. See Robert Lucas, *Frieda Lawrence,* trans. Geoffrey Skelton (New York, 1973).

2. See Montague Weekley, "Ernest Weekley: A Biographical Memoir," in Ernest Weekley, *An Etymological Dictionary of Modern English* (New York, 1967), pp. i–v.

3. Frieda Lawrence, *Memoirs and Correspondence,* p. 84.

4. Aldous Huxley, *Letters,* ed. Grover Smith (New York, 1969), p. 813; Interview with Barbara Weekley Barr, Chestfield, Kent, March 12, 1980.

5. Quoted in Alfred Alvarez, "Lawrence and Frieda," *Life After Marriage* (London, 1982), pp. 80–81.

6. Lawrence, *Mr. Noon,* p. 127.

7. Garnett, *Golden Echo,* p. 243; Ottoline Morrell, *Ottoline at Garsington, 1915–1918,* ed. Robert Gathorne-Hardy (London, 1974), pp. 94, 77.

8. Huxley, *Letters,* p. 832; Brett, *Lawrence and Brett,* p. 256; Dorothy

Brett, "Autobiography: My Long and Beautiful Journey," *South Dakota Review,* 5 (1967), 67.

9. Garnett, *Golden Echo,* pp. 241–242; Taped interview with John Middleton Murry in "Son and Lover" (1955), National Sound Archive; Carswell, *Savage Pilgrimage,* p. 15.

10. *Letters:* Cambridge, 2.224; Barbara Weekley Barr, in Nehls, *Composite Biography,* 2.294; Davies, *Print of a Hare's Foot,* p. 138.

11. Brewster, *Reminiscences,* p. 17.

12. Knud Merrild, *A Poet and Two Painters* (London, 1938), p. 102; Carlton Beals, *Glass Houses* (Philadelphia, 1938), p. 186.

13. Lawrence, *Sons and Lovers,* p. 306; D. H. Lawrence, "The Captain's Doll," *Four Short Novels* (New York, 1965), p. 189.

14. Frieda Lawrence, *Not I, But the Wind,* pp. 4–5.

15. *Letters:* Cambridge, 1.384, 1.415.

16. Lawrence, "Love Among the Haystacks," *Four Short Novels,* p. 27; Lawrence, *The Rainbow,* p. 24.

17. Frieda Lawrence, *Not I, But the Wind,* pp. 56–57; *Letters:* Cambridge, 2.73.

18. Frieda Lawrence, Foreword to *The First Lady Chatterley* (New York, 1973), pp. 13–14; Frieda Lawrence, *Memoirs and Correspondence,* p. 104; *Letters:* Cambridge, 1.439. See Molly's explanation of her attraction to Leopold Bloom in James Joyce, *Ulysses* (New York, 1986), p. 643: "I liked him because I saw he understood or felt what a woman is."

19. Lawrence, *Complete Poems,* p. 204.

20. Interview with Barbara Weekley Barr; Montague Weekley, "The Unexpected Step-Father" (n.d.), National Sound Archive; D. H. Lawrence, *The Virgin and the Gipsy* (New York, 1968), pp. 2–3.

21. Else von Richthofen Jaffe, in Nehls, *Composite Biography,* 1.165; Frieda Lawrence, *Not I, But the Wind,* p. 7.

22. *Letters:* Cambridge, 1.394–395; 1.429.

23. *Ibid.,* 1.393; 1.401, 1.403.

24. Lawrence, "A Propos of *Lady Chatterley's Lover,*" *Phoenix II,* p. 500; *Letters:* Cambridge, 1.406–407, 1.404.

25. David Garnett, "Frieda and Lawrence," *D. H. Lawrence: Novelist, Poet, Prophet,* ed. Stephen Spender (New York, 1973), p. 39; Huxley, *Letters,* pp. 831–832. Barbara Weekley Barr denied that the incident with the woodcutter occurred, but Garnett was on the scene at the time, heard about it from Lawrence and seems the more reliable informant.

26. Lawrence, *Mr. Noon,* pp. 276–277.

27. *Letters:* Cambridge, 1.402–403; William Hopkin, in Nehls, *Composite Biography,* 1.74; Interview with Barbara Weekley Barr.

28. Quoted in Lucas, *Frieda Lawrence,* p. 80; *Letters:* Cambridge, 1.388.

29. Frieda Lawrence, *Memoirs and Correspondence,* p. 108; *Letters:* Cambridge, 2.288.

30. *Letters:* Cambridge, 2.244; Barbara Barr, "I Look Back," *Twentieth Century,* 165 (March 1969), 254, 257; A. C. Wood [a Nottingham colleague], "Ernest Weekley," *Guardian,* May 10, 1954.

31. Frieda Lawrence, *Not I, But the Wind,* p. 40; Quoted in Lucas, *Frieda Lawrence,* p. 97.

32. *Letters:* Cambridge, 2.345.

33. *Letters:* Cambridge, 1.463; D. H. Lawrence, *Study of Thomas Hardy and Other Essays,* ed. Bruce Steele (Cambridge, England, 1985), p. 180. Even Tolstoy has second thoughts about Anna's morality and later said: "There was nothing else she could do—struggling her whole life through with that tedious Karenin" (quoted in A. N. Wilson, *Tolstoy,* New York, 1988, p. 308).

CHAPTER EIGHT: ITALY

1. Frieda Lawrence, *Not I, But the Wind,* p. 70; *Letters:* Cambridge, 1.441.

2. Johann Wolfgang von Goethe, *Italian Journey,* trans. W. H. Auden and Elizabeth Mayer (New York, 1968), pp. 24–25, 31–32.

3. *Letters:* Cambridge, 1.453.

4. *Ibid.,* 1.474; 1.544.

5. *Letters:* Moore, p. 951.

6. *Letters:* Cambridge, 2.78; 2.164; 2.118.

7. *Ibid.,* 1.503.

8. D. H. Lawrence, *Aaron's Rod,* ed. Mara Kalnins (Cambridge, England, 1988), p. 103; Lawrence, *The Lost Girl,* p. 285; Lawrence, *The Rainbow,* p. 240.

9. *The Letters of D. H. Lawrence, Volume IV: 1921–1924,* ed. Warren Roberts, James Boulton and Elizabeth Mansfield (Cambridge, England, 1983), 4.286; Lawrence, *Phoenix,* p. 343.

10. *Letters:* Cambridge, 4.234, 4.239.

11. Lawrence, *Twilight in Italy,* in *D. H. Lawrence and Italy,* p. 31.

12. *Ibid.,* pp. 68, 45, 136.

13. *Ibid.,* pp. 154, 165.

14. *Letters:* Cambridge, 1.490.

15. D. H. Lawrence, *Fantasia of the Unconscious* (New York, 1962), p. 169; *Letters:* Huxley, p. 563.

16. Frieda Lawrence, *Not I, But the Wind,* p. 55; Quoted by Barbara Barr, in Nehls, *Composite Biography,* 3.58; *Letters:* Huxley, p. xxxi; Frieda Lawrence, *Memoirs and Correspondence,* p. 440.

17. Frieda Lawrence, *Memoirs and Correspondence,* p. 354.

18. After Lawrence's death, Bernard Shaw wrote a letter to *Time and Tide,* 13 (August 6, 1932), 863, praising another of his plays, *The Widowing of Mrs. Holroyd* (1914): "In my ignorance, I attached no importance to Lawrence until one afternoon at the Stage Society [in December 1926], when I saw a play by him which rushed through in such a torrent of profuse yet vividly effective dialogue, making my own seem archaic in comparison, that I was strongly interested technically."

19. William Hopkin, in Nehls, *Composite Biography,* 1.71; Frieda Lawrence, *Not I, But the Wind,* p. 34.

20. Frieda Lawrence, *Not I, But the Wind,* pp. 56, 35; *Letters:* Cambridge, 1.550, 1.503.

21. Lawrence, *Complete Poems,* p. 191.

22. Lawrence, Foreword to *Fantasia of the Unconscious,* p. 57; Lawrence, "Poetry of the Present," *Complete Poems,* pp. 183–185.

23. Lawrence, "Preface to *Collected Poems*" (1928), *Complete Poems,* p. 27; Amy Lowell, "A New English Poet," *New York Times Book Review,* April 20, 1919, p. 25; Lawrence, "Argument" to *Look! We Have Come Through!, Complete Poems,* p. 191.

24. Lawrence, *Complete Poems,* p. 217; Lawrence, *Twilight in Italy,* pp. 57–58; Lawrence, "The Reality of Peace," *Reflections on the Death of a Porcupine,* p. 51; Lawrence, *Complete Poems,* p. 250.

25. Julian Morrell Vinogradoff, in Nehls, *Composite Biography,* 1.310; Quoted in John Jones, "The Prose and the Poetry," *New Statesman,* 54 (July 6, 1957), 23; W. H. Auden, "D. H. Lawrence," *The Dyer's Hand* (New York, 1968), p. 288; *Letters:* Cambridge, 3.178.

26. *Letters:* Cambridge, 4.25; Lawrence, *Lady Chatterley's Lover,* p. 80.

27. Brett, *Lawrence and Brett,* p. 247; *Letters:* Moore, p. 840; *Letters:* Cambridge, 2.90.

28. *Letters:* Cambridge, 1.476–477.

29. *Letters:* Huxley, p. 104; Lawrence, *Fantasia of the Unconscious,* p. 160.

30. Lawrence, *Sons and Lovers,* p. 251.

31. *Letters:* Cambridge, 1.531n, 1.553n; Frieda Lawrence, *Not I, But the Wind,* p. 56.

CHAPTER NINE: LITERARY LONDON

1. The connections between Lawrence's circle of friends were extremely complex. Dorothy Brett as well as Cynthia Asquith's sister-in-law, who was married to a Rumanian prince, became Murry's mistresses in 1919–20. Cynthia's future father-in-law had been Ottoline's suitor, and Ottoline had had an affair with J. A. Cramb, who had been Mansfield's German teacher at Queen's College, London. E. M. Forster had been tutor in Germany to the children of Mansfield's cousin Elizabeth von Arnim, who later married Bertrand Russell's older brother.

2. Diana Cooper, *Autobiography* (New York, 1985), p. 78; Lawrence, "The Ladybird," *Four Short Novels,* p. 46.

3. Interview with Michael Asquith, London, August 3, 1988. *Letters:* Cambridge, 2.198 n2, states that Michael died in 1960, but he was certainly alive in 1988.

4. Taped interview with Lady Cynthia Asquith, National Sound Archive; Quoted in Nicola Beauman, *Cynthia Asquith* (London, 1987), pp. 160, 164.

5. *Letters:* Cambridge, 2.337, 3.118, 3.201.

6. D. H. Lawrence, "The Rocking-Horse Winner," *The Portable D. H. Lawrence,* ed. Diana Trilling (New York, 1954), p. 47. John Asquith, the model for Paul, died of a heart attack in a mental home at the age of twenty-six.

7. This account of Catherine Carswell is based on interviews with her son, John Carswell, London, August 9, 1988, with Enid Hopkin Hilton and with Yvonne Kapp, London, August 16, 1988; and on John Carswell, Introduction to Catherine Carswell's autobiographical novel, *Open the Door!* (London, 1986), pp. v–xvii.

8. Carswell, *The Savage Pilgrimage,* p. 63.

9. Diana Farr, *Gilbert Cannan* (London, 1978), pp. 35, 113.

10. *Letters:* Cambridge, 3.677. See *The Letters of D. H. Lawrence and Amy Lowell, 1914–1925,* ed. Claire Healey and Keith Cushman (Santa Barbara, 1985).

11. John Manchester, Prologue to Dorothy Brett's *Lawrence and Brett* (Santa Fe, 1974), p. vii.

12. D. H. Lawrence and M. L. Skinner, *The Boy in the Bush* (Harmondsworth, 1963), pp. 390, 386; Faith Compton Mackenzie, *More Than I Should* (London, 1940), p. 33.

13. Quoted in F. A. Lea, *The Life of John Middleton Murry* (London, 1959), p. 44; Brett, *Lawrence and Brett,* p. 17.

14. D. H. Lawrence, *Kangaroo* (New York, 1976), p. 105.

15. Leonard Woolf, *Beginning Again* (London, 1964), pp. 251, 249.

16. Beatrice Glenavy, *Today We Will Only Gossip* (London, 1964), p. 161.

17. Quoted in Mark Gertler, *Selected Letters,* ed. Noel Carrington (London, 1965), p. 162n; *Letters:* Cambridge, 2.305.

18. As Kot grew older, his dark moods developed into depressions that could last for months at a time. His melancholy was intensified by poverty and poor health, by the death of Mansfield in 1923 and of Lawrence in 1930, by the suicide of Gertler in 1939, by the persecution of the Jews and the Nazi occupation of Europe. After a nervous breakdown in the 1940s, he tried to kill himself by cutting his throat. He was persuaded to undergo electroshock treatment and was cared for by H. G. Wells' daughter-in-law, Marjorie. He died in London in 1955 and bequeathed his valuable papers to the British Museum.

   This account of Kot is based on George Zytaruk, Introduction to *The Quest for Rananim: D. H. Lawrence's Letters to S. S. Koteliansky, 1914–1930* (Montreal, 1970), pp. xi–xxxvii; John Carswell, *Lives and Letters* (New York, 1978); Juliette Huxley, *Leaves of the Tulip Tree* (London, 1986).

19. Aldous Huxley, *Crome Yellow* (Harmondsworth, 1972), p. 15; *The Letters of Roger Fry,* ed. Denys Sutton (London, 1972), p. 417; Quoted in John Rothenstein, "Mark Gertler," *Modern English Painters* (London, 1956), p. 213.

20. Gertler, *Selected Letters,* pp. 56, 47.

21. *Letters:* Cambridge, 3.44; 3.136–137; 3.144.

22. *Letters:* Moore, p. 938; *Letters:* Cambridge, 3.242–243.

23. Apart from Kot, Gertler and Eder, his Jewish friends and colleagues included William Heinemann, his first publisher; Edgar Jaffe, his brother-in-law; Ivy Low, who had visited him in Italy and later married Maxim Litvinov, Stalin's future foreign minister and ambassador to Washington during World War II; and Ivy's aunt, Barbara Low, an early psychoanalyst in England. Lawrence was also friendly with the barrister Montague Shearman, who lent him money and helped him after he had been expelled from Cornwall during the war;

and with three of his American publishers: Ben Huebsch (who took
over his works after Lawrence had been swindled out of the royalties
of *Sons and Lovers* by a gentile, Mitchell Kennerley), Thomas Seltzer
and Alfred Knopf. In the 1920s Lawrence also became friends with
the actress Ida Rauh, the former wife of Max Eastman and a Taos
friend of Mabel Luhan.

24. Helen Thomas, "Two Pieces of Advice from D. H. Lawrence," *Times,*
February 13, 1963, p. 12; Richard Aldington and Lawrence Durrell,
Literary Lifelines, ed. Ian MacNiven and Harry Moore (New York,
1981), p. 42; Lawrence, *Women in Love,* pp. 129–130.

25. *Letters:* Moore, p. 899; Interview with William Hopkin (1949),
National Sound Archive.

Beginning with himself and Frieda, Lawrence eventually used
most of his friends as models for characters in his fiction. Paul Morel,
Gilbert Noon, Rupert Birkin, Rawdon Lilly, Richard Lovat Somers
and Oliver Mellors were self-portraits; Johanna Keighley, Ursula
Brangwen, Tanny Lilly, Harriet Somers, Kate Leslie, Connie Chat-
terley (and many women in his paintings) were modeled on Frieda.
He used Jessie Chambers, Alan Chambers and George Neville in *The
White Peacock;* George Neville in *Mr. Noon;* Helen Corke in *The
Trespasser;* his parents, siblings, the Chambers family and Alice Dax
in *Sons and Lovers;* Willie Hopkin in *Touch and Go* and *Mr. Noon;*
Louie Burrows and her father in *The Rainbow;* Ernest and Barbara
Weekley in *The Virgin and the Gipsy;* Baron von Richthofen in "The
Thorn in the Flesh"; Florence Cullen, her parents and Maurice Mag-
nus in *The Lost Girl;* Cynthia Asquith in "The Ladybird" and "The
Rocking-Horse Winner"; Catherine Carswell in "The Blind Man";
Katherine Mansfield in *Touch and Go, Women in Love,* "Mother and
Daughter" and *John Thomas and Lady Jane;* Middleton Murry in
Women in Love, "Smile," "The Border Line," "Jimmy and the Desper-
ate Woman," "The Last Laugh" and *David;* Kot and David Eder in
Kangaroo; Ottoline, Russell, Gertler and Philip Heseltine in *Women
in Love;* Brett in *The Boy in the Bush,* "The Princess," "The Last
Laugh" and "Glad Ghosts"; Wyndham Lewis and Michael Arlen in
Lady Chatterley's Lover; Percy Lucas and his family in "England,
My England"; Compton Mackenzie in "Two Blue Birds" and "The
Man Who Loved Islands"; Norman Douglas, Richard Aldington,
Reggie Turner, Hilda Doolittle and Cecil Gray in *Aaron's Rod;* Earl
and Achsah Brewster in "Things"; Witter Bynner and Spud Johnson
in *The Plumed Serpent;* Mabel Luhan in "The Woman Who Rode

Away," "None of That" and *St. Mawr;* and Frederick Carter in *St. Mawr.*

26. Warren Roberts, Introduction to *Letters:* Cambridge, 4.3.

CHAPTER TEN: MANSFIELD AND MURRY

1. Lawrence, *Women in Love,* p. 10; Dorothy Brett and John Manchester, "Reminiscences of Katherine Mansfield," pp. 85–87.

2. Lea, *Life of Murry,* p. 7; Quoted in Colin Murry, *I at the Keyhole* (New York, 1975), p. 86; *The Letters of John Middleton Murry to Katherine Mansfield,* ed. C. A. Hankin (London, 1983), p. 238; *Letters:* Moore, p. 821.

3. Brett, *Lawrence and Brett,* p. 18; John Middleton Murry, *Between Two Worlds* (London, 1935), p. 80.

4. Murry, *Between Two Worlds,* p. 232; Quoted in *Ottoline at Garsington,* p. 188.

5. *The Letters of Virginia Woolf: Volume II, 1912–1922,* ed. Nigel Nicolson and Joanne Trautmann (New York, 1976), pp. 546, 515, 540; Letter from Gerald Brenan to Jeffrey Meyers, October 3, 1975; Bertrand Russell, *Autobiography, 1914–1944* (New York, 1969), p. 58.

6. *Letters:* Cambridge, 1.519; Frieda Lawrence, *Not I, But the Wind,* pp. 67–68; *Letters:* Cambridge, 2.290.

7. *Letters:* Cambridge, 2.110.

8. *Ibid.,* 2.110–111; *The Letters of Katherine Mansfield,* ed. J. Middleton Murry (London, 1928), 2.138.

9. Quoted in Lea, *Life of Murry,* p. 42; *Katherine Mansfield's Letters to John Middleton Murry, 1913–1922* (New York, 1951), p. 431; Murry, *Between Two Worlds,* p. 344; Quoted in Jeffrey Meyers, *Katherine Mansfield: A Biography* (London, 1978), pp. 82–83.

10. *Letters:* Cambridge, 2.160.

11. Carswell, *Savage Pilgrimage,* pp. 22, 199; John Middleton Murry, *Reminiscences of D. H. Lawrence* (London, 1933), pp. 88–89.

12. Quoted in Antony Alpers, *The Life of Katherine Mansfield* (London, 1980), p. 170.

13. Lea, *Life of Murry,* p. 31; *Letters of Murry to Mansfield,* p. 55.

14. *Journal of Katherine Mansfield,* ed. J. Middleton Murry (London, 1954), pp. 67–69; Quoted in Leonard Woolf, *Beginning Again,* p. 252.

15. *Letters:* Cambridge, 2.333.

16. Lawrence, "Note to 'The Crown,'" *Reflections on the Death of a Porcupine*, p. 249.

17. *Letters:* Cambridge, 2.481–482.

18. *Letters of Murry to Mansfield*, p. 79; *Letters:* Cambridge, 2.473.

19. *Letters:* Cambridge, 2.549; 2.569; 2.576; *The Collected Letters of Katherine Mansfield: Volume One, 1903–1917*, ed. Vincent O'Sullivan and Margaret Scott (Oxford, 1984), p. 248.

20. Frieda Lawrence, *Not I, But the Wind*, p. 84; *Letters:* Cambridge, 2.591.

21. *Letters:* Cambridge, 3.302; *Collected Letters of Mansfield*, 1.261–262.

22. Murry, *Between Two Worlds*, pp. 413, 288; *Collected Letters of Mansfield*, 1.264.

23. *Collected Letters of Mansfield*, 1.263–264.

24. *Ibid.*, 1.261; 1.292. Lawrence was influenced by Nietzsche's hostility to Christianity, ideas about will and sexuality, emphasis on body, instinct and heredity against mind, reason and consciousness, self-overcoming, revaluation of values, and the role of women.

25. *Ibid.*, 1.280, 1.267–268; 1.360; Mansfield, *Journal*, p. 146.

26. Murry, *Reminiscences*, p. 73; Murry, *Between Two Worlds*, p. 417. In a letter to Kot of May 11, 1916, Katherine reported that Lawrence used this parasitic metaphor to describe Frieda as "a bug who has fed on my life" (*Collected Letters of Mansfield*, 1.263).

27. *Letters:* Cambridge, 2.610; *Collected Letters of Mansfield*, 1.272; *Letters:* Cambridge, 2.623.

28. Murry, *Between Two Worlds*, p. 411; Quoted in Frank Swinnerton, *Figures in the Foreground* (London, 1963), p. 102; Quoted in Meyers, *Katherine Mansfield*, p. 93.

CHAPTER ELEVEN: WAR

1. John Keegan, *The Mask of Command* (New York, 1987), pp. 71–72, 240, 243; A. J. P. Taylor, *The First World War* (New York, 1972), p. 134; B. H. Liddell Hart, *History of the First World War* (1930; London, 1972), p. 332.

2. *Letters:* Cambridge, 1.478; Lawrence, "Review of John Oman's *The Book of Revelation*," *Phoenix II*, p. 273.

3. Henry James, *Letters*, ed. Percy Lubbock (London, 1920), 2.398; Leonard Woolf, *Downhill All the Way* (New York, 1967), p. 9.

4. *Letters:* Cambridge, 2.339; 2.431–432.

5. *Ibid.*, 2.218; Lawrence, "Adolf," *Phoenix,* p. 7; *Letters:* Cambridge, 3.32.

6. Sigmund Freud, *Civilization and Its Discontents,* trans. James Strachey (New York, 1961), p. 59; Frieda Lawrence, "A Bit about D. H. Lawrence," *Memoirs and Correspondence,* p. 443; Unpublished letter from Lawrence to Alfred Sutro, September 10, 1914, copy in my possession.

7. Osbert Sitwell, *Laughter in the Next Room* (Boston, 1951), p. 18.

8. Quoted in Michael Holroyd, *Lytton Strachey* (Harmondsworth, 1968), pp. 599, 597.

9. Huxley, *Crome Yellow,* p. 9; Osbert Sitwell, "Triple Fugue," *Triple Fugue* (New York, 1925), p. 255; D. H. Lawrence, *Women in Love,* ed. David Farmer, Lindeth Vasey and John Worthen (Cambridge, England, 1987), p. 15.

10. Interview with Lady Juliette Huxley, London, August 2, 1988; Williams, *The Derbyshire Miners,* p. 444; Interview with Julian Morrell Vinogradoff, Banbury, England, July 24, 1988; Taped interview with Julian Morrell Vinogradoff, Nottingham County Library.

11. Morrell, *Ottoline at Garsington,* pp. 70, 66.

12. *Ibid.*, pp. 143, 59, 36n, 37, 78.

13. *Letters:* Cambridge, 2.359; 2.433; 3.216.

14. Morrell, *Ottoline at Garsington,* pp. 233–234, 128–129.

15. *Letters:* Huxley, pp. 740, 742.

16. E. M. Forster, *Selected Letters,* ed. Mary Lago and P. N. Furbank (London, 1983), 1.218; *Letters:* Cambridge, 2.280, 2.283; 2.293; Forster, *Selected Letters,* 1.219. The editors identify "Hilda" as Hilda Doolittle, whom Forster did not know and would be unlikely to refer to by her first name. Hilda, as the context suggests, was more probably Hilda Jones, the little daughter of Lawrence's landlord in Croydon, where he wrote *The White Peacock.*

17. *Ottoline at Garsington,* p. 55; Bertrand Russell, "D. H. Lawrence" (1953), *Portraits from Memory* (New York, 1956), p. 112; Alan Ryan, *Bertrand Russell: A Political Life* (London, 1988), pp. 49, 22.

18. *Letters:* Cambridge, 2.282; Quoted in Ronald Clark, *The Life of Bertrand Russell* (New York, 1976), p. 261.

19. *Letters:* Cambridge, 2.309; 2.320–321; Interview with David Garnett, Montcuq, France, August 17, 1977.

20. Quoted in Sandra Darroch, *Ottoline: The Life of Ottoline Morrell* (New York, 1975), p. 137; John Maynard Keynes, "My Early Beliefs" (1938), *Essays and Sketches in Biography* (New York, 1956), p. 256.

21. Russell, *Autobiography,* p. 9; *D. H. Lawrence's Letters to Bertrand Russell,* ed. Harry Moore (New York, 1948), p. 79. A page of Russell's typescript, with Lawrence's corrections, is reproduced in *Lawrence's Letters to Russell,* opposite p. 88.

22. *Letters:* Cambridge, 2.361; 2.364–366, 2.370–371.

23. *Letters:* Cambridge, 2.392; Russell, "D. H. Lawrence," *Portraits from Memory,* p. 115.

24. Paul Delany, *D. H. Lawrence's Nightmare* (New York, 1978), pp. 121, 135, 207.

25. Moore, *Priest of Love,* p. 300; Lawrence, "Note to 'The Crown,'" *Reflections on the Death of a Porcupine,* p. 249.

26. *Letters:* Cambridge, 2.470; Lawrence, *Women in Love,* pp. 83, 98; Russell, "D. H. Lawrence," *Portraits from Memory,* pp. 112, 114.

27. Unpublished letter from Richard Aldington to Edward Nehls, February 7, 1958, University of Texas.

28. *Memoirs of Lady Ottoline Morrell,* ed. Robert Gathorne-Hardy (New York, 1964), p. 276.

29. Samuel Taylor Coleridge, "*The Friend,*" no. 11 (October 26, 1809), in *Collected Works,* ed. Barbara Rooke (London, 1969), 4.146; *Letters:* Cambridge, 2.259.

30. *Letters:* Moore, p. 928; Lawrence, *Aaron's Rod,* p. 246; *Letters:* Cambridge, 3.226.

31. Interview with Dr. Mary Saleeby Fisher, Greatham, Sussex, August 23, 1988 (this interview was conducted in the same room and at the same table where Lawrence had tutored Mary in 1915); Dr. Mary Saleeby Fisher, in Nehls, *Composite Biography,* 1.304. Katherine Mansfield met her first husband, George Bowden, at the house of Mary Saleeby's father in St. John's Wood. The song about President McKinley is printed in *Letters:* Cambridge, 2.332. Mary's exercise book is now at the University of Texas.

32. Audrey Lucas, *E. V. Lucas: A Portrait* (London, 1939), p. 133; Viola Meynell, *Alice Meynell: A Memoir* (New York, 1929), pp. 310–313, 291.

33. Sylvia had many operations, lost the flexibility of her knee and walked with a stiff leg. She later married a Canadian soldier named Mulvey, had children, led a normal life and was still living in a cottage in Greatham in 1988. Interview with Dr. Mary Saleeby Fisher.

34. The biblical references in "England, My England," *Complete Short Stories,* vol. 2, include snakes in the Garden of Eden, pp. 303, 306 (Genesis 3:1), lilies of the valley, p. 311 (Matthew 6:28), the sacrifice

of Isaac, p. 315 (Genesis 22:10), "a little child shall lead them," p. 315 (Isaiah 11:6), Lot's wife, p. 315 (Genesis 19:26), the *Mater Dolorata,* p. 317 (i.e., the grieving Virgin Mary), Ishmael the wandering outcast, p. 325 (Genesis 16:11), the pagan gods Baal and Ashtaroth, p. 326 (Numbers 22:41 and Deuteronomy 1:4), God brooding on the face of the uncreated flux, p. 330 (Genesis 1:2), the four horses of the Apocalypse, p. 330 (Revelation 6:8) and the fidelity of Ruth, p. 331 (Ruth 1:16).

35. *Letters:* Cambridge, 2.635; Interview with Dr. Mary Saleeby Fisher. Seventy years later Sylvia, still embittered by Lawrence, was unwilling to see me.

36. Richard Aldington, *Death of a Hero* (Garden City, New York, 1929), p. 131; See Violet Hunt, *I Have This to Say* (New York, 1926), p. 259; Ford, *Portraits from Life,* pp. 118–119.

37. Frieda Lawrence, in Nehls, *Composite Biography,* 2.412–413; Quoted in Mabel Luhan, *Lorenzo in Taos* (New York, 1932), p. 325; Frieda Lawrence, *Memoirs and Correspondence,* p. 389. Harry Moore agreed with Frieda and maintained that Ford, who was not appointed an officer until August 1915, could not have been wearing a uniform at the time. For this reason, he dismissed Ford's story as pure fantasy. But Arthur Mizener showed that Ford *could* have been in uniform in March and takes his memoir more seriously. See Moore, *Priest of Love,* pp. 296–297, and Arthur Mizener, *The Saddest Story: A Biography of Ford Madox Ford* (New York, 1971), p. 596 n10.

38. Unpublished letter from David Garnett to Edward Nehls, August 1, 1957, University of Texas; Aldington, *Literary Lifelines,* p. 149; Quoted in Harry Moore, *Richard Aldington: An Intimate Portrait,* ed. Alister Kershaw and F.-J. Temple (Carbondale, Illinois, 1965), p. 91.

39. Interview with Dr. Mary Saleeby Fisher.

CHAPTER TWELVE: THE SUPPRESSION OF
THE RAINBOW

1. *Letters:* Cambridge, 2.182–183; Mark Schorer, "*Women in Love* and Death," *The World We Imagine* (New York, 1968), p. 108.

2. Lawrence, *The Rainbow,* pp. 494–495. For a thorough discussion of the novel, see Meyers, "Fra Angelico and *The Rainbow,*" *Painting and the Novel,* pp. 53–64.

3. D. H. Lawrence, *The Rainbow* (Harmondsworth: Penguin, 1949), p. 344 (Methuen edition, p. 318; the italicized passage was omitted from the Viking paperback edition, p. 339); Lawrence, *The Rainbow* (Penguin ed., pp. 485–486; Methuen ed., pp. 448–449; Viking ed., p. 479).

4. Lawrence, *The Rainbow* (Penguin ed., p. 241; Viking ed., p. 235), my italics; *Letters:* Cambridge, 3.459.

Lawrence cut at least six other passages from the American edition:

—3 lines from Methuen, p. 220 (Penguin, p. 239, omitted from Viking, p. 234): Will's desire to lick Anna with a lascivious tongue and bury himself in her flesh.

—1 line from Methuen, p. 300 (Penguin, p. 325, omitted from Viking, p. 320): Ursula's passionate sexual plea: "Let me come—let me come."

—4 lines on Ursula's love-making with Winifred Inger.

—24 lines from Methuen, p. 425 (Penguin, p. 460, omitted from Viking, p. 455): Ursula and Anton's nonphysical intimacy when bathing and getting into bed.

—5 lines from Penguin, p. 468 (omitted from Viking, p. 462): " 'Don't I satisfy you?' he asked of her, again going white to the throat. 'No,' she said. 'You've never satisfied me since the first week in London. You never satisfy me now. What does it mean to me, your having me—?' "

—30 lines from Methuen, p. 446 (Penguin, p. 483, omitted from Viking, p. 477): a much tamer love scene between Ursula and Anton, just before the amphibious one, in which "She let him take her, and he seemed mad, mad with excited passion."

5. *The Collected Letters of Joseph Conrad,* ed. Frederick Karl and Laurence Davies (Cambridge, England, 1988), 3.154; *Letters:* Cambridge, 2.327; Quoted in John Carter, "*The Rainbow* Prosecution," *TLS,* February 27, 1969, p. 216.

6. Quoted in R. P. Draper, *D. H. Lawrence: The Critical Heritage* (London, 1970), pp. 96; 93–95. Wilde had called homosexuality "the love that dare not speak its name" and had wittily defined fox hunting as "the unspeakable in full pursuit of the uneatable."

7. See *Letters:* Cambridge, 2.477.

8. Quoted in Viscount Brentford (William Joynson Hicks), *Do We Need A Censor?* (London, 1929), p. 11; Frank Swinnerton, *Background with Chorus* (London, 1956), p. 151.

9. Quoted in *"The Rainbow:* Destruction of a Novel Ordered," *The Times,* November 15, 1915, p. 3; Quoted in "An Objectionable Novel: Messrs. Methuen Summoned," *Daily Telegraph,* November 15, 1915, p. 12.

10. Lawrence, "Introduction to Edward McDonald's *A Bibliography of D. H. Lawrence," Phoenix,* p. 234; Pound, *Selected Letters,* p. 81; Ezra Pound, *Pound/Joyce,* ed. Forrest Read (New York, 1967), pp. 282–283. It was typical of the hypocrisy of the time that Augustine Birrell, father of the flagrant homosexual Frankie Birrell, should be arbiter of public morality.

11. *Letters:* Cambridge, 2.429.

12. *Ottoline at Garsington,* p. 38; Quoted in Nehls, *Composite Biography,* 1.333–335. In July 1922 copies of *Women in Love* were seized in the office of Lawrence's American publisher, Thomas Seltzer, by John Sumner, secretary of the New York Society for the Suppression of Vice. Sumner prosecuted Seltzer, who successfully defended the book in court in September. Lawrence might well have had similar success if he had had the financial means to defend *The Rainbow.*

13. Register of Bow Street Police Court, November 13, 1915, Greater London Record Office.

14. Home Office Papers HO45/13944, November 1915; March 10, 21 and 25, 1930, Public Record Office, Kew, London.

15. Cynthia Asquith, *Diaries, 1915–1918,* ed. E. M. Horsley (London, 1968), p. 85.

16. Lawrence, *The Rainbow* (Penguin ed., p. 330; Viking ed., p. 325); Richard Aldington, *Life for Life's Sake* (New York, 1941), pp. 229–230.

17. Richard Aldington, Introduction to D. H. Lawrence's *Apocalypse* (New York, 1932), p. vi; Quoted in Moore, *Priest of Love,* p. 311; Richard Aldington, *Portrait of a Genius, But* (New York, 1950), pp. 172–173.

CHAPTER THIRTEEN: CORNWALL

1. John Wade [pseud. of C. J. Stevens], "D. H. Lawrence in Cornwall: An Interview with Stanley Hocking," *D. H. Lawrence Review,* 6 (1973), 253; Lawrence, "Education of the People," *Reflections on the Death of a Porcupine,* p. 91; Lawrence, "Autobiographical Sketch," *Phoenix II,* p. 594.

2. *Letters:* Cambridge, 3.289; Cynthia Asquith, *Remember and Be Glad* (London, 1952), p. 149.

3. Emily Martin, Biographical Sketch of Robert Mountsier, December 8, 1971, pp. 2, 3–5, courtesy of Silas Mountsier III (*Letters:* Cambridge, 3.24n, incorrectly states that Mountsier earned a doctorate from the University of Michigan); Letter from Silas Mountsier III to Jeffrey Meyers, March 28, 1988.

4. *Letters:* Cambridge, 3.27, 3.25; Lawrence, *Kangaroo,* pp. 228–229. The factual basis of this passage is confirmed by *Letters:* Cambridge, 3.65, and by eight letters from Andrews to Mountsier at the University of Texas.

5. *Letters:* Cambridge, 3.678; 4.113; Letter from Silas Mountsier III to Jeffrey Meyers, March 28, 1988.

6. *Letters:* Cambridge, 3.27, 3.72; 3.180.

7. Carswell, *Savage Pilgrimage,* pp. 86–87.

8. Letter from Betsey Harries to Jeffrey Meyers, February 28, 1989; Letter from Andrews Wanning to Jeffrey Meyers, March 20, 1989; Luhan, *Lorenzo in Taos,* pp. 41, 51.

9. Letter from Wanning to Meyers; John Dos Passos, *The Best Times* (New York, 1966), pp. 135–136. References to Esther also appear in Hutchins Hapgood, *A Victorian in the Modern World* (1939; Seattle, 1972), pp. 558–559; in John Dos Passos, *The Fourteenth Chronicle: Letters and Diaries,* ed. Townsend Ludington (Boston, 1973), pp. 303, 315, 359, 392, 467, 476, 482; in Edmund Wilson, *The Thirties,* ed. Leon Edel (New York, 1980), pp. 353–354; and in Ernest Hemingway, *Selected Letters, 1917–1961,* ed. Carlos Baker (New York, 1981), pp. 355–356, 435, 447.

Esther and Canby were together for some time before he contracted polio and became paralyzed from the hips down. They moved from New York to Key West. Canby's "exercise was swimming, and he swam every day in Hemingway's pool. (Ernest had gone to Cuba with Martha Gellhorn, but Pauline, his previous wife, was very kind and hospitable.) After his polio, he took to drink as a panacea and, in fact, became an alcoholic. His life became a round of drinking broken by drying out in the local hospital."

"Esther inherited a considerable amount of money from her uncle and built a house in Key West in 1939–40. The sad irony is that she, who loved to spend money generously, got rich after she was in no condition to spend it. The end of her life was rather sad. She must have begun to lose her immediate memory in the late 1940s." Her close friends Charles and Lorine Thompson who were also friends of Hemingway, could no longer take care of her after Canby's death. So she was put into a Quaker hospital and died there on December 22, 1962 (Letter from Wanning to Meyers).

10. Morrell, *Ottoline at Garsington,* pp. 143, 59, 36n, 37; Quoted in Vincent Brome, *Ernest Jones: Freud's Alter Ego* (New York, 1982), p. 103.

11. Compton Mackenzie, *My Life and Times: Octave Five, 1915–1923* (London, 1966), pp. 167–168; Aldous Huxley, *Antic Hay* (1923; Harmondsworth, 1948), p. 45; Cecil Gray, *Musical Chairs* (London, 1948), p. 138.

12. Letter from D. H. Lawrence to Emily Lawrence King, June 14, 1926, omitted from *Letters:* Moore, p. 919, University of Nottingham.

For the refutation of the theory that Lawrence was H.D.'s lover and the father of the child born in 1919, see Jeffrey Meyers' review of Janice Robinson's *H.D.: The Life and Work of an American Poet, Hudson Review,* 34 (Winter 1982–83), 628–632. In the Introduction to the Virago edition of her mother's novel, *Bid Me to Live* (London, 1984), p. ix, Perdita Schaffner categorically states that her father was Cecil Gray.

13. F. D. Chambers, in Nehls, *Composite Biography,* 1.548 n99; Lawrence, "Study of Thomas Hardy," *Study of Thomas Hardy,* p. 94.

14. D. H. Lawrence, *"David," Complete Plays* (London, 1965), p. 106 (the covenant is sworn in I Samuel 20:16–17); *Letters:* Cambridge, 2.115.

15. *The Letters of Gerard Manley Hopkins to Robert Bridges,* ed. C. C. Abbott (London, 1955), p. 155; *Letters:* Cambridge, 3.478; D. H. Lawrence, *Studies in Classic American Literature* (London, 1924), pp. 167–168.

16. Merrild, *A Poet and Two Painters,* pp. 91–92; *Letters:* Cambridge, 3.302. The passage from Nietzsche comes from the chapter "Of the Love of One's Neighbor" in *Thus Spake Zarathustra* (1883–84). It attacks the concept in Leviticus 19:18—"thou shalt love thy neighbor as thyself"—and characterizes it as perverted self-love and hypocritical selflessness. Nietzsche denies the love of the neighbor and advocates love of the distant friend, which requires an overflowing heart and provides "a foretaste of the Superman."

17. *Letters:* Cambridge, 2.323; 2.331.

18. *Ibid.,* 2.650, 3.160; Lawrence, *Women in Love,* p. 127; *The Letters of T. E. Lawrence,* ed. David Garnett (1938; London, 1964), pp. 420, 669.

19. *Letters:* Cambridge, 2.285; Lawrence, "The Noble Englishman," *Complete Poems*, pp. 446–447.

20. See C. J. Stevens, *Lawrence at Tregerthen* (Troy, New York, 1988), pp. 46–54.

21. David Chambers and Stanley Hocking, in Nehls, *Composite Biography*, 1.47, 1.367.

22. *Letters:* Cambridge, 2.642, 2.664; D. H. Lawrence, "Prologue to *Women in Love*," *Texas Quarterly*, 6 (Spring 1963), 110.

23. Quoted in Stevens, *Lawrence at Tregerthen*, p. 33; Quoted in Robinson, *H.D.*, p. 250; *Frieda Lawrence and Her Circle*, ed. Harry Moore and Dale Montague (Hamden, Conn., 1981), p. 93; Unpublished letter from Barbara Weekley Barr to Edward Nehls, August 29, [early 1950s], University of Texas.

24. *Ottoline at Garsington*, p. 93; Cecil Gray, *Peter Warlock: A Memoir of Philip Heseltine* (London, 1934), p. 114n; Frieda Lawrence, *Not I, But the Wind*, p. 115; Lawrence, *Kangaroo*, p. 250.

25. Lawrence, *Women in Love*, pp. 480–481; Lawrence, "Prologue to *Women in Love*," pp. 107–110.

26. Lawrence, "Tortoise Shout," *Complete Poems*, p. 366.

27. John Middleton Murry, *Son of Woman* (London, 1931), p. 119.

28. Merrild, *A Poet and Two Painters*, p. 104.

29. Lawrence, *Women in Love*, pp. 199–201.

30. Plato, *The Symposium*, trans. Benjamin Jowett, *The Portable Plato*, ed. Scott Buchanan (New York, 1948), p. 144; Murry, *Between Two Worlds*, pp. 409, 412; F. A. Lea, *Lawrence and Murry: A Twofold Vision* (London, 1985), p. 64; Frieda Lawrence, *Memoirs and Correspondence*, pp. 295, 360.

31. Lawrence, *Women in Love*, pp. 268–271, 273, 275.

32. *Ibid.*, p. 314; *Letters:* Cambridge, 1.99; Lawrence, *Women in Love*, p. 353.

33. Quoted in Gray, *Peter Warlock*, p. 106; *Letters:* Cambridge, 2.526.

34. Lawrence, *Kangaroo*, pp. 258, 261.

35. David Garnett, "A Whole Hive of Genius," *Saturday Review of Literature*, 9 (October 1, 1932), 142.

36. Richard Aldington, "Son and Lover" (1955), National Sound Archive; Gray, *Musical Chairs*, p. 120.

37. Frieda Lawrence, *Not I, But the Wind*, p. 86; Quoted in Stevens, *Lawrence at Tregerthen*, pp. 101, 99; *Letters:* Cambridge, 3.188.

38. Quoted in Stevens, *Lawrence at Tregerthen*, pp. 108–111; *Crockford's Clerical Directory* (London, 1916), p. 1567.

39. Frieda Lawrence, *Not I, But the Wind*, p. 90; Asquith, *Diaries*, pp. 356–357.

40. Aldington, "Introduction" to *Apocalypse*, p. xi; Lawrence, *Kangaroo*, p. 220.

41. Vivian de Sola Pinto, "Notes on Interview with Emily Lawrence King," University of Nottingham; Frieda Lawrence, *Not I, But the Wind*, p. 80.

42. Cecily Lambert Minchin, in Nehls, *Composite Biography*, 1.465, 505, 503; 1.463–464, 466–467; Lawrence, "Ego-Bound Women," *Complete Poems*, p. 475.

43. Lawrence, "The Fox," *Portable Lawrence*, pp. 223, 236, 265, 304.

44. *Letters:* Cambridge, 3.215; *Hansard,* November 11, 1918; Quoted in David Garnett, *The Flowers of the Forest* (London, 1955), p. 190.

CHAPTER FOURTEEN: CAPRI AND TAORMINA

1. *Letters:* Cambridge, 3.417; Quoted in Mark Holloway, *Norman Douglas: A Biography* (London, 1976), pp. 39, 102.

2. D. H. Lawrence, Introduction to *Memoirs of the Foreign Legion* by M[aurice] M[agnus] (London, 1924), pp. 11–12, 15; Lawrence, *Aaron's Rod,* pp. 233, 238, 216, 218.

3. Lawrence, Introduction to *Memoirs*, pp. 12–13; Edward Craig, *Gordon Craig: The Story of His Life* (London, 1968), pp. 203–206; Richard Ellmann, *Oscar Wilde* (New York, 1987), p. 415.

4. Garnett, *Golden Echo*, pp. 239, 167; *Letters:* Cambridge, 3.431–432.

5. Anthony Burgess, *Flame into Being: The Life and Work of D. H. Lawrence* (New York, 1985), p. 136; Conrad, *Collected Letters*, 3.230, 3.239, 3.241. Capri continued to attract many writers after Lawrence: Sinclair Lewis, Scott Fitzgerald, Thornton Wilder, Curzio Malaparte, Graham Greene, Jean-Paul Sartre, Mario Soldati, W. H. Auden, Roger Peyrefitte and Theodore Roethke.

6. *Letters:* Cambridge, 3.443; Quoted in interview with Compton Mackenzie, National Sound Archives; Quoted in Compton Mackenzie, "Memories of D. H. Lawrence," *Moral Courage* (London, 1962), pp. 107–108.

7. *Letters:* Cambridge, 3.481.

8. *Ibid.,* 3.23; 3.83; 3.90; 3.663. The anonymous review, "Real Life and Dream Life," *Nation,* 28 (February 5, 1921), 639–640, was by Katherine's friend H. M. Tomlinson.

9. Carswell, *Savage Pilgrimage,* p. 198; Lawrence, *Women in Love,* p. 263.

10. *Collected Letters of Mansfield,* 1.306; 1.325; 2.279, 2.282. Katherine had also criticized Murry as a feeble John the Baptist—a voice crying in the wilderness.

11. *Collected Letters of Mansfield,* 2.284; *Letters:* Cambridge, 3.301–302.

12. *Letters:* Cambridge, 3.346; *Collected Letters of Mansfield,* 2.309, 2.314.

13. *Letters:* Cambridge, 3.343; 3.335.

14. *Letters:* Cambridge, 3.467; Mansfield, *Journal,* p. 198; *Letters:* Cambridge, 3.469.

15. *Mansfield's Letters to Murry,* p. 470; Quoted in Lea, *Life of Murry,* p. 83. Lawrence used similar words—"stewpot" and "stewing"—to describe both Capri and Katherine. In the French Alps in June 1928, Lawrence would also be forced to leave a hotel when his tubercular cough alarmed the other guests.

16. *Mansfield's Letters to Murry,* p. 473; *Letters of Murry to Mansfield,* p. 268; *Mansfield's Letters to Murry,* p. 505.

17. Mansfield, *Journal,* p. 207; Interview with Barbara Weekley Barr.

18. Mansfield, *Journal,* p. 146; *Letters:* Cambridge, 3.675; 4.114; Katherine Mansfield, *Scrapbook,* ed. J. Middleton Murry (New York, 1940), p. 135. Clement Shorter's *The Sphere* had published his damaging review of *The Rainbow* in October 1915.

19. *Letters of Mansfield,* 2.223; 2.230.

20. *Ibid.,* 2.175, 2.267.

21. *Letters:* Cambridge, 4.241; *Letters of Mansfield,* 2.234; *Mansfield's Letters to Murry,* pp. 671, 688.

22. D. H. Lawrence, *Letters to Thomas and Adele Seltzer,* ed. Gerald Lacy (Santa Barbara, 1976), p. 64; *Letters:* Cambridge, 4.375.

23. Lawrence, "Smile," *Complete Short Stories,* 2.584; D. H. Lawrence, *John Thomas and Lady Jane* (Harmondsworth, 1973), pp. 61, 72–73; *Letters:* Cambridge, 4.555.

24. Giuseppe Tomasi di Lampedusa, "The Professor and the Siren," *Two Stories and a Memory,* trans. Archibald Colquhoun (Harmondsworth, 1966), pp. 84–85.

25. *Letters:* Cambridge, 3.489; Lawrence, "Introduction to *Mastro-don Gesualdo,*" *Phoenix,* p. 230.

26. Lawrence, *Sea and Sardinia,* p. 182; Interview with Jan Juta, Mendham, New Jersey, June 28, 1988 (Juta's painting is now in the National Portrait Gallery, London); Carlo Levi, *Words Are Stones,* trans. Angus Davidson (1951; New York, 1958), pp. 116, 120, 124.

27. Denis Mack Smith, *Italy: A Modern History,* revised edition (Ann Arbor, 1969), pp. 372, 341, 412, 410; *Letters:* Cambridge, 4.226.

28. Lawrence, *Sea and Sardinia,* pp. 26, 123, 3, 60.

29. *Ibid.,* pp. 53, 57, 80, 150, 163; *Letters:* Cambridge, 3.676.

30. Interview with Harwood Brewster Picard, Fairfax, Virginia, June 24, 1988.

31. Brett, *Lawrence and Brett,* pp. 267–268; *Letters:* Moore, pp. 1215, 1221; Lawrence, "Return to Bestwood," *Phoenix II,* p. 265; *Letters:* Moore, p. 851.

32. Interview with Harwood Brewster Picard.

33. Quoted in Lawrence, *Letters to Seltzer,* pp. 185–186, 188; Quoted in unidentified bookseller's catalogue sent to me by John Martin of Black Sparrow Press on November 16, 1988; *Letters:* Moore, pp. 839, 855.

34. Lawrence, *The Lost Girl,* pp. 83, 34, 338.

35. *Ibid.,* pp. 86, 102, 104, 246; *Sea and Sardinia,* p. 123.

36. Lawrence, *Aaron's Rod,* pp. 293, 89.

37. *Ibid.,* p. 96.

38. Murry, *Son of Woman,* pp. 210, 212.

39. Quoted in Carswell, *Savage Pilgrimage,* p. 117; Lawrence, Introduction to *Memoirs,* p. 26; Norman Douglas, *D. H. Lawrence and Maurice Magnus: A Plea for Better Manners* (Florence, 1924), p. 33.

40. Lawrence, Introduction to *Memoirs,* pp. 77–78, 83; Graham Greene, "Frederick Rolfe," *Collected Essays* (London, 1969), p. 176; Lawrence, Introduction to *Memoirs,* p. 84.

41. D. H. Lawrence, *Memoir of Maurice Magnus,* ed. Keith Cushman (Santa Rosa, Calif., 1987), pp. 141, 144, 94–95.

42. Douglas, *Lawrence and Magnus,* pp. 6, 26, 41.

43. *Letters:* Moore, pp. 834, 836, 841, 890.

44. Lawrence, "Accumulated Mail," *Phoenix,* p. 800; Aldington, *Life for Life's Sake,* p. 376; *Letters of Virginia Woolf,* 3.361.

45. *Letters:* Cambridge, 4.105–106; Thomas Bergin, *Giovanni Verga* (New Haven, 1931), p. 107; Unpublished letter from Lawrence to H. Herlitschka, November 25, 1929, University of Nottingham.

46. Lawrence, *Phoenix,* p. 240; Brewsters, *Reminiscences and Correspondence,* p. 250.

47. *Letters:* Cambridge, 3.534, 3.624, 3.695, 4.143.

48. *Ibid.,* 4.198, 4.95, 4.205, 4.312; *Letters:* Moore, p. 814.

CHAPTER FIFTEEN: CEYLON AND AUSTRALIA

1. *Letters:* Cambridge, 2.330.
2. *Ibid.,* 4.447; Quoted in Brewsters, *Reminiscences and Correspondence,* p. 153; *Letters:* Moore, pp. 1155, 1221.
3. *Letters:* Cambridge, 4.208; Leonard Woolf, *Growing* (New York, 1961), pp. 134, 150; Interview with Harwood Brewster Picard.
4. *Letters:* Cambridge, 4.215–216; Lawrence, *Complete Poems,* pp. 390, 392; Quoted in Brewsters, *Reminiscences and Correspondence,* p. 258.
5. *Letters:* Cambridge, 4.224–225; Quoted in Brewsters, *Reminiscences and Correspondence,* p. 47; Lawrence, *The Plumed Serpent,* pp. 188, 332–333; Brigit Patmore, in Nehls, *Composite Biography,* 3.259.
6. Mary Durack, Foreword to Mollie Skinner, *The Fifth Sparrow: An Autobiography* (Sydney, 1972), pp. ix, 116; Lawrence, "Preface to *Black Swans,*" *Phoenix II,* p. 294; Carswell, *Savage Pilgrimage,* p. 201.
7. Quoted in Robert Darroch, *Lawrence in Australia* (London, 1981), p. 10; *Letters:* Cambridge, 2.241.
8. *Letters:* Cambridge, 4.263.
9. Russel Ward, *A History of Australia: The Twentieth Century, 1901–1975* (London, 1978), p. 141; Lawrence, *Kangaroo,* pp. 189, 157, 190.
10. Lawrence, *Kangaroo,* pp. 160–161, 200, 208.
11. Graham Hough, *The Dark Sun* (New York, 1959), p. 104; D. H. Lawrence, *Mornings in Mexico* (London, 1974), p. 42; Lawrence, *Kangaroo,* p. 264.
12. Lawrence, *Kangaroo,* pp. 321, 326, 347.
13. *Ibid.,* pp. 177, 335, 98.
14. *Letters:* Cambridge, 4.239; 4.286; 3.549; R. L. Stevenson, *Letters,* ed. Sidney Colvin (London, 1911), pp. 306–397.
15. R. L. Stevenson, *Travels with a Donkey* (London, 1929), p. 57.
16. Stevenson, *An Inland Voyage* (London, 1911) pp. 165, 13; R. L. Stevenson, "On the Enjoyment of Unpleasant Places," *Essays of Travel* (London, 1912), p. 224.
17. Quoted in Carswell, *Savage Pilgrimage,* p. 190.

CHAPTER SIXTEEN: TO THE NEW WORLD

1. Luhan, *Lorenzo in Taos,* p. 3; *Letters:* Cambridge, 4.111.
2. Quoted in Carswell, *Savage Pilgrimage,* p. 199; *Letters:* Cambridge, 4.226.

3. Witter Bynner, *Journey with Genius* (New York, 1951), p. 2; See Lois Rudnick, *Mabel Dodge Luhan* (Albuquerque, 1984).

4. Quoted in Laurie Lisle, *Portrait of an Artist: A Biography of Georgia O'Keeffe* (New York, 1981), p. 220; Interview with Enid Hopkin Hilton.

5. Luhan, *Lorenzo in Taos,* p. 134; Meyers, *Katherine Mansfield,* p. 222.

6. Interview with Enid Hopkin Hilton; Quoted in *Letters:* Cambridge, 4.450; Luhan, *Lorenzo in Taos,* p. 63.

7. *Letters:* Cambridge, 4.351; Luhan, *Lorenzo in Taos,* pp. 69–70, 270.

8. *Letters:* Cambridge, 4.337; Luhan, *Lorenzo in Taos,* p. 72, 89; Quoted in Rudnick, *Mabel Dodge Luhan,* p. 198; Frieda Lawrence, *Memoirs and Correspondence,* p. 250.

9. Quoted in Merrild, *Poet and Two Painters,* pp. 239–240; D. H. Lawrence, *St. Mawr and The Man Who Died* (New York, 1960), pp. 95, 136.

10. Lawrence, "Indians and an Englishman," *Phoenix,* p. 92; *Letters:* Moore, p. 804.

11. Merrild, *Poet and Two Painters,* p. 92. Götzsche was born in Aarhus, the son of an engineer, and married in 1926. Merrild, born in Ødum, the son of a teacher, was dismissed from the Arts and Crafts School in Copenhagen in 1916 for his outspoken advocacy of modern art, withdrew from the Royal Academy of Fine Arts in 1917 because of the stifling atmosphere, won the backstroke championship of Scandinavia in 1919 and married in 1926. He became a friend of Henry Miller, had a successful career in America and lived in Los Angeles until 1952, when he returned to Copenhagen. See *Weilbachs Kunstnerleksikon,* ed. Merete Bodelsen and Povl Engelstoft (København, 1947, 1949), 1.417–418, 2.369–370; Letter from Vibeke Merrild to Jeffrey Meyers, April 27, 1989; Henry Miller, "Knud Merrild: A Holiday in Paint," *Circle,* 6 (1945), 41–47.

12. Merrild, *Poet and Two Painters,* p. 94; Interview with Rachel Hawk, San Cristobal, New Mexico, March 29, 1988. Sixty-six years after Lawrence first arrived, Rachel Hawk was still living on the Del Monte ranch.

13. Joseph Foster, *D. H. Lawrence in Taos* (Albuquerque, 1972), p. 309; Merrild, *Poet and Two Painters,* pp. 343, 157, 173; Lawrence, "Bibbles," *Complete Poems,* pp. 399–400.

14. Brett, *Lawrence and Brett,* p. 75; Interview with Enid Hopkin Hilton.

15. Interview with Rachel Hawk; Lawrence, "New Mexico," *Phoenix,* p. 142.

16. In 1928, five years after Lawrence saw the bullfights, the rules were changed; the horses were provided with protective pads to prevent goring and the most unpleasant aspect of the *corrida* was eliminated.

17. Lawrence, *The Plumed Serpent*, pp. 52–53, 62; Carlos Fuentes, *The Death of Artemio Cruz*, trans. Sam Hileman (London, 1964), p. 156.

18. *Letters:* Cambridge, 4.419, 4.430, 4.463.

19. Lawrence, *The Plumed Serpent*, p. 28; Bynner, *Journey with Genius*, p. 109; Quoted in William Gerhardie, *Memoirs of a Polyglot* (New York, 1931), p. 234.

20. *Letters:* Cambridge, 4.442; Bynner, *Journey with Genius*, pp. 151, 31; Frederick Leighton, in Nehls, *Composite Biography*, 2.229–230.

21. *Frieda Lawrence and Her Circle*, p. 99.

22. *Letters of Lawrence and Amy Lowell*, pp. 108, 92; Carswell, *Savage Pilgrimage*, p. 190.

23. *Letters:* Cambridge, 4.506; 4.512; 4.527.

24. *Ibid.*, 4.532; Frieda Lawrence, *Not I, But the Wind*, pp. 141, 144.

CHAPTER SEVENTEEN: LONDON, TAOS AND
OAXACA

1. *Letters:* Cambridge, 3.127; Alpers, *Life of Mansfield*, p. 160.

2. Murry, *Reminiscences*, pp. 211–213, 215–218, 223; *Letters:* Cambridge, 5.94.

3. Mansfield, *Journal*, p. 296; Aldous Huxley, *Point Counter Point* (Harmondsworth, 1965), pp. 170–172 (Lawrence appears in this novel as Rampion); Lawrence, "Smile," *Complete Short Stories*, 2.584. For a full discussion of this subject, see Jeffrey Meyers, "Murry's Cult of Mansfield," *Journal of Modern Literature*, 7 (February 1979), 15–38.

4. Letter from Lawrence to H. Herlitschka, December 26, 1929, University of Nottingham: Quoted in Bynner, *Journey with Genius*, p. 150.

5. *Letters:* Cambridge, 4.480; Quoted in Lea, *Life of Murry*, pp. 117–118.

6. Carswell, *Savage Pilgrimage*, p. 192; Lawrence, "The Border Line," *Complete Short Stories*, 3.589; John Carswell, *Lives and Letters*, p. 202.

7. Lea, *Life of Murry*, p. 120; E. W. Tedlock, *D. H. Lawrence: Artist and Rebel* (Albuquerque, 1963), p. 160; Carswell, *Savage Pilgrimage*, p. 212.

8. Murry, *Reminiscences*, p. 196; *Letters:* Cambridge, 5.205; 5.313; *Letters:* Moore, p. 1136. Murry was actually born in 1889 (also a lying year).

9. Quoted in Richard Rees, "John Middleton Murry," *Dictionary of National Biography, 1951–1960* (Oxford, 1971), p. 761; *The Letters of T. S. Eliot: Volume 1, 1898–1922*, ed. Valerie Eliot (London, 1988), p. 433; *Letters of Virginia Woolf*, 4.315; 4.312; Frieda Lawrence, Manuscript on Murry's *Son of Woman*, UCLA.

10. *Letters:* Cambridge, 5.273. Mabel later gave the manuscript to her psychoanalyst, A. A. Brill, to settle her medical bills, and he sold it to the University of California at Berkeley. Frieda gave the ranch to the University of New Mexico, and it is now used as a residence for visiting writers.

11. *Letters:* Cambridge, 5.47, 5.28, 5.148; 5.109.

12. Quoted in Brett, *Lawrence and Brett*, p. 104; William Gerhardie, in Nehls, *Composite Biography*, 3.12; Brett, *Lawrence and Brett*, pp. 31, 272.

13. Luhan, *Lorenzo in Taos*, p. 166; Brett, "Autobiography," *South Dakota Review*, p. 31.

14. Harvard University, Class of 1922, 25th Anniversary Report, p. 1018; Foster, *Lawrence in Taos*, pp. 156, 160.

15. Brett, *Lawrence and Brett*, p. 109; Luhan, *Lorenzo in Taos*, pp. 226–227.

16. Brett, *Lawrence and Brett*, p. 128; Luhan, *Lorenzo in Taos*, p. 173.

17. Brett, *Lawrence and Brett*, p. 208; *Letters:* Cambridge, 5.192; 5.203–204; Interview with Barbara Weekley Barr.

18. Quoted in Manchester, Epilogue to *Lawrence and Brett*, p. III. The variant phrase is quoted by Sean Hignett (who believes her fantasy) in *Brett* (New York, 1984), p. 192. In Wyndham Lewis' *Tarr* (New York, 1918), p. 171, Kreisler, dancing with a buxom woman at Frau Liepmann's ball, also finds her "boobs are all wrong" and says: "Excuse me! It's awkward—. More to the left—so! Clumsy things, and women are so proud of them!"

19. See Morrell, *Ottoline at Garsington*, p. 145, and Catherine Carswell, "D. H. Lawrence," *Time and Tide*, 11 (March 14, 1930), 342, who attest to Lawrence's fidelity; *Letters:* Moore, p. 898.

20. Frieda Lawrence, *Not I, But the Wind*, p. 147; *Letters:* Cambridge, 5.157; Lawrence, *Phoenix*, p. 387.

21. *Letters:* Cambridge, 5.162–164. For a good account of this period, see Ross Parmenter, *Lawrence in Oaxaca* (Salt Lake City, 1984).

22. Wyndham Lewis, *Paleface* (London, 1929), pp. 176–177, 173, 175; Lawrence, *Mornings in Mexico*, p. 55; Lawrence, *Phoenix*, p. 301.

23. *Letters:* Cambridge, 2.193; Letter from Wyndham Lewis to Newman Flower, Cornell University; Lewis, *Paleface*, p. 180.

24. See Garnett, *Flowers of the Forest,* p. 37; Lawrence, *Lady Chatterley's Lover,* p. 268; Lawrence, *Phoenix,* p. 271.

25. Wyndham Lewis, *Hitler* (London, 1931), p. 109; Wyndham Lewis, *The Roaring Queen,* ed. Walter Allen (London, 1973), p. 71.

26. Frank Tannenbaum, *Mexico: The Struggle for Peace and Bread* (New York, 1950), p. 65; See Frank Brandenburg, *The Making of Modern Mexico* (Englewood Cliffs, New Jersey, 1964), pp. 74–75.

27. *Letters:* Cambridge, 5.167–168; D. H. Lawrence, *Movements in European History* (1921; Oxford, 1971), p. 306; Lawrence, *Fantasia of the Unconscious,* p. 210.

28. Quoted in Bynner, *Journey with Genius,* p. 47.

29. Lawrence, *Plumed Serpent,* pp. 70, 439, 58, 135.

CHAPTER EIGHTEEN: TUBERCULOSIS

1. Thomas Mann, *The Magic Mountain,* trans. H. T. Lowe-Porter (London, 1957), p. 432. For a discussion of this novel and treatment of this subject, see Jeffrey Meyers, *Disease and the Novel* (London, 1985); *Letters of John Keats,* ed. Robert Gittings (Oxford, 1970), p. 385; Witter Bynner, Foreword to Nehls, *Composite Biography,* 2.ix.

2. Walter Pagel, *Pulmonary Tuberculosis,* 4th ed. (London, 1964), p. 428; F. B. Smith, *The Retreat of Tuberculosis, 1850–1950* (New York, 1988), p. 166. My discussion of tuberculosis has drawn on: S. Vere Pearson, "The Psychology of the Consumptive," *Journal of State Medicine,* 40 (1932), 477–485; René and Jean Dubos, *The White Plague* (Boston, 1952); Phineas Sparer, ed., *Personality, Stress and Tuberculosis* (New York, 1956); Selman Waksman, *The Conquest of Tuberculosis* (Berkeley, 1964); Lester King, "Consumption: The Story of a Disease," *Medical Thinking* (Princeton, 1982), pp. 16–72; Stefan Grzybowski, *Tuberculosis and Its Prevention* (St. Louis, 1983); Linda Bryder, *Below the Magic Mountain: A Social History of Tuberculosis in Twentieth-Century Britain* (New York, 1988).

3. Quoted in Stanley Weintraub, *Beardsley* (1967; Harmondsworth, 1972), p. 208; Mansfield, *Scrapbook,* pp. 134–135; Katherine Mansfield, *Novels and Novelists* (1930; Boston, 1959), p. 282.

4. Mansfield, *Journal,* p. 207; Mansfield, *Collected Letters,* 2.254.

5. Lawrence shared Anton Ferge's attitude, though not Mann's ironic tone, in *The Magic Mountain,* p. 310: "The pleura [the membrane covering the lung], my friends, is not anything that should be felt of;

it does not want to be felt of and it ought not to be. It is taboo. It is covered up with flesh and put away once and for all; nobody and nothing ought to come near it."

6. *Letters:* Cambridge, 5.632; Quoted in Brewsters, *Reminiscences and Correspondence,* p. 171; Aldous Huxley, *Writers at Work: The "Paris Review" Interviews: Second Series* (New York, 1963), p. 210.

7. Quoted in Carswell, *The Savage Pilgrimage,* p. 77.

8. "The Letters of Anton Tchehov," trans. Katherine Mansfield and S. S. Koteliansky, *Athenaeum,* 1 (June 6, 1914), 441; Quoted in Lord Houghton, *The Life and Letters of John Keats* (1848; London, 1963), p. 200.

9. Frieda Lawrence, *Not I, But the Wind,* pp. 149–151. Lawrence's "Sun" (1928), *Complete Short Stories,* 2.528, echoes these words and begins: " 'Take her away, into the sun,' the doctors said."

10. *Letters:* Cambridge, 5.289; Parmenter, *Lawrence in Oaxaca,* p. 318, also cited in *Letters:* Cambridge, 5.211n. See *Manson's Tropical Diseases,* 19th ed. (London, 1987), p. 6.

11. *Letters:* Cambridge, 5.229. See Grummon's obituary in the *New York Times,* June 3, 1960, p. 31.

12. *Letters:* Cambridge, 5.545; 5.578, 5.630. Gertler, depressed by his unsuccessful career and by the fate of the European Jews, gassed himself in 1939. Gertie Cooper recovered and lived until 1942.

13. William Ober, *Boswell's Clap,* p. 108; Lawrence, "The Reality of Peace," *Reflections on the Death of a Porcupine,* p. 34; Lawrence, "Basta!" *Complete Poems,* p. 508. Thomas Carlyle, John Ruskin, James Barrie and Edward Marsh were impotent for psychological reasons.

14. Lawrence, "The Flying Fish," *Phoenix,* pp. 780, 783, 785; Brewsters, *Reminiscences and Correspondence,* p. 288.

15. Lawrence, *St. Mawr and The Man Who Died,* p. 165; Quoted in Brewsters, *Reminiscences and Correspondence,* p. 18.

16. *Letters:* Cambridge, 5.268; Interview with Rachel Hawk.

17. Ross Parmenter, notes on his interview with Friedel Jaffe, January 1974, and letter from Friedel Jaffe to Ross Parmenter, October 7, 1973, courtesy of Mr. Parmenter; Phone conversation with Friedel Jaffe (now Frederick Jeffrey), June 5, 1988.

18. *Letters:* Cambridge, 5.126; 5.300n; 5.347.

CHAPTER NINETEEN: SPOTORNO AND SCANDICCI

1. *Letters:* Cambridge, 5.321; Barbara Weekley Barr, in Nehls, *Composite Biography,* 3.8; William Gerhardie, in Nehls, *Composite Biography,* 3.11.
2. Fredric Warburg, *An Occupation for Gentlemen* (Boston, 1960), p. 155; *Letters:* Cambridge, 5.377.
3. Catherine Carswell, *Savage Pilgrimage,* p. 227; Letter from Yvonne Kapp to Jeffrey Meyers, April 14, 1988.
4. *Letters:* Cambridge, 5.376; 5.372–373.
5. Lawrence, "The Border Line," *Complete Short Stories,* 3.588; Interview with Barbara Weekley Barr.
6. Huxley, *Point Counter Point,* p. 98; Frieda Lawrence, *Not I, But the Wind,* pp. 179–181.
7. *Letters:* Cambridge, 5.411; 5.420; 2.215; 5.350.
8. Lucas, *Frieda Lawrence,* pp. 242–243; Interview with Barbara Weekley Barr.
9. Harry Moore, in *Aldington: An Intimate Portrait,* p. 85; Interview with Lady Juliette Huxley.
10. Unpublished letter from Lawrence to Mrs. Otway, June 7, 1927, courtesy of Gene DeGruson; *Letters:* Cambridge, 5.486; 5.472; 5.474.
11. Norman Douglas, *Together* (1923; New York, 1931), p. 3; *Letters:* Moore, p. 1172 (the old baroness outlived Lawrence by eight months and died in November 1930); *Letters:* Cambridge, 5.509.
12. *Letters:* Huxley, p. 713. Richard Griffiths, *Fellow Travellers of the Right: British Enthusiasts for Nazi Germany, 1933–1939* (London, 1980), pp. 143, 145, writes: "Gardiner's views, in the twenties and thirties, were an amalgam of youth movementry, 'organic' agricultural theory, folk-dance and folk-song enthusiasm, and ethnic theories about Britain and Germany, combined with the usual interest, in such circles, in Social Credit.... The Nazi Revolution, once it had succeeded, found in him an ardent admirer"—right through the 1930s.
13. *Letters:* Cambridge, 5.380; Murry, *Reminiscences,* pp. 249, 254, 269.
14. Ottoline Morrell, *Ottoline at Garsington,* p. 78; Huxley, *Letters,* pp. 288, 332; Aldous Huxley, Introduction to *Letters of Lawrence,* p. xxx. Richard Aldington, in *Life for Life's Sake,* p. 334, echoed Huxley's eulogy and called Lawrence "the most interesting human being I have known."
15. Quoted in Luhan, *Lorenzo in Taos,* p. 326; Frieda Lawrence, *Not I, But the Wind,* p. 195; Unpublished letter from Lawrence to Pino Orioli, [early July 1927], UCLA.

16. *Letters:* Moore, pp. 991–992; 1005; Franz Schoenberner, *Confessions of a European Intellectual* (1946; New York, 1965), p. 305; Huxley, Introduction to *Letters of Lawrence,* p. xxxii.

17. *Letters:* Moore, pp. 1015, 1028; Letter from Carlo Carlucci, Managua, Nicaragua, to Jeffrey Meyers, February 17, 1988, describing his interview with Signora Mirenda in the fall of 1973.

18. Brewsters, *Reminiscences and Correspondence,* p. 284; *Letters:* Moore, p. 1065. The same thing had happened to Katherine Mansfield in San Remo in 1919. When she began to cough, the guests discovered she had tuberculosis, the manager asked her to leave and she had to pay to have the room disinfected. See Meyers, *Katherine Mansfield,* p. 186.

19. Quoted in Brewsters, *Reminiscences and Correspondence,* p. 182; Aldington, *Portrait of a Genius, But,* p. 337; *Letters:* Moore, pp. 1102, 1135–1136.

20. Lawrence, *Etruscan Places,* pp. 29, 40.

21. *Ibid.,* pp. 49–50, 76, 109, 29.

CHAPTER TWENTY: *LADY CHATTERLEY'S LOVER* AND THE PAINTINGS

1. *Letters:* Cambridge, 5.205, 5.322; Quoted in Brett, *Lawrence and Brett,* p. 240; Lawrence, "Introduction to These Paintings," *Phoenix,* p. 569; Lawrence, *Apocalypse,* p. 149.

2. Lawrence, "Sun," *Complete Short Stories,* 2.533, 2.541, 2.544–545; D. H. Lawrence, *Sun* (Paris, 1928), p. 38.

3. Harry Crosby, *Shadows of the Sun: The Diaries of Harry Crosby,* ed. Edward Germain (Santa Barbara, 1977), p. 241; Unpublished letter from Lawrence to Caresse Crosby, August 8, 1929, University of Texas; Quoted in Brewsters, *Reminiscences and Correspondence,* p. 308; *Letters:* Moore, p. 1224. After Crosby's death, and Lawrence's own, four other friends and acquaintances killed themselves: Philip Heseltine, a friend of Cecil Gray, who once planned to publish a private edition of *The Rainbow* and was later satirized as Halliday in *Women in Love,* in 1930; Dora Carrington, a painter in the Garsington circle, in 1932; Mark Gertler in 1939; and the American publisher Mitchell Kennerley in 1950.

4. *Letters:* Cambridge, 5.479, 5.533, 5.536; Lawrence, *Women in Love,* p. 115; Lawrence, *Lady Chatterley's Lover,* pp. 143, 149.

5. The three versions are *The First Lady Chatterley* (1944), *John*

Thomas and Lady Jane (1972) and *Lady Chatterley's Lover* (1928). For a discussion of these works, see Michael Squires, *The Creation of "Lady Chatterley's Lover"* (Baltimore, 1983) and Derek Britton, *Lady Chatterley: The Making of the Novel* (London, 1988).

6. The photograph and Lawrence's comment are printed in Harry Moore, *D. H. Lawrence and His World* (New York, 1966), p. 19; Lawrence, *Lady Chatterley's Lover*, pp. 187, 263.

7. William Blake, "The Marriage of Heaven and Hell," *The Poetical Works*, ed. John Sampson (Oxford, 1958), p. 250; Friedrich Nietzsche, *Ecce Homo*, trans. and ed. Walter Kaufmann (New York, 1967), p. 268; Lawrence, "A Propos of *Lady Chatterley's Lover*," *Phoenix II*, pp. 508, 510.

8. Lawrence, *Lady Chatterley's Lover*, p. 20; Quoted in A. S. Frere, Introduction to Michael Arlen, *The Green Hat* (1924; London, 1968); Ottoline Morrell, *Ottoline at Garsington*, p. 77; Gray, *Peter Warlock*, p. 119. In *The London Venture* (New York, 1920), pp. 10–13, Arlen describes Lawrence as bitter, arrogant, shameless and malicious.

9. Lawrence, *Lady Chatterley's Lover*, p. 107.

10. W. B. Yeats, *Letters*, ed. Allan Wade (London, 1954), p. 810. Unlike Mellors, Connie—the proper lady—does not use four-letter words. He praises her cunt and arse, but she does not commend his cock and balls.

11. Dylan Thomas, *Collected Letters*, ed. Paul Ferris (New York, 1985), p. 50; Unpublished letter from Lawrence to Christine Hughes, April 25, 1927, University of Texas.

12. Holloway, *Norman Douglas*, p. 310; *Letters:* Huxley, p. 717; Lawrence, "A Propos of *Lady Chatterley's Lover*," *Phoenix II*, p. 515.

13. *Letters:* Huxley, p. 792.

14. Brentford, *Do We Need a Censor?*, pp. 9, 24; Evelyn Waugh, *Vile Bodies* (New York, 1960), p. 23.

15. *Letters:* Huxley, p. 781.

16. Unpublished letter from Lawrence to "Arabella" Yorke, August 4, 1928, Stanford University; Quoted in Richard Ellmann, *James Joyce*, revised edition (New York, 1982), p. 615n; Quoted in Brett, *Lawrence and Brett*, p. 81; Quoted in Mackenzie, *My Life and Times: Octave Five*, p. 167; Crosby, *Shadows of the Sun*, p. 245. For Lawrence's criticism of Joyce, see *Phoenix*, pp. 250, 270, 517–518.

17. "Famous Novelist's Shameful Book," *John Bull*, October 28, 1928, p. 11, in Draper, *Lawrence: The Critical Heritage*, p. 278; James Drawbell, *An Autobiography* (New York, 1964), pp. 281–282.

18. Huxley, Introduction to *Letters of Lawrence,* p. xiii.

19. Nietzsche, *The Antichrist,* in *The Portable Nietzsche,* pp. 585–586; Gabriele D'Annunzio, *The Maidens of the Rocks,* trans. Anna and Giuseppe Antona (New York, 1926), pp. 20–21.

20. *Letters:* Cambridge, 1.236; Lawrence, *The Rainbow,* pp. 283, 272; D. H. Lawrence, *The Symbolic Meaning,* ed. Armin Arnold (London, 1962), p. 255.

21. *Letters:* Moore, p. 1115; Lawrence, "The Risen Lord," *Phoenix II,* p. 575; *Letters:* Moore, p. 975.

22. Lawrence, *The Man Who Died,* pp. 165, 174, 205, 168.

23. *Ibid.,* pp. 172, 177, 193.

24. Lawrence, *Etruscan Places,* p. 10; Lawrence, "The Ship of Death," *Complete Poems,* pp. 716–720.

25. Lawrence, "Making Pictures," *Phoenix II,* p. 602; *Letters:* Cambridge, 5.585, 5.637; Lawrence, "Making Pictures," *Phoenix II,* pp. 603–604.

26. Lawrence, *Etruscan Places,* p. 68; See Raymond Bloch, *Etruscan Art* (Greenwich, Conn., 1959), plates 32, 48, 34, 55; Lawrence, *Etruscan Places,* pp. 46–47.

27. *Letters:* Cambridge, 5.637; Herbert Read, "Lawrence as a Painter," *The Paintings of D. H. Lawrence,* ed. Mervyn Levy (London, 1964), p. 63.

28. *Letters:* Cambridge, 5.648; 5.576.

29. Interview with Yvonne Kapp; Interview with Julian Morrell Vinogradoff; Roger Berthoud, *The Life of Henry Moore* (New York, 1987), p. 90. For Lawrence's influence on Moore, see p. 54.

30. Interview with Enid Hopkin Hilton; Quoted in Stephen Spender, "The Erotic Art of D. H. Lawrence," *Vanity Fair,* 49 (January 1986), 93; Lawrence, *Phoenix,* pp. 567–568; "Paintings Seized by London Police as Indecent," *New York Times,* July 6, 1929, p. 4; *Letters:* Moore, p. 1164.

31. Metropolitan Police Papers, MEP02/9428: "Indecent Exhibition of Pictures by D. H. Lawrence at the Warren Gallery, 39A Maddox Street, W1," Public Record Office, Kew.

32. Quoted in Harry Moore, "D. H. Lawrence and the 'Censor-Morons,'" in D. H. Lawrence, *Sex, Literature and Censorship* (New York, 1959), p. 21; Quoted in *Frieda Lawrence and Her Circle,* p. 11.

33. *Letters:* Moore, pp. 1164, 1176, 1180; Lawrence, *Complete Poems,* pp. 579–580; Metropolitan Police Papers.

34. Frieda Lawrence, *Not I, But the Wind,* p. 73.

CHAPTER TWENTY-ONE: BANDOL AND VENCE

1. *Letters:* Moore, pp. 1135, 1142; Gertler, *Selected Letters,* p. 228.
2. Aldington, *Portrait of a Genius, But,* p. 111; Huxley, *Letters,* p. 364.
3. "D. H. Lawrence Sees New Civilization," *New York Evening Post,* August 20, 1923, p. 4.
4. Frieda Lawrence, *Not I, But the Wind,* p. 199; Huxley, *Letters,* pp. 313–314; Frieda Lawrence, *Memoirs and Correspondence,* p. 233.
5. Mohr, a gentile anti-Nazi, published a novel about Lawrence, *Philip Glenn* (1932). Three years later he emigrated to Shanghai, where he practiced medicine and lived in poverty until his death, at the age of fifty-three, in 1944.
6. *Letters:* Huxley, p. 847; *Letters:* Moore, p. 1212.
7. Frederick Carter, *D. H. Lawrence and the Body Mystical* (London, 1932), p. 51; Barbara Weekley Barr, in Nehls, *Composite Biography,* 3.427–428.
8. Lawrence's doctors included William Addey in Croydon (November 1911), Maitland Radford in Padstow (February 1916), Mullan-Feroze in Ripley (February 1919), Dr. Martin in Taos (August 1924), Sydney Uhlfelder in Mexico City (February 1925), Dr. Giglioli in Florence (July 1927 and July 1929), Hans Carossa in Irschenhausen (September 1927), Max Mohr in Irschenhausen and Rottach (September 1927 and September 1929).
9. Andrew Morland, in Nehls, *Composite Biography,* 3.424–425; Andrew Morland, "The Last Days of D. H. Lawrence: Hitherto Unpublished Letters of Dr. Andrew Morland," ed. George Zytaruk, *D. H. Lawrence Review,* 1 (1968), 46–47. See also, Andrew Morland, "The Mind in Tubercule," *Lancet* (January 23, 1932), 176–178, and Andrew Morland, *Pulmonary Tuberculosis in General Practice* (London, 1933).
10. *Letters:* Moore, pp. 1231–1232; 1241, 1243–1245; "Letters of Morland," *D. H. Lawrence Review,* p. 48.
11. Quoted in Weintraub, *Beardsley,* p. 214; *Letters:* Cambridge, 5.632; Frieda Lawrence, *Not I, But the Wind,* pp. 288–289.
12. Huxley, *Letters,* pp. 330–331; Quoted in Sybille Bedford, *Aldous Huxley: A Biography* (New York, 1974), p. 226.
13. Frieda Lawrence, *Not I, But the Wind,* p. 295; Frieda Lawrence, Untitled manuscript relating to Lawrence's will, c.1930, Bancroft Library, University of California, Berkeley; Lawrence, "Prayer," *Complete Poems,* p. 684.

14. Interview with Margaret King Needham; Interview with Harwood Brewster Picard; Quoted in Bedford, *Huxley,* p. 225.

15. Frieda Lawrence, *Memoirs and Correspondence,* p. 236; Quoted in Forster, *Selected Letters,* 2.91.

EPILOGUE

1. Catherine Carswell, "D. H. Lawrence," *Time and Tide,* p. 342; Forster, *Selected Letters,* 1.249; E. M. Forster, "D. H. Lawrence," *Listener,* 3 (April 30, 1930), 753; E. M. Forster, "D. H. Lawrence," *Nation and Athenaeum,* 46 (March 29, 1930), 888. Forster echoed the judgment of Francis Brett Young, who, in "A Note on D. H. Lawrence," *The Borzoi, 1925* (New York, 1925), p. 235, wrote that Lawrence is "the only authentic literary genius, in my opinion, of the generation to which we belong."

2. Lea, *Life of Murry,* p. 165; Huxley, *Letters,* pp. 352–353; Wyndham Lewis, "The Son of Woman," *Time and Tide,* 12 (April 18, 1931), 470. For a discussion of books on Lawrence by his friends, see Jeffrey Meyers, "Memoirs of Lawrence: A Genre of the Thirties," *D. H. Lawrence Review,* 14 (1981), 1–32.

3. *Frieda Lawrence and Her Circle,* p. 20. See Lucas, *Frieda Lawrence,* pp. 256–257, and Alvarez, *Life After Marriage,* p. 84.

4. *Nettles, Assorted Articles, The Virgin and the Gipsy, A Propos of "Lady Chatterley's Lover"* and *Love Among the Haystacks* were published in 1930; *Apocalypse* in 1931; *Etruscan Places* and the *Letters* in 1932.

5. Lawrence's death certificate of June 5, 1930, and *The Times,* June 12, 1930, p. 16, list the value of his estate at £2,438. Frieda's letter to Bynner of March 13, 1930, in *Journey with Genius,* p. 344, Moore, *Priest of Love,* p. 635, and J. W. Saunders, *The Profession of English Letters* (London, 1964), p. 219, list the value as £4,000.

6. Huxley, *Letters,* p. 364; Bynner, *Journey with Genius,* p. 347. Frieda left one half of Lawrence's increasingly lucrative and now immensely valuable estate to her three children and the other half to Ravagli, so that, by a strange irony, fifty percent of Lawrence's royalties continue to go to the children of the man who cuckolded him in his lifetime.

7. *Frieda Lawrence and Her Circle,* pp. 43, 50; Interview with Rachel Hawk; Huxley, *Letters,* p. 422.

8. Letter from Frank Waters to Jeffrey Meyers, April 18, 1988; Letter

from Dorothy Brett to Edward Nehls, University of Texas; Lisle, *Georgia O'Keeffe,* p. 281.

9. *Letters:* Cambridge, 1.478; 5.408; Carswell, "D. H. Lawrence," *Time and Tide,* p. 342. "The husband of one wife" alludes to 1 Timothy 3:2. For Lawrence's influence on English and American writers, see Jeffrey Meyers, ed., *The Legacy of D. H. Lawrence* (London, 1987).

Bibliography

Brett, Dorothy. *Lawrence and Brett*. Philadelphia, 1933.

Brewster, Earl and Achsah. *D. H. Lawrence: Reminiscences and Correspondence*. London, 1934.

Bynner, Witter. *Journey with Genius*. New York, 1951.

Carswell, Catherine. *The Savage Pilgrimage*. New York, 1932.

Chambers, Jessie. *D. H. Lawrence: A Personal Record* (1935). 2nd edition, ed. Jonathan Chambers. London, 1965.

Darroch, Sandra. *Ottoline: The Life of Ottoline Morrell*. New York, 1975.

Delany, Paul. *D. H. Lawrence's Nightmare*. New York, 1978.

Delavenay, Emile. *D. H. Lawrence: The Man and His Work*. Trans. Katherine Delavenay. London, 1972.

Draper, R. P., ed. *D. H. Lawrence: The Critical Heritage*. London, 1970.

Lawrence, Ada, and Stuart Gelder. *Young Lorenzo* (1931). New York, 1966.

Lawrence, Frieda. *Not I, But the Wind*. New York, 1934.

————. *The Memoirs and Correspondence*. Ed. E. W. Tedlock. New York, 1964.

Lea, F. A. *The Life of John Middleton Murry*. London, 1959.

Lucas, Robert. *Frieda Lawrence*. trans. Geoffrey Skelton. New York, 1973.

Luhan, Mabel Dodge. *Lorenzo in Taos*. New York, 1932.

Merrild, Knud. *A Poet and Two Painters*. London, 1938.

Meyers, Jeffrey. *Katherine Mansfield: A Biography*. London, 1978.

————. *D. H. Lawrence and the Experience of Italy*. Philadelphia, 1982.

————, ed. *D. H. Lawrence and Tradition*. London, 1985.

————, ed. *The Legacy of D. H. Lawrence*. London, 1987.

Moore, Harry. *The Priest of Love* (1974). Harmondsworth, 1976.

Morrell, Ottoline. *Ottoline at Garsington, 1915–1918*. Ed. Robert Gathorne-Hardy. London, 1974.

Murry, J. M. *Son of Woman*. London, 1931.

————. *Reminiscences of D. H. Lawrence*. London, 1933.

————. *Between Two Worlds*. London, 1935.

Nehls, Edward, ed. *D. H. Lawrence: A Composite Biography*. 3 vols. Madison, 1957–59.

Parmenter, Ross. *Lawrence in Oaxaca*. Salt Lake City, 1984.

Roberts, Warren. *A Bibliography of D. H. Lawrence*. 2nd ed. Cambridge, England, 1982.

Sagar, Keith. *D. H. Lawrence: A Calendar of His Works*. Manchester, 1979.

Spencer, Roy. *D. H. Lawrence Country*. London, 1980.

Stevens, C. J. *Lawrence at Tregerthen*. Troy, New York, 1988.

Index

—Compiled by Valerie Meyers

ACKNOWLEDGMENTS

Grateful acknowledgment is made to the following for permission to reprint previously published material:

Alfred A. Knopf, Inc. and *Laurence Pollinger Limited:* Excerpts from *The Man Who Died* by D. H. Lawrence. Copyright 1928 by Alfred A. Knopf, Inc. Excerpts from *The Virgin and the Gipsy* by D. H. Lawrence. Copyright 1930 by Alfred A. Knopf, Inc. Excerpts from "The Woman Who Rode Away" by D. H. Lawrence. Copyright 1928 by D. H. Lawrence. Excerpts from *St. Mawr* by D. H. Lawrence. Copyright 1925 by Alfred A. Knopf, Inc. Excerpts from *Pornography and Obscenity* by D. H. Lawrence. Copyright 1930 by Alfred A. Knopf, Inc. Excerpts from *The Plumed Serpent* by D. H. Lawrence. Copyright 1926 by Alfred A. Knopf, Inc. Excerpts from *Mornings in Mexico* by D. H. Lawrence. Copyright 1927 by D. H. Lawrence. Rights in the British Commonwealth controlled by Laurence Pollinger Limited. Reprinted by permission of Alfred A. Knopf, Inc. and Laurence Pollinger Limited and the Estate of Mrs. Frieda Lawrence Ravagli.

Laurence Pollinger Limited: Excerpts from the books *David, Pansies, Assorted Articles,* and *Lady Chatterley's Lover,* and letters of D. H. Lawrence. Reprinted by permission of Laurence Pollinger Limited and the Estate of Mrs. Frieda Lawrence Ravagli.

Viking Penguin and *Laurence Pollinger Limited:* Excerpts from *Phoenix: The Posthumous Papers of D. H. Lawrence,* edited by Edward D. McDonald. Copyright 1936 by Frieda Lawrence. Copyright renewed 1964 by the Estate of Frieda Lawrence Ravagli. Excerpts from *Phoenix II: Uncollected, Unpublished, and Other Prose Works* by D. H. Lawrence, edited by Warren Roberts and Harry T. Moore. Copyright © 1959, 1963, 1968 by the Estate of Frieda Lawrence Ravagli. Excerpts from *Aaron's Rod* by D. H. Lawrence. Copyright 1922 by Thomas Seltzer, Inc. Copyright renewed 1950 by Frieda Lawrence. Excerpts from *Apocalypse* by D. H. Lawrence. Copyright 1932 by the Estate of D. H. Lawrence. Excerpts from "Fanny and Annie" in *The Complete Short Stories of D. H. Lawrence,* Volume II. Copyright 1922 by Thomas Seltzer, Inc. Copyright renewed 1950 by Frieda Lawrence. Excerpts from *The Rainbow* by D. H. Lawrence. Copyright 1915 by David Herbert Lawrence. Copyright renewed 1943 by Frieda Lawrence. Excerpts from *Kangaroo* by D. H. Lawrence. Copyright 1923 by Thomas Seltzer, Inc. Copyright renewed 1951 by Frieda Lawrence. Excerpts from *Sons and Lovers* by D. H. Lawrence. Copyright 1913 by Thomas Seltzer, Inc. Excerpts from *Women in Love* by D. H. Lawrence. Copyright 1920, 1922 by D. H. Lawrence. Copyright renewed 1948, 1950 by Frieda Lawrence. Excerpts from *The Complete Poems of D. H. Lawrence,* collected and edited by Vivian de Sola Pinto and F. Warren Roberts. Copyright © 1964, 1971 by Angelo Ravagli and C. M. Weekley, Executors of the Estate of Frieda Lawrence Ravagli. Excerpts from *Etruscan Places* by D. H. Lawrence. Originally published in 1932 by The Viking Press, Inc. All rights reserved. Rights outside the U. S. and Canada controlled by Laurence Pollinger Limited, London. Reprinted by permission of Viking Penguin, a division of Penguin Books USA Inc. and Laurence Pollinger Limited and the Estate of Mrs. Frieda Lawrence Ravagli.